THE CAMBRIDGE COMPANION TO
KANT AND MODERN PHILOSOPHY

The philosophy of Immanuel Kant is the watershed of modern thought, which irrevocably changed the landscape of the field and prepared the way for all the significant philosophical movements of the nineteenth and twentieth centuries. This volume, which complements *The Cambridge Companion to Kant*, covers every aspect of Kant's philosophy, with an expanded focus on his moral and political philosophy. It also provides detailed coverage of Kant's historical context and of the enormous impact and influence that his work has had on the subsequent history of philosophy. The bibliography provides extensive and organized coverage of both classical and recent books on Kant in the main languages of Kant scholarship. This volume thus provides the broadest and deepest introduction to Kant and his place in modern philosophy currently available. It makes the philosophical enterprise of Kant accessible to those coming to his work for the first time.

Paul Guyer is Florence R. C. Murray Professor in the Humanities at the University of Pennsylvania. The editor and translator of three volumes in the *Cambridge Edition of the Works of Immanuel Kant*, he is the author of more than 150 articles and six books. He has held fellowships from the John Simon Guggenheim Memorial Foundation, the National Endowment for the Humanities, and at the Princeton University Center for Human Values. He is a member of the American Academy of Arts and Sciences.

OTHER VOLUMES IN THE SERIES OF CAMBRIDGE COMPANIONS:

AQUINAS *Edited by* NORMAN KRETZMANN *and* ELEONORE STUMP
HANNAH ARENDT *Edited by* DANA VILLA
ARISTOTLE *Edited by* JONATHAN BARNES
AUGUSTINE *Edited by* ELEONORE STUMP *and*
    NORMAN KRETZMANN
BACON *Edited by* MARKKU PELTONEN
BERKELEY *Edited by* KENNETH P. WINKLER
DESCARTES *Edited by* JOHN COTTINGHAM
DUNS SCOTUS *Edited by* THOMAS WILLIAMS
EARLY GREEK PHILOSOPHY *Edited by* A. A. LONG
FEMINISM IN PHILOSOPHY *Edited by* MIRANDA FRICKER *and*
    JENNIFER HORNSBY
FOUCAULT *Edited by* GARY GUTTING
FREUD *Edited by* JEROME NEU
GADAMER *Edited by* ROBERT J. DOSTAL
GALILEO *Edited by* PETER MACHAMER
GERMAN IDEALISM *Edited by* KARL AMERIKS
HABERMAS *Edited by* STEPHEN K. WHITE
HEGEL *Edited by* FREDERICK BEISER
HEIDEGGER *Edited by* CHARLES GUIGNON
HOBBES *Edited by* TOM SORELL
HUME *Edited by* DAVID FATE NORTON
HUSSERL *Edited by* BARRY SMITH *and*
    DAVID WOODRUFF SMITH
WILLIAM JAMES *Edited by* RUTH ANNA PUTNAM
KANT *Edited by* PAUL GUYER
KIERKEGAARD *Edited by* ALASTAIR HANNAY *and*
    GORDON MARINO
LEIBNIZ *Edited by* NICHOLAS JOLLEY
LOCKE *Edited by* VERE CHAPPELL
MALEBRANCHE *Edited by* STEVEN NADLER
MARX *Edited by* TERRELL CARVER
MILL *Edited by* JOHN SKORUPSKI
NEWTON *Edited by* I. BERNARD COHEN *and*
    GEORGE E. SMITH
NIETZSCHE *Edited by* BERND MAGNUS *and*
    KATHLEEN HIGGINS
OCKHAM *Edited by* PAUL VINCENT SPADE
PLATO *Edited by* RICHARD KRAUT
PLOTINUS *Edited by* LLOYD P. GERSON
ROUSSEAU *Edited by* PATRICK RILEY
SARTRE *Edited by* CHRISTINA HOWELLS
SCHOPENHAUER *Edited by* CHRISTOPHER JANAWAY
SPINOZA *Edited by* DON GARRETT
WITTGENSTEIN *Edited by* KANS SLUGA *and*
    DAVID STERN

The Cambridge Companion to

KANT AND MODERN PHILOSOPHY

Edited by

Paul Guyer
University of Pennsylvania

CAMBRIDGE
UNIVERSITY PRESS

CAMBRIDGE UNIVERSITY PRESS
Cambridge, New York, Melbourne, Madrid, Cape Town, Singapore, São Paulo

Cambridge University Press
32 Avenue of the Americas, New York, NY 10013-2473, USA

www.cambridge.org
Information on this title: www.cambridge.org/9780521823036

First published 2006
Reprinted 2007

Printed in the United States of America

A catalog record for this publication is available from the British Library.

Library of Congress Cataloging in Publication Data

The Cambridge companion to Kant and modern philosophy / edited
by Paul Guyer.
    p.   cm.
Includes bibliographical references and index.
ISBN-13: 978-0-521-82303-6 (hardback)
ISBN-10: 0-521-82303-x (hardback)
ISBN-13: 978-0-521-52995-2 (pbk.)
ISBN-10: 0-521-52995-6 (pbk.)
    1. Kant, Immanuel, 1724–1804.   2. Philosophy, Modern.   I. Guyer, Paul,
1948–   II. Title.
B2798.C365   2006
193 – dc22   2005029335

ISBN   978-0-521-82303-6 hardback
ISBN   978-0-521-52995-2 paperback

CONTENTS

Foreword   *page* vii

Contributors   ix

Method of Citation   xiii

Introduction: The starry heavens
and the moral law   I
PAUL GUYER

1. *"A Priori"*   28
    PHILIP KITCHER

2. Kant on the perception of space (and time)   61
    GARY HATFIELD

3. Kant's philosophy of mathematics   94
    LISA SHABEL

4. Kant on *a priori* concepts: The metaphysical
    deduction of the categories   129
    BÉATRICE LONGUENESSE

5. Kant's philosophy of the cognitive mind   169
    PATRICIA KITCHER

6. Kant's proofs of substance and causation   203
    ARTHUR MELNICK

7. Kant and transcendental arguments   238
    RALPH C. S. WALKER

v

8. The critique of metaphysics: The structure
    and fate of Kant's dialectic   269
    KARL AMERIKS

9. Philosophy of natural science   303
    MICHAEL FRIEDMAN

10. The supreme principle of morality   342
    ALLEN W. WOOD

11. Kant on freedom of the will   381
    HENRY E. ALLISON

12. Mine and thine? The Kantian state   416
    ROBERT B. PIPPIN

13. Kant on sex and marriage right   447
    JANE KNELLER

14. Kant's theory of peace   477
    PAULINE KLEINGELD

15. Kant's conception of virtue   505
    LARA DENIS

16. Kant's ambitions in the third *Critique*   538
    PAUL GUYER

17. Moral faith and the highest good   588
    FREDERICK C. BEISER

18. Kant's critical philosophy and its
    reception – the first five years (1781–1786)   630
    MANFRED KUEHN

    Bibliography   665
    Index   709

FOREWORD

The Cambridge Companion to Kant was published in 1992. Since that time, interest in Kant has remained strong and Kant scholarship has continued to flourish. When the late and dearly missed Terry Moore, at that time Executive Editor of the Humanities at Cambridge University Press, first proposed this volume, he may have had in mind that the authors of the 1992 text would update their essays and that I would update the bibliography. But it seemed to me that it would be more interesting to produce a very different volume that would supplement rather than supplant the earlier book. I have been fortunate to be able to recruit new essays from some of the contributors to *The Cambridge Companion to Kant*, although in many cases they have written on topics different from those they addressed in that volume. And I have been equally fortunate in signing up a healthy number of new contributors, including both senior members of the community of Kant scholars and several of the brightest new lights in the field.

This new volume is larger than the earlier book primarily because it includes more extensive coverage of Kant's moral and political philosophy. The aims of this *Companion* are also somewhat different than those of the first. To write the history of the position of Kant in modern philosophy, that is, of both his response to previous philosophy and his impact on the subsequent history of philosophy, would be tantamount to writing a comprehensive history of modern philosophy, and at this point in time may well be beyond the capacity of any single person. But I thought that this volume could make at least a start on such a project, and accordingly asked that each essay address both the historical context and the historical impact of the particular topic in Kant that it concerns. Contributors have responded to this charge in different ways, but all have done so in interesting ways. I therefore hope that this volume will not only introduce readers to the extraordinary breadth as well as depth of Kant's thought, but also make a start on the project of assessing the extraordinary breadth and depth of Kant's influence on the entire course of modern philosophy.

In addition to Terry Moore, who has left the whole series of *Cambridge Companions* to the philosophers as one among the many lasting monuments to his life's work at Cambridge University Press, two of the contributors to the earlier *Companion*, Eva Schaper and J. Michael Young, have also passed away since 1992. They are all remembered here with affection and gratitude. I am also grateful to Beatrice Rehl for her unstinting support in spite of the circumstances in which she inherited this project.

PAUL GUYER
February, 2005

CONTRIBUTORS

HENRY E. ALLISON is Professor of Philosophy at the University of California, Davis. His books include *Lessing and the Enlightenment* (1966), *The Kant-Eberhard Controversy* (1973), *Benedict de Spinoza: An Introduction* (1975; revised edition, 1987), *Kant's Transcendental Idealism: An Interpretation and Defense* (1983; revised and enlarged edition, 2004), *Kant's Theory of Freedom* (1990), *Idealism and Freedom* (1996), and *Kant's Theory of Taste: A Reading of the* Critique of Judgment (2001). He also edited Kant's *Theoretical Philosophy after 1781* (2002, with Peter Heath).

KARL AMERIKS is McMahon-Hank Professor of Philosophy at the University of Notre Dame. He is the author of *Kant's Theory of Mind* (1982; second edition, 2000), *Kant and the Fate of Autonomy* (2000), and *Interpreting Kant's Critiques* (2003). He has edited and translated Kant's *Lectures on Metaphysics* (1997) and Karl Leonhard Reinhold's *Letters on the Kantian Philosophy* (2005). He also edited *The Cambridge Companion to German Idealism* (2000).

FREDERICK C. BEISER is Professor of Philosophy at Syracuse University. His books include *The Fate of Reason: German Philosophy from Kant to Fichte* (1987), *Enlightenment, Revolution, and Romanticism: The Genesis of Modern German Political Thought, 1790–1800* (1992), *The Sovereignty of Reason: The Defense of Rationality in the Early English Enlightenment* (1996), *German Idealism: The Struggle against Subjectivism, 1781–1801* (2002), *The Romantic Imperative: The Concept of Early German Romanticism* (2003), and *Hegel* (2005). He has also edited *The Cambridge Companion to Hegel* (1993) and *The Early Political Writings of the German Romantics* (1996).

LARA DENIS is Associate Professor of Philosophy and Director of the Ethics Program at Agnes Scott College. She is the author of *Moral Self-Regard: Duties to Oneself in Kant's Ethics* (2001) and has edited a new version of Thomas K. Abbott's 1873 translation of Kant's *Groundwork for the Metaphysics of Morals* (2005).

MICHAEL FRIEDMAN is Frederick P. Rehmus Family Professor of Humanities at Stanford University. His publications include *Foundations of Space-time Theories: Relativistic Physics and Philosophy of Science* (1983), *Kant and the Exact Sciences* (1992), *Reconsidering Logical Positivism* (1999), *A Parting of the Ways: Carnap, Cassirer, and Heidegger* (2000), and *Dynamics of Reason* (2001). He has also translated Kant's *Metaphysical Foundations of Natural Science* (2004).

PAUL GUYER is Professor of Philosophy and Florence R. C. Murray Professor in the Humanities at the University of Pennsylvania. He has written *Kant and the Claims of Taste* (1979; second edition, 1997), *Kant and the Claims of Knowledge* (1987), *Kant and the Experience of Freedom* (1993), *Kant on Freedom, Law, and Happiness* (2000), *Kant's System of Nature and Freedom* (2005), and *Values of Beauty: Historical Essays in Aesthetics* (2005). He has translated Kant's *Critique of Pure Reason* (1998, with Allen W. Wood), *Critique of the Power of Judgment* (2000, with Eric Matthews), and *Notes and Fragments* (2005, with Curtis Bowman and Frederick Rauscher). In addition to *The Cambridge Companion to Kant*, he has also edited *Essays in Kant's Aesthetics* (1982, with Ted Cohen), *Pursuits of Reason: Essays in Honor of Stanley Cavell* (1993, with Ted Cohen and Hilary Putnam), and volumes of critical essays on Kant's *Groundwork for the Metaphysics of Morals* (1998) and *Critique of the Power of Judgment* (2003).

GARY HATFIELD is Adam Seybert Professor of Moral and Intellectual Philosophy at the University of Pennsylvania. His books include *The Natural and the Normative: Theories of Spatial Perception from Kant to Helmholtz* (1990) and *Descartes and the* Meditations (2003). He has translated Kant's *Prolegomena to any future Metaphysics* (1997; revised edition, 2004).

PATRICIA KITCHER is Professor of Philosophy and Mark Van Doren Professor of Humanities at Columbia University. Her books include

Kant's Transcendental Psychology (1990) and *Freud's Dream* (1992). She has also edited *Kant's Critique of Pure Reason: Critical Essays* (1998).

PHILIP KITCHER is John Dewey Professor of Philosophy at Columbia University. His books include *Abusing Science: The Case against Creationism* (1982), *The Nature of Mathematical Knowledge* (1984), *Vaulting Ambition: Sociobiology and the Quest for Human Nature* (1984), *The Advancement of Science: Science without Legend, Objectivity without Illusions* (1993), *Science, Truth, and Democracy* (2001), *In Mendel's Mirror: Philosophical Reflections on Biology* (2003), and *Finding an Ending: Philosophical Reflections on Wagner's Ring* (2004, co-authored with Richard Shacht). He has also written a number of articles on Kant.

PAULINE KLEINGELD is Professor of Philosophy at the University of Leiden, the Netherlands. She is the author of *Fortschritt und Vernunft: Zur Geschichtsphilosophie Kants* (1995) and the editor of a volume of essays on Kant's *Toward Perpetual Peace* (2005).

JANE KNELLER is Professor of Philosophy at Colorado State University. She has edited *Autonomy and Community: Readings in Contemporary Kantian Social Philosophy* (1998, with Sidney Axinn), and translated Klaus Reich's *The Completeness of Kant's Table of Categories* (1992, with Michael Losonsky) and Novalis's *Fichte Studies* (2003).

MANFRED KUEHN is Professor of Philosophy at Boston University. His works include *Scottish Common Sense in Germany, 1768–1800: A Contribution to the History of Critical Philosophy* (1987) and *Kant: A Biography* (2001). He has also edited an extensive compilation of papers on Kant, *Kant: Theoretical Philosophy* and *Kant: Practical Philosophy* (1999, with Heiner Klemme).

BÉATRICE LONGUENESSE is Professor of Philosophy at New York University. She is the author of *Hegel et la Critique de la Métaphysique* (1981), *Kant et le Pouvoir de Juger* (1993), translated and expanded as *Kant and the Capacity to Judge* (1998), and *Kant on the Human Standpoint* (2005).

ARTHUR MELNICK is Professor of Philosophy at the University of Illinois, Urbana-Champaign. He is the author of *Kant's Analogies of*

Experience (1973), *Space, Time, and Thought in Kant* (1989), *Representation of the World: A Naturalized Semantics* (1996), and *Themes in Kant's Metaphysics and Ethics* (2004).

ROBERT B. PIPPIN is the Raymond W. and Martha Hilpert Gruner Distinguished Service Professor in the Committee on Social Thought, Department of Philosophy, and the College at the University of Chicago. His books include *Kant's Theory of Form: An Essay on the Critique of Pure Reason* (1982), *Hegel's Idealism: The Satisfactions of Self-Consciousness* (1989), *Modernism as a Philosophical Problem: On the Dissatisfactions of European High Culture* (1991), *Idealism as Mondernism: Hegelian Variations* (1997), *Henry James and Modern Moral Life* (2000), *The Persistence of Subjectivity: On the Kantian Aftermath* (2005), *Die Verwirklichung der Freiheit* (2005), and *Nietzsche, moralist français: La conception nietzschéenne d'une psychologie philosophique* (2005).

LISA SHABEL is Associate Professor of Philosophy at the Ohio State University. She is the author of *Mathematics in Kant's Critical Philosophy: Reflections on Mathematical Practice* (2003).

RALPH C. S. WALKER is Fellow and Tutor in Philosophy, Magdalen College, the University of Oxford. He is the author of *Kant* (1978), *The Coherence Theory of Truth* (1988), and *Kant and the Moral Law* (1998). He has also edited *Kant on Pure Reason* (1982) and *The Real in the Ideal* (1989).

ALLEN W. WOOD is the Ward W. and Priscilla B. Woods Professor of Philosophy at Stanford University. His books include *Kant's Moral Religion* (1970), *Kant's Rational Theology* (1978), *Karl Marx* (1981; second edition, 2004), *Hegel's Ethical Thought* (1990), *Kant's Ethical Thought* (1999), *Unsettling Obligations* (2002), *Immanuel Kant: Grundlegung zur Metaphysik der Sitten. Ein einführender Kommentar* (2002, with Dieter Schönecker), and *Kant* (2004). He has translated Kant's *Lectures on Philosophical Theology* (1978, with Gertrude M. Clark), Kant's *Writings on Religion and Rational Theology* (1996, with George di Giovanni), Kant's *Critique of Pure Reason* (1998, with Paul Guyer), and Kant's *Groundwork for the Metaphysics of Morals*, with critical essays (2002). He has also edited *Self and Nature in Kant's Philosophy* (1984), *Marx: Selections* (1988), Hegel's *Elements of the Philosophy of Right* (1991), and The *Philosophy of Immanuel Kant* (2001).

METHOD OF CITATION

Citations to Kant's texts are generally given parenthetically, although additional references are often included in the endnotes to the essays. Two forms of citation are employed. Citations from the *Critique of Pure Reason* are located by reference to the pagination of Kant's first ("A") and/or second ("B") editions. All other passages from Kant's works are cited by the volume and page number, given by arabic numerals separated by a colon, in the standard edition of Kant's works, *Kant's gesammelte Schriften*, edited by the Royal Prussian, later German, then Berlin-Brandenburg Academy of Sciences, 29 volumes (volume 26 not yet published) (Berlin: Georg Reimer, later Walter de Gruyter & Co., 1900–). Where Kant divided a work into numbered sections, his section number typically precedes the volume and page number. These references are preceded by a short title for the work cited, except where the context makes that obvious. Since standard translations of the *Critique of Pure Reason* provide the "A" and "B" page numbers and modern editions of Kant's other works always give the Academy edition pagination, page numbers for translations have been omitted. Unless otherwise indicated in the individual essays, all translations are from the *Cambridge Edition of the Works of Immanuel Kant* (1992–).

The following lists, in alphabetical order, the short titles of Kant's works, with date of original publication in parentheses, that are used throughout the volume.

Conflict	*Conflict of the Faculties* (1798)
Correspondence	*Kant's correspondence*, in volumes 10–13 of the Academy edition or in Zweig (see Bibliography)

Directions	*Concerning the Ultimate Ground of the Differentiation of Directions in Space* (1768)
Dissertation	Inaugural dissertation *On the Form and Principles of the Sensible and Intelligible Worlds* (1770)
Dreams	*Dreams of a Spirit-Seer* (1766)
Enlightenment	"Answer to the Question: What is Enlightenment?" (1784)
False Subtlety	*On the False Subtlety of the Four Syllogistic Figures* (1762)
FI	First Introduction to the *Critique of the Power of Judgment* (posthumous)
Groundwork	*Groundwork for the Metaphysics of Morals* (1785)
Judgment	*Critique of the Power of Judgment* (1790)
Living Forces	*On the True Estimation of Living Forces* (1747)
Logic	*Immanuel Kant's Logic: A Handbook for Lectures,* edited by G. B. Jäsche (1800)
Metaphysical Foundations	*Metaphysical Foundations of Natural Science* (1786)
Morals	*Metaphysics of Morals* (1797)
Negative Magnitudes	*Attempt to Introduce the Concept of Negative Magnitudes into Philosophy* (1763)
New Elucidation	*A New Elucidation of the First Principles of Metaphysical Cognition* (1755)
Observations	*Observations on the Feeling of the Beautiful and Sublime* (1764)
Only Possible Argument	*The Only Possible Argument in Suppport of a Demonstration of the Existence of God* (1763)
Orientation	"What Does It Mean to Orient Oneself in Thought?" (1786)

Perpetual Peace	*Toward Perpetual Peace* (1795)
Physical Monadology	*The Employment in Natural Philosophy of Metaphysics combined with Geometry, of which Sample I Contains the Physical Monadology* (1756)
Practical Reason	*Critique of Practical Reason* (1788)
Prize Essay	*Inquiry concerning the Distinctness of the Principles of Natural Theology and Morals* (1764)
Progress	*What is the Real Progress that Metaphysics has made in Germany since the Time of Leibniz and Wolff*, edited by F. T. Rink (1804)
Prolegomena	*Prolegomena to Any Future Metaphysics That Shall Come Forth as Scientific* (1783)
Pure Reason	*Critique of Pure Reason* (1781, 1787)
R	*Reflexionen* (Kant's notes and marginalia in volumes 14–20, 23 of the Academy edition)
Religion	*Religion within the Boundaries of Mere Reason* (1793)
Theodicy	"On the Failure of all Philosophical Attempts at a Theodicy" (1791)
Theory and Practice	"On the common saying: That may be correct in theory but it is of no use in practice" (1793)
Universal History	"Ideas toward a Universal History from a Cosmopolitan Point of View" (1784)
Universal Natural History	*Universal Natural History and Theory of the Heavens* (1755)

Introduction
The starry heavens and the moral law

In what may be his single most famous passage, the first sentence of which was even inscribed on his tombstone, Immanuel Kant concluded his *Critique of Practical Reason* (1788) thus:

Two things fill the mind with ever new and increasing admiration and awe, the more often and steadily we reflect upon them: *the starry heavens above me and the moral law within me.* I do not seek or conjecture either of them as if they were veiled obscurities or extravagances beyond the horizon of my vision; I see them before me and connect them immediately with the consciousness of my existence. The first starts at the place that I occupy in the external world of the senses, and extends the connection in which I stand into the limitless magnitude of worlds upon worlds, systems upon systems, as well as into the boundless times of their periodic motion, their beginning and continuation. The second begins with my invisible self, my personality, and displays to me a world that has true infinity, but which can only be detected through the understanding, and with which . . . I know myself to be in not, as in the first case, merely contingent, but universal and necessary connection. The first perspective of a countless multitude of worlds as it were annihilates my importance as an *animal creature*, which must give the matter out of which it has grown back to the planet (a mere speck in the cosmos) after it has been (one knows not how) furnished with life-force for a short time. The second, on the contrary, infinitely elevates my worth, as an *intelligence*, through my personality, in which the moral law reveals to me a life independent of animality and even of the entire world of the senses, at least so far as may be judged from the purposive determination of my existence through this law, which is not limited to the conditions and boundaries of this life but reaches into the infinite.

(*Practical Reason,* 5:161–2)

Like many philosophers from the time of René Descartes and Thomas Hobbes onward, Kant tried to explain both the possibility of the new scientific knowledge, which had culminated in the mathematical worldview of Isaac Newton, and the possibility of human freedom. Unlike mechanists and empiricists from Hobbes to David Hume, Kant did not try to reduce human freedom to merely one more mechanism among those of a predictable nature. But unlike rationalists from Descartes to Gottfried Wilhelm Leibniz and Christian Wolff, Kant was not willing to ground human freedom on an alleged rational insight into some objectively perfect world only confusedly grasped by the senses. Instead, Kant ultimately came to see that the validity of both the laws of the starry skies above and the moral law within had to be sought in the legislative power of human intellect itself. It took Kant a long time to transcend the solutions of his predecessors, and perhaps he never fully clarified the nature of his own solution. Nonetheless, the idea to which he was ultimately drawn was the recognition that we can be certain of the foundations of physical science because we ourselves impose at least the basic form of scientific laws upon the nature that is given to us by our senses, yet that precisely because we ourselves impose the basic laws of science upon our world, we are also free to look at the world from a standpoint in which we are rational agents whose actions are chosen and not merely predicted in accordance with deterministic laws of (as we would now say) biology, psychology, or sociology. But in neither case, Kant ultimately came to recognize, is our freedom complete. Although we can legislate the basic forms of laws of nature, and indeed bring those laws ever closer to the details of nature through increasingly concrete conceptualizations, we can do so only asymptotically and must wait upon nature itself to fill in the last level of detail – which, because of the infinite divisibility and extendability of matter in space and time, nature will never quite do. And although we can autonomously legislate laws of reason for our actions, we must ultimately also look to nature, not only outside us but also within us, for cooperation in realizing the ends of those actions.

For Kant, then, his profound recognition of our legislative power in both science and morals, in both theoretical and practical reason, always had to be reconciled with an equally deep sense of the contingency of our success in both theory and practice. Even though he was hardly a conventionally religious thinker, Kant retained a sense of the limits of human powers of mind that is often missing from the wilder optimism of some of his rationalist predecessors and idealist successors. In spite of his sense of human limits, however, Kant radically and irreversibly transformed the nature of Western thought. After he wrote, no one could ever again think of either science or morality as a matter of the passive reception of entirely external truth or reality. In reflection upon the methods of science, as well as in many particular areas of science itself, the recognition of our own input into the world we claim to know has become inescapable. In the practical sphere, few can any longer take seriously the idea that moral reasoning consists in the discovery of external norms – for instance, objective perfections in the world or the will of God – as opposed to the construction for ourselves of the most rational way to conduct our lives both severally and jointly. Of course not even a Kant could have single-handedly transformed the self-conception of an entire culture; but at least at the philosophical level of the transformation of the Western conception of a human being from a mere spectator of the natural world and a mere subject in the moral world to an active agent in the creation of both, no one played a larger role than Immanuel Kant.

This extraordinary revolution was accomplished by a most unlikely individual. Unlike his predecessors such as Leibniz or John Locke who were men of means familiar with the corridors of power in the great European capitals and active in the political and religious struggles of their day, Kant was born into narrow straits in a small city virtually at the outermost limits of European civilization. Although Königsberg, where Kant was born into an artisan family in 1724, was a Hanseatic trading city with British connections as well as the administrative center of East Prussia, it was hardly London or Paris or Edinburgh or Amsterdam (the German city of Königsberg no longer exists, having been leveled in World War II and replaced with the Russian naval base Kaliningrad). Its university, which Kant entered at the age of sixteen after a preparatory education financially supported by the family's Pietist pastor and where he then spent most of his life, was barely more than a glorified high school, and even so Kant had to struggle in the poverty of a *Privatdozent* paid by the head (he quickly learned how to make his lectures very popular, however) until he was finally appointed to a proper chair in metaphysics at the age of forty-six. And after the decade of frequent publication that led to that appointment in 1770, Kant fell into a decade of silence that must have persuaded many that his long wait for a chair even at such a provincial university had been fully deserved. Yet from this dreary background there erupted a philosophical volcano the likes of which the world has rarely seen. Beginning in 1781, when he was already fifty-seven years old, Kant published a major work almost every year for more than a decade and a half. Foremost, of course, are his three great *Critiques*, the *Critique of Pure Reason* (1781, substantially revised in 1787), offering a new foundation for human knowledge and demolishing virtually all of traditional metaphysics; the *Critique of Practical Reason* (1788), inextricably linking human freedom to the moral law while attempting to reconstruct the most cherished ideas of traditional metaphysical belief on a practical rather than theoretical foundation; and the *Critique of the Power of Judgment* (1790), ostensibly bringing the seemingly disparate topics of aesthetic and teleological judgment into Kant's system but also struggling to refine and even substantially revise some of Kant's most basic conceptions about theoretical and practical reason and the relation between them. But these works were accompanied by a flood of others: In the *Prolegomena to Any Future Metaphysics That Shall Come Forth as Scientific* of 1783, Kant attempted to make the ideas of the first *Critique* accessible to a broader public while defending them from the first onslaught of criticism. He wrote several essays on the nature of enlightenment and the role of reason in history, including "Ideas towards a Universal History" and "What Is Enlightenment?" in 1784 and the "Conjectural Beginning of Human History" and "What Does it Mean to Orient Oneself in Thought?" of 1786. In the *Groundwork for the Metaphysics of Morals* of 1785, he made his boldest brief for the purity of the moral law and the certainty of human freedom. In the *Metaphysical Foundations of Natural Science* of 1786, he attempted to reconstruct Newtonian physics on the *a priori* basis offered by the principles of human knowledge demonstrated in the *Critique of Pure Reason*. In *Religion within the Boundaries of Mere Reason* of 1793 and *Conflict of the Faculties* of 1798, Kant argued firmly for the primacy of philosophy over religion in both its theoretical and institutional forms. And finally, in 1797, in the work at which he had been aiming most of his life, the *Metaphysics of Morals*, divided into a *Theory of Right* or political philosophy and *Theory of Virtue* or normative ethics, Kant demonstrated that his formal principle of morality justifies the use of coercion in the state yet simultaneously places strict limits on the ends the state can justifiably pursue by coercive means. He also demonstrated that the same principle implies a detailed series of ethical duties to ourselves and others that go beyond the limits of positive legislation in such a state. Even after all this work had been done, Kant continued to work at the foundations of scientific theory, trying to bring the basic principles of the *Metaphysical Foundations of Natural Science* into closer contact with physical reality, as well as with the latest advances in the sciences of chemistry and physics. The book that was to result from this work, however, remained incomplete before the wane of his powers and his death a few weeks short of his eightieth birthday in 1804. (The surviving sketches of this work have been known as the *Opus postumum* since their publication early in the last century.) Any one of these works – produced in spite of a daily load of three or four hours lecturing on subjects like anthropology and geography as well as metaphysics, ethics, and rational theology – would have made Kant a figure of note in the history of modern philosophy; together, they make him the center of that history.

As the whole of the book that follows can serve as only an introduction to the great range of Kant's work, it would certainly be hopeless to attempt to introduce the reader to all of it here. What follows will be only the briefest of sketches of the evolution of Kant's thought to help the reader situate what is offered in the essays of this collection.

Kant first came to attention with several scientific works: on graduation from the university in 1747 he published *On the True Estimation of Living Forces*, a piece on the debate between Leibnizians and Cartesians on the proper measure of forces; and at the time of his return to the university as a *Privatdozent* in 1755, after eight years as a household tutor for several East Prussian landowners, he published two more scientific works, the *Universal Natural History and Theory of the Heavens*, in which he showed how a system of heavenly bodies could have arisen out of an unformed nebula by purely mechanical means (what later became known as the Kant–Laplace cosmology), as well as a less important Latin dissertation on fire. In that same year he also published his first philosophical work, another Latin treatise, the *Principiorum primorum cognitionis metaphysicae nova dilucidatio* or *New Elucidation of the First Principles of Metaphysical Cognition*. This treatise, only thirty pages in length, is pregnant with Kant's philosophical future, for in it Kant revealed what was to become his lifelong preoccupation with the fundamental principles of natural science on the one hand and the problem of human freedom on the other. The positions for which the then thirty-one-year-old philosopher argued were far from his mature positions, but of great significance nonetheless. On the theoretical side, Kant accepted the basic rationalist enterprise of deriving the principle of sufficient reason from purely logical considerations (although he departed from the details of the proofs offered by Wolff and his follower Alexander Gottlieb Baumgarten, on whose textbooks of metaphysics and ethics Kant was to lecture for his entire career), but he also tried to show that this principle led to results precisely the opposite of those Leibniz and his followers had drawn from it. In particular, manifesting his future concern with the justification of the concept and principle of causation long before he had become familiar with Hume, Kant argued that the principle of sufficient reason implied rather than excluded real causation and interaction among substances, and that it even gave rise to a refutation of idealism. In this work Kant also introduced the first version of his critique of the ontological argument, that paradigmatic rationalist attempt to move directly from the structure of concepts to the structure of reality itself. On the practical side, Kant took the side of Leibnizian compatibilism between free will and determinism rather than the radical incompatibilism of the anti-Wolffian Pietist philosopher Christian August Crusius. (Kant's mature work on freedom of the will consists of a perhaps never quite completed attempt to reconcile the Leibnizian insight that we can only be responsible for actions produced in accordance with a law with the Crusian insight that responsibility requires a radical freedom of choice not compatible with the thoroughgoing predictability of human action.) Kant's major works of the 1750s were completed with another Latin scientific treatise, the *Physical Monadology*, in which he introduced the conception of attractive and repulsive forces that was to be essential to his attempts to provide a foundation for physical theory for the remainder of his life.

The philosophical work of the 1750s pointed Kant in the direction of a number of conclusions he subsequently wanted to establish. It turned out, however, that this work could not serve as a foundation for the later version of those conclusions, because Kant came to reject completely the rationalist methodology on which that work was based. Much of the 1760s was devoted to the demolition of rationalism, particularly of its two assumptions that all philosophical principles could be discovered by essentially logical methods alone and that the principles thus arrived at automatically give us insight into the ontology of objective reality. Kant's search for an alternative philosophical method in this decade was less successful than his demolition of all previous methods, however. In a work published in 1763, *The Only Possible Argument in Support of a Demonstration of the Existence of God*, Kant deepened the critique of the ontological argument already suggested in 1755. He accompanied that critique with an attack upon the two other forms of proof of the existence of God that had still enjoyed currency in eighteenth-century debates: the argument from the existence of a contingent creation to some necessary cause of it (what he called the "cosmological" argument), and the argument from design, according to which the orderly form of the world we observe around us can be explained only by the activity of an intelligent designer (what he called the argument from "physicotheology"). Yet Kant still argued that there was an *a priori* proof for the existence of God available, which had been overlooked by his predecessors: God could be demonstrated as the necessary ground of even the mere possibility of existence. Kant's confidence in this argument turned out to be a last gasp of rationalism. Later that same year, in his *Attempt to Introduce the Concept of Negative Magnitudes into Philosophy*, Kant introduced a fundamental distinction between *logical* and *real* opposition – a distinction of the kind that exists between a proposition and its negation on the one hand, and two physical forces trying to push a single object in opposite directions on the other. He intimated not only that this could be extended into a general distinction between logical and real relations, but also that all causal and existential relations would have to be understood as real rather than logical relations, and so could never be demonstrated by any purely logical means alone. But this result, reminiscent of Hume but more likely to have been influenced by Crusius at this point in time, left room for the conclusion that philosophy could have no distinctive nonanalytical yet not merely empirical methodology at all, a danger evident in Kant's essay *Inquiry concerning the Distinctness of the Principles of Natural Theology and Morals* published the following year (1764). Here Kant argued that, contrary to the dream of all rationalist philosophers since Descartes, philosophy could not use the same method as mathematics. Mathematics could begin with definitions and then prove indubitable results by constructing objects in accordance with those definitions and performing various operations upon them; philosophy, however, could never begin with definitions but only with "certain primary fundamental judgments" the analysis of which could lead to definitions as its conclusion, not its commencement. The origin and source of the certainty of these fundamental judgments remained obscure. In language reminiscent of both Crusius and British moral sense philosophers such as Francis Hutcheson (both of whom were influential for Kant at this time), he could say only that metaphysics had to begin with "certain inner experience, that is, by means of an immediate evident consciousness" that could give reliable information about the nature of a reality without immediately yielding "the whole essence of the thing" (2:286). At this point, it seems fair to say, Kant had hardly replaced the rejected method of the rationalists with a concrete proposal of his own for grounding first principles of either theoretical or practical reasoning.

This embarrassment remained evident in Kant's peculiar *Dreams of a Spirit-Seer* of 1766, which engaged in a lengthy examination of the spiritualist fantasies of the Swedish mystic Emanuel Swedenborg for the polemical purpose of showing that rationalist arguments for the simplicity, immateriality, and immortality of the soul offered by such philosophers as Wolff and Baumgarten were not any better grounded in empirical evidence. Like the essay *Negative Quantities*, the *Dreams of a Spirit-Seer* then concluded with the negative result that only empirical claims about "relations of cause and effect, substance, and action" could serve as starting points for philosophy, "but that when one finally comes to fundamental relations, then the business of philosophy is at an end, and we can never understand through reason how something can be a cause or have a force, but these relations must merely be derived from experience" (2:370). However, Kant completed this work with one point that was to remain unchallenged in all his subsequent thought about morality. All the metaphysical attempts to prove the immortality of the soul have been motivated by the need to allow for the reward of virtuous deeds performed in ordinary life, he argued, but are entirely unnecessary because only a morality that can motivate us to perform our duty without either promise of reward or fear of punishment is truly virtuous. Kant asked,

Is it good to be virtuous only because there is another world, or are actions rather not praised because they are good and virtuous in themselves? Does not the heart of man contain immediate moral precepts, and must one in order to motivate his disposition in accordance with all of these here always set the machinery of another world to work? Can one properly be called upright and virtuous who would gladly yield to his favorite vices if only he were not terrified of a future punishment, and would one not rather say that he avoids the expression of evil but nourishes a vicious disposition in his soul, that he loves the advantage of the simulation of virtuous action but hates virtue itself?

Obviously these questions needed no answer; so Kant could conclude that it is "more appropriate for human nature and the purity of morals to ground the expectation of a future world on the sensations of a well-disposed soul than to ground its good behavior on the hope of another world" (2:372–3). This insistence that virtue must move us by itself and that faith in religious doctrines of immortality and providence must not be the basis for morality but only a consequence of it were to reverberate in Kant's work for the rest of his life.

The *Dreams of a Spirit-Seer* thus reduced the need for a new method for metaphysics by freeing morality from the need for a positive metaphysical foundation altogether, although Kant was subsequently to recognize that morality requires at least a metaphysical proof that freedom is not impossible and that at least a "groundwork" for the metaphysics of morality was required. And the task of providing certain foundations for the Newtonian worldview without appealing to the method of mathematics still remained. Kant took a first step toward providing the latter if not the former in his next two works, an essay *Concerning the ultimate Ground of the Differentiation of Directions in Space* in 1768 and the dissertation *On the Form and Principles of the Sensible and Intelligible Worlds*, which he defended on his inauguration, at long last, as Professor of Metaphysics in 1770. In the first of these, Kant argued that the fact that two objects such as right- and left-handed gloves or screws could be described by identical conceptual relations but nevertheless be incongruent demonstrated that their orientation toward the axes of an absolute space was an irreducible fact about them, and thus proved the validity of the Newtonian conception of absolute space rather than the Leibnizian reduction of space to more primary and independent properties of substances. But the metaphysical possibility as well as the epistemology of Newtonian absolute space remained a mystery until Kant solved it in the inaugural dissertation by arguing that the human mind possesses two fundamentally distinct capacities of sensibility and intellect, not the single faculty for more or less clear and distinct thought that Leibniz and Wolff and all their followers had supposed, and that the existence of a unique and absolute space – and time – in which all the objects of our experience can be ordered reflects the inherent form of our capacity for sensible experience itself. Thus Kant took the fateful first step of arguing that the possibility and indeed the certainty of the spatiotemporal framework of Newtonian physics could be secured only by recognizing it to be the form of our own experience, even though this meant that the certainty of the foundations of Newtonian science could be purchased only by confining them to objects as we experience them through the senses – "appearances" or "phenomena" – rather than those objects as they might be in themselves and known to be by a pure intellect – "noumena." Thus Kant argued that absolute space is "not some adumbration or schema of the object, but only a certain law implanted in the mind by which it coordinates for itself the sensa that arise from the presence of the object" (§4, 2:393). As for the further principles of the scientific worldview as well as the metaphysics of morality, however, the *Dissertation* did not merely fail to demonstrate any progress, but in some ways even regressed from the critical position of the 1760s. A metaphysical insight that all of the substances of the world constitute a single whole could be grounded, Kant claimed, in intellectual insight into their dependence on a common extramundane cause (God, of course). More purely intramundane or immanent foundations for science, such as the maxims that "*All things in the universe take place in accordance with the order of nature*," "*Principles are not to be multiplied beyond what is absolutely necessary*," and "*No matter at all comes into being or passes away*," he could only introduce as mere "*principles of convenience*" (§30, 2:419). Morality, finally, Kant was suddenly prepared to treat as a matter requiring metaphysical, indeed "dogmatic" insight into "some exemplar only to be conceived by the pure intellect and which is a common measure for all other things insofar as they are realities." Kant continued:

This exemplar is NOUMENAL PERFECTION. This perfection is what it is either in a theoretic sense or in a practical sense. In the first sense it is the highest being, GOD, in the second sense it is MORAL PERFECTION. So *moral philosophy*, in as much as it supplies the first *principles of critical judgment*, is cognized only by the pure intellect and itself belongs to pure philosophy. And the man who reduced its criteria to the sense of pleasure or pain, Epicurus, is very rightly blamed.   (§9, 2:396)

Kant was certainly to retain the idea that morality could not be grounded in empirical facts about what is pleasurable and what is painful, and that its principle must come from pure reason instead; but any sense that recognition of such a principle required metaphysical cognition of a reality lying beyond ourselves, as knowledge of God does, was ultimately to be banished from his thought. This meant that the inaugural dissertation had left entirely untouched all the work of grounding foundational principles for scientific knowledge beyond its abstract spatiotemporal framework, as well as the task of explaining both the nature of moral knowledge and the possibility of freedom in spite of the scientific worldview.

Kant struggled with these unresolved difficulties for a decade and then adopted the extraordinary objective of eliminating the lingering noumenal metaphysics of the inaugural dissertation from the foundations of both science and morality and showing how all of the fundamental principles of both science and morality, like the form of space and time, are products of our own thought alone, although we cannot just ruthlessly impose these principles upon the data of our senses but must engage in a never-ending task of accommodating them to the particularity of experience. It would be misleading to suppose, however, that Kant had clearly formulated the idea of accomplishing this objective in his three great *Critiques* before commencing their composition; in fact, the evidence strongly suggests that Kant had no idea that a *Critique of Practical Reason* would be required when he first finished the *Critique of Pure Reason*, and still had no idea that a *Critique of the Power of Judgment* would be needed even when the *Critique of Practical Reason* had been finished. Each of the latter two *Critiques* revises as well as extends the insights of its predecessors. Indeed, for all its appearance of systematicity,

Kant's thought was in a state of constant evolution throughout his life.

The evolution of Kant's mature thought obviously begins with the *Critique of Pure Reason* as first published in 1781, which turned out not to be the complete foundation for both science and morality that Kant originally intended it to be, but which certainly remained the basis for all that followed. The agenda for this work is enormous but can be brought under the two headings suggested by our opening quote. On the one hand, Kant aims to provide a general foundation for the laws of science, a metaphysics of experience that will generalize the approach taken to space and time alone in the *Dissertation* by showing that there are also concepts of the understanding and principles of judgment, including general forms of the laws of the conservation of matter, universal causation, and universal interaction, that can be shown to be certain by their *a priori* origin in the structure of human thought itself, although the cost of this certainty is that we must also recognize "that our representation of things, as they are given to us, does not conform to these things as they are in themselves, but rather that these objects, as appearances, conform to our manner of representation" (B xx). On the other hand, the very fact that the universal validity of the foundational principles of the scientific worldview, including that of universal causation, can be proved only for the appearances of things means that we can at least coherently consider the possibility that things as they are in themselves may not be governed by these laws, indeed may be governed by other laws; in particular, we can coherently consider that at the deepest level we ourselves are free agents bound only by the laws of morality and not by the deterministic laws of nature. Kant sums up this complex result thus:

On a hasty overview of this work one will believe himself to perceive that its use is only *negative*, namely that we can never dare to exceed the bounds of experience with speculative reason, and that is indeed its first use. But this then becomes *positive* if one becomes aware that the principles with which speculative reason dares to exceed its bounds would not in fact have the inevitable result of *extending* but, more closely considered, that of *restricting* our use of reason, in that they would really extend the bounds of sensibility, to which they actually belong, to everything, and so threaten to obstruct the pure (practical) use of reason. Thus a critique, which limits the former, is so far to be sure *negative*, but, insofar as it also removes a hindrance that threatens to restrict or even destroy the latter use of reason, is in fact of *positive* and very important use, as soon as one is convinced that it yields an entirely necessary practical use of pure reason (the moral use), in which it is unavoidably extended beyond the limits of sensibility, but thereby requires no help from speculative reason, but must nevertheless be secured from its opposition in order not to land in contradiction with itself.   (B xxiv–xxv)

Or as Kant more succinctly but also more misleadingly puts it, "I must therefore suspend *knowledge* in order to make room for *belief*," or, as it is often translated, *"faith"* (B xxx). This is misleading if it is taken to mean that Kant intends to argue that knowledge must be limited in order to allow us some nonrational basis for belief about important matters of morality. Rather, what Kant means is that the limitation of the foundational principles of the scientific worldview to the way things appear to us is necessary not only to explain its own certainty but also to allow us to conceive of ourselves as rational agents who are not constrained by the deterministic grip of nature but can freely govern ourselves by the moral law as practical reason (although certainly not all forms of religious faith) requires.

The steps that Kant goes through to secure this result are intricate, and some of them will be treated in much more detail in what follows. The barest sketch will have to suffice here. Kant begins in the "Transcendental Aesthetic," or theory of sensibility, by reiterating the argument of 1770 that all of our particular experiences of objects, or empirical intuitions, necessarily come to us in spatiotemporal form, and also that we have *a priori* insight into the uniqueness and infinitude of space and time, both of which can be explained only on the supposition that space and time are the pure forms of our intuition of all objects, forms originating in the structure of our own sensibility and not anything derived from the independent properties of objects as they are in themselves. In the *Prolegomena* of 1783 and the second edition of the *Critique* of 1787, Kant supplements this with a specific argument that the propositions of mathematics, especially geometry, are nontautologous and informative, or synthetic rather than analytic, yet are known *a priori*, which can also be explained only on the supposition that they describe the structure of subjective forms of intuition rather than independent properties of objects (see especially A 47–8/B 64–5).

In the "Transcendental Analytic," or theory of understanding, Kant extends this argument by showing that in addition to *a priori* forms of intuition there are *a priori* concepts of the pure understanding, or categories, as well as *a priori* principles of judgment that are necessary conditions for our own thought of objects rather than principles derived from any particular experience of those objects. Kant's argument for this result proceeds through several stages. First, he argues that the fact that our knowledge of objects always takes the form of *judgment* and that judgment has certain inherent forms, discovered by logic, implies that there must be certain basic correlative concepts necessary for thinking of the *objects* of those judgments (the "metaphysical deduction"). Next, he tries to argue that our very certainty of the numerical identity of our self throughout all our different experiences implies that we must connect those experiences according to rules furnished by the understanding itself, which are none other than the same categories required by the logical forms of judgment (the "transcendental deduction"). Finally, and most convincingly, he tries to show in detail that the ability to make objective judgments about objects given in space and time (which are missing from most of the transcendental deduction) requires that we bring them under concepts of extensive and intensive magnitude and under principles of conservation, causation, and interaction (the "system of principles," especially the "analogies of experience"). And indeed, Kant finally argues, the ability to make determinate temporal sense of our own experiences, considered even as merely subjective states, requires that we see them as caused by such a law-governed realm of external objects (the "refutation of idealism"). Kant describes the underlying assumption of this extended argument thus:

However exaggerated, however absurd it may sound to say that the understanding is itself the source of the laws of nature, thus of the formal unity of nature, such an assertion is nevertheless right and appropriate to the object, namely experience. To be sure, empirical laws as such can by no means derive their origin from pure understanding, just as little as the immeasurable multiplicity of appearances can be adequately comprehended from the pure form of sensible intuition. But all empirical laws are only particular determinations of the pure laws of understanding, under which and in accordance with the norm of which they are first possible and the appearances assume a lawful form, just as all appearances, in spite of the diversity of their

empirical form, must nevertheless always be in accord with the conditions
of the pure form of sensibility.   (A 127–8)

In the longest part of the work, the "Transcendental Dialectic," Kant
then argues that most of the doctrines of traditional metaphysics are
fallaciously derived by attempting to use concepts of the understanding without corresponding evidence from sensibility. These are fallacies, he adds, into which we do not just happen to fall but to which
we are pushed by reason's natural inclination to discover a kind of
completeness in thought that the indefinitely extendable bounds of
space and time can never yield. Thus we mistake the logical simplicity of the thought of the self for knowledge of a simple, immaterial,
and immortal soul (the "paralogisms of pure reason"), and we think
that the mere idea of a ground of all possibility (the "ideal of pure reason") is equivalent to knowledge of the necessary existence of such a
ground. (Kant now brings his critique of the ontological argument to
bear on the one possible basis for a demonstration of the existence of
God that he had spared in his work of that title of 1763.) Little can be
salvaged from these misguided metaphysical doctrines, but the case
is somewhat different with the metaphysical paradoxes that Kant
describes under the title of "antinomies of pure reason." Operating
without any notice of the need for evidence from the senses and thus
of the limits of sensibility, pure reason manages to convince itself
both that the world must be finite in space and time and that it must
also be infinitely extended in both dimensions, that the division of
substances must yield the smallest possible particles and yet that
it cannot, that there must be a causality of freedom in addition to
the mechanism of nature and yet that there can be no such thing,
and finally that there must be a necessary being at the ground of the
series of contingent existences and yet again that there cannot be
any such thing. The first two paradoxes may simply be set aside by
recognizing that space and time are, again, nothing but the forms of
our own intuitions, and that things as they are in themselves, which
reason takes itself to know, are thus neither spatially nor temporally
finite nor infinite. But the case is different with the last two antinomies. Here, no longer dealing with quantitative concepts that are
necessarily linked to the structure of sensibility, Kant argues that
while we can conceive of the empirical or phenomenal world only as
a realm of contingent existences entirely governed by causal laws of

nature, we can at least coherently consider that the realm of things in themselves lying behind the appearances of the empirical world not only contains a necessary being but, more important, contains free and not merely determined actions. Thus, Kant claims, the critique of traditional metaphysics at least leaves open the *possibility* of freedom. Then he can conclude:

We require the principle of the causality of appearances among themselves in order to seek and to be able to provide natural conditions for natural occurrences, i.e., causes in appearance. If this is conceded and is not weakened through any exception, then the understanding, which in its empirical employment sees in all events nothing but nature and is justified in so doing, has everything that it can require, and physical explanations can proceed unhindered on their way. Now it does not do the least violence to this, if one assumes, even if it is otherwise only imagined, that among natural causes there are also some that have a faculty that is intelligible only in that their determination to action never rests on empirical conditions, but on mere grounds of reason, though in such a way that the *action in the appearance* from this cause is in accord with all the laws of empirical causality.

(A 545/B 573)

Kant concludes, therefore, that we can at least consistently conceive of events that fit into the seamless web of natural causality yet are also the products of the free exercise of the rational agency of natural agents considered as they are in themselves. In thinking of ourselves as moral agents, we can think of ourselves in precisely this twofold way.

It is not clear whether Kant thought it would be necessary to say more about freedom when he finished the *Critique of Pure Reason*, but he shortly realized that it was. A further proof, indeed a theoretical proof, that freedom is not just possible but actual is one of the two main items on the agenda of the *Groundwork for the Metaphysics of Morals* of 1785, along with a clear formulation of the fundamental law of morality itself and a sketch of how such a principle would give rise to the specific set of duties that Kant had always intended to describe in a metaphysics of morals. Kant argued that not only the concepts of good will and duty, which could be derived from ordinary consciousness, and the concept of a categorical imperative, which could be derived from more technical moral philosophy, but also his own conception of humanity as an end in itself whose free agency must always be preserved and when possible enhanced, all give rise to the fundamental moral principle that one should act only on maxims or policies of action that could be made into a universal law or assented to, made into an end of their own, by all agents who might be affected by the action. Such a principle Kant characterizes as the law of pure practical reason, reflecting the requirements that are imposed on actions not from any external source but from the nature of reason itself. But he also argued that to know that we are actually bound by such a moral principle, we must know that we really are rational agents capable of freely acting in accordance with the principle of pure reason regardless of what might be predicted on the basis of our passions and inclinations, indeed our entire prior history and psychology. Kant thus now felt compelled to prove that human freedom is not just possible but actual. Although he initially suggests that the very idea of ourselves as agents implies that we conceive of ourselves as acting under rules of our own choice, he attempts to go beyond this in order to deliver a metaphysical proof of the actuality of freedom. He argues that in ourselves as well as all other things we must distinguish between appearance and reality. He then equates this distinction with one between that which is passive and that which is active in ourselves, which he in turn equates with the distinction between sensation and reason. Thus Kant infers that we must assign to ourselves a faculty of reason rooted in our nature as things in themselves and thus free to act without constraint by the causal laws governing mere appearance. Kant concludes:

A rational being must therefore regard itself as an *intelligence* (therefore not from the side of its lower powers) as belonging to the world of understanding, not of sense; thus it has two standpoints from which it can consider itself and know the laws of the use of its powers, thus of all of its actions, *first*, insofar as it belongs to the world of senses, under natural laws (heteronomy), *second*, as belonging to the intelligible world, under laws which, independent from nature, are not empirical but grounded in reason alone.   (4:452)

Unfortunately, in spite of his attempt to avoid such a problem, Kant's argument is circular. It derives our possession of a spontaneous and efficacious faculty of reason from our membership in the world of things in themselves precisely by construing that world as an *intelligible* world – that is to say, nothing less than a world conceived to be essentially rational and understood by reason itself. In other words, Kant's argument – not for the content but for the actuality and efficacy of pure practical reason – violates one of the most fundamental strictures of his own *Critique of Pure Reason*. It depends on interpreting our ultimate reality not as noumenon in a merely *"negative* sense" but as noumenon in a *"positive* sense," that is, not just something that is *not* known through sensibility but something that *is* known through pure reason (B 307).

Kant never doubted that he had correctly formulated the content of pure practical reason through the requirement of the universal acceptability of the maxims of intended actions, but he quickly recognized the inadequacy of the *Groundwork*'s proof that we actually have a pure practical reason. He thus radically revised his approach to the problem of freedom in the *Critique of Practical Reason*, published only three years later in 1788. Kant does not call this work a critique of *pure* practical reason, like the earlier critique of pure theoretical reason, because whereas the point of the former work was to show that theoretical reason oversteps its bounds when it tries to do without application to empirical data, in the case of practical reason the point is precisely to show that it is *not* limited to application to empirically given inclinations and intentions but has a pure principle of its own. Kant now surrenders the objective of giving a theoretical proof of the efficacy of pure practical reason, however. While both the *Groundwork* and the new *Critique* agree that a will bound by the moral law must be a free will and that only a free will can be bound by the moral law – what has come to be known as his "reciprocity thesis" (5:28–9) – Kant's strategy is now not to prove that we are bound by the moral law by offering a theoretical proof that we possess a free will but rather simply to argue that we must possess a free will because of our indubitable recognition that we are in fact bound by the moral law. "The thing is strange enough and has no parallel in the entire remainder of practical reason," Kant admits; nevertheless, he insists:

The *a priori* thought of a possible universal law-giving ... without borrowing anything from experience or any external will, is given as an unconditioned law. .... One can call the consciousness of this fundamental law a fact of reason, since one cannot speciously derive it from any antecedent data of reason, e.g., the consciousness of freedom (since this is not antecedently given to us), rather since it presses itself upon us as a synthetic *a priori* proposition, which is not grounded in any intuition, whether pure or empirical, although it would be analytic if one presupposed the freedom of the will. . . . But in order to regard this law as *given* without misinterpretation one must well note that it is not an empirical fact but the sole fact of pure reason.   (5:31)

Theoretical philosophy can prove the possibility of freedom of the will, Kant continues to believe, but not its actuality; this can follow only from our firm consciousness – our conscience, one might say – of being bound by the moral law itself. If we have a pure practical reason, there is no problem explaining how it binds us, precisely because the law that binds us comes from within ourselves and not from anywhere else, not from any other will, not the will of a Hobbesian sovereign nor even from the will of God; but our proof that we have such a pure practical reason is precisely our recognition that we bind ourselves by its law.

Although the proof of the actuality of freedom can only appeal to our conviction of our obligation under the moral law, Kant has no hesitation about the power of our freedom. Kant is more convinced than ever that the scope of our freedom is unlimited, that no matter what might seem to be predicted by our prior history we always retain the freedom to make the morally correct choice, even if the very history of our empirical character itself must be revised in order to make our freely chosen action compatible with natural law:

The same subject, who is also conscious of himself as thing in himself, considers his own existence, *so far as it does not stand under conditions of time*, as itself determinable only through laws that he gives himself through reason, and in this his existence nothing is antecedent to his determination of his will, but every action and every determination of his existence changing in accord with his inner sense, even the entire course of his existence as a sensible being is never to be regarded in his consciousness of his intelligible existence as anything but the consequence and never the determining ground of his causality as *noumenon*.   (5:97–8)

The *Critique of Practical Reason* also includes Kant's attempt to reconstruct two of the most cherished doctrines of traditional metaphysics, the existence of God and the immortality of the soul. He argues that morality enjoins on us not just the effort to be motivated by duty alone but also the end of attaining happiness in proportion to our virtue. Moral motivation alone may be the sole unconditioned good, but it is not the complete or highest good until happiness in proportion to our worthiness to be happy through our virtue is added to it. But we have no reason to believe that we can approach purity of will in our terrestrial life spans alone, or that our virtue will be accompanied with proportionate happiness by natural mechanisms alone. We must thus postulate, although always as a matter of practical presupposition and never as a theoretical doctrine, that our souls can reach purity in immortality and that there is a God to redress the natural disproportion between virtue and happiness. But Kant insisted always that these practical postulates could never enter into our motivation to be moral, and that they would undermine the purity of that motivation if they did; they rather flesh out the conditions presupposed by the rationality of moral action and so allow us to act on that pure motivation without threat of self-contradiction.

Kant remained content with this doctrine for the remainder of his life, but the problem of freedom continued to gnaw at him; and as he refined his solution to the problem of freedom he refined his theory of the foundations of science as well. The evidence for this further struggle is found in his last great critique, the *Critique of the Power of Judgment* of 1790. This work ostensibly deals with the rational foundations of two forms of judgment not considered in Kant's previous work, aesthetic judgments of taste about natural or artistic beauty and sublimity, and teleological judgments about the role of purpose in natural organisms and systems; but Kant's reflections on these two species of what he calls reflective judgment touch on larger issues as well.

Kant begins the work with a reflection upon the role of the ideal of systematicity in the attempt to move from the abstract level of the categories to concrete knowledge of empirical laws of nature. Whereas the *Critique of Pure Reason* had assigned the search for systematicity to the faculty of reason, suggesting that it is required for the sake of completeness but has nothing to do with the truth of empirical laws themselves, the *Critique of the Power of Judgment* assigns it to the faculty of reflective judgment, suggesting that we can never get from the categories to particular empirical laws except by trying to place individual hypotheses in the context of a system of such laws. Because such a system is always an ideal that is never actually completed, however, this implies that the search for empirical law is necessarily open-ended. Thus we can approach but never actually reach certainty about any individual law of nature, and the same limitation applies also regarding the completeness in the whole system of such laws. This was a perspective that Kant attempted to explore further in his *Opus postumum*, which fittingly itself remained incomplete.

Kant then introduces the more specific subjects of aesthetic and teleological judgment with the claim that there is a "great abyss" between the concepts of nature and of freedom that must yet be bridged (5:195). Since in the *Critique of Practical Reason* he had argued that the domination of reason over the world of sense must be complete, it is not immediately apparent what gulf Kant has in mind, but his meaning gradually emerges. In the first half of the work, the "Critique of Aesthetic Judgment," Kant is concerned to show that the existence and power of freedom are not just accessible to philosophical theory but can be made palpable to us as embodied and therefore feeling human beings as well. His argument in the case of the experience of the sublime is obvious. Vast and powerful objects in nature exceed the grasp of our imagination and understanding, but our indifference to their threats of intellectual and even physical injury is an exhilarating revelation of the power and primacy of practical reason within ourselves. Kant's argument about beauty is more complex, however. The experience of beauty is initially characterized as one in which sensibility or imagination and understanding reach a state of harmony without the constraint of any concept, moral concepts of the good included. But then it turns out that in virtue of its very freedom from constraint by such concepts the experience of beauty can serve as a symbol of our freedom in morality itself and make this freedom palpable to us. In addition, although our first layer of pleasure in natural beauty is free of any antecedent interests, the very fact that nature offers us beauty without intervention of our own is some evidence that it is hospitable to our own interests, those of morality included, and we take additional pleasure in the realization of this fact. Here Kant does not treat us as simply dominating nature by our reason, but rather more contingently finding that our reason allows us to be at home in nature.

Kant's argument about teleological judgment is even more complicated, and, although the force of Kant's treatment of organisms has certainly been undercut by the success of the Darwinian theory of evolution, the "Critique of Teleological Judgment" remains profoundly revealing of Kant's philosophical sensibility. Kant argues that organisms require us to see the parts as the cause of the whole but also the whole as the cause of its parts. The latter requirement violates the unidirectional nature of our conception of mechanical causation – we cannot conceive how a whole that comes into being only gradually from its parts can nevertheless be the cause of the properties of those parts (here is where the theory of natural selection removes the difficulty). And so, Kant argues, we can explain the relation only by supposing that the nature of the parts is determined by an antecedent *conception* of the whole employed by a designer of the organism, although we can never have theoretical evidence of the existence of such an intelligence. Next Kant argues that we cannot suppose an intelligent designer to have acted without a *purpose* as well as a *plan*, but that the only kind of nonarbitrary purpose that we can introduce into natural systems and indeed into nature as a system as a whole is something that is an end in itself – which can be nothing other than human freedom, the sole source of intrinsic and unconditioned value. Besides all of humankind's merely natural ends, desires, and conceptions of happiness that are of no more value than any other creature's and to which nature is not in any case particularly hospitable, "there remains as that which in respect to nature can be the final purpose that lies beyond it and in which its ultimate purpose can be seen only [mankind's] formal, subjective condition, namely [our] capacity to set our own ends in general" (§83, 5:431). Mankind is "the only natural being in whom a supersensible faculty (of *freedom*) can be known," and only as "the subject of morality" can humanity constitute a "final purpose to which the whole of nature is teleologically subordinated" (§84, 5:435–6). Again, Kant subtly revises his earlier point of view: Human freedom is not to be seen just as a force entirely external to nature, but as the ultimate aim of nature itself.

Kant is still careful to insist that this is not a perspective that can be justified by theoretical or scientific reasoning, but rather a point of view that is at least compatible with scientific reasoning and recommended for its value to practical reason. But his expression of this caution in the *Critique of the Power of Judgment* also suggests a subtle shift in his view of the status of scientific law itself. In his first two critiques, Kant had argued that the application of the fundamental principles of theoretical knowledge and thus the foundations of science to the world of experience was without exception, indeed as he called it "constitutive" of the phenomenal realm, and that there could be room for a conception of human freedom only because we could also regard ourselves as things in themselves whose nature is not determined by the laws of appearance. Now, however, Kant suggests another view, namely, the idea that *both* the causal laws of nature *and* the laws of reason that guide our freely chosen actions are "regulative principles" that we bring to nature. He argues that an antinomy can be avoided only by supposing that the "maxim of reflection" that "All generation of material things and their forms must be estimated as possible according to merely mechanical laws" and the maxim that "Some products of material nature cannot be estimated as possible according to merely mechanical laws," that they instead require "an entirely different law of causality, namely, that of final causes," are both "regulative principles for the investigation" of nature (§70, 5:387). He thus suggests that the deterministic perspective of the mechanical worldview is not something that we can simply impose on nature, but a perspective that we bring to bear on it just as we do the perspective of freedom itself. The latter perspective Kant now also explicitly describes as a regulative ideal:

Although an intelligible world, in which everything would be actual solely because it is (as something good) possible, and even freedom itself as the formal condition of such a world, is an excessive concept, which is not suitable to determine any constitutive principle, an object and its objective reality: Nevertheless in accordance with the constitution of our (partially sensible) nature and faculty it serves for us and all rational creatures standing in connection with the sensible world, insofar as we can represent ourselves in accordance with the constitution of our reason, as a universal *regulative* principle, which does not determine the constitution of freedom as the form of causality objectively, but rather, and with no less validity than if this were the case, makes the rule of actions in accordance with this idea a command for everyone.   (§76, 5:404)

Here Kant not only suggests that we cannot give a theoretical proof of the existence of freedom, but also that we do not even have to regard it as a metaphysical fact about some purely noumenal aspect of our being at all, and can instead bring the principle of practical reason as a rule for actions to bear on our natural existence, something we can do precisely because the deterministic picture of natural causation necessary for scientific explanation and prediction is also only a perspective that we ourselves bring to bear on nature. Because the presuppositions of both science and morality are principles that we ourselves bring to bear on nature, Kant finally recognizes, they must ultimately be compatible.

Having finally reached this recognition so late in his career, Kant never worked out the details, although that may have been the last thing he was trying to do in the latest stage of his work on the *Opus postumum* just before his death. Nor is it clear that any philosopher since has taken up the challenge of fleshing out this suggestion. Perhaps that is the most vital task Kant leaves for us.

I will end this Introduction with a brief guide to the essays that follow.

The first nine chapters concern Kant's theoretical philosophy, that is, his theory of knowledge in general and of mathematics and natural science in particular as well as his critique of previous metaphysics – the central subjects of the *Critique of Pure Reason*. In Chapter 1, Philip Kitcher explores Kant's conception of *a priori* knowledge, the term Kant introduced to capture the idea that genuine philosophical knowledge, if such exists, possesses a kind of universality and necessity that can never be derived from any particular experiences of objects. In Chapter 2, Gary Hatfield situates Kant's views on space and time, but primarily space, in their historical context. As Hatfield argues, Kant successfully demonstrated the intuitional character of our representation of space, but his view that we have an *a priori* intuition of space as Euclidean cannot survive the mathematical and physical revolutions of the nineteenth and twentieth centuries. In Chapter 3, Lisa Shabel examines in detail Kant's arguments that mathematical cognition is not only *a priori* but also synthetic, that is, it does more than merely explicate the meaning of our mathematical concepts. She then discusses the role of this position in Kant's arguments for transcendental idealism, his doctrine that our synthetic *a priori* cognition must be confined to the appearances of things and does not characterize them as they are in themselves. In Chapter 4, Béatrice Longuenesse turns from Kant's theory of the pure intuitions that underlie mathematics to the pure concepts of the understanding that underlie all of our cognition. She describes Kant's conceptions of logic and judgment, or his attempt to derive a complete list of the pure conceptions of the understanding or fundamental categories for conceiving of objects from the fundamental characteristics of judgment in the so-called "Metaphysical Deduction of the Categories," and examines the impact of Kant's thought on these matters on such later thinkers as Hegel, Heidegger, and Frege. In Chapter 5, Patricia Kitcher turns to a central theme of Kant's "Transcendental Deduction of the Categories," namely, his conception of the human mind as actively imposing the categories identified in the "Metaphysical Deduction" on our experience. Kant's conception of the mind as actively constituting knowledge rather than passively receiving it has been extraordinarily influential on subsequent philosophy, as Kitcher suggests. In Chapter 6, Arthur Melnick offers a distinctive reconstruction of Kant's central arguments for the indispensable role of the categories of substance and causation in our experience of a world of determinate objects, and argues that Kant's position provides the basis for an argument against W. V. O. Quine's well-known doctrine of "ontological relativity." In Chapter 7, Ralph Walker turns to the question of whether Kant introduced a general style of "transcendental argument" to answer skepticism, and argues that Kant's method of transcendental argument ironically undermines his own transcendental idealism. In Chapter 8, Karl Ameriks contrasts Kant's critique of traditional metaphysics as a purported source of theoretical cognition to his novel alternative, a metaphysics based on practical rather than theoretical grounds, and examines the revival of speculative metaphysics that immediately followed Kant's critique of it. This chapter could provide the transition to the second half of the collection, but before we turn to Kant's practical philosophy Michael Friedman examines the work that Kant himself wrote before turning the major part of his energy to the latter, namely, the *Metaphysical Foundations of Natural Science*. Friedman argues that though Kant in this work was attempting to establish the foundations of Newtonian science in particular, his method of identifying the constitutive presuppositions of science is by no means completely undermined by the subsequent revision of Newtonianism in the nineteenth and twentieth centuries.

The next six chapters deal with Kant's practical philosophy, that is, his moral and political thought. In Chapter 10, Allen Wood demonstrates how Kant's various formulations of the "categorical imperative," that is, the supreme principle of morality as it presents itself to human beings, all depend upon his central conception of autonomy, and should be understood collectively as a systematic presentation of the normative implications of this conception. In Chapter 11, Henry Allison examines the relationship between the normative notion of autonomy and the metaphysical conception of the freedom or spontaneity of the will. The next four essays turn to specific types of duty that arise from the fundamental principle of morality in the concrete circumstances of human life. Kant divided these duties into duties of right or justice, that is, those that can and should be enforced through the instrument of the polity or state, and duties of virtue or ethics, that is, our obligations to ourselves and those of our obligations to others that can be enforced only through our own consciences and should not be coercively enforced through juridical and political institutions. In Chapter 12, Robert Pippin examines Kant's foundation of both the necessity and the limits of the state in the conception of external freedom or freedom of action. In Chapter 13, Jane Kneller unpacks Kant's convoluted thought about human sexuality and its impact on his conception of the legal rights associated with marriage, an area in which Kant's thought is both liberal and conservative. In Chapter 14, Pauline Kleingeld turns to Kant's influential thought on peace and international law, examining the difficult question of whether Kant thought that peace could be guaranteed by an international league of free republics or only by a single although still republican international government. Finally, in Chapter 15, Lara Denis provides a sympathetic interpretation of Kant's thought about virtue, showing how Kant grounded the various human virtues in the fundamental principle of morality without succumbing to the unrealistic rigorism of which some subsequent advocates of "virtue ethics" accuse him.

The next two chapters turn to Kant's two other great concerns after the *Critique of Pure Reason*, the theory of aesthetics and teleology on the one hand, and the philosophy of religion on the other. In Chapter 16, Paul Guyer suggests that the three apparently diverse topics of the *Critique of the Power of Judgment* – the systematicity of scientific concepts, the universal validity of judgments of taste, and the possibility of a teleological as well as a mechanical conception of nature – can all be related as part of Kant's lifelong debate with David Hume. In Chapter 17, Frederick Beiser defends an interpretation of Kant's "moral faith" or practical belief according to which Kant by no means completely rejects traditional religious belief.

Finally, in Chapter 18, Manfred Kuehn gives us a fascinating glimpse into the immediate reception of Kant's *Critique of Pure Reason*, showing how the response of Kant's contemporaries both spurred Kant's enormous productivity in the years following 1781 and helped shape the further course of Kant's thought as well as the form of its expression. This essay could have been placed at several points in the volume, at the beginning or between the essays on Kant's theoretical philosophy and his practical philosophy; but coming at the end it can serve as a concluding reminder of the profound unity of Kant's thought in spite of the immense diversity of his philosophical subjects.

1 "A Priori"*

I. ORIGINS

Although Kant introduced many pieces of technical terminology to articulate the themes of his critical philosophy, perhaps none is more pervasive than "*a priori.*" The initial care, and apparent precision, with which the term enters the *Critique of Pure Reason* quickly gives way to profligacy, as all sorts of things come to be hailed as *a priori.* My aim in this essay is to bring some order to Kant's many-sided usage.

One source of Kant's conception is evident. Many of his predecessors had recognized that there are apparently items of human knowledge that do not rest upon our everyday processes of sensory observation, and had supposed that there must be other sources that deliver knowledge of these types. In the more ambitious versions of this idea, there is a rich collection of "truths of reason," among which earlier philosophers had sometimes counted controversial metaphysical principles, as well as generalizations they took to be fundamental to nascent physical science.[1]

Even those most firmly committed to empiricism, and to the thesis that human knowledge is based upon sensory observation, made a place for something like *a priori* knowledge. The classical British Empiricists were unwilling to grant that our knowledge of logical truths and of the principles of mathematics – by which they understood basic arithmetical identities and Euclidean geometry – is justified by some process of sensory experience. What types of experience might be pertinent here? Instead, they endeavored to reconcile the distinctive status of logic and mathematics with the general empiricist commitment by proposing that these areas of our knowledge were, in an important sense, not genuinely concerned with the world, but rather unfolded relations among our concepts.[2] Believing that subjects who have a particular concept in their repertoire are able to produce for themselves an image associated with that concept, they suggested that those who have acquired the logical, arithmetical, and geometrical concepts are able to display to themselves appropriate images and discern "with the mind's eye" the relations that logical, arithmetical, or geometrical truths embody. This account is most plausible for the case of geometry, where, we may suppose, the aspiring geometer, equipped with the concepts of line, point, circle, and so forth, will be able to generate images from which the standard Euclidean axioms can be read off.

We can thus envisage Kant reading his predecessors, identifying a broad consensus on the view that logical and mathematical knowledge is not justified on the basis of sensory experience, as well as recognizing a swirl of controversy about whether nonempirical sources – perhaps just like those that allow for knowledge of logic and mathematics, perhaps distinctive – generate other types of knowledge (metaphysical principles, foundations for physical science, or whatever). Kant's own conception of apriority could then be seen as an attempt to deal systematically with the contrast between the empirical and the nonempirical that earlier philosophers had employed, to focus issues about logical and mathematical knowledge, to classify the empiricist and rationalist strategies for delineating the kinds of nonempirical knowledge, and to resolve the disputes about the extent of our nonempirical knowledge. From this perspective, the strategy of the *Prolegomena* appears quite straightforward: previous philosophy has failed to understand the crucial question that underlay these disputes, namely, the problem of how synthetic *a priori* knowledge is possible.

Matters are, however, much more complicated. Kant's distinctive epistemological program not only takes up the traditional questions about the scope of nonempirical knowledge, it also transforms epistemology more generally through the insertion of the notion of apriority into a far wider range of discussions. I shall try to explain how this occurs, but, before we attend to the full complexities, it is worth trying to achieve a clear vision of one important facet of Kant's thought about the *a priori*, that which responds to the earlier debates about the scope of nonempirical knowledge.

2. THE OFFICIAL EPISTEMOLOGICAL NOTION

The early pages of the Introduction to the first *Critique* provide an account of what I shall call "the official epistemological notion of the *a priori*." Kant explains that knowledge that is independent of the senses is *a priori*, that such knowledge is distinguished from the empirical, which has its "sources" in experience, and that *a priori* knowledge is not simply independent of the subject's current experience but of the stream of experiences that the subject has had (B 2). The last point is made with the help of a simple example: we are asked to imagine a man who has undermined the foundations of his house; this man, Kant points out, might have known in advance that the house would fall, but this would not count as an item of *a priori* knowledge because the advance knowledge would be based on earlier experiences of the behavior of objects that come to lack physical supports. The illustration is immediately followed with an explicit definition:

In the sequel therefore we will understand by *a priori* cognitions not those that occur independently of this or that experience, but rather those that occur *absolutely* independently of all experience.   (B 2–3)[3]

If this definition is to help his readers, we shall need a clear account of what is meant by "independence from experience."

There are two obvious ways of explicating this phrase, one that links independence to the *genesis* of the item of knowledge and the other that connects independence with the *justification* of the knowledge. According to the former, we would say that a piece of knowledge is independent of experience if experience plays no role in generating it; according to the latter, a state of knowledge would be independent of experience if experience is not involved in the justification. The simplest (and crudest) elaboration of the genetic approach is to suppose that there are things that subjects know at birth (or even earlier?), before their sensory experience begins. A more refined version would suppose that subjects are born with some developmental program whose typical unfolding will deliver, at some later stage of their lives, particular kinds of knowledge; for that program to run properly, experiential stimulation may prove necessary, but the exact character of this experience is completely irrelevant (just as, to obtain certain configurations inside a computer, the computer may have to be plugged in to a power source, although the location of the plug does not matter).

The genetic approach to *a priori* knowledge treats the subject as passive: certain kinds of knowledge will arise within us provided that we live in a normal way (and the range of the normal is extremely wide). By contrast the justificationist view regards the subject as more active. As we undergo the stream of experiences that constitute our lives, we are able to engage in certain kinds of processes that justify us in holding particular beliefs, and we can do this whatever specific form the stream of experience takes. In his talk of "sources" of knowledge, Kant seems to envisage us as having faculties that are able to provide us with justifications against the background of any experience whatsoever. Indeed, it seems to me that the official epistemological notion of the *a priori* is obtained by reading the phrase "independent of experience" in the justificationist way, and that the idea of an active, justifying subject pervades the Introduction to the *Critique*.[4]

For the moment, then, I shall set aside the genetic approach to *a priori* knowledge (whether crude or refined),[5] and concentrate on the justificationist mode of explication. Even here, things are not as straightforward as I have hitherto suggested. For Kant introduces a division *within* those parts of knowledge he takes as *a priori*. Immediately following the explicit definition, he distinguishes *pure a priori* knowledge by explaining that such knowledge involves only concepts that are not derived from experience (B 3). He asserts that the proposition "Every alteration has its cause" can be known *a priori*, but denies that it is pure, on the grounds that we have to acquire the concept of an alteration through experience. This means that *a priori* knowledge cannot be viewed as that knowledge that could be obtained given *any* experience, since, in some instances, a stream of experience might not allow a subject to have the concepts needed for entertaining the pertinent proposition. Plainly, Kant wants to distinguish two roles that experience might play in our knowledge, one of enabling us to have particular concepts and the other as serving as an essential ingredient in our justification; in the case of *a priori* knowledge, experience is not to play the latter role, but it is allowed to fulfill the former.

Here, then, is a picture of *a priori* knowledge. Such knowledge arises when a subject has a stream of experience that allows for acquisition of the appropriate concepts and when the subject goes through some process that justifies a belief in the relevant proposition; whatever alternative stream of experience the subject had had, provided only that it allowed for the acquisition of the concepts, would have enabled the subject to know the proposition, and, indeed, to know it in the same way. That is, the type of process that the subject uses to justify the belief would have been available against the background of the envisaged alternative stream of experience.

We can make this picture more precise as follows.[6] Let us call the total stream of experience that a subject has had the subject's *life*. A life will be said to be sufficient for the proposition *p* just in case it would allow the subject to acquire the concepts needed to entertain *p*. We can now define *one* notion of *a priori* knowledge by introducing the concept of an *a priori warrant* (a justifying process) as follows:

α is an *a priori* warrant for the belief that *p* just in case

(i) given the subject's actual life, undergoing α justifies the subject in believing that *p*

(ii) α would be available to the subject given any life sufficient for *p*.

A subject knows *a priori* that *p* if and only if the subject knows that *p* on the basis of a process that is an *a priori* warrant for it.

At first glance, this account seems to capture what Kant has in mind when he talks of knowledge independent of all experience. As things stand, the subject justifies her knowledge in a particular way, a way that cannot depend on the particularities of her experience, for she must be able to do the same thing whatever alternative stream of experiences she has, provided only that that stream enables her to acquire the relevant concepts. So, when we imagine her undergoing an alternative (sufficiently rich) life, we can envisage her as doing exactly what she does in the actual circumstances, producing the justification that actually gives her knowledge.

What this shows, then, is that the definitions provided so far capture the idea that a process *that actually serves as a justification* is independent of experience. But this isn't quite the same as demonstrating that the *justifying power* of the process or the state of *knowledge* is independent of experience. Even though the subject can do the same thing against the background of a different life (one sufficient for the proposition in question), it might be the case that behaving as she does would not generate knowledge under those rival conditions. It seems appropriate to take the notion of *a priori* knowledge encapsulated in the definitions given so far as *weak a priori* knowledge, for the definitions allow for the *revisability* of items of *a priori* knowledge. To see this, we need suppose only that, on the basis of a certain stream of experiences, a particular kind of process justifies a belief and that, given more extensive experiences, although that kind of process remains available, it no longer justifies the subject in the belief.

Any number of passages in Kant's writings, especially those in which he connects *a priori* knowledge with "apodictic certainty," make it plain that he aims to exclude revisable *a priori* knowledge. Not only must the processes that serve as justifications be available given alternative (sufficiently rich) experiences, but they must retain their justifying power, and the belief states they support must maintain their status as items of knowledge. It is not hard to see how to modify the notion of *weak a priori* knowledge to a concept of *strong a priori* knowledge that will satisfy these requirements. Instead of the previous conditions on *a priori* warrants, we adopt

α is an *a priori* warrant for the belief that p just in case

(i) α would be available to the subject given any life sufficient for p

(ii) given any life sufficient for p, α would justify the subject in believing that p

(iii) given any life sufficient for p, p.[7]

The notion of *strong a priori* knowledge just introduced comes close, I believe, to capturing Kant's official epistemological notion.

What kinds of processes, and what types of knowledge might count as *a priori* according to this strong conception? Kant's Introduction to the *Critique* continues by specifying his version of the distinction between analytic and synthetic propositions. He characterizes (affirmative) analytic judgments as "those in which the connection of the predicate [with the subject] is thought through identity" (A 7/B 10), a formulation that, as Frege rightly pointed out, is restricted to a very specific form of judgment.[8] I interpret Kant as attempting to find a place within his views about *a priori* knowledge for the identification of conceptual connections that had been crucial to his empiricist predecessors in formulating their claims about mathematical and logical knowledge. On the face of it, reflection on and analysis of our concepts looks like an obvious source of *a priori* knowledge of the strong type. Let us suppose that anyone who has a concept in his repertoire can present that concept to himself and identify its contents, and call the processes of conceptual presentation and content identification *conceptual unfolding*. Then if *p* is an analytic truth (in Kant's sense), anyone who grasps *p* can know *a priori* that *p*. For, if you grasp *p*, there is a process of conceptual unfolding you can undergo, a process that will justify belief that *p*, and moreover this process will be available to you whatever life you have (provided it is sufficient for *p*), and it will justify belief that *p*, given that you have that life (and, of course, in worlds where you have that life, *p* will obtain).

There are many passages in Kant's writings where he seems to hold that *a priori* knowledge of analytic truths is not epistemologically interesting, and there are some places in the *Critique* where he appears to be drawn toward an even stronger position on *a priori* knowledge, one in which our knowledge of analytic truths would not always be *a priori*.[9] In contrasting the role of definitions in mathematics and in other discussions, he places great emphasis on the idea that the concepts of mathematics are not "arbitrarily thought" and that we have an *a priori* assurance that we have defined a "true object" (A 729/B 757). The same theme is sounded much earlier, when he announces that a requirement on genuine knowledge is that the concepts we apply be applicable in experience. So, for example, there is an important task that needs to be undertaken with respect to mathematics, namely, that of establishing the "objective validity" of mathematical concepts (A 156/B 195), and this task seems to be taken up in the Axioms of Intuition.

One way[10] of reading these passages is to view Kant as haunted by a concern about the status of analytic truths. The simple argument for supposing that analytic truths could always be known *a priori* rested on the supposition that conceptual unfolding would always justify belief in the truth, whatever the character of the experience that supplied us with the concepts. Suppose that we now think of the "objective validity" of a concept as consisting in the fruitfulness of that concept for the description of experience. Then it might happen that some experiences that were sufficient to enable us to acquire a concept also justified us in believing that those concepts were *not* apt for the description of our experience. Under these conditions, we might go ahead with our process of conceptual unfolding, but the result might seem, in Kant's phrase, "senseless and meaningless." So one might judge that the justificatory power of the process of conceptual unfolding is compromised, and that, under these experiential conditions, the process no longer satisfies condition (ii) on *a strong priori* warrants.

We could guard against this apparently possible form of experiential undermining by insisting that the aptness of our concepts be able to survive, come what may. One sense that Kant seems to give to his locution "*a priori* concept" is that of a concept for which we have a guarantee that it will always prove fruitful in our classification of our experiences. If we adopt this interpretation, then his account of *a priori* knowledge is even more stringent than initially appeared, for, implicit in the requirements of *a priori* warrants is the condition that the concepts that figure in the propositions known *a priori* be such that no experience can undermine claims as to their aptness. If Kant is read in this way, we obtain not only an interpretation of his insistence on defending the special status of certain concepts (mathematical concepts, the categories), but also an explanation of why simple analyticity is not his concern. For, on this approach, analytic truths are only *a priori* if they meet the very special condition of containing only *a priori* concepts (that is, concepts whose usefulness experience cannot impugn).

Let us turn now to the possibility of synthetic *a priori* knowledge, which is, of course, far more prominent in the *Critique* than any account of our knowledge of analytic truths. What kind of procedure can serve as an *a priori* warrant for belief in synthetic truths? Kant poses the problem in the Introduction:

> If I am to go beyond the concept *A* in order to cognize another *B* as combined with it, what is it on which I depend and by means of which the synthesis becomes possible, since I here do not have the advantage of looking around for it in the field of experience? (A 9/B 13)

This "third thing," the "unknown = X" (A 9/B 13), cannot be experienced, for that would be incompatible with the apriority of the knowledge. From the perspective of the official epistemological notion, Kant's answer is clearest in the case of mathematical knowledge. Here, he suggests, a process of construction in pure intuition functions as the justifying process.[11]

Unlike many authors who have written on the ways in which people can come to elementary mathematical knowledge, Kant is admirably straightforward about the processes he views as epistemologically fundamental. We convince ourselves of the principles of Euclidean geometry, or of the basic arithmetical identities, by constructing mental representations – diagrams in the geometrical case, something like assemblages of strokes or dots in arithmetic – and by inspecting their properties. This sounds very much like the mode of basic mathematical knowledge recognized by Kant's empiricist predecessors – who believed, of course, that what we learn in this way are relations among concepts ("analytic truths" in Kant's favored idiom); but Kant maintains that such processes deliver knowledge of *synthetic* truths, and how that can be is initially quite puzzling.

The puzzle is resolved by Kant's theory of space and time as forms of intuition, and, indeed, it is precisely the power of this theory of space and time to yield the needed explanation that serves as a central argument in the theory's favor. Committed to the claim that propositions of mathematics are synthetic, Kant maintains that there are possible worlds in which those propositions are false. Yet, in an important sense, those propositions are necessary, for they hold in all those worlds of which we, constituted as we are, can have experience. Mathematical truths obtain in all such worlds because, in experience, our minds impose a particular mathematical structure on the phenomena. Now in the special kind of process that counts as construction in pure intuition, we illuminate to ourselves just those structural features that the mind imposes on all experience. To use a simple analogy, it is as if all our sensory experience were to consist in images flashed upon a surface, so that some of the properties of the images we received embodied the structure of the surface. Independently of experience, we have a way to reveal the character of that structure, and thus to learn propositions that must hold in any world of which we can have experience, because we can always block out the sensory channels, construct figures in imagination, and inspect their properties. To use Kant's preferred terminology, the images so generated count as the "third thing(s)" that make the connection of subject and predicate possible.

This is an ingenious account of mathematical knowledge, one that has the genuine virtue of specifying, with some clarity and precision, how basic *a priori* mathematical knowledge might be gained. In the end, I believe, it cannot succeed, because Kant cannot distinguish those properties of the images we generate in imagination that are accidents of the particular construction from those that genuinely reflect the structure that our minds impose on experience.[12] For the purposes of understanding Kant's official epistemological notion of *a priori* knowledge, however, this defect does not matter. The account of construction in pure intuition can serve as a paradigm for those processes that subjects can carry out, given any sufficiently rich experience, processes that are supposed to justify the beliefs they generate.

3. THE "MARKS" OF THE *A PRIORI*

I have been trying to clarify a conception of *a priori* knowledge that both emerges from Kant's official definition and relates to the issues about knowledge of "truths of reason" that had occupied Kant's predecessors. Immediately after the discussion of knowledge independent of all experience, however, he offers criteria that seem to be intended to be more readily applicable than the definition itself. So, with the apparent goal of showing that we do have some *a priori* knowledge, Kant suggests that there are clear "marks" of apriority. These are announced in a famous equivalence:

Necessity and strict universality are therefore secure indications of an *a priori* cognition, and also belong together inseparably.   (B 4)

Unfortunately, there are quite powerful reasons for thinking that this equivalence is faulty, at least if we suppose that the idea of apriority in question is the official epistemological notion.

Let us start with a simple approach to the notions of necessity and universality: the necessary truths are just those that obtain in all possible worlds; the universal truths are those that express generalizations about all entities of a particular kind. Anything so simple will surely fail to honor Kant's thesis about the "marks" of *a priori* knowledge, for the obvious reason that these notions of necessity and universality are hardly "inseparable from one another" (there are contingent universal truths, as well as necessary truths that are not of universal form). Furthermore, we can apparently know, independently of experience, some propositions that fail to be necessary: given any stream of experience sufficient for you to entertain the thought that you exist, it seems that you can know that you exist, even though your existence is a contingent matter. Finally, there are necessary truths that are too complex for human beings ever to formulate, others, perhaps, that we can formulate but could never come to know, and, on the prevalent approaches to necessity, some necessary truths that can only be known with the aid of experience (for example, the proposition that water is H_2O).[13]

Although Kant's suggestion about the marks of *a priori* knowledge may look as though it is a straightforward equivalence between propositions that can be known *a priori*, necessary truths, and universal truths, his text belies both that interpretation and the readings of necessity and universality proposed in the last paragraph. The first thing to notice is that he appears to collapse the concept of universality into the notion of necessity, telling us that if

a judgment is thought in strict universality, i.e., in such a way that no exception at all is allowed to be possible, then it is not derived from experience, but is rather valid absolutely *a priori*.   (B 4)

There are two important aspects of this clarification, a first that contrasts strict universality with merely accidental generalities (propositions that look as though they are of universal form but that just happen to be true), and a second that introduces the idea of *thinking* a proposition as universal. Together, these points identify the universal propositions in which Kant is interested as those that legislate for all possible cases, ruling out worlds in which there are counterexamples. So conceived, universal propositions seem to be just those that are *recognized* by the subject who entertains them as holding necessarily.

Indeed, Kant sets out his argument for the existence of *a priori* knowledge by introducing the idea of a proposition that "is thought along with its **necessity**" (B 3), declaring that such propositions have to be *a priori*. Plainly, it will not do to suppose that if someone *believes* that p and it is necessary that p, then the subject must *know a priori* that p, since people can come to hold propositions in bizarre ways. Nor is it enough to require that propositions known to be necessary must be known *a priori*, for it seems possible to decompose the knowledge into subsidiary parts, not all of which are *a priori*: I might know that if *p* then it is necessary that *p*, and gain the knowledge that *p* empirically, for example. I think we do most justice to Kant's approach by supposing that in those instances where someone knows a necessary proposition and knows that it is necessary, there must be some ingredient in the subject's knowledge that is *a priori*. More exactly, in any instance in which a person knows a necessary proposition and knows that the proposition is necessary there is some proposition (perhaps, for example, the claim that propositions of a particular type are necessary) that the subject could have known *a priori*.

This is, I believe, as far as we can go to make sense of Kant's thesis about the marks of *a priori* knowledge – at least so long as we confine ourselves to the official epistemological conception. Yet in trying to identify what might be going on in his defense of apparently problematic equivalences, we have uncovered a different perspective on *a priori* knowledge. The notion of "ingredients in knowledge," just introduced in the last paragraph, is a vague gesture towards an idea that is central to his epistemology, an idea that leads to a very different approach to apriority.

4. *A PRIORI* INGREDIENTS

Even before the Introduction, Kant has already prepared his reader for the view that there are *a priori* ingredients in human knowledge. In the Preface to the Second Edition, we are told that "[i]nsofar as there is to be reason in these sciences, something in them must be cognized *a priori*" (B ix). In the celebrated discussion of Galileo, Torricelli, Stahl, and the experimental method, which occurs two pages later, Kant is more explicit about what he has in mind, and his explanation relates directly to the treatment of necessity and universality in the Introduction.

Accidental observations, made according to no previously designed plan, can never connect up into a necessary law, which is yet what reason seeks and requires. Reason in order to be taught by nature must approach nature with its principles in one hand, according to which alone the agreement among appearances can count as laws, and, in the other hand, the experiments thought out in accordance with these principles – yet in order to be instructed by nature not like a pupil, who has recited to him whatever the teacher wants to say, but like an appointed judge who compels witnesses to answer the questions he puts to them.   (B xiii).

Plainly, Kant is suggesting that there is some ingredient in – or contribution to – our ordinary empirical and scientific knowledge that stems from us, from our faculties, here designated as "reason" but later to be partitioned among the forms of sensibility, the categories of the understanding, and the regulative use of the ideas of pure reason. A naïve reading of his view would be to propose that people have to know *explicitly* the principles that are embodied in all our experience, and that this knowledge is *a priori* in the sense of the official epistemological notion we have already reviewed; that wildly implausible suggestion invites the ironic comment that, if that were so, we would hardly need Kant's dense arguments to bring the principles in question to light. An alternative interpretation would deny that the psychological contributions that shape our experience are matters of cognition at all; the character of our experience may cause us to represent the world in a particular way, but this does not entail that we *know* the principles that describe the distinctive features we impose. Although this would make Kant's position neater and more coherent, I do not believe it does justice to the passages already quoted from the Preface, with their clear suggestion that subjects' knowledge of certain principles is being deployed in the genesis of their empirical knowledge, nor with passages I shall consider shortly.[14]

There is an intermediate view, one that makes use of the idea of *tacit* knowledge. Suppose we think of subjects as having knowledge that they cannot articulate, knowledge which they use in arriving at judgments about the physical world. You look ahead and come to believe that there is a vast array of daffodils before you. Your senses have been stimulated in various ways, but the sensory input, by itself, could not justify a judgment about the independent existence of enduring objects in a particular complex of spatial relations. To arrive at your knowledge of the daffodils, you have to deploy, unconsciously, principles of a very general kind; to put the point negatively, someone who lacked the knowledge of those principles would be quite unable to arrive at the judgment you make – and indeed make without any conscious effort.

To bring the view I am attributing to Kant into clearer focus, it helps to recall a celebrated contemporary use of similar ideas. From the 1960s on, Noam Chomsky and his many followers have argued that it would be impossible for children to acquire the ability to speak grammatically unless they already had tacit knowledge of the principles of universal grammar.[15] As Chomsky formulates the project of learning a language, the young child's task is to acquire knowledge of the grammatical principles underlying that language (the fluent child, or adult speaker, cannot typically articulate this knowledge, so it too is tacit). Children accomplish this by hearing the utterances of those who talk to, at, or around them, but, in Chomsky's view, the collection of such utterances is too scanty and debased to allow for any process of selecting the appropriate grammatical principles unless the child already knows the very general and abstract principles that characterize all grammars. So, he claims, we must all start with innate (tacit) knowledge of the general features of the grammars of all learnable languages, and, as the corrupt data roll in, we use them, together with our store of innate knowledge, to arrive at the grammar of the language those around us speak. Once the process is finished, we are able to speak fluently because we unconsciously use our tacit knowledge of the grammar of our native language. That tacit knowledge in turn is the product of the particular stream of linguistic performances we have heard (the "matter of sensation") and the innate knowledge of principles that govern all grammars of learnable languages (the "principles of reason").

This skeletal account of an influential contemporary view about language-learning helps us to see what Kant might be proposing when he claims that there is a certain type of knowledge that is prior to experience (and my parenthetical remarks attempt to indicate how to draw the analogy).[16] Suppose that our judgments about the world are the product of a causal process in which physical nature makes an impact upon us through our senses and in which we make unconscious use of principles that we know, but which we cannot articulate fully, so as to make inferences from unconscious judgments about the character of the sensory information presented to us to full-fledged judgments about objects in space and time. Before we have sensory experience we have no explicit knowledge – and, indeed, Kant might even maintain that we have no tacit knowledge either, if he were to argue that experience were required as a trigger to transform the precursors of our innate tacit knowledge into genuine states of knowing. The tacit knowledge that enables us to go beyond the bare materials given us through sensation to knowledge of the world that we actually experience is both causally crucial to the process of arriving at explicit judgments and epistemically required for them to be justified. So, even if by some miraculous means a subject lacking the tacit knowledge of the principles that guide the unconscious inferences were to arrive at a belief of the kind we fluently and typically acquire in response to sensory stimulation, that subject's belief would be unjustified.

With this picture in mind, let us return to the Introduction and consider an alternative approach to the notion of apriority. In the famous first sentence of the second edition, Kant commits himself to the idea that "all our cognition begins with experience" (B 1), and we can understand this either as a claim about the origins of our explicit knowledge, or (as I suggested in the last paragraph) as a more ambitious thesis concerning both tacit and explicit knowledge. In the equally famous sentence that opens the second paragraph, Kant writes: "But although all our cognition commences **with** experience, yet it does not on that account all arise **from** experience" (B 1). Even though one might read this in terms of the official epistemological notion, it is equally (if not more) easily construed as indicating the picture of empirical knowledge I have been sketching. Moreover, the sentences that follow are more obviously in tune with that picture, for Kant goes on to write of empirical knowledge as "a composite of that which we receive through impressions and of what our own cognitive faculty (merely prompted by sensible impressions) provides out of itself" (B 1), and immediately raises the question of how the respective contributions (in particular, the "addition" due to our faculty of knowledge) can be separated.

This is the context in which Kant introduces the notion of independence from experience, and that context suggests a different reading from the one introduced in section 2. To know something independently of experience is to have tacit knowledge that is not justified by experience but is put to work in all one's empirical knowledge. This is not to declare that there is some non-empirical mode of justification (something like an *a priori* warrant, as section 2 understood it) of which we are typically unconscious, but simply to sidestep questions about justification altogether. Knowledge of this sort is true belief, with the added twist that such beliefs must hold true of any world we can experience.

Before we raise obvious questions about whether the true beliefs that are "independent of experience" in this sense genuinely constitute knowledge, it is worth recognizing that the tacit knowledge picture provides Kant with a much more plausible defense of his "marks" of *a priori* knowledge than that derived from the official epistemological notion. If *a priori* knowledge comprises principles that we have to use in arriving at and justifying any claim we make about the world, then it is easy to see that they have to be thought of as necessary and universal: in the unconscious inferential work that the knowing subject does, the necessity and universality of the principles tacitly known is taken for granted. We saw in section 3 that the official epistemological notion makes Kant's claimed equivalences among apriority, necessity, and universality look problematic, and we struggled to find some thesis in the vicinity that could be sustained – the result of the efforts being a view that broaches the idea of a "decomposition" of knowledge into "ingredients," an idea that is central to the tacit knowledge picture.

Why, then, did I begin with the official epistemological notion? Why not reject this as a misnomer and explicate Kant's conception of apriority in terms of the tacit knowledge picture? To answer these questions, which naturally arise at this stage of the discussion, it will be worth reflecting on some peculiarities of the notion of tacit knowledge.

Start with an explicit definition of tacit *a priori* knowledge.

A subject tacitly knows *a priori* that *p* just in case

(i) the subject believes that *p*

(ii) the subject would come to believe that *p* given any empirical stimulus

(iii) the subject's state of belief that *p* is necessarily used in arriving at and justifying empirical judgments

(iv) the content of that state of belief, the state employed in arriving at and justifying empirical judgments, is not fully accessible to the subject, so that that state cannot lead the subject to a full articulation of the belief that *p*[17]

(v) *p* obtains in any world of which the subject can have experience.

Quite evidently, this definition diverges from accounts of *a priori* knowledge that use the standard framework for understanding knowledge – knowledge is true belief *that is justified* (or that meets some other "third condition") – and that try to specify the constraints on *a priori* justification. Should it count as a definition of any kind of *knowledge* at all? In response to that query, one might respond that for states of belief that are triggered in cognitive subjects come what may, questions of origins are unimportant, and for states of belief that have to be deployed in a subject's empirical knowledge questions of justification are unimportant; in effect, these states are the unmoved movers of the business of justification. Justification, it is conceded, is crucial to ordinary sorts of knowledge, but the heart of Kant's epistemological position is that there is a kind of knowledge that is required for any justification to proceed. In my view, this is a plausible reply to the skeptical query.

Yet it seems to me absolutely crucial that the knowledge in question is *tacit*. Suppose we tried to arrive at an account of *explicit a priori* knowledge by building on the definition just given. It would plainly not do to declare that whenever a subject has tacit *a priori* knowledge that *p* and also has an explicit belief that *p* the latter state of belief counts as *a priori* knowledge. For, once we start talking about explicit knowledge, questions of origins and justification really do matter. If the state of explicit belief comes about in the wrong way, and if the subject can say nothing in support of the explicit belief, then all our normal reservations about equating knowledge with mere true belief come flooding in. Moreover, if the subject has a state of explicit belief whose content is that of an item of tacit *a priori* knowledge, and if the state of explicit belief is justified by some sort of empirical investigation, then there is an obvious way to evaluate the overall epistemic situation: the tacit belief is *a priori* knowledge, the explicit belief is empirical knowledge. This is of course precisely the attitude that we're encouraged to take in the case of our linguistic knowledge – all of us have tacit knowledge of the principles of universal grammar. This knowledge does not depend on our experiences, and (with luck) a few grammarians may come to have explicit knowledge of those same principles. But that explicit knowledge will be thoroughly empirical, based on their intricate investigations.

Hence, to the extent that Kant wants to make room for explicit *a priori* knowledge, he cannot simply extend the tacit knowledge picture. Instead, he veers to the official epistemological notion, with its account of special *a priori* modes of justification, and this will generate his discussions of the unfolding of concepts that provide us with explicit knowledge of analytic truths, as well as the doctrine that there must be some "third thing" that enables us to justify synthetic propositions *a priori*. In revisiting the early pages of the Introduction, we have ignored these parts of his endeavor.

But perhaps explicit *a priori* knowledge is not important to the Kantian enterprise? After all, the definition of tacit *a priori* knowledge will allow for elaborating all sorts of themes that are central to the *Critique*, themes that mark out Kant's distinctive epistemological position, the transcendental psychology that makes him a precursor of contemporary cognitive science.[18] The trouble is that this will leave him unable to complete another aspect of his enterprise, namely, the proper delineation of those problematic areas of knowledge that had puzzled his epistemological predecessors.

This is, of course, where we came in. Empiricists and rationalists had pondered the status of logical and mathematical knowledge, and had wondered whether there was a wider class of propositions (truths of reason) of which we have explicit knowledge that is not based upon our experience. Kant wants to settle these issues as well, and, as soon as he has laid out his basic approach to *a priori* knowledge, he wants to identify our *explicit* mathematical knowledge and our *explicit* knowledge of some very general propositions about the world (for example, the principles of substance and causation) as *a priori* and to show how the possibility of this knowledge can be explained. The *Critique* plainly aspires to completeness – all our knowledge is to be pigeonholed and accounted for. So the option of simply deploying the notion of tacit *a priori* knowledge is not open to Kant.

Yet, as I suggested above, there are many discussions in the book, not only in the early pages of the Introduction but also in the theory of our empirical knowledge adumbrated in the Analytic, in which the tacit knowledge picture appears paramount. I conclude that Kant is committed to *two* notions of apriority, both the official epistemological account and the definition of tacit *a priori* knowledge that I have offered. But this leaves us with an obvious interpretative puzzle, the puzzle of reconciling what I have taken to be separate strands in his thinking (strands possibly intertwined at crucial points in his discussion by the rich ambiguities of terms like "independent of experience").

I conjecture that Kant might have hoped to connect the two different approaches to the *a priori* by what I shall call the "Disclosure Thesis."

(DT)   For any *p*, if we have tacit *a priori* knowledge that *p*, then there is a possible process of disclosure that will generate explicit *a priori* knowledge that *p* (that is, explicit knowledge that satisfies the conditions for the official epistemological notion).

So, for example, in advertising the project of the *Critique*, Kant tells us that the possibility of a system of *a priori* principles should appear quite plausible to us. For the task is not to fathom "the nature of things, which is inexhaustible, but the understanding, which judges about the nature of things, and this in turn only in regard to its *a priori* cognition, the supply of which, since we do not have to seek for it externally, cannot remain hidden from us, and in all likelihood is small enough to be completely recorded, its worth or worthlessness assessed, and subjected to a correct appraisal" (A 13/B 26–7). Even earlier, at the end of the discussion of the "marks" of *a priori* knowledge, he links the explicit ("official") conception to the idea of ingredients in empirical knowledge by offering first as examples explicit mathematical knowledge and subsequently the "rules" according to which our experience proceeds (B 5).

Now even if the Disclosure Thesis could be established, that would not be enough to show the equivalence of the two approaches to *a priori* knowledge, for it would allow for the possibility that some items of explicit *a priori* knowledge had no counterpart in the system of tacit knowledge that guides all our experience. Central to Kant's enterprise is the denial of this possibility, his insistence that all *a priori* knowledge should have a real application. So we find passages that claim something like the following, which I call "Real Application":

(RA)   For any *p*, if we have explicit *a priori* knowledge that *p* (knowledge satisfying the official epistemological conception), then there must be some item of empirical knowledge in which tacit *a priori* knowledge that *p* plays an essential role.

So, for example, in the heart of the Transcendental Deduction (in the second edition), Kant tells us that "[t]he pure concepts of the understanding, consequently, even if they are applied to *a priori* intuitions (as in mathematics), provide cognition only insofar as these *a priori* intuitions, and by means of them also the concepts of the understanding, can be applied to empirical intuitions" (B 147). The theme is developed in the Analytic of Principles, where Kant writes

A priori principles bear this name not merely because they contain in themselves the grounds of other judgments, but also because they are not themselves grounded in higher and more general cognitions. Yet this property does not elevate them beyond all proof. For although this could not be carried further objectively, but rather grounds all cognition of its object, yet this does not prevent a proof from the subjective sources of the possibility of a cognition being possible. (A 149/B 188)

This, I take it, announces that Kant intends to disclose particular principles that we know tacitly *a priori* by revealing them as conditions of the possibility of empirical knowledge, and that his process of disclosure will constitute a proof of them. Conversely, in the case of mathematics, where we already have a means of arriving at explicit *a priori* knowledge – through the procedure of construction in pure intuition – the task will be to identify the ways in which tacit knowledge of mathematics functions in our experience. So Kant announces the project of the Axioms of Intuition:

The mathematical principles do not constitute any part of this system, since they are drawn only from intuition, not from the pure concept of the understanding; yet their possibility, since they are likewise synthetic *a priori*, necessarily finds a place here, not in order to prove their correctness and apodictic certainty, which is not at all necessary, but only to make comprehensible and to deduce the possibility of such evident cognitions *a priori*. (A 150/B 188–9)

A few pages later, he reminds us of his central theme about empirical knowledge, that the understanding must be "the source of the principles in accordance with which everything (that can even come before us as an object) necessarily stands under rules" (A 159/B 198), which I interpret as the claim that we have tacit *a priori* knowledge of such principles. In the next paragraph, Kant points out that we have explicit *a priori* knowledge of mathematical principles, based on our pure intuition. But there is still an incompleteness in our understanding of these, for they have not yet been connected with the compendium of rules that underlie all experience. So there remains the question of "their application to experience, thus their objective validity," and hence "the possibility of such synthetic *a priori* cognition (its deduction) still always rests on the pure understanding" (A 160/B 199). The Axioms of Intuition are intended to help establish something like (RA) and connect the two conceptions of *a priori* knowledge in the case – mathematics – that Kant uses as a major exemplar.

The obvious trouble, however, is that the theses required to link the conceptions look highly dubious. Consider, first, the Disclosure Thesis. What sort of process could yield us explicit knowledge of the principles that we tacitly know and bring to all our experience? Here it is useful to remind ourselves of the early discussion of how synthetic *a priori* knowledge comes to be possible. In answer to his own question – "If I am to go beyond the concept A in order to cognize another B as combined with it, what is it on which I depend and by means of which the synthesis becomes possible, since I here do not have the advantage of looking around for it in the field of experience?" (A 9/B 13) – he tells us that we always need to identify a third thing "on which the understanding depends when it believes itself to discover beyond the concept of A a predicate that is foreign to it" (A 9/B 13); in the parade case of mathematics, pure intuition comes in to save the day, for it is a process we may carry out against the background of any sufficiently rich experience. How are we to apply this model to the disclosure of those principles that are known tacitly *a priori*?

In many places, Kant explains his method – the Transcendental Method – and I think it eminently reasonable to suppose that his actual discussions that aim to disclose various principles to his readers follow the method he describes. *Transcendental* knowledge is concerned with identifying the mind's contribution to our various modes of knowing, or more exactly with isolating the tacit knowledge that is put to work when we know anything (A 11–12/B 25). To arrive at items of transcendental knowledge, we look for the conditions on which the possibility of experiential knowledge depends, and the key is to find what remains "if one abstracts from every-thing empirical in the appearances" (A 96). Hence the general fea-ture of Kant's "proofs" of the principles he hails as *a priori* lies in their starting with some form of knowledge and using some sort of abstraction or isolation method to strip away the contributions of experience and leave some element that could not have been sup-plied by experience. It is hardly surprising that when Kant inquires after the "third something" (A 155/B 194) that yields the synthetic *a priori* knowledge of the Principles of the Analytic, he explains that "The **possibility of experience** is therefore that which gives all of our cognitions *a priori* objective reality" (A 156/B 195).

At this point, it is useful to recall the example used to introduce and motivate the idea of tacit *a priori* knowledge. To fathom the principles of grammar that fluent adult speakers tacitly know surely takes a significant amount of empirical research, and even more data will be required to identify the universal grammatical principles tacit knowledge of which guides the process of language acquisition. It looks, then, as though the method to which Kant commits himself may embroil him in some dubious armchair psychology. The idea of generating substantial conclusions about the character of our fac-ulties from the comfort of his armchair may seem bad enough, but for our purposes the critical deficiency lies elsewhere. For even the schematic description of the transcendental method offered in the last paragraph, where the principles that will guide the process of abstraction out of which the items of tacit *a priori* knowledge will be distilled are left in an obligingly soft focus, makes it plain that Kant will require some premises about our actual capacities, their range of operation, and the potential contributions of experience. The prob-lem for reconciling the two notions of *a priori* knowledge is not that the alleged modes of disclosing the tacit principles have to involve *armchair* psychology, but rather that empirical assumptions, even if they are relatively commonplace claims that Kant can reflect on in his armchair, are at the heart of the psychology he must use. Nor is the situation alleviated when we move from Kant's advertisement of what he will do to his actual practice, for, throughout the Analytic of Principles, he begins with a claim (an empirical claim) about our having a mode of knowledge of a particular kind, and the analysis of the cognitive preconditions of this knowledge invariably intro-duces further (albeit usually highly general) empirical assumptions.

I see no way of reconstructing the arguments that supposedly disclose the tacit knowledge we bring to experience in such a way that the process of following them could be conceived as satisfying the conditions imposed on explicit *a priori* knowledge in the official epistemological conception.

The tensions at the heart of Kant's enterprise are evident when one juxtaposes the attempts to establish the principles of the analogies of experience (both in the general discussion [A 177/B 218ff.], and in the proofs of the principles of substance and causation) with occasions on which he introduces the principles as examples in general discussions of *a priori* knowledge. It is very hard not to read the detailed proofs as anything other than accounts of how our minds tacitly deploy general principles in building up a world of spatiotemporally connected objects and events. Yet, as we have already seen, Kant uses the principle of causation to draw a distinction between those propositions known *a priori* that contain only pure concepts and those that include some concept drawn from experience (B 3). To make sense of these passages, Kant must think that people (all people? most people? scientists? studious readers of the *Critique*?) have explicit *a priori* knowledge of the principle of the second analogy. How do they arrive at it? Presumably through the sort of analysis delineated in the proof of the second analogy.[19] But, when we reflect on some of the premises Kant needs for that proof – premises about the existence of particular types of knowledge and about our limitations in perceiving time – it is hard to suppose that constructing and following the proof would meet the conditions on *a priori* warrants. My suspicion is that Kant is led into epistemological tangles because, at different places in the *Critique*, different approaches to apriority are uppermost in his mind, and because he makes an (unwarranted) assumption, the Disclosure Thesis, that helps support him in thinking that his fundamental conceptions of the *a priori* are equivalent.

Nor are matters any better when we turn to the converse of the Disclosure Thesis, namely, RA. For, although it is entirely possible that a sophisticated psychological investigation might reveal that some items of explicit *a priori* knowledge – some parts of mathematical or logical knowledge, say – are used tacitly in the everyday empirical judgments that we all make, it would be hard to suppose that *all* theorems of mathematics are so deployed. (I should note, in passing, that a serious case for identifying some pieces of mathematical knowledge as tacitly put to work in empirical knowledge, in the construction of representations of three-dimensional objects from the patterns of retinal stimulation, for example, would appear to depend on a very different style of argumentation than that offered us by the *Critique*; Kant's achievement here – and it is no mean accomplishment – consists in recognizing the possibility of a certain kind of cognitive reconstruction, rather than delivering the full psychological details.) Already in Kant's time, the scope of mathematics (indeed of "pure" mathematics) included much more than the two disciplines, arithmetic and Euclidean geometry, that figure in his arguments: Leibniz's successors, most notably Euler, had amassed a rich collection of results on integrals and the sums of infinite series, while the theory of numbers had extended the theorems proved by Fermat in the seventeenth century. There is little reason to think that *every* piece of eighteenth-century mathematical knowledge (such as theorems to the effect that numbers of a particular form are invariably prime) is tacitly put to work in some item of empirical knowledge. Yet even if we restrict our attention to arithmetic and geometry, it seems highly likely that there will be some truths that we can come to know *a priori* by engaging in what Kant would count as a proof – for example, theorems about the sums of very large numbers or the properties of polygons with many sides – for which there would be no tacit counterpart with a use in our ordinary knowledge. The basic trouble is evident. At most, Kant can hope to establish that empirical knowledge of particular types requires the tacit use of certain mathematical concepts and the deployment of very basic principles involving these concepts. That by no means requires that we make tacit use of the consequences that can be drawn from those basic principles by processes that Kant would count as genuine mathematical proofs. If the basic principles that are tacitly deployed are not explicitly known *a priori*, then the equivalence of the two concepts fails in one way. If they are explicitly known *a priori*, then the equivalence must be violated in another way, for we can use our *a priori* knowledge of the principles as a starting point for a proof that will yield explicit *a priori* knowledge of consequences that are not items of tacit *a priori* knowledge. Explicit *a priori* knowledge is closed under a class of procedures, but tacit *a priori* knowledge is not closed under those very same procedures.

Let us take stock. I suggest that Kant operates with two conceptions of the *a priori*. Passages in his writings indicate that he thinks of these as equivalent. But when the conceptions are made relatively precise, it appears that he has no right to the assumption of equivalence. Thus, in my judgment, the epistemology of the *Critique* falls apart in a quite fundamental way. I now want to consider the interpretative possibilities that this unfortunate situation allows.

5. THREE WAYS OF MENDING KANT

The approach I favor is to leave Kant unmended, to recognize that he has two non-equivalent conceptions of *a priori* knowledge, and to pick through the *Critique* with caution, asking on each specific occasion which notion is primary and whether Kant's faulty assumption of equivalence is infecting his reasoning. (In fact, this will be more complicated than I have hitherto noted because of the tendency of the tacit knowledge approach to become wilder and woollier as "*a priori*" becomes attached to a variety of constituents of the psychological processes that underlie cognition – not only to principles and concepts, but to syntheses; not only as an adjective, but as an adverb, modifying such verbs as "determine," "relate," "give," and "combine." These usages can be reconstructed by carefully extending the tacit knowledge conception.) Previous sections have marked the poles of Kant's discussions. Typically, when he is concerned with mathematical knowledge, the official epistemological conception is paramount; when he is applying the transcendental method and analyzing the preconditions of cognition, as in the Analytic, the tacit knowledge conception comes to the fore. In a significant number of passages, however, there is flux between the two, and the assumed equivalence leads the argument astray.

Can one do better by picking one of the two notions as primary and reading the *Critique* in light of it? I think not. Emphasis on the official epistemological conception makes good sense of large segments of the Introduction, of parts of the Aesthetic, and of the Transcendental Methodology; with some strain it can yield a reading of the Axioms of Intuition. The cost, however, is obvious. Most of the Analytic becomes utterly mysterious (and, arguably, important themes in the Aesthetic are also slighted).

A second try at mending Kant does better. If one adopts the tacit knowledge conception as primary, the projects of the Analytic (and some of those of the Aesthetic) come into much clearer focus. The price is that Kant's discussions of our explicit mathematical knowledge – especially in the Introduction, the Aesthetic, and the Methodology – now become as incomprehensible as the investigations of the Analytic were on the approach considered in the last paragraph. Although mathematical knowledge is his principal example for motivating the account of *a priori* knowledge, this is surely a relatively small price to pay. This way of mending Kant detaches him from the debates about the "truths of reason," but it does make him an interesting precursor to contemporary cognitive science.

A third approach has been more popular than either of the two just mentioned. Many of Kant's interpreters have wanted to talk about "*a priori* knowledge" by detaching knowledge from the subject.[20] In effect, they view "*a priori*" as primarily a predicate of propositions, and try to characterize it by considering the logical relations among various types of propositions. So, for example, *a priori* propositions might be viewed as necessary presuppositions of truths that identify general features of the world, or of experience of the world; or, perhaps, *a priori* truths are those that hold across a particular class of worlds (worlds of which we, constituted as we are, could have experience).

I do not doubt that the concepts generated in this way are often philosophically interesting, or that some of them figure in Kant's work. But these approaches, inspired by the thought that proper epistemological interpretation can liberate itself from the psychological speculations that seem to clutter Kant's discussions, do violence to the *Critique*. For, as he makes clear from the beginning, Kant is interested in human *knowledge*, and there is no way to generate a conception of *a priori* knowledge without attention to the psychological processes that occur in the knowing subject. To see this, suppose that we were offered an account of the form:

A subject knows *a priori* that *p* just in case

(a) *p*
(b) the subject believes that *p*
(c) *p* is a presupposition of some body of truths *B*.

If this is an account of explicit knowledge – one appropriate to understand Kant's treatment of mathematics – then it is plainly insufficient, for genuine knowledge does not require simply that the proposition believed have some status, but that the subject's belief be formed and sustained in the right way. Kant is clear, and clearly right, in seeing that theses about someone's *a priori* knowledge require an explanation of how the person comes to know. On the other hand, if it is supposed that this is an item of tacit knowledge, it fails to distinguish *a priori* knowledge from all sorts of true unconscious beliefs we might happen to have – fails in effect to indicate why the investigation of our *a priori* knowledge is so important for understanding our empirical knowledge. This failure surfaces when we consider Kant's protracted struggles to understand how items of tacit knowledge are used in our everyday empirical knowledge.

The de-psychologized approach to *a priori* knowledge thus seems to me to inherit the vices of both the previous attempts at mending Kant, serving neither of his epistemological projects. This is not to deny that considering the presuppositions of certain propositions (say the principles of Newtonian science) might not illuminate some *metaphysical* projects in which Kant engaged.[21] The point is that it ignores the concern with human knowledge that is so central to the *Critique*.

6. KANT'S LEGACIES

Discussions of *a priori* knowledge after Kant have been shaped largely first by Frege's influential explorations of the foundations of mathematics, second, by the development of logical positivism and its metamorphosis into logical empiricism, and third, by Quine's reaction to the positivist/empiricist tradition. In closing, I want to look briefly at these developments.

In approaching issues about mathematical knowledge, Frege placed Kant in a line of thinkers who had discussed the status of logic, mathematics, and the "truths of reason," a thinker who had refined the categories introduced by his predecessors. So, from Frege's perspective, Kant had been insightful in having formulated the *a priori/a posteriori* distinction and the analytic/synthetic distinction, and in taking the notion of the *a priori* to involve the idea of a justification that is independent of experience – in effect, Frege understood

Kant as advancing the official epistemological conception of the *a priori*.[22] But, he believed, Kant had made two important mistakes, the more obvious in his assignment of arithmetic to the synthetic *a priori* and the more fundamental in his inadequate method of formulating the fundamental distinctions, an inadequacy born of Kant's impoverished view of the scope of logic. Proposing that propositions are *a priori* just in case they admit of a special kind of justification (one that does not appeal to sensory experience), Frege granted that one source of such justification is Kantian pure intuition (and that Kant was correct to suppose that geometry allowed for this style of justification), while another is justification from basic laws of logic "that neither need, nor admit of, proof"[23] (and, of course, Frege's brilliant articulation of mathematical logic was devoted to the cause of showing that such justifications could be provided in the case of arithmetic and analysis).

Late nineteenth-century and early twentieth-century investigations of the foundations of geometry and of the use of geometrical representations in theories of physical space led to the repudiation of Kant's claims about the synthetic *a priori* status of Euclidean geometry. Armed with the distinction between "pure geometry" (in which the primitive notions like *point* and *line* are not given physical interpretations) and "applied geometry" (in which lines might be identified with the paths of light rays), Frege's successors came to regard the former as analytic (and thus *a priori*) and the latter as synthetic *a posteriori*. In the English-speaking world, the renaissance of empiricism came to identify itself with the denial of the synthetic *a priori*. Once Kant's pair of distinctions had become aligned – analytic with *a priori*, synthetic with *a posteriori* – the predominant mode of drawing them substituted the precision and clarity of logical formulations for apparently cloudy references to "knowledge independent of experience" and "ideal sources of justification." Frege's characterization of the basic laws of logic as neither needing nor admitting proof inspired, in the heyday of logical empiricism, a steadfast refusal to ask how the basic principles of logic or mathematics might be known, or in what ways their justification is independent of experience.[24] Although the label "*a priori*" continued to be used, its sole epistemological import seemed to be that *a priori* principles were unrevisable in the course of experience.

Quine's celebrated attack on the analytic/synthetic distinction is, at least in part, a critique of this epistemological vestige.[25] Quine argues that there is no important difference between those modifications of one's corpus of beliefs that occur when one abandons a particular concept and those that obtain in revision of allegedly "substantive" claims. From one perspective, this might be viewed as removing the last traces of Kant's doctrines about *a priori* knowledge; from another, it can be seen as teasing out those themes in Kant that make him insist on the importance of showing the legitimacy of our concepts.

Recent decades have seen both a more sympathetic return to the epistemological notion of the *a priori* and the exploration of a variety of concepts that descend from Kant's. In seminal work, Saul Kripke argued that "*a priori*" is primarily an epistemological predicate and that it is not simply to be definitionally equated with "analytic" or "necessary."[26] His arguments have provoked further scrutiny of the official epistemological notion, and of the idea of "independence from experience." The result has been a distinction of the weak and strong notions of apriority (see section 2), and investigation of whether our mathematical knowledge can be defended as *a priori* in either sense.[27]

As I have suggested in the last section, it would be wrong to insist on this conception as the only approach to the *a priori* that is valuable for articulating Kantian themes in contemporary philosophy. There has been a rich tradition of Kantian philosophy that has pursued the post-Fregean line of treating epistemological issues in the spare idiom of logical relations, considering whether there are presuppositions of ordinary conceptions of the world or of scientific inquiry that resemble the principles Kant hailed as privileged; in recent explorations, what used to be seen as the embarrassment of Kant's commitment to the apriority of Euclidean geometry has been transformed into the development of an idea of the "relativized *a priori*," which can illuminate the ways in which abstract principles frame the project of physical inquiry at different times.[28] Further, although it has been relatively neglected, the "tacit knowledge" conception of the *a priori* serves as a basis for pursuing Kantian themes in the context of the burgeoning cognitive sciences. The burden of this essay has been that no one of these approaches can do justice to the tangle of ideas about the *a priori* that we find in the first *Critique*.

By the same token, the different strands in that tangle can provide us with resources for addressing a variety of enduring philosophical questions.

NOTES

*Thanks to Christia Mercer for some helpful advice. I am especially grateful to Paul Guyer for his thoughtful and constructive suggestions about an earlier draft.

1. For important pre-Kantian examples, see the discussion of axioms in Antoine Arnauld, *The Art of Thinking* (1662; Indianapolis: Bobbs-Merrill, 1964) Part IV, Chapter 6; and Leibniz's accounts in the *New Essays on Human Understanding* (1765; Cambridge: Cambridge University Press, 1982), particularly in the explicit drawing of an *a priori/a posteriori* distinction in Book IV, Chapter 9. Leibniz's approach to these questions is given a valuable, if brief, discussion in Robert Merrihew Adams, *Leibniz: Determinist, Theist, Idealist* (New York: Oxford University Press, 1994) 109–10; less focused on the epistemological issues that concern me here, but still illuminating, is Margaret Wilson, "On Leibniz's Explication of 'Necessary Truth'," in Harry Frankfurt (ed.), *Leibniz: A Collection of Critical Essays* (Notre Dame: Notre Dame University Press, 1976), 401–19.

   In the *Principles of Philosophy*, Descartes seems to commit himself to an ambitious program of arriving at basic laws of the physical sciences on the basis of reason alone; thus, he maintains that the fundamental principles that govern the motions of bodies can be established on the basis of reason, and that we need only experiments to determine the particular configurations that God has actually brought about. See Descartes' *The Philosophical Writings of Descartes*, John Cottingham, Robert Stoothoff, and Dugald Murdoch, (eds.) (Cambridge: Cambridge University Press, 1985), Volume I, 256–7; see also 245. The same attitude is developed also in Section 6 of his *Discourse on Method* (Indianapolis: Hackett, 1993), 36–8; this discussion corresponds to pages 64–8 in volume 6 of the standard French edition of Descartes' works, *Oeuvres*, M. Adam and M. Tannery (eds.) (Paris: Vrin, 1965).

2. See John Locke, *Essay Concerning Human Understanding*, Book IV, Chapter IV, Section 7; George Berkeley, A Treatise Concerning the *Principles of Human Knowledge*, Sections 118–32; David Hume, *A Treatise of Human Nature*, Book I, Part iii, Section 1 (Hume, unlike Locke and Berkeley, has concerns about the certainty of our geometrical knowledge, but he joins the empiricist consensus with respect to arithmetic).

3. Here and elsewhere I shall quote from the translation of Kant's *Critique of Pure Reason* by Paul Guyer and Allen Wood (Cambridge: Cambridge University Press, 1998). In discussing Kant, however, I shall use the term "knowledge" (and "items of knowledge") rather than talking about "cognitions."

4. Indeed, even earlier in the book; see, for example, the specification of the project in the Preface to the First Edition, where Kant takes the question to be "how much we can hope to achieve by reason, when all the material and assistance of experience are taken away" (A xiv).

5. Issues about origins of knowledge will reemerge in section 4.

6. For a more detailed account of the notions of apriority sketched in the following paragraphs, see my essays "*A Priori* Knowledge," *Philosophical Review* 89 (1980), 3–23, and "*A Priori* Knowledge Revisited," in Paul Boghossian and Christopher Peacocke (eds.), *New Essays on the A Priori* (Oxford: Oxford Univesity Press, 2000) 65–91.

7. Without this last condition, the processes allegedly producing *a priori* knowledge might generate *false* beliefs; hence the status of the belief states as items of *knowledge* would not be maintained under rival experiences.

8. Gottlob Frege, *Foundations of Arithmetic* (Oxford: Blackwell, 1950), 99–100.

9. I consider this Kantian position in much more detail in "How Kant Almost Wrote 'Two Dogmas of Empiricism' (And Why He Didn't)," *Philosophical Topics* 12 (1981), 217–49.

10. I shall consider an alternative below in section 4.

11. I have discussed this at greater length in "Kant and the Foundations of Mathematics," *Philosophical Review* 84 (1975), 23–50 and in *The Nature of Mathematical Knowledge* (New York: Oxford University Press, 1983), Chapter 3.

12. See my "Kant and the Foundations of Mathematics." For an important and different line of critical analysis of Kant's position, see Charles Parsons, "Infinity and Kant's Conception of the 'Possibility of Experience'," *Philosophical Review* 73 (1964), 183–97.

13. See Saul Kripke, *Naming and Necessity* (Cambridge, MA: Harvard University Press, 1980).

14. The line of interpretation I'm rejecting here pervades my previous work on Kant's treatment of the *a priori*. It has the advantage of reserving a single conception of *a priori* knowledge – the official epistemological interpretation – and the disadvantage of fitting very badly with large parts of Kant's usage of "*a priori*" and cognate terms when he is not discussing logic, mathematics, and other "truths of reason."

15. This view is defended in many of Noam Chomsky's writings. See for example his *Reflections on Language* (New York: Pantheon, 1975).

16. Here I have been helped by Patricia Kitcher's discussions of the *a priori*, both in Chapter 1 of her *Kant's Transcendental Psychology* (New York: Oxford University Press, 1990), and in her "Revisiting Kant's Epistemology: Skepticism, Apriority, and Psychologism," *Noûs* 29 (1995), 285–315. I should note that she does not present this approach to apriority in quite the way I do here.

17. This somewhat convoluted formulation is needed to allow for the possibility that the same proposition could be known both tacitly *a priori* and also explicitly in some independent way. In cases where there is no such explicit knowledge of *p*, conditions (iii) and (iv) can be replaced by (iii') the subject's belief that *p* is necessarily used in arriving at and justifying empirical judgments, and (iv') the subject cannot fully articulate the belief that *p*. Quite evidently, in cases where there's both tacit and explicit knowledge, (iv') will be false. To cope with those cases, one needs a way of identifying the independence (causally and justificationally) of different states with the same content. Hence, the more complicated formulation of the text.

18. See Patricia Kitcher, *Kant's Transcendental Psychology*.

19. In my judgment, the best reconstruction of this proof is that given by Paul Guyer, *Kant and the Claims of Knowledge* (Cambridge: Cambridge University Press, 1987), 241–59, although I am not sure that Guyer would agree with my claims about the status of the premises.

20. Two outstanding examples of this tradition are Peter Strawson, *The Bounds of Sense* (London: Methuen, 1966) and Michael Friedman, *Kant and the Exact Sciences* (Cambridge, MA: Harvard University Press, 1992).

21. Indeed, I believe that Friedman provides considerable illumination of Kant's efforts to identify the presuppositions of Newtonian accounts of space and time. See Friedman, *Kant and the Exact Sciences*.

22. See Frege, *Foundations of Arithmetic*. I have discussed the relation between Frege's views about mathematical knowledge and those of Kant in "Frege's Epistemology," *Philosophical Review* 88 (1979), 235–62. For a different perspective, see Tyler Burge, "Frege on Apriority," in Boghossian and Peacocke (eds.), *New Essays on the A Priori*.

23. This phrase is from the Preface to Frege's *Basic Laws of Arithmetic*.

24. See, for example, Rudolf Carnap, *The Logical Syntax of Language* (London: Routledge and Kegan Paul, 1937) and A. J. Ayer, *Language, Truth, and Logic* (London: V. Gollancz, 1936).

25. See W.V.O. Quine, "Two Dogmas of Empiricism," in his *From a Logical Point of View* (Cambridge, MA: Harvard University Press, 1953), especially the final section.

26. See Kripke, *Naming and Necessity.*

27. For illuminating exploration of these issues, see Laurence Bonjour, *In Defense of Pure Reason* (Cambridge: Cambridge University Press, 1998), the essays collected in Boghossian and Peacocke (eds.), *New Essays on the A Priori*, and Albert Casullo, *A Priori Justification* (New York: Oxford University Press, 2003). My own skepticism about the apriority of mathematics is articulated in *The Nature of Mathematical Knowledge*, and in "*A Priori* Knowledge Revisited."

28. For elaboration of this approach to Kant, and for links to Thomas Kuhn's ideas about scientific change, see Michael Friedman, *Dynamics of Reason* (Stanford: CSLI Publications, 2001).

2 Kant on the perception of space (and time)

Although the "Transcendental Aesthetic" is the briefest part of the first *Critique*, it has garnered a lion's share of discussion.[1] This fact reflects the important implications that Kant drew from his arguments there. He used the arguments concerning space and time to display examples of synthetic *a priori* cognition, to secure his division between intuitions and concepts, and to support transcendental idealism. Earlier, in the years around 1770, Kant's investigations into space and time had facilitated his turn toward "critical" philosophy. Prior to that time, Kant's main interests in space and time pertained to physics and metaphysics. As he entered the critical period, he delved into the cognitive basis of our experience of space (and time), and drew his conclusions about their ideality.

Kant's doctrines of space and time provoked extensive response in his own time and throughout the nineteenth century. These responses variously concerned the metaphysics, physics, epistemology, psychology, and geometry of space. Throughout the nineteenth century, philosophers, physiologists, and psychologists sought to extend or to refute Kant's theories of space. By the last decades of the nineteenth century, many had rightly concluded that the existence of non-Euclidean geometry as a candidate description of physical space refuted Kant's full doctrine of space – though some have hoped that his position might be saved by restricting it to "visual space."

This chapter first examines the background to Kant's work on space (and time) in the writings (primarily) of Descartes, Leibniz, Wolff, and Crusius. It then follows the development of Kant's own views, from his first writings through the second edition of the *Critique of Pure Reason*. Finally, it surveys the reception of his mature views in the nineteenth and twentieth centuries.

Space and time, or the related concepts of extension and duration, attained special prominence in early modern philosophy because of their importance in the new science. Prior to Newton, the mechanical philosophies of Descartes, Galileo, Gassendi, Boyle, and others designated a subset of the Lockean "primary qualities" as the fundamental properties of matter: size, shape, position, and motion. Size and shape are, in early modern parlance, "modes" or "modifications" of extension or space; position is a spatial relation; and motion requires space and time. Subsequently, the absolute space and time of Newtonian mechanics sparked further debate, most notably the *Leibniz–Clarke Correspondence* (published in 1717).

Metaphysical questions surrounding the new science pertained to the nature of space and time and their relation to matter. Epistemological questions pertained to the cognition of space itself or extension in general (including geometry, understood to be the science of extension), and also to the operation of the senses in perceiving the actual spatial order of things. Various positions emerged in both domains, and debate continued to the time of Kant.

In the *Principles of Philosophy*, Descartes staked out a bold new position, which equated space with matter.[2] Famously, he held that the essence of matter is *extension*: spatial extension in three dimensions. There is no distinction between matter and space. Matter is not *in* space; rather, its own extension is required for there to be any spatiality at all. Consequently, Descartes ruled out, on metaphysical grounds, the existence of a true vacuum. He maintained that the world is a plenum, that is, it is completely filled with matter, which is infinitely divisible. Some of this matter is a fine dust called the aether, which fills in between larger particles (with no gaps). Descartes held a relational view of position, according to which the positions of bodies are defined in relation to other bodies. There is no coordinate system of spatial positions independent of material things.

The extension that constitutes the essence of matter was, in Descartes' view, the object of geometry. He held that the truths of geometry are known innately by the human mind, through the "pure intellect" operating independently of the senses. In perceiving these geometrical truths, the intellect perceives also the essence of matter, and therefore comes to know what properties matter can and cannot have (independently of matter's existence). For instance, any matter that takes the shape of a right triangle must exhibit the Pythagorean relations between sides and hypotenuse. In this way, the pure intellect knows the real possibilities of bodies as they are in themselves.[3]

Descartes distinguished the purely intellectual apprehension of extension from the perception of the shape, size, and distances of extended things by means of the senses. Sense-perception depends on bodily organs. The mind must be affected so as to experience sensations and perceptions of spatial properties. In vision, the primary sensations are produced by a two-dimensional pattern in the brain that echoes the retinal image. The sensation itself is of a two-dimensional array of light and color. These sensations are altered into perceptions by a variety of psychological mechanisms, including unnoticed judgments that infer the distant sizes and shapes of things. Sense-perceptions are adequate for everyday life, but not for metaphysics. Indeed, Descartes described sensations of qualities such as color as "obscure and confused," because we are unable to tell from them whether there is a property in bodies resembling the color we experience. The pure intellect must tell us the essential properties of bodies as they are in themselves, which are modes of extension (primary qualities) only.[4]

Descartes' metaphysics of space was set against the doctrines of ancient atomism, as revived and promoted by Pierre Gassendi and others. According to atomism, matter comes as small, indivisible particles or "atoms." These are distributed through space itself, conceived as an empty container. Where there are no atoms, there is a vacuum (empty space).

Newton was an atomist who posited an absolute space and time as a (potentially empty) container.[5] He held that the containing space provides an absolute framework for motion. According to Newton's laws of motion, any change in motion (defined as an acceleration) requires a cause (an acting force). However, the changes involved pertain to absolute motion in relation to space, not merely to the motion of one body in relation to another. To see this, consider two bodies that are accelerating away from one another. There are three possibilities for the true story about their absolute motions (and hence about the true forces): (1) one body is at rest (or in inertial motion) and the second is accelerating (which requires that it is acted upon by force); (2) they are both accelerating (both are acted upon by forces); or (3) the first body is accelerating and the second is at rest (or in inertial motion). A gap between two bodies (considered to be alone in the universe, if you like) that widens at a given rate is consistent with three different causal scenarios.

Newton's postulation of an invisible, homogeneous, and potentially empty space (and time) was subject to criticism. Leibniz, in correspondence with Samuel Clarke (who acted as Newton's mouthpiece), advanced both metaphysical and epistemological objections. Epistemologically, he objected that absolute motion in relation to a containing space could not be discerned. (Suppose first that the universe is at rest in relation to absolute space, and then instead that it is in inertial motion; the difference is undetectable according to Newton's theory.) Metaphysically, he appealed to the principle of sufficient reason (among other arguments). He argued that God would have no reason to place the universe (holding its internal spatial relations constant) in one position in absolute space rather than another (or to create it at one instant rather than another in time). But, in his view, God always acts for a (nonarbitrary) reason. Further, he asked what the (potentially empty) containing space is supposed to be. If it is a substance, would it be coeternal with God? If it is a property, what is it a property of? Clarke wrote as if it were a property of God, or of God's sensorium, to which Leibniz responded scornfully that this would make God an extended thing, or at least give him extended parts or organs.[6]

Leibniz's own position, which is only partially revealed in the Leibniz–Clark correspondence, was that space is relational, phenomenal, and ideal. Leibniz argued that the essence of matter could not be extension, as Descartes had maintained, but must also include force. He also held that anything composite (as bodies are) must be constituted from, or at least based upon, simples. In positing his (infinity of) simple substances, or "monads," he conceived of them by analogy with minds, as immaterial (or "metaphysical") points, which have internal states but no external relations – causal, spatial, or otherwise (no windows or doors). The internal states are perceptions, which mirror the whole universe from a point of view. That is, they portray a spatially extended universe of bodies that can be described, in accordance with the mechanical philosophy, as matter in motion (in a plenum). But those bodies are phenomenal and ideal: they are "well-founded phenomena," founded in their agreement with the perceptions of other individual substances (and with the divine vision of the universe).[7]

In the Leibniz–Clarke correspondence, without revealing his position that bodies are phenomena, Leibniz argued that space is constituted by relations among bodies. Space is the perception of the order of coexistences – or rather, of possible relations of coexistence. Bodies at an instant have a set of actual relations among themselves; the idea of space comes from recognizing that they could be otherwise ordered (switching two small bits of matter, or reordering it all). The mind thus recognizes space as the set of possible relations among bodies. Space is ideal just in the sense that it abstracts away from the actual relations among really existing bodies (in the language of the *Correspondence*) to represent possible relations.

This point about the ideality of space is consistent with but independent of the claim that bodies are phenomenal (i.e., are well-founded phenomena). It is also independent of Leibniz's claim that there are neither direct causal interactions nor actual external relations between the monads themselves. Among this group of doctrines, some were better known in the eighteenth century than others. Leibniz discussed the ideality of space at length in the *Correspondence*. His system of preestablished harmony, as an alternative to mind–body interaction, had been published in 1695, and he referred to it in the *Correspondence*. However, the *Correspondence* is written as if the relations among material bodies are real, and as if material bodies causally interact with one another.[8] The *Correspondence* maintains the ideality of space without the *Monadology*'s noninteracting immaterial substances lacking external relations. (As should be apparent, Leibniz's "ideality" of space is not equivalent to Kant's transcendental idealism; but Kant's position has similarity with Leibniz's phenomenalism.)

Leibniz's account of sensory representations of space suggests that they are confused representations of the underlying reality (the monads), though this aspect of his phenomenalism about body was not well represented in his eighteenth-century published works. In published works, he affirmed the Cartesian point that the senses present confused images of things, at least as regards secondary qualities. He did not hold that these images should themselves be clarified by analyzing them; rather, clear ideas should be used to draw conclusions about their causes. Sensory images, even involving secondary qualities such as color, may have a regular relation to the cause of color in objects (a structure that reflects light in a certain way), but we cannot discern this fact by attending carefully to the sensory ideas. Rather, we must come to understand how light works and how it affects our nerves.[9]

If space is ideal and phenomenal, what implications does this have for geometry as the science of extension? It might seem as if Leibniz would adopt an abstractionist view of extension and geometry. Aristotelian philosophy had held that the object of geometry, "intelligible extension," is abstracted from sensory experience. This abstractionist position was challenged by Descartes and others (and later by Kant) to show how the cognitive basis of mathematics could be empirical, since mathematics achieves demonstrative certainty about perfect shapes, which are not found in sensory images.[10] Leibniz offered a version of this challenge, but he did not affirm Descartes' contention that the pure intellect can contemplate a purely intelligible extension. He agreed with Descartes that the intellect possesses innate ideas, or "seeds of eternity," that can serve to establish the universal, necessary truths of geometry.[11] By contrast with Descartes, who held that these ideas can be found by turning away from the senses, Leibniz held that they are awakened by sensory images. And yet Leibniz distinguished such ideas from sensory images, thereby affirming that there are thoughts without images – without suggesting that these thoughts directly present an intelligible extension. He gave a hint in the *New Essays* that geometry might be based on number and logic. In unpublished papers, he offered the hope that geometry could be reduced to logical identities without a need for spatial images.[12]

Christian Wolff was the dominant philosopher in Germany at mid-century. In some ways a follower of Leibniz, he did not adopt Leibniz's positions wholesale. He accepted that composite things are constituted from simples (though finite in number). He agreed that the simple substances are indivisible and unextended. He also adopted the relational view of space. However, unlike Leibniz's actual position (but more like the position Leibniz took in the *Correspondence*), Wolff held that (a finite number of) simple substances are aggregated to form continuously extended bodies. He affirmed real relations among simples, both spatial and causal. Contra Leibniz, he held that bodies causally influence one another directly. He merely tentatively endorsed Leibniz's "preestablished harmony" for mind–body relations.[13] By contrast, Alexander Baumgarten, a Wolffian philosopher of sorts, adopted a pre-established harmony for both body–body and mind–body interaction.[14]

As regards the ontology and epistemology of space, Wolff held that space is ideal but not merely phenomenal (in Leibniz's sense). Bodily extension is composed of unextended simple substances. Our perceptions of those substances represent their coexistent order as a spatial order, which it is (that is, it is a set of actual external relations among simples). Perceived space represents the real relations among things. Yet it does so only confusedly. We are in fact unable to understand how unextended simples can be composed to form continuously extended bodies. Accordingly, our spatial perceptions must be considered as confused. If they represented the simple substances clearly, we would be able to "see" or understand how unextended simples can yield extension.[15]

Christian August Crusius (whose work Kant admired in his early years) pounced on this implication of the Wolffian position, complaining that the relational view of space rendered it into a "*Götze*" (false idol) of the imagination.[16] Crusius aimed to establish a metaphysical basis for absolute space and to show how extended things could be composed of simple substances. He considered space to be neither a substance nor a property. As he put it, "substances must be in space"; space is not in the substances. Space is not an inhering property of anything; rather, properties inhere in the things that are in space. Neither is space a set of relations, for there are many relations – even of "next-to-ness" (as in a melody) – that are not spatial. Rather, spatial relations arise because things are *somewhere* in space.[17]

Crusius considered space to be an aspect of the reality of things as they really are. He held that the finite world of matter is composed of indivisible parts (substances) that fill space. From this merely finite world, we would not derive an infinite, absolute spatial framework. But Crusius sided with Newton and Clarke in holding that there is an infinite absolute space into which the finite world could be placed in one location or another. This infinite space is an abstraction from the existence of God, or from his omnipresence. Crusius held that God "fills" space, but is not extended (and that unextended souls "fill space" too). He sustained his distinction between being extended and being space-filling by defining an extended thing as something that has "actual parts." But God is indivisible and has no actual parts, hence is (in this technical sense) not extended, even though he fills space. Crusius also held that the elemental parts of matter (simple substances) fill space but are not extended. According to Crusius, there is no truly empty space (God is everywhere), but the infinite space abstracted from God's being can be empty of matter, or not.[18]

Through his unextended but space-filling material elements, Crusius claimed to show how extension can arise from unextended parts (thereby countering Wolff's claim that the spatial representations are inherently confused). The unextended (indivisible but space-filling) elements of matter, when put alongside one another, form a composite thing, which is divisible and so extended. Because the elements are already spatial, they can be composed to yield a continuous space, actually divisible into simples, and infinitely divisible in thought. He also claimed to provide a basis for cognizing infinite, absolute space, by abstraction from an unextended but space-filling God. He further held that magnitude, as the object of mathematics, is an abstraction from existing things: God and bodies.[19] This makes geometry rely for its object on content abstracted from the reality of things. However, Crusius (by contrast with Kant's subsequent critical attitude) held that mathematics could nonetheless achieve perfectly general definitions that would apply to all instances (and support demonstrative reasoning). It could do so because, in abstracting its object, it pays attention solely to magnitude itself. By contrast, philosophy treats of things together with their accidents. Crusius therefore reasoned that in mathematics alone, a single instance could provide the exemplar for mathematical definitions that would apply to all other instances.[20]

The theory of the senses, and especially vision, attracted philosophical discussion throughout the eighteenth century, stimulated by Descartes' Dioptrics and Berkeley's New Theory of Vision, among others. The psychological process of spatial perception was widely discussed in Germany. While Kant was working on his first Critique, J. N. Tetens published an extensive discussion of the perception of size in individual objects by means of the senses.[21]

A central problem in these discussions was to explain why we experience objects at close range to remain a constant size, even at different distances. If an object is seen at four and then at eight paces from the viewer, the size of its image on the retina is reduced by half (along any axis). Most eighteenth-century theorists held that we nonetheless experience the object as of a constant size. Tetens agreed, and suggested that in the second case the sensation is altered to produce an image of the full-sized object. He observed that some theorists ascribed this alteration to associative processes in which true sizes are associated with various projected sizes and cues for distance, while others ascribed it to a process of reasoning, in which projected size and distance are combined according to geometrical relations. Tetens rejected both types of theory. Instead, he described the process as a kind of abstraction from variations in projected size. In the normal course of things, we come to recognize objects when they are near to us and fill the visual field. When the object is further away, we recognize it as the same object, but do not notice its small projected size. We abstract from the small size, and experience the object as we did under the circumstances in which we first came to recognize it, with its "normal" size. As in the other accounts, the result of this psychological operation is phenomenally immediate, and we do not even notice that the sensation has been altered.

Without entering further into the details of Teten's position, we may note that Kant was aware of the fact that typical accounts of perception posited association or judgment – or, in Teten's case, a sensory act of abstraction – to underlie visual appearances. This is apparent from his discussion of the moon illusion, which he ascribes to the influence of imagination (presumably, through association) in making the moon appear larger at the horizon than overhead (A 295–7/B 351–4).

2. KANT'S EARLY WRITINGS ON SPACE
AND SPATIAL COGNITION

Kant discussed space and spatiality in his early works on physics and metaphysics, adopting a quasi-Leibnizian, relational view of space. He considered himself to have solved certain problems that plagued the positions of Leibniz, Wolff, and the Wolffians. In essence, he came to see space as an appearance of real relations, but one that was neither merely ideal nor confused. He arrived at these improvements by applying Crusius's ideas to the question that Wolff had found insoluble: how simple substances might fill space without being rendered divisible.

The *New Elucidation* of 1755 examined the "first principles of metaphysical cognition."[22] It first covered the principle of contradiction and the principle of a "determining ground" or sufficient reason, before turning to the principles of succession and coexistence. These latter two principles concern the causal sequence of changes of states in substances over time, and the basis of the coexistent relations of states and so the basis of space. In the section on the principle of succession, Kant argued that changes depend on the "reciprocal dependency" of substances on one another. If individual substances were in causal isolation (as Baumgarten in fact argued), they would have no impetus to change states and would therefore remain always in the same condition (1:410–11). (Once an isolated substance was in one state, it would have no basis for determining itself to change states.) Change arises through the interaction of substances, or their mutual causal dependence. These interactions establish the relations that exist among coexistent substances, as well. In this way, Kant considered himself to have overturned the Wolffians (in fact, his position on causal influence goes against Baumgarten, but not Wolff himself), and also Leibniz's preestablished harmony between soul and body (1:411–12).

Kant held that substances would not, merely in virtue of their existence, stand in any relation to one another. Rather, it is only through real reciprocal causal relations (grounded in a divine conception of their mutual relations) that things obtain real relations among themselves.[23] These relations then constitute the space of the substances, as in the Leibnizian relational view of space. As Kant put it, "place, position, and space are relations of substances, in virtue of which substances, by means of their reciprocal determinations, relate to other substances which are really distinct from themselves and are in this way connected together in an external connection" (1:414). In the work of 1755, Kant said little about the cognition of space, merely observing that the "concept of space" is constituted by cognition of "the interconnected actions of substances," that is, their reciprocal actions (1:415).

In the *Physical Monadology* of 1756, Kant advanced a conception of space as an appearance. The work was devoted to the problem of reconciling the infinite divisibility of space as posited by geometry with the simple substances advanced by the metaphysicians (including Leibniz, Wolff, Baumgarten, and, in his own way, Crusius). Kant accepted that space is infinitely divisible. He also accepted that bodies are constituted from simples, though he specified that their number should be finite. He departed from Leibniz and Wolff in saying that "each monad is not only in space; it also fills a space" (1:480). Talk of simple substances "filling space" was of course applied by Crusius to God, souls, and the simple substances constituting matter.

Kant developed and altered Crusius's position, combining the relational view of space found in Leibniz and Wolff with talk of "monads," now conceived in Crusian fashion. He treated monads as "filling space" without being (physically or metaphysically) divisible. Crusius had said that the space of simple, indivisible substances is technically not extended (because indivisible), but Kant dropped this definition of extension. However, again echoing Crusius,[24] he held that the monads stand in real relations through causal interaction. But departing from Crusius, he held that space arises solely from these interactions (rather than the monads being in a space provided by God's omnipresence). As Kant saw things, in the light of his relational view of space, each monad determines "the little space of its presence" (1:480) through forces that it exerts on the substances next to it. As in the *New Elucidation*, an order of relations among coexistent things arises from causal relations of mutual dependence among substances, though now these relations are explained as interactive forces.

Space is "the appearance of the external relations of unitary monads" (1:479). With this doctrine, Kant in effect claimed to solve Wolff's problem of how to derive a continuous space from indivisible simples, thereby avoiding the bane of previous supporters of monads, who had "regarded it as their duty to maintain that the properties of geometrical space were imaginary" (1:480). Although he did not mention names, his position departed from both the phenomenal space of Leibniz and the confused representations of Wolff. Contrary to Leibniz, Kant's space is not merely phenomenal; it is the appearance of real relations (that form a real external space). But contrary to Wolff, this appearance need not be regarded as confused, because Kant has claimed to solve the problem of how a finite composition of simples could yield a continuous space.

In 1756, when Kant described space as an appearance, it may seem as if he was asserting its phenomenality (in Leibniz's sense) or ideality (in his later sense). He says that the continuously divisible space of mathematics arises as "an appearance of the external relations" among indivisible simples (1:479). But he also says that these simple substances "fill space" through their "sphere of activity" (1:480–1). The divisibility found in appearance is grounded in the continuous space-filling actions of simple substances. The space of appearance echoes the space created by the monads.

3. THE SHIFT TO ABSOLUTE SPACE, AND THE CRITICAL TURN

Having started with a relational view of space, Kant changed his mind by 1768, when his *Concerning the Ultimate Ground of the Differentiation of Directions in Space* appeared. He now advocated an "absolute and original space" in which physical things are located (2:383). His arguments for this space hinged largely on the consideration of incongruent counterparts. The arguments did not directly establish a mind-independent absolute space, but they revealed that the Leibnizian or relational view, as Kant had understood it, could not capture certain distinctions that exist in our descriptions of space. By contrast, a view of space as an empty, absolute container could account for these distinctions.

Incongruent counterparts are spatial structures (shapes) in which all internal sizes and relations are identical, but which cannot be made to coincide spatially. Typical examples include objects that are (precise) mirror images of one another, such as left and right hands, or left and right ears. For true counterparts, if one measured all the relations among the fingers of left and right hands and wrote them down, the listed measurements would be identical: the thumb would be x units long and its joint would be y units from the knuckle of the index finger. Although the listed measurements for each hand would not differ, a right hand will not fit into the space of a left hand (or into its glove).

Kant's argument that a relational theory is precluded by the existence of incongruent counterparts depends partly on his conception of the relational view. He has in mind a view in which space is constituted from relations among simples. His argument also depends on what should be asked of a theory. Kant expects the theory to account for our "intuitive judgments about extension" (2:378). That is, he expects a metaphysical theory of space to account for the descriptive judgments we make about space. Now Kant asks: from describing relations among simples, without orienting them to directions in space, can we distinguish the description of two actually distinct (according to our perception), incongruent counterparts? Kant correctly answered "no."[25]

To see this, continue the set of measurements on your hands, seeking a description that someone else (or you on another occasion) could use to construct a congruent hand. Holding the position of one hand fixed, measure the length of each finger, the distances between each pair of adjacent joints, the distance from the wrist knob to each knuckle, and so on, and then go on to the other. Considered purely as internal relations defined by the structure of each hand, these two sets of measurements cannot be distinguished. To distinguish them, one must orient the hands in space, and note that on the left hand (as viewed from above with palm down) the index finger is to the left of the thumb, whereas on the right hand it is to the right. Such descriptions use the orienting directions of *up*, *down*, *right*, and *left*. To convey these directions in a description, they must be related either to the directionality in our individual perceptual spaces to a common external frame (absolute space). This can be verified by trying to use one of the descriptions to construct a specific hand. Failing an appeal to an external frame (to right and left, up and down), one will be unable to provide distinct instructions for constructing either a left or a right hand.

In 1768, Kant's conclusion was that "the ground of the determination of a corporeal form does not depend simply on the relation and position of its parts to each other; it also depends on the reference of that physical form to universal absolute space, as it is conceived by the geometers" (2:381). This is the universal and absolute space of Newton. Bodies possess a distinctive structure in the relations among their parts that can be described only by appeal to directions defined within this encompassing space. If, as in Kant's conclusion just quoted, the "ground of the determination" pertains to our descriptions or cognitions of space, then his argument is unassailable. But if he means to say that an existing thing could not exhibit handedness independently of our ability to distinguish that handedness descriptively, then the argument fails. A set of oppositely handed relations might exist, whether we are able to find a framework for describing them or not. Kant's metaphysical argument depends on an epistemic argument about what can be conveyed cognitively in descriptions of parts and their relations.

Two years later, when he presented his inaugural *Dissertation*, Kant again supported an absolute spatial framework, but he now denied that such a space exists apart from our perceptions – a conception that he had, in 1768, already described as involving "difficulties" (2:383). He rejected both the relational view of Leibniz and the "English" view of space as an "*absolute* and boundless *receptacle* of possible things" (2:403). He now asserted that "Space is not something objective and real, nor is it a substance, nor an accident, nor a relation; it is, rather, subjective and ideal; it issues from the mind in accordance with a stable law as a scheme, so to speak, for co-ordinating everything which is sensed externally" (2:403). Kant now asserts the *ideality* of space in his critical sense of that term. He also holds that "the concept of space" is an "intuition" (2:402), which means that the representation of space is a concrete image (not a discursive concept).[26]

Kant's absolute spatial framework is no longer a Newtonian container, but is now a phenomenally given appearance. He sought to support this position by undermining attempts (which he associated with Leibnizian and Wolffian views) to abstract spatial representation from sensory experience. He contended that the concept of space is "presupposed" by the perceptions of the external senses; sensations can be located outside us, and next to one another, only if a space exists for so ordering them (2:402). This space is "a singular representation," embracing all spaces within itself, unlike an abstract concept, under which instances fall. It is "a pure intuition," which means it is not compounded from sensations. It provides the "form" or the structure in which all sensations are ordered. (We will return to similar arguments in the next section.)

To support the point that space is a pure intuition, Kant again employed the argument from incongruent counterparts, now restricted to the cognition and description of an ideal or phenomenal space (which suits the argument). Kant argued that our discursive description of an incongruent counterpart could be made determinate so as to distinguish left and right hands only if spatial intuition were already given with the directions up and down, right and left. That is, any merely conceptual description of the counterparts could not supply a directional framework; our spatial representations must arise as a concrete intuition or image. From this argument, he also concluded that geometry cannot content itself with mere discursive descriptions and universal concepts, but must appeal to concrete or "singular" intuitions (2:403). Discursive descriptions would be unable to capture directions in space without an ostensive basis (in an imagistic representation).

Kant's argument that "space is not something objective and real" (whether "substance," "accident," or "relation"), but "is, rather, subjective and ideal," depended on ruling out the two alternative theories named above: that space exists apart from perceptions as an absolute container or as relations among elements. He baldly described real absolute space (apart from perception) as "a fable" because "it invents an infinite number of true relations without there being any beings which are related to one another" (2:404). This is a version of the arguments found in Leibniz and Crusius, namely, that absolute space considered as an infinite receptacle cannot be a substance (otherwise it would compete with God as an infinite substance), nor an accident or relation, since by hypothesis there is no substance for it to be an accident or relation of. Further, Kant could not accept the Crusian abstraction of space from the omnipresence of God, for it spatializes God, whom he placed outside time and space (2:297, 414).

Kant offered an epistemological objection to relational space: it could not account for the necessity of geometry. In his view, if space were abstracted from the given relations of things, our knowledge of space would be empirical and so could not support apodictic certainty. However, geometry provides us with apodictic knowledge of spatial structure. This would be explained if our spatial representations were subjective and ideal (on the assumption that they must conform uniformly to Euclid's geometry). Hence, our subjective space is "the foundation of all truth in outer sensibility" (2:404). Because all spatial perceptions are constructed according to the same laws of sensibility, the properties of pure intuition (as described by geometry) must apply to all empirical intuition. Hence, the applicability of geometrical descriptions to the physical world (as experienced) is guaranteed.

With these arguments and conclusions, many of which will reappear in the "Transcendental Aesthetic" of the *Critique of Pure Reason*, Kant has begun his critical turn. Missing is the limitation of the intellect or understanding to possible experience. In the *Dissertation* (2:392, 402–5), Kant still held that the form of the intelligible world can be understood through causal relations (though no longer through spatial relations, which do not apply to intelligible beings). Once he had achieved the critical restriction of all cognition to actual or possible experience, the previously secured ideality of space and time entailed his mature position of transcendental idealism, thereby also entailing the impossibility of traditional metaphysical knowledge of things as they are in themselves.

4. SPACE (AND TIME) IN THE "TRANSCENDENTAL AESTHETIC"

Kant's arguments in the "Transcendental Aesthetic" of the *Critique of Pure Reason*, first published in 1781 and then revised in 1787, are intended to establish the ideality of an absolute (as opposed to relational) space and time. More precisely, he intended to establish the transcendental ideality of space, which meant that it was not only dependent on human perception, but was also an *a priori*, necessary, and universal representation. He employed several arguments to achieve this aim. Some of the arguments were conceptual: he contended that spatiality was presupposed by spatial representation, and that empty space was a more fundamental representation than space with objects. Other arguments were epistemological. Drawing on his conceptual arguments, he contended that the representation of space could not arise from experience (by abstraction from things as given in space). It is difficult to see how these arguments could establish Kantian ideality of space (that it pertains to perception only, not to things in themselves), at least not without other premises. Kant also maintained that the necessary and universal cognitions found in geometry could be explained only if space was an *a priori* form of representation that universally structures all intuition, and hence that also accounts for the conformity of physical objects in experience to the geometry of that *a priori* spatial structure. This argument, if correct, might establish ideality.

These arguments appear in both the first and second editions of the Aesthetic, though in the second edition the argument from geometry is separated from the conceptual (and related epistemological) arguments. Here we follow the second version, in which Kant offers four numbered arguments in the "metaphysical exposition" of the concept of space. By establishing that our representations of space and time are fundamentally intuitions and not general concepts, these four arguments are intended to refute metaphysical and epistemological implications of the relational view of space – as well as, to a lesser extent, those of the (Newtonian) absolute view – and also to establish Kant's fundamental distinction between intuitions and concepts.

In preparation for his numbered arguments, Kant draws several key distinctions. He distinguishes *sensibility*, as a passive faculty of receiving representations, from the *understanding*, as the faculty of thought. He calls the "immediate" representations of sensibility *intuitions*, as distinct from *concepts* employed by the understanding. Within intuitions, he distinguishes the sensations proper (for vision, color, and intensity), which he calls the *matter* of sensory appearance, from the *form* of the appearance, which is "that which makes it that the manifold of appearance can be ordered in specific relations" (A 20/B 34). (Soon he will speak of the "form of intuition" in addition to the form of appearance.)

With this terminology in hand, Kant goes on to ask a set of questions regarding the status of space and time, laying out several alternative positions for consideration.

What, now, are space and time? Are they actual beings? Are they mere determinations or else relations of things, but nonetheless of a sort that would in themselves belong to such things if they were not being intuited; or are they such that they inhere only in the form of intuition, and hence in the subjective constitution of our mind, in the absence of which these predicates could not be ascribed to anything whatsoever?   [A 23/B 37–8]

The alternatives offered here are Newtonian absolute space and time (actual beings independent of objects in space); Crusian absolute spatial extension as a "determination" of God, or Cartesian spatial

extension as a determination of matter; Leibnizian or Wolffian relational views; and Kant's own view. We should note that the first
three are realist theories of space, according to which either space is
a real being in itself or spatiality is a real property based in things. In
Kant's own view, space is transcendentally ideal, that is, it inheres
only in "the subjective constitution of our mind."

In the arguments of the Aesthetic, Kant purports to decide among
these alternatives through arguments about the "concept of space"
(the metaphysical exposition) and about the possibility of geometrical cognition. As he has done from 1768 onward, he seeks to draw
conclusions about the ontological status of space (and time) from
arguments about spatial (and temporal) cognition.

The first of his numbered arguments holds that "space is no empirical concept, which has been abstracted from outer experiences"
(A 23/B 38). One potential origin for the representation of space
would be that it arises empirically from the experience of objects
in space. An advocate of a relational view of space might hold that
space is constituted out of relations among things in themselves
that cause the representation of space to arise in us through experience. A Newtonian absolute view also permits an empirical origin
for our spatial representations, through interaction with objects in
absolute space. In either case, Kant argues that we could not in fact
acquire the representation of space by means of experience because
any representation of sensations as spatially related already presupposes a capacity for spatial representation. It is this capacity – for
representing sensations as "in another position in space from that in
which I am located," and also for representing them "as outside and
alongside one another" (A 23/B 38) – that already requires "the representation of space" as a ground for presenting the sensations with
spatial relations. Whatever may be the status of space itself, spatial
representation cannot be acquired as a result of experience.

The second argument is also intended to support the view that
the representation of space cannot be acquired from the experience
of bodies because it is prior to or more fundamental than that experience. Kant expresses this point by asserting that "space is a necessary
representation, *a priori*, which underlies all outer intuitions" (A 23/
B 38). It *underlies* all outer intuitions because "one can never form
a representation of the absence of space, though one can very well
conceive that no objects are to be found in it." It is therefore "the

condition for the possibility of appearances." That is, no objects can be represented except as in space. Since space is required for the very possibility of appearances (of objects), it is a (conditionally) *necessary* representation (relative to appearances). As a condition of appearances, it is not "a determination that is dependent on appearances"; hence, it is not empirical but *a priori*. Finally, Kant would seem to assert also that space is a necessary feature of any human consciousness, for he says that we can "never form a representation of the absence of space"; this phrase suggests that all our (sensory, or world-related?) representations contain a spatial element.

The third argument is intended to show that "space is no discursive, or, as one says, general concept of the relations of things in general, but rather is a pure intuition" (A 24–5/B 39). This argument opposes the conclusion that space is an intuition to the notion that space is a "concept of the relations of things in general." By contrast with the fourth argument, the third one does not seem to rely on a conception of concepts as applying to many independent instances (as the concept *dog* is related to many dogs). Rather, this argument opposes the notion that space is a representation that arises empirically from the consideration of numerous elements (or "parts") of space, as in the Wolffian theory that Kant himself had previously embraced. Kant contends that the parts of space presuppose a single, all-encompassing space. They are created by introducing limitations into (or carving up) the continuous, concrete, unitary space of intuition. Kant does not explain why this unitary space must itself be an intuition rather than a type of concept that is not relational. Presumably, it has to do with the fact that "intuitions," in contrast with Kantian concepts, are "immediately given" and concrete representations (A 19/B 33), as elaborated in the subsequent argument. Finally, because the representation of space cannot be derived from relations among previously given elements or parts, it must be *a priori*. As such, Kant observes, it is able to sustain apodictic geometrical propositions about spatial relations (A 25/B 39).

The fourth argument is intended to establish as a general point that space is an intuition (a pure, *a priori* one), and not a concept. It does so by asserting that "space is an infinite *given* magnitude" (B 39). As suggested by the wording of the first-edition version, the infinity of this magnitude is not to be understood as something given all at once; rather, it amounts to "boundlessness in the progress of intuitions" (A 25). Presumably, this boundlessness occurs in the fact that (1) the space of intuition is given without a boundary, and so we can continuously traverse into new space in thought (or imagination), and (2) we can divide all finite parts of space *ad infinitum* (i.e., without ever coming to an indivisible part). In this potential sense, "all parts of space, to infinity, exist simultaneously" (B 40). This notion that the parts of space are represented as being "in it" (as parts to be carved out of a single, continuous space) marks the contrast between intuition and concept. For, as Kant explains, a concept can represent an infinity of instances "under it," which means that it applies to an infinity of independent, discrete objects. The parts of space are not represented apart from the one embracing space, nor as independent constituent parts of it; rather, they are dependent parts of that space and are found (potentially) in it. Again, because the representation of space precedes its parts or elements, Kant claims that it is *a priori*.

The first-edition version of the Aesthetic contained another numbered argument concerning the basis for geometrical cognition. This topic was transferred into a newly titled section of the Aesthetic in the second edition, called the "Transcendental Exposition," immediately following the four numbered arguments just discussed. This section addresses (for sensory representation) what was, according to both the first- and second-edition versions of the Introduction, the central problem of the *Critique*: "to uncover the ground of the possibility of synthetic *a priori* judgments with appropriate generality, to gain insight into the conditions that make every kind of them possible, and not merely to designate this entire cognition (which comprises its own species) in a cursory outline, but to determine it completely and adequately for every use in a system in accordance with its primary sources, divisions, domain, and boundaries" (A 10; see also B 14–24). Hence, while the previous arguments lay the groundwork by explicating the cognitive origins and status of space (and time, in the subsequent section), the "Transcendental Exposition" uses these results to explain the possibility of a domain of synthetic *a priori* cognition, namely, that found in geometry, and thereby fulfills a central mission of the Aesthetic.

The way in which the *a priori* representation of space enters into geometrical demonstration is treated by Lisa Shabel in the following chapter. Here we should note that Kant's explication of the possibility of geometrical knowledge helps us to understand his distinction between concepts and intuitions; to the extent that his explication is accepted, it serves to support that distinction. In his explication, Kant invokes the account of mathematical methodology found in the "Transcendental Doctrine of Method": the "construction of concepts" "in intuition" (A 713–17/B 741–5). Two points are especially important for our purposes. First, to sustain geometrical demonstrations, intuition must provide representations that are "*a priori*" and "immediate" (B 41); this latter condition, as articulated in the "Doctrine of Method," means that intuitions are "individual," "concrete," and "particular." Unlike the philosophical use of concepts, which "considers the particular only in the general," that is, in a general concept that applies to many discrete and independently given particulars, the mathematical construction of concepts in intuition "considers the general in the particular, nay, even in a single instance" (A 714/B 742). These instances are intuitions that "display" the objects of mathematical cognition "in concreto," though of course also *a priori* (A 715–16/B 743–4).

Second, the wording of the "Transcendental Exposition," with its talk of "the properties of space" and of "objects" that pertain to "outer intuition" (B 40–1), suggests that Kant takes geometrical knowledge to apply to physical space and objects in space. Indeed, elsewhere Kant makes clear that he considered geometry to apply to physical space and objects in space (A 27–8/B 43–4, A 40–1/B 57–8, A 157/B 196, A 165/B 206, A 224/B 271, A 240/B 299, B 147; 4:283–4, 287–8). This means that any explanation of the possibility of geometrical cognition not only would need to explain what kind of representation is needed for geometrical cognition, but also must answer the question: "how can outer intuition inhabit the mind that precedes the objects themselves, and in which the concept of the latter can be determined *a priori*?" (B 41). The answer here is that the "concept" or representation (that is, space as a form of intuition) must have "its seat merely in the subject, as its formal constitution for being affected by objects" (B 41). In other words, the *a priori* applicability of geometrical judgments and principles to all objects of cognition is to be secured by the transcendental ideality of space as a form of intuition. (This also supports Kant's "empirical realism" regarding our knowledge of objects in space [A 28/B 44].)

The arguments of the metaphysical and transcendental exposi-tions are successful to various degrees. The conceptual point that the capacity for spatial representation is presupposed for the spatial ordering of sensations held up well against onslaughts in the nine-teenth century (discussed below). The claim that space is prior to its parts accorded with the geometrical knowledge of its time, but was challenged by subsequent models of geometrical extension as com-posed of points. The conception of the basis of geometrical proof also was challenged by the algebraization of geometry and the discovery of non-Euclidean geometries in the nineteenth century.

The most pressing question concerns whether the arguments really show that space itself is ideal and *a priori*, that is, whether they effectively support Kant's preferred option among those named above. Suppose that the numbered arguments are effective in show-ing that the *representation* of space is prior to the presentation of spatially ordered sensations. That, by itself, would not show that *space* is a mere representation (would not establish transcendental idealism). Neither, presumably, would the conclusion that Euclid's diagrammatic proofs require an *a priori* spatial medium to capture their apodictic certainty.

The argument from geometry, when extended to geometrical claims about space itself, might well do the trick. Suppose one took it to be certain that geometry must apply (with necessity) to physical space (as Kant thought). Then the argument would succeed if it could be shown that such applicability can be explained only if physical space is itself ideal and the product of a subjective form of intuition that underwrites geometrical demonstration. This would sustain the conclusion that space and the objects in it are ideal.[27]

Moreover, one can understand why Kant might have believed that the numbered arguments, which purport to show that the represen-tation of space cannot be acquired from objects, would bear on the status of space. Kant's "critical question" as related to Marcus Herz in 1772 (10:130), which informs the first *Critique* at crucial junctures and underlies Kant's Copernican revolution (B xvi–xvii), inquired after the ground of the relation between objects and representa-tions. In the *Critique*, Kant identified only two possibilities for this relation: either "the object alone makes the representation possible," or "the representation alone makes the object possible" (A 92/B 124). These alternatives do not allow that the representation and the object would independently establish the same possibilities (e.g., would independently establish the properties of space). Kant presumably ruled out that option because he was interested in the necessary applicability of representations to objects, and he saw his transcendental idealism as the only way to achieve that. Under these circumstances, in showing that the representation of space must be *a priori*, he might well have considered himself to have established that it is not made possible by objects (and does not pertain to objects). Hence, it must make objects possible (as in transcendental idealism). Even if one does not share Kant's goal (of necessary applicability) or his parsing of the alternatives, one can see how Kant could believe that with this added premise about the alternatives, his numbered arguments would support the transcendental ideality of space (and time) – though in any case he considered the explanation of the applicability of geometrical knowledge to physical objects as the real clincher (A 40–1/B 57–8; 4:287–8, 292).

5. SPACE AS AN OBJECT (SECOND-EDITION "TRANSCENDENTAL DEDUCTION")

Once we have been told that space and time are *a priori* forms of intuition, the question remains of what exactly we have been told. Does this mean that our sense perceptions present us with a world of objects in space and time, without any other cognitive activity? Clearly not. The Kantian notions of "cognition" and of "experience" require that our cognition and experience of a world of objects is mediated by concepts that synthesize intuitions to yield judgments (A 50–1/B 74–5, A 156/B 195). But what about our knowledge of space as an *a priori* form of intuition? Does that arise from intuitions that are given to us already presenting the properties of space, or must the understanding be involved in synthesizing the spatial structures we know in intuition?

Kant made clear in both the first- and second-edition versions of the "Transcendental Deduction of the Pure Concepts of the Understanding" (i.e., the categories) that in order to be cognized, spatial structures must be subject to synthesis by the understanding (A 99, 115–25; B 137–8, 147, 150–6, 160–2). In the second-edition Deduction he explained that in the Aesthetic he had not properly expressed this requirement, but that he now was in a position to qualify and correct what he said there. This passage, which occurs as a footnote to §26, is worth quoting in full:

Space, represented as *object* (as is really required in geometry), contains more than the mere form of intuition, namely the *comprehension* of the manifold given in accordance with the form of sensibility in an *intuitive* representation, so that the *form of intuition* merely gives the manifold, but the *formal intuition* gives the unity of representation. In the Aesthetic I ascribed this unity merely to sensibility, only in order to note that it pre-cedes all concepts, though to be sure it presupposes a synthesis, which does not belong to the sense but through which all concepts of space and time first become possible. For since through it (as the understanding determines the sensibility) space or time are first *given* as intuitions, the unity of this *a priori* intuition belongs to space and time, and not to the concept of the understanding (§24).   [B 160-1]

The distinction here between the "form of intuition" and "formal intuition" implies that space, as an object, is cognized or known only through the synthetic activity of the understanding. In two earlier passages in the second-edition Deduction, Kant had explained that space can be known only through the synthetic activity of producing objects in intuition. The first passage says that

the mere form of outer sensible intuition, space, is not yet cognition at all; it only gives the manifold of intuition *a priori* for a possible cognition. But in order to cognize something in space, e.g., a line, I must *draw* it, and thus synthetically bring about a determinate combination of the given manifold, so that the unity of this action is at the same time the unity of consciousness (in the concept of a line), and thereby is an object (a determinate space) first cognized.   [B 137-8]

In §24, he says that "we cannot think a line without *drawing* it in thought, we cannot think a circle without *describing* it, we cannot represent the three dimensions of space at all without *placing* three lines perpendicular to each other at the same point" (B 154). He is not of course here talking about things that we are forced to do by habit; rather, the "drawing," "describing," and "placing" are *requirements* for "thinking" the objects in question.

Interpreters have long puzzled over Kant's picture of the inter-action between the understanding and sensibility in synthesiz-ing spatial objects such as lines or circles. Of particular interest here are questions concerning what is given in the "manifold" of spatial (or temporal) intuition from the senses, and what is provided by the understanding's synthesis. Three positions have been formulated about how the "forms" of intuition deliver material to the understanding. According to one position, called "forms as mechanisms," the forms of intuition are laws or rules for ordering the matter of sensations into spatial and temporal structures. According to a second, called "forms as representations," space and time are empty representations, independent of matter, into which the matter of sensation is arranged. According to a third, called "forms as orders of intuited matter," intuitions initially come with the matter ordered in a spatiotemporal manner. This third position requires no laws of or rules for this ordering. Further, because spatial and temporal structures are orders of matter, it does not allow the possibility of empty spatial and temporal forms into which matter would be placed in a spatial or temporal arrangement.[28]

Many questions arise in any attempt to decide among these views of what space and time as forms of intuition might be. One question concerns where the synthetic activity of the understanding fits into the various positions. In the forms as mechanisms view, would the understanding apply the laws or rules, or would sensibility do it? And if the understanding was responsible for the synthesis, would it supply the laws or rules, or follow laws or rules prescribed by sensibility? Further, if, as in the third view, sensibility simply provides ordered, intuited matter, does that mean it directly yields perceptions of a spatially ordered world? But why then does Kant suggest that empirical perception of objects depends on the activity of understanding in the "figurative synthesis" of the imagination (B 151–2)?

We will not be able to sort out these various positions here. However, there is greater commonality among (the more reasonable versions of) these positions than may at first be apparent. First, all three positions allow that form and matter are in some way distinct; matter by itself would not be spatially or temporally ordered. Second, they all agree that the synthetic activity of the understanding is required for cognizing objects, as objects, in space. Third, they all agree that the forms of intuition are responsible in some way for the constraint that intuitions can be ordered (or are ordered) with spatial and temporal relations. The constraint that human intuitions are spatial and temporal is provided by sensibility, whether in the way in which it passively creates ordered intuitions ("orders" view), in the rules by which it constrains the synthetic activity of the understanding (reasonable version of the "mechanisms" view), or through forms as containing representations into which matter is placed by sensibility or the understanding ("representations" view). Hence, on all views, sensibility yields (by itself or jointly with the understanding) intuitions as spatially continuous and infinitely divisible images (occurring in temporal succession). In cognizing these images in an *a priori* manner, through its own imaginative activity (drawing lines and the like), the understanding can explore the properties of space and time and achieve *a priori* knowledge of them (B 152, 155; A 157/B 196). Since, on all views, perceptual experience of objects is constrained by the forms of intuition, this exploration yields knowledge of the spatial and temporal properties of all possible objects of experience. That, in the end, was the conclusion Kant wished to highlight, and it must constrain any attempt to sort out his theory of the relation between the forms of intuition and the synthetic activity of the understanding, whether in pure *a priori* or empirical cognition.

Kant took up issues surrounding space and time again in two later sections of the *Critique*, the "Amphiboly of the Concepts of Reflection," where he criticized the Leibnizian theory, and in the "Antinomy of Pure Reason," where he sought to show the impossibility of ever decisively deciding the cosmological questions of whether the world is infinite in space and time or finite, and whether it consists of simple parts, or not. The Antinomies are treated in Chapter 8 of this volume.

6. RECEPTION OF KANT'S CRITICAL THEORY OF SPACE

Kant's theory of space has been continuously discussed from the time of its publication. These discussions have questioned all aspects of the theory: his transcendental idealism, his theory of space and time as *a priori* forms of intuition, and his conception of the epistemic basis of (Euclidean) geometry and its applicability to physical space and the objects in it.

Among the many discussions, I will consider some representative instances and main trends. One trend in German metaphysics of the nineteenth century, represented by J. F. Herbart and R. H. Lotze, was to view the universe as constituted of simple substances called "reals." This was a return to a Leibnizian (and early Kantian) metaphysics. The positions of these two authors differed in their conformity to Leibniz's actual doctrines and offered opposing evaluations of Kant's theory of space. Herbart chastised Kant's argument for the ideality of space as based on explaining the possibility of geometrical cognition, and contended that metaphysics must come before geometry. In his metaphysics, he posited reals as simple substances in causal interaction. He considered these causal interactions to provide the basis for an intelligible space (graspable independently of the senses), and also as the basis for sensory space. The capacity for spatial representation arises from experience (though no one, including Herbart, ever successfully explained how), by contrast with what he took to be Kant's nativism about space and time as *a priori* forms. Geometry takes as its object the continuous spaces abstracted from experience and certified by metaphysics.[29] By contrast, Lotze posited reals as simple substances that do not interact, accepted Kant's conclusion of the ideality of space, but provided his own arguments for that conclusion, stemming from the unreality of external relations and the subsequent need to see space as arising from the mind's imposition of relations onto its representation of the reals. He accorded geometry its own authority, independent of metaphysics.[30]

Many German sensory physiologists and psychologists in the nineteenth century viewed Kant's doctrine of space as a psychological thesis about the innateness of spatial perception. They then lined up in support or opposition to Kant's (alleged) nativism. In the first part of the nineteenth century, Johann Georg Steinbuch developed a radically empiricist theory of sensory perception, according to which even the bare capacity for spatial representation is acquired through experience (involving ideas arising from muscular activity, a theory developed cleverly but in the end not convincingly).[31] A few years later, Caspar Theobald Tourtual argued in favor of a Kantian nativism as regards spatial representation itself and the localization of objects in space through sensory perception.[32] Both Steinbuch and Tourtual rejected Kant's transcendental idealism, and asserted that spatial perception reveals the real spatial properties of physical objects as they are in themselves. A third sensory physiologist, Johannes Müller, developed a nativistic position distinct from Tourtual's. Tourtual had considered himself to be true to the Kantian form–matter distinction in treating sensations as nonspatial and positing an ordering activity of the mind that innately places this matter into spatial order.[33] Müller considered the sensations of vision to be spatial from the beginning. In effect, he posited that the retina feels its own spatiality, so that the spatiality of sensations is based on the spatiality of the human body (considered as a thing in itself). Müller explicitly rejected Kant's theory that geometry requires an *a priori* basis, and contended, with Herbart, that geometry could achieve necessity even while working by abstraction from an empirically based representation of space.[34]

The single most important event for the evaluation of Kant's theory of space was the discovery of non-Euclidean geometries in the nineteenth century and the subsequent conclusion that physical space-time is non-Euclidean in the twentieth. Kant had contended not merely that the space of experience is Euclidean and grounds Euclidean demonstrations, but that (owing to transcendental idealism) we can therefore know *a priori* that physical space and physical objects are described by Euclid's geometry with apodictic certainty. In Kant's view, Euclid's description of spatial structure provides universal and necessary principles of the structure of physical space and physical objects. Generations of scientists and philosophers, including Hermann Helmholtz and Rudolf Carnap, challenged Kant's position. Helmholtz argued that the existence of non-Euclidean geometries, and the fact that we might make measurements that, given certain assumptions, would yield the conclusion that space is non-Euclidean, refuted Kant's claim that Euclid's geometry necessarily describes physical space.[35] The question of the structure of physical space then becomes a matter of empirical investigation. Even if each geometry were found to be a deductive system with its own internal necessity, the question of the fit between a given geometrical structure and the physical structure of the world would be empirical. Henri Poincaré later contended that the choice of geometry was conventional: one might choose always to posit an Euclidean space, and revise mechanics in the light of that choice (a position suggested by Lotze).[36] But as Carnap observed, even in that case the very possibility of choosing a non-Euclidean convention refutes the Kantian claim to necessity. Moreover, Einstein decided in favor of a realistic, not conventionalist, claim about the structure of physical space-time, according to which it is non-Euclidean. That conclusion directly contradicts Kant's claims about physical space and time.[37]

In the twentieth century there was some tendency among Anglo-American analytic commentators to seek to defend Kant's theory of geometry from refutation by advances in mathematics and physics. One strategy is to suggest that Kant's position was not refuted, because the view that geometry intrinsically describes physical space differs in conception from the internally consistent but abstract mathematical geometries of the nineteenth century.[38] It is true that the understanding of geometry as a mathematical discipline changed in the nineteenth century, and that a new distinction arose between abstract mathematics and its application to nature. Further, it may be granted that Kant was a good expositor of the role of spatiality in the geometrical demonstrations of his day. Nonetheless, he did assert that Euclid's geometry necessarily describes physical space, and that is wrong.

Another strategy is to retreat to the claim that Kant could be right about Euclid's geometry applying to our own subjective spatial representations, including our "visual space." P. F. Strawson, in particular, has sought a notion of "phenomenal geometry" to which Kant's theory might apply. Strawson would abandon Kant's theory that Euclid's geometry necessarily describes physical space, but retain it for phenomenal space. Strawson, however, gives up on the idea that this "phenomenal geometry" describes the phenomenal space of visual perception – which in any case may not be a standard Euclidean space.[39] There remains very little for Kant to be right about, as regards the necessary relation of Euclid's geometry to any aspect of our experience. In the end, we are better off acknowledging the insightfulness of Kant's philosophical reconstruction of the actual Euclidean proof procedures, while allowing that Kant's theory that physical (or visual) space is necessarily Euclidean should be abandoned.

NOTES

1. Scaled to its relative size within the first *Critique*, the Aesthetic received exceptional attention in the older, monumental commentaries: H. Vaihinger, *Commentar zu Kants Kritik der reinen Vernunft*, 2 vols., incomplete (Stuttgart: Union deutsche Verlagsgesellschaft, 1881–1892), N. Kemp Smith, *A Commentary to Kant's "Critique of Pure Reason"*, 2d edn. (London: Macmillan, 1923), H. J. Paton, *Kant's Theory of Experience*, 2 vols. (New York: Macmillan, 1936). Most recently: Lorne Falkenstein, *Kant's Intuitionism: A Commentary on the Transcendental Aesthetic* (Toronto: University of Toronto Press, 1995); also Arthur Melnick, *Space, Time, and Thought in Kant* (Dordrecht: Kluwer Alcademic Publishers, 1989).

2. René Descartes, *Principles of Philosophy*, tr. V. R. Miller and R. P. Miller (Dordrecht: Kluwer, 1983), Pt. 2, arts. 1–25. On the mechanical philosophy more generally, see R. S. Westfall, *Construction of Modern Science: Mechanisms and Mechanics* (Cambridge: Cambridge University Press, 1971), chap. 2, and Gary Hatfield, "Metaphysics and the New Science," in D. Lindberg and R. Westman, eds., *Reappraisals of the Scientific Revolution* (Cambridge: Cambridge University Press, 1990), pp. 93–166.

3. Descartes, *Meditations on First Philosophy*, tr. J. Cottingham (Cambridge: Cambridge University Press, 1996), Fifth Meditation.

4. Descartes, *Principles*, Pt. 1, arts. 63–74. On Descartes' theory of the senses, see Hatfield, "Descartes' Physiology and Its Relation to His Psychology," in J. Cottingham, ed., *Cambridge Companion to Descartes* (Cambridge: Cambridge University Press, 1992), pp. 335–70; on his theory of intellect in relation to the senses, see Hatfield, "The Senses and the Fleshless Eye: The *Meditations* as Cognitive Exercises," in A. Rorty, ed., *Articles on Descartes' Meditations* (Berkeley: University of California Press, 1986), pp. 45–79.

5. On Newton's atomism, see Alan E. Shapiro, "Newton's optics and atomism," in I. B. Cohen and George E. Smith, eds., *Cambridge Companion to Newton* (Cambridge: Cambridge University Press, 2002), pp. 227–55, on pp. 245–51; on space and time, see Robert DiSalle, "Newton's philosophical analysis of space and time," in the same volume, pp. 33–56.

6. G. W. Leibniz and S. Clarke, *Leibniz–Clarke Correspondence*, tr. H. G. Alexander (Manchester: Manchester University Press, 1956), pp. 16–17, 25, 66, 68.

7. Among Leibniz's works discussing these positions and available in the eighteenth century, the best known is the *Monadology*, which, along with many other writings, is translated in G. W. Leibniz, *Philosophical Papers and Letters*, 2d edn., tr. L. E. Loemker (Dordrecht: Reidel, 1969). Phenomenalism about matter, a doctrine Leibniz held from the time of his correspondence with Arnauld (1686), is only implicit in the *Monadology*; the doctrine was published in 1698 and 1720 (*Philosophical Papers*, pp. 496, 623). Leibniz's more limited position positing a pre-established harmony between mind and body was published in 1695, in subsequent defenses, and in the *Leibniz–Clarke Correspondence*, pp. 18, 41, 84.

8. *Leibniz–Clarke Correspondence*, p. 12. If bodies are phenomena, the ideality of space arises among phenomenal material entities. On pre-established harmony, see the previous note.

9. Leibniz, *New Essays on Human Understanding*, tr. P. Remnant and J. Bennett (Cambridge: Cambridge University Press, 1981), pp. 132–3, 382–3, 403–4 (originally published in French in 1765). If bodies are

well-founded phenomena, then these causal hypotheses will be descriptions of fine-grained relations among actual or possible bodily phenomena, in accordance with a mechanistic approach.

10. On Aristotelian abstraction and intelligible matter, see Hatfield, "Metaphysics and the New Science," pp. 98–9. On Descartes' challenge, see the Fifth Meditation.

11. Leibniz, *New Essays*, pp. 49–50; also, p. 74.

12. Leibniz, *New Essays*, pp. 137, 266; see also his *Philosophical Papers*, pp. 248–58. See also Shabel's chapter in this volume.

13. On extension, C. Wolff, *Cosmologia generalis*, new edn. (Frankfurt am Main: Renger, 1737), §§184, 221–30. On cause, Wolff, *Philosophia prima, sive ontologia*, new edn. (Frankfurt am Main: Renger, 1736), §§713–14, 880–2. On pre-established harmony as merely the best hypothesis, Wolff, *Psychologia rationalis*, new edn. (Frankfurt am Main: Renger, 1740), §§638–9. (All cited works are reprinted in C. Wolff, *Gesammelte Werke* [Hildesheim: Olms, 1962].)

14. A. G. Baumgarten, *Metaphysica*, 7th edn. (Halle: Hemmerde, 1779), §463, 762.

15. Wolff called space a "phenomenon," which he took to imply that it represents the properties and relations of substances in a confused manner (*Cosmologia*, §224–6). Wolff's term does not carry the implications of Leibniz's "well-founded phenomena." In Leibniz's phenomenalist position, spatial representations are not founded upon actual external relations (as in Wolff), but on other perceptions representing a common (intentional) spatial world.

16. C. A. Crusius, *Entwurf der nothwendigen Vernunft-Wahrheiten* (Leipzig: J. F. Gleditsch, 1745), §§48–50.

17. Crusius, *Vernunft-Wahrheiten*, §§48–53, 253, 351–6.

18. Crusius, *Vernunft-Wahrheiten*, §§52, 108–19, 252–3, 351–6, 440.

19. Crusius, *Vernunft-Wahrheiten*, §§1, 114–19.

20. Crusius, *Weg zur Gewissheit und Zuverlässigkeit der menschlichen Erkenntniss* (Leipzig: J. F. Gleditsch, 1747), §§5–10.

21. J. N. Tetens, *Philosophische Versuche über die menschliche Natur und ihre Entwicklung*, 2 vols. (Leipzig: Weidmann, 1777), pp. 431–59. On early modern theories of vision prior to Kant, see Hatfield, *The Natural and the Normative: Theories of Spatial Perception from Kant to Helmholtz* (Cambridge, MA: MIT Press, 1990), chap. 2.

22. Citations to Kant's works are explained in the frontmatter to this volume. I have used the translations of the various volumes of the Cambridge Edition, except for passages appearing in *Prolegomena to Any Future Metaphysics with Selections from the Critique of Pure Reason*, tr. G. Hatfield, rev. edn. (Cambridge: Cambridge University Press, 2004).

23. Kant distinguished his position from "physical influence" (*influxus physicus*), pre-established harmony, and occasionalism. Like the true Leibnizian doctrine of pre-established harmony (applied to all monads), he grounded mutually harmonious states of individual substances in the divine understanding. But unlike the Leibnizian position, he considered this harmony to arise "by means of efficient causes" and through a "universal interaction of substances" (1:415). He distinguished it from a physical influence arising from the individual substances themselves by arguing that his substances depend for their interaction on "the connection, by means of which they are linked together in the ideas entertained by the Infinite Being" (1:415). God decrees an order of efficient causal relations among the substances, establishing their relations of mutual dependency. Left to themselves, they could not interact with other things nor be in relation to them.

24. Crusius, *Vernunft-Wahrheiten*, §§350, 359.

25. For further discussion of this answer, see Martin Gardner, *Ambidextrous Universe* (New York: Basic Books, 1964).

26. As Falkenstein observes (*Kant's Intuitionism*, p. 394, n. 10), the fact that Kant contrasts intuitions with concepts (here and in the Aesthetic) does not mean that he denies we have concepts of space and time; rather, his point is that our spatial and temporal representations cannot be accounted for by general or abstract concepts; rather, our "original" and primary representations of space and time are intuitions (B 40).

27. Commentators have long suspected that Kant overlooked a "neglected alternative," that the space of intuition is *a priori* but that things in themselves are also spatial and in fact conform to the space of intuition. This alternative would be excluded by the present argument, unless one wanted to distinguish (in the neglected alternative) between physical objects and things in themselves while still ascribing spatiality to the latter. But then this alternative would rightly be neglected as arbitrary foot stomping. See also Paul Guyer, *Kant and the Claims of Knowledge* (Cambridge: Cambridge University Press, 1987), pp. 362–9.

28. These positions are reviewed (with citations) in Falkenstein, *Kant's Intuitionism*, chap. 2 (he favors the third one). On this topic, see also Melnick, *Space, Time, and Thought in Kant*.

29. J. F. Herbart, *Lehrbuch zur Einleitung in die Philosophie*, 4th edn. (Königsberg: Unzer, 1837), secs. 137, 157, 160; *Allgemeine Metaphysik* (Königsberg: Unzer, 1828–1829), secs. 142–3, 243–4, 258–60.

30. R. H. Lotze, *Metaphysic*, tr. B. Bosanquet, 2 vols. (Oxford: Clarendon, 1887), Bk. 2, chaps. 1–2.

31. J. G. Steinbuch, *Beytrag zur Physiologie der Sinne* (Nurnberg: Schragg, 1811).

32. C. T. Tourtual, *Die Sinne des Menschen* (Münster: Regensberg, 1827).

33. Tourtual, *Sinne des Menschen*, pp. 175–86.

34. J. Müller, *Elements of Physiology*, tr. W. Baly, 2 vols. (London: Taylor and Walton, 1838–1842); see Hatfield, *Natural and the Normative*, pp. 152–6.

35. H. Helmholtz, "Origin and Meaning of Geometrical Axioms," *Mind* 1 (1876), pp. 301–21.

36. H. Poincaré, *Science and Hypothesis*, tr. G. B. Halstel (New York: Dover, 1952), chaps. 3–5. Lotze, *Metaphysic*, 1:293.

37. R. Carnap, *Philosophical Foundations of Physics* (New York: Basic, 1966), chaps. 15–18.

38. D. P. Dryer, *Kant's Solution for Verification in Metaphysics* (London: Allen & Unwin, 1966), pp. 160–9.

39. P. F. Strawson, *Bounds of Sense* (London: Methuen, 1966), pt. 5. On the geometry of visual space as not standardly Euclidean, see Gary Hatfield, "Representation and Constraints: The Inverse Problem and the Structure of Visual Space," *Acta Psychologica* 114 (2003), pp. 355–78.

3   Kant's philosophy
of mathematics

In his *Critique of Pure Reason*, Kant proposes to investigate the
sources and boundaries of pure reason by, in particular, uncovering the ground of the possibility of synthetic *a priori* judgments:
"The real problem of pure reason is now contained in the question:
How are synthetic judgments *a priori* possible?" (*Pure Reason*,
B 19). In the course of answering this guiding question, Kant defends
the claim that all properly mathematical judgments are synthetic
a priori, the central thesis of his account of mathematical cognition,
and provides an explanation for the possibility of such mathematical
judgments.

In what follows I aim to explicate Kant's account of mathematical cognition, which will require taking up two distinct issues. First,
in sections 2 and 3, I will articulate Kant's philosophy of mathematics. That is, I will identify the conception of mathematical reasoning and practice that provides Kant with evidence for his claim
that all mathematical judgments are synthetic *a priori*, and I will
examine in detail the philosophical arguments he gives in support
of this claim. Second, in section 4, I will explain the role that
Kant's philosophy of mathematics – and, in particular, his claim
that mathematical judgments are synthetic *a priori* – plays in his
critical (transcendental) philosophy. That is, I will identify the way
in which Kant's philosophy of mathematics informs his arguments
for transcendental idealism, and thus serves his larger philosophical
goals.

It will be helpful to begin in section 1 with some historical background.

I. BACKGROUND

Despite his commitment to the importance of the synthetic *a priori* to both mathematical and metaphysical inquiry, Kant conceives the mathematical method to be distinct and different from the philosophical. In holding this view (which I will discuss in section 2 and 4) Kant departs from the received wisdom of his predecessors and contemporaries, many of whom were actively engaged in considering the question of the relation between mathematical and philosophical demonstration. In particular, Leibniz, Wolff, and Mendelssohn all contributed to the debate on this question and their views, taken together, constitute a rationalist philosophy of mathematics that dominated in the period prior to and contemporary with Kant. Because Kant conceives his own view to displace that of the "dogmatic metaphysicians," theirs must briefly be considered before we turn to Kant.

Christian Wolff argues that because both mathematics and philosophy seek certitude, their ideal methods are identical: "both philosophy and mathematics derive their methods from true logic."[1] The method so derived depends upon the accurate determination of the subject and predicate of demonstrable propositions, which are "rigorously demonstrated from previously established definitions and propositions" in a proper order.[2] Certitude is the result of following such a method: one is guaranteed that a mathematical proposition demonstrated in this manner can be known with certainty, in part because our access to mathematical concepts is via clear and distinct ideas. Wolff thus articulates a philosophy of mathematics according to which the rigorous logical analysis of mathematical concepts and propositions is sufficient to account for mathematical truth. Moreover, philosophical inquiry is to be modeled on the prototype of mathematical analysis.

Wolff holds this view with respect to all mathematical inquiry, including geometry, despite his use of diagrams to support geometric proof in his own mathematical work. That is, Wolff takes every step of a mathematical demonstration to rest on conceptual analysis and syllogistic inference, and thus conceives of diagrammatic evidence as reducible to logical evidence.[3] Wolff here follows Leibniz, who conceives every mathematical proposition to express an identity,[4] every step in the demonstration of which depends on the Law of Non-Contradiction. For Leibniz, even the propositions of geometry rest on the general principles of logic, and not on the singular evidence provided by geometric diagrams:

> You must understand that geometers do not derive their proofs from diagrams, although the expository approach makes it seem so. The cogency of the demonstration is independent of the diagram, whose only role is to make it easier to understand what is meant and to fix one's attention. It is universal propositions, i.e. definitions and axioms and theorems which have already been demonstrated, that make up the reasoning, and they would sustain it even if there were no diagram.[5]

The view evinced here makes clear why Leibniz's philosophy of mathematics, as well as that of his follower Wolff, might aptly be called a formalist and logicist account of mathematical reasoning.

Moses Mendelssohn, a contemporary of Kant's, follows in the Leibniz-Wolffian tradition and presents perhaps the clearest statement of the rationalist philosophy of mathematics in his so-called "prize essay."[6] Despite the fact that his account of mathematical reasoning is more subtle than Wolff's, and also that his acceptance of the substantive use of diagrams, or signs *in concreto*, in a mathematical context is a departure from Leibniz, nevertheless Mendelssohn is committed to the rationalist tenet that mathematical truth and metaphysical truth are equally certain due to their common method of reasoning, namely, conceptual analysis. The evidence for mathematical truth is obtained by "unpacking" and thereby making distinct the content of our mathematical concepts. Once mathematical concepts are sufficiently "unpacked," their contents can be compared, causing underlying identities to surface:

> The certainty of mathematics is based upon the general axiom that nothing can be and not be at the same time. In this science each proposition such as, for example, "A is B," is proven in one of two ways. Either one unpacks the concepts of A and shows "A is B," or one unpacks the concepts of B and infers from this that not-B must also be not-A. Both types of proof are thus based upon the principle of contradiction, and since the object of mathematics in general is magnitude and that of geometry in particular extension, one can say that in mathematics in general our concepts of magnitude are unpacked and analyzed, while in geometry in particular our concepts of extension are unpacked and analyzed.[7]

About the "unpacking" process Mendelssohn claims that the mathematician examines the "real and essential signs" of given concepts to reveal the order of our thoughts and the necessary connection between the subject and predicate of a mathematical proposition. The technique of conceptual analysis that one employs to accomplish this process is

for the understanding nothing more than what the magnifying glass is for sight.... [The analysis of concepts] makes the parts and members of these concepts, which were previously obscure and unnoticed, distinct and recognizable, but it does not introduce anything into the concepts that was not already to be found in them.[8]

He claims further that this process is similar to that famously described by Plato in the *Meno*, without the "mystical aspect." So, for Mendelssohn, the natural unfolding of concepts in the human soul is the source of our ability to achieve mathematical certainty.[9]

I will show that Kant is concerned with the same issues about the mathematical method and the certainty of mathematical propositions as are his predecessors. But he is concerned to show, contrary to the views of his predecessors, that the method that yields mathematical certainty is unique and cannot be assimilated to the conceptual analysis that occupies philosophy. In the course of so distinguishing the mathematical from the philosophical method, Kant articulates a coherent and compelling philosophy of mathematics that engages with the mathematical practice of his time and that moreover serves his own metaphysical and epistemological purposes in a variety of ways. It is to Kant's view that I now turn.

2. THE SYNTHETICITY OF MATHEMATICS

Kant agrees with his rationalist predecessors that mathematical propositions are expressed as judgments that relate a subject concept to a predicate concept. For instance, Proposition I.32 in Euclid's *Elements* says that the three interior angles of any triangle are equal to two right angles.[10] In this case, the concept of being equal to two right angles is predicated of the subject concept, the interior angle sum of any triangle. But Kant disagrees that such propositions can be understood by virtue of conceptual analyses of the subject and predicate concepts. That is, Kant rejects the idea that mathematical judgments are *analytic*.[11] For Kant, mathematical propositions involve conceptual *syntheses*: a predicate concept not already contained in the subject concept is shown to "belong to" the subject concept nonetheless, thus issuing in a true mathematical judgment. In order to defend this view, Kant must provide a complete account of such mathematical syntheses by identifying the cognitive grounds for nonanalytic mathematical judgments.

Central to this account is Kant's claim that the mathematical method is distinguished from the philosophical by virtue of its dependence on the *construction* – and not the analysis – of concepts: "Philosophical cognition is rational cognition from concepts, mathematical cognition that from the construction of concepts" (A 713/B 741). To understand this claim, and Kant's thesis that mathematical concepts and propositions are constructible, we must first understand Kant's taxonomy for pure concepts:

Now an *a priori* concept (a non-empirical concept) either already contains a pure intuition in itself, in which case it can be constructed; or else it contains nothing but the synthesis of possible intuitions, which are not given *a priori*, in which case one can well judge synthetically and *a priori* by its means but only discursively, in accordance with concepts, and never intuitively through the construction of the concept.   (A 719–20/B 747–8)

Here Kant conceives an exhaustive division between those pure concepts that contain pure intuitions in themselves and are thereby constructible, and those that are not. What this comes to becomes clear given what he says next, namely, that the pure sensible concepts that provide the form of appearances are constructible: "space and time, and a concept of these, as *quanta*, can be exhibited *a priori* in pure intuition, i.e., constructed, together with either its quality (its shape) or else merely its quantity (the mere synthesis of the homogeneous manifold) through number" (A 720/B 748). Because mathematical concepts are derived from the combination of the categories of quantity with space and time, "the *modis* of sensibility" (A 82/B 108), mathematical concepts are precisely those concepts that Kant conceives to be constructible. The constructibility of mathematical concepts, and the nonconstructibility of the categories, thus provides the basis for Kant's distinction between mathematical and philosophical cognition.

Now we must consider more precisely what it means to construct a mathematical concept. Early in the Preface to the second edition of the *Critique*, Kant characterizes mathematics as having found the "royal path" to the secure course of a science as the result of an ancient geometer's realization: the key to mathematical demonstration is the mathematician's ability to produce figures via construction according to *a priori* concepts (B xii). Later, in the Discipline of Pure Reason, he says that "to construct a concept means to exhibit *a priori* the intuition corresponding to it" (A 713/B 741) and, further, that only mathematics has the means to so construct, and thereby define, its concepts (A 729/B 757). Taking these comments together suggests that Kant conceives mathematics to have a unique ability to define its concepts by constructing them, which amounts to exhibiting their content in the form of a singular representation, or intuition. In producing a figure in intuition, the mathematician defines a mathematical concept by constructing an individual figure to correspond to that concept.

For example, to attempt to define the concept *triangle* one considers the possibility of constructing a three-sided rectilinear figure. Kant thinks of this concept as "arbitrary" in the following sense: in considering such a concept, one knows precisely what its content is since one "deliberately made it up," and, moreover, the concept was not "given through the nature of the understanding or through experience" (A 729/B 757). Mathematical concepts thus contain an "arbitrary synthesis": in the case of a triangle, one considers the concept *figure* (that which is contained by any boundary or boundaries) together with the concepts *straight line* and *three*, and then proceeds to effect the synthesis of these concepts by exhibiting an object[12] corresponding to this new concept, namely, by constructing a triangular figure, either in imagination or by rendering a drawn diagram. In either case, the triangle so constructed and exhibited is presented intuitively, that is, as a singular and immediate mental representation. Mathematical concepts are thus given through synthetic definitions, which prescribe a rule or pattern for constructing a corresponding intuition.[13] Geometric concepts in particular provide us with the rule or pattern for constructing sensible intuitions of the spatial magnitudes of objects of outer sense.

Even in the case of nongeometric concepts, such as the numeric concept *five*, one must still "**make** an abstract concept **sensible**," that is, "display the object that corresponds to it in intuition, since without this the concept would remain (as one says) without **sense**, i.e., without significance" (A 240/B 299). Numeric concepts provide us with the rule or pattern for constructing sensible intuitions of the magnitudes of objects in general, that is, of the quantitative measures of objects of both inner and outer sense. These "seek their standing and sense" in "the fingers, in the beads of an abacus, or in strokes and points that are placed before the eyes" (A 240/B 299). Thus, the concept *five* can be constructed by representing five discrete units in the following way: |||||.

Both geometric and arithmetic concepts are exhibited via "ostensive" constructions, which show or display the content of the concepts to which they correspond. The geometer's triangular figure and the arithmetician's five strokes serve to make manifest the sensible content of the concepts *triangle* and *five*, respectively, and to connect abstract mathematical concepts to the sensible intuitions of space and time. The arithmetician's strokes differ from the geometer's figure in that the former use spatial distinctness not to represent qualitative spatial magnitudes, such as shapes, but only to represent discrete quantitative units. Thus the stroke, despite being ostensive, is nevertheless a more abstract mathematical tool than might appear from its sensible rendering.[14] Arithmetic construction represents features of our temporal intuition by displaying number as the result of a (temporal) counting process, but this process includes the use of spatial intuition: the construction of a numeric magnitude as a temporal sequence requires the use of spatial intuition to exhibit discrete and countable objects. Likewise, geometric construction represents features of our spatial intuition by displaying shapes as the result of a (spatial) drawing or mapping process, but this process includes the use of temporal intuition: the construction of a geometric magnitude as a spatial figure requires the use of temporal intuition to exhibit continuous and extended objects.[15]

Kant contrasts such ostensive constructions with the "symbolic" constructions of algebra:

Mathematics does not merely construct magnitudes (*quanta*) as in geometry, but also mere magnitude (*quantitatem*), as in algebra, where it entirely abstracts from the constitution of the object that is to be thought in accordance with such a concept of magnitude. . . . [Algebra] thereby achieves by a symbolic construction equally well what geometry does by an ostensive or geometrical construction (of the objects themselves), which discursive cognition could never achieve by means of mere concepts.   (A 717/B 745)

Kant does not mean to draw a strict distinction here between two *kinds* of mathematical construction. For Kant, the algebraist's "symbolic" construction is that which symbolizes an ostensive construction, as described above. So, an algebraic symbol, such as the variable "x," can be used to represent a concretely constructible entity, such as a line segment. In such a case, the variable symbolically constructs the concrete object by symbolizing the ostensive construction of that object. Thus, Kant does not use "symbolic construction" to designate a category of mathematical constructions that are constructed out of symbols, and thereby distinct from ostensive constructions. He rather uses "symbolic construction" to designate that which symbolizes ostensive constructions. If we fail to regard symbolic construction as a species of ostensive construction, it is difficult to see how a symbolic construction of, say, an algebraic variable could be the exhibition of an intuition in Kant's sense, for the display of an algebraic variable does not in itself reveal anything about the spatio-temporal forms of objects.[16] Thus, the procedure and result of *all* mathematical construction is, for Kant, fundamentally ostensive: to construct a mathematical concept one necessarily exhibits an intuition that displays its features manifestly.[17]

According to Kant's account, then, one defines a mathematical concept by constructing it, that is, by exhibiting its content ostensively in intuition. One might suspect that such an ability to construct definitions for our mathematical concepts would render our mathematical propositions analytic: because the precise and determinate content of our mathematical concepts is available to us via construction, one might suppose that we can determine the truth of a mathematical proposition by analyzing the relation between perfectly well-defined subject and predicate concepts. Of course, Kant rejects this inference: Kant's theory of the constructibility of mathematical concepts is the basis for his claim to the contrary that mathematical propositions are *synthetic*, and is thus the ground for his rejection of his predecessors' views. I will now consider his arguments for the syntheticity thesis, and see how, in particular, these arguments depend on the constructibility thesis.

In the second-edition Introduction, Kant claims that "Mathematical judgments are all synthetic" (B 14).[18] He begins his defense of this claim by dismissing unnamed opponents, the "analysts of human reason," who argued that because the certainty of any particular mathematical inference is assured only if it proceeds in accordance with the principle of contradiction, the principles and propositions of mathematics could be "cognized from the principle of contradiction," and thus are analytic. Kant concedes the analysts' claim that mathematical propositions are deduced in accordance with the law of contradiction but denies that this shows that mathematical propositions are analytic. He proceeds to an argument in favor of his contrary view, namely, that mathematical propositions are synthetic.[19]

Kant argues for the general claim that mathematical propositions are synthetic in two cases, the arithmetic case and the geometric case.[20] This strategy reflects his understanding of the elementary mathematics of his day, which took mathematics to be the science of discrete and continuous magnitudes (number and extension, respectively). Arithmetic and geometry, the most basic mathematical sciences, are thus those to which Kant here directs his philosophical attention. Beginning with the arithmetic case, Kant asks us to consider the proposition "$7 + 5 = 12$" and argues first that the proposition is not analytic. He claims that in thinking the subject concept, the sum of 7 and 5, one thinks "nothing more than the unification of both numbers in a single one," but does not think what this single number is (B 15). That is, the concept of a sum of two numbers contains only the concepts of each of the two numbers, together with the concept of summing them, but does not contain the number that is their sum: "no matter how long I analyze my concept of such a possible sum I will still not find twelve in it" (B 15). Here Kant argues against the analyticity of all arithmetic propositions by arguing against the analyticity of a representative numerical formula. The basis for his argument is a challenge to the opponent: if one could provide an analysis of the concept of the sum of 7 and 5 that yields the concept of equal to 12, then one would have to grant that the proposition is analytic. But, no such analysis is possible.[21] Therefore, by definition of analyticity, the proposition is not analytic.

On its own this argument is clearly insufficient to defend Kant's claim that mathematical propositions are synthetic since he has not examined any candidate analyses of the relevant concepts but has merely declared such analyses to be impossible. He thus needs a positive argument in favor of syntheticity to support his denial of analyticity. The positive argument for the syntheticity of arithmetical propositions begins with a claim that depends on Kant's constructibility thesis, discussed earlier: to grasp the relation between the subject and predicate concepts of an arithmetic proposition, one must "go beyond" the subject concept to the intuition that corresponds to it and identify properties that are not analytically contained in the concept, yet still belong to it (B 15; A 718/B 746). Kant holds therefore that *construction* of the concept of the sum of 7 and 5 is necessary if we are seeking grounds for judging whether the proposition "$7 + 5 = 12$" is true or false. By constructing the concept of the sum, we are able to judge that the concept of the sum of 7 and 5 has the property of being equal to 12, even though that property is not analytically contained in the concept of the sum of 7 and 5:

For I take first the number 7, and, as I take the fingers of my hand as an intuition for assistance with the concept of 5, to that image of mine I now add the units that I have previously taken together in order to constitute the number 5 one after another to the number 7, and thus see the number 12 arise.   (B 16)

Whether one uses fingers, strokes, points, or the beads of an abacus to represent the content of the number concepts 7 and 5, one must put the intuition of 7 together with the intuition of 5 to represent their sum to determine that, taken together, they come to 12:

$$||||||| + ||||| = ||||||||||||$$

Importantly, Kant takes the content of the concept 12 to "arise" from this intuitive computation: the construction and summing of the concepts comprising the subject concept is a process that generates the properties of that very concept, expressed in the predicate concept. Kant concludes from this that "The arithmetical proposition is therefore always synthetic" (B 16) since it is a judgment whose predicate concept is not "covertly contained" in its subject concept but rather "lies entirely outside" the subject concept while still standing "in connection with it" (A 6/B 10). In proceeding "outside" of the subject concept to discover the properties that are connected with it, we are constrained by the general conditions of sensible intuition: it is due to features of our sensible faculty and its original *a priori* representations of space and time that the sum should be determined in exactly the way that it is.[22]

Before proceeding to the geometric case, Kant adds one final consideration to support his argument for the syntheticity of arithmetical propositions. He claims that one is made more "distinctly aware" of the syntheticity of arithmetical propositions upon considering large number calculations, "for it is then clear that, twist and turn our concepts as we will, without getting help from our intuition we could never find the sum by means of the mere analysis of our concepts" (B 16). Kant cannot mean to suggest that we actually mark off strokes or points in intuition in order to calculate the sum of, say, 7,007 and 5,005 and determine the truth of the proposition "7,007 + 5,005 = 12,012." His idea is rather that such strokes or points are, ultimately, the justification for the truth of the large number proposition because our methods for performing large number calculations depend on our methods for performing small number calculations; that is, they depend on the use of intuition to display or exhibit the content of our small number concepts. Kant's point is that, even if we have a shortcut (perhaps symbolic) method for performing large number arithmetic calculations, the relations among large number concepts must be justified on intuitive, and thus synthetic, grounds.[23]

Kant's next move is to argue for syntheticity in the geometric case. In the second-edition Introduction, as noted, he considers geometric principles, or axioms, as examples of synthetic propositions. Elsewhere, he argues in favor of the syntheticity of geometric theorems. Taken together with his arguments in favor of the syntheticity of arithmetic just discussed, these arguments complete his defense of the syntheticity of mathematics.

Beginning with the geometric principles, Kant considers as an example the proposition that the straight line is the shortest line between two points (B 16).[24] He says that because the "concept of the straight contains nothing of quantity, but only a quality," so "the concept of the shortest is therefore entirely additional to it, and cannot be extracted out of the concept of the straight line by any analysis" (B 16). In other words, the concept of the straight line between two points A and B does not analytically contain the concept of the shortest line between A and B, since it speaks only of the shape of the line between them and not the measure of the line between them; it follows that the straight line between A and B cannot be judged to be the shortest line between A and B merely by conceptual analysis. In order to judge the identity between the straight line and the shortest line between two points, one must synthesize the concept of the straight line with the concept of the shortest line by seeking "help" from intuition (B 16). Kant takes this particular judgment to be axiomatic because the synthesis between the concepts is immediately evident: upon constructing a straight line between two points, and thereby exhibiting the content of the subject concept of the proposition, one judges immediately, without any mediating inferences, that the straight line so constructed likewise exhibits the content of the predicate concept. Again, features of our sensible faculty determine this identity: on Kant's view, were we to connect A to B by constructing a line longer than the straight line between A and B, our line so constructed would either be curved or bent. Kant reiterates this point in the Axioms of Intuition where he writes that geometry and its axioms are "grounded" on the "successive synthesis of the productive imagination, in the generation of shapes" and "express the conditions of sensible intuition" (A 163/B 204).[25] The synthetic activity of shape construction is our means for displaying the features of our original spatial intuition. It thus makes evident the spatial forms that we are warranted and constrained to represent.[26]

Finally, Kant provides an argument in favor of the syntheticity of geometric theorems, an argument that makes especially clear the role that constructibility plays in his account of syntheticity and the understanding of mathematical proof. This argument occurs in the Discipline of Pure Reason, where Kant considers Euclid's proposition I.32[27] in the context of his comparison of the mathematical to the philosophical method.[28] Here Kant contrasts the fortunes of the philosopher and the mathematician when faced with the task of determining the relation between the sum of the interior angles of a triangle and a right angle. This contrast is meant to emphasize that the analytic tools of the philosopher are inadequate to the task, whereas the synthetic and constructive tools of the mathematician are adequate. To make this point, Kant notes first the weakness of the philosopher's position, who faces the task armed only with the technique of conceptual analysis and the concept of a figure that is both tri-lateral and tri-angular: "[The philosopher] can analyze and make distinct the concept of a straight line, or of an angle, or of the number three, but he will not come upon any other properties that do not already lie in these concepts" (A 716/B 744). As before, Kant declares the impossibility of using conceptual analysis to extract from a mathematical concept any properties that are not given discursively in its definition, and as before, he must supplement this declaration with an argument in favor of the role of intuitive synthesis in the identification of such properties.

The geometer, by contrast to the philosopher, "begins at once to construct a triangle" (A 716/B 745). To construct the concept *triangle*, the geometer displays an intuitively accessible three-sided rectilinear figure: Δ. The proof can then be effected in several simple steps, as Kant describes:

Since [the geometer] knows that two right angles together are exactly equal to all of the adjacent angles that can be drawn at one point on a straight line, he extends one side of his triangle, and *obtains* two adjacent angles that together are equal to two right ones. Now he divides the external one of these angles by drawing a line parallel to the opposite side of the triangle, and sees that here *there arises* an external adjacent angle which is equal to an internal one, etc. In such a way, through a chain of inferences that is always guided by intuition, he arrives at a fully illuminating and at the same time general solution of the question.   (A 716/B 744, *emphasis added*)

We will take up the question of what makes this solution general in section 3. Here I must emphasize Kant's insight that the construction of the triangle, and the auxiliary constructions of the lines and angles adjacent to the triangle, provide information to the geometer that was not contained within the concepts that compose the proposition to be proved, namely, that the three interior angles of a triangle are equal to two right angles. That this proposition *cannot* be deduced by analysis of the concepts of angle, triangle, etc., but *can* be deduced by construction of those same concepts, Kant gleans from the geometer's own practice. In particular, Kant observes that from the geometer's construction of two lines auxiliary to the original triangle there "arise," first, one new angle, exterior and adjacent to the triangle, and second, the two angles that are its parts. The geometer thus "obtains" these new angles as intuitive representations that are connected to but not contained in the concept of the original triangle. Moreover, the geometer's technique of displaying the intuition of the triangle and its adjacent angles makes available diagrammatic information that is indispensable for the ensuing demonstration. In particular, the diagram so constructed witnesses the part-whole relations among the triangle and its adjacent angles, and so testifies to the relevant spatial containments, namely, that the exterior adjacent angle is equivalent to the two opposite interior angles of the triangle and thus, together with the adjacent interior angle, sums to two right angles.

The key point here is Kant's recognition that the geometer's proof cannot succeed without information about the relations among the spatial regions delimited by the triangle and its external angles, information that is unavailable to the philosopher examining the bare concept of a triangle. Kant understood that the constructed figure in Euclid's proof is not a heuristic aid to understanding, but rather an essential and ineliminable component of the reasoning that leads the geometer from the interior angles of a triangle, "through a chain of inferences that is always guided by intuition," to the sum of two right angles. The syntheticity of the resulting theorem is due to the fact that the relation between its subject and predicate concepts (the three interior angles of a triangle and two right angles, respectively) is discovered via a deduction that depends on the construction of each concept and the additional intuitive information that each concept thereby reveals.[29]

The syntheticity of geometry and arithmetic is ultimately due to the fact that their propositions codify and describe the content of our original *a priori* representations of space and time, which are presented in intuition and not through mere concepts. The construction of mathematical concepts in intuition thus serves more generally to reveal or exhibit the sensible conditions that warrant and constrain mathematical judgment. Because Kant takes mathematics to be built upon the basic propositions of arithmetic and geometry, he takes his arguments for the syntheticity of the propositions of arithmetic and geometry to constitute an argument for the syntheticity of all mathematical propositions. Having rehearsed those arguments, I must now consider the second part of the central thesis of Kant's philosophy of mathematics, namely, that all mathematical cognition is *a priori*.

3. THE APRIORITY OF MATHEMATICS

Just prior to presenting his arguments for the syntheticity of mathematics in the second-edition Introduction, Kant offers a brief argument in support of what appears to be a background assumption, namely, that math is *a priori*:

Properly mathematical judgments are always *a priori* judgments and are never empirical, because they carry necessity with them, which cannot be derived from experience. But if one does not want to concede this, well then, I will restrict my proposition to pure mathematics, the concept of which already implies that it does not contain empirical but merely pure *a priori* cognition.   (B 14–15)

Here Kant claims that the apparent necessity of mathematical propositions is sufficient evidence of their apriority; this follows from his equation, offered earlier, that "Necessity and strict universality are therefore secure indications of an *a priori* cognition, and also belong together inseparably" (B 4). But his subsequent arguments for the syntheticity of mathematical propositions make it difficult to accept such a terse defense of apriority since Kant's conception of the construction of mathematical concepts, on which the syntheticity arguments rest, suggests that mathematical reasoning depends on *singular* and *concrete* representations. This leads to the worry that mathematical constructions cannot possibly support reasoning that is fully general or universal, and further, that mathematical judgments justified with such reasoning are neither necessary nor *a priori*. For Kant to provide a coherent philosophy of mathematics and defend his central thesis that mathematical cognition is synthetic and *a priori*, he owes us an account of how the mathematician's constructive practices can provide evidence for and support arguments that lead to fully general and universal mathematical propositions.

Kant's main argument in support of the claim that mathematical propositions are fully general and universal is that the concept constructions on which they rest, despite producing singular and concrete intuitions, are *themselves* fully general and universal processes resulting in fully general and universal representations. It will follow that mathematical propositions relating such constructible concepts are fully general and universal. The question is: What makes concept construction a fully general and universal process resulting in fully general and universal representations?

An important passage that is relevant to Kant's answer to this question is worth quoting in full:

For the construction of a concept, therefore, a **non-empirical** intuition is required, which consequently, as intuition, is an individual object, but that must nevertheless, as the construction of a concept (of a general representation), express in the representation universal validity for all possible intuitions that belong under the same concept. Thus I construct a triangle by exhibiting an object corresponding to this concept, either through mere imagination, in pure intuition, or on paper, in empirical intuition, but in both cases completely *a priori*, without having had to borrow the pattern for it from any experience. The individual drawn figure is empirical, and nevertheless serves to express the concept without damage to its universality, for in the case of this empirical intuition we have taken account only of the action of constructing the concept, to which many determinations, e.g., those of the magnitude of the sides and the angles, are entirely indifferent, and thus we have abstracted from these differences, which do not alter the concept of the triangle.   (A 713–4/B 741–2)

Here Kant addresses how a single intuition can represent all possible intuitions that fall under the same concept – for example, how a particular triangular figure can serve to represent all triangles and so be thought to construct the general concept of triangle. Kant's first point is that whether the triangle is constructed in empirical intuition, by sketching it on paper or with a stick in the sand, or in pure intuition using only the imagination, the triangle so constructed is exhibited *a priori*. This is because its pattern is not borrowed from experience. That is, the shapes we construct in a mathematical context are not abstracted from our sensible impressions of shaped objects, such as plates or tables. Rather, on Kant's view, our empirical intuitions of shaped objects borrow *their* patterns from our pure intuitions of shapes in space.[30] So, an empirical intuition of a triangle can function in a mathematical context because it itself relies on a prior ability to construct shapes *a priori* with the productive imagination, and thus on a pure intuition of space. Constructed figures thus need not (but can) be rendered empirically to serve their indispensable role in mathematical reasoning: if such figures *are* rendered empirically, the apriority of the reasoning they support is not surrendered.

There remains the question how an intuition, pure *or* empirical, can represent the general content of a concept. This is addressed in the second point Kant makes in the passage above, where he distinguishes the act of construction from the constructed object: in constructing the intuition that corresponds to a mathematical concept, we attend not to the particular features of the resultant figure, but to the act that produced it. So, in constructing the concept *triangle* one might produce a scalene or an equilateral figure; either way, one has produced a representation of all possible triangles by producing a single paradigm triangle. That one figure has unequal and another equal sides is irrelevant: one abstracts from the particular magnitudes of the sides and angles in order to recognize the relevant feature of the figure, namely, three-sidedness. And this recognition is effected by taking account of the act of constructing a three-sided rectilinear figure "to which many determinations . . . are entirely indifferent."

As Kant sees it, then, the act of construction is the ultimate source of the full generality and universality of intuitive mathematical representations. In the next passage, he points us to the Schematism for an explanation of the universality of the act of construction:

Mathematical cognition considers the universal in the particular, indeed even in the individual, yet nonetheless *a priori* and by means of reason, so that just as this individual is determined under certain general conditions of construction, the object of the concept, to which this individual corresponds only as its schema, must likewise be thought as universally determined.
(A 714/B 742)

And later:

By means of [geometrical construction] I put together in a pure intuition, just as in an empirical one, the manifold that belongs to the schema of a triangle in general and thus to its concept, through which general synthetic propositions must be constructed.   (A 718/B 746)

In these passages, Kant suggests that in constructing the concept *triangle* we produce an individual triangle that, because it is determined under certain general conditions, provides the pattern for triangles in general, and thus provides the pattern for *all* triangular objects of sensation. The "general conditions of construction" that determine the features of our pure intuition of a triangle include the general features of our pure intuition (the "infinite given magnitudes" of space and time described in the Metaphysical Exposition) together with the general features of our pure sensible concepts, in this case triangularity, as given by the definition of triangle.[31] That mathematical concepts can be synthetically defined and constructed makes it possible for us to have direct cognitive access to such general mathematical patterns; to construct a triangle by acting in accordance with general conditions of construction while ignoring the particular determinations of the constructed figure is to cognize the general pattern for *any* three-sided rectilinear figure.

Kant fills out this picture in the Schematism, where he argues that schemata are the mediating representations that are needed to link pure concepts to appearances.[32] In the case of the concept *triangle*, the schema – a product of pure imagination – is the determinate procedure for constructing a three-sided rectilinear figure, a procedure which must itself be consistent with universal spatiotemporal conditions of construction. Because Kant construes mathematical concepts like *triangle* to *contain* such determinate construction procedures, mathematical concepts like *triangle* provide us with rules for representing the objects that instantiate them. Thus, there is no heterogeneity between mathematical concepts and the intuitions that directly correspond to them via construction: the pure mathematical concept *triangle* is homogeneous with all pure and empirical intuitions of triangles, and so with all triangular objects of experience, since the concept *triangle* provides us with the rule for representing *any* three-sided rectilinear object.[33] In the case of mathematical concepts, then, schemata are strictly redundant: no "third thing" is needed to mediate between a mathematical concept and the objects that instantiate it since mathematical concepts come equipped with determinate conditions on and procedures for their construction.[34]

Mathematical schemata thus have the generality of a concept (since they represent the general content of a mathematical concept) but the particularity of an intuition (since they issue in a concrete display of that content). Kant denies, however, that such schemata are *images*:

In fact it is not images of objects but schemata that ground our pure sensible concepts. No image of a triangle would ever be adequate to the concept of it. For it would not attain the generality of the concept, which makes this valid for all triangles, right or acute, etc., but would always be limited to one part of this sphere. The schema of the triangle can never exist anywhere except in thought, and signifies a rule of the synthesis of the imagination with regard to pure shapes in space.   (B 180)

Ultimately, then, the generality and universal applicability of a concept like *triangle* is due not to the individual triangle that is produced in constructing that concept, but to the awareness that the production of such a concrete representation of the general concept *triangle* depends on a general "rule of synthesis" for the production of any such figure, that is, its schema. This rule of synthesis has its source in our own cognitive faculties and explains why Kant holds that in performing acts of mathematical construction, we must take account of the act itself, noting what we contribute to the constructed figure:

[The geometer] found that what he had to do was...to produce the [properties of the figure] from what he himself thought into the object and presented (through construction) according to a priori concepts, and that in order to know something securely a priori he had to ascribe to the thing nothing except what followed necessarily from what he himself had put into it in accordance with its concept.   (B xii)

To "take account only of the action of constructing" a shape, and thereby to ascribe features to the shape not only as it is given in its general *a priori* concept but also as it is determined by more general features of the spatial mode of construction, is to display the *general* content of a mathematical concept in a particular concrete entity. The general cognitive conditions that govern mathematical thought and ground mathematical reasoning are thus accessible via the performance of mental acts that produce singular and concrete representations.

The generality of mathematical construction becomes a bit more clear, perhaps, in the arithmetical case. A number concept can be constructed ostensively with strokes or points, but what allows any number concept so constructed to represent that number universally, in abstraction from some particular set of numbered things, is the mental act we perform in exhibiting the strokes or points. The schema of any number concept includes the representation of a general counting procedure: "if I only think a number in general, which could be five or a hundred, this thinking is more the representation of a method for representing a multitude (e.g., a thousand) in accordance with a certain concept than the image itself" (A 140/B 179). Moreover, such a procedure requires the generation of "time itself" (A 142/B 182) and so provides insight into the general temporal conditions that govern numeric operations.

As Kant sees it, the generality of mathematical representations is due to the fact that both mathematical concepts and the pure intuitions that correspond to those concepts depend on universal and necessary features of our pure cognitive faculties of sensibility, imagination, and understanding.[35] A mental act of mathematical construction must accord with a rule of synthesis prescribed by a pure concept of understanding, though under the constraints imposed by the pure intuitions of sensibility. For example, the act of constructing a triangle accords with the geometric concept of a triangle given in its definition by synthesizing (or "putting together the manifold" of) three straight lines in the space of pure intuition, of which the resulting triangle is merely a limitation. Thus, the act of constructing a singular and concrete triangle serves to exhibit the general features of any three-sided rectilinear figure, the spatial relations among the parts of any such figure, and the general features of the space in which it is constructed. These features and relations include, for example, that any three-sided rectilinear figure has also three interior angles, that the three sides of a triangle bound a region of space, that there is an inside and an outside of the region so bounded, and so on. Likewise, the act of constructing the concept *five* by representing "the successive addition of one (homogeneous) unit to another" (A 142/ B 182) accords with both the general concept of magnitude and the pure intuition of time, as well as with the arithmetic concept *five*: the act of constructing the number five exhibits not only the features of five-unit quanta but also the general features of magnitude and the temporal conditions under which such magnitudes can be counted or measured.

On Kant's view, then, the act of construction in accordance with a rule transmits generality and universality to mathematical representations. It follows that the mathematical judgments that relate such general and universal mathematical representations themselves hold generally and apply universally. For the same reasons, mathematical judgments are known with apodictic certainty and so are *a priori*: because Kant takes the pure spatiotemporal intuition on which mathematical propositions are grounded to be both a "subjective condition regarding form" and a "universal *a priori* condition" of experience, mathematical propositions are necessarily true. Thus, on Kant's view, we can be apodictically certain that the synthetic propositions of pure mathematics are generally true of and apply universally to all spatiotemporal objects of experience.[36]

4. MATHEMATICS IN SERVICE
OF THE CRITICAL PHILOSOPHY

As we have seen, Kant denies that mathematics and philosophy share a method; this is the thrust of his rejection of the views of his predecessors, who argued that both mathematics and philosophy proceed by the analysis of concepts. Kant has argued, on the contrary, that mathematics proceeds by the construction of concepts, which is a synthetic and not an analytic exercise. Despite this methodological difference, mathematics and its distinctive style of reasoning nevertheless play the role of a paradigm for Kant's philosophical investigations and are pivotal elements of his arguments for transcendental idealism. In this final section, I will discuss, albeit briefly, the role that the synthetic apriority of mathematics plays in Kant's critical philosophy.[37]

In the Transcendental Aesthetic Kant argues, first, that space and time are *a priori* intuitions. By this he means that we possess original nonconceptual representations of space and time that have their source in pure sensibility, that mental faculty that enables our cognitive receptivity of objects. He argues further that these representations provide the pure form for all sensible intuition, that is, that they provide us with a structure for cognizing empirical objects. The synthetic *a priori* propositions of mathematics, he claims, are "derived from" these *a priori* intuitions of space and time and so are grounded by our pure sensible faculty.[38] That geometry is the science of space thus means for Kant that geometry, and mathematics more generally, at the very least codifies and describes the original intuitive representations afforded by pure sensibility.

This conception of the relation between pure sensibility and the science of mathematics, which science (as we have seen) Kant takes to comprise a set of synthetic *a priori* propositions, provides Kant with an argument for transcendental idealism, according to which the pure intuitions of space and time and the pure concepts of the understanding apply to all – but only – appearances, and not to things as they are in themselves.[39] In the particular case of space, transcendental idealism amounts to the claim that space is itself nothing over and above the original sensible representation described and codified by geometry, that is, that space is not a property inhering in objects independent of our cognitive contact therewith. So, Kant takes the transcendental ideality of space to follow from the previously defended premises that space is a pure intuition and that mathematical cognition is synthetic *a priori*. His argument is a *reductio* of the supposition that space is *not* transcendentally ideal: suppose that "space and time are in themselves objective and conditions of the possibility of things in themselves"; then one cannot account for the "large number of *a priori* apodictic and synthetic propositions about [space]" (A 46/B 64). That is, the doctrine of transcendental realism contradicts the synthetic apriority of mathematics, which itself rests on the *a priori* intuitivity of space and time. Therefore, transcendental realism must be rejected in favor of transcendental idealism.⁴⁰

Kant fills out the argument by sketching a possible account of the synthetic apriority of the propositions of mathematics on the assumption that space and time are transcendentally real. He first shows with an argument from elimination that realist and idealist alike must concede that mathematical cognition is attained via pure intuition. Mathematical cognition, like any cognition, is attained via either concepts or intuitions, both of which are either pure or empirical. But mathematics cannot be based on empirical concepts or empirical intuitions, for such representations "cannot yield any synthetic proposition except one that is also merely empirical" and so "can never contain necessity and absolute universality of the sort that is nevertheless characteristic of all propositions of geometry" (A 47/B 64). There remains the possibility that mathematics be based on pure concepts or intuitions. Pure concepts are ruled out on the grounds that "from mere concepts no synthetic cognition but only merely analytic cognition can be attained" (A 47/B 65). The mathematician must therefore "take refuge in intuition . . . give your object *a priori* in intuition, and ground your synthetic proposition on this" (A 47–8/B 65).⁴¹

Kant next introduces the consequences of pairing transcendental realism about space with this account of mathematics: given the *reductio* assumption that space is transcendentally real, it follows that the object represented in pure intuition for the purposes of geometric reasoning, such as a triangle, is "something in itself without relation to your subject," and moreover that the latter is "given prior to" the former, and not "through it" (A 48/B 65). If this is the case – if the triangle in itself is cognized independent of the triangle constructed in pure intuition for the purposes of mathematical reasoning – then what mathematics shows with necessity to lie in the subjective conditions for constructing a triangle cannot be shown with necessity to apply to the triangle in itself. That is, the mathematical method of construction required for mathematical proof cannot be brought to bear on the triangle in itself. Thus, on the assumption that space is transcendentally real, one can "make out absolutely nothing synthetic and *a priori* about outer objects" (A 48/B 66) since outer objects are taken to be objects in themselves.

But this result directly contradicts the premises of the argument, which take mathematics (geometry) to be the synthetic *a priori* science of space, and space to be an original representation of "outer sense." In short, transcendental realism entails that the science of space cannot yield synthetic *a priori* propositions about outer objects, but mathematics apparently provides us with just such propositions. So it is inconsistent to suppose both that mathematics is synthetic *a priori* cognition of space *and* that space is transcendentally real. Thus, the *reductio* assumption that space is transcendentally real is rejected in favor of the view that space is transcendentally ideal:

It is therefore indubitably certain and not merely possible or even probable that space and time, as the necessary conditions of all (outer and inner) experience, are merely subjective conditions of all our intuition, in relation to which therefore all objects are mere appearances and not things given for themselves in this way; about these appearances, further, much may be said *a priori* that concerns their form but nothing whatsoever about the things in themselves that may ground them.   (A 48–9/B 66)

Here Kant concludes that space and time are *merely* the forms of intuition, that is, that space and time are nothing over and above the way we represent them in pure intuition, and so are not properties of things as they are in themselves, as the transcendental realist had supposed.[42] He has thus used the synthetic apriority of mathematics to defend the broad doctrine of the transcendental ideality of space and time.[43]

Kant's account of mathematics and its relation to the pure intuitions of space and time plays an equally important role in a variety of arguments that occur after the Transcendental Aesthetic. In the first section of the Deduction, Kant states that all pure concepts require a transcendental deduction, that is, an explanation of the way in which such concepts relate to objects *a priori* (A 85/B 117). In the case of the pure cognitions of space and time, however, it is enough to have shown in the Transcendental Aesthetic that these are pure intuitions that "contain *a priori* the conditions of the possibility of objects as appearances," which exercise has already served to explain and determine their *a priori* objective validity (A 89/B 121). Because space and time are forms of sensibility, they "determine their own boundaries" and "apply to objects only so far as they are considered as appearances, but do not present things in themselves. Those alone are the field of their validity, beyond which no further objective use of them takes place" (A 39/B 56). Space, time, and the mathematical cognition that is grounded thereon, are thus guaranteed to apply to all and only objects of experience, or appearances, for these are first given through the pure forms of sensibility. In other words, the mathematical propositions that derive from the pure forms of sensibility are necessarily applicable to all and only those objects that appear to us by means of space and time.

Space, time, and the mathematical concepts thereof thus provide a point of contrast as well as a sort of paradigm for the deduction of the pure concepts of understanding, or categories. Because mathematical concepts "speak of objects" through "predicates of intuition," sensibility itself is the source of their relation to objects in general; by contrast, the categories "speak of objects not through predicates of intuition and sensibility but through those of pure *a priori* thinking" and so must "relate to objects generally without any conditions of sensibility" (A 88/B 120). Accordingly, the categories cannot use pure sensibility to "ground their synthesis prior to any experience" (A 88/B 120), as can mathematical concepts, and so "do not represent to us the conditions under which objects are given in intuition at all" (A 89/B 122). It follows that, despite the fact that objects *cannot* appear to us without necessarily having to be related to the forms of sensibility, and so cannot be objects for us without having mathematical properties, "objects can indeed appear to us without necessarily having to be related to functions of the understanding" (A 89/B 122). Thus, although the objects of experience necessarily possess the sensible features we represent them to have, and so are necessarily mathematically describable, such objects do not necessarily possess the conceptual or categorical features we represent them to have, at least without further argument. That is, though the results of the Transcendental Aesthetic assure us that our sensible concepts are objectively valid, we have no such assurance in the case of pure concepts of understanding: "Thus a difficulty is revealed here [in pure understanding] that we did not encounter in the field of sensibility, namely how **subjective conditions of thinking** should have **objective validity**, i.e., yield conditions of the possibility of all cognition of objects" (A 90/B 122). Kant of course resolves this difficulty and demonstrates the transcendental ideality of the categories with the Transcendental Deduction. In some sense, then, the project of demonstrating the objective validity of the categories can be seen as modeled on, or at least as motivated by, the successful prior demonstration of the objective validity of space, time, and mathematics.

Kant revisits the objective validity of mathematical concepts and propositions in the Axioms of Intuition, where he identifies and defends the synthetic *a priori* judgment that he claims is the principle of the possibility of all mathematical principles, including the axioms of geometry.[44] Here he answers for the specific case of mathematics the guiding question with which this essay began, namely, "How are synthetic judgments *a priori* possible?" Synthetic judgments are *a priori* possible in mathematics only given the prior synthetic *a priori* principle that "All intuitions are extensive magnitudes"[45] (B 202). The sense in which mathematical judgments are thereby made possible is quite specific: only the principle that all intuitions are extensive magnitudes can make it possible for each and every mathematical judgment to apply to – and thereby provide synthetic and *a priori* cognition of – the objects of experience, or appearances.[46] Kant claims that the principle that all intuitions are extensive magnitudes, what he calls the "transcendental principle of the mathematics of appearances,"

yields a great expansion of our *a priori* cognition. For it is this alone that makes pure mathematics in its complete precision applicable to objects of experience, which without this principle would not be so obvious, and has indeed caused much contradiction.[47]   (A 165/B 206)

Kant's argument in support of this claim begins with a restatement of the central thesis of transcendental idealism, defended earlier: "Appearances are not things in themselves. Empirical intuition is possible only through the pure intuition (of space and time)" (A 165/B 206). He then notes that if objects of the senses – which are given in empirical intuition – were not in complete agreement with the mathematical rules of ostensive construction – which are given in pure intuition – then mathematics would not be objectively valid. That is, the objective validity of mathematics depends on such agreement between pure and empirical intuition, and on the fact that "what geometry says about the latter is therefore undeniably valid of the former" (A 165/B 206). But this agreement is precisely what is expressed by the principle that "All intuitions are extensive magnitudes," which means that as intuitions all appearances "must be represented through the same synthesis as that through which space and time in general are determined" (B 203). Therefore, the objective validity of mathematics, and the possibility that the synthetic *a priori* propositions of mathematics are applicable to the appearances, is explained by the transcendental "axiom" of intuition.

This "axiom" clarifies Kant's reasons for denying, contra his predecessors, that philosophy and mathematics can share a methodology. Mathematics is distinguished from philosophy by virtue of its constructive procedure, which is the cause of its "pertaining solely to quanta": because mathematics constructs its object *a priori* in intuition, and because the only concept that can be so constructed is the concept of magnitude, mathematics necessarily takes quantity as its object (A 714/B 742). But, according to the Axioms of Intuition, such constructed quanta make possible the apprehension of appearances and the cognition of outer objects. Thus, "what mathematics in its pure use proves about the former is also necessarily valid for the latter" (A 166/B 207). That is, our mathematical cognition of purely constructed quanta is likewise cognition of the quantitative form of empirical objects. Philosophical cognition, by contrast, cannot construct and exhibit qualities in an analogous way and so cannot hope to achieve rational cognition of objects of experience via a mathematical method.

5. CONCLUSION

Kant, a long-time teacher and student of mathematics, developed his theory of mathematics in the context of the actual mathematical practices of his predecessors and contemporaries, and he produced thereby a coherent and compelling account of early modern mathematics.[48] As is well known, however, mathematical practice underwent a significant revolution in the nineteenth century, when developments in analysis, non-Euclidean geometry, and logical rigor forced mathematicians and philosophers to reassess the theories that Kant and the moderns used to account for mathematical cognition. Nevertheless, the basic theses of Kant's view played an important role in subsequent discussions of the philosophy of mathematics. Frege defended Kant's philosophy of geometry, which he took to be consistent with logicism about arithmetic;[49] Brouwer and the Intuitionists embraced Kant's idea that mathematical cognition is constructive and based on mental intuition;[50] and Husserl's attempt to provide a psychological foundation for arithmetic owes a debt to Kant's characterization of mathematics as providing knowledge of the formal features of the empirical world.[51]

In the later twentieth century, by contrast, most philosophers accepted some version of Bertrand Russell's withering criticism of Kant's account, which he based on his own logicist program for mathematics.[52] But now it is clearly time to reassess the relevance of Kant's philosophy of mathematics to our own philosophical debates. For just a few examples, contemporary work in diagrammatic reasoning and mereotopology raise issues that engage with Kant's philosophy of mathematics;[53] Lakatos-style antiformalism is arguably a descendant of Kant's constructivism;[54] and our contemporary understanding of the relation between pure and applied mathematics, especially in the case of geometry, is illuminated by Kant's conception of the sources of mathematical knowledge. More generally, because we persist in considering mathematics to be a sort of epistemic paradigm, our current investigations into the possibility of substantive *a priori* knowledge would surely benefit from reflection on Kant's own subtle and insightful account of mathematics.

I hope to have shown that Kant's account is not an isolated philosophy of mathematics, developed only to make sense of early modern practices and as a tangent to his primary purposes, but is rather a crucial component of his broader philosophical project. It is impossible to appreciate fully Kant's thesis that all mathematical cognition is synthetic and *a priori*, and the arguments that he offers in its support, in isolation from his theory of pure sensibility, doctrine of transcendental idealism, and views on appropriate and successful methods of reasoning. Likewise, the general aims of Kant's broad and deep critical project are themselves much easier to appreciate given the insights afforded by his philosophy of mathematics. Further, I would argue that understanding Kant's philosophy of mathematics, despite its association with his own mathematical and historical context, speaks directly to our own views about the relation between philosophical and mathematical reasoning.[55]

NOTES

1. Christian Wolff, *Preliminary Discourse on Philosophy in General* (Indianapolis: Bobbs-Merrill Co, Inc., 1963 [1779]), p. 77.
2. Wolff, *Preliminary Discourse*, p. 76.
3. For a detailed discussion of Wolff's philosophy of mathematics and, in particular, his conception of analysis, see Lanier Anderson, "The Wolffian Paradigm and its Discontents: Kant's Containment Definition of Analyticity in Historical Context," *Archiv für Geschichte der Philosophie* (forthcoming).
4. That, for Leibniz, every mathematical proposition expresses a demonstrable identity is no surprise, given his more general predicate containment theory of truth. For discussion, see G. H. R. Parkinson, "Philosophy and Logic," in Nicholas Jolley, ed., *The Cambridge Companion to Leibniz* (Cambridge: Cambridge University Press, 1995).
5. G. W. Leibniz, *New Essays in Human Understanding*, Peter Remnant and Jonathan Bennett, eds. and trans. (Cambridge: Cambridge University Press, 1996 [1704]), IV, I, pp. 360–1.
6. Moses Mendelssohn, "On Evidence in Metaphysical Sciences," in Daniel Dahlstrom, ed., *Philosophical Writings* (Cambridge: Cambridge University Press, 1997 [1763]). Mendelssohn's was the prize winning essay in a contest held by the Royal Academy on the question of the relation between mathematical and metaphysical truth. The second place essay was Kant's *Inquiry concerning the Distinctness of the Principles of Natural Theology and Morals*. For a thorough and helpful discussion of both essays, see Paul Guyer, "Mendelssohn and Kant: One Source of the Critical Philosophy," *Philosophical Topics*, 19:1 (1991), reprinted in his *Kant on Freedom, Law, and Happiness* (Cambridge: Cambridge University Press, 2000).
7. Mendelssohn, "On Evidence," p. 257.
8. Mendelssohn, "On Evidence," p. 258.
9. Because of space limitations, I have not discussed the relation between mathematical concepts and the sensible world on the rationalist view. For some further discussion of these issues see Lisa Shabel, "Apriority and Application: Philosophy of Mathematics in the Modern Period," in

Stewart Shapiro, ed., *The Oxford Handbook of Philosophy of Math and Logic* (Oxford: Oxford University Press, 2005).

10. Euclid, *The Elements*, T. L. Heath, ed. and trans. (New York: Dover, 1956), p. 316.

11. For a fascinating discussion of Kant's notion of analyticity, and the related notion of concept containment, see Anderson, "Wolffian Paradigm," and Lanier Anderson, "It Adds Up After All: Kant's Philosophy of Arithmetic in Light of the Traditional Logic," *Philosophy and Phenomenological Research*, LXIX:3 (2004).

12. Kant's use of "object" to describe a geometric figure is in tension with his commitment to the idea that a pure geometric figure is the form of an empirical object of the same shape. Technically, a pure geometric figure is not itself an "object" in Kant's sense.

13. For a discussion of Kant on definition, see Lewis White Beck, "Kant's Theory of Definition," in Hoke Robinson, ed., *Selected Essays on Kant* (Rochester: University of Rochester Press, 2002). For a discussion of Kant on mathematical definitions in particular, see Emily Carson, "Kant on the Method of Mathematics," *Journal of the History of Philosophy*, 37:4 (1999).

14. This makes plain another difference between our construction of geometric and arithmetic concepts. In constructing the concept *triangle*, one could produce a right or scalene triangle, an equilateral or isosceles. That is, there are multiple distinct and different three-sided rectilineal figures that count as triangles, in the relevant sense. However, there is only one way to construct the concept *five*, by counting out five discrete units of some uniform kind. Thus our intuitive representation of any particular number concept is unique in a way that our intuitive representation of any particular shape concept is not. Whether the concept *five* is represented with strokes, points, or fingers, there is only one way to count to five; this fully general procedure is captured by an intuitive representation of number. Kant owes us an explanation, then, of how a particular geometric figure can attain the generality necessary to adequately represent a general spatial concept. I will return to this in the next section.

15. Kant discusses this in the A-Deduction where he writes: "Now it is obvious that if I draw a line in thought, or think of the time from one noon to the next, or even want to represent a certain number to myself, I must necessarily first grasp one of these manifold representations after another in my thoughts. But if I were always to lose the preceding representations (the first parts of the line, the preceding parts of time, or the successively represented units) from my thoughts and not reproduce them when I proceed to the following ones, then no whole

representation and none of the previously mentioned thoughts, not even the purest and most fundamental representations of space and time, could ever arise" (A 102).

16. The same follows for numerals.

17. For the details of this interpretation of symbolic construction see Lisa Shabel, "Kant on the 'Symbolic Construction' of Mathematical Concepts," *Studies in History and Philosophy of Science*, 29:4 (1998). For alternative interpretations of Kant on symbolic construction, see Michael Friedman, *Kant and the Exact Sciences*. (Cambridge, MA: Harvard University Press, 1992), Chapter 2, and articles by Gordon Brittan, Jaako Hintikka, Philip Kitcher, Charles Parsons, Manley Thompson, and J. Michael Young collected in Carl Posy, ed., *Kant's Philosophy of Mathematics: Modern Essays* (Dordrecht: Kluwer Academic Publishers, 1992).

18. The corresponding argument in the *Prolegomena* occurs in the Preamble (at 4:269–71).

19. Kant moves back and forth inconsistently between discussing "principles" ("Grundsätze") and "propositions" ("Sätze") in this passage. In the succeeding passages, his argument for the syntheticity of geometry is directed at principles, or axioms, whereas his argument for the syntheticity of arithmetic is directed at propositions. Though he has further arguments in support of the syntheticity of geometric propositions or theorems, which I will discuss later in this section, he does not have further arguments in support of the syntheticity of arithmetic principles, for he denies that arithmetic has principles, or axioms (A 164/B 205). The reason for this denial is that the "numerical formulas" of arithmetic are synthetic but singular, and thus not general like the synthetic principles of geometry. Kant takes the singularity of a numerical formula such as "7 + 5 = 12" to be captured by the fact (mentioned above in note 14) that "the synthesis here can take place only in a single way, even though the subsequent use of these numbers is general" (A 164/B 205).

20. Before moving to the arguments for syntheticity, Kant makes a very brief remark about the apriority of mathematical judgments. I come back to this claim, and his arguments in support of it, in the next section.

21. The impossibility of such an analysis may be best understood as a function of the traditional logic. See Anderson, "It Adds Up After All."

22. I will say more about these general conditions of sensible intuition later.

23. Kant's philosophy of arithmetic has been discussed by many commentators. See, in particular, Charles Parsons's "Kant's Philosophy of Arithmetic" and "Arithmetic and the Categories," both reprinted in Posy, *Kant's Philosophy of Mathematics*, and Béatrice Longuenesse, *Kant and*

the Capacity to Judge (Princeton: Princeton University Press, 1998), Chapter 9.

24. This is not an axiom in Euclid's *Elements*, but it was included as an axiom in many early modern treatments of Euclidean geometry.

25. In this passage, Kant gives two more examples of synthetic geometric axioms: between two points only one straight line is possible, and two straight lines do not enclose a space. It is harder to make out Kant's claim for these two examples since one would have to take intuition to display not merely the possibility of constructing lines, but rather the *impossibility* of constructing a second straight line between two points, as well as the *impossibility* of a space enclosed by two straight lines. Despite the obvious difficulty, I think that Kant holds that the conditions of sensible intuition make these impossibilities apparent: one would fail were one to attempt construction of multiple straight lines between two points, or of a figure bounded by two straight lines. The failure would be the result of contradicting one's own prior definitions. In the first case, if one were to construct multiple lines between two points, all but one of them would fail to be straight, by definition of straight; in the second case, if one were to construct a figure bounded by two lines, one of the boundary lines would fail to be straight, by definition of straight. He discusses mathematical axioms further at A 47/B 65 and A 732/ B 760.

26. Kant follows this discussion of the syntheticity of the axioms of geometry with a caveat that would seem to defeat his claim that *all* mathematical propositions are synthetic: "To be sure, a few principles that the geometers presuppose are actually analytic and rest on the principle of contradiction" (B 16). Here he mentions identities that Euclid took to be "common notions," or logical principles that apply to any scientific discipline (e.g., the whole is greater than the part). Kant proceeds to defend the idea that these are not true principles and that, in any case, one must exhibit their concepts in intuition actually to think them.

27. "In any triangle, if one of the sides be produced, the exterior angle is equal to the two interior and opposite angles, and the three interior angles of the triangle are equal to two right angles." Euclid, *Elements*, p. 316.

28. Because of space limitations, I will not be able here to discuss all of the reasons why philosophy can never appropriate the mathematical method. The bulk of the argument is at A 727–35/B 755–63. The discussion concludes with Kant's proclamation that "it is not suited to the nature of philosophy, especially in the field of pure reason, to strut about with a dogmatic gait and to decorate itself with the titles and ribbons of

mathematics, to whose ranks philosophy does not belong, although it has every cause to hope for a sisterly union with it" (A 735/B 763). For discussion, see Carson, "Kant on the Method of Mathematics."

29. There is a great literature on the role of intuition in Kant's theory of mathematics. Roughly speaking, commentators have divided on whether that role is primarily logical, or primarily phenomenological. I intend for my explication of the syntheticity of mathematical propositions to suggest that constructed geometric diagrams play both roles: they provide phenomenological evidence that warrants the logical inferences of a deductive proof. For further discussion of the role of the Euclidean diagram in Euclidean proof, see Lisa Shabel, *Mathematics in Kant's Critical Philosophy: Reflections on Mathematical Practice* (New York: Routledge, 2003), Part I. For further discussion of Kant's interpretation of Euclid I.32, see Lisa Shabel, "Kant's 'Argument from Geometry,'" *Journal of the History of Philosophy*, 42:2 (2004). See also Longuenesse, *Kant and the Capacity to Judge*, pp. 287–291, and Friedman, *Kant and the Exact Sciences*, Chapter 1. For sources relevant to the debate between the logical and the phenomenological interpretation of the role of intuition in Kant's theory of mathematics, see articles by Hintikka, Parsons, and Friedman in Posy, *Kant's Philosophy of Mathematics*, as well as Emily Carson, "Kant on Intuition in Geometry," *Canadian Journal of Philosophy*, 27:4 (1997), and Michael Friedman, "Geometry, Construction and Intuition in Kant and his Successors," in Gila Sher and Richard Tieszen, eds., *Between Logic and Intuition: Essays in Honor of Charles Parsons* (Cambridge: Cambridge University Press, 2000).

30. This step requires a result from the Transcendental Aesthetic, namely, that pure intuition is the form of empirical intuition. I will discuss this briefly in section 4.

31. Since "the concept is first given through the definition, it contains just that which the definition would think through it" (A 731/B 759). As I mentioned earlier, spatial concepts derive from the combination of a pure concept of quantity with space, a mode of sensibility.

32. For discussion of the Schematism and its particular relation to Kant's philosophy of mathematics, see J. Michael Young's "Construction, Schematism and Imagination," in Posy, *Kant's Philosophy of Mathematics*, and Longuenesse, *Kant and the Capacity to Judge*, Chapters 8 and 9.

33. Kant uses the example of a pure concept of a circle and a plate. See (A 137/B 176).

34. In other words, mathematical concepts are unique among pure concepts for being, strictly speaking, identical to their schemata. On this point I

concur with Paul Guyer, who writes that "[Kant's] view of [pure sensible] concepts is that they basically *are* rules for applying predicates to particular objects or their images, and thus virtually identical to schemata." Paul Guyer, *Kant and the Claims of Knowledge* (Cambridge: Cambridge University Press, 1987), p. 159.

35. For a detailed discussion of these and related issues, see Longuenesse, *Kant and the Capacity to Judge*, especially Chapters 8 and 9.

36. This last move requires additional arguments in favor of Kant's theory of transcendental idealism, the structure of which I will discuss briefly in section 4.

37. Many commentators, of course, have addressed the question of the role of mathematics in Kant's critical philosophy. See, in particular, Friedman, *Kant and the Exact Sciences*, especially Chapter 1, and Longuenesse, *Kant and the Capacity to Judge*, Chapters 8 and 9. Also, on the particular topic of the problem of incongruent counterparts (which I have not addressed here) and its role in Kant's arguments for transcendental idealism, see Jill Vance Buroker, *Space and Incongruence: The Origin of Kant's Idealism* (Dordrecht: D. Reidel, 1981). For a less recent but classic discussion of the relation between Kant's philosophy of mathematics and his doctrine of transcendental idealism, see P. F. Strawson, *The Bounds of Sense* (London: Routledge, 1995 [1966]), Part 5.

38. At (A 29/B 44) Kant says explicitly that the synthetic *a priori* propositions of mathematics "derive" from the intuition of space. There he refers back to the Transcendental Exposition of the Concept of Space, where he uses the metaphor that the synthetic *a priori* cognitions of mathematics "flow from" the representation of space (A 25/B 40). Later he uses another metaphor, saying that the synthetic cognitions of mathematics "can be drawn *a priori*" from the representation of space (A 39/B 55). For discussion of the relation between the original representation of space and the cognitions of geometry, see Shabel, "Kant's 'Argument from Geometry'."

39. Kant has, of course, a variety of arguments in defense of transcendental idealism. For a helpful introductory discussion of his different argumentative strategies, see Sebastian Gardner, *Routledge Philosophy Guidebook to Kant and the Critique of Pure Reason* (New York: Routledge, 1999), Chapter 5. For further discussion, see Henry Allison, *Kant's Transcendental Idealism* (New Haven: Yale University Press, 1983), and Guyer, *Kant and the Claims of Knowledge*, Part V. The exegesis of Kant's arguments that I offer in what follows is similar in spirit, if not in detail, to Guyer's analysis in *Kant and the Claims of Knowledge*, pp. 354 ff.

40. Of course, this only follows given Kant's further supposition that transcendental realism and transcendental idealism are the only two possible philosophical positions to take with respect to the status of space and time.

41. Up to this point in the argument, Kant basically has reiterated support for his premises that mathematics (geometry) is the synthetic *a priori* science of space, a pure intuition. What he must do next is show that the *reductio* supposition contradicts these premises.

42. In the course of the argument, Kant offers various formulations of the doctrine of transcendental idealism, not identical to the one just quoted. For example: the "subjective condition regarding form" is "at the same time the universal *a priori* condition under which alone the object of this (outer) intuition is itself possible"; and, "space (and time as well)" is "a mere form of your intuition that contains *a priori* conditions under which alone things could be outer objects for you, which are nothing in themselves without these subjective conditions" (A 48/B 66). Note too that his argument is specifically focused on the case of space, yet he draws his conclusion with respect to the ideality of both space and time.

43. The structure of Kant's arguments in the *Prolegomena* of course differ from those in the *Critique*, and the way in which Kant uses the thesis that mathematical cognition is synthetic *a priori* to support the doctrine of transcendental idealism is likewise different. A comparison of these texts is unfortunately beyond the scope of this paper.

44. Kant explains that mathematical principles, such as the axioms of geometry, are not themselves included in the "analytic of principles" that includes the Axioms of Intuition, and "do not constitute any part of this system, since they are drawn only from intuition, not from the pure concept of the understanding." Nevertheless, it is necessary to identify the *principle* of these principles, that is, the synthetic *a priori* judgment that makes possible the synthetic *a priori* mathematical principles, such as the axioms of geometry (A 149/B 188–9).

45. In the A-edition the principle reads "All appearances are, as regards their intuition, **extensive magnitudes**" (A 162).

46. In a sense, the A-edition version of the principle makes this move more perspicuous than does the B-edition version, since the A-edition version confirms that it is our intuitions of *appearances* that are extensive magnitudes.

47. Kant takes contradiction to arise from the failure to identify the proper bounds of cognition. In particular, the failure to identify the proper "field of validity" for mathematical cognition has, according to Kant, led his predecessors to develop accounts of mathematical cognition that are

in direct conflict with the "principles of experience." I explore Kant's account of this conflict, and his proposed resolution thereof, in Shabel, "Apriority and Application."

48. For further discussion, see Shabel, "Kant on the 'Symbolic Construction'" and *Mathematics in Kant's Critical Philosophy*.

49. See Gottlob Frege, *On the Foundations of Geometry and Formal Theories of Arithmetic* (New Haven, CT: Yale University Press, 1971 [1903–1906]).

50. See L. E. J. Brouwer, *Collected Works 1. Philosophy and Foundations of Mathematics*, A. Heyting, ed. (Amsterdam: North Holland Publishing Company, 1975) and L. E. J. Brouwer, *Brouwer's Cambridge Lectures on Intuitionism*, D. van Dalen, ed. (Cambridge: Cambridge University Press, 1981).

51. See Edmund Husserl, *Philosophy of Arithmetic: Psychological and Logical Investigations with supplementary texts from 1887–1901*, Dallas Willard, ed. and trans. (Dordrecht: Kluwer Academic Publishers, 2003).

52. See Bertrand Russell, *An Essay on the Foundations of Geometry* (New York: Dover, 1956), Chapter 2, and Bertrand Russell, *Principles of Mathematics* (New York: Norton, 1938), Chapter LII.

53. For a comprehensive bibliography of sources, see http://www.hcrc.ed.ac.uk/gal/Diagrams/biblio.html.

54. See Imre Lakatos, *Proofs and Refutations: The Logic of Mathematical Discovery* (Cambridge: Cambridge University Press, 1976).

55. This material is based upon work generously supported by the National Science Foundation under Grant No. SES-0135441.

4   Kant on *a priori* concepts

The metaphysical deduction of the categories

In Chapter One of the Transcendental Analytic in the *Critique of Pure Reason*, Kant establishes a table of the categories, or pure concepts of the understanding, according to the "leading thread" of a table of the logical forms of judgment. He proclaims that this achievement takes after and improves upon Aristotle's own endeavor in offering a list of categories, which Aristotle took to define the most general kinds of being. Kant claims that his table is superior to Aristotle's list in that it is grounded on a systematic principle.[1] This principle is also what will eventually ground, in the Transcendental Deduction, the *a priori* justification of the objective validity of the categories: a justification of the claim that all objects (as long as they are objects of a possible experience) do fall under those categories.

Kant's self-proclaimed achievement is the second main step in his effort to answer the question: "How are synthetic *a priori* judgments possible?" The first step was the argument offered in the Transcendental Aesthetic, to the effect that space and time are *a priori* forms of intuition. As such, Kant argued, they make possible judgments (propositions) whose claim to truth is justified *a priori* by the universal features of our intuitions. Such propositions are thus both *synthetic* and *a priori*. They are *synthetic* in that their truth does not rest on the mere analysis of the subject-concept of the proposition. They are *a priori* in that their justification does not depend on experience but on *a priori* features of our intuitions that make possible any and all experience. However, space and time, as forms of intuition, do not suffice on their own to account for the content of any judgment at all, much less for our forming or entertaining such judgments. Kant's second step in answering the question "how

129

are synthetic *a priori* judgments possible?" consists in showing that conceptual contents for judgments about objects of experience are provided only if categories guide the ordering of our representations of those objects so that we can form concepts of them and combine those concepts in judgments.

The two aspects of Kant's view (we have *a priori* forms of intuition, we have *a priori* concepts whose table can be systematically established according to one and the same principle) gradually took shape during three decades of Kant's painstaking reflections on issues of natural philosophy and ontology. His questions about natural philosophy include, for instance, the following: how can we reconcile the idea that the reality of the world must be reducible to some ultimate components, and the idea that space is infinitely divisible? Are there any real interactions between physical things, and if so, what is the nature of those interactions? Such questions call upon the resources of an ontology, where Kant struggles with questions such as the following: what is the nature of space and time? How does the reality of space and time relate to the reality of things? Do we have any warrant for asserting the universal validity of the causal principle? Is the causal principle just a variation on the principle of sufficient reason, and if so, what is the warrant for the latter principle?

Kant's argument for his table of the categories (what he calls, in the second edition of the *Critique of Pure Reason* [B 159], the "metaphysical deduction of the categories") is one element in his answer to these questions, as far as the contribution of pure concepts of the understanding is concerned. Further elements will be the transcendental deduction of the categories, in which Kant argues that the categories whose table he has set up do have objective validity; and the system of principles of pure understanding, where Kant shows, for each and every one of the categories, *how* it conditions any representation of an object of experience and is thus legitimately predicated of such objects. From these proofs it follows, as Kant maintains in the concluding chapter of the Analytic of Principles, that "the proud name of an ontology, which presumes to offer synthetic *a priori* cognitions of things in general in a systematic doctrine . . . must give way to the more modest one of a mere analytic of the pure understanding" (A 247/B 303). In other words, whereas the ontology of Aristotelian inspiration defended by Kant's immediate predecessors in German school-philosophy purported to expound, by *a priori* arguments, universal features of things as they are in themselves, Kant's more modest goal is to argue that our understanding is so constituted that it could not come up with any objective representation of things as they present themselves in experience, unless it made use of the concepts expounded in his table of the categories.

It would be futile to try to summarize even briefly the stages through which Kant's view progressed before reaching its mature formulation in the *Critique of Pure Reason*. Nevertheless, it will be useful for a proper understanding of the reversal that Kant imposes on the ambitions of traditional ontology, it will be useful to recall a few of the early formulations of the problems he tries to address in the metaphysical deduction of the categories.

I. HISTORICAL BACKGROUND

In the 1755 *New Elucidation of the First Principles of Metaphysical Cognition*, Kant offered a "proof" of the principle of sufficient reason (or rather, as he defined it, of the principle of *determining* reason) understood inseparably as a logical and an ontological principle, as were also the principle of identity and the principle of contradiction (see *New Elucidation*, 1:388–94). From this general "proof" he then derived a proof of the principle of determining reason *of every contingent existence* (of every existing thing that might as well have existed as not existed) (1:396–8). And finally he derived a proof of the "principle of succession" (there is a sufficient reason for any change of state of a substance) and a "principle of coexistence" (the relations between finite substances do not result from their mere coexistence, but must have been instituted by a special act of God) (1:410–16). Although these proofs differed from those provided by Christian Wolff and his followers, they nevertheless had the same general inspiration. They rested on a similar assumption that logical principles (defining the relations between concepts or propositions) are also ontological principles (defining the relations between existing things and states of affairs), and that one can derive the latter from the former.

In his lectures on metaphysics from the early 1760s, as well as in the published works of the same period, Kant expresses doubts on precisely this point. In the 1763 *Attempt to Introduce the Concept of Negative Quantities into Philosophy*, he distinguishes between *logical* relations and *real* relations. And he formulates the question that he will later describe, in the Preface to the *Prolegomena*, as "Hume's Problem": how are we to understand a relation in which "if something is posited, something else also is posited"? (See *Prolegomena*, 4:257; cf. *Negative Quantities*, 2:202–4.) It is important to note that the question is formulated in the vocabulary of the school logic in which Kant was trained. The relation between something's "being posited" and something else's "being posited" is just the logical relation of *modus ponens*, according to which if the antecedent of a hypothetical judgment *is posited*, then the consequent *should also be posited*. In his *Lectures on Metaphysics* of the 1760s, Kant notes that the logical *ratio ponens* or *tollens* is *analytic*, but the real *ratio ponens* or *tollens* is synthetic – empirical. By this he means that *in an empirical hypothetical judgment, the relation between the antecedent and consequent of the judgment is synthetic*: the consequent is not conceptually contained in the antecedent. Kant's question follows: what, in such a case, grounds the connection between antecedent and consequent and thus the possibility of concluding from the antecedent's *being posited* that the consequent *should also be posited*? (See *Metaphysics Herder*, 28:12; *Negative Quantities*, 2:202–3.)[2]

During the same period of the 1760s, Kant becomes interested also in the difference between the method of metaphysics and the method of mathematics. Metaphysics, he says, proceeds by analysis of confused and obscure concepts. Mathematics, in contrast, proceeds by synthesis of clear, simple concepts. In the same breath, Kant expresses scepticism with respect to the Leibnizian project of solving metaphysical problems with a universal combinatoric. This would be possible, Kant says, if we were in a position to completely analyze our metaphysical concepts. But they are far too complex and obscure for that to be possible (*Prize Essay*, 2:276–91, especially 283).

Note that the notions of *analysis* and *synthesis* by which Kant contrasts the respective methods of metaphysics and mathematics are not the same as the notions of analytic and synthetic connections at work in the reflections on *ratio ponens* and *tollens* mentioned earlier. The latter describe a relation of concepts in a (hypothetical) proposition. The former characterize a method. Nevertheless, the two uses of the notions are, of course, related. Just as mathematics proceeds by synthesis in that it proceeds by combining concepts that were not contained in one another, similarly a synthetic *ratio ponens* is a relation between antecedent and consequent that does not rest on the fact that the concepts combined in the latter are contained in the concepts combined in the former (as in, for instance, "if God wills, then the world exists," or "if the wind blows from the West, then rain clouds appear"). (Cf. *Negative Quantities*, 2:202–3.) Just as metaphysics proceeds by analysis in that it proceeds by clarifying what is contained, or thought, in an initially obscure concept, similarly an analytic *ratio ponens* is a relation between antecedent and consequent that rests on the fact that the concepts combined in the latter are contained in the concepts combined in the former. It is also worth noting that in both cases, analysis and synthesis, and analytic and synthetic connection, respectively, are defined with respect to *concepts*. There is no mention of the distinction between two kinds of representations (intuitions and concepts) that will play such an important role in the critical period.

That distinction is introduced in the 1770 inaugural dissertation *On the Form and Principles of the Sensible and Intelligible Worlds*. There Kant maintains that all representations of spatio-temporal properties and relations of empirical objects depend on original *intuitions* of space and time, in which objects can be presented and related to one another. These objects are themselves objects of particular intuitions. All intuitions differ from concepts in that they are *singular*: they are representations of individuals, or, as we might say in the case of particular intuitions, they are the representational counterparts of demonstratives. And they are *immediate*: they do not require the mediation of other representations to relate to individual objects. Concepts, in contrast, are *general*: they are representations of properties common to several objects. And they are *mediate* or *reflected*: they relate to individual objects only through the mediation of other representations, that is, intuitions. In saying that space and time themselves are intuitions, Kant is saying that they are representations of individual wholes (the representation of one space *in which* all particular spaces and spatial positions are included and related, and the representation of one time *in which* all particular durations and temporal positions are included and related) that are prior to, and a condition for, the acquisition of any *concepts* of spatial

and temporal properties and relations. And this in turn allows him
to distinguish two kinds of synthesis: the classically accepted synthesis *of concepts*; and the *synthesis of intuitive representations of
things, and parts of things, individually represented* in space and in
time.[3]

The *Dissertation* thus has the resources for solving many of the
problems that occupied Kant over the preceding twenty years. In particular, because space and time are characterized not only as intuitions, but as intuitions *proper to our own sensibility* or ability to
receive representations from the way we are affected by things, their
property of infinite divisibility makes it the case that things *as they
appear to us* can be represented as susceptible to division *ad infinitum*. But from this, one need not conclude that there are no ultimate
components of the world *as a world of purely intelligible things*,
things independent of their representation in our sensibility (see *Dissertation*, 2:415–16).

Moreover, Kant asserts that in addition to space and time as forms
of our sensibility, that is, original intuitions in which things given
to our senses are related to one another, we also have concepts "born
from laws innate to the mind" that apply universally to objects.
Among such concepts, he cites those of cause, substance, necessity,
possibility, and existence (see *Dissertation*, 2:395). It is our use of
such concepts that allows us to think the kinds of connections that
befuddled Kant in the 1760s. For instance, in applying the concept of
cause to objects, whether given to our senses or merely thought, we
come up with the kind of synthetic *modus ponens* Kant wondered
about in the essay on negative magnitudes and the related lectures
on metaphysics.

However, in a well-known letter to Marcus Herz of February 1772,
Kant puts this last point into question: how can concepts that have
their origin in our minds be applied to objects that are given? This
difficulty concerns both our knowledge of the sensible world and our
knowledge of the intelligible world. For in both cases, things, on the
one hand, and our concepts of them, on the other hand, are supposed
to be radically independent of one another. Having thus radically
divided them, how can we hope to put them back together? In that
same letter, Kant announces that he has found a solution to this
quandary, and that it will take him no more than three months to
lay it out (see *Correspondence*, 10:132). In fact, it took him almost

a decade. The result of that effort is the *Critique of Pure Reason*, its metaphysical deduction of the categories, and the two related components in Kant's solution to the problem laid out in the letter to Herz: the transcendental deduction of the categories, and the proofs of the principles of pure understanding (cf. *Pure Reason*, A 50–234/ B 74–287).

Of these three components, the first – the metaphysical deduction of the categories, that is, the establishment of their table according to a systematic principle – has always been the least popular with Kant's readers. In the final part of this essay, I shall consider some of the objections that have been raised against it, from the time the *Critique* first appeared to more recent times. Whatever the fate of those objections, it is important to keep in mind that the key terms and themes at work in the metaphysical deduction – the relation between logic and ontology, the distinction between analysis and synthesis and between synthesis *of concepts* and synthesis *of intuitions* – are all part of Kant's effort to find the correct formulation for questions that preoccupied him since the earliest years of his philosophical development.

II. KANT'S VIEW OF LOGIC

The metaphysical deduction of the categories is expounded in Chapter One of the Transcendental Analytic in the *Critique of Pure Reason*, entitled "On the Clue to the Discovery of All Pure Concepts of the Understanding."[4] This chapter is preceded by a fairly long Introduction to the Transcendental Analytic as a whole, where Kant explains what he means by "logic." This is worth noticing. For as we saw, one main issue in his precritical investigations was that of the relation between logic and ontology, and the capacity of logic to capture fundamental features of the world. But now Kant puts forward a completely new distinction, that between "general pure logic" (which he also sometimes calls "formal logic," e.g., at A 131/B 170) and "transcendental logic" (A 50–7/B74–81). In putting forward this distinction, Kant intends *both* to debunk the Leibnizian-Wolffian direct mapping of forms of thought upon forms of being, *and* to redefine, on new grounds, the grip our intellect can have on the structural features of the world. As we shall see, establishing a new relation between logic and ontology is also what guides his "metaphysical deduction of the categories," namely, his suggestion that a complete and systematic table of *a priori* concepts of the understanding, whose applicability to objects given in experience is impervious to empirical verification or falsification, can be established according to the "leading thread" of logical forms of judgment.

Kant's primary tool for his twofold enterprise – first prying apart logic and ontology, but then finding new grounds for the grip our intellect has on the world – is the distinction between two kinds of access that we have to reality: our being affected by it or being "receptive" to it, and our thinking it or forming concepts of it. Each of these two kinds of access, he says, depends on a specific capacity: our acquiring representations by being affected depends on "receptivity" or sensibility, and our acquiring concepts depends on "spontaneity" or understanding. Kant differentiates these capacities primarily by way of the contrast just mentioned, between *receiving* (through sensibility) and *thinking* (through understanding). But they are also distinguished by the *kinds of representations* they offer, and by the *ways in which they order and relate these representations to one another*. Sensibility offers intuitions (singular and immediate representations), understanding offers concepts (general and reflected representations). As beings endowed with sensibility or receptivity, we relate our intuitions to one another in one and the same intuition of space and of time. As beings endowed with understanding, we relate concepts to one another in judgments and inferences. These modes of ordering representations are what Kant calls the "forms" of each capacity: space and time are forms of sensibility, the logical forms of judgment are forms of the understanding (cf. *Pure Reason*, A 19–21/B 33–5, A 50–2/B 74–6).

These initial distinctions have important consequences for Kant's characterization of logic. Logic, he says, is "the science of the rules of the understanding in general," to be distinguished from aesthetic as "the science of the rules of sensibility" (A 52/B 76). Characterizing logic in this way is surprising for a contemporary reader. We are used to characterizing logic in a more objective way, as a science of the relations of implication that hold between propositions. Learning logic is of course learning to *make use* of these patterns of implication in the right way for deriving true proposition from true proposition, or for detecting the flaw in a given argument. But that is not what the proper object of logic is, or what logic is *about*.[5] Now,

Kant's more psychological characterization of logic is one he shares with all early modern logicians, influenced by Antoine Arnauld and Pierre Nicole's *Logic or the Art of Thinking*, also known as the *Port-Royal Logic*. However, as the very title of Arnauld's and Nicole's book shows, even their logic is not just preoccupied with the way we happen to think, but establishes norms for thinking *well*.[6] But Kant is more explicit than they are about the normative character of logic: logic, he says, does not concern the way we think but the way we ought to think. It "derives nothing from psychology" (*Logic*, 9:14; *Pure Reason*, A 54/B 78). More precisely, logic so considered is what Kant calls "pure" logic, which he distinguishes from "applied" logic where one takes into account "the empirical conditions under which our understanding is exercised, e.g. the influence of imagination, the laws of memory, the power of habit, inclination, and so on" (A 53/B 77). Logic properly speaking, or "pure" logic, has no need to take these psychological factors into account. Rather, its job is to consider the patterns of combination of concepts in judgments that are possible by virtue of the mere form of concepts (i.e., their universality); and the patterns of inference that are possible by virtue of the mere forms of judgments.

The idea of taking into account the "mere form" of concepts, judgments, and inferences rests in turn on another distinction, that between the logic of the "general use" and the logics of the "particular use" of the understanding. A logic of the particular use of the understanding is a science of the rules the understanding must follow in drawing inferences in connection with a particular content of knowledge – each science, in this way, has its particular "logic."[7] But the logic of the general use of the understanding is the logic of the rules presupposed in *all* use of the understanding, whatever its particular domain of investigation.

Kant has thus identified "general pure" logic: a logic that, as "pure," does not derive anything from psychology; and as "general," defines the most elementary rules of thought, rules that any use of the understanding must follow. Now, that he also defines this logic as *formal* is where his radical parting of ways with his Leibnizian-Wolffian rationalist predecessors is most apparent. For the latter – just as for the early Kant of the 1750s – the most general principles of logic also defined the most general structural features of *being*. But as we saw, ever since he distinguished relations of concepts and relations of existence (in his metaphysical essays of the early 1760s), Kant no longer took the identity of logical and real connections for granted. This being so, forms of thought are just this: forms of thought. And the question arises: just what is their relation to forms of being, or to the way things are? Logic, as "general and pure," is thus *only* formal.[8]

On the other hand, the distinction between the forms of sensibility and the forms of understanding helps delineate the domain for a logic that is just as *pure* as formal logic, because it does not derive its rules from empirical-psychological considerations of the kind described earlier; but that is not as *general* as formal logic, in that the rules it considers are specified by the *content* of thought they are relevant for. They are the rules for combining representations *given in sensibility*, whatever the empirical (sensory) content of these representations may be. Those rules are thus not merely *formal* (concerning only the forms of thought in combining concepts and judgment for arriving at valid inferences), but they concern the way a *content* for thought is formed by ordering manifolds in intuition (multiplicities of qualitatively determined spatial and temporal parts). These rules are the rules of "transcendental" logic.

I now turn to Kant's argument for his table of the logical forms of judgment, in Section One of the chapter on the "Leading Thread for the Discovery of all Pure Concepts of the Understanding" (A 67–9/B 92–4), and to the table itself, expounded in Section Two (A 70–6/B 95–101).

III. THE LEADING THREAD: KANT'S VIEW OF JUDGMENT AND THE TABLE OF LOGICAL FORMS OF JUDGMENT

In the 1770 *Dissertation*, Kant distinguished what he called the "logical use" and the "real use" of the understanding. In the real use, he said, concepts of things and of relations are given "by the very nature of the understanding" (2:394). In the logical use, "the concepts, no matter whence they are given, are merely subordinated to each other, the lower, namely, to the higher concepts (common characteristic marks) and compared with one another in accordance with the principle of contradiction" (2:393). The real use is what we saw Kant put into question in the letter to Herz of February 1772: How could concepts that have their origin in the laws of our understanding be applicable to objects independent of our understanding? (Cf. 10:125.)

But the logical use remained unscathed, and it is precisely what Kant describes again in Section One of the *Leitfaden* chapter under the title: "On the logical use of the understanding in general" (A 67/B 92). By "logical use of the understanding," it is thus clear we should not understand the use of understanding *in logic* – whatever that might mean. Rather, it is the use we make of the understanding according to the rules of logic when we subsume sensible intuitions under concepts and subordinate lower concepts to higher concepts, in accordance with the principle of contradiction, thus forming judgments and inferences. As we shall see, Kant argues that considering precisely this "logical use of the understanding" gives him the clue or leading thread (*Leitfaden*) he needs for a solution to the problem he raised about its "real use." For the very acts of judging by which we subsume intuitions under concepts and subordinate lower concepts to higher concepts *also* provide rules for ordering manifolds in intuition and thus eventually for subsuming objects of sensible intuition under the categories. Or so Kant will argue in Section Three of the *Leitfaden* chapter.

But before we reach that point, we need to consider the "logical use" in more detail, to see how Kant thinks he can derive from it his table of the logical forms of judgment.

The key term, in Kant's exposition of the "logical use of the understanding," is the term *function*.

All intuitions, as sensible, rest on affections, concepts therefore on functions [*Begriffe also auf Funktionen*]. By a function, however, I understand the unity of the action of ordering different representations under a common one.

(A 68/B 93)

The term "function" belongs to the vocabulary of biology and the description of organisms. Kant talks of the "function" of mental capacities as he would talk of the "function" of an organ. In this very general sense, sensibility too has a "function." Indeed, in the Introduction to the Transcendental Logic Kant writes:

The two capacities or abilities [*Beide Vermögen, oder Fähigkeiten*] cannot exchange their functions. The understanding is not capable of intuiting anything, and the senses are not capable of thinking anything.   (A 51/B 76)

However, in the present context, Kant employs "function" in a more restricted sense. Concepts, he says, rest on functions, *as opposed* to intuitions, which, as sensible, rest on affections. More precisely: *because* intuitions rest on affections or depend on receptivity, concepts have to rest on functions, that is, namely, they depend on our unifying representations (intuitions) that are given in a dispersed, random order in sensibility. In this context, function is (as quoted above) the "unity of the action of ordering different representations under a common representation." Another possible analogue for the notion of function in this context, besides the biological one, is then the notion of a mathematical function. The "function" we are talking about here would map given representations – intuitions – on to combinations of concepts in judgments.[9]

The "action" mentioned in the citation given earlier should not be understood as a temporally determined psychological event.[10] What Kant is describing are universal modes of ordering our representations, whatever the empirically determined processes by which those orderings occur. They consist in subsuming individuals under concepts, and subordinating lower (less general) concepts under higher (more general) concepts. These subsumptions and subordinations are themselves structured in determinate ways, and each specific way in which they are structured constitutes a specification of the "function" defined earlier. Interestingly, introducing the term "function" in Section One of the *Leitfaden* chapter to describe the logical employment of the understanding is already making space for what will be the core argument of the metaphysical deduction of the categories:

The same function that gives unity to different representations in a judgment also gives unity to the mere synthesis of different representations in an intuition, which, expressed universally, is called the pure concept of the understanding.   (A 79/B 104–5)

I will return to this point in a moment.

The "function" in question is from the outset characterized as a function of judging. This is because we can make no other use of concepts than subsuming individuals under them, or subordinating lower concepts under higher concepts, that is, forming (thinking) judgments. This being so, the "unity of the action" or function by way of which we acquire concepts results in judgments that have a determinate form (a determinate way of combining the concepts they unite). There is thus an exact correspondence between the *functions* ("unity of the action of ordering different representations") the understanding exercises in judging, and the forms of the judgments that result from the functions. Unlike the functions, the forms are manifest in the linguistic expression of the judgments.[11]

In Section One of the "Leading Thread," Kant makes use of two examples of actual judgments to further elucidate the function of judging. The first is "All bodies are divisible." He insists that in this example, the concept "divisible" is related to the concept of "body" (or the latter is subordinated to the former), and *by way of this relation*, the concept "divisible" is related to all objects thought under the concept "body" (or all objects thought under the concept "body" are subsumed under the concept "divisible"). A similar point is made again later in the paragraph, when Kant explains that the concept "body" means something, for instance, "metal," which thus can be known by way of the concept "body." In other words, in saying "Metal is a body," I express some knowledge about what it is to be a metal, and thus also a knowledge about everything that falls under the concept "metal." The two examples jointly show that whatever position a concept occupies in a judgment (the position of subject or the position of predicate, in a judgment of the general form "S is P"), in its use in judging a concept is always, ultimately, a predicate of individual objects falling under the subject-concept of the judgment. This in turn makes every judgment the major premise of an implicit syllogistic inference whose conclusion asserts the subsumption, under the predicate-concept, of some object falling under the subject concept (e.g., the judgment "all bodies are divisible" is the implicit premise of a syllogistic inference such as: "all bodies are divisible; this x is a body; so, this x is divisible." Or again: "All bodies are divisible; metal is a body; so, metal is divisible; now, this is metal; so, this is a body; so, this is divisible." And so on). If it is true to say that we make use of concepts only in judgments, it is equally true to say that the function of syllogistic inference is already present in any judgment by virtue of its form. For asserting a predicate of a subject is also asserting it of every object falling under the subject-concept.

This is why, as Kant maintains in what is undoubtedly the decisive thesis of this section, and perhaps of the whole *Leitfaden* chapter:

We can, however, trace all acts of the understanding back to judgments, so that the understanding in general can be represented as a capacity to judge [*ein Vermögen zu urteilen*]. (A 69/B 94)

By "understanding" he means here the intellectual capacity as a whole, what he has described as *spontaneity* as opposed to the *receptivity* or passivity of sensibility. In agreement with a quite standard presentation of the structure of intellect in early modern logic textbooks, Kant divides the understanding into the capacity to form concepts (or understanding in the narrow sense), the capacity to subsume objects under concepts and subordinate lower concepts to higher concepts (the power of judgment, *Urteilskraft*), and the capacity to form inferences (reason, *Vernunft*). He is now telling us that all of these come down to one capacity, the capacity to judge. The latter is not the same as the power of judgment (*Urteilskraft*). One way to present the relation between the two would be to say that the *Urteilskraft* is an actualization of the *Vermögen zu urteilen*. But for that matter, so are the two other components of understanding. So the *Vermögen zu urteilen* is that structured, spontaneous, self-regulating capacity characteristic of human minds that makes them capable of making use of concepts in judgments, of deriving judgments from other judgments in syllogistic inferences, and of systematically unifying all of these judgments and inferences in one system of thought.[12]

This explains why Kant concludes Section One with this sentence: "The functions of the understanding can therefore all be found if we can completely present the functions of unity in judgments" (A 69/B 94) If the understanding as a whole is nothing but a *Vermögen zu urteilen*, then identifying the totality of functions ("unities of the act") of the understanding amounts to nothing more and nothing less than identifying the totality of functions present *in judging*, which in turn are manifest by linguistically explicit *forms* of judgments. Kant adds: "That this can easily be accomplished will be shown in the next section." The "next section" is the section that expounds (as its title indicates) "the logical function of understanding in judgments" by laying out a table of logical forms of judgments.

But of course, even if we grant Kant that he has justified his statement that "the understanding as a whole is a capacity to judge," this by itself does not suffice to justify the table he presents. How is the table itself justified?

Kant's explanation of the function of judging decisively illuminates the table he then goes on to set up. First, if the canonical form of judgment is a subordination of *concepts* (as in the two examples analyzed above), then this subordination can be such that either *all* or *part* of the extension of the subject-concept is included in the extension of the predicate-concept: this gives us the quantity of judgments, specified as universal or particular. Moreover, the extension of the subject can be included in or *excluded from* the extension of the predicate-concept. This gives us the title of quality, specified as affirmative or negative judgment. The combination of these two titles and their specifications provides the classical Aristotelian "square of opposites": universal affirmative, universal negative, particular affirmative, and particular negative judgments.

Within each of these first two titles, however, Kant adds a third specification, which does not belong in the Aristotelian square of opposites: "singular" judgment under the title of quantity, and "infinite" judgment under the title of quality. In both cases he explains that these additions would not belong in a "general pure logic" strictly speaking. For as far as the forms of judgment relevant to forms of syllogistic inference are concerned, a singular judgment can be treated as a universal judgment, where the totality of the extension of the subject concept is included in the extension of the predicate concept. Similarly, an infinite judgment (in Kant's sense: a judgment in which the predicate is prefixed by a negation) is from the logical point of view an affirmative judgment (there is no negation appended to the copula). But those two forms do belong in a table geared toward laying out the ways in which our understanding comes up with knowledge of objects. In this context there is all the difference in the world between a judgment through which we assert knowledge of just one thing (singular judgment) and a judgment through which we assert knowledge of a complete set of things (universal judgment). Similarly, there is all the difference in the world between including the extension of a subject-concept in that of a determinate predicate-concept, and locating the extension of a subject-concept in the indeterminate sphere that is outside the limited sphere of a given predicate (see A 72–3/B 97–8, where Kant distinguishes the infinite judgments from both the affirmative and the negative judgments). Now it is significant that Kant should thus add, for the benefit of his transcendental inquiry, the two forms of singular and infinite judgment to the forms making up the classical square of opposites. It shows that if the logical forms serve as a "leading thread" for the table of categories, conversely the goal of coming up with a table of categories determines the shape of the table of logical forms.

This is even more apparent, I suggest, if we consider the third title, that of relation. It should first be noted that this title does not exist in any of the lists of judgments presented in the logic text-books with which Kant was familiar.[13] On the other hand, the three kinds of relation in judgments (relation between a predicate and a subject in a categorical judgment, relation between a consequent and an antecedent in a hypothetical judgment, relation between the mutually exclusive specifications of a concept and that concept in a disjunctive judgment) determine the three main kinds of inferences, from a categorical, a hypothetical, or a disjunctive major premise. This is in keeping with what emerged as the most important thesis of Section One: the understanding as a whole was characterized as a *Vermögen zu urteilen* because *in the function of judging as such* were contained the other two functions of the understanding – acquiring and using concepts and forming inferences. This being so, it is natural to include in a table of logical forms of judgment meant to expound the features of *the function of judging* the three forms of relation that govern the three main forms of syllogistic inference.

Still, as many commentators have noted, it is somewhat surprising to see Kant include, as equally representative of forms of judgment that govern forms of inference, the categorical form that is the almost exclusive concern of Aristotelian syllogistic, and the hypothetical and disjunctive forms that find prominence only with the Stoics. Does this not contradict Kant's (admittedly shocking) statement that logic "has been unable to make a single step forward" since Aristotle (B viii)?

I think there are two answers to this question. The first is historical: the forms of hypothetical and disjunctive inference (*modus ponens* and *tollens, modus ponendo tollens* and *tollendo ponens*) are actually briefly mentioned by Aristotle, developed by his followers (especially Galen and Alexander of Aphrodisias) and present in the Aristotelian tradition as Kant knows it.[14] The second answer takes us back to the remark I made earlier. Kant's table is not *just* a table of logical forms. It is a table of logical forms motivated by the initial analysis of the *function* of judging and by the goal of laying out which aspects of the "unity of the act" (the function) are relevant to our eventually coming up with knowledge of objects. In this regard, it is certainly striking that Kant should have developed the view that in the "mediate knowledge of an object," that is, judgment, we not only predicate a concept of another concept *and thus of all objects falling under the latter* (categorical judgment), but we also predicate a concept of another concept and thus of all objects falling under the latter, *under the added condition that some other predication be satisfied* (hypothetical judgment), and we think both categorical and hypothetical predications *in the context of a unified and, as much as possible, specified conceptual space* (expressed in a disjunctive judgment). These added conditions for predication (and thus for knowing objects under concepts) find their full import when related to the corresponding categories, as we shall see in a moment.

The fourth title in the table is that of modality. Kant explains that this title "contributes nothing to the content of the judgment (for besides quantity, quality and relation there is nothing more that constitutes the content of a judgment), but rather concerns only the value of the copula in relation to thinking in general" (A 74/B 100). The formulation is somewhat surprising since, after all, none of the other titles were supposed to have anything to do with content either: they were supposed merely to characterize the *form* of judgments, or the ways concepts were combined in judgments, whatever the contents of these concepts. But what Kant probably means here is that modality does not characterize anything further *even with respect to that form*. Once the form of a judgment is completely specified as to its quantity, quality, and relation, the judgment can still be specified as to its modality. But this specification concerns not the judgment individually, but rather its relation to other judgments, within the systematic unity of "thinking in general." Thus a judgment is problematic if it belongs, as antecedent or consequent, in a hypothetical judgment, or if it expresses one of the divisions of a concept in a disjunctive judgment. It is assertoric if it functions as the minor premise in a hypothetical or disjunctive inference. It is apodeictic (but only conditionally so) as the conclusion of a hypothetical or disjunctive inference. Such a characterization of modality is strikingly anti-Leibnizian since for Leibniz the modality of a judgment would have entirely depended on the content of the judgment itself: whether its predicate is asserted of its subject by virtue of a finite or an infinite analysis of the latter. Note, therefore, that Kant's characterization of modality from the standpoint of "general pure" logic confirms that the latter is concerned only with the *form* of thought, not with the particular content of any judgment or inference.

So the table, in the end, is fairly simple: it is a table of forms of concept subordination (quantity and quality) where, to the classical distinctions (universal and particular, affirmative and negative), is added under each title a form that allows special consideration of individual objects (singular judgment) and their relation to a conceptual space that is indefinitely determinable (infinite judgment). And it is a table where judgments are taken to be possible premises for inferences (relation) and are taken to derive their modality from their relation to other judgments or their place in inferences (modality). Kant's claim that the table is systematic and complete is not supported by any explicit argument. Efforts have been made by recent commentators to extract such an argument from the first section of the *Leitfaden* chapter, the most systematic effort being Michael Wolff's. Even he, however, recognizes that the full justification of Kant's table of logical forms comes only with the *transcendental* deduction.[15] My view is that although Kant's analysis in Section One gives strong leads for the table as it is set up, the table in its detail can only have emerged from Kant's painstaking reflections about the relation between the forms according to which we relate concepts to other concepts, and thus to objects (forms of judgment, which as we shall see shortly, Kant also characterizes as forms of analysis) and forms according to which we may combine manifolds in intuition *so that* they may fall under concepts: forms of synthesis, in the new sense of this term we encountered in the *Dissertation*. Indeed it is a striking fact that the first mature version of Kant's table of logical forms appeared not in his reflections on logic, but in his reflections on metaphysics. This seems to indicate that the search for a systematic list of the categories and a justification of their relation to objects determined the establishment of the table of logical forms of judgment just as much as the latter served as a leading thread for the former.[16]

I now turn to the culminating point of this whole argument: Kant's argument for the relation between logical forms of judgment and categories, and his table of the categories.

IV. KANT'S ARGUMENT FOR THE TABLE OF THE CATEGORIES

I said earlier that the fundamental thesis of Section One of the *Leitfaden* chapter is that "Understanding as a whole is a capacity to judge." I might now add that the fundamental thesis of Section Three ("On the pure concepts of the understanding or categories") is that judgments presuppose synthesis.

In a way, this statement is a truism. After all, "synthesis" means nothing more than "positing together" or "combination," and it is obvious that any judgment of the traditional Aristotelian form "S is P" is a positing together or combination of concepts. Indeed, Aristotle defined it in just this way, and the Aristotelian tradition followed suit all the way down to Kant, including in the early modern version of Port-Royal's logic of ideas.[17] What is new, however, in Kant's notion of synthesis, is that it does not mean only or even primarily a combination of concepts. As far as concepts of objects given in sensibility are concerned, the combining (synthesis) of those concepts in judgments can occur only under the condition that a combining of *parts* and *aspects* of the objects given in sensibility and potentially thought under concepts also occur. The rules for *these* combinings is what transcendental logic is concerned with.

But why *should* there be syntheses of parts and aspects of objects presented to our sensibility? Why should it not be the case that empirically given objects *just do* present themselves as spatio-temporal, qualitatively determined wholes that have their own presented boundaries? Kant does not really justify the point in Section Three of the *Leitfaden* chapter. The furthest he goes in that direction is to explain that in order for *analysis* of sensible intuitions into concepts to be possible, *synthesis* of these same intuitions (or of the "manifold [of intuition], whether it be given empirically or *a priori*" [A 77/B 102]) must have occurred. The former operation, as we saw from Section One of the *Leitfaden* chapter, obeys the rules of the logical employment of the understanding. The latter operation must present the sensible manifold in such a way that it *can* be analyzed into concepts susceptible to being bound together in judgments according to the rules of the logical employment of the understanding.

Here it will be useful to recall the problem laid out in the letter to Herz mentioned in part I of this essay. Mathematical concepts present their own objects by directing the synthesis of an *a priori* (spatial) manifold according to rules provided by the relevant concept (e.g., a line, a triangle, or a circle). But we cannot do that in metaphysics because there the objects of our concepts are not just constructed in pure intuition. They are supposed to be independently existing things, so that in this case we just do not see how *a priori* concepts might relate to objects.[18] But here in Section Three of the *Leitfaden* chapter, Kant is telling us that a function of the understanding, specifically the function of judging, is not arbitrarily producing (constructing) representations of objects, as in geometry or even in arithmetic, but at least *unifying according to rules the presented manifold of intuition*, so that it can be analyzed into (empirical) concepts and thought about in judgments.

Thus he writes:

Synthesis in general, as we shall subsequently see, is the mere effect of imagination, a blind, though indispensable function of the soul, without which we would have no cognition at all, but of which we are seldom even conscious. Yet *to bring this synthesis to concepts is a function that pertains to the understanding* [my emphasis] and by means of which it first provides cognition in the proper sense.   (A 78/B 103)

What might it mean to "bring synthesis to concepts"? I suggest the following. What is given to us in sensibility is given in a dispersed way – spread out in space and time, where similar things do not present themselves to us at the same time but rather need to be recalled in order to be compared. Moreover, the variety and variability of what does present itself is such that *which* pattern of regularity should be picked out might be anybody's guess. Even the way we synthesize or bind together the manifold might itself be quite random, obeying here some rule of habitual association, there some emotional connection, and so on. So, ordering *the synthesis itself* under systematic rules so that the components of intuition can be thought under common concepts in a regular fashion is the work of the understanding. The understanding thus "brings synthesis *to* concepts." It makes it the case that synthesis *does* give rise to, opens the way for, conceptualization.

The analogy with the mathematical case is only partly helpful here. Kant writes:

Now pure synthesis, universally represented, yields the pure concept of the understanding. By this synthesis, however, I understand that which rests on a ground of synthetic unity *a priori*: thus our counting (as is especially noticeable in the case of larger numbers) is a synthesis in accordance with concepts, since it takes place in accordance with a common ground of unity (e.g. the decimal). Under this concept, therefore, the synthesis of the manifold becomes necessary.   (A 78/B 104)

In counting, we add unit to unit, and then units of higher order (a decade, a hundred, a thousand, and so on) that allow us to synthesize (enumerate) larger and larger collections (of items, of portions of a line, etc.). The idea is that similarly, in ordering empirical manifolds, we make use of grounds of unity of these manifolds (e.g., whenever event of type A occurs, then event of type B also occurs), which we think under concepts or "represent universally" (in the case at hand, under the concept of cause). We thus form chains of connections between these manifolds, in an effort to unify them in one space and one time, in the context of one and the same totality of experience. But of course, whereas it is always possible to enumerate a collection of things or parts of things once one has arbitrarily given oneself a unit for counting or measuring, in contrast, actually *finding* repeated occurrences of similar events depends on what experience presents to us. Because of this difference, Kant distinguishes the former kind of synthesis, which he calls "mathematical" synthesis, from the latter, which he calls "dynamical," and he accordingly distinguishes the corresponding categories by dividing them along the same line (see B 110; A 178–9/B 221–2). Nevertheless, in the latter case just as in the former, a "ground of unity" that has its source in the understanding is at work in our synthesizing (combining, relating) the objects of our experience or their spatiotemporal parts. This ground of unity, says Kant, is a pure concept of the understanding.

This reasoning leads to the core statement of all three sections of the *Leitfaden* chapter:

The same function that gives unity to the different representations *in a judgment* also gives unity to the mere synthesis of different representations *in an intuition*, which, expressed generally, is called the pure concept of understanding. The same understanding, therefore, and indeed by means of the very same actions through which it brings the logical form of a judgment into concepts by means of the analytical unity, also brings a transcendental content into its representations by means of the synthetic unity of the manifold in intuition in general, on account of which they are called pure concepts of the understanding that pertain to objects *a priori*; this can never be accomplished by general logic.   (A 79/B 104–5)

I indicated earlier how the introduction of the term *function* at the beginning of Section One already foreshadowed the argument of Section Three: the very same "unity of the act" that accounts for the unity of concepts of judgments also accounts for there being just those forms of unity in our intuitions that make them liable to being reflected under concepts in judgment. The concepts that reflect those forms of unity in intuition are the categories. But they do not just *reflect* those forms of intuitive unity. As the mathematical analogue made clear (cf. A 78/B 104, cited earlier), they originally *guide* them. So for instance, as we just saw, the concept of magnitude is that concept that guides the operation of finding (homogeneous) units (say, points, or apples) or, as the case may be, units of measurement (say, a meter), and adding them to one another in enumerating a collection or in measuring a line. The end result of this operation is the determination of a magnitude, whether discrete (the number of a collection) or continuous (the measurement of a line), as when we say that the number of pears on the table is seven or the measurement of the line is four meters. Here we *reflect* the successive synthesis of homogeneous units under the concept of a determinate magnitude (seven units, four meters). Similarly, the concept of cause (the concept of some event's being such as to be adequately or "in itself" reflected under the antecedent of a hypothetical judgment with respect to another event, adequately or "in itself" reflected under the consequent) *guides* the search for some event that might always precede another in the temporal order of experience. Once such a constant correlation is found, we say that event of type *a* is the *cause* of event of type *b*. In other words, the sequence is now reflected under the concept of a determinate causal connection.[19]

The two aspects in our use of categories are explicitly mentioned in §10. Kant says, on the one hand, that categories "*give* this pure synthesis *unity*" (A 79/B 104). He says, on the other hand, that the pure concepts of the understanding are "the pure synthesis *universally represented*" (A 78/B 104; see also A 79/B 105, quoted earlier, where both aspects are present in one and the same sentence: "the same function … *gives unity* which *expressed generally*, is the pure concept of the understanding"). These two points are fully explained only in Book Two of the Transcendental Analytic, The Analytic of Principles. There Kant explains that categories, insofar as they determine *rules for synthesis* of sensible intuitions, have *schemata*

(Chapter One of Book Two, A 137/B 176). Being able to pick out instances of such schemata allows us to subsume our intuitions under the categories (Chapter Two, A 148–235/B 187–287). Only in those chapters does Kant give a detailed account of the way in which each category both *determines* and *reflects* a specific rule (a schema) for the synthesis of intuitions.

As far as the metaphysical deduction is concerned, Kant is content with making the general case that

In such a way there arise [*entspringen*] exactly as many pure concepts of the understanding which apply to objects of intuition *a priori*, as there were logical functions of all possible judgments in the previous table: for the understanding is completely exhausted and its capacity is entirely measured by these functions.   (A 80/B 106)

Kant does *not* mean that every time we make use of a particular logical function/form of judgment, we *thereby* make use of the corresponding category. True, absent a sensible manifold to synthesize, all that remains of the categories are logical functions of judgment. But the logical functions of judgment are not, on their own as it were, categories. They become categories (categories "arise" or *entspringen*, as Kant says in the text just cited) only when the understanding's capacity to judge is applied to sensible manifolds, thus synthesizing them (combining them in intuition) for analysis (into concepts) and for synthesis (of concepts in judgments). And even then, there remains a difference between the category's *guiding* the synthesis of manifolds, and the manifolds' being correctly subsumed under the relevant category. For instance, it may be the case that the understanding's effort to identify what might fall under the antecedent and what might fall under the consequent of a hypothetical judgment leads it to recognize the fact that *whenever* the sun shines on the stone, the stone gets warm. This by itself does not warrant the claim that there is an objective connection (a causal connection) between the light of the sun and the warmth of the stone. Only some representation of the overall unity of connections of events in the world can give us at least a provisional, revisable warrant that this connection is the right one to draw (on this example, see *Prolegomena*, 4:312–13).

Kant is not yet explaining how his metaphysical deduction of the categories might put us on the way to resolving the problem left open after the 1770 *Dissertation*, namely, how do concepts that have their source in the understanding apply to objects that are given? All we have here is an exposition of the table of the categories as a system "from a common principle, namely the capacity to judge" (A 80–1/ B 106), and an explanation of the role they perform in synthesizing manifolds so that the latter can be reflected under concepts combined in judgments. To respond to the problem he set himself, Kant will need to argue that those combining activities are necessary conditions for any object at all to become an object of cognition for us. And as I suggested earlier, only the later argument will provide a full justification of the table of logical forms itself: it is a table making manifest just those functions of judging that are necessary for any empirical concept at all to be formed by us, and thus for any empirical object to be recognized under a concept. This confirms again that the "leading thread" from logical forms to categories is precisely no more (but no less) than a "leading thread." Its actual relevance will be proved only when the argument of the transcendental deduction is expounded and, in turn, opens the way to the Schematism and System of Principles.

V. THE IMPACT OF KANT'S METAPHYSICAL DEDUCTION OF THE CATEGORIES

The history of Kant's metaphysical deduction of the categories is not a happy one. Kant's idea that a table of logical functions of judgments might serve as a leading thread for a table of the categories was very early on an object of suspicion, on three main grounds. First, Kant's careless statement that he "found in the labors of the logicians," namely, in the logic text-books of the time, everything he needed to establish his table of the logical forms of judgment raises the obvious objection that the latter is itself lacking in systematic justification (see *Prolegomena*, 4:323–4). This in turn casts doubt on Kant's claim that unlike Aristotle's "rhapsodic" list (A 81–2/B 106–7), his table of the categories is systematically justified. Second, even if one does endorse Kant's table of the logical forms of judgment, this does not necessarily make it an adequate warrant for his table of the categories. And finally, once the Aristotelian model of subject-predicate logic was challenged by post-Fregean truth-functional, extensional logic, it seemed that the whole Kantian enterprise of establishing a table of categories according to the leading thread of forms pertaining to the old logic seemed definitively doomed.

1. An early and vigorous expression of the first charge mentioned above was Hegel's. In the *Science of Logic*, Hegel writes:

> Kantian philosophy ... borrows the categories, as so-called root notions for transcendental logic, from subjective logic in which they were adopted empirically. Since it admits this fact, it is hard to see why transcendental logic chooses to borrow from such a science instead of directly resorting to experience.[20]

Note, however, that it is not Kant's table of logical forms *per se* to which Hegel objects. Rather, it is the way the table is justified (or rather, *not* justified) and the random, empirical way in which the categories themselves are therefore listed. Nevertheless, in the first section of his Subjective Logic, Hegel too expounds four titles and for each title, three divisions of judgment that exactly map the titles and divisions of Kant's table, although Hegel starts with the title of quality rather than quantity. Moreover, the names of each title are changed, although the names of the divisions remain the same. Kant's title of "quality" becomes "judgment of determinate-being" (*Urteil des Daseins*), with the three divisions of positive, negative, and infinite judgment. "Quantity" becomes "judgment of reflection," with the three titles of singular, particular, and universal. "Relation" becomes "judgment of necessity" (*sic*), with the three titles of categorical, hypothetical, and disjunctive. And finally "modality" becomes "judgment of the concept," with the three divisions of assertoric, problematic, and apodeictic.[21] Of course, the change in nomenclature signals fundamental differences between Hegel's and Kant's understanding of the four titles and their twelve divisions. The most important of those differences is that for Hegel, the four titles and three divisions within each title do not list mere *forms* of judgment, but forms *with a content*, where *content* and *form* are mutually determining. So, for instance, the *content* of "judgments of determinate-being" (affirmative, negative, or infinite) is the immediate, sensory qualities of things as they present themselves in experience. The *content* of "judgments of reflection" (singular, particular, or universal) is what Hegel calls "determinations of reflections," namely, general representations, or representations of common properties as they emerge for an understanding that compares, reflects, and abstracts. The content of "judgments of necessity" (categorical, hypothetical, or disjunctive) is the relation between essential and accidental determinations of things. And finally the content of "judgments of the concept" (assertoric, problematic, or apodeictic) is the normative evaluation of the adequacy of a thing to what it *ought to be*, or its *concept*. So certainly Hegel's interpretation of each title radically transforms its Kantian ancestor. Nevertheless, despite his criticism of Kant's empirical derivation, Hegel maintains the structure of Kant's divisions, which indicates that Hegel's intention is not to criticize the classifications themselves, but rather to denounce the cavalier way in which Kant asks us to accept them as well as Kant's shallow separation between form and content of judgment.[22]

Nor is Hegel's intention to challenge the relation between categories and functions of judgment. In the *Science of Logic*, categories of quantity and quality are expounded in Part One (*Being*) of Book One (*The Objective Logic*); those of relation and modality are expounded in Part Two (*The Doctrine of Essence*) of Book One. Logical forms of judgment and syllogistic inference are expounded in Section One of Book Two (The Subjective Logic or the Doctrine of the Concept). If we accept, as I suggest we should, that Book Two expounds the activities of thinking that have governed the revelation of the categorial features expounded in Parts One and Two of Book One, then Hegel's view of the relation between categories and forms of judgment is similar to Kant's at least in one respect: there is a fundamental relation (in need of clarification) between the structural features of the acts of judging and the structural features of objects. The difference between Hegel's view and Kant's view is that Hegel takes this relation to be a fact about being itself, and the structures thus revealed to be those of being itself, whereas Kant takes the relation between judging and the structures of being to be a fact about the way human beings relate to being, and the structures thus revealed to be those of being *as it appears* to human beings.

2. Hegel's grandiose reinterpretation of Kant's titles of judgments did not have any immediate posterity, and his speculative

philosophy was soon superseded by the rise of naturalism in
nineteenth-century philosophy.[23] When Hermann Cohen, reacting against both the excesses of German Idealism and the rampant
naturalism of his time, undertook to revive the Kantian transcendental project, he declared that his goal was to "ground anew the
Kantian theory of the *a priori*" ("die Kantische Aprioritätslehre
erneut zu begründen").[24] By this he meant that, against the
vagaries of Kant's German Idealist successors, he intended to lay
out what truly grounds Kant's theory of the categories and *a priori*
principles. According to Cohen, Kant's purpose in the *Critique of
Pure Reason* is to expound the presuppositions of the mathematical science of nature founded by Galileo and Newton. The leading thread for Kant's pure concepts of the understanding or categories (expounded in Book One of the Transcendental Analytic)
is really Kant's discovery of the principles of pure understanding
(expounded in Book Two), and the leading thread for the latter
is Newton's principles of motion in the *Principia Mathematica
Philosophiae Naturalis*. Thus the true order of discovery of the
Transcendental Analytic leads from the Principles of Pure Understanding (Book Two), to the Categories (Book One). In Cohen's
eyes, this does not make the logical forms of judgment irrelevant.
For the latter formulate the most universal patterns or models
of thought derived from the unity of consciousness, which for
Cohen is nothing other than the epistemic unity of all principles
of experience, where experience means scientific knowledge of
nature expounded in Newtonian science. So it is quite legitimate
to assert that the categories depend on these universal patterns.
But the systematic unity of the categories *and* of the logical forms
can be discovered only by paying attention to the unity of the *principles* of the possibility of experience, that is, of the Newtonian
science of nature.[25]

Cohen follows up on his interpretative program by showing how
Kant's systematic correlation between logical forms of judgment
and categories can be understood in the light of the distinction he
offers in the *Prolegomena* between judgments of perception and judgments of experience. Cohen then proceeds to explain and justify
Kant's selection of logical forms by relating each of them to the

corresponding category and to its role in the constitution of experience. In other words, he implements the very reversal in the order of exposition that he argues is faithful to Kant's true method of discovery: moving from the *a priori* principles that may ground judgments of experience, to the categories present in the formulation of these principles, to the logical forms of judgment.[26]

Cohen's achievement is impressive. But it is all too easy to object that his reducing Kant's unity of consciousness to the unity of the principles of scientific knowledge, as well as his reducing Kant's project to uncovering the *a priori* principles of Newtonian science, amount to a very biased reading of Kant's *Critique of Pure Reason*. In fairness to Cohen, his interpretation of Kant's critical philosophy did not stop there. In *Kants Begründung der Ethik*, he considered Kant's view of reason and its roles in morality. And this in turn led him to give greater consideration, in the second and third editions of *Kants Theorie der Erfahrung*, to Kant's theory of the ideas of pure reason and the bridge between knowledge and morality.[27] Nevertheless, as far as the metaphysical deduction of the categories is concerned, his interpretation remained essentially unchanged.

That interpretation found its most vigorous challenge in Heidegger's reading of Kant's first *Critique*. Heidegger urges that Kant did not *primarily* intend his *Critique of Pure Reason* to clarify the conceptual presuppositions of natural science. Rather, Kant's goal was to question the nature and possibility of metaphysics. According to Heidegger, this means laying out the ontological knowledge (knowledge of being as such) that is presupposed in all ontic knowledge (knowledge of particular entities). Kant's doctrine of the categories is precisely Kant's "refoundation" of metaphysics, or his effort to find for metaphysics the grounding that his predecessors had been unable to find. This refoundation consists, according to Heidegger, in elucidating the features of human existence in the context of which human beings' practical and cognitive access to being is made possible.

What does this have to do with Kant's enterprise in the Metaphysical Deduction of the categories? In the *Phenomenological Interpretation of the Critique of Pure Reason* (a lecture course delivered at Marburg in 1927–8, and first published in 1977) and in *Kant and the Problem of Metaphysics* (1st edition, 1929), Heidegger develops the following view. Kant's groundbreaking insight was to discover that the unity of our intuitions of space and of time, and the unity of concepts in judgments, have one and the same "common root": the synthesis of imagination in which human beings develop a unified view of themselves and of other entities as essentially temporal entities. Now, categories, according to Heidegger, are the fundamental structural features of the unifying synthesis of imagination, which results, on the one hand, in the unity of time (and space) in intuition, and, on the other hand, in the unity of discursive representations (concepts) in judgments. This being so, the fundamental nature of the categories is expounded *not* in the metaphysical deduction, which relates categories to logical forms of judgments, but rather in the transcendental deduction and even more in the chapter on the Schematism of the Pure Concepts of the Understanding. For it is in these two chapters that the role of the categories as structuring human imagination's synthesizing (unifying) of time is expounded and argued for. This does not mean that the metaphysical deduction is a useless or irrelevant chapter of the *Critique*. For if it is true that the unity of intuition and the unity of judgments have one and the same source in the synthesis of imagination according to the categories, then the logical forms of judgment *do* give a clue to a corresponding list of the categories. But this should not lead to the mistaken conclusion that the categories have their *origin* in logical forms of judgment. Rather, logical forms of judgment give us a clue to those underlying forms or structures of unity because they are the surface effect, as it were, of forms of unity that are also present in sensibility (where they are manifest as the schemata of the categories) by virtue of one and the same common root in imagination.[28]

Note that Heidegger agrees with Cohen at least in maintaining that logical forms of judgment can provide a leading thread to a table of categories just because forms of judgment and categories have one and the same ground, the unity of consciousness. Their difference consists in the fact that Cohen understands that unity as being the unity of thought expressed in the principles of natural science. Heidegger understands it as the unity of human existence projecting the structures of its own temporality.

3. The readings of Kant's metaphysical deduction we have considered so far offer challenges only to Kant's motivation and method

in adopting a table of logical forms of judgment as the leading thread to his table of categories. What they do not challenge is the relevance of Kant's Aristotelian model of logic in developing the argument for his table of the categories. A more radical challenge, of course, comes from the idea that contrary to Kant's claim, logic did not emerge in its completed and perfected form from Aristotle's mind.[29] Here we have to make a quick step back in time. For the initiator of modern logic, Gottlob Frege, wrote his *Begriffschrift* (1879) several decades before Heidegger wrote *Being and Time* (1927). By far the more threatening challenge to Kant's Metaphysical Deduction came from Frege's *Begriffschrift* and its aftermath.

As we saw, Kant takes logic to be a "science of the rules of the understanding." But Frege takes logic to be the science of objective relations of implication between thoughts, or what he calls "judgeable contents."[30] Against the naturalism that had become prevalent in nineteenth-century views of logic, Frege defends a radical distinction between the subjective conditions of the act of thinking and its objective content. Logic, according to him, is concerned with the latter, psychology with the former. In spite of his declared intention not to mix general pure (= formal) logic with psychology, Kant, according to Frege, is confused in maintaining that logic deals with the rules *we* (human beings) follow in thinking, rather than with the laws that connect thoughts independently of the way any particular thinker or group of thinkers actually think.[31]

According to Frege, Kant's subservience to the traditional, Aristotelian model of subject-predicate logic is grounded on that confusion. For the subject-predicate model really takes its cue from the grammatical structure of sentences in ordinary language. And ordinary language is itself governed by the subjective, psychological intentions and associations of the speaker addressing a listener. But again, what matters to logic are the structures of thought that are relevant to valid inference, nothing else. Those structures, for Frege, include the logical constants of propositional calculus (negation and the conditional), the analysis of propositions into function-argument rather than subject-predicate, and quantification.[32]

In §4 of the *Begriffschrift*, Frege examines "the meaning of distinctions made with respect to judgments." The distinctions in question are clearly those of the Kantian table, which have become classic in Frege's time. Frege first notes that those distinctions apply to the "judgeable content" rather than to judgment itself.[33] This being said, he retains as relevant to logic the distinction between "universal" and "particular" judgeable contents (Kant's first two titles of quantity), but leaves out "singular." He retains negation (Kant's second title of quality, negative judgment) and thus the contrasting affirmation (which does not need any specific notation), but leaves out infinite judgments. He declares that the distinction between categorical, hypothetical, and disjunctive judgments "seems to me to have only grammatical significance." Meanwhile, he introduces his own notation for conditionality in the next section, §5 of the *Begriffschrift* (more on this in a moment). Finally, he urges that the distinction between assertoric and apodeictic modalities (which alone, he says, characterize judgment rather than merely the judgeable content) depends only on whether the judgment can be derived from a universal judgment taken as a premise (which would make the judgment apodeictic), or not (which would leave it as a mere assertion, or assertoric judgment), so that this distinction "does not affect the conceptual content." Frege presumably means that the distinction between assertoric and apodeictic judgments does not call for a particular notation in the *Begriffschrift*. As for a proposition "presented as possible," Frege takes it to be either a proposition whose negation follows from no known universal law, or a proposition whose negation asserted universally is false. Although this last characterization differs from Kant's characterization of problematic judgments (as components in hypothetical or disjunctive judgments), it remains that Frege's view of modality is similar to Kant's own view, and indeed seems inspired by it. For as we saw, Kant thinks that modality does not concern the content of any individual judgment, but only its relation to the unity of thought in general. However, Kant does not think that what we might call this "holistic" view of modality makes it irrelevant to logic. This point would be worth pursuing, but we cannot do it here.

In short, according to Frege one need retain from the Kantian table only the first two titles of quantity, the first two titles of quality, and the second title of modality (assertion expressed by the judgment stroke). To these he adds his own operator of conditionality, which one might think has a superficial similarity to Kant's hypothetical judgment. However, Frege makes it clear they are actually quite different. He recognizes explicitly, for instance, that his conditional is not the hypothetical judgment of ordinary language, which he identifies with Kant's hypothetical judgment. And he states that the hypothetical judgment of ordinary language (or Kant's hypothetical judgment) expresses causality.[34] However, his view on this point does not seem to be completely fixed, at least in the *Begriffschrift*, since elsewhere in this text he urges that the causal connection is expressed by a universally quantified conditional.[35] In any event, Kant would not accept any of those statements. For as we saw, he would say that although the hypothetical judgment does express a relation of *Konsequenz* between antecedent and consequent, this relation is not by itself sufficient to define a causal connection. As for the universal quantification of a conditional, it would even less be sufficient to express a causal connection, precisely because the conditional bears no notion of *Konsequenz*. So even Frege's (very brief) discussion of hypothetical judgment and causality bears very little relation to Kant's treatment of the issue.

This might just leave us with Frege's general complaint against Kant's table: the reason this table can have only very little to do with Frege's forms of propositions is that it is governed by models of ordinary language. Consequently, Frege's selective approach to Kant's table does not merely consist in getting rid of some forms and retaining others. Rather, it is a drastic redefinition of the forms that are retained (such as the conditional, generality, and assertion as expressed by the judgment stroke). And this, Frege might urge, is necessary to purify logic definitively of the psychologistic undertone it still has in Kant. But then one needs to remember what the purpose of Kant's table is, as opposed to the purpose of Frege's choice of logical constants for his propositional calculus. Frege sets up his list so that he has the toolbox necessary and sufficient to expound patterns of logical inference, where the truth-value of conclusions is determined by the truth-value of premises, and the truth-value of premises is determined by the truth-value of their components (truth-functionality). Kant's logic, on the other hand, is a logic of the combination of concepts as "general and reflected representations."

And we might say that his setting up a table of elementary forms for that logic should help us understand how the very states of affairs by virtue of which Frege's propositions stand for True or False are perceived and recognized as such. In fact, I suggest that Frege's truth-functional propositional logic captures relations of co-occurrence or non-co-occurrence of states of affairs that Kant would have no reason to reject, but which for him would take secondary place with respect to the relations of subordination of concepts that, when related to synthesized intuitions, allow us to become aware of those states of affairs and their co-occurrence in the first place.

What about Frege's challenge to the subject-predicate model of judgment and his replacement of it by the function-argument model?[36] Here one might think that the modern logic of relations (n-place functions) is anticipated by Kant's *transcendental* logic, which thus overcomes the limitations of his "general pure" or "formal" logic. For transcendental logic is concerned *not* with mere concept-subordinations, but with the spatiotemporal mathematical and dynamical relations by means of which objects of knowledge are constituted and individuated. Indeed, the most prolific of Hermann Cohen's neo-Kantian successors, Ernst Cassirer, advocated appealing to a logic of *relations* to capture the Kantian "logic of objective knowledge," or transcendental logic.[37] Examining this suggestion would take us beyond the scope of the present essay. In any case, two points should be kept in mind. The first is that according to Kant, the relational features of appearances laid out by transcendental logic are made possible by synthesizing intuitions under the guidance of logical functions of judgment as he understands them. In other words, the source of the relations in question is itself none other than the very elementary discursive functions (functions of concept-subordination) laid out in his table and the guiding syntheses of *a priori* spatiotemporal manifolds. The second point to keep in mind is that however fruitful a formalization of Kant's principles of *transcendental* logic in terms of a modern quantificational logic of relations might be, it does not by itself accomplish the task Kant wants to accomplish with his transcendental logic and his account of the nature of categories, which is to explain how our knowledge of objects is possible in general, and thus explain why any attempt at *a priori* metaphysics on purely conceptual grounds is doomed to fail.

NOTES

1. The principle that determines the completeness and systematic unity
    of the table of categories is the fact that the latter have their origin in the
    understanding as a "capacity to judge." This point will be expounded
    and analyzed in part III of this essay.

2. Note that Kant's hypothetical judgment thus differs from our mate-
    rial conditional: for the *modus ponens* Kant mentions here has to be
    grounded on a connection, which Kant, like his contemporaries, calls
    consequentia (in Latin) or *Konsequenz* (in German) between antecedent
    and consequent (on this point see also Part Five of this essay). Kant's
    question is: in cases where the consequent in the hypothetical judgment
    is not conceptually contained in the antecedent, and so the relation
    between antecedent and consequent is synthetic, *what is the nature of
    the connection?* To my knowledge, this 1760s *Reflection* on the nature of
    the causal connection understood as a synthetic *ratio ponens* is Kant's
    first mention of the distinction between analytic and synthetic judg-
    ments that will become so prominent in the critical period. It is inter-
    esting that it should occur in the context of what will become, in Kant's
    terms, "Hume's problem," and thus in considering a kind of judgment
    that is not of the form "S is P," but "If S is P, then Q is R" (a hypothetical
    judgment). Contrary to a widely held view and *pace* the characteriza-
    tion given in the Introduction to the *Critique of Pure Reason* (A 6–10/
    B 10–14), Kant does not restrict the distinction between analytic and
    synthetic judgments to *categorical* judgments.

3. In the *Dissertation*, the distinguishing feature of intuition, in contrast
    with concepts, is their singularity: see *Dissertation*, 2:399, 402. How-
    ever, the contrast between intuitions and concepts is not firmly fixed:
    Kant also calls intuitions "singular concepts" (ibid., 2:397). In the *Cri-
    tique of Pure Reason*, Kant emphasizes not only the singularity, but also
    the *immediacy* of intuitions: see *Pure Reason*, A 19/B 33. For a discus-
    sion of these two features of intuition in the critical period, see Charles
    Parsons, "The Transcendental Aesthetic," in *The Cambridge Compan-
    ion to Kant*, Paul Guyer, ed. (Cambridge: Cambridge University Press,
    1992), p. 64. On the two kinds of synthesis in the inaugural dissertation,
    see 2:387–8.

4. A 66/B 92. Here as elsewhere I am following the translation by
    Paul Guyer and Allen Wood in the *Cambridge Edition of the Works
    of Immanuel Kant* (Cambridge: Cambridge University Press, 1992–).
    "Clue" is their choice for translating Kant's "Leitfaden." It is certainly
    correct, but I prefer "leading thread," which captures better what Kant
    is doing: following the lead of logical forms of judgment to establish his
    table of the categories. In citations I will follow Guyer and Wood, but in

the main text I will adopt "leading thread." The reader should be aware that both words translate the German "Leitfaden."

5. On this point, see Gilbert Harman, "Internal Critique: A Logic is not a Theory of Reasoning and a Theory of Reasoning is not a Logic," in D. M. Gabbay, R. H. Johnson, H. J. Ohlbach, and J. Woods, eds., *Handbook of the Logic of Argument and Inference: The Turn Towards the Practical*. Volume 1 in *Studies in Logic and Practical Reasoning* (Amsterdam: Elsevier Science B.V., 2002), pp. 171–86. On the contrast between Kantian and Fregean logic with respect to this point (does logic have anything to do with the way we think or even ought to think?), see John McFarlane, "Frege, Kant, and the Logic in Logicism," *Philosophical Review* 111 (2002), pp. 32–3.

6. Antoine Arnauld and Pierre Nicole, *La Logique ou l'art de penser*, P. Clair and F. Girbal, eds. (Paris: Vrin, 1981). English translation by Jill Vance Buroker, *Logic or the Art of Thinking* (Cambridge: Cambridge University Press, 1996). The full title contains, after the subtitle ("or the Art of Thinking"), the further precision: "containing, in addition to the common rules, several new observations proper to form judgment" (*propre à former le jugement*).

7. Kant was quite aware, for instance, that mathematical proof has rules of its own: see *Pure Reason*, A 716–18/B 744–6. Similarly, the mathematical science of nature has to combine the constructive methods of mathematics, the inductive methods of empirical inquiry, and the deductive methods of syllogistic inference.

8. Michael Wolff notes that Kant is not the first to make use of the expression "formal logic." He cites Joachim Jungius's *Logica Hamburgensis* (Hamburg, 1638) as an earlier source for this expression. See Michael Wolff, *Die Vollständigkeit der Kantischen Urteilstafel: Mit einem Essay über Freges Begriffschrift* (Frankfurt: Vittorio Klostermann, 1995), p. 203 fn. He is clearly correct on this point. Nevertheless, Kant's emphasis on the idea that "general pure logic" is *merely* formal, as opposed to the various "logics of the special use of the understanding" (including transcendental logic), which are specified by the particular *content* of thought they take into consideration, seems to be proper to him and certainly does not play anywhere else the ground-breaking role it plays in Kant's critical philosophy. On this point, see again John McFarlane, "Frege, Kant, and the Logic in Logicism," pp. 44–57.

9. For a historical survey of the term "function," its twofold meaning (biological and mathematical) for Leibniz, for Kant's immediate predecessors, and finally for Kant himself, see Peter Schulthess, *Relation und Funktion: Eine systematische und entwicklungsgeschichtliche Untersuchung zur theoretischen Philosophie Kants* (Berlin: Walter de Gruyter, 1981), pp. 217–47.

10. Michael Wolff maintains that according to Kant, the *functions* are not temporal, but the *actions* (*Handlungen*) are (see Wolff, *Die Vollständigkeit*, p. 22). I do not think that is correct. To say that the actions by which representations are unified are temporal would be to say that they are events in time. But surely this is not what Kant means. When he talks of actions of the understanding, what he means to point out is that the unity of representations is not *given* with them but depends on the thinking subject's *spontaneity*. What particular events and states of affairs in time might be the empirical manifestations of that spontaneity are not questions he is concerned with. I would add that the actions in question are no more noumenal than they are phenomenal: the concept "action" here does not describe a property or relation of things, but only the status we can grant to the unity of our representations: the latter is not "given" but "made," or it is a contribution of the representing subject to the structuring of the contents of his/her representations.

11. Both Michael Wolff and Reinhart Brandt have drawn attention to the fact that for Kant, there is no thought without language (see Wolff, *Die Vollständigkeit*, pp. 23–4; Reinhart Brandt, *Die Urteilstafel: Kritik der reinen Vernunft A67–76; B92–101*. Kant-Forschungen Band 4 [Hamburg: Felix Meiner Verlag, 1991], pp. 42, 110). In the *Jäsche Logic*, Kant opposes the distinction that is usual in logic textbooks of his time, namely, between judgments and propositions, according to which judgments are mere thoughts, whereas propositions are thoughts expressed in language. Such a distinction is wrong, he says, for without words "one simply could not judge at all" (9:109). Instead, he distinguishes judgment and proposition as problematic versus assertoric judgment (9:109). But in fact, with a few exceptions Kant uses the term "judgment" to refer to all three kinds of modally qualified judgments (problematic, assertoric, apodeictic). Note also that in his usage "judgment" refers, on the one hand, to the *act of judging*, and on the other hand, to the *content* of the act (what we would call the proposition). This is consistent with the fact that the *function* of judging finds expression in a *form* of judgment (inseparably belonging to thought and language).

12. Above I have translated *Vermögen zu urteilen* as *capacity to judge*. Guyer and Wood have translated it as *faculty of judging*. Although their translation is certainly justified if one considers that the Latin counterpart to *Vermögen* is *facultas*, I still prefer "capacity to judge" both because it avoids the connotation of faculty psychology carried by "faculty of judging" and because it better emphasizes the idea of a mere *potentiality* that gets *realized* when we actually judge or form inferences. On this point, see my *Kant and the Capacity to Judge*

(Princeton: Princeton University Press, 1998), pp. 7–8. On judgments and inferences, see ibid., pp. 90–3.

13. Early modern logicians typically distinguish between *simple* and *composite* propositions, and their list of composite propositions includes many more besides Kant's hypothetical and disjunctive judgments. More important, the distinction between simple and composite propositions puts Kant's categorical judgment on one side of the divide, and Kant's hypothetical and disjunctive judgments on the other side. Only Kant includes categorical, hypothetical, and disjunctive judgments under one and the same title, that of relation. For more details about early modern lists of propositions, see *Kant and the Capacity to Judge*, p. 98, fn. 44. Note that Kant uses the term "judgment" to refer mostly to the content of the act of judging (an act which is also called "judgment"), but he sometimes insists that when the judgment is assertoric, it should be called a proposition. See *Logic*, §§30–3, 9:109.

14. See Michael Wolff, *Die Vollständigkeit*, p. 232.

15. Ibid., pp. 45–195, esp. p. 181.

16. The *Logik Blomberg* (1771) and the *Logik Philippi* (1772) give a presentation of judgments that remains closer to Meier's text-book, which Kant used for his lectures on logic, than to the systematic presentation of the first *Critique*. See 24:273–9 and 461–5; *Logic Blomberg*, in *Lectures on Logic*, 220–5. For an occurrence of the two tables in the lectures on metaphysics of the late 1770's, see *Metaphysik L1*, 28:187. But see also *Reflexion* 3063 (1776–78), in *Reflexionen zur Logik*, 16:636–38. For a more complete account of the origins of Kant's table, see Tonelli, "Die Voraussetzungen zur Kantischen Urteilstafel in der Logik des 18. Jahrhunderts," in Friedrich Kaulbach, and Joachim Ritter, eds., *Kritik und Metaphysik: Heinz Heimsoeth zum achtzigsten Geburtstag* (Berlin: Walter de Gruyter, 1966). Also Schulthess, *Relation und Funktion*, pp. 11–12, and Longuenesse, *Kant and the Capacity to Judges*, p. 77 fn. 8, p. 98 fn. 44.

17. See Aristotle, *De Interpretatione*, 16a11; Antoine Arnauld and Pierre Nicole, *Logique*, Volume II, Chapter 3. As we saw in the previous section, Kant nevertheless gives new meaning to the idea of judgment as a combination of concepts since in his view the activity of judging determines the formation of concepts. Thus, the unity of judgment is, strictly speaking, prior to what it unites, namely, concepts. Note also that in the main text I write that "synthesis" means *positing together* as well as combination. In saying this I would like to emphasize the fact that as with all of Kant's terms pertaining to representation, one should give "synthesis" the sense of the *act* of synthesizing as much as that of the *result* of the act. Similarly, "combination" means *combining*

as much as the result thereof. Depending on the context, it is sometimes helpful to use the term expressly connoting the *action* of the
mind rather than the term connoting the result or intentional correlate of the action. In any event, both dimensions are always present for
Kant.

18. See letter to Herz, 10:125; Cf. *Correspondence*, 10:131.

19. In the chapter on the Schematism of the Pure Concepts of the Understanding, Kant maintains that the schema of the concept of cause is "the
real upon which, when it is posited, something else always follows" (A
144/B 183). This means that it is by apprehending the regular repetition of a sequence of events or states of affairs ("the real upon which,
whenever posited, something else follows") that we recognize in experience the presence of a causal connection. But conversely, we *look for*
such constant conjunctions because we *do* have a concept of cause as
the concept of something that might be thought under the antecedent
of a hypothetical judgment, with respect to something else that might
be thought under the consequent. Of course, Kant's point is also that
we can always be mistaken about what we so identify. Some repeated
sequence is warranted as a true causal connection only if it can be
thought under a causal *law*, and this involves the application of mathematical constructions that allow us to anticipate the continuous succession and correlation of events in space and in time. However, here I am
anticipating developments of Kant's argument that go way beyond the
metaphysical deduction properly speaking. See my "Kant on Causality:
What was he trying to prove?," in Christia Mercer and Eileen O'Neill,
eds., *Early Modern Philosophy: Mind, Mattler, and Metaphysics*
(Oxford University Press, 2005).

20. G. W. F. Hegel, *Wissenschaft der Logik*, II: *Die subjective Logik*, in
Gesammelte Werke (Hamburg: Felix Meiner, 1981), XII, pp. 253-4; *Science of Logic*, English translation by A. V. Miller (Atlantic Highlands,
N.J.: Humanities Press International, 1989), p. 613. What Hegel means
here by "subjective logic" is what Kant called "pure general logic,"
namely, the logic of concepts, judgments, and syllogistic inferences. But
unlike Kant's "pure general logic," Hegel's subjective logic is definitely
not "merely formal." More on this shortly.

21. See *Die subjective Logik*, pp. 59-90; Engl. transl., pp. 623-63.

22. On this point see my "Hegel, Lecteur de Kant sur le jugement," in
Philosophie 36, October 1992, pp. 62-7.

23. On this point, see Hans D. Sluga, *Gottlob Frege* (London: Routledge and
Kegan Paul, 1980), pp. 8-35.

24. Hermann Cohen, *Kants Theorie der Erfahrung* (Berlin: Bruno Cassirer,
1st ed. 1871, 2nd ed. 1885, 3rd ed. 1918, 4th ed. 1925). The citation is
from the Preface to the first edition (included in the fourth edition), p. ix.

25. Ibid., p. 229.
26. See ibid., pp. 245–8.
27. See ibid., Preface to the second edition, p. xiv.
28. See Martin Heidegger, *Phänomenologische Interpretation der Kritik der reinen Vernunft*, Gesamtausgabe Band 25 (Frankfurt am Main: Vittorio Klostermann, 1977), pp. 257–303, English translation by Parvis Emad and Kenneth Maly, *Phenomenological Interpretation of the Critique of Pure Reason* (Bloomington: Indiana University Press, 1995), pp. 175–207; and *Kant und das Problem der Metaphysik*, Gesamtausgabe Band 3 (Frankfurt am Main: Vittorio Klostermann, 1991), pp. 51–69, English translation by Richard Taft, *Kant and the Problem of Metaphysics* (Bloomington: Indiana University Press, 1990), pp. 34–46.
29. See *Pure Reason*, B viii.
30. Gottlob Frege, *Begriffschrift, eine der arithmetischen nachgebildete Formelsprache des reinen Denkens*, in *Begriffschrift und andere Aufsätze* (Hildesheim: Olms, 1964), English translation by Stefan Bauner-Mengelberg, *Begriffschrift, a formula language for pure thought, modeled upon that of arithmetic*, in *Frege and Gödel. Two Fundamental Texts in mathematical logic*, Jean van Heijenhoort, ed. (Cambridge, MA: Harvard University Press, 1970). On the distinction between judgment and judgeable content, see §2, p. 2; English translation, p. 11: "A judgment will always be expressed by means of the sign ⊢, which stands to the left of the sign, or the combination of signs, indicating the content of the judgment. If we *omit* the small vertical stroke at the left end of the horizontal one, the judgment will be transformed into a *mere combination of ideas* [*Vorstellungsverbindung*], of which the writer does not state whether he acknowledges it to be true or not." Frege later renounces the expression "Vorstellungsverbindung" as too psychological, and talks instead of "Gedanke" to describe the judgeable content to the right of the judgment stroke. See the 1910 footnote Frege appended to §2; English translation, p. 11 fn. 6.
31. On the rise of nineteenth-century naturalism about logic and Frege's conception of logic as reacting against naturalism, see Hans Sluga, *Frege* (London: Routledge and Kegan Paul, 1980), especially chapters 1 and 2. In fairness to Kant, it should be recalled that he does distinguish logic from psychology: he maintains that contrary to the latter, the former is concerned not with the way we think, but with the way we ought to think. But this distinction can have little weight for Frege, who wants to free logic from any mentalistic connotation, whether normative or descriptive.
32. Strawson's criticism of the redundancies of Kant's table is clearly inspired by Frege's. See P. F. Strawson, *The Bounds of Sense: An Essay on Kant's Critique of Pure Reason* (London: Methuen, 1966), pp. 78–82.

33. It is worth noting that Frege reverses the Kantian terminology and calls "proposition" the *judgeable* content and "judgment" the *asserted* content, whereas Kant reserved the term "proposition" to assertoric judgment: see fn. 11 above, and Frege's *Begriffschrift*, §2, §4. These are mere terminological differences, but they need to be kept in mind to avoid confusions.

34. *Begriffschrift* §5, p. 7; English translation, p. 15.

35. Ibid., §5, p. 6; English translation, p. 14; §12, p. 23; English translation, p. 27.

36. Ibid., §9. English translation, pp. 21–3.

37. See Cassirer, *Substanzbegriff und Funktionsbegriff: Untersuchungen über die Grundfragen der Erkenntniskritik* (Berlin: Bruno Cassirer, 1910), English translation, published as *Substance and Function*, translated by William and Marie Swabey (Chicago: Open Court, 1923). Peter Schulthess has defended the view that Cassirer's emphasis on the *relational* nature of Kant's transcendental logic, as well as his emphasis on the ontological primacy of relations, not substances, is in full agreement with Kant's own view, including his view of logic. See Peter Schulthess, *Relation und Funktion*. Michael Friedman has defended the relevance of Cassirer's version of neo-Kantianism for contemporary philosophy of science: see Michael Friedman, *A Parting of the Ways: Carnap, Cassirer and Heidegger* (Chicago and La Salle, IL: Open Court, 2000), especially Chapter 6, pp. 87–110; and "Transcendental Philosophy and A Priori Knowledge: a Neo-Kantian Perspective," in Paul Boghossian & Christopher Peacocke, eds., *New Essays on the A Priori* (Oxford: Clarendon, 2000), pp. 367–84.

5 Kant's philosophy of the cognitive mind

Kant's contributions to our understanding of the mind came largely in the course of pursuing other projects. The *Critique of Pure Reason* was intended to determine what we can know. In trying to answer that question Kant was led to consider what minds must be like to be capable of knowledge. His search for a sound basis for ethics included an investigation of the nature of a being who could be a morally responsible agent. He offered hypotheses about how observers appreciate beauty and sublimity in order to clarify the significance of the aesthetic appreciation of art and nature. By investigating what we could do or what he thought we could do, he developed theories about who or what we are.

The task of integrating the aspects of mind that Kant believed are required for knowledge, morality, and aesthetic sensibility in a consistent portrait of a subject has yet to be carried out. In this chapter, I focus exclusively on his depictions of the mind as a subject of knowledge in the *Critique of Pure Reason*. His theory of the active cognizer stands behind his most arresting philosophical doctrine, namely, the thesis that "we ourselves bring into the appearances that order and regularity in them that we call **nature**, and moreover we would not be able to find it there if we, or the nature of our mind, had not originally put it there" (*Pure Reason*, A 125).[1]

Kant presented the *Critique* as the culmination of the efforts of seventeenth- and eighteenth-century philosophers to determine the scope and limits of human knowledge. Whether or not one agrees with that immodest assessment, it is almost impossible to understand the reasoning behind his views, and sometimes the views themselves, without considering the predecessors whom he hoped to surpass. Since the topic of this chapter is not his theory of cognition *per se*, but his understanding of a mind or self capable of cognition, I will consider only the explicit or implicit theories of mind contained in his forerunners' theories of cognition.

I. DESCARTES' COGITO AND NATIVISM

Kant owned Latin versions of Descartes' *Meditations on First Philosophy* and his *Principles of Philosophy*,[2] and he explicitly criticized the reasoning of the *cogito* in both the Paralogisms chapter of the *Critique* and in his lectures on anthropology (25:14). In trying to determine whether any part of knowledge is secure, Descartes had famously argued that there were two propositions that could be known with absolute certainty, "I think" and "I exist." But he had also said a great deal more about thinking. Affirming, doubting, imagining, and sensing are species of thinking and as certain as thinking itself. Someone who perceives his two hands before him might doubt that they are real, but he could not doubt either that he is perceiving in a particular way – having a "two-hand" perception – or that he is doubting the veridicality of his perception. The various actions or conditions of the mind are transparent to it and so known with complete certainty.

Beyond the certainty of the mental, Descartes was widely known for reviving the thesis of nativism. He maintained that the empiricist *credo* that nothing is in the mind that was not first in the senses could not possibly be true for mathematical ideas or for the idea of God. Our senses do not present us with examples of infinities or, for that matter, with instances of mathematical figures of any sort (e.g., sets of points that are perfectly equidistant from one point). In his polemic against Eberhard (*On a Discovery*), Kant tried to distinguish his position from Descartes as clearly as possible: "The Critique admits absolutely no divinely implanted or innate **representations**" (8:221).

2. LOCKE ON "INTERNAL" SENSE AND SAMENESS OF PERSON

Descartes' reintroduction of the hypothesis of innate ideas inspired a lengthy rebuttal from John Locke in the *Essay Concerning Human Understanding*.[3] The *Essay* was widely known in Germany and

Locke had been officially approved by all Prussian faculties as a source to follow in metaphysics.[4] He took up the challenge of showing how seemingly difficult cases could be understood as ideas originating in sensory experience. A crucial move was his introduction of a second "fountain" of sensory experience. Beyond the universally acknowledged five senses, Locke posited an "internal sense":

> the other fountain . . . is, – the perception of the operations of our own mind within us, as it is employed about the ideas it has got; – which operations, when the soul comes to reflect on and consider, do furnish the understanding with another set of ideas, which could not be had from things without. And such are *perception, thinking, doubting, believing, reasoning, knowing, willing,* and all the different actings of our own minds. . . . This source . . . though it be not sense, as having nothing to do with external objects, yet it is very like it, and might properly enough be called *internal sense.*   (*Essay,* 2.1.4)

In a stroke, the hypothesis of an internal sense solved the problem of the origin of our ideas of thinking, imagining, judging, and the like. Although these might be invisible to other senses, each of us could acquire ideas about the mind from inner observation of our own mental activities.

Locke's view of how the "internal sense" or "reflection" worked was not completely clear. The preceding passage suggests a two-stage process: we perceive mental operations and then reflect on what we have perceived in order to form the idea of, for example, willing. But just after that passage, Locke gave an explicit account of his understanding of "reflection" that suggested that it happens in a single stage. Reflection is that notice that the mind takes of its own operations (*Essay,* 2.1.4).

Beyond providing ideas of mental activities, Locke thought the internal sense also provides knowledge of the fact of our own existence.

> It is evident to any one who will but observe what passes in his own mind, that there is a train of ideas which constantly succeed one another in his understanding. . . . For whilst we are thinking, or whilst we receive successively several ideas in our minds, we know that we do exist. (*Essay,* 2.14.3)

Did Locke's view that the internal sense gives us knowledge of the fact of our existence contradict or reaffirm the doctrine of the *cogito*?

Locke suggested that knowledge of our existence comes with the observing of our thoughts. So the question of his agreement or disagreement with the *cogito* turns on whether Descartes understood knowledge of existence to come with awareness of thinking or to be an inference from that awareness. Scholars disagree on how best to read the *Meditations*, but Descartes' own rehearsal of the argument in the *Principles of Philosophy* presented it in its classic inferential form: I am thinking, therefore I exist.[5] Kant understood it that way and, in his early lectures on anthropology (winter 1772–3), seemed to take Locke's side: "I am, that is an intuition and not a conclusion as Descartes believed" (25:14).[6]

In addition to introducing the important, if not entirely clear, notion of an "internal sense," Locke moved the issue of the self and its identity to the center of philosophical discussions of mind. Having rejected the Scholastic notion of "substance," he needed to provide some other basis for the fundamental legal and moral assumption that persons persist through time, so that the one who committed the crime was the same person as the one who receives the punishment.[7] Locke began his celebrated account of personal identity with an account of what "person" stands for:

a thinking intelligent being, that has reason and reflection, and can consider itself as itself, the same thinking thing, in different times and places; which it does only by that consciousness which is inseparable from thinking.

(*Essay*, 2.27.9)

Here again, it is not obvious how we are to take some of his key mental terms. He seemed to distinguish reasoning from reflecting, but is the latter the same as the consciousness that is inseparable from thinking? In maintaining that consciousness is inseparable from thinking, Locke offered a very strong claim: you could not sometimes perceive outer objects and other times perceive your own mind; rather, whenever you look at this page in this book, for example, you would be simultaneously aware of your own perceiving of the page. Because he took thinking always to involve consciousness of yourself thinking, Locke also believed that consciousness provides a criterion for personal identity: sameness of person extends as far as "consciousness can be extended backwards to any past action or thought" (*Essay*, 2.27.9). Since this backwards extension of consciousness seems very like remembering, Locke's theory of personal identity is usually understood as proposing a "memory" criterion: you are the same person as the one who did or thought things you remember doing or thinking.

3. LEIBNIZ ON PERSONS, NATIVISM, AND "APPERCEPTION"

In 1704, Gottfried Wilhelm Leibniz completed the *New Essays Concerning Human Understanding*,[8] an odd work that presented Locke's ideas, in roughly the order they appeared in the original *Essay*, interwoven with his own commentaries and criticisms. To begin where we left off with Locke, Leibniz offered what he took to be a friendly amendment to the memory criterion. He agreed with Locke's fundamental point that the moral identity of a person is preserved through consciousness of past and present thoughts and actions, but he suggested that although it is logically possible that consciousness could be extended in the absence of what he called "real identity,"

[he] should have thought that, according to the order of things, an identity which is apparent to the person concerned – one who senses himself to be the same – presupposes a real identity obtaining through each immediate temporal transition accompanied by reflection, or by the sense of *I*.

(*New Essays*, 236)

For Leibniz, the "real identity" of real substances requires neither continuity of atoms, nor continuity of organization. Rather, it depends on an "enduring principle of life" or "monad" containing the entire history of the substance in such a way that its stages unfold one after another (*New Essays*, 231). His view was not that if the continuity established by memory diverges from the real identity of a subject, the latter consideration is decisive; it was that in an orderly world the sorts of divergences Locke imagined between memory and substance would not arise.

The *New Essays* also offered a critique of Locke's rejection of innate ideas and principles. Leibniz argued that since the principles of logic and mathematics are *necessarily* true, they cannot be established by experience. He countered Locke's objection that principles such as "everything that is, is" cannot be innate (because they are unknown to children) with the hypothesis that our minds have many ideas and principles of which we are not conscious. To take his classic, if not entirely convincing, example: when we are aware of the roar of the ocean, we are not conscious of (cannot distinguish) the sound of the individual waves. Yet we must be aware of the sounds of the individual waves in some sense or we would not hear the combination of these sounds as a roar (*New Essays*, 54). He explained that children and the unschooled operate on logical principles without recognizing them as such. Ever the diplomat, Leibniz presented his rebuttal to Locke again in the form of an amendment: nothing is in the mind that was not first in the senses – except the mind (and its principles) itself (*New Essays*, 110–11).

The question of whether all thinking is conscious was frequently debated between the followers of Locke and Leibniz, but there is no question where Kant stood. He devoted a section of his anthropology lectures to "the ideas we have without being aware of them," and he compared conscious thoughts to a few illuminated points on a vast map of the mind (7:135). Having trumpeted the existence of unconscious or *"petites"* perceptions, Leibniz needed to distinguish those perceptions from conscious ones. The citation that follows is from the "Principles of Nature and Grace," a work that Kant referred to towards the end of the *Critique* (*Pure Reason*, A 813/B 841, A 815/B 843):

So it is well to make a distinction between perception, which is the inner state of the monad representing external things, and *apperception*, which is consciousness or reflective knowledge of this inner state itself and which is not given to all souls or to any soul all the time.[9]

Notice, however, that this account of the difference between perception and apperception suggests that there might be three different cases: an inner state that represents the sound of a single wave, an inner state that represents it in a way that enables you to be conscious of the sound of a single wave (in that you clearly distinguish it from other things) and reflection on your inner state itself. Or are there just two, unconscious perceptions and conscious perceptions, which are also always reflective?

Leibniz's failure to clarify the relation between conscious perception and reflective perception is evident in his treatment of animals. Animals have feelings. So if apperception were required for conscious perception, they would sometimes apperceive. Still, he maintained that human minds are importantly different. Since we have knowledge of necessary or eternal truths, such as those of logic, number, and geometry, we can rise to reflective acts, acts "which enable us to think of what is called *I* and to consider this or that to be in us...these reflective acts provide the principal objects of our reasonings" (*Monadology*, §30, see also "Principles of Nature and Grace", §5, and *New Essays*, 50–1).[10] For obvious reasons, scholars have been perplexed about exactly how Leibniz understood "apperception" and "reflection." Without trying to advance this difficult issue, I will just note that Leibniz appeared to agree with Locke that our cognitive access to the "I" is through reflection. On Locke's view, we know that we exist through observing the succession of our states. According to Leibniz, we come to think about the "I" through reflective acts involving necessary truths.

4. HUME'S BUNDLES AND THE "GENTLE FORCE" OF ASSOCIATION

Restricting ourselves to the views of Locke and Leibniz, Kant's empiricist and rationalist predecessors seem to be in substantial, if hardly complete, agreement about our knowledge of our own minds or selves: we have it and it comes from reflection. But this common wisdom was shattered by Locke's more consistent empiricist successor, David Hume. Hume applied Locke's project of tracing every idea to a sensory impression to the idea of the "self." And he drew an infamous conclusion:

What we call a *mind* is nothing but a heap or collection of different perceptions...which succeed each other with inconceivable rapidity, and are in a perpetual flux and movement....There is properly no simplicity in [the mind] at one time, nor identity in different [times], whatever natural propension we have to imagine that simplicity and identity....They are the successive perceptions only that constitute the mind.[11]

That is, Hume maintained that, in providing awareness of a succession of mental states, the internal sense does not inform us of the existence of any self or mind, but only of the states themselves.

Presumably Hume used the term "heap" to bring out the contrast between his view and that of his opponents. Where they saw a simple, unified immaterial substance going through a succession of different perceptions or thoughts, he saw only the collection of perceptions itself. Even for Hume, however, the collection is not as disorderly as "heap" might suggest. He believed that ideas and perceptions more generally are subject to the "gentle force" of association (*Treatise*, 10). When two sorts of perceptions, say perceptions of apples and perceptions of sweetness, have often co-occurred, then future perceptions of apples will call up ideas of sweetness.

For many years scholars believed that Kant was unaware of Hume's attack on the notion of a single mind or self. Dissatisfied with the account in the *Treatise of Human Nature*, Hume did not refer to it in the *Enquiry Concerning Human Understanding*, which Kant owned in a German translation.[12] The *Treatise* itself was not translated into German until 1791, and by all accounts Kant did not read English. It turns out, however, that Kant nevertheless had several means of access to Hume's "no self" theory. James Beattie cited long swaths of the *Treatise*'s account of the self (including the citations above),[13] and both J. C. Lossius and J. N. Tetens discussed Hume's view and various criticisms of it.[14] Remarkably, Kant may have learned about the option of a "no self" theory from a completely different source.[15] During the 1760s he read *Emile*, where Rousseau presented the Savoyard Vicar as engaging in a Cartesian exercise of doubting. His efforts led quickly to Humean skeptical doubt about our knowledge of a self distinct from its states:

Who am I? . . . I exist. . . . Do I have particular sentiments of my existence, or do I sense it only through my sensations? This is my first doubt, which it is for the present impossible for me to resolve; for as I am continually affected by sensation whether immediately or by memory, how can I know whether the sentiment of the *I* is something outside these same sensations and whether it can be independent of them?[16]

5. RATIONAL AND EMPIRICAL PSYCHOLOGY

In addition to the theories of mind and self (or no self) that followed from various seventeenth- and eighteenth-century epistemologies, Christian Wolff (1679–1754) and his followers tried to establish more or less independent disciplines devoted to the study of mind, "Empirical" and "Rational" Psychology. The data of Empirical Psychology were to be supplied by "attending to those occurrences in our souls of which we are conscious,"[17] bringing them under accurate definitions, and then determining the sufficient reason for their occurrence. Although Empirical Psychology was based on observation, it included demonstrations, and most important, a demonstration of the existence of the soul:

Whatever being is actually conscious of itself and other things exists. I am actually conscious of myself and other things. Therefore, I exist.[18]

In our post-Kantian epistemological framework, Wolff's inclusion of demonstrations in an empirical science seems jarring. But his understanding of Rational Psychology is even more alien. This discipline began from the data of Empirical Psychology and so was less reliable than that science; but it was also somewhat unreliable because it rested on ontology and cosmology. Starting from the fact of the soul's existence, Rational Psychology appealed to ontology to try to establish propositions about it that are true of being in general; it appealed to cosmology to try to understand the soul in relation to the theory of body. As Wolff presented Rational Psychology (somewhat defensively), it cleaved to the method that Bacon had unfavorably contrasted with the experimental method (*New Organon*, 1620):[19] "[this method] flies from the senses and particulars to the most general axioms, and from these principles, the truth of which it takes for settled and immovable, proceeds to judgment and to the discovery of middle axioms." At least by the time he wrote the *Critique*, Kant had firmly rejected this method; the Preface to the second edition lauds Bacon for putting science on the right path (*Pure Reason*, B xii).

6. KANT'S EARLY VIEWS ABOUT MIND AND SELF

In his earliest philosophical tract, *A New Elucidation of the First Principles of Metaphysical Cognition* (1755), Kant offered a criticism of Wolff and Leibniz that remained a staple of his metaphysical views about the succession of mental states. Leibniz had abstracted from his distinctive metaphysical position for the purpose of debating Locke in the *New Essays*, but Kant's audience was very familiar with the theory of the *Monadology*. In that work, Leibniz maintained that the basic constituents of reality are "monads," simple noninteracting substances whose existence could be understood in terms of the changing perceptions of a mind.[20] Kant's objection was straightforward: if a simple, causally isolated substance contained the determining ground or sufficient reason for its own changing perceptions, then at T_1 it would have to contain the determining ground for whatever perception it would have at T_2, for example, the perception of the roar of the ocean. If it contained the determining ground for this perception at T_1, however, then it must have that perception at T_1: "it is necessary that whatever is posited by a determining ground be posited simultaneously with that determining ground" (*New Elucidation*, 1:411). From this metaphysical argument, Kant concluded that changes in the soul establish the existence of objects outside the soul in which it stands in reciprocal connection and that it is necessary for souls to be connected with bodies (*New Elucidation*, 1:412).

Kant made other important claims about the mind in the service of offering a metaphysical account of two different worlds, those of sense and intellect, in the *Dissertation*. The concepts that apply to the real, intellectual or intelligible world "are given by the very nature of the understanding; they contain no form of sensitive cognition and they have been abstracted from no use of the senses" (*Dissertation*, 2:394). By contrast, our sensory representations present things as they appear. These representations include, first, sensation, which Kant believed could be understood as their matter, and also a "form," "the aspect of things which arises according as the various things which affect the senses are coordinated by a certain natural law of the mind" (*Dissertation*, 2:393). The formal aspects of the world of appearance or the "phenomenal" world are space and time. In Kant's view, every object represented by our senses appears in space and time because our minds have a lawful propensity to take the materials received from objects through sensation and to form from them representations of whole objects in a unitary space and time.

The *Dissertation*'s account of the intelligible world was philosophically unsatisfactory in two important ways. How do we know that fashionable metaphysical concepts such as "substance" and "perfection" reflect the basic laws of the understanding? Even if they do, why should principles that govern the way we think be considered as true of the real world of objects? These questions did not just bother Kant's critics; they provided the impetus for the intense philosophical investigations that culminated in the *Critique*. Despite its failings, the *Dissertation* offers a window into Kant's understanding of the intimate relation between cognition and the mind: some aspects of the world as we cognize it reflect the "stable and innate" laws of the mind (2:393).

7. KANT'S LECTURES ON METAPHYSICS AND ANTHROPOLOGY

The *Dissertation* was occasioned by Kant's appointment as a professor of logic and metaphysics, and although he did not publish any substantive philosophical work between 1770 and 1781, he gave many courses from which student lecture notes have been preserved.[21] In his metaphysics and anthropology courses during the mid-1770s, he appeared to accept many central arguments from Rational Psychology: the soul is a substance, it is simple, single, and spontaneous (*Lectures on Metaphysics*, 28:266):

> It is remarkable that we represent so much under the I, for by analysis we find that under the I we think the following parts... the simplicity of the soul,... the substantiality of the soul,... a rational substance, for because I think the I, I feel that I can make myself the topic of my thoughts,... the freedom of the soul.   (*Lectures on Anthropology*, 25:244–5)

In his (reported) discussions of Empirical Psychology in the metaphysics and anthropology courses, he maintained up through the mid-70s that we intuit the I (*Lectures on Anthropology*, 25:14, 474; *Lectures on Metaphysics*, 28:244). Kant's presentation of Rational Psychology and his claim for the intuitive status of the "I think" in these recently published lecture notes stand in stark contrast to his treatment of these issues in the *Critique*. There he repeats many times that we do not intuit a self (e.g., *Pure Reason*, A 107, B 134, B 157, A 382). And one chapter of the *Critique*, the Paralogisms of Pure Reason, is devoted to criticizing the discipline of Rational Psychology. These texts raise a fascinating philosophical and historical puzzle: how and when did Kant discover that the arguments of Rational Psychology were "paralogisms," that is, fallacies?

8. THE ELEMENTS OF COGNITION

Much of the central argumentation of the *Critique of Pure Reason* is dedicated to resolving the problem revealed by the *Dissertation*: why should the laws of human thinking find application in the natural world? The outlines of Kant's solution will be clearer if we consider the dispute between rationalists and empiricists about universal and necessary principles. Both groups and Kant agreed on an essential point: it is impossible to establish universal and necessary principles or laws on the basis of experience. Given that realization, consistent empiricists concluded that we have no cognition of necessary and universal laws. By contrast, rationalists argued that universal and necessary laws are essential to cognition, but that they need not be acquired through experience.

Many arguments of the first half of the *Critique* are intended to reveal the inadequacy of the empiricist theory of cognition. As Kant understood that view, cognitions arise in us through the actions of objects causing representations in our minds via our outer senses or our internal sense (which he called "inner sense"). The representations received are connected via the law of association. Thus, the connections among representations in our minds reflect the patterns of our sensory experiences: we would think early dusk together with ice and snow if we had frequently experienced ice and snow on the shortest days of the year (*Pure Reason*, A 100). For one type of cognition after another, Kant argued that mere association is insufficient to explain the ways in which representational elements are connected in empirical cognitions that all acknowledge we possess.

In the case of perception, Kant maintained that we could not achieve a perceptual image solely through receiving and associating sensory impressions (*Pure Reason*, A 121). Some of his metaphysics lectures provide a helpful illustration of the issue.

> When I see a city, my mind then forms itself an image of the object which it has before it while it runs through the manifold.
>
> (*Lectures on Metaphysics*, 28:235)

Suppose I take in part of the Manhattan skyline, by looking first at the Empire State Building and then at the Chrysler Building. To form the whole image, I must reproduce, for example, the visual materials acquired from the interaction of my senses and (light rays from) the Empire State Building. Following then-standard psychology, Kant characterized the capacity to represent in perception objects that were not or were no longer present to the senses as the "imagination." He noted that although an imagination that reproduced previously acquired visual material is necessary to form such an image, it is not sufficient.

> If, however, representations reproduced one another without distinction, just as they fell together, there would in turn be no determinate connection, but merely unruly heaps of them, and no cognition at all would arise.
>
> (*Pure Reason*, A 121)

The problem is that I cannot form an image of this part of the sky-line merely by reproducing the different pieces in the order I took them in. Rather, the imagination must create an order among the representational elements that represents the *simultaneous* spatial positions of the landmarks.

Despite his legendary obscurity, Kant could not have been clearer on the new role for imagination in his epistemology:

> No psychologist has yet thought that the imagination is a necessary ingredient of perception itself. This is so partly because this faculty has been limited to reproduction, and partly because it has been believed that the senses do not merely afford us impressions but also put them together, and produce images of objects, for which without doubt something more than the receptivity of impressions is required, namely a function of the synthesis of them.   (*Pure Reason*, A 122n.)

In the first edition, Kant provided an explicit account of the crucial activity of synthesizing:

> By **synthesis** in the most general sense, however, I understand the act of putting different representations together with each other and comprehending their manifoldness in one cognition.... The synthesis of a manifold...is what first brings forth a cognition...[it] is that which properly collects the elements for cognition and unifies them into a certain content.
>
> (*Pure Reason*, A 77/B 103)

That is, synthesis is an activity of the mind whereby elements contained in diverse representations are brought together and represented as unified (in various ways) in a further representation. We have seen why he thought that a synthesis is involved in perception. To produce an image, various perceptual elements that were taken in sequentially must be put together in some way other than by repeating the sequence given in sense. The citation makes the sweeping claim that a synthesis of diverse elements is what first gives rise to (any) cognition. If we make a rough division of the cognitive into perception and conception, as he did, then the other case would be cognition through concepts.

It is not obvious that a synthesis is needed to recognize an object as falling under a concept. Why can't we do this simply by association? If a number of features occurred together in our experience, these would become associated in a single representation and we could then compare the items in that representation with the properties of the object before us. To get a sense of why Kant believed that this is insufficient and so that another synthesis is necessary for conception, it may be useful to consider an example and a variation on it. Macbeth thought that he saw a dagger floating in the air, but when he tried to grasp it, he felt nothing. Suppose instead that he thought he saw a smoke ring and that it too seemed nothing to his grasp. In the latter instance, he could perfectly well conclude that his original judgment that there is a smoke ring before him was correct; in the former, he came to doubt his judgment (and his sanity).

Kant's explanation for the difference between the two cases would be that the different concepts are associated with different *rules*. The rules associated with the concept "smoke ring" allowed smoke rings to produce no tactile sensations; but if something falls under the concept "dagger," then it must have a distinctive feel. To conceive of an object as a dagger involves connecting representational elements in a way that they were not and could not have been connected in the senses: various *possible* visual and tactile sensations *must be* connected with the object and so with each other.

We find, however, that our thought of the relation of all cognition to its object carries something of necessity with it ... since insofar as they are to relate to an object our cognitions must also necessarily agree with each other in relation to it, i.e. they must have that unity that constitutes the concept of an object.   (*Pure Reason*, A 104–5, cf. A 197/B 242)

At least when we stick to particular examples, Kant's claim seems eminently plausible. Insofar as representations are to be representations of a single object, then they *must* agree with each other. To switch examples, two representations could not represent the same object as being entirely red and entirely green at the same time.

When we consider the issue more generally, as Kant did, the picture is, however, considerably murkier. What, exactly, is "that unity that constitutes the concept of an object" (any object)? Although, as we have seen, Kant believed that different objects have different sorts of unity (or are associated with different rules), he also believed that all concepts of objects are governed by a common set of rules, rules associated with special concepts, the "categories." So, for example, he argued that any object that we perceive through inner or outer sense must have extensive magnitude; its spatial and/or temporal extent must be measurable (*Pure Reason*, A 161/B 202). He also maintained that everything that we encounter through perception must obey the principle that the quantity of basic substances must be conserved (A 182/B 224). Most famously, he argued that any change that we can perceive must be understood as occurring in accordance with the law of cause and effect (A 188/B 232).

It may seem a long way from these highly general principles to the claim that it is part of the concept of a "dagger" that certain tactile and visual representations must be connected in the overall perceptual representation of a dagger – as indeed it is. Although Kant offered almost no details about how this is supposed to work, his idea seems to have been that the rules associated with particular (noncategorial) concepts represent different specifications of the very general rules, specifications made in light of sensory experience. So daggers take up a certain amount of space (they are neither two inches nor two miles long); they are brought into being through, for example, the shaping of steel; they cause cuts, and so forth. Although smoke is an odd kind of object, it still obeys the principle of conservation, so we can determine the weight of some smoke by subtracting the weight of the ash from the initial weight of the wood (*Pure Reason*, A 185/B 228). Where empiricists understood the concept of a "dagger" as being built up by abstracting features from instances that had been encountered in experience, Kant believed that such a concept has to be associated with rules that are experiential specifications of highly general principles (A 126, A 128, B 164–5). Only in that way can concepts be associated with universal and necessary rules (since such rules cannot be based on experience).

As in the case of perceptual images, conceptual representations do not (merely) reflect the patterns in which the particular elements were taken in by the senses. They too have to be produced by synthesis, by the active (as opposed to merely receptive or passive) faculties of a cognizer creating relations among representational elements that were not given by their association in sensory experience. Kant labeled the faculty involved in the syntheses required by concept use the "understanding." Haphazard or arbitrary combinings of sensory elements would hardly produce representations of objects that conform to the very general rules associated with the categories. He seemed to think that the understanding synthesizes conceptual representations of objects that conform to categorial principles by making implicit use of those principles themselves in the synthesizing (*Pure Reason*, A 105).

Kant agreed with the rationalists that the empirical cognitions we enjoy presuppose universal and necessary metaphysical principles, such as the principle that all changes have causes, but he disagreed about the source of these principles. They are neither divinely implanted innate principles nor intellectual insights into the structure of reality. He agreed with the empiricists that our only avenues to outside sources of cognition are our senses. According to his "third way," the source of these principles is the understanding itself. He drew attention to his "third way" at the beginning of the Introduction to the *Critique*. Although all cognition begins with objects rousing our faculties into action,

It could well be that even our experiential cognition is a composite of that which we receive through impressions and that which our own cognitive faculty (merely prompted by sensible impressions) provides out of itself....
It is therefore at least a question requiring closer investigation ... whether there is any such cognition independent of all experience and even of all impressions of the senses [because it is supplied by the cognitive powers]. One calls such **cognitions *a priori*** and distinguishes them from **empirical** ones, which have their sources *a posteriori*, namely, in experience.

(*Pure Reason*, B 1–2)

That is, his empiricist predecessors erred in not recognizing that what they took to be merely empirical or sensory cognition is in fact a composite of *a posteriori* (from the senses) and *a priori* (from the actions of the mind) elements and thus is already infused with principles deriving from the understanding.

We can now return, at last, to the key question raised by the *Dissertation*. Why do the universal and necessary laws that govern the objects we cognize as part of the natural world agree with the laws governing our understanding? In briefest form, Kant's answer was that the only representations – and hence cognitions – that we can have of objects are representations produced by the synthesizing activities of the understanding according to its categorial principles. Hence all the objects of our cognition must agree with those principles. (We have not considered any of the complex and controversial arguments that he offered to support this claim, because the focus of the chapter is not his theory of cognition, but the theory of the cognitive mind that he extracted from it.)

9. THE PROPERTIES OF COGNITIVE SUBJECTS

Even this skeletal account of Kant's theory of cognition enables us to start filling in the corresponding pieces of his theory of the subject of cognition. Where the *Dissertation* had the lower faculty of sensation producing representations of a world of appearances and the higher faculty of understanding laying down the laws of the real intelligible world, the signature theme of the first *Critique* is that even empirical cognition is possible only through the cooperation of our faculties (*Pure Reason*, A 51/B 75–6), that is, through imagination and understanding organizing the materials supplied through sensibility.

Kant's view that our faculties contribute to the production of cognition extended even to the target of his critique, reason itself. Although he intended to demonstrate that reason has limits and that much metaphysical confusion can be traced to failures to heed those limits, he assumed that, as a natural faculty, reason must also have some positive purpose (*Pure Reason*, A 642–3/B 670–1). In the light of considerations we need not explore here, he believed that the distinctive contribution of reason is to unify all our cognitions in a systematic hierarchy of principles. On his model of cognition, then, sensory elements come in through sensibility (outer and inner sense) and are combined by the understanding into concepts and judgments; those concepts and judgments are in turn organized by reason into a unified system of cognition, in which (ideally) concepts and principles are arranged in hierarchies from the specific to the most general (*Pure Reason*, A 298–9/B 355). As with the relation between sensibility and understanding, he argued that reason's ability to fulfill its purpose of systematizing cognition implies that it must be coordinate with the understanding (*Pure Reason*, A 651/B 679).

If we were to stop at this point, with the faculties of sensibility, imagination, understanding, and reason, Kant's portrait of a cognitive subject would be reasonably clear. The obscurity that constantly threatens to engulf his entire theory of mind arises because he maintains that a further fundamental power or faculty is required for cognition, the power of "apperception." As we have seen, Leibniz introduced this term into the philosophical lexicon, but seemed to use it equivocally, to stand for (at least) conscious perception and reflection. Kant first employed the term in some unpublished argument sketches in the mid-1770s. Although there is some interpretive controversy on this point, his contextual definitions seem to align it with Lockean "internal sense." Apperception is the intuition of ourselves as opposed to objects (R 4675, 17:651); "apperception is the consciousness of thinking, that is of representations, in so far as these are set in the mind" (R 4674, 17:647). By the time he wrote the *Critique*, it was clear to him that the faculties of apperception and inner sense must be "carefully distinguished" since the latter is "receptive" (*Pure Reason*, A 19/B 33, B 157n.) or "passive" (B 153), whereas the faculty of "apperception" is active. It brings about "the unity of this synthesis [of the various sensory materials]" (A 94); it makes out of all appearances "a connection or coherence according to laws" (A 108).

In the more extensive discussion of cognitive faculties in the first edition of the *Critique*, the power of apperception entered the argument as Kant explored our ability to recognize objects under concepts. To return to our example, suppose that you judge, on the basis of observation, that there is a dagger before you. In so doing, you are relating your visual images and your tactile images in the way required by the concept – one object is being represented as simultaneously having a certain look and feel. Since these representations were not united in the senses as they are in the conceptual representation (as necessarily connected), Kant maintained that the unified representation in question is possible only through

that unity of consciousness that precedes all data of the intuitions, and in relation to which all representation of objects is alone possible. This pure, original, and immutable consciousness I will now name **transcendental apperception**.   (*Pure Reason*, A 107).

In the second edition as well, "transcendental apperception" was introduced as a solution to the problem of the unity of combination:

The concept of combination also carries with it the concept of the unity of the manifold... we must seek this unity... in that which itself contains the ground of... unity.   (*Pure Reason*, B 130-1)

The succeeding section concerns "the original synthetic unity of apperception."

From the beginning Kant's readers have been baffled by his doctrine of transcendental apperception. About the only clear point is that "*transcendental* apperception" was intended to contrast with "*empirical* apperception" (which is sometimes called "empirical consciousness") and that the latter referred to Lockean internal sense (e.g., *Pure Reason*, A 107). Although both "transcendental" and "apperception" are complex and contested technical terms, there is substantial agreement on one aspect of the former. It is widely believed that Kant's distinctive method of "transcendental" proof sought to establish the legitimacy or necessity of presuming various faculties, principles, and aspects of representations or concepts by arguing that those items are necessary for the "possibility of [cognitive] experience."[22] So, for example, he tried to show that it is legitimate to use the concept of "cause" by arguing that unless we conceive of changes in terms of laws of cause and effect, we cannot have cognitive experience of the changes at all. If we adopt this relatively well-accepted meaning of "transcendental," then "transcendental apperception" (henceforth "TA") would seem to indicate an apperception that is necessary for the possibility of cognitive experience or empirical cognition.

From the textual indications given above (from both editions), TA seems to be concerned with the unity required for synthesizing representations out of the materials of sense. As we have seen, however, Kant connects "unity" with two rather different sorts of things. When referring to the "unity that constitutes the concept of an object," he seems to mean the unity provided by a *rule* (section 8). When discussing the unification of the faculties of intuition and understanding required for the possibility of cognition, he seems to refer to the *coordination* of the faculties (section 9). But he also refers to apperception itself as a "faculty" or power (*Pure Reason*, A 94, A117n.)!

Despite the appearance of inconsistency and confusion, I think it is possible both to disentangle and to relate many of Kant's claims about apperception. The question of whether "apperception" names a faculty or refers only to the unification of faculties can be resolved somewhat by noting that he sometimes thought of apperception as a fundamental or root faculty (*Radicalvermögen*)[23] (*Pure Reason*, A 114). On that picture, "apperception" would refer to a faculty, but a faculty of a special sort. Other faculties would be different manifestations of that single faculty – which would explain why the various non-fundamental cognitive faculties work so well together. Still, he knew that he did not have adequate grounds for claiming that cognition requires one underlying capacity (A 682–3/B 710–11). All that he could argue was that cognition requires the *coordination* or *cooperation* of the faculties that receive sensory materials and combine them for cognition (see A 353). Under these circumstances it seems best to understand one strand of the doctrine of the transcendental unity of apperception as maintaining that cognition requires coordinated faculties.

Kant also believed that the unity of syntheses – the fact that they are not haphazard or arbitrary – is a function of the rules by which they are (implicitly) carried out. At first glance, the unity provided by a rule would seem very different from the unity provided by a fundamental faculty or a coordination of faculties. In fact, Kant linked cognitive powers and rules or principles explicitly in 1790 in the *Critique of the Power of Judgment*: "no use of the cognitive powers can be permitted without principles" (*Judgment*, 5:385). The first *Critique* made the related claim that "every effective [or efficient] cause must have a character, i.e., a law of its causality, without which it would not be a cause at all" (*Pure Reason*, A 539/B 567). I take Kant's point to be that insofar as a cognitive faculty is a power (an efficient cause), it must operate in a definite way that can be specified in a principle. Notice, however, that the bald claim that any cognitive faculty must operate by principles appears to be just the sort of unsupported metaphysical claim that Kant wrote the *Critique* to protest.

Kant could have forged connections across several of his claims about the "transcendental unity of apperception" had he been willing to make two metaphysical moves: a coordination of faculties could be explained by an underlying root faculty, *therefore* we have such a faculty, "apperception"; faculties may not operate without principles, *therefore* the root faculty of apperception operates according to a principle or rule. Since he did not feel such metaphysical arguments are legitimate, he argued instead that certain conditions are necessary for the possibility of empirical cognition. As we have seen, he argued that cognition requires the coordination of faculties. He offered separate considerations to show that *all* synthesizing of representations into cognitions must be subject to a principle.

Kant's insight may be easier to grasp via an example. Consider again the delusional Thane of Cawdor. For reasons we have seen, Kant maintained that insofar as they are to represent an object, the *contents* of representations must present a coherent portrait of an *object* (hence Macbeth's realization that he was seeing things when his visual dagger perceptions did not agree with his tactile perceptions). Kant also recognized, however, that representations *qua* representations or *vehicles* of content must present a coherent portrait of a *subject* of representations. After all, had Macbeth suddenly been replaced by some other cognitive subject or been instantly transported to a different location, the visual dagger perception at one time and the empty tactile perception at another would reveal nothing about the presence or absence of a dagger in his original location. For cognition to be possible, any representation that purports to provide cognition of *objects* must also be able to be represented as the state of a single *continuing subject* of cognition.

Even though Kant maintained that the syntheses of representations in various object are subject both to different rules and to several common rules about objects, he also came to believe that all cognitive syntheses are subject to an overarching rule or principle: it must be possible to understand all the representations involved in cognition as representations of a single subject of experience (or different sets of representations must be understood as belonging to different subjects of cognitive experience). Thus, "the synthetic proposition that all the varied *empirical consciousness* [consciousness of particular representations] must be combined in one single self-consciousness is the absolutely first and synthetic principle of all our thought as such" (*Pure Reason*, A 117n.). Although I have offered an example to illustrate why Kant's "absolutely first" principle might seem plausible, that hardly amounts to an argument for this sweeping and controversial claim. A full-scale evaluation of this cardinal principle of Kant's epistemology is beyond the scope of the present essay, but I will try to give a somewhat fuller picture of how he understood the principle and of the sort of argument he thought could be given for it.

Where did this principle come from? As with the principles that must be involved in cognition of objects through concepts, Kant maintained that the principle of transcendental apperception could not come from the senses.

In inner perception, consciousness of oneself in terms of the determinations of one's state...is merely empirical and always changing...it can give us no constant and abiding self in this flow of inner appearances. It is usually called **inner sense** or **empirical apperception**.   (*Pure Reason*, A 107)

In this passage, Kant appeared to agree with Hume that inner sense divulges no self, but he did not conclude that our belief in a continuing self rests on a confusion. In a famous later passage, he located the source of this principle in our own active or spontaneous faculties:

The **I think** must be **capable** of accompanying all my representations, for otherwise something would be represented in me that could not be thought at all.... This representation [i.e., the **I think**], is an act of **spontaneity**; i.e., it cannot be regarded as belonging to sensibility.   (*Pure Reason*, B 132)

(To say that "I think" must be able to accompany all my representations is just to say that all my representations must be able to be referred to a single I that thinks.) That is, as our active faculties are the source of connections among elements in a representation of an object, so too are they the source of the connection of representations, as such, to an I that has representations.

But has Kant simply begged the question against Hume? Even if our active faculties bring forth the representation of a self, how could that justify *using* that concept in the absence of any sensory impression of the self? In the passage where Kant agreed with Hume about the absence of such an impression, he went on to criticize the empiricist approach and to stake out his novel argumentative strategy:

That which is **necessarily** to be represented as numerically identical cannot be thought as such through empirical data. A condition that is to validate such a transcendental presupposition must be one that precedes all experience and that makes experience itself possible.
            (*Pure Reason*, A 107, amended translation, cf. B 134)

Although Hume was right that the senses furnish no evidence for a self or for the relation of representations to a self, that does not mean we could not have other grounds for holding that different representations must belong to a continuing self. In particular, it might be possible to establish that empirical cognition is possible only if that principle is presupposed. And that was exactly how Kant argued for the concept of a self. Different representations must all be understood as belonging to a single **I think**, because a "representation" that did not belong with others to a continuing self would be impossible as a representation (that is, as a representation of an object [*Pure Reason*, B 132, A 112]); such a state would be "a blind play of representations, i.e., less than a dream" (A 112). As we saw in the case of Macbeth, a "representation" that did not belong to an ongoing subject could yield no cognition about a dagger – or even about a hallucination.

At this point, we have two interpretations of "transcendental apperception." Kant used this phrase to indicate a necessary-for-cognition coordination of the faculties and to indicate a necessary-for-cognition principle that all cognitive states must belong to ongoing subjects of cognition. Other passages present the unity of apperception in a different guise: all my representations must be "brought under" the "original synthetic unity of apperception...by means of a synthesis" (*Pure Reason*, B 135–6); the "synthetic unity of the manifold of intuition...is the ground of the identity of apperception itself" (*Pure Reason*, B 134). Here the suggestion seems to be not that apperception is a mind-generated principle governing syntheses or a coordination or faculties, but something that is *achieved* through the activity of synthesizing representations. In this sense, "apperception" indicates the connection or connectability of different representations through acts of synthesis in the representation of a continuing subject. I take his point to be that even if cognizers possess coordinated faculties and an implicit principle governing their synthesizing (the principle that all representations must belong to on-going cognizers), they might still lack the unity of apperception if their representations cannot be connected as states of an ongoing subject. His view is that if our sensory experiences were so chaotic that we could not combine them into cognitions (perceptions or conceptions) of objects, then we could not combine our representations into a coherent history of a subject of cognition either. That is, although apperception is necessary for cognition, cognition of objects is also necessary for the unity of apperception!

We may seem to have a hopeless chicken and egg problem. For, it is not just that "apperception" in the sense of "coordination" or "principle" is necessary for cognition. "Apperception" in the sense of "connection" or "connectability" is also necessary for cognition. On Kant's theory, we cannot cognize objects unless we can represent the representations through which we know objects as states of an ongoing subject, but we cannot represent ourselves as ongoing subjects and our representations as parts of those cognitive lives without cognizing objects. Whether or not this view is correct, it is, I believe, coherent. Kant's position was that cognition of objects and cognition, or even consciousness, of ourselves have to go hand in hand. He had already made this point in his metaphysics lectures in the mid-1770s when considering the possibility of the existence of the soul before birth. Suppose one assumed that the soul always exists and so existed before being joined with a body.

It does not at all follow that it had in it such a full use of its powers and faculties...rather, it follows that [it]...already possessed all abilities and faculties; but such that these developed only through the body, and that it acquired all the cognition that it has of the world only through the body.... *The state of the soul before birth was thus without consciousness of the world and of itself.*   (*Lectures on Metaphysics*, 28:284)

It is interesting to note that if Kant's position is correct here, then the situation that Descartes envisioned at the end of the *Meditations*, where the protagonist knows nothing about the world around him, but only his own existence as a thinking self, would be impossible.

In another central text, Kant offered what appears to be a direct criticism both of Locke's view that we get our idea of the self from inner sense and also of his theory of personal identity. No names are mentioned, but this is what Kant wrote:

The empirical consciousness that accompanies different representations is intrinsically scattered and without relation to the identity of the subject. This relation [to an identical subject] does not yet come about through my accompanying each representation with consciousness, but through my **adding** one representation to another, and being conscious of the synthesis of them.   (*Pure Reason*, B 133, amended translation)

That is, the ability to extend consciousness to a variety of representations does not establish that they belong to an identical subject. Kant's positive proposal here, with its emphasis on *adding* or combining, suggests a somewhat different foundation for the doctrine of apperception and so a different interpretation of TA. Perhaps the most important implication of his theory of cognition for the cognitive subject is simply that cognition requires more than just passive reception; it also requires activity. The passage just considered (*Pure Reason*, B 132–3) is not unique in tying apperception to activities and, indeed, to a consciousness of mental acts or activities. In another crucial but equally enigmatic passage (*Pure Reason*, B 158), he proclaimed that "I exist as an intelligence that is conscious solely of its power of combination" (amended translation, see also *Pure Reason*, A 103, A 108, B 134, B 135).

In the Second Analogy, Kant laid out a line of reasoning that would lead from activity to something like a cognitive subject: "[the concept of] action leads to the concept of force and thereby to the concept of substance" (*Pure Reason*, A 204/B 249). That is, where there is activity, there must be some substance that carries out the activity. As with the hypothesis of TA as a root faculty, however, he explicitly retreated from the speculation that the thinking I is a substance – one of the basic sorts of thing in the universe – so this fourth gloss on TA should offer a more muted thesis: "transcendental apperception" refers to the creative powers that must be involved in cognition whether or not those powers resided in basic substances.

To recap, Kant seems to use "transcendental apperception"[24] to indicate four rather different sorts of things:

1. a *unity* or *coordination* of the various cognitive faculties that is necessary for cognition;
2. the *principle* that diverse mental states must be able to be represented as combined in one single I that thinks, which is necessary for cognition;
3. the *connections* among mental states produced by the synthesizing activities of the faculties that are necessary for cognition of objects and ourselves;
4. the *creative powers* that must be involved in cognition whether or not those powers reside in basic substances.

Although these glosses differ about what sort of thing transcendental apperception is supposed to be – a unity of faculties, a principle about a relation among cognitive states, a relation of connection among mental states, or a creative faculty or faculties – they emerge from a univocal cognitive theory. And each doctrine presents a presupposition or a consequence of the central claim of Kant's theory that empirical cognition requires creative syntheses. Interpretations 1 and 4 can be read as emphasizing different aspects of the necessary syntheses. They are *both* coordinated and creative. Interpretations 2 and 3 highlight, respectively, the most general principle to which the results of the syntheses have to conform and the relations that result from the necessary syntheses. Weaving these strands together in one complex statement of his analysis, we get something like this: empirical cognition is possible only because we have a capacity for combining the contents of cognitive states in (later) cognitive states according to an overarching principle that all the states can themselves be represented as states of a single on-going cognitive subject.

Kant often used "apperception" as interchangeable with "self-consciousness" (e.g., *Pure Reason*, B 139). For all its length, the preceding discussion may appear to have overlooked his central clue about what he meant. Unfortunately, the clue is misleading. If we understand "self-consciousness" in one of its normal senses – as a "consciousness" or "awareness" of a "self" – then it cannot be equated with Kantian "apperception." As we have seen, Kant came to distinguish "apperception" from the faculty by which we are aware of inner happenings, "inner sense." (Further, he explicitly denied that we are aware of a self through inner sense.) Rather than trying to get a grip on the doctrine of "apperception" through appealing to our pre-theoretical grasp on "self-consciousness," it is probably better to use the former to try to figure out his novel understanding of "self-consciousness." Given interpretations 1 through 4 above, apperceptive self-consciousness might be understood as a consciousness of the activity of synthesizing, as a number of texts suggest, or it might be understood as the recognition that various cognitive states must be understood as states of a single cognizer.[25] Here again, although the glosses on apperceptive self-consciousness are quite different, the doctrines are compatible. We could be self-conscious both in being (implicitly) aware of our synthesizing activities and in recognizing the necessity of our different states as belonging to a single enduring cognitive subject. Perhaps Kant wished to link his views about apperception explicitly to the notion of "self-consciousness" because it followed from his theory that previous notions of self-consciousness were badly mistaken. We are not at all conscious of a self in the way that Locke suggested; but we still know that there is a continuing self and there are several senses in which we could truly be said to be "self-conscious."

Although Kant rejected the Humean claim that the "I think" represents a fiction and the Lockean claim that our knowledge of our existence derives from inner sense, he did not understand the mind as a Leibnizean monad either. As we saw in section 6, he did not believe that the succession of mental states could be understood as the unfolding of a monad's "principle of life"; causal interaction with other substances is required for a simple substance to alter. We have also seen that, despite his temptation to view the necessary cooperation of cognitive faculties as indicating that they are diverse manifestations of an underlying fundamental faculty of representation (as the Wolffians thought), he resisted this speculation as well as the one that the mind is a basic substance. His rejection of arguments purporting to show that the mind is a substance was part of his systematic critique of metaphysical speculations about the mind or soul in the Paralogisms of Pure Reason. In his view, Rational Psychologists had erred because they had failed to see the limitations of their cognitive theories. He argued, for example, that although it is true that cognition requires the "absolute unity of the subject" (*Pure Reason*, A 353), it does not follow that thought can inhere only in a simple substance: "since the thought consists in many representations, its unity is collective and can . . . refer just as well to the collective unity of the substances cooperating on the thought" (*Pure Reason*, A 353). He criticized another "paralogism" on the grounds that it purports to infer from the fact that the "*I* is in all thoughts" to the conclusion that the soul is a permanent substance (*Pure Reason*, A 350). The problem is that from the fact that diverse mental states must refer to a single I, nothing follows about the composition of the I, about how it must be constituted (*Pure Reason*, A 350, A 398). More generally, Kant believed that it is impossible to infer from the highly general characteristics that could be attributed to the I to account for the possibility of cognition to *any* claims about the constitution of the I. As we cannot answer the question "what must a thing be to be movable?," we cannot answer the question of what something must be to be a thing that thinks (*Pure Reason*, A 398). Although he had taught some of the principles of Rational Psychology in both his metaphysics and anthropology courses, his critique of this discipline marked its end. Serious scholars no longer believed that it was possible to establish theologically interesting conclusions by starting with premises about the requirements of cognition.

10. THEORY OF COGNITION OR COGNITIVE THEORY?

Kant's theory of cognition clearly had implications about the cognitive mind, but a number of critics have thought that that was exactly what was wrong with it. These implications flowed from it, they maintain, because the theory was more speculative psychology than philosophy. At one level, this long-standing criticism is irrefutable. Psychological faculties appear on virtually every page of the positive, first half of the book. In this regard, the *Critique of Pure Reason* fits into the epistemological genre of its time. Locke's and Leibniz's essays were about human *understanding*, Hume's treatise was about human *nature*, and so forth. Kant may inspire more criticism on this point than his contemporaries because he frequently protested that he was not engaged in a psychological pursuit, but in a logical one. What he meant by "psychology" and by "logic," however, is not what we mean by these terms. The "psychology" he disavowed was the Empirical Psychology of introspection and the Rational Psychology of speculation; the "logic" he embraced was the "self-cognition of the understanding and of reason" (*Logic*, 9:14). For him, as for his contemporaries, questions about cognition were inextricably intertwined with hypotheses about cognitive powers.

The issue of whether a theory of cognition can be divorced from cognitive theories goes beyond the bounds of this essay. I will just note, however, that several important contemporary trends in epistemology, including "reliabilism" and "social epistemology," depend openly on assumptions about cognitive capacities. Even if Kant's appeal to cognitive faculties was unavoidable, however, serious questions remain about the particular claims he made. In the space remaining, I will lay out two important sets of issues that have emerged from his treatment of the cognitive mind: the unity of the faculties (and cognition), and the nature of self-consciousness and self-knowledge.

Both topics were highlighted in the immediate reactions to Kant and both have been widely discussed in contemporary philosophy and psychology. Kant took himself to have made a fundamental advance in clearly distinguishing the faculties that receive sensory information from those that combine it in conceptual representations.

> Only from their [sensibility and understanding] union can cognition arise. This fact, however, must not lead us to confuse their respective contributions; it provides us, rather, with a strong reason for carefully separating and distinguishing sensibility and understanding from each other. Hence we distinguish the science of the rules of sensibility as such, i.e. aesthetic, from the science of the rules of the understanding as such, i.e. logic.
>
> (*Pure Reason*, A 51/B 75)

(The rules of sensibility are, roughly, that all objects must be represented in space and time.) The problems that concerned his immediate successors and also trouble some influential recent philosophers are not hard to see: if sensory information is received in terms of one set of rules (everything must appear in space and time), what reason is there to believe that it can be organized according to a distinct set of rules, the general principles governing concepts of objects?[26] If sensory data include qualities such as color and texture, how can these things be said either to accord with or not to accord with principles such as "all events have causes"?

Critics from Salomon Maimon[27] in the eighteenth century to Wilfrid Sellars[28] in the twentieth have rejected Kant's dualistic epistemology – sensations received by one faculty and organized by other faculties involved with concept use – on the grounds that, once made, a division between what is without and what is within the province of rules governing concepts can never be bridged. As we have seen, Kant believed that however difficult it might be to spell out the exact nature of the coordination, the possibility of cognition requires coordinated faculties. How else could claims couched in concepts partially arise from and be (partially) supported by appeal to sensory evidence? Toward the end of the twentieth century, cognitive scientists returned to the essential Kantian problem of relating sensory evidence to conceptual representations and tried, again, to bridge the gap, sometimes by appealing to an intermediary sort of information, "non-conceptual content."[29] Almost immediately, philosophers, including many inspired by Sellars, raised the objection of Kant's early critics on the other side: how can non-conceptual representations, representations not governed by the rules of concept use, ever form the basis of concept use?[30]

Given the complexities and obscurities of Kant's discussion of apperceptive self-consciousness, it is hardly surprising that his successors immediately offered criticisms and clarifications. One way to appreciate a central difficulty is to recall that Kant believed that cognition comes in two basic flavors, perception and conception. But how did he understand self-consciousness? Through inner sense, we perceive our states, but not our selves; in apperceptive self-consciousness, we are (perhaps) implicitly aware of acts of thinking, but we have no conception of whatever performs these acts. Johann Gottlieb Fichte thought the only way to render the Kantian position consistent was to posit a third sort of cognition, "intellectual intuition."[31] Although this amendment may capture some of what Kant wanted to say about self-consciousness, it does not provide a satisfactory resolution of the issue. A central tenet of Kantian epistemology, which he went to considerable efforts to underline in the second edition, is that human beings lack intellectual intuitions; they receive information only through their senses (e.g., *Pure Reason*, B xl, B 68, B 72, B 159, B 307).

The issue of the unity of the mind or person (personal identity) and our knowledge of that unity returned to the forefront of philosophical discussion in the 1960s, thanks largely to Sydney Shoemaker's recasting of the Lockean position.[32] Twentieth- and twenty-first-century discussions in both philosophy and psychology have presupposed the Humean view that we have no inner or introspective access to a self. This has led a number of psychologists to consider why the ordinary person believes in a unified self at all. Rather than asking what a self is, they have raised such questions as 'what are subjects' theories of the self or self-constructs?," "how do self-constructs arise?," and "what is their function in the mental economy?"

At first glance, it might appear that Kant also held that we do not so much discover as construct selves. On his view, all we sense through inner sense are our states; the conception of various states as all belonging to a single, ongoing self arises through the spontaneous activities of our faculties. Notice, however, that Kant's theory of our knowledge of our selves – that it is a composite of sensory information received through inner sense and *a priori* concepts produced by the understanding – is, in this respect, exactly on a par with his view of our knowledge of everything else. This was his "third way" of steering between the limitations of empiricism and the excesses of rationalism. So he would not regard the self as a "construct" – something that is believed to exist but does not – anymore than he would take a dagger or gravity to be a construct. Rather, the self, with its various passive and active capacities, is what constructs knowledge out of the sensory information it receives. To put the point somewhat paradoxically, Kant maintained that the self partially constructs cognitions of the world and of itself, but that the resulting cognitions are cognitions of objects, not of mere constructs, mere objects of belief. His question to contemporary psychologists would be: who or what constructs these self-constructs?

For Kant, a unified self is an ineliminable element in explaining our cognition of the world (including ourselves). It is ineliminable both because its unified capacities produce cognitions and because every cognition of an object involves a simultaneous explicit or implicit cognition of the states of an on-going subject of cognition. In this respect, Kant regarded our knowledge of ourselves as very different from our knowledge of other sorts of objects (including our bodies). Among contemporary philosophers, Peter Strawson,[33] Hector-Neri Castañeda,[34] Gareth Evans,[35] Sydney Shoemaker,[36] and others have developed Kantian themes about the ineliminability of the self in knowledge and some of the resulting peculiarities of self-knowledge. Their work serves as a counterpoint to the popular "no self" theories espoused by such recent Humeans as Derek Parfit[37] and Daniel Dennett.[38]

NOTES

1. I will use the standard "A" and "B" pagination for references to the *Critique of Pure Reason*. References to Kant's other works will be to *Kants Gesammelte Schriften, Akademie Ausgabe*, edited by the *Königlichen Preussischen Akademie der Wissenschaften*, 29 vols. (Berlin: Walter de Gruyter and predecessors, 1900–), and will be cited in the text by the volume and page numbers. Except as noted, and where they are available, the translations will be from *The Cambridge Edition of the Works of Immanuel Kant* (Cambridge: Cambridge University Press, 1992–).

2. Kant's books were catalogued after his death, and the list can be found in Arthur Warda, *Bibliographien und Studien*, 3, Immanuel Kants Bücher (Berlin: Verlag von Martin Breslauer, 1922), p. 47.

3. Alexander Campbell Fraser, ed. (New York: Dover, 1959). References to this work will be cited in the text in parentheses with "*Essay*" and the book, chapter, and section numbers.

4. Reinhard Brandt, "Materialien zur Entstehung der *Kritik der reinen Vernunft*," in I. Heidemann and W. Ritzel, eds., *Beiträge zur Kritik der reinen Vernunft* (Berlin: Walter de Gruyter, 1981), p. 45.

5. John Cottingham, Robert Stoothoff, and Dugald Murdoch, trans., *The Philosophical Writings of Descartes* (Cambridge: Cambridge University Press, 1984), vol. 1, p. 196.

6. This comment appears in student notes from Kant's lectures on anthropology. Scholars are not of one mind on the reliability of the notebooks that were created from his courses. Material from them lacks the authority of works that Kant prepared for publication; nonetheless, the lecture notes can be useful in elaborating or illustrating the published doctrines.

7. Edwin McCann argues this point in "Locke on Identity: Matter, Life, and Consciousness," in Margaret Atherton, ed., *The Empiricists: Critical Essays* (Lanham, MD: Rowman and Littlefield, 1999), pp. 63–88.

8. Posthumously published in 1765; translated and edited by Peter Remnant and Jonathan Bennett (Cambridge: Cambridge University Press, 1981). References to this work will be cited in the text in parentheses by "*New Essays*" and the page number.

9. Leroy E. Loemker, trans. and ed., *Gottfried Wilhelm Leibniz, Philosophical Papers and Letters* (Dordrecht: D. Reidel, 1965), p. 637.

10. For first two references, see Loemker, *Leibniz*, pp. 646, 638.

11. *Treatise of Human Nature*, L. A. Selby-Bigge, ed. (Oxford: Oxford University Press, 1888), pp. 207, 253. Future references to this work will be cited in the text in parentheses by *Treatise* and the page number.

12. Hume's first *Enquiry* appeared in German translation in 1755 in the second volume of his miscellaneous writings, edited by Johann Georg Sulzer. See Warda, *Bibliographien*, p. 50.

13. These citations appear on pp. 70, 249–50 of his *Essay on the Nature and Immutability of Truth*, in *Beattie's Works* (Philadelphia: Hopkins and Earle, 1809).

14. Manfred Kuehn documents these connections in *Scottish Common Sense in Germany, 1768–1800* (Montreal: McGill-Queen's University Press, 1987), pp. 92–5.

15. Reinhard Brandt offers evidence of the possible influence of Rousseau on Kant's views about the self in "Rousseau und Kants 'Ich Denke'," in R. Brandt and W. Stark, eds., *Autographen, Dokumente und*

Berichte. Zu Edition, Amtsgeschäften und Werk Immanuel Kants, Kant–Forschungen, Band 5 (Hamburg: Felix Meiner Verlag, 1994), pp. 1–18.

16. *Emile*, Allan Bloom, trans. (New York: Basic Books, 1979), p. 270.

17. See Robert J. Richards, "Christian Wolff's Prolegomena to Empirical and Rational Psychology: Translation and Commentary," *Proceedings of the American Philosophical Society*, 124, 3 (1980): 227–39, at p. 231.

18. Cited in Richard J. Blackwell, "Christian Wolff's Doctrine of the Soul," *Journal of the History of Idea XXII* 1 (1961): 339–54, at p. 341.

19. Reprinted in *Modern Philosophy: An Anthology of Primary Sources*, R. Ariew and E. Watkins, eds. (Indianapolis: Hackett Publishing Company, 1998), pp. 4–8, at p. 5.

20. Loemker, *Leibinz*, pp. 633–4.

21. See note 5.

22. See, for example, Norman Kemp Smith, *A Commentary to Kant's 'Critique of Pure Reason,'* 2nd ed. (London: Macmillan, 1923), p. 45.

23. While perfectly reasonable, I think that Guyer and Wood's rendering of this term as "radical faculty" does not capture Kant's view of apperception as the most fundamental active faculty.

24. Andrew Brook, in *Kant and the Mind* (Cambridge: Cambridge University Press, 1994), has suggested that the A and B editions differ in that the former emphasizes apperception as an activity where the latter stresses apperception as a consciousness of the unity of the self. Although I think Brook's teasing out of the different strands of the doctrine of apperception is extremely helpful and have drawn on some of his views, both themes seem to be present in both editions.

25. Henry Allison recommends the second account in *Kant's Transcendental Idealism* (New Haven: Yale University Press, 1983), p. 140.

26. As the attentive reader will have noticed, this criticism is predicated on the assumption that Kant failed in the central mission of the *Critique* to show why the laws of the understanding apply to all objects of cognition.

27. Paul Franks offers a brief account of Maimon's objection in Karl Ameriks, ed., *The Cambridge Companion to German Idealism* (Cambridge: Cambridge University Press, 2000), pp. 105ff.

28. Sellars's most prominent statement of this problem is in "Empiricism and the Philosophy of Mind," reprinted in his *Science, Perception, and Reality* (London: Routlege and Kegan Paul, 1963), pp. 127–96.

29. Non-conceptual content is discussed in several papers in Tim Crane, ed., *The Contents of Experience* (Cambridge: Cambridge University Press, 1994).

30. See, for example, John McDowell's *Mind and World* (Cambridge, MA: Harvard University Press, 1994).

31. Frederick Neuhouser offers a particularly clear and helpful account of this issue in chapter 3 of *Fichte's Theory of Subjectivity* (Cambridge: Cambridge University Press, 1990).

32. In *Self-Knowledge and Self-Identity* (Ithaca, NY: Cornell University Press, 1963).

33. See Part Three, section 2.1 of *The Bounds of Sense* (London: Methuen, 1966).

34. In, for example, "'He': A Study in the Logic of Self-Consciousness," *Ratio* 8 (1966): 130–57.

35. *The Varieties of Reference* (Oxford: Oxford University Press, 1982).

36. *The First-Person Pespective and Other Essays* (Cambridge: Cambridge University Press, 1996).

37. *Reasons and Persons* (Oxford: Oxford University Press, 1984).

38. "The Self as a Center of Narrative Gravity," in Frank Kessel, P. Cole, and D. Johnson, eds., *Self and Consciousness: Multiple Perspectives* (Hillsdale, NJ: Erlbaum, 1992), pp. 103–15.

6 Kant's proofs of substance and causation

I. PRELIMINARY REMARKS

Kant's views on the nature of causation and substance do not depend on any compromise between or any combination of rationalism and empiricism, but on what he calls a "third thing," the pure intuition of time, which is completely missing in both rationalism and empiricism.

For Kant the empiricist position on causation fails to establish the necessary connection between events, that one event "arises out of" or "emerges" from another. Besides constant conjunction in experience, Kant grants the empiricist "empirical" universality through induction (*Pure Reason*, A 91/B 124),[1] or completely universal generalization. This universality, however, implies only that all events of a certain type are followed by events of a second type – but not that any particular event of the first type *forces, produces, or necessarily yields* an event of the second type. The regularity theory that defines causation in terms of subsumption under inductively allowable universal generalization[2] simply fails to account for the connection in singular causation. For Kant the rationalist position on causation is that the causal connection is a connection of inference in the intellect, namely, that the existence of a second event can be inferred or deduced from a first event (A 243/B 301).[3] But now for Kant this idea of inferring existence makes no sense apart from causation (one event's producing or yielding another) and so cannot explain it.[4]

A variant of the rationalist view is that causation is to be understood in terms of explanation. Thus, if we have an explanatory theory according to which an event explains another event, that is all there is to the first event causing the second one. If we combine this rationalism with the empiricist's regularity theory, we simply get as an analysis of causation that events come under a universal regularity that is also explanatory (a consequence of an explanatory theory). Such a combination is not Kant's view. If we cannot get the necessity of singular causation from regularity or explanation alone, we cannot get it by combining them.

I will argue that Kant derives the nature and universal existence of causation from its function or role in constituting the necessary advance of time and so that Kant holds his own unique version of what later came to be called a causal theory of time. He locates the source of necessary connection then neither in the inferences of the intellect (rationalism), nor in the features and patterns of events (empiricism), nor in both together. Rather, he finds it in a "third thing," which is the nature of pure time.

For Kant an empiricist conception of substance is impossible. He says the concept of substance is what is left "if we remove from our concept of any object . . . all properties which experience has taught us" (B 6). For Hume, roughly, aspects of experiences such as uniformity of features or continuity of change are the sole (objective) basis of the concept of substance or of identity through time. As even Hume recognizes, however, these are not sufficient since they are compatible with the existence of a series of connected but distinct momentary objects. For Kant, the rationalist conception of substance is the intellectual concept of a subject that is not also a predicate.[5] This concept, Kant says, is "ignorant of any conditions under which this logical pre-eminence may belong to anything" (A 243/B 301). In particular, this rationalist conception does nothing to determine a singular use of subject term (pertaining to a substance existing through time) as opposed to a plural use of subject terms (pertaining to momentary existents). Nor will combining the rationalist's logical concept of a subject with the empiricist's constancy or continuity of variation determine any application of the concept of substance that neither determines on their own.

Kant, I will argue, derives the determinate existence of substances from their role or function in constituting the "permanence" or the ongoing nature of time, that is, the fact that the present does not begin time, but continues an already existing duration. Kant holds what can be called a "substance-theory" of the ongoing-ness or last-ingness of time. He locates the source of substantial identity, then, neither in the individuative apparatus of the intellect (rationalism), nor in the steady qualities of experience (empiricism), nor in both together. Rather, he finds it in the "third thing," which is the nature of time itself.

2. KANT'S PROOF OF CAUSATION

In the Second Analogy Kant claims to derive causation from objective succession by showing that the representation of objective succession entails that every event has a preceding condition that necessitates the event. The argument, then, is meant to answer Hume's skepticism regarding the nature of causation itself (of the causal tie or the necessary bond between events), and his skepticism regarding the universal applicability of causation. My contention is that Kant's derivation turns on his holding what may be called a "partial causal theory" of time,[6] so that it is this theory that is the crux of Kant's answer to Hume.

The Second Analogy begins (A 190–1/B 235–6) with a discussion of what objectivity means, if appearances alone are "what can be given us to know." For present purposes we can understand this to mean that all we have to deal with are sensory representations. I shall call these representations "reactions" or "responses" to emphasize their passivity, but so far there is no implication that these are reactions or responses to entities outside us. Now objectivity, for Kant, requires a distinction between our representations, on the one hand, and that which they agree with (or fail to agree with), on the other. Indeed for Kant truth consists "in the agreement of knowledge with its object," and so the question becomes "what is there for our actual reactions or responses to agree with?" Kant's answer is that our reactions may agree with, or fail to agree with, a *rule* for reacting. Thus, I may in fact first react r_1 (where r_1 is, for example, ship-upstream) and then react r_2 (ship-downstream). This actual sequence of reactions may or may not agree with how it is proper or legitimate to react. How it is legitimate or proper to react is a constraint on our actual reactions, since we can fault our actual reactions for not being faithful to how it is proper to be reacting. The notion of a rule, then, takes over the function of some actual entity outside our actual representations, of being a constraint on those representations.[7] As an analogy, consider making an actual move in a chess game. The move may agree or not, or may correspond or not, to how it is then legitimate or legal to move. Thus, without going outside an ontology of moves, one has a distinction between actual moves and what constrains actual moves, namely, legitimate moves.

Kant next (A 191–3/B 236–8) applies this notion of objectivity to the case of succession, and finds that the rule for an objective succession is irreversibility of the order of reacting. The rule, that is, is that it is legitimate or proper to first react r_1 and then r_2, but not legitimate to first react r_2 and then r_1. To think our actual successive reactions as subject to, or governed by, such a rule is to think of them as not only being successive, but also representing what is successive. Equivalently, it is only when we think the order of reacting as necessary or required, in the sense in which it is necessary to move a bishop only diagonally, that we think of the succession as something more than the order in which we happen to react. For Kant, the objective succession is then the necessary order of proper reactions. Lovejoy[8] and Strawson[9] charge Kant with a non sequitur in arguing from the order of our reactions being necessitated by the sequence of states constituting the event outside us to the necessity of the order of that sequence of states itself. This, however, is to miss Kant's point that the only "states" that stand against our actual reactions are proprieties of reacting. My apprehension of the ship being upstream and then downstream is not bound by necessity to the order of a distinct sequence of states (ship upstream, ship downstream) whose order is definable apart from necessity (as simply being the order of states that are outside my apprehension). Rather, necessity is built into the very conception of that which constrains my apprehension, namely, the rule of how it is necessary or required to react. To think of my apprehension as bound at all is to think of it already as bound or constrained by what has a necessary order (viz., the rule), and so there is no non sequitur over the notion of necessity. An objective succession is just a rule containing a necessary or required order of reaction.

The charge of a non sequitur by Lovejoy and Strawson depends on attributing to Kant a kind of realist view that he does not hold. This has been pointed out by various commentators.[10] The point remains, however, that the supposed necessity in the order of reacting that avoids the non sequitur is still not sufficient for any sort of causal connection. From the fact that it is legitimate or required to react r_1 and then r_2, but not vice versa, it does not follow that the legitimacy of reacting r_2 is due to (or forced or determined by) the legitimacy of reacting r_1. From the fact that it is legitimate to react ship-upstream only before ship-downstream, it does not follow that its being legitimate to react ship-upstream makes it the case that it is legitimate then to react ship-downstream. The rule says only that if I now have both sensible reactions, I can have them only in one order, not that the second reaction has to happen at all.[11] Thus, suppose I see ship-upstream. The rule as yet is not even operative, since it is a rule only for thinking a necessary order when I have both successive reactions. The rule then does not even imply that if it is proper to react ship-upstream, then it is also proper to react ship-downstream. Since it does not even imply that the second reaction is proper after the first one, it certainly does not imply that the propriety of the second reaction is caused by or forced by the propriety of the first reaction. Fortunately, however, it is not Kant's contention that irreversibility is causation. Rather, in the paragraph at A 194/ B 239 Kant says not that the rule of irreversibility is causation, but that in conformity with it there must (also) be a causal connection.

Recall that the rule of irreversibility is supposed to express or represent objective succession. But now there is more to the idea of objective succession than that it is distinct from objective coexistence (the distinction expressed in the rule of irreversibility). An objective succession, further, must have existence in the time-series, that is, exist at a stage in the previously ongoing course of time.[12] What is this time-series like? Kant says here that "The advance, on the other hand, from a given time to a determinate time that follows is a necessary advance" (A 194/B 239). The series of times, that is, is such that earlier times necessarily advance to later times. Given earlier times, the later times *must* happen. Later times fully *emerge from* earlier times. Earlier times *force or determine* the existence of times afterward. All this is just to say that further later times do not *just happen* to come after preceding times – they necessarily do. Now it is on this character of the time-series that Kant bases his conclusion that there must be something that determines the succession expressed in the rule of irreversibility. Equivalently, it is from the necessary advance of time that Kant concludes to the existence of a preceding causal or determining condition of that succession. Kant's argument is that since time itself is not an object of perception, the necessary advance in the time-series has to be represented by, or within, the series of objective occurrences themselves. Thus, he says later on, "Now since absolute time is not an object of perception, this determination of position [in time] cannot be derived from the relation of appearances [reactions or legitimate reactions] to it. On the contrary, the appearances must determine for one another their position in time, *and make their time-order a necessary order*" (A 200/B 245; italics mine). In other words, Kant is holding that the necessary time order (that previous times force, or necessarily advance to, succeeding times) has to be represented within or between occurrences.

Let us put this all together now. I must represent the succession expressed by the rule of irreversibility as occurring in the already ongoing time-series. This series is one in which preceding times necessarily advance to succeeding times. But this necessary advance itself has to be represented within or between occurrences. Therefore, the succession expressed by the rule of irreversibility has to be represented as necessarily advancing from a preceding occurrence (which occurrence, likewise, to be placed in the time-series, has to be represented as advancing from an occurrence preceding it, etc.). Indeed, the preceding occurrence must *determine* or *force* the succession. The succession must *emerge from* or *arise out of* the preceding occurrence. In sum, it cannot be that the succession *just happens* to come after the preceding occurrence if the necessary advance of times is to be represented in the series of occurrences themselves. But the idea of a preceding occurrence determining or forcing what comes after is just the idea of a causal connection. In this way it follows that if the succession expressed by the rule of irreversibility is to be an objective succession (viz., a succession determined in the time series), then "I must refer it necessarily to something which precedes it, and upon which it follows . . . of necessity" (A 194/ B 239), hence representing it as in causal connection.

Let us try to formulate Kant's conclusion now in terms of his conception that occurrences or states are appearances. Recall that an occurrence, as opposed to its apprehension, is simply a proper reaction as opposed to an actual reaction. The purported objective succession, then, that has to be placed in the time-series is simply that it is legitimate to first react r_1 and then to react r_2. To place it in a series that represents the necessary advance of time requires a preceding condition, say r_0, which forces or determines it; that is, it must be that the propriety of reacting r_0 forces or determines the propriety of reacting r_1 and then r_2. There is then a necessary tie or bond between proper reactions so that succeeding proper reactions emerge from or necessarily arise from preceding ones, as opposed to just happening to arise after preceding ones. The relata then of causal connections are proper reactions. These are acceptable as relata since, for example, I can say that it is proper or legitimate to react "smoke" because it was proper or legitimate to react "fire," and in saying this I am expressing a causal connection.

The same now is true of the propriety of reacting r_0 (the reaction preceding the original succession). It too must be placed in the time-series (which then places the original succession in a longer time series), which entails that for some r_{-1} the propriety of reacting r_{-1} forces the propriety of reacting r_0. In this manner not only is it shown that the original succession is caused, but that all members of the ongoing objective series are caused. In sum, from the very notion of an objective succession, we have the conclusion that *all* objective occurrences (occurrences in the time-series) have a necessary tie or bond to preceding occurrences that determine or force them. The causal bond, that is, is universally applicable.

One might think there is the following gap in Kant's argument for the universality of the causal principle. A proper reaction, say r, might exist simultaneously, and even in the same object, as another proper reaction r*. The one reaction r could have a place in the necessary advance of the time series by arising together with r*, which latter is causally tied to a preceding series of reactions (and so has a place in the time-series), without r being causally tied. In this way r inherits a place in the necessary advance without itself being caused. This gap, I believe, is closed by being careful as to what it means for proper reactions to represent the necessary advance of time. If the later *moment*, as opposed to one particular proper reaction at that moment, is to be represented as emerging from or being determined by the earlier moment, then *every possible* proper reaction at that later moment must emerge from or be determined by a reaction at the earlier moment. Otherwise, it is not the later moment that emerges or is determined, but only some reactions at it. Roughly, properties such as emergence characterize the moment exactly by characterizing the equivalence class of all possible reactions taking place at it. As an analogy, something is a feature or property of the property *wise,* not if some wise things have the feature, but if all possible wise things have it. Similarly, if we speak abstractly and say "The bird comes from the dinosaur," we mean that all birds are descended from dinosaurs. Now to say "The present necessarily emerges from the preceding" is to speak abstractly, and means likewise that all present occurrences necessarily emerge from earlier preceding ones. If this is correct, then the scope of the causal principle is shown to be absolutely universal, extending to all possible proper reactions whatsoever. Kant seems to be making just this point at A 199/B 244, where he says, "If then . . . the preceding time necessarily determines the succeeding . . . it is also an indispensable law of *empirical representation* of the time series that the appearances of past [preceding] time determine *all existences* [italics mine] in the succeeding time."

3. REMARKS ON KANT'S ACCOUNT OF CAUSATION

Kant's argument, as we have presented it, depends on his holding a version of the causal theory of time, namely, the theory that time relations are not something over and above causal relations. That Kant does hold such a theory is made completely clear in the passage just cited at A 199/B 244. He there says that time has the characteristic "that the preceding time necessarily determines the succeeding." Because of this, he says, "it is also an indispensable law of *empirical* representation of the time series that the appearances of past time [necessarily] determine all existence in the succeeding time." He is arguing, then, that the characteristic of preceding times determining the succeeding has to be represented in terms of (is nothing over and above) a relationship of appearances determining later existence, and so in terms of causal relationships. It is not that moments or stages of time determine one another alongside appearances that determine one another, but rather "since absolute time is not an object of perception . . . the appearances must determine for one another their position in time and *make their time-order a necessary order*" (A 200/B 245; italics mine). In other words, it is between the appearances alone that the relation of the preceding determining the succeeding holds.

Although Kant holds a causal theory of time, it is, in fact, a partial causal theory since not all characteristics of time are reduced to characteristics of appearances. In particular, Kant is not defining the relation of earlier-to-later itself in terms of occurrences. It is only the necessary-determination aspect, not the serial-order aspect, of this relation that Kant claims must be found in the appearances alone. Kant holds, indeed, that causation itself can be understood only in terms of the earlier-to-later relation. Thus the schema of causation involves succession (A 144/B 183), and it is this notion, not some pure atemporal notion of causation or determination, that Kant argues must apply to experience. He says that "in applying it [the pure category] to appearances, we substitute for it its schema as the key to its employment, or rather set it alongside the category" (A 181/B 224). Succession (the schema) is applied, then, *alongside* or together with the pure atemporal notion of determination (the concept of ground and consequent expressed in the hypothetical judgment). Kant is certainly not defining the schema of succession in terms of the pure category. The schema, rather, is something added. This is made clear when he says that "pure *a priori* concepts, *in addition to* the function of understanding expressed in the category, must contain *a priori* certain formal conditions of sensibility" (A 190/ B 179; italics mine), that is, time-relations not definable in terms of the understanding.

Kant is allowing that I can represent succession (temporal order) without thinking of causation, as when I formulate the rule of irreversibility. Here I am representing that it is legitimate only to react r_1 before r_2. I can further think there are other proper reactions that precede my apprehension, so that it is also legitimate (though too late for me) to react r_0 before reacting r_1 and r_2. Kant's point is that all of this is still not sufficient for representing succession in a time-series where the preceding time determines the succeeding. This latter aspect of the relation of succession or temporal order, namely, its necessary advance, is what is representable for Kant only in terms of a relation between the occurrences themselves (and which requires, alongside the schema of succession or order, the concept of determination or of ground and consequent). To place the legitimacy of reacting r_1 before r_2 in a time-series where the earlier determines the later, that is, I must represent not only that it is legitimate to react r_0 before it is legitimate to react r_1 and then r_2, but that the legitimacy of reacting r_0 earlier determines, or has as a consequence, the legitimacy of reacting r_1 and then r_2.

Kant's partial causal theory of time differs radically from Leibniz's full causal theory. For Leibniz, the law of activity of a substance or monad, according to which its states determine one another in an atemporal (although asymmetrical) sense of determination, founds well the phenomenal (temporal) order. In other words, some non-temporal sense of determination is the fundamental order in terms of which there is temporality at all. In Kant's terms Leibniz is apply-ing a non-schematized concept of causation (determination of ground to consequent according to a law) to determine the temporal order. It should be clear that such a view goes against all the fundamentals of Kant's thinking. Understanding the difference between Kant's partial causal theory and Leibniz's total causal theory enables us to avoid the objections Suchting makes[13] to attributing the causal theory of time to Kant. Suchting recognizes the two paragraphs at A 199–200/B 244–5 as apparently expressing a causal theory of time, but he rejects them as incompatible with Kant's thinking since Suchting understands them as an attempt to derive the form of sensibility (time) from the form of understanding (causation). Further, he holds that such a the-ory is circular since the notion of causation makes reference to the notion of succession it is trying to define. Each of these objections would be relevant if these paragraphs were expressing a Leibnizian version of the causal theory but are irrelevant against the partial causal theory we have attributed to Kant.

According to Kemp Smith[14] and Suchting,[15] the two paragraphs at A 199–200/B 244–5, which focus almost entirely on expressing a causal theory of time, constitute an argument distinct and sepa-rate from the rest of the Second Analogy. On their view Kant's main argument for causation is quite separate from having to represent the necessary advance of time in the appearances themselves. A careful reading of the text, however, shows that in each and every presenta-tion of the argument Kant includes a reference to the nature of the time-series. Thus, in the paragraph at A 194/B 239, where he first con-cludes (in the first edition) to the existence of causal connections, a premise is that "The advance, on the other hand, from a given time to the determinate time that follows is a necessary advance." In the paragraph at A 196/B 241, after making his second conclu-sion to causal connections, he explains the nature of his argument by saying, "Nevertheless the recognition of the rule [that everything that happens has a cause] as a condition of the synthetic unity of appearances in time, has been the ground of experience itself." In the paragraph beginning at A 198/B 243, where he makes his third conclusion to causal connections, he says the determining cause is required for "connecting the event [the succession] in necessary relation with itself in the time-series." The two paragraphs that follow, which focus on the causal theory of time, do not then constitute a separate argument, but make clear in a general manner the issue (representing the necessary advance of time) that is involved in each of the presentations of the argument. The introductory statement to the Analogies likewise expresses that in each of the Analogies the proof of the category depends on the fact that "time, however, cannot itself be perceived [and so] the determination of the existence of objects in time can take place only through their relation [to one another] in time in general . . . through a representation of necessary connection of perceptions" (B 219).[16]

4. CAUSATION AND TIME AS A PURE INTUITION

A key premise of Kant's argument is that time itself cannot be perceived (so that the necessary advance of time has to be represented within or via the connection of legitimate or proper reactions). Of course Kant, in the Aesthetic, has already argued that time is not an objective, self-subsistent entity (A 32/B 49). Roughly, then, the reason he holds that time itself cannot be perceived is because time itself as an object does not exist. Indeed, time exists for Kant only as a pure intuition. In the Aesthetic Kant holds a constructivist theory of space and time that is somewhat parallel to a constructivist theory of number. Just as for the constructivist numbers exist only as termini of counting procedures, so too for Kant space and time exist only in flowing procedures or flowing constructions. The reason for this is that any space or time is a continuous expanse or extent. This, for Kant, implies that it is a whole that is prior to its parts or elements (A 25/B 39), rather than composed out of them. Indeed, the "seamlessness" of a continuous expanse is just this fact that it is so seamless that it cannot be constituted out of elements. Now an objective whole exists only by all its elements existing, and so is composed of them. On the other hand, a flowing construction, such as sweeping out a line, is not composed out of any cuts or stops that construct parts of the flow. Only as flowing constructions, then, or motions of the subject (B 155), can stretches of space and time be continuous. An example of a temporal construction, or what we may call "temporizing," would be a conductor who paces or tempers the orchestra's playing of a note by a downbeat gesture that is, indeed, a flowing performance. For something to be given in intuition, for Kant, is for it to be immediately presented. Space and time, being immediately presented by constructing or performing, rather than by sensing, are thus given in *pure* intuition. Moments of time, now, are limits or cuts of the flow. Thus, the start of the downbeat and the terminus constitute the construction of successive moments of the extensivity that time is. This supports our contention that Kant is not holding a causal theory of the successive order of time (of the earlier-to-later relation of moments) since this order is given in pure intuition (in construction).

Let us suppose then that in the Aesthetic Kant is holding a constructivist theory of space and time. How does this theory cohere with the partial causal theory that we claim he holds in the Second Analogy?[17] To begin with, different aspects of time are involved in the two accounts. Whereas the expansiveness of time and its seriality is constructed, it is the necessary advance of the seriality that is represented causally.[18] Second, the necessary advance cannot be represented in construction. Construction is not such that having constructed an extent forces or determines a further construction. Nor does the propriety or legitimacy of one construction force or make a second construction proper. The legitimacy of my now going ahead to temporize is not forced or determined by the propriety of preceding constructions. Indeed, each construction is proper or legitimate on its own. The order of proper constructions may be irreversible, but, as we have seen, irreversiblity is not sufficient for determination. It is only proprieties of reacting or responding (via causation) that can force or produce subsequent proprieties. The causal theory of the Second Analogy then is not redundant. Thirdly, a causal theory does not represent moments of substantival time, or even temporal relations as with relational time. The causal theory adds only a *dynamical* relation of production or necessary advance among occupants (proper reactions) to the aspects of time represented in construction. In other words, *nothing specifically temporal that exists objectively* (or outside of construction) is added. Space and time for Kant, recall, are not only pure intuitions, but are also forms of empirical intuition (reacting or responding perceptually). It is, so to speak, by proper reacting being tied to (being in the course of) proper constructing that reactions "inherit" successive order separated by expanse. But now, in the Second Analogy, it is by proper constructing being tied to (or encompassing) proper reacting (in accord with the determination by causation) that the successive order (of constructing) inherits necessary advance from the earlier to the later. Thus, in the Second Analogy Kant is adding a dynamical dimension (causation) to the representation of reacting in the course of constructing, which is not adding any extra-constructive ontological time (whether relational or absolute).[19] In this fashion, I believe, the partial causal theory Kant is holding in the Second Analogy is fully consistent with his account of time in the Aesthetic that time is merely a pure intuition that is the form of empirical intuition. The account in the Aesthetic also explains, I believe, why Kant can argue from the unperceivability of time to causation, despite the fact that he explicitly holds that causal necessity is likewise unperceivable. Time is unperceivable because it exists only constructively, not objectively. Causation, on the other hand, is a dynamical notion, not a constructive one. The crux is not unperceivability, but extra-constructive existence, which causation has, but which time lacks.

5. KANT'S ANSWER TO HUME

On our account so far, Kant's argument is that objective succession requires, first, rules for reacting, since objectivity concerns the propriety or legitimacy of reacting. Second, it requires a connection of necessary advance between such proper reactions, in order to represent the necessary advance of the time-series within which any objective succession takes place. Embedded in this account is Kant's answer to Hume. First, proper reactions are connected by a tie or nexus of producing, forcing to happen, determining, necessarily emerging into, and so forth. This bond derives from the nature of the time-series that the relation among proper reactions has to represent, namely, that the earlier time determines or forces or necessarily advances to the later time. In particular, the bond or connection is completely independent of Humean propensities to transfer force and vivacity upon associating ideas with impressions. Kant, that is, "finds" the singular causal nexus in the nature of time, not in mental habits. Second, this causal (productive, determining) connection must pertain to every proper (objective) reaction whatsoever since all such reactions have a place in the time series. In other words, both the causal nexus and the universality of the causal principle are conditions of the possibility of experience (or of the representation of objective succession). Kant is clearly addressing Hume in the paragraph at A 196/B 241, where he begins by saying that the concept of cause does not depend on repeated succession of events; that is, it does not depend on constant conjunction in experience. Of course, on Hume's analysis it does, since constant conjunction is involved in association and so in transference of force and vivacity. Kant says that such a concept of cause would be merely empirical. Notice that on his view the concept of cause (production, necessary determination) derives not from constant conjunction, but from the nature of the time-series. Kant further says that Hume's account makes the principle "that everything which happens has a cause" contingent (viz., it would be accidental depending on how much regularity there happens to be in experience). Kant's proof of the principle, rather, is that "experience itself is brought about only by [its] means" (viz., the representation of the universal necessary advance of the time-series requires universal causation, or that every proper reaction whatsoever emerges from, or is produced by, a preceding proper reaction). Indeed, this "rule determining the series of events" (that each event emerges or is produced from something preceding) is said by Kant to be "a condition of the synthetic unity of appearances in time." In this paragraph then Kant is holding that regularity (uniformity, constant conjunction) is irrelevant to establishing either the nature of the causal bond itself or the universal causal principle (that this bond is universally applicable). Nevertheless, Kant does believe that the causal relation involves universality (that events similar to the cause are always followed by events similar to the effect). This strict universality follows, I believe, not from any inductive inference based on regularity, but from the necessity that holds between cause and effect.[20] The necessity with which a preceding time emerges into the succeeding is an absolute or unrestricted necessity, as opposed to a necessity limited in some regard or fashion. But now suppose A causes B only in the present case, or only in some cases. Then the necessity by which A emerges into B would be restricted or conditional. It would not be absolutely necessary that B follows A, but only now (or in some cases) necessary. Thus, the relation between A and B could not carry or represent the absolute necessity of the advance of the time-series. Alternatively, the necessity in the advance of time has a constant character at all times. Each moment flows from or emerges from preceding time in the same way as any other moment. This homogeneity in the way time necessarily unfolds has to be represented by a homogeneity in the way events necessarily unfold into other events, namely, by this necessary unfolding having always the same character. But this universality of the character of causation is just the same cause/same effect principle, or the principle that all causes and effects come under universal laws of what causes what. Thus, although regularity may be an empirical criterion for ascertaining what specifically causes what, it is not a basis for the strict universality that holds between cause and effect, which has its basis rather in the homogeneous nature of the necessary advance of time.

So far Kant's answer to Hume has not taken Kant outside the realm of proper reactions or proper perceptions. So far, that is, Kant like Hume is a phenomenalist; in other words, the ontology includes only perceptions and related notions such as either imaginative propensities regarding perceptions (as with Hume) or else rules of proper perceptions (as with Kant). However, in the very first paragraph of the Second Analogy, and again in the paragraphs beginning at A 204/B 249, Kant makes clear that causation requires or involves substances, thus going beyond any version of phenomenalism. I shall consider first, in some detail, Kant's proof of substance in the First Analogy and then return to his claim that causation imputes substances.

6. KANT'S PROOF OF SUBSTANCE

In the First Analogy Kant says (B 225) that the time (as form of intuition) in which all time relations are thought is permanent. Further, since time itself (as objective time) cannot be perceived, the "substratum" that represents time in general must be found in the objects of perception, and this permanent thing is substance. Note that he says that time is the permanent form of intuition. If permanence is in time as a form of intuition, however, then why must it also be represented in the objects of perception? Suppose we accept that Kant is a constructivist regarding time. I can now carry out a temporizing construction or procedure such as marking time. But time exists prior to any such construction I can now carry out. My constructions, that is, do not begin a new time, but continue the flow of an already ongoing time. What this means is that *if* time as a form of intuition (as construction) is to be "permanent" (a continuation), then there must be some way of representing construction prior to any that I can go ahead and perform. Of course, besides actual constructing, there are rules of how it is proper to construct (whether one actually does so or not). Such rules, however, will not enable a representation of earlier construction if they are simply rules for how it is proper or legitimate to go ahead and temporize. What I suggest, now, is that it can be presently proper or legitimate to be *in the course of* (at a middle or end stage of) procedures or constructions, whether or not one has actually performed the initial stages. Thus, suppose I have a rule for (a procedure of) baking a cake. I shall presume this is an ordered step-by-step procedure for adding ingredients, mixing ingredients, etc. Now suppose I come into a room and find that the first three ingredients are sitting in the bowl. Then I claim it is proper for me presently to be up to stage 4 in the cake-baking procedure, even though I have not added the first three ingredients. Note that it is only something in my present circumstance that can "make it" proper to be so far along in the procedure, rather than at the beginning. If I represent that it is thus legitimate to presently be up to the fourth ingredient in the procedure, then I represent my present performance of putting in the fourth ingredient as a *continuation* of preceding stages of a larger procedure.

To represent temporizing, then, as a continuation (rather than the construction of a new time), I must represent that it is legitimate for me to be up to a certain stage of a larger temporizing procedure, rather than at the beginning. Let the temporizing procedure be to mark time by a series of downbeat gestures, where each such flowing gesture is accompanied by reciting a numeral. Such a procedure would begin with reciting "1" at the end of a downbeat, then reciting "2" at the end of the next downbeat, etc. Then the representation of its being presently legitimate to be up to "k" in such a procedure would represent that a present construction I can perform (a downbeat together with a recitation of k + 1) is a continuation of a larger temporizing construction. In this manner, time *as a form of intuition* (as constructive) would be "permanent" (viz., it would be a continuation of constructive time). But now like the cake-baking case, something in my present circumstance must "make it proper" to be so far along in the temporizing procedure, rather than at the beginning. After all, a procedure is always to do first things first (put in the first ingredient first, recite "1" at a downbeat first, etc.) *unless* something presently sets me ahead in the procedure.

Let us recapitulate. If time *as a form of intuition* is to be permanent (not something begun anew with a present construction), then it must be presently proper or legitimate to be *in the course of* a constructive temporizing procedure. But then something in the present circumstance must make it legitimate to be beyond or past earlier stages of the procedure (despite not having performed them); that is, something present must be the basis or "substratum" of the permanence of time. Now this something cannot be objective time itself. It is not, that is, that objective time is presently so far along in its unfolding that "to keep up with it" it is legitimate to be presently so far along in a temporizing procedure. Hence, it must be rather that something real is presently so far along in its existence that "to keep up with it" it is proper to be so far along in a temporizing procedure geared to its existence. Existence or reality for Kant pertains to that which affects us. And continued existence then pertains to continued affection. Continued affection is what obtains in keeping track of what affects. What the temporizing procedure keeps up with then is tracking, so that we have finally the following representation of the substratum or basis of the permanence of time:

With respect to what presently affects (the real), it is proper to be so far along (up to k) in a temporizing-cum-tracking procedure (a procedure that marks time while keeping track).

But now this represents what presently affects as being something proper to *have been* tracking. It represents, that is, that what is presently real is also what is proper to be *in the course of (at a non-beginning stage of)* tracking. But this is exactly to represent the presently real as having previous existence, or as being "permanent" (its "permanence" extending back as far as the tracking procedure that is presently up to k). Permanence of the real, of course, is just substance for Kant, and so the substratum or basis of representing (past) time is substance.[21]

Note that on our account of the argument, substance is, as Kant says it is, the condition of time magnitude (A 183/B 226; A 177/B 219) or time duration. Our temporizing or marking time construction, in numbering the flows (the downbeats), makes that flow a unit for measuring an extent of time or duration of time. The extensivity (continuity) of time is exactly what exists for Kant only in flowing construction. The point of the argument, then, is not that continuity (and with it, duration or magnitude) is represented outside of flowing constructions in substance. Rather, the point is that representing past extensivity or duration is a matter of representing myself as being in the course of (past or beyond stages of) extensive flowing construction, and that this requires a basis in my present circumstance, and so it requires substance. Substance, that is, is required to extend the scope of construction "into the past." Just as in the Second Analogy, the necessary advance of the time-series goes beyond constructive time, and requires gearing the time-order (succession) to dynamical causation, so too here in the First Analogy, past duration (extensivity) of time goes beyond constructive time, *unless it can be proper to be in the course of such construction*, which requires gearing the construction of magnitude to tracking in regard to what presently affects. In both cases the representation of a mode of time (past duration in the case of the First Analogy, and necessary advance of the time-series in the case of the Second Analogy) is made possible without adding objective (extra-constructive) temporality (but rather adding existence in the one case and causation in the other).

On our reading of the paragraph at B 225 so far, the real that presently affects is the substratum or basis of the permanence of time as a form of intuition (viz., of constructive time). Kant holds also, however, that only in this permanent form of intuition "can either coexistence or succession be represented." In other words, the time-series or time-order is represented as within the extensivity that time is. Kant goes on to say now that "all that belongs to existence can be thought only as a determination of substance." What belongs to existence are appearances or proper reactions. Suppose then that I want to represent that the propriety of a certain reaction arises in past time. I must represent myself as presently being beyond or past so reacting. This, in turn, requires representing myself as being beyond or past an extensivity of time at which the reaction is proper. But we have just seen that this requires representing myself, based on present reality, as being beyond a temporizing-cum-tracking procedure. It requires, that is, representing myself, with respect to what presently affects, as being up to k in marking time while tracking. It is this that represents the "permanence" of time *as a form of intuition* (ongoing temporizing). To represent the appearance (the proper reaction) in relation to the permanent form of intuition, then, is just to represent the reaction as what is proper at the beginning of the procedure. We have then the following representation of appearance in the "permanence" of time as a form of intuition:

With respect to what presently affects, it is legitimate to be up to k in temporizing-while-keeping-track-from-first-reacting-r.

This represents the propriety of reacting r as something proper upon initially tracking what presently affects me (though I am now up to k in tracking it). But this is just to say that the appearance (reacting r) pertains to *this which is before me*, only I am past or beyond so reacting (temporally separated from so reacting by being in the course of a temporizing procedure rather than at the beginning where the reaction is proper). In this way, the appearance (the proper reaction) is a "determination of substance" (of that which is before me), where, roughly, "determination" means that the reaction is to be had with or upon keeping track. Not only, then, is substance the basis of representing past time, but it is the basis of representing proper reactions in past time, which are represented, indeed, as pertaining to (determinations of) trackable existence. Thus, Kant can say, "the permanent is the object itself . . . ; everything on the other hand which changes or can change [proper reactions] belongs only to the way in which substance or substances exist, and therefore to their determinations" (A 184/B 227).[22]

7. THE RELATION OF CAUSATION TO SUBSTANCE

We return now to the relation of causation to substance in the Second Analogy (A 202–5/B 248–51). We begin with Kant's illustrative example of a ball hollowing out a cushion. There is a succession of states in a substance (the cushion) – from being flat to then being hollowed out – and an influence of a second substance (the ball being placed on the cushion). Involved in the transition of states then is both the nature of the substance that undergoes it (its being a soft cushion) and the nature of a second substance that influences it (its being a hard ball). Note that the second state of hollowed out *emerges from* or *necessarily advances from* the first state; that is, the key relationship of necessary advancement between states (between proper reactions) required for representing the necessary advancement of time still obtains. Now, however, it obtains because they are states of a substance with a nature under the influence of a second substance with a nature. The example, that is, does not overturn the key relationship of a necessary succession of states that is the crux of the argument of the Second Analogy.[23] What I wish to suggest is that this model of causation follows from the fact that the time-series that causation is supposed to represent is itself also limited to individual substances. Kant holds, that is, what can be called a "substance-based" theory of time, according to which the time-series exists basically or fundamentally in relation to individual substances.[24] This substance-based theory is akin to the modern idea that time basically is "proper time" holding along individual world-lines, each world-line having its own proper time. The necessary advance in a time-series, then, is an advance in regard to an individual substance. Further, this substance-based theory follows from the fact the time-series unfolds in relation to the extensivity that time is, and such time-duration or time-magnitude (as per the First Analogy) is itself representable as a procedure only in relation to individual substances. Thus Kant's model of causation as involving a necessary succession of states of a single substance coheres with his understanding of the very nature of the time-series that causation is meant to represent.

One may ask, now, how this model of causation is compatible with objective successions between states of different substances. Thus, first a ship is upstream, and then a bell on the shore rings. This succession of states is objective, but there is no causal connection between them according to the model of causation in the Second Analogy.[25] The ship upstream, to be an objective occurrence, must be represented in a necessarily advancing time-series *with regard to a single substance*, and similarly for the bell ringing in regard to a second such series. It is only when they are each thus represented as being two objective occurrences (two occurrence arising in time) that any issue of their relationship (their succession) comes up. It is only in the Third Analogy that this subsequent issue of objective temporal relations between states of different substances is considered.

Kant's representation of the causal series can be set out as follows:

With respect to what presently affects me, it is legitimate to be in the course of a series of successive reactions, each of which necessarily advances to the next.

Since this series supposedly ends with present "irreversible" reactions (like ship-upstream, ship-downstream), this present objective succession is thus represented within a necessary advance of time-order. Note that it is still a representation of *proper reactions* necessarily advancing. Despite the fact that substance is now invoked, there is not for Kant a second series of states of substance outside of proper reactions.[26] The proper reactions themselves (as per the First Analogy) are the determinations of the substance. Thus, the Lovejoy–Strawson[27] charge of a non sequitur is still bogus, even though, by now, Kant is not a phenomenalist.

8. THE RELATION OF CAUSATION AND SUBSTANCE TO THE TRANSCENDENTAL DEDUCTION

Kant's answer to Hume, then, is not only that the universal applicability of the causal tie or bond is required for representing proper reactions in time (for representing objective succession), but also that substances, which are enduring realities and not proper perceptions, are required as well. Not only is causation or necessary connection not a "fiction" of the (empirical) imagination, but substance (or identity through time of reality) is not such a fiction either. Indeed, these are two concepts that must be applicable if possible appearances (proper reactions) are to be represented objectively in time. Kant says in a famous sentence that "The *a priori* conditions of a possible experience in general are at the same time conditions of the possibility of objects of experience" (A 111). This, I suggest, is neither a trivial claim, nor a mere reminder of Kant's Copernican revolution. Rather, it is a statement of Kant's refutation of phenomenalism. "Possible experience" signifies all possible perceptions (all proper reactions), which includes not just further perceptions we can locally and presently have, but perceptions remote in past time and in far away space.[28] What Kant is saying is that although the purport of representation or cognition is just proper reaction in the full scope of space and time, this cognition requires objects of experience (indeed, substances). In other words, phenomenalism is incoherent since in order to represent the full scope of possible perception, substantial entities are necessary. Indeed, we have seen in our account of the First Analogy that to represent a proper past reaction as in past extensive time requires representing it as a reaction at an initial stage of a procedure of tracking what is present (which procedure we are now in the course of rather than at the initial stage). The proper reaction, that is, has to be represented as a reaction proper *to* what is presently real, only not now, but formerly. What Kant is saying then in this sentence is that concepts of objects (the relational categories) are necessary conditions of representing possible experience (the full propriety of reacting).

On our account, both the concepts of substance and of causation are required to bring all proper reactions (appearances) to the unity of apperception. Apperception, for Kant (A 119), is the faculty of understanding (cognition via concepts, or thought), and the understanding is the faculty of rules (A 126; A 118). To bring remote proper reactions to my present apperception, then, is to have rules which encompasses those reactions. This, in turn, is by having rules that encompass the spatio-temporal manifold, which in turn encompasses all proper reactions. This manifold is a matter of constructions by the *productive* imagination (B 155)[29] involving essentially "motion as an act of the subject" (B 155). The rules then are rules for spatio-temporal constructions or procedures, within which reactions are proper. This much, I claim, constitutes Kant's account of what cognition is.[30] Any concepts, now, that are required for bringing the full spatiotemporal manifold to present rules will necessarily apply to proper reactions (appearances), for only by these concepts are those proper reactions anything to my present cognition. Kant, indeed, characterizes the categories just this way, when he says that they are concepts "which contain the necessary unity of the pure synthesis of imagination in respect of all possible appearances" (A 119). The necessary unity, I suggest, is the unity of a rule, which is how it is proper to construct and react.

The Transcendental Deduction, I believe, is a recipe or method for establishing the applicability of pure concepts to cognizable reality. The method is to show that such concepts effect (are required for) cognition. The heart of the Deduction is not to prove any categories, but to give the account of cognition, in relation to which, then, the categories might be required. Kant hearkens back to this same account in his summary of the Analogies. He says, "Our analogies therefore really portray the unity of nature in the connection of all appearances [all possible or all purportedly proper reactions] under certain exponents [the categories] which express nothing save the relation of time [in so far as time comprehends all existence] to the unity of apperception [to my present cognitive ability to represent rules] – such unity being possible only in synthesis according to rules" (A 216/B 263).

On our account, now, the concept of substance is required to bring a pure synthesis of imagination (viz., time-extensivity in the past), and so proper reactions (past appearances) to rules. As we have said, substance makes possible rules for being in the course of temporizing, and so being in the course of temporizing procedures that begin with a proper reaction. This proof of substance, then, in the First Analogy exactly fits the recipe for proving a category outlined in the Transcendental Deduction. Likewise, causation makes possible rules for being in the course of a series of successive reactions (while tracking), which reactions necessarily advance to one another, and so it is via causation that the necessary advance of the manifold of time (the time-series) is brought to present rule.

If I am on the right track, then neither the proof of substance nor the proof of causation makes any sense at all, unless one starts with the theory of cognition set out in the Transcendental Deduction, according to which all cognition is a matter of presently representing myself as variously "situated" with respect to proper reactions. This representation can be, for example, that I am situated as "too late" for a proper reaction (as in being at the tail end of a procedure that begins with the reaction), or it can be that I am situated "too far" from the reaction (as in being at the beginning of a spatial procedure that ends with the reaction), and so forth. In each case, my representation of my situation with respect to proper reactions is via presently operative rules for spatial and temporal constructions. Our reconstruction of the two Analogies has turned entirely on this account of cognition.

We note finally that with respect to substance Kant is not deducing that there is trackable reality (which is an empirical factor). Rather, he is legitimating our right to think of that which is trackable (if such there be) as one enduring entity, as opposed, say, to a succession of continuously successive replacements. Because this latter thought of one enduring entity is not a thought of any further feature reality may present or not, thinking it (justifiably because of its necessity for cognition) is no different than its "really" pertaining or being so. It cannot fail to pertain for failing to pick out what reality is like. Similarly, with respect to causation Kant is not deducing that there is orderly, regular, constant reality, which is an empirical feature. Rather, he is legitimating our right to think of regularity (if such there be) that it is a regularity in (or of) a necessary succession. Thus, if smoke regularly follows fire, we are entitled to think of it as regularly emerging from fire. Because this latter thought does not pertain to a feature that events present, thinking that it pertains (justifiably so because of its requirement for cognizing the unfolding of time) is no different than its "really" pertaining. It cannot fail to pertain for (regular) reality failing to incorporate some further feature. In this way Stroud's objections to the force of transcendental arguments[31] fail, since for pure *a priori* concepts there is no such thing as their application to reality failing because reality lacks some feature that they supposedly depict. There is no difference, that is, between having to believe they apply (having to apply them for cognition to be possible) and their "really" applying.

In sum now, Kant's proof of causation, on our account, turns fundamentally on a partial causal theory of time. This account makes the Second Analogy basically one single argument where objective succession is first distinguished from objective coexistence, and then placed in a time series where the earlier necessarily advances to the later. It answers Hume both as to the nature of the causal tie or nexus (the necessary connection), and as to the universality of the causal principle. It is consistent with (indeed depends on) Kant's theory of time as a pure intuition (something immediately presentable by construction) in the Aesthetic, and it coheres with (indeed depends on) Kant's theory of cognition in the Deduction (bringing all possible appearances to the unity of apperception, by that unity governing the transcendental synthesis of imagination). The account is also consistent with (indeed demands) a rejection of phenomenalism via the connection of causation to substance. Despite this rejection of phenomenalism, it is consistent with Kant's transcendental idealism, according to which space and time are *mere* forms of intuition (are exclusively constructions within which proper reactions arise) and the categories (substance and causation), by being required for rules for spatiotemporal constructions, pertain only to possible appearances (proper reactions). Indeed the causal relation holds between proper reactions (the propriety of reacting one way necessarily advancing to the propriety of then acting another way), and states of substances are proper reactions (had in the course of keeping track of what affects).

9. MODERN DEVELOPMENTS IN CAUSATION

The modern version of a causal theory of time is developed in great detail by Reichenbach.[32] Unlike Kant's, his is a total causal theory where the causal relation fully constitutes time-order itself, not any necessary advance of an already given order. He can thus use a probabilistic conception of causation as long as he can recover the order and direction of time from it. For Kant, on the other hand, the exact role of the causal relation is to constitute the earlier time as necessarily advancing to or determining the later time, and hence causation must be deterministic. The "direction" of the causal relation (that what causes or produces precedes what is effected or produced) derives as well from this same exact role. Since the earlier time determines or yields the later, the relation that constitutes this must likewise be asymmetric. In sum, the relation between events whose role is to constitute the necessary advance of time must be both an asymmetric and deterministic one (the determining cause prior to the effect). Mackie is exactly wrong, then, when he says, regarding Kant, "Surprisingly, in view of the importance which it would appear to have for his thesis that objective time order depends upon causation, Kant has little to say about causal priority [the direction of causation]."[33]

Although the priority of cause to effect follows from Kant's view, it does so only to the extent that the linear advance of time is itself necessary. The necessary advance of such linear time-order can be regarded simply as the existence of that order in a set of possible worlds. This family of possible worlds, for Kant at least, is characterizable as constituting the "real" possibilities. Kant's view on the direction of causation does not apply outside this family of worlds. Thus, where time is cyclic or branching, a relation between events that constitutes or represents this order would likewise be cyclic or branching, violating respectively the direction and deterministic nature of causation.[34]

Kant's view depends essentially on the idea that time "advances," that the present "emerges" out of the past, and so forth. These features belong to what McTaggart[35] called the "A-series" and are features of time that many philosophers find troublesome. Mellor, for example, says, "I shall therefore ignore all accounts of causation which . . . involve time's flow, e.g., by using the way it 'fixes' events as they become present to say how causes fix their effects . . . for . . . time does not flow."[36] Now on Kant's view it is not how time fixes events as they become present, but how preceding time fixes present time that is used to say how causes fix their effects. Clearly though, Kant's is an account of causation that involves time's flow. I cannot go into a general discussion of McTaggart's arguments against time-passage, but I will note that the arguments are framed in terms of objective time, and seem not to apply to Kant's constructivist account of time. The reason is that on Kant's account, before and after (i.e., McTaggart's B-series) are not "constructible" apart from my presently being up to a certain stage in temporizing (the "cut" between the past and the present that belongs to McTaggart's A-series). Since the B-series exists in construction only as dependent on and fixed in terms of the A-series, McTaggart's argument, which depends in effect on an independent B-series, is blocked. It is nevertheless true that Kant's entire theory of causation, not just the direction of causation as on Mackie's account,[37] depends on time's "passage" or "flow."

What I wish to argue next is that Kant's view can incorporate or contain the view defended by Fair[38] and Salmon[39] that causation in the actual world is just transference of energy or momentum in processes or interactions. We note that Kant's causal theory of (the necessary advance of) time constitutes a functional analysis of the notion of causation. Causation is not taken as a primitive notion and then employed to constitute time-order. Rather, causation itself is defined by its role or function of being that connection of events that represents or constitutes the necessary advance of time. The fact that the cause produces or determines the effect or that the effect emerges or derives from the cause is a consequence of that role or function. Since the bond derives from the role or function, it holds between events insofar as these events play this role or serve this function. This leaves open what event pairs in fact play this role in the actual world, and whether those same pairs play it in all (really) possible worlds.[40] Thus it may be that in the actual world causation is always transference of energy or momentum. However, on Kant's view such transference is not definitive of causation per se, but simply characterizes what actually plays the role. It is the role itself that *defines* causation. In the *Metaphysical Foundations of Natural Science* (1786) Kant himself allows for a universal but *empirical* applicability of matter in motion as the causal connection in the actual world. The separation between this and the *Critique*'s account of causation is just the separation between the essential nature of causation per se and what causes what in actuality.

The contemporary view[41] of probable causation, or causation without determination, is of course incompatible with Kant's account. Anscombe contends that causation goes with notions such as "derives from," "comes from," "arises out of," and that these notions do not involve necessitation.[42] In Kant's theory, however, they do involve necessitation since the source of these notions is the advance of time-order, which is also a necessitating advance. Anscombe gives as an example of such non-necessitating causation a bomb connected to a Geiger counter. She says, "There would be no doubt of the cause of the reading or of the explosion if the bomb did go off."[43] But exactly what does she think the cause of the reading is? The particle having left the nucleus? There is some reason to hold that *until the reading* there is no event going on that leads to the reading. In other words, there is no preceding cause of the reading. This is just the standard understanding that in quantum mechanics there are not well-defined events that occur to produce the probable outcome. Mellor[44] gives the example of enough fissionable material causing the explosion although it only makes it incredibly probable. It seems to me that enough fissionable material precisely does not *make* the explosion happen; it only *makes* it incredibly probable. Hence, at best, it causes it to be highly probable for there to be an explosion, but not the explosion (the event) itself. Even if there is no such thing as probabilistic causation, the lack of causation in quantum mechanics should, on Kant's view, imply the failure of the necessary advance of time-order. The many-worlds interpretation of quantum mechanics comes closest to such a view if we think of the branching of the worlds as also being a branching of time.[45]

The contemporary regularity theory, according to which singular causation is simply a matter of falling under nomic generalizations, has its source in Hume. Mackie goes so far as to attribute such a view to Kant. According to Mackie, Kant "has nothing to say about any intimate tie between an individual cause and its effect."[46] Now Kant does hold that cases of causation always come under universal laws. He holds this by deriving *both* the intimate tie between a cause and its effect and the universality of causes (same cause/same effect) from the role of causation in representing the necessary advance of time. As we have seen, that advance is not only necessary (determining, yielding) from moment to moment, but the necessity itself has the same character universally for all transitions in time. The upshot, for Kant, is a singular causal tie that is also universally generalizable. The singular tie is not defined in terms of a nomic law, for the law itself is a law of the universality of the singular tie. Thus, the law would state something to the effect that an event of a certain type always yields or produces or necessitates an event of a second type. If anything, nomic lawfulness, as opposed to "accidental" universality, is to be defined in terms of the singular bond of causation rather than vice versa.

Kant's account of causation, as opposed to contemporary accounts, has all the advantages and disadvantages of being an account embedded in a more general metaphysical theory. The advantage I believe is obvious. Kant is able to derive (explain) the singular bond between cause and effect, the universality of particular causal connections (same cause/same effect), and the universal law of causation (every event has a cause) all from the role causation has in his account of the representation of reality. No contemporary theory I believe comes close to such a derivation of any of these three matters. The disadvantage is equally obvious. One must accept Kant's specifically constructivist view of time and the features he attributes to time (necessary advance) or his whole account collapses.

10. MODERN DEVELOPMENTS REGARDING SUBSTANCE

The most important contemporary view on the nature of substance derives from Quine's account of reference. First, on Quine's account reference to substances is a "posit" that is underdetermined by experience or by the data.[47] As such, there is no "flat-out" truth to the existence of substances in the world, but only truth relative to some theory, decision, language, and so forth. Second, for Quine, apart from analytical hypotheses (which do not derive from anything about a person), there is no sense to the idea of a person's referring to or using the concept of a substance.[48] Hence there is no "flat-out" truth to a person's having the concept of a substance, but only truth relative to a choice of analytical hypotheses.

To the idea of substance, all Quine finds is our use of the individuative apparatus of our language, consisting of "plural endings, pronouns, numerals, the 'is' of identity and its adaptations 'same' and 'other.'"[49] It is this apparatus that is undetermined as to its truth and inscrutable as to its employment in cognition. This individuative apparatus essentially corresponds to Kant's logical function of subject-predicate in being the "judgmental" or "intellectual" component of the notion of substance. Quine is surely right, as against Kant, that various aspects and components of judgment (not just subject-predicate) go with reference to substances. Now Quine looks for an empirical basis for the use of the individuative apparatus and finds none. In Kant's terms, the trouble is that the apparatus and the empirical are "heterogeneous," requiring the intermediation of a schema. Without schemata the functions of judgment for Kant are empty or represent no object (A 147/B 187). The schemata give both significance and applicability to the judgmental apparatus (A 146/B 186). The schemata, lastly, are determinations of time. What Quine lacks, then, and what keeps him from finding significance and applicability for the individuative apparatus is its use in the determination of time. Let us see how this works for the schema of substance.

The schema of substance for Kant is the permanence of the real functioning to represent the permanence of time, that is, to represent the fact that present time is a continuation of ongoing past time. As we have seen on a constructivist view of time, this representation involves being in the middle of a temporizing construction, which in turn requires that something present puts us beyond the beginning of the construction or procedure. But to say that it is proper to be at the mid-stage of a procedure tracking what is now present is eo ipso to say that what is now present is a substance (viz., something that has a past or that was), since a temporally extended procedure is proper with respect to it (the very reality that is present).

So, in particular, I cannot be in the middle of tracking a present "slice" or "stage." Since such a slice is a momentary existent, it cannot be proper to be so far along in keeping track of *it*. Nor can I presently be in the course of tracking a series of such slices or stages the last of which is now present, because this would require there being past stages (stages existing in the past) that only *subsequently* are represented by being in the course of a temporizing procedure. But then there would be pastness pertaining to things antecedent to being in the course of temporizing procedures with regard to them, which would take us beyond constructivist time (the *only time* Kant allows).

That there are substances as opposed to slices, then, may be underdetermined by the empirical data, but it is not underdetermined by the necessity of the existence of past time. The pure functional role of substance in determining time to have a past (on a constructivist construal of time) ensures that there are substances, not slices. It ensures, that is, the "flat-out" truth of the existence of substances in the world.

A person has a concept or a thought of what is present to him as being a substance if he thinks of himself as properly being up to a mid-stage in the procedure of tracking it. The concept of substance is "scrutable" then to the extent that there is evidence for thoughts of being at mid-stages of procedures. Suppose now that a person who has a procedure for baking a cake in ordered steps when he starts from scratch on his own comes into a room and sees the first three ingredients mixed in. Instead of putting in the fourth ingredient right away,[50] suppose he first quickly goes through the motions of putting in the first three ingredients. Then he evidences that he thinks of himself as being up to putting in the fourth ingredient in a procedure that begins with the first three. Similarly, suppose a person first quickly goes through the motions of timing to k and keeping track of what is present before he tracks while marking time at a slow pace from k+1. The person evidences that he thinks of himself as being up to k in tracking and keeping time (at a slow pace) with what is present. Hence he evidences that he thinks of what is present as a substance. In this way there is a "flat-out" truth (apart from analytical hypotheses) to a person's having the concept of a substance.[51]

NOTES

1. All parenthetical references are to *Critique of Pure Reason,* translated by Norman Kemp Smith (London: Macmillan, 1933).

2. For Kant a "true" (as opposed to an inductive) universal would hold that all events of a certain type *force or produce* events of a second type, and so would contain necessity.

3. For this view, see for example Spinoza's *Ethics,* Book I, Axioms IV, V, and Proposition III where the effect is said to be "apprehended" or "understood" by means of the cause.

4. For example, transformations between mathematical equations have to be *interpreted* as signifying real causal processes before the mathematical deducibility counts as an explanation of a transition in existence.

5. I believe Kant has in mind that the substantiality of something is not any property or feature of it (but rather the support or basis of all properties, as in Locke), and so the subject that pertains to the substantiality itself cannot also be any predicate (which pertains to features).

6. For the causal theory of time, see H. Mehlberg; *Time, Causality, and the Quantum Theory* (Dordrecht: D. Reidel, 1980).

7. See Kant's discussion of objectivity in the A Edition Deduction at A104–5, which is of a piece with his discussion in the Second Analogy.

8. A. J. Lovejoy, "On Kant's Reply to Hume," in *Kant: Disputed Questions,* edited by M. S. Gram (Chicago: Quadrangle Books, 1967).

9. Peter Strawson; *The Bounds of Sense* (London: Methuen & Co, 1966).

10. See, for example, James Van Cleve, "Four Recent Interpretations of Kant's Second Analogy," *Kant-Studien,* 64 (1973), p. 84. See also Henry Allison, *Kant's Transcendental Idealism* (New Haven: Yale University Press, 1983), p. 233.

11. This point is made both by Jonathan Bennett, *Kant's Analytic* (Cambridge: Cambridge University Press, 1966), p. 221, and James Van Cleve, "Four Recent Interpretations of Kant's Second Analogy," p. 80.

12. That objective succession itself involves, besides irreversibility, a connection to what precedes, is made clear in the paragraph at A 195/B240, where Kant says "For mere succession in my apprehension, if there be no rule determining the succession *in relation to something that precedes,* does not justify me in assuming any succession in the object" (italics mine). Kant here is saying clearly that some relationship to what precedes the succession (and hence something beyond the irreversibility in regard to the apprehension) is required for objective succession.

13. W. A. Suchting, "Kant's Second Analogy of Experience," in *Kant Studies Today,* edited by L. W. Beck (La Salle, IL: Open Court, 1969).

14. Norman Kemp Smith, *Commentary to Kant's Critique of Pure Reason*, 2nd ed. (London: Macmillan, 1923) pp. 363, 375.

15. See also A. C. Ewing, *Kant's Treatment of Causality* (London: K. Paul, Trench, Trubner & Co, 1924), p. 73, and Henry Allison, *Kant's Transcendental Idealism*, p. 222.

16. See also the formulation of the principle of the Analogies at A 177.

17. For the contention that his theory in the Analogies is inconsistent with his account in the Aesthetic, see for example T. K. Swing, *Kant's Transcendental Logic* (New Haven: Yale University Press, 1969), pp. 151–2, and R. P. Wolff, *Kant's Theory of Mental Activity* (Cambridge, MA: Harvard University Press, 1963), p. 263.

18. Toward the end of the Second Analogy (A 207/B 253), Kant argues that alterations are continuous *because* time is a continuous magnitude; that is, the alterations do not represent continuity but conform to the distinct continuity of time. This shows that Kant does not hold a causal theory of time magnitude.

19. The causal theory, *in this sense*, is not a version of the relational theory since it does not add any specifically temporal objective relations to time-construction. Rather, it adds the causal relation among proper reactions *instead of* any objective temporal relations. Equivalently, it adds a *dynamical* component to the constructivist account of time. As an analogy, adding a dynamical component to the notion of straightness (geodesic) in terms of force-free motion, is not adding a further (relational or substantival) spatial component to that notion. Likewise, adding a dynamical component in terms of causation to the notion of time-order or time-series (specifically to its aspect of necessary advance) is not adding a further (relational or substantival) temporal component.

20. See B 4, where Kant says "Necessity and strict universality are thus sure criteria of *a priori* knowledge, and are inseparable from one another."

21. Once again the fact that substance (permanence of the real) is no more perceivable than time itself is no objection to Kant's argument. For this objection, see Paul Guyer, *Kant and the Claims of Knowledge* (Cambridge: Cambridge University Press, 1987), p. 219. There is no objective continuous flow of time to keep up with, while tracking what is real (what affects) is holding or moving attention continuously. That Kant has to go to something objectively dynamical rather than objectively temporal is required by time's being *merely* a form of intuition.

22. This answers Guyer's second objection (*Kant and the Claims of Knowledge*, pp. 220–1) that Kant equivocates in going from substance as permanent (or enduring) to substance as the bearer of properties. There is no "too hasty" transition here. The only way to represent past

appearances (proper reactions) is to represent them in past time. The only way to represent past time is by its being geared to trackable existence (the permanent). Hence, past appearances can be represented at all only as geared to trackable existence (= as determinations of the permanent). There is a difference between focusing on what is real and keeping track of it, versus specifically reacting to it. This, I claim, is the difference between substance and the "properties" (proper reactions) it bears.

23. Paul Guyer (*Kant and the Claims of Knowledge*, p. 260) makes the point clearly and definitively that the connection of causation to substance is compatible with the argument of the Second Analogy.

24. That Kant holds such a substance-based theory of time is clear from the paragraph at A 189/B 232 of the First Analogy (beginning "Substances in the field of appearances . . ."). Each substance is a substratum of time determination. He does believe that the time series relative to various substances must also be relatable to one another, but this is a further matter.

25. Schopenhauer considers such cases to be coincident successions (as when I first leave a house and then a tile falls on my head). He thinks they are therefore not causal, but nevertheless objective, thereby refuting Kant's Second Analogy. For this objection of Schopenhauer's as well as a reply, see Norman Kemp Smith, *Commentary to Kant's Critique of Pure Reason*, pp. 378–9.

26. This is shown, I believe, by what Kant holds about the series of appearances in past time in the First Antinomy. Objective states of substances would have to form a finite or an infinite series, whereas the propriety of reacting can be limitless without being a finite or infinite totality. See, for example, A 495/B 523.

27. See footnotes 8 and 9 above.

28. In the paragraph at A 110, Kant has said there is *one single experience* that encompasses all (proper) perception, just as "there is only one space and time in which all modes of appearance . . . occur." It is this single experience (viz., the entire spatio-temporal scope of appearances) that is signified by "a possible experience in general" in the sentence we have quoted.

29. The imagination is characterized by Kant as "the faculty of representing in intuition an object that is *not itself present*" (B 151). If so, then *pure* imagination must be a faculty of representing in *pure* intuition what is not present or what is remote. This is exactly our contention that the spatio-temporal manifold is required not basically for organizing what is presently given, but more fundamentally for representing what is not present at all (remote appearances).

30. For a more detailed discussion of his theory of cognition, see chapters 3 and 4 in my book *Themes in Kant's Metaphysics and Ethics* (Washington, DC: Catholic University Press, 2004).

31. Barry Stroud, "Transcendental Arguments" (1968), reprinted in *Kant on Pure Reason*, edited by R.C.S. Walker (Oxford: Oxford University Press, 1982). Although it is true that there are empirical elements (trackability, regularity) that are necessary for cognition, it is also true that Kant is not deducing these elements. For an interesting discussion of such empirical elements of cognition, see Kenneth R. Westphal, "Affinity, Idealism, and Naturalism: The Stability of Cinnabar and the Possibility of Experience," *Kant-Studien*, 88, 2 (1997).

32. Hans Reichenbach, *The Direction of Time* (Berkeley: University of California Press, 1956).

33. J. L. Mackie, *The Cement of the Universe* (Oxford: Clarendon Press, 1974), p. 90.

34. This is just to say that for Kant "backwards causation" and non-deterministic causation are logically possible. General Relativity, though perhaps allowing for cyclic time, does not allow for branching time. Since *locally everywhere* the earlier necessarily advances to or determines the later, the relation between events constituting such advance would still be universal deterministic causation.

35. J. M. E. McTaggart, *The Nature of Existence* (Cambridge: 1927), Book 5, Chapter 33.

36. D. H. Mellor, *The Facts of Causation* (London and New York: Routledge, 1995).

37. J. L. Mackie, *The Cement of the Universe*, Chapter 7.

38. David Fair, "Causation and the Flow of Energy," *Erkenntnis*, 14 (1979).

39. Wesley Salmon, "Causality, Production and Propagation" (1980), reprinted in *Causation*, edited by Ernest Sosa and Michael Tooley (New York: Oxford University Press, 1993).

40. A necessary connection between cause and effect deriving from its role leaves it open as to what causes what, just as an "authority connection" between sergeant and private leaves it open as to who (which person) has authority over whom.

41. G. E. M. Anscombe, "Causality and Determination," (1971), in *Causation*, edited by Ernest Sosa and Michael Tooley (New York: Oxford University Press, 1993). See also D. H. Mellor, *The Facts of Causation*.

42. G. E. M. Anscombe, "Causality and Determination," pp. 91–2.

43. G. E. M. Anscombe, "Causality and Determination," p. 101.

44. D. H. Mellor, *The Facts of Causation*, Chapter 5. Again, as in the Anscombe example, no exact events go on between stages of the explosion process and so there is no causal chain from the sufficient material to stages and from stages to other stages.

45. For Kant, however, such branching is not "really" possible since there are *no constructions* for going off into incompatible future times.

46. J. L. Mackie, *The Cement of the Universe*, p. 90.

47. See Willard Van Orman Quine, *Word and Object* (Cambridge, MA: MIT Press, 1960), p. 22.

48. W.V.O. Quine, *Word and Object*, p. 73.

49. W. V. Quine, *Ontological Relativity and Other Essays* (New York: Columbia University Press, 1969), p. 33.

50. By itself, this might only be evidence that he has the thought of beginning with a later series of ingredients when certain ingredients are already mixed.

51. I deal with the "scrutability" of substance in detail in *A Representation of the World: A Naturalized Semantics* (New York: Peter Lang, 1996).

7 Kant and transcendental arguments

The idea of a transcendental argument has sometimes been held to be Kant's greatest contribution to philosophy. Such arguments can be found before Kant, but nobody was so clear about them or gave them such a central role. Many of Kant's transcendental arguments have been criticised and reconstructed again and again, and new arguments have been devised along similar lines. But there has also been debate about what exactly transcendental arguments are, how they work, and what they can hope to achieve. There is room too for dispute about their role in Kant's own thought. Here an important question concerns the relation between transcendental arguments and transcendental idealism. It is a mistake to think Kant's transcendental arguments led him into transcendental idealism, but it remains interesting to ask how far the use of transcendental arguments does lead toward idealist conclusions. Kant's followers are still divided between those who reject and those who defend the connection.

Kant does not use the term "transcendental argument" in the way we do, so we cannot look to him for a definition.[1] He does call transcendental some of the types of argument he uses, notably transcendental deductions and transcendental expositions, but as people use the term nowadays Kant's transcendental expositions are not really transcendental arguments, since their premises assume too much. His transcendental deductions are (or most of them), but his terminology is never very consistent, and what matters is the type of argument and not what name he gives it. Roughly, transcendental arguments are arguments of the form "There is experience; it is a condition of the possibility of experience that P; therefore, P." Kant sometimes substitutes "cognition" for experience, and other writers start from "conscious awareness" or "intelligible thought" instead. On other occasions experience (or cognition, etc.) is specified as being of a certain general kind, and Kant is often interested in the conditions required for experience of a *spatiotemporal* character. In all versions, though, "conditions of the possibility" (Kant's usual phrase) must mean "necessary conditions," and these conditions are understood not to be empirical conditions (like the need for oxygen) but conditions that can be shown to be required *a priori*. This fits with Kant's own remark, "I call all cognition transcendental that is occupied not so much with objects but rather with our mode of cognition of objects insofar as this is to be possible *a priori*" (A 11–12/B 25):[2] in other words, transcendental knowledge has to do with the *a priori* necessary conditions under which cognition is possible.

Transcendental arguments matter to Kant, and to many of those who have used them more recently, because they offer a way of answering the sceptic and providing a justification for knowledge claims – which is why he often calls them "deductions," meaning by that, justifications of legitimacy (cf. A 84f./B 116f.).[3] Some people have seen their function as lying elsewhere, in delineating our conceptual scheme and determining which of its elements are the most basic, but these are complementary functions, and Kant was concerned with both of them.[4] But why, one might ask, should arguments against scepticism be important? It may seem eccentric to spend time trying to answer the sceptic who doubts the existence of the external world, for such doubts can seem rather foolish.

The attempt to answer scepticism is trying to do two things. One is to understand how scepticism can be tackled in general. Some kinds of scepticism need to be taken seriously: there are plenty of sceptics about God, about morality, about aesthetic value; and if we can see how to tackle doubts about the external world, we may be better able to see whether there is an answer to people like these. The second aim is to see how our beliefs relate to the evidence we receive through our senses; and this is of interest for its own sake. Kant thought it could be understood only by seeing that certain particular synthetic *a priori* principles are at work, principles that can be justified by their indispensability for any experience or knowledge of the world. Some philosophers have tried to dispense with this notion of justification, but it is not dispensable.[5] The need to distinguish beliefs that are justified from those that are not is essential to everyday practice, to scientific theorising, to questions about God and morality, and other disputed matters.

It is worth mentioning two examples of pre-Kantian arguments to show that something must be so, because otherwise experience or knowledge would not be possible. One is Aristotle's argument for the principle of non-contradiction: someone may profess to doubt the principle, but anyone with whom we can have an argument must treat it as reliable; anyone who makes an assertion must thereby exclude its negation, and is thus committed to the principle.[6] A similar argument is used by the rationalists to defend their reliance on reason. Descartes describes the "natural light" as the ultimate faculty we have to rely on, and Spinoza, more explicitly, says that sceptics who doubted the initial clear and distinct idea could know nothing, would lack self-consciousness, and would have to "be regarded as automata, completely lacking a mind."[7]

Kant made transcendental arguments central to philosophy. They did not, however, lead him to transcendental idealism. It is sometimes thought that he argued first that certain conditions – spatiotemporal ordering, the applicability of the categories – are required for experience to be possible; and that he then reflected that there would be no *guarantee* of the possibility of experience unless the world as we know it, the world of appearances, were transcendentally ideal, constituted in part by our minds' supplying these conditions to it.[8] There are passages that do support such a reading (perhaps A 114, B 167), but this would be a poor argument for idealism of any kind. There is no reason why the possibility of experience should have to be guaranteed; indeed not even transcendental idealism could guarantee it, for our minds might cease to exist or might never have existed. To show that space, time, and the categories are required for experience is only to show that unless the world had this character we should not be able to experience it. It is to say nothing about how it is that the world comes to have this character.[9]

So far from grounding his transcendental idealism on transcendental arguments, Kant became a transcendental idealist before he thought of transcendental arguments. Thus he uses transcendental arguments within a context that is already committed to transcendental idealism. This is not to say that his real reason for transcendental idealism was a convincing one. Ironically enough, he showed its inadequacy himself, and precisely by his discovery of transcendental arguments. But he never noticed that.

I

Kant's fundamental concern was with how we can have knowledge that is genuinely about the world, and yet independent of experience: the problem of how synthetic *a priori* knowledge is possible. It is hard to see how we can know things about the world that we have not learned empirically. What distinguishes such knowledge from pure prejudice? This has seemed to some people a good ground for rejecting the possibility of synthetic *a priori* knowledge altogether. Kant was in no doubt that it was possible, partly because Hume's attempt at a consistent empiricism had led to an intolerable scepticism. One cannot avoid some reliance on *a priori* principles in getting to know the world, for what is given in experience constantly requires interpretation, and to interpret it we must have principles that cannot themselves be derived from experience. These principles must be true to the world if our interpretations are to be reliable, but their truth cannot be established empirically, for it is only through relying on just such principles that we can test against experience a claim that does more than reflect the content of the experience.[10]

But if we know truths about the world without deriving them from experience, and without being able to verify them empirically, how is this knowledge possible? Plato had suggested, perhaps without complete conviction, that we know them through recollection of the Forms. Descartes thought our clear and distinct convictions were guaranteed true by God. Kant did not take Plato's idea seriously, and he rejected Descartes', because it rested on circular reasoning and because it would remove from these *a priori* truths the necessity they must possess in their own right (B 167).[11] With even more vigour he rejected a simple reliance on self-evidence. His predecessor Crusius had claimed that "whatever we can only think as true is true, and what we simply cannot think, or can only think as false, is false."[12] But Crusius himself believed that claims like "God is in space" were amongst the things that can only be thought of as true. Kant objected that Crusius' position "encourages all sorts of wild notions and every pious and speculative brainstorm" (10:131). Claims of self-evidence will not help us.

As Kant saw the matter, the position was simply this:

There are only two possible cases in which synthetic representation and its objects can come together, necessarily relate to each other, and, as it were, meet each other. Either if the object alone makes the representation possible, or if the representation alone makes the object possible. If it is the first, then this relation is only empirical, and the representation is never possible *a priori*.   (A 92/B 124–5)

The *a priori* elements in our knowledge must therefore be brought to experience by us, and the world that we know by their means must be transcendentally ideal: its reality is dependent on us and on these *a priori* conditions that have their origin in us.

This was, of course, a radical position to adopt and a surprising one. Kant thought there was no alternative, given the bankruptcy of the empiricist approach. It took him some time, however, before he was prepared to adopt this solution in its full generality.[13] Initially he thought of the problem as particularly pressing for mathematics, and above all for geometry, which he took to be a body of *a priori* truths about the nature of space. In 1768 he had concluded that the difference between a left and a right hand can be understood only if space has its own nature that we are somehow aware of *a priori*, so that we can recognise the different relationships of the hands to space as a whole. Thus he thought we know about space *a priori*, and indeed know it to be Euclidean; and he thought analogous considerations applied to time. But if space and time are independent of us, how can we know about them *a priori*?

In his *Dissertation* of 1770 he resolved the problem, so far as space and time were concerned, by saying that space and time are not "objective and real," but arise "from the nature of the mind" (2:400, 403). They are not for that reason fictions. They are "formal principles of the sensible world," the world that we can know through our senses, for only under these forms, due to ourselves, can we know it (2:402, 405). They are not, however, features of the underlying intelligible world: that we can know only through our rational faculties.

As he soon came to recognise, though, this is not satisfactory. It provides an explanation of how we can have synthetic *a priori* knowledge about space and time: space and time are not independent of us, but read into the sensible world by us. Yet it also asserts that there are other things we can know about the world by using our rational faculties, that is, other synthetic *a priori* truths. There have to be, if we are to apply concepts that take us beyond what is given to us, like the concepts of causality and objectivity, or substance. In retrospect, it may seem obvious to try the same solution for these principles as for space and time, and that is what Kant does in the *Critique of Pure Reason*. But it seemed far from obvious to him at first, and his letter to Marcus Herz of 21 February 1772 shows him finding the problem hard to resolve. This was partly because he had come to the conclusion that there was a sharp and radical difference to be drawn between space and time, on the one hand, and our concepts, on the other; contrary to Leibniz's idea that sensation was just "confused thought," there was a difference of kind between sensibility and understanding, with space and time being the forms of sensibility. The solution worked for space and time, the forms of sensibility: they are our means of ordering what is given to us. But how could one go further and account for our knowledge of these other principles?

The answer of the *Critique* is that concepts like causality and substance also supply us with ways to order experience. Such fundamental concepts he calls categories. These concepts we ourselves supply in the ordering of what is given to us in sensation, and they are therefore conditions on which the nature of the sensible or phenomenal world depends. This world is objective in an everyday sense, in that everyone can make mistakes about it, so that it is no mere figment of anyone's imagination, and it is shared by all of us. It does not, however, have a reality wholly independent of our minds and our cognitive capacities. It is therefore "transcendentally ideal," and must be contrasted with things as they are in themselves, wholly independently of us. About these no synthetic *a priori* knowledge is possible, and therefore no knowledge at all. For knowledge about them cannot be read off from experience – the object alone does not make the representation possible; nor does the representation make the object possible, since their nature is entirely independent of our ways of thinking and experiencing the world.

One problem that had to be overcome, if this solution was to work, was of how to avoid the conclusion that we could read into the world whatever concepts we felt like. It is here that transcendental arguments come in. They did not appear in the *Dissertation*. In the *Critique of Pure Reason* Kant sets the problem out explicitly, by asking how we are to show that *a priori* concepts like those of substance and cause do apply to the world, in contrast to those of fortune and fate (A 84/B 116–17). We cannot read off from experience that there are substances and causes. The categories require instead a transcendental deduction, a proof of legitimacy. The deduction that he offers is a transcendental argument. It contains a good many obscurities, so there is room for dispute about exactly how it goes, but its aim is to show that experience is possible only if the categories do have application in the experienced world. "They must be recognized as *a priori* conditions of the possibility of experience.... Concepts that supply the objective ground of the possibility of experience are necessary just for that reason" (A 94/B 126). To show them necessary is to show them legitimate.

A key step in the argument is to show that all experience requires synthesis, "the action of putting different representations together with each other and comprehending their manifoldness in one cognition" (A 77/B 103). Judgement involves synthesis, and Kant argues that all experience requires a capacity to ascribe one's experiences to a unitary subject, which in turn requires a capacity to judge how things are as opposed to how they seem. These arguments have been highly influential, from Fichte's contention that consciousness requires the positing of the self and the not-self through to Wittgenstein's argument against a private language and his thoughts about rule-following. Kant uses them to show the need to apply categories by observing that judgement can only take place in accordance with the forms of judgement revealed by logic, for "the **categories** are nothing other than these very functions for judging, insofar as the manifold of a given intuition is determined with regard to them" (B 143). He argues also that even where judgement is not involved, in the most elementary kind of concept-application and in pre-conceptual awareness, synthesis is still required and must be category-governed (B 161). His account of the synthetic character of concept-application has also been a decisive contribution, rendering permanently untenable the British empiricists' quasi-pictorial account of ideas as copies of sense-impressions.

It might be said that in giving so large a part to synthesis Kant is using at least *this* transcendental argument to make a case for transcendental idealism. Synthesis is "a blind though indispensable function of the soul, without which we would have no cognition at all" (A 78/B 103); an act of synthesis is "an action of the understanding," and "we cannot represent anything as combined in the object without having previously combined it ourselves" (B 130). But that would be a bad argument for transcendental idealism, and Kant does not offer it as such. The considerations about synthesis can support idealism only *given* the argument for idealism Kant has already used, the argument that what we do not read off from the world we must supply to it. They have no independent force at all.

Certainly, synthesis is carried out by the mind, but the question is whether the mind puts things together in a way that corresponds to a reality independent of it. Since (as Kant says) in making any judgement we are putting items together in thought, this is the same question as we had with judgements. Kant's solution there was to say that either the object makes the representation possible, or else the representation makes the object possible. With empirical judgements the object makes the representation possible. The same will be true with empirical synthesis: here the mind's putting-together will be guided by experience. If there is such a thing as *a priori* synthesis – and Kant argues that there must be – then, certainly, Kant will say that the representation makes the object possible; our synthesis contributes to that ordering of things that constitutes the world we can know about, the world of appearances. But his reason for saying this rests entirely on his principle that since the object does not make the representation possible, the representation must make the object possible. The discovery that synthesis, even *a priori* synthesis, plays so large a role in our knowledge provides no new argument for transcendental idealism, though some have thought it did.[14]

In the Transcendental Aesthetic Kant had already set out his case for transcendental idealism, but without relying – at least consciously – on transcendental arguments. As in the *Dissertation*, his case rests on the thesis that since we have nonempirical knowledge about space and time, it must be provided through our ordering of the world of appearances. He does claim at A 87/B 119–20 to have given a transcendental deduction of space and time, but all he seems to mean is that he has shown that our knowledge of them is legitimate because of their status as transcendentally ideal. It is true that the Aesthetic contains arguments called transcendental expositions, but these are not transcendental arguments in our sense, for they *start* from the assumption that we have synthetic *a priori* knowledge about space and time, and so have no force against anyone who is not prepared to concede that we do have the synthetic *a priori* knowledge in question.

In the Aesthetic Kant feels no need for transcendental arguments, for there is no need – as there is with the categories – to show that space and time are not mere fictions like "fortune" or "fate." He does raise the question whether space and time are the *only possible* forms of intuition, but says that "we cannot decide this" (B 72, cf. A 27/ B 43). He does not appear much interested in the question: what matters is that they are *our* forms of intuition. Others, more recently, have taken the question up, and argued that without space and time – or something very like them – experience would not be possible because there would be no way of distinguishing or interrelating the items experienced. Thus Strawson argued that all experience must be temporal, but tentatively canvassed the possibility of some alternative order to space. Bennett took the idea further. Others have disagreed, in particular Evans, who has argued that spatial as well as temporal order is indispensable for any experience in which particulars can be reidentified. But this is to go well beyond Kant himself.[15]

Because it treats the categories in a highly abstract way, the transcendental deduction of the categories does not fully discharge its task of showing the legitimacy of our ordinary concepts of cause, substance, objectivity, and so forth, thereby distinguishing them from the concept of witchcraft. The argument is carried through in the Analytic of Principles by a further set of transcendental arguments, in which the abstract categories are considered as applying to spatiotemporal experience. Kant argues that synthetic *a priori* principles are needed to govern this application. The abstract category of cause, for example, is just the concept of something depending on another,[16] but in spatiotemporal experience it must be applied through the experience of constant conjunctions of event-types, where we take the constancy to be governed by a rule. Otherwise we could not distinguish objective from subjective time-series in the way that spatiotemporal experience requires. The principle underlying this is that of the Second Analogy: "All alterations occur in accordance with the law of the connection of cause and effect" (B 232). Similar arguments are offered for the other categories, but it seems reasonably clear that it was the three categories of relation, namely, substance, cause, and community that Kant was most concerned about. Certainly it is his arguments about substance and cause that have attracted most attention since. Critics have often felt that there is something in these arguments, but usually that they prove less than Kant claims for them; they remain the subject of much discussion.

Later in the *Critique* Kant gives us another transcendental deduction: the deduction of the ideas of pure reason. It is developed more clearly in the *Critique of the Power of Judgment*, where it is described as the deduction of the "transcendental principle" of "the formal purposiveness of nature" (5:181).[17] Until recently it has been less studied than the deduction of the categories, but Kant thought it very important. It is a transcendental argument of a different kind, because it is not meant to establish a truth about the empirically real (and transcendentally ideal) world. The ideas of pure reason are concepts of unity and completeness that extend beyond what any amount of experience can exhibit, and their deduction does not seek to show that the world actually contains these kinds of unity and completeness – which would amount to its being systematically governed by unitary and comprehensible laws, as though purposively designed. Instead, it aims to show that we are justified in proceeding as if it did, and indeed that we must believe (or "presuppose") that it does.

[T]he law of reason to seek unity is necessary, since without it we would have no reason, and without that, no coherent use of the understanding, and, lacking that, no sufficient mark of empirical truth; thus in regard to the latter we simply have to presuppose the systematic unity of nature as objectively valid and necessary. (A 651/B 679)[18]

Science can only approximate towards finding this unity, and its approximations are always tentative. The complete unity could only be found in a totality that goes beyond all possible experience, and the order concerned is one that we could never ourselves supply: it depends on how things turn out empirically, and so on the character of the data that our minds have to deal with. Yet Kant denies that reason gives us only a methodological principle, requiring us to look for unity: we must also assume that unity is there to be found (A 661/B 689).[19] His argument is that we have no other way to think: that is, if we are to think consistently and coherently.

The earlier arguments showed that certain principles were straightforwardly true, within the world of appearances. What made it possible for Kant to say that was his transcendental idealism. The principles established were constitutive of the world of appearances. This time, the principle is called regulative, not constitutive, and the argument gives us a conclusion about what we must believe. Kant thinks we cannot get beyond belief to truth, because the truth of the belief cannot be secured by his transcendental idealism. However, we must notice that there are (though not very explicitly) other arguments present in the *Critique* to conclusions that go beyond the world of appearances. These are the arguments to show that there must be a subject of experiences that does not itself belong to the world of appearances, and that there must be things in themselves.[20] Kant never spells these out clearly enough, but his transcendental idealism depends on them. He might have found it hard to say why in these cases we can show how things must be, whereas in the deduction of the ideas we can show only how we must believe them to be.

He has often been construed as doubting that there are things in themselves, but the evidence of his commitment to them is very strong.[21] Without things in themselves there would be nothing to supply the data that our minds can order, nothing *a posteriori* in experience, nothing that does not have its origin in our mental activity. The subject in itself is equally indispensable. He says that "the subject of the categories cannot, by thinking them, obtain a concept of itself as an object of the categories; for in order to think them, it must take its pure self-consciousness . . . as its ground," though nothing can be known about this subject (B 422). It seems obvious that we must know that it exists and is, indeed, a subject; and that is something. Without a subject there would have been no experience. Kant is keen to point out that, given transcendental idealism, there is no way to know anything about conditions for the identity of the subject, and so no way to know that the subject is coterminous with what we think of as a human being. We can grant him that. However, without a subject of experience there could not be experience; this seems to be a very straightforward transcendental argument. Kant never calls it such, and is embarrassed by it, because it shows something that he was never prepared clearly to recognise. In establishing synthetic *a priori* propositions, transcendental arguments can have a life of their own. They do not depend on transcendental idealism. If it is really a necessary condition for experience that *p*, then *p* must be true, even though *p* is neither read off from the world nor made constitutive of it.

Kant is unnecessarily obscure about this in the *Critique* because
he originally invoked transcendental arguments just to show which
a priori requirements held within the world of appearances. He took
himself to have established already that synthetic *a priori* judgements are confined to the world of experience, by means of his thesis that either "the object alone makes the representation possible"
(as in the case of *a posteriori* knowledge) or else "the representation
alone makes the object possible" (A 92/B 124–5). He failed to see that
transcendental arguments provide a way of establishing synthetic *a
priori* truths that belong to neither category: they can be known to
be true because without them experience would not be possible at
all. There is no reason why these truths should not concern things
as they are in themselves.

This puts in question the whole basis for transcendental idealism. Kant's case for it was that knowledge must either be read off
from the world empirically, or read into it by us. If transcendental
arguments provide a way of justifying synthetic *a priori* knowledge,
independently of transcendental idealism, that case has gone.

II

Kant's immediate successors had doubts about his use of transcendental arguments, and their primary interest focussed largely on idealism and the dispensability of things in themselves. In Reinhold and
Fichte there are arguments we could call transcendental, but they
demand more than Kant does for the first premise, since they require
it to be self-grounding; and increasingly amongst Kant's successors
it is the ontological considerations that come to dominate rather
than the attack on scepticism.[22] It never occurred to Kant's realist
opponents that it might be possible to use transcendental arguments
against transcendental idealism and in defence of the principles concerned. This strategy was not properly worked through until com-
paratively recently: it was given its fullest development by Strawson.

Strawson and others aimed to reconstruct Kant without the idealism. Transcendental arguments could show us how the world must
be, if experience is to be possible. It must be a world of objects,
extended in time and arguably in space (or something like it), reasonably regular and causally ordered; it must contain subjects of
experience, who however need not be mysterious or unknowable,

since they can just be embodied human persons. Kant, they felt, had got the transcendental arguments very nearly right, except for the mistake of transcendental idealism. When they work, they establish conclusions about reality – the only reality there is. Strawson thought that many of Kant's arguments do not quite work, but are closely related to arguments that do. Thus Kant failed to show that every event must have a cause, but a related argument does show that most events must have causes. Likewise Kant failed to establish that there must be something that is absolutely permanent through time, as he claimed in the First Analogy, but did show that there must be relatively permanent objects. Otherwise experience would not be possible. And there is no way for us to play a part in guaranteeing the possibility of experience by somehow reading these things into the world. Unless the world were this way, experience would not be possible and we would not be here.[23]

The main objection to this approach was raised by Stroud. He contended that transcendental arguments do not establish conclusions about the world. They may be able to show that it is a condition of our having experience that we must have certain beliefs, or deploy certain concepts. But to go on from there, and show that the world must match those beliefs, or contain instances of those concepts, requires an extra step, to ensure that our ways of thinking match the way the world is. That could be achieved by using some sort of verification principle, to the effect that the intelligibility of our thoughts depends on our capacity to establish whether or not they are true to the real world. But then there would be no need for transcendental arguments since the verification principle itself would show that the world must meet the appropriate conditions.[24]

Stroud did not try to *prove* that no transcendental argument can establish conclusions about how the world really is; he argued that the transcendental arguments people have produced do not take us beyond conclusions about the concepts and beliefs we must have about the world. Cassam clarified the situation further, by suggesting that a transcendental argument can be divided into two elements, a Conceptual Component and a Satisfaction Component. The Conceptual Component would show that if experience is to be possible, there are certain distinctions we must draw or certain concepts we must use. The Satisfaction Component would show that the world must be of a certain character if we are to be able to draw these distinctions or apply these concepts: it would show "that *only* a world of this kind could satisfy the requirements elaborated in the Conceptual Component."[25] It is natural to see the first component as essentially internal to one's conceptual system, while the second seeks to step outside it. A merit of this formulation is that it states the Conceptual Component not in terms of what we must believe, but in terms of the concepts and distinctions we must draw. The concept of belief is a complex one, but it is not immediately obvious that there is anything people *have* to believe as a condition of having experience. The sceptic who claims to believe nothing may be very irrational, but then some people are.

Put like this, it does seem unclear how the Satisfaction Component could ever be supplied, except by adopting either verificationism, or else an idealism that equates the world of appearances with the world as we take it to be. As verificationism seemed unsustainable, this line of thought began to make it seem plausible that transcendental arguments do lead to transcendental idealism after all.

Yet we did have a transcendental argument to show that there must be at least one subject of experience. It is not clear why there could not also be other arguments to conclusions about how the world must really be. There is, of course, a sense in which any argument whatever must move within a system of thoughts and concepts, but if there were a general concern about whether our system of thoughts and concepts can ever be true to the world, no argument at all could ever answer it. It would be a concern that we could never take seriously. It is important, though sometimes difficult, clearly to distinguish this quite general concern from the more specific worries that arguments can answer; and there seems to be no reason in principle why transcendental arguments should not establish truths about fully independent reality, in any sense in which any argument can. It is partly the failure to distinguish clearly between these concerns that explains why people have been so willing to accept Stroud's suggestion that transcendental arguments can only establish conclusions about what we must believe.

It is not the only reason, though. Many transcendental arguments have depended at the final stage, the stage that takes us from concepts or beliefs to how things are, on a semantic step that looks dubious. To say they must rely on some form of verification principle is not quite right. They depend on a step that says: "Unless the world were thus and so, we could not deploy the concept C" or " ... we could not distinguish A from B," where it has been argued that experience requires that we have the concept C or distinguish A from B. *One* way of making this step is to bring on a verification principle that says that we could not have the concept, or make the claimed distinction, except in a world that would allow us the empirical means to decide whether the concept has application or verify the claim. But usually people do not rely on anything so general as a principle of verification. They argue directly that we could not possess the concept, or the make the claim, unless (in one version) the world itself contained real instances of the concepts involved; or (in another version) the world itself provided us with adequate grounds for applying them.

One form the argument has taken recently is to say that our concepts are "not in the head," and that the very possession of a concept like "water" depends on there being water in the real world. If this theory of concept-possession could be substantiated, it would encourage a range of arguments from premises like "I am imagining water" to the reality of water. That, however, would not be a good way of proving the existence of water, for the premise is now less evident than it appears: if there is no such thing as water, my thought cannot have been rightly expressed (it cannot have been water that I was imagining). Where the Conceptual Component shows that a concept is necessary for experience, it is hard to see much plausibility in the idea that any such theory of concept-possession applies to it.[26]

In an alternative form, the argument is that the concept concerned could not "get a grip" on the world unless certain conditions were met by the world. The concept of causality could not "get a grip" unless there were regularities on which one could rely.[27] The idea of something existing unperceived could not "get a grip" except in a spatial world that provides some other place for the unperceived thing to occupy.[28] And unless the concept could "get a grip" in this way, we could not possess it. But here it seems proper to ask why we could not. Just *how much* regularity is supposed to be required before the concept of causality can get its grip – or *how much* of the appropriate patterning of experience is needed to provide for existence unperceived?[29] There can be no clear answer to this. What I will need must depend on my background information and my willingness to make assumptions about how my experience fits together. But more importantly, this approach leaves it unclear why the use of the concept makes any demand at all on what the world is like. To employ the concept in describing my experience, my *experience* must exhibit some pattern, but nothing follows about the world; unless we can assume that my experience somehow matches the world. So we are still left with a conclusion about our concepts and beliefs, and not about the way the world is.

However, setting these issues aside, we need to have a closer look at the structure of transcendental arguments. There are difficulties here that threaten the whole method, whether as used by Kant or by recent philosophers. First, it is unclear where the argument is supposed to start. Kant starts with the claim that there is experience, or cognition, but it is not obvious what this amounts to, nor why it is the right place to start. He sometimes says that experience is the self-conscious knowledge of objects of the senses,[30] but could there not be a kind of experience that is not self-conscious? And could there not be a kind of experience that is not of *objects*, at least if objects are taken to have an independent existence? In fact the deduction of the categories includes a step that seems designed to show that experience must be self-conscious, and then another to show that it must allow for a conception of objectivity, but it would have been helpful if the initial conception of experience had been made clearer at the outset. Strawson starts from the sort of awareness that one can make sense of to oneself; Wittgenstein and Davidson and others look for the conditions of intelligible thought. It is not evident what dictates, or should dictate, the choice of starting point. And is it supposed to be an empirical fact that there is experience, or intelligible thought? Kant wants his transcendental arguments to establish synthetic *a priori* truths, but an *a priori* conclusion cannot be derived from an empirical premise.

The second premise says "If there is experience (or whatever), then...." Is this supposed to be analytic? Conceptual analysis can reach surprising and important conclusions, as (for example) in yielding Gödel's theorem, but if the conclusion of a transcendental argument is supposed to follow analytically from its first premise, precision about the first premise is all the more important. If it is vague, there is the risk that we can make it precise only by building the conclusion into the premise and so trivializing the argument. Yet there are difficulties also in the idea that the second premise is not analytic. Kant himself insists that synthetic *a priori* propositions outside mathematics can be warranted only by transcendental arguments (A 737/B 765, A 783/B 811). The second premise must, as we have seen, be *a priori*, and if it is not to be analytic, it must be synthetic. But if it is itself to be synthetic *a priori*, it can be warranted only by another transcendental argument, which itself must be warranted by another, and so on: a vicious regress.[31]

In any case, the first premise must evidently start with some claim, and draw out its necessary conditions, whether they be analytically necessary or not. It therefore operates, as all arguments do, within a particular conceptual scheme, and whatever conclusions it yields can hold only within that conceptual scheme. So it is objected that Kant's claim to the universality of his categories must be unfounded. All he can do is delimit the requirements of his own conceptual system. He has no way to show that they must be shared by other conceptual systems, and he has no way to show that his own conceptual system may not change over time and be succeeded by another with quite different conditions.[32]

Historically the last of these objections has been quite prominent. One reason why transcendental arguments fell out of fashion after Kant was that few people thought there could be one fixed set of categories, shared by all conceptual schemes at every time. If transcendental arguments are *not* capable of exhibiting factors that must be shared by all experience at every time, they degenerate into observations about how we do think, not arguments about how we must think. Observations of that kind have their place, and they may play quite a significant role in showing which elements in our conceptual scheme depend on others, and which are the most basic. In fact Strawson's revival of transcendental arguments started with just that as its goal: descriptively to delineate the features of our conceptual scheme, without denying the possibility of alternatives.[33] Its appeal, however, lay in its promise to do more than that, and something much more Kantian.

III

What could determine the *right* premise to start from? It seems plain that there must be some first principles that are not susceptible of proof, and also that to rest on self-evidence would return us to Crusius' position. Aristotle points out that no defence of the law of non-contradiction could avoid relying on the law of non-contradiction, but says that all the same an "*ad hominem* proof" may be possible: a proof that works by getting one's sceptical opponent to say something, and that goes on from there.[34] This is a promising idea, though it is not immediately clear quite what he has in mind. One suggestion might be Strawson's, that because the sceptic's doubts "amount to the rejection of the whole conceptual scheme within which alone such doubts make sense," we can show them to be "unreal."[35]

But in what sense exactly are such doubts unreal? Even ordinary people have unreasonable doubts, and our sceptic could go on doubting despite all arguments. It would be possible even to doubt while accepting that the doubt does not make sense. That might be irrational, but the sceptic might be quite unmoved by rationality: people sometimes are. People can also be mad. In the First Meditation Descartes simply dismisses the suggestion that he might be mad, like people who think they are pumpkins, or made of glass.[36] The dismissal is not unduly brusque, as has sometimes been thought. Rather, the point is that there is no way of arguing against such a suggestion because someone who is mad will not be convinced by any argument. There is no way of arguing against someone who is completely unreasonable. But what is it to be unreasonable?

What Aristotle does, in his "*ad hominem* proof" of the law of non-contradiction, is to get the sceptic to say something meaningful, and to argue that in doing so his opponent is already committed to rejecting the negation of what was asserted. Aristotle recognises that his interlocutor might refuse to say anything, but in that case we could not argue with him, any more than if he were a vegetable. Equally, Aristotle recognises that the sceptic might refuse to accept the argument, or deny the possibility of meaningful discourse, but then "how could there be any common discussion between them?"[37] He would be refusing to let anything count as an argument against him. Thus the sceptic must at least be prepared to assume that his thoughts are intelligible (which is not of course to imply that he must have a concept of intelligibility), and must accept rational arguments; rational arguments will just be those that turn on those fundamental principles of argument without which argument is not possible at all. This,

I think, gets us quite close to seeing what the appropriate premises for a transcendental argument must be like. Kant does not spell it out like this, but he was, after all, imbued with Aristotle's ideas.

Aristotle's proof is thought of as an argument with a person, not as an abstract piece of reasoning. Of course all real arguments are like that, but philosophers often consider arguments in the abstract, regardless of whether they could play a part in any real debate. This can cause confusion in the present area. But even when we see that the argument must be placed in context, it is easy to misunderstand how to do this. It is sometimes suggested that we should find a proposition the assertion of which would involve the sceptic in a pragmatic self-contradiction: the utterance of it being incompatible with its truth. "There are no meaningful judgements" or "I do not exist" cannot be uttered without being false. So it is thought their negations could be starting-points for our arguments. But this will not do. It is not because their utterance would involve a pragmatic self-contradiction that we cannot reasonably doubt them. The fact that an utterance is pragmatically self-contradictory has nothing to do with whether it is known to be such, or is epistemologically safe from doubt. My present utterance "These words are not English words" is pragmatically self-contradictory, as is "I am not Ralph Walker"; these particular utterances, as made by me, could not be true. But although in both cases I do in fact know this, they are both matters about which I could be in doubt (and I did once forget my own name).

Aristotle must be essentially right: transcendental arguments should start from premises that everyone must accept if it is to be possible for us to enter into an argument with them. "Argument" here must mean "rational argument"; one could always exchange insults with anyone. We cannot get any further. The premises of a transcendental argument should be premises anyone must be prepared to accept if we are to be able to have a serious debate with them, the sort of debate that can convince them provided that they think rationally. Those who are mad, or inaccessible to reason, are not our concern.

The point is *not* that the argument should start from premises all sensible people would think obvious; this would limit the value of transcendental arguments considerably, though it is close to the position Strawson has come to adopt in recent years.[38] It is that there are premises that anyone must grant to enter into argument with us at all, and it is these that are the proper starting-points of transcendental arguments. It does not seem unreasonable to call them *a priori*, since they are presuppositions of our discourse, but it should be clear this does not imply that they are necessary truths. Indeed, Kant himself says that the fact that we have experience is contingent (A 737/ B 765).

Kant's transcendental arguments typically start from the premise that there is experience, or cognition. Someone who insisted on doubting that there was experience, if that just means some sort of awareness, would be beyond the reach of argument: to be able to talk or think intelligibly one must have some level of awareness, at least of what one is thinking or trying to say. Such an awareness amounts to a kind of cognition. The deduction of the categories seems intended to start from just this minimal premise. The same applies to the deduction of the ideas, which justifies our search for systematic and comprehensible unity.[39] Other arguments start from less minimal premises, and in particular from the claim that there is spatiotemporal experience – experience presented as spatially and temporally ordered. But here, too, and even if other forms of intuition might be possible for other beings, the premise is secure in the same sort of way: someone who denied it could not be argued with. We could get nowhere with a being that denied that its experience was spatiotemporally arrayed.

The same considerations will apply to the second premise of the argument – the premise that says that *p* is a condition of the possibility of experience, or cognition – as indeed they will for the mode of inference on which the argument itself relies. The second premise, and the mode of inference, must be of a kind that anyone must be prepared to accept, if we are to be able to argue with them. That will be true for the elementary kinds of logical inference;[40] it will be true for premises that can be shown to be analytic. But there is no reason in principle why it should not be true for other modes of inference, and for second premises that are not analytic. There is a difficulty in practice, in that the nonanalytic second premises that are offered are often not convincing. But then the second premises that philosophers put forward as analytic are often not convincing either. Again the point is not that these are things we find psychologically compelling, but that someone who did not accept them (or could not be brought to accept them) could not enter into argument with us. For the same reason as before, it seems appropriate to call such premises, and modes of inference, *a priori*. This will allow us to call their conclusions *a priori* also. And if these conclusions tell us that experience requires us to have certain concepts or beliefs, these concepts or beliefs will themselves be *a priori* in a clear sense: they cannot be derived from experience nor can they be open to empirical confirmation or refutation, since the holding of them is a condition of experience itself.

This has a bearing on the suggestion that our conceptual scheme may be only one among others. Those transcendental arguments that start from the minimal premise that there is experience or cognition leave no scope for the idea that there might be alternative conceptual schemes for which their conclusions did not hold. For the conditions of experience or cognition in the minimal sense, which must include a preparedness to be guided by the most basic logical rules, are required for anything that could be called a conceptual scheme. People sometimes suggest that there is a circularity in saying this because I am using the concepts and modes of inference that belong to our conceptual scheme. But so does the concept of a concept, of a conceptual scheme, of thought, of the world. If the suggestion is that despite this, there might be beings who did not exactly have thought, or rationality, or concepts, but something equally legitimate, one can only reply that there could be beings that lacked thought and rationality and concepts; indeed there are, and vegetables are such; but no clear meaning attaches to the idea that they might have "something equally legitimate."

Transcendental arguments with less minimal premises, premises that cannot (or arguably cannot) be shown to be themselves required for anything that could be called experience or cognition, do allow us to ask whether there might not be a place for alternative conceptual schemes. Kant raises this himself, in saying that "we cannot decide" whether there may be finite thinking beings whose intuition is not spatio-temporal (B 72). Perhaps there might be beings with different forms of intuition, or who synthesised differently from us, while still meeting the fundamental requirements for concept possession. To such beings the arguments of the Analytic of Principles would not apply, for they start from the premise that intuition is spatio-temporal, and that the basic categorical concepts have to be applied to experience – "schematised" – in a certain sort of way. These beings could perhaps communicate with one another, though not with us, and they might be able to argue with one another and talk about philosophy; for they would of course have to recognise the basic principles of logic, and in some way unify their experience under concepts, in order to be thinking about the world at all.

We need to be careful about what is being suggested here. If the idea is just that there might be an alternative universe in which things were different, then perhaps we can accept that. No evident contradiction is involved. If on the other hand the suggestion is that these people might live in our world, and yet see it in a radically different way from us – but one that is just as good as ours – then we cannot take it seriously.[41] Patently, our experience *is* spatiotemporally arrayed, and nobody who denied that, or the consequences of that, could be taken seriously, any more than the proponent of the *malin génie* idea, of which this is just a variant. That we are radically wrong about everything remains a bare logical possibility, and one that we can do nothing with. So does the suggestion that we are radically wrong about the spatial order.

Some of those who talk about alternative conceptual schemes are just pointing out that concepts change, and our ways of thinking about the world change with them. Of course that is right. It is also arguable that some of Kant's key concepts are not, as he thought, indispensable to all thought at all times and all places. But to admit that is only to say that Kant chose the wrong set of categories, and perhaps that he chose concepts insufficiently fundamental. The concepts of objectivity, or of "if . . . then . . . ," do seem clearly indispensable (though this is not the place to go into detail on such matters). There are limits to how different conceptual schemes can be, and transcendental arguments reveal them.

There remains the concern that most transcendental arguments find it difficult, or impossible, to get beyond the Conceptual Component. They can show that experience requires us to use certain concepts and to draw certain distinctions, but they do not yield results about what the world must be like – at least, unless we rely on a kind of idealism, or coherence theory of truth, according to which reality is a construction out of our ways of thinking.[42] They start from premises that people must accept if they are to be able to argue with us, but it is not even clear that from premises like "there is experience" or "there is spatio-temporal experience" anything further follows about people's actual beliefs. Arguably they must deploy concepts like those of causality and objectivity, but they might do this without actually believing that there are causes and objects; they might, for example, be philosophers. What the argument does allow us to infer, however, is that they *ought* to believe that there are causes and objects, the "ought" here being a rational "ought": the norms of rationality require that they should. For if they must make use of these concepts in ordering our experience – not just as a psychological necessity, but as a transcendental requirement – they have the best possible justification for believing that there are causes and objects: there is no rationally coherent way of ordering experience other than this. We could certainly formulate this by saying "We must believe that there are causes" (etc.), but here what is meant by "must" is not that we inevitably do, but that we ought to: it would be irrational not to.

No doubt we might have hoped to get further than this, and if we cannot, that is a limitation. But it is not a very great one. Every good argument that establishes anything, whether it is transcendental or not, starts from premises that are taken to be satisfactory, and proceeds by steps we find compelling to a conclusion we ought therefore to accept if we are to be rational. To "prove" something is simply to show that rationally we ought to accept it. Given that there is experience, we ought, by the norms of rationality, to accept that there is some subject of experience. We might not accept it, of course, but if so, then (assuming the argument is a good one) we should be flouting those norms.

Now as we have just seen, the Conceptual Component of a transcendental argument can, sometimes at least, be formulated "We must believe that *p*," where the "must" is again normative. Supposing Kant and Strawson are right in saying that we must deploy the concept of cause for experience to be possible, it follows that everyone must apply the concept in practice, and that even our doubting philosopher *ought* to believe there are causes: he will do so if he attends to the argument and reacts to it rationally. For the argument shows that the concept is indispensable for experience, and thereby justifies us in using it to describe the world. There is no rational alternative.

Thus the two kinds of transcendental argument, those that establish *p* to be true and those that only entitle us to infer "We must believe that p," are similar in their effect. The difference is that the first kind shows that we rationally ought to accept that p; the other kind shows that we rationally ought to accept that we must believe that p. But in this context "we must believe that p" means, "we rationally ought to believe that p." So the second kind of transcendental argument, the one that is said to establish a conclusion not about the world but about what we must believe, shows that we rationally ought to accept that we rationally ought to accept that p, whereas the first kind, the kind that includes the argument to the subject of experience, shows that we rationally ought to accept that p.

How much significance is there in this distinction between "We rationally ought to accept that p" and "We rationally ought to accept that we rationally ought to accept that p"? Very little, I suggest. That is not to say there is none at all, but there is not enough to warrant the idea that arguments of the second kind do not entitle us to make claims about the way the world is (and thereby to claim truth). In both types of case the arguments justify us in asserting something, and they justify us in the most effective way – by showing that it is rationally required of us that we should do so. Of course none of these arguments will guarantee for us that the world is the way we are justified in taking it to be, but then no argument will ever do that. Every argument must turn on principles that are rationally required of us; and the *génie* reminds us that what is required by the principles that govern thought may always fail to match the independent world.

Kant would not have agreed. His deduction of the categories establishes truth about the world (of appearances). His deduction of the ideas establishes only that we must believe in the systematic unity of things – or that we ought to believe in it, insofar as we are rational. It is his transcendental idealism, however, that makes this distinction possible for him. It is this that makes him think that our belief in systematic unity can only be a "presupposition": it takes us beyond the realm of possible experience, about which alone knowledge is supposedly possible. But if one can argue for a subject and for things in themselves, where the conclusions go beyond possible experience, why should one not accept this argument also as giving us as good a justification as we can ever have for taking the belief to be true? Assuming, that is, that we accept his contention that we do have to believe in the systematic unity of nature. It is not his best argument.

There is nothing wrong with the method of transcendental arguments. It does not push us towards idealism, transcendental or otherwise. The main problem with transcendental arguments is just that many of the examples proposed, by Kant and by others, do not seem to be good arguments when they are examined carefully; often the proposed second premise is unconvincing.[43] But some have made important contributions to epistemology and to metaphysics, and the question remains open how much more headway can be made. Can transcendental arguments help us with doubts about God, freedom, and morality? In the *Groundwork* there is a brief argument, to the effect that every rational being must think of itself as free both in judging and in acting, and "the author of its principles independently of alien influences" (4:448), hence, apparently, as a moral agent. Kant seems to be sketching the outline of a transcendental deduction of moral obligation, though if that was his intention here he abandoned it later. The argument is far from convincing, but the idea of providing a transcendental defence of morality is very tempting. Perhaps transcendental arguments can answer the sceptic who doubts the reality of the moral law. In recent years several attempts have been made to supply a transcendental argument along these lines, notably by Gewirth and Apel.[44]

A worry may remain over just how much is established by those transcendental arguments that yield conclusions about what we ought to believe. Stroud holds that they can show that certain of our beliefs are indispensable, in the sense that they "could not be abandoned consistently with our having a conception of the world at all," and that these beliefs would therefore be *invulnerable*, in the sense that they "could not be found to be false consistently with [their] being found to be held by people."[45] Now normally, as I have said, we have every reason to call these beliefs *true*, since we have the best possible justification for doing so. But another possibility remains (besides the tiresome *génie*). Stroud is right to say that these beliefs could not be found to be false, but his choice of the word "invulnerable" may not have been quite right. What if we found ourselves rationally obliged to hold two incompatible beliefs: both, perhaps, necessary for experience or cognition? We could regard neither as refuting the other, but in a sense both would have been "wounded." Kant came close to this, with his argument that every event must have a cause, on the one hand, and on the other, the argument just mentioned from the *Groundwork*, that we must be free in a sense that precludes external causes. Neither of these arguments is very satisfactory. But it does not seem absurd to think that someone might provide convincing transcendental arguments to show both that we must think of the world as a unitary deterministic system, and also that we must think of ourselves as free. Where should we then stand?

Everything we say and think depends on our cognitive powers, and when these powers mislead us they generally provide us also with the capacity to get back onto the right track. If it could be shown that we are rationally compelled to hold two conflicting beliefs, things would have gone badly wrong. It would be as if logic, or mathematics, had turned out to contain contradictions. I can only make two comments. First, there is no serious reason to think any such disaster will happen; we are some way from a plausible transcendental argument either for free will or for determinism. Second, if such a situation did arise, we should just have to limit the damage. Kant indicates one way to do it: we could adopt a transcendental idealism, whereby determinism could (perhaps) hold in the world of appearances, with free will available at the level of things in themselves. This is emphatically *not* how Kant himself reached transcendental idealism: he thought there were powerful arguments for freedom and for determinism, but he did not think they were transcendental arguments. If we did have compelling transcendental arguments for such an antinomy, then our transcendental arguments might impel us towards transcendental idealism. But not otherwise.

NOTES

1. He has often been thought not to use it at all, but Paul Franks reports David Bell as pointing out that it occurs at A 627/B 655 for an argument that transcends the proper limits of our understanding – not what is standardly meant. See Paul Franks, "The Origins of Post-Kantianism," in Robert Stern, ed., *Transcendental Arguments: Problems and Prospects* (Oxford: Oxford University Press, 1999), p. 112n.
2. Cf. also *Critique of the Power of Judgement*, 5:181.
3. On their use against scepticism see also A 154–8/B 193–7; B 168; A 736f./B 769; A 758/B 786,–A 769/B 797; *Prolegomena*, Preface, 4:258–60; *Real Progress*, 20:263.

4. The view that Kant's aim is essentially descriptive has been defended with vigour by Graham Bird in his *Kant's Theory of Knowledge* (London: Routledge & Kegan Paul, 1962). He accepts that Kant is concerned with certain "local scepticisms," in arguing for example that it is a mistake to see our knowledge of the external world as based on a questionable inference, but rejects the idea that Kant has the more general concerns about radical scepticism that are often ascribed to him, and are ascribed in this paper. See his "Kant and the Problem of Induction," in Stern, ed., *Transcendental Arguments: Problems and Prospects*.

5. Hume is often interpreted in this way. More recently the view has been put forward by W. V. O. Quine, in (for example) "Epistemology Naturalized," in his *Ontological Relativity and Other Essays* (New York: Columbia University Press, 1969), pp. 69–90. The objection that Quine cannot consistently sustain it has often been made, for example, by Hilary Putnam, "Why Reason Can't be Naturalized," in his *Realism and Reason* (Cambridge: Cambridge University Press, 1983), pp. 229–47. The issues are too large, however, to be pursued here.

6. Aristotle, *Metaphysics* Γ4 and K5.

7. Descartes, *Meditation* III, in C. Adam and P. Tannery, eds, *Oeuvres de Descartes* (Paris: Vrin/C.N.R.S., revised ed. 1964–76), VII:38; English translation by J. Cottingham, R. Stoothoff, and D. Murdoch, *The Philosophical Writings of Descartes* (Cambridge: Cambridge University Press, 1984), vol. II; Spinoza, *Tractatus de Intellectus Emendatione*, in C. Gebhardt, ed., *Spinoza: Opera* (Heidelberg: C. Winter, 1925), II:18; English translation by E. Curley, *The Collected Works of Spinoza* (Princeton: Princeton University Press 1985), vol. I.

8. Cf. Ross Harrison, "Transcendental Arguments and Idealism," in G. Vesey, ed., *Idealism Past and Present* (Cambridge: Cambridge University Press, 1982), and Quassim Cassam, "Transcendental Arguments, Transcendental Synthesis and Transcendental Idealism," *Philosophical Quarterly* 37 (1987).

9. This point is made by Harrison and Cassam; cf. also Paul Guyer, "The Rehabilitation of Transcendental Idealism?," in Eva Schaper and Wilhelm Vossenkuhl, eds., *Reading Kant* (Oxford: Blackwell, 1989).

10. Cf. Larry BonJour, *In Defense of Pure Reason* (Cambridge: Cambridge University Press, 1998), pp. 1–11.

11. See also his letter to Herz of 21 February 1772, 10:131.

12. C. A. Crusius, *Weg zur Gewissheit und Zuverlässigkeit der menschlichen Erkentniss* (Leipzig: Gleditsch, 1747), § 256.

13. On the development of Kant's thought in the pre-critical period see Paul Guyer, *Kant and the Claims of Knowledge* (Cambridge: Cambridge University Press, 1987), chs. 1 and 2.

14. Thus T. H. Green, *Prolegomenon to Ethics* (Oxford: Oxford University Press, 2nd ed., 1884), ch. 1; H. H. Joachim, *The Nature of Truth* (Oxford: Oxford University Press, 1906); and in recent years it has become a common thought that because classification is something that we do, our knowledge must be confined to the world as we have ordered it. Cf. John McDowell, *Mind and World* (Cambridge, MA: Harvard University Press, 1994), though McDowell would certainly resist being called an idealist himself.

15. Their arguments do start, however, from the line of thought developed (or half-developed) by Kant in the first two arguments of the metaphysical expositions of space and time. See P. F. Strawson, *Individuals* (London: Methuen, 1959), ch. 2, and *The Bounds of Sense* (London: Methuen, 1968), pp. 47–51; Jonathan F. Bennett, *Kant's Analytic* (Cambridge: Cambridge University Press, 1966), ch. 3; Gareth Evans, "Things Without the Mind," in Zak van Straaten, ed., *Philosophical Subjects* (Oxford: Oxford University Press, 1980).

16. He says at the end of the chapter on Schematism that the significance of the pure categories must be "only…logical" (A 147/B 186). However, this example does not contradict that: the if-then relation in Kant's Aristotelian logic would be one of dependence, a much stronger relationship than material (or even strict) implication.

17. Paul Guyer sees more of a discontinuity than I do between the two *Critiques*; he also finds the passage in the first *Critique* to be inconsistent, and concerned with a requirement that is at best methodological. See his "Kant's Conception of Empirical Law," *Proceedings of the Aristotelian Society*, Supplementary vol. lxiv (1990), and my reply (ibid.). On the relation between the two *Critiques* on these matters, see also Béatrice Longuenesse, *Kant and the Capacity to Judge* (Princeton: Princeton University Press, 1998), esp. pp. 163ff.

18. Cf. also *Critique of the Power of Judgment*, 5:180, 182ff.

19. Henry Allison makes a strong case for treating the argument, at least in the form in which it appears in the *Critique of the Power of Judgment*, as a transcendental defence against Hume's inductive scepticism: "Reflective Judgement and the Application of Logic to Nature," in H.-J. Glock, ed., *Strawson and Kant* (Oxford: Oxford University Press, 2003). As he puts it elsewhere, "it is *right*, that is, rationally justified, to presuppose the principle": Henry E. Allison, *Kant's Theory of Taste* (Cambridge: Cambridge University Press, 2001), p. 41. Cf. also my "Induction and Transcendental Argument," in Stern, ed., *Transcendental Arguments: Problems and Prospects*. There is some unclarity as to just what is involved in "presupposing," and this supports accusations of inconsistency against Kant. Cf. Guyer, "Kant's Conception of Empirical Law,"

and Philip Kitcher, "Projecting the Order of Nature," in Robert E. Butts, ed., *Projecting the Order of Nature* (Dordrecht: Reidel, 1986).

20. There are various passages in the *Critique* and elsewhere that could be taken as elaborating the bare statement that "it follows naturally from the bare concept of an appearance in general that something must correspond to it which is not in itself appearance" (A 251, cf. B xxvi f.). The only passage that can be construed as an extended argument to this conclusion is the Refutation of Idealism. In Guyer's interpretation the Refutation of Idealism is designed to establish that ontological conclusion, while at the same time showing that the independence of things in themselves can be presented to us only through their appearance in space. See Guyer, *Kant and the Claims of Knowledge* Part IV, and his "Kant's Intentions in the Refutation of Idealism," *Philosophical Review* 92 (1983).

21. It is set out very fully by Erich Adickes, *Kant und das Ding an Sich* (Berlin: Pan, 1924).

22. See especially Paul Franks, "Transcendental Arguments, Reason, and Scepticism: Contemporary Debates and the Origins of Post-Kantianism," in R. Stern, ed., *Transcendental Arguments: Problems and Prospects*. The role of transcendental arguments in Hegel is disputed: see Charles Taylor, "The Opening Arguments of the *Phenomenology*," in A. MacIntyre, ed., *Hegel* (Notre Dame: University of Notre Dame Press, 1976), and Robert Stern, *Transcendental Arguments and Scepticism* (Oxford: Oxford University Press, 2000), chs. 4 and 5. In his article "Modest Transcendental Arguments and Sceptical Doubts," in Stern, ed., *Transcendental Arguments: Problems and Prospects*, Christopher Hookway draws attention to the use of transcendental arguments by Charles Sanders Peirce and Josiah Royce.

23. Strawson, *Individuals*, Part I; *The Bounds of Sense*, esp. Part II ch. 3. Since then Strawson has lost faith in transcendental arguments; see his *Skepticism and Naturalism: Some Varieties* (London: Methuen, 1985).

24. Barry Stroud, "Transcendental Arguments," *Journal of Philosophy* 65 (1968), reprinted in his *Understanding Human Knowledge* (Oxford: Oxford University Press, 2000).

25. Quassim Cassam, "Transcendental Arguments, Transcendental Synthesis and Transcendental Idealism," *Philosophical Quarterly* 37 (1987); quotation from p. 358.

26. It would apply in the extreme form in which it is put forward by Hilary Putnam, in his *Reason, Truth and History* (Cambridge: Cambridge University Press, 1981), ch. 1, or in *Realism and Reason*. But (setting aside the fact that Putnam's argument has been widely attacked) the trouble with that is that it then establishes not the realist conclusions that

Strawson and others were hoping for, but a sort of transcendental idealism, as Putnam admits. On this style of argument more generally, see A. Brueckner, "Transcendental Arguments from Content Externalism," in Stern, ed., *Transcendental Arguments: Problems and Prospects*.

27. Strawson, *Bounds of Sense*, p. 144.

28. Gareth Evans, "Things without the Mind," in Z. van Straaten, ed., *Philosophical Subjects*.

29. Cf. Bennett, *Kant's Analytic*, ch. 3.

30. 20:274; cf. B 161, B 218f.

31. On this problem see esp. Guyer, *Kant and the Claims of Knowledge*, pp. 417–21, and Franks, "The Origins," pp. 117–21.

32. This argument has been popular lately, and had many precursors in the 19th century. For a good statement of it, see Stefan Körner, "The Impossibility of Transcendental Deductions," *Monist* 51 (1967); reprinted in Lewis White Beck, ed., *Kant Studies Today* (La Salle, IL: Open Court, 1969).

33. Strawson, *Individuals*, pp. 9, 247.

34. Aristotle, *Metaphysics* Γ4 and K5; "apodeixis...pros tonde," 1062a3, cf. 1062a31. T. H. Irwin is very helpful on this, in his *Aristotle's First Principles* (Oxford: Oxford University Press, 1988), ch. 9.

35. Strawson, *Individuals*, p. 35.

36. Descartes, *Oeuvres*, VII:19.

37. *Metaphysics*, 1062a14.

38. Strawson, *Skepticism and Naturalism*.

39. The argument turns not just on how human beings reason, but on the nature of reason itself, as required for any possible experience: cf. A 651/B 679; *Critique of the Power of Judgment*, 5:182, and more fully in the First Introduction to the *Critique of the Power Judgment*, 20:213–6. Whether Kant is right to make so strong a claim is, of course, a different matter. See my "Induction and Transcendental Argument," in Stern, ed., *Transcendental Arguments: Problems and Prospects*.

40. Including no doubt *modus ponens* and the principle of noncontradiction in some form, though not controversial principles like the law of the excluded middle.

41. Kant, on the other hand, can take it seriously, and does, in *What Real Progress*, 20:267. It is of course his transcendental idealism that makes this possible: if we represent things in themselves spatially, we cannot exclude the possibility that "some beings in the world might intuit the same objects under another form [of intuition]." Given transcendental idealism, this is no threat to the thesis that the world we live in is spatial and temporal. Conversely, someone inclined to realism, but who was converted by Kant on this matter, would thereby be converted to transcendental idealism.

42. Putnam's attempt at defeating the *génie*, in his *Reason, Truth and History* (Cambridge: Cambridge University Press, 1981), ch.1, leads him to a kind of idealism, but it fails in any case. The most it shows – even granting his questionable causal theory of reference – is that if I am a brain in a vat, I am mistaken about the content of many of my own thoughts, for I am not capable of thinking about things like vats. Putnam's argument, one of the more influential (if less successful) recent attempts at a transcendental argument, has been widely discussed; for a summary of the discussion see Stern, *Transcendental Arguments and Scepticism*, pp. 133–7.

43. For an excellent recent study of how well particular transcendental arguments fare, see Stern, *Transcendental Arguments and Scepticism*.

44. Alan Gewirth, *Reason and Morality* (Chicago: University of Chicago Press, 1978); Karl–Otto Apel, "The *A Priori* of the Communication Community and the Foundation of Ethics," in G. Adey and D. Frisby, eds, *Towards a Transformation of Philosophy* (London: Routledge & Kegan Paul, 1980). For a critical discussion of these ideas and an attempt to achieve the same result while avoiding their difficulties, see C. Illies, *The Grounds of Ethical Judgement* (Oxford: Oxford University Press, 2003).

45. Barry Stroud, "The Goal of Transcendental Arguments," in Stern, ed., *Transcendental Arguments: Problems and Prospects*, p. 158; see also his "Kantian Argument, Conceptual Capacities, and Invulnerability," in P. Parrini, ed., *Kant and Contemporary Epistemology* (Dordrecht: Kluwer, 1994). Both these papers are reprinted in Stroud's *Understanding Human Knowledge*.

8 The critique of metaphysics
The structure and fate of Kant's dialectic

The impact of Kant's critique of metaphysics is deeply ambiguous. A vivid assessment by a distinguished and relatively sympathetic British reader in the mid-nineteenth century may still reflect the opinion of most analytic philosophers today. According to Sir William Hamilton, "Kant had annihilated the older metaphysic, but the germ of a more visionary doctrine of the absolute, than any of those refuted, was contained in the bosom of his own philosophy. He had slain the body, but had not exorcised the spectre of the absolute; and this spectre continued to haunt the schools of Germany even to the present day."[1]

Hamilton's words still provide a helpful structure for trying to understand and evaluate the full effect of Kant's treatment of metaphysics. They raise a set of unavoidable questions:

1) What is the "older metaphysic" under attack by the *Critique*, and how does it express what can appear to be the "body" of the "absolute"? (See below, I, The Prelude of Kant's Critique.)
2) How does Kant's attack proceed?
3) Does it truly "annihilate" this "body"? (See below, II and III, The Process of Kant's Critique and The Result of the Dialectic.)
4) What is the "germ" in the "bosom" of Kant's own philosophy that can appear as a "spectre of the absolute," an absolute "more visionary" than anything in the "older metaphysic"? (See below, IV, The Poison of Kant's Critique.)
5) How did this "spectre" develop after the *Critique*, and what is the relation of that development to the *Critique*'s

own basic position on metaphysics? (See below, V, Kantian Postlude.)

I. THE PRELUDE OF KANT'S CRITIQUE OF METAPHYSICS

The complexity of the aftermath of Kant's critique of metaphysics is due at least in part to the fact that his own project is fundamentally ambiguous from the start. The very first pages of the first edition *Critique of Pure Reason* use the term "metaphysics" in contrasting ways. On the one hand, as signifying "the older metaphysic," it stands for a traditional "battlefield of endless controversies" (A viii) because it concerns questions that "by its very nature" theoretical reason "cannot answer" (A vii).[2] On the other hand, "metaphysics" also stands for a fruitful new discipline, "the only one of all the sciences that may promise that little but unified effort [namely, the effort of the Critical philosophy itself]... will complete it" (A xx). Similarly, the Preface to the second edition explicitly separates the successful first "part" of metaphysics covered in the *Critique*'s Transcendental Analytic of experience, which has "the secure course of a science," from the troublesome second "part" of metaphysics, which, according to the Transcendental Dialectic, fails in its attempt to fly "beyond the boundaries of possible experience" (B xix). No wonder Kant frequently compared overly ambitious forms of rationalism – what Hamilton called "the body of the absolute" – to a vain flapping of wings.

From the beginning, different schools of interpretation have focused primarily on one or the other of these two aspects of Kant's concern with metaphysics. In the eighteenth century, Moses Mendelssohn expressed lament in characterizing Kant as the "destroyer" of traditional metaphysics, whereas Karl Reinhold and his Jena successors heralded the *Critique* as the starting point for a new and completely scientific metaphysics.[3] More recently, W. H. Walsh presented a sympathetic study of the *Critique* under the negative title, *Kant's Criticism of Metaphysics*, while his illustrious predecessor H. J. Paton organized an apologetic commentary under the positive title, *Kant's Metaphysic of Experience*. In general, mainline twentieth-century philosophers tended to praise rather than lament Kant's attack on transcendent metaphysics and to endorse a relatively modest "descriptive" version of his immanent meta-physics of experience.

These different reactions, more often than not, still follow famil-iar national patterns, although, from the very beginning, there were also significant empiricist critiques of Kant offered from within Germany as well as influential speculative appropriations of his thought proposed from outside Germany (e.g., Coleridge and the American transcendentalists).[4] One reason for this variety of reac-tions has to do with complications concerning central notions such as the determination of "conditions of experience." There is a basic ambiguity already in Kant's famous statement that metaphysics con-cerns that which reason claims "independently of all experience" (A xii). The term "independent" can be used in different ways, as sig-nifying partial or total independence. When it is understood as indi-cating total independence, the statement signals the idea that what we are to learn about metaphysics is negative, namely, that we must always guard against any wholly "nonexperiential use" (A xii) of the-oretical reason. But Kant uses the statement positively when speak-ing of what is a less than total independence, namely, a justificatory independence from any particular path of experience but not from the context of possible experience altogether (B 2). In this case it points to the "transcendental" task of finding what is necessary in general for our experience, that is, for our being able to make empirical knowl-edge claims.[5] More specifically, the main task of the Transcendental Analytic is the establishment of the *a priori* principles needed if sensible beings like us, in space and time, are to be able to make warranted theoretical claims about determinate objects at all.

An obvious problem here is that such claims, which are sup-posedly immanent and yet "partially" independent of experience, can seem to empiricists in many ways just as questionable as the transcendent claims that Kant means to criticize. Kant's immedi-ate reply, no doubt, would be that the main traditional claims are the theoretical assertions of the "Ideas of Reason" – God, freedom, and immortality – and that these all go clearly "beyond all bounds of experience" because they involve concepts "to which no correspond-ing object at all can be given in experience" (A 3/B 6). A difficulty with this reply by itself is that a reader who recalls the details of the *Critique*'s positive metaphysics of experience could object that

Kant himself makes many *a priori* "immanent" claims about ("permanent") substance, ("universal" and "necessary") causality, ("infinite") space and time in such a way that it is also *not* the case that these items are themselves literally "given" as "objects." Instead, these concepts stand for general rules, ordering principles, or special frameworks with which certain ("objective") combinations of representations are claimed necessarily to agree – in a way that is, at best, evident only after considerable abstract argument. But, similarly, it would seem that, without relying literally on reference to any "given object," many traditional metaphysicians of the kind Kant is criticizing (and this would include positions found throughout his own pre-Critical works) could claim as much for their favorite so-called transcendent concepts. For Descartes, Malebranche, Leibniz, and others, rigorous metaphysics implies that there can be our kind of experience only with God, freedom, and other unique features of subjectivity.

At this point Kant might add that his claim is more than simply that our experience will have to "agree" with these principles. The *Critique*'s distinctive point is that our experience is "constituted" by them because they are directly essential to the construction of the spatiotemporal determinations that alone "make" our (objective) experience possible, whereas it is supposedly not clear how this could be the case for the Ideas of Reason of traditional theoretical metaphysics (whatever their value may be for "regulative," "reflective," or practical claims[6]). But this response in turn leads to at least two further worries. First, it might be countered that there are ways – that Kant has not considered or adequately acknowledged – in which these Ideas, or ones like them, turn out to be transcendentally necessary after all. It might, for example, be argued that Kant's own arguments point to something like a theoretical vindication of freedom in the sense of an unconditional presence of spontaneity in knowing, for how else are we to understand his own notion of rational argumentation and of a basic kind of "synthesis" that is needed by all human understanding and "can never come to us through the senses" (B 129)?[7] There is little in the Transcendental Analytic that clearly shows why such a strategy *must* be forever rejected at the same time that never-directly-given but supposedly-always-required notions such as substance and cause can be allowed.

Second, a traditional metaphysician could in any case retreat and argue that even if Ideas of Reason do not have a clear role in constituting, that is, ordering, our spatiotemporal experience as such, they, or some other special metaphysical notions, might still have some other kind of warrant. Kant does insist that all proper philosophical assertions must be objective, not merely formal, and therefore must be synthetic, must use intuition, and must depend on our forms of space and time and all the restrictions that they involve – but each of these claims is very controversial, especially if one is willing to retreat from the demand for certainty, which Kant cannot in any case easily claim for his own methodology. Contemporary metaphysics continues to thrive with rigorous general arguments concerning matters such as universals, substrata, properties, modality, essence, identity, and realism.[8] Precisely because most metaphysical terms have a meaning that seems independent of any ordinary spatiotemporal characterization of objects, one would not at first expect them to have to be justified in terms of some kind of transcendental role in structuring spatiotemporal determinations. That by itself would not prove they are illegitimate, however, unless we *already* have in hand some general and non-question-begging "principle of significance" that restricts the claims of theoretical philosophy to concepts justified by reflecting on such a role. It has in fact been contended, by leading eighteenth-as well as twentieth-century interpreters (e.g., Jacobi, Hamann, and Hegel; Strawson, Bennett, and Rorty), that Kant was relying on such a principle – but this contention has also been roundly disputed, and it is very hard to see how it can be relied on at the outset without imposing a kind of dogmatism (or concept phenomenalism) on Kant that would be just as questionable as whatever the *Critique* meant to criticize.[9] It is striking in any case that "successors" of Kant such as Hegel came to insist that, even after the *Critique*, numerous metaphysical notions, including versions of "infinite Ideas" such as God, world, and mind, can be legitimated by theoretical philosophy for reasons that are not simply a matter of grounding spatiotemporal determinations – and that only a lingering empiricism kept Kant from acknowledging this himself.[10] For these reasons, it should be clear, even if one has no sympathy with figures such as Hegel, that if Kant's philosophy is to have any chance of "complete" and "scientific" success in curbing metaphysics in a bad sense, the *Critique* needs at the very least to offer a systematic examination of all the Ideas of Reason allegedly central to metaphysics. Fortunately, this appears to be exactly why the largest part of the *Critique* is devoted to an extensive Transcendental Dialectic, and it is to a brief review of this section that we now turn.

II. THE PROCESS OF KANT'S CRITIQUE OF METAPHYSICS: THE STRUCTURE OF THE DIALECTIC

The Dialectic proposes a general pattern for the errors of transcendent metaphysics. The pattern is not exactly what one might first expect, namely, the error of simply employing categories apart from their specific spatiotemporal schematization, for example, by making claims about substance without considerations of permanence. This is an error, but by itself it is accidental in the double sense of being neither fully systematic nor imposed by any special force. For Kant, dialectical errors are anything but accidental. They involve very special representations, designated as Ideas of Reason, which are systematically organized and give rise to inferences with a unique force, as if they were a *"natural* and unavoidable *illusion"* (A 298/B 355).[11]

The content of the Ideas is determined by ordered variations of the notion of something unconditioned, an idea which comes from making into a "real principle" what is only a general "logical maxim" of reason, namely, to seek the condition of any particular conditioned judgment, so that "a unity [of reason] is brought to completion." This step involves the assumption that "when the conditioned is given, then so is the whole series of conditions...which is itself unconditioned, also given (i.e., contained in the object and its connection)" (A 308/B 364). The analytic connection of a given concept and its logical ground is, of course, not the same as the synthetic connection of a given thing and its real ground. Nonetheless, Kant claims there is a force making this assumption "unavoidable" for reason, namely, the naturalness of taking "the subjective necessity of a certain connection of our concepts on behalf of the understanding...for an objective necessity, the determination of things in themselves" (A 297/B 353).

The "connection of concepts" Kant has in mind here comes from what he takes to be the peculiar office of reason to connect representations in chains of syllogisms: "we can expect that the form of the syllogisms [*Vernunftschluss*]...will contain the origin of special concepts *a priori* that we may call pure concepts of reason, or

transcendental ideas, and they will determine the use of the understanding according to principles in the whole of an entire experience"
(A 321/B 378). The "determination of things in themselves" that he
has in mind here amounts to the thought of an unconditioned item,
or set of items, corresponding to each of the syllogistic "forms,"
namely, an unconditioned (i.e., unpredicable) *subject* of *categorical*
syllogisms, an unconditioned (i.e., first) item for "the *hypothetical*
synthesis of the members of a *series,*" and an unconditioned (i.e.,
exhaustive) source for "the *disjunctive* synthesis of the parts in a
system" (A 323/B 379).

To this ambitious scheme Kant immediately adds a further systematic proposal. He holds that the "unconditioned subject" corresponds to the absolute *"unity* of the *thinking subject,"* the unconditioned first item of the series of hypothetical syllogisms corresponds
to the "absolute *unity* [i.e., either an absolutely first item or a total
series] of the *series* of *conditions of appearance,*" and the unconditioned ground of the disjunctive syntheses is "the absolute *unity* of
the *condition of all objects of thought* in general" (A 334/B 391).
Even more specifically, the thought of an unconditioned subject is
taken to lead to the Idea of an immortal self, that of the unconditioned appearance is taken to lead to the contradictory notion of a
completely given whole of spatiotemporal appearances (and thereby
to allow some undefeated conceptual space for the Idea of our transcendental freedom), and the notion of an unconditioned source for
all thought is taken to lead to the Idea of "a being of all beings," God
(A 336/B 393; cf. B 395n.).[12]

These proposed connections are only the first layers of Kant's ingenious architectonic. The Ideas are each determined further by the
table of categories, so that the subject is considered as unconditioned
qua substance, quality, quantity, and modality (hence there are four
paralogisms of rational psychology), and the whole of appearances as
unconditioned qua quantity, quality, causality, and modality (hence
there are four antinomies of rational cosmology).

More specifically, in the Paralogisms Kant challenges rationalist
arguments from the mere representation of the I to *a priori* claims
that the self is substantial, simple, identical over time, and independent of other beings. Kant's ultimate concern is with showing
that the unique and ever-available character of the representation
of the I, which is central to his own philosophy as an indication of
the transcendental power of apperception, should not mislead us into

claims that it demonstrates a special "spiritual" object, that is, something that necessarily can exist independent of whatever underlies other things. But although Kant properly stresses that our theoretical representation of the I does not by itself provide a determinate intuition of the soul as a special phenomenal or noumenal object, it is not clear that his exposure of certain fallacies directly undermines *all* traditional rationalist claims about the self.[13]

In the attack on rational cosmology in the Antinomies, Kant "skeptically" contrasts opposing sets of *a priori* claims about the division, composition, origination, and relation of dependence of existence "of the alterable in appearance" (A 415/B 443). The theses are: The set of appearances is finite in age and spatial extent, composed of simples, containing uncaused causality and a necessary being. The antitheses are: It is given as infinite in age and extent, divisible without end, and without uncaused causality or a necessary being underlying it. Kant challenges these particular assertions by pointing out ways that the indirect arguments for them fail, since the denial of the opposite claim does not entail the assertion of the original claim. Thus, one can escape the antinomies by avoiding the general assumption that either, because no endless series is given, there must be an absolute end in composition, division, generation, and so forth, or, because no end can be given as unconditioned, there must be a series given absolutely without end. (Here Kant is relying on a distinction between coming to an end in fact, and knowing that there must be a final end, as well as between being able to continue a series *in infinitum* and having an actual infinity in one's total grasp.)

In the last two Antinomies Kant discusses the causal and modal status of an appearance in general in the same kind of "open-ended" way that he treats the phenomenal characterization of the self: It is an *a priori* truth that we can go on without end in seeking empirical acts of causality impinging on it, and empirical beings upon which it is dependent, and yet this does not yield a *given unconditioned* series but always leaves open a possible involvement with some (non-given) non-empirical causality and non-dependent being.[14] Thus, while Kant can distinguish this result from dogmatic claims that there must be, or that there cannot be, a first causality and a non-dependent being, he still leaves open (for grounding elsewhere) both the assertion that there must be *a priori* laws governing phenomena and the idea that there is some ground for assuming something beyond phenomena. His discussions fit the metaphysical tradition insofar as they still entail, as Leibniz would want, that all items within the spatiotemporal field are thoroughly governed by a principle of sufficient reason, and also, as Newton would want, that they are located in irreducible (although not absolutely real) forms of space and time.

Just as one should not be wholly taken in by the anti-rationalist tone of the Dialectic, one also should not assume that its architectonic has a sacrosanct structure. Like much of the Dialectic, it may have been the product of a series of hasty rearrangements,[15] and its final form contains some surprising oddities. The discussion of the Idea of God largely ignores the table of categories, while the treatments of the self and of the world seem to pick arbitrarily from that table, each using only four of the six main headings (quantity, quality, substance, cause, community, and modality). Thus the issue of the agency of the self, which was considered a proper categorial topic in notes prior to the *Critique*, mysteriously disappears from the discussion of rational psychology, whereas the very basic question of the substantiality of phenomena in general is not posed directly (A 414/ B 441). It is unclear why the notion of an unconditioned starting point for categorical syllogisms should lead to an ultimate subject considered only in terms of the psychological capacity for thinking, just as it is unclear why the nature of the thinking subject should not be considered (as it was by many rationalists) as a part of the general theory of the world. The discussion of rational cosmology supposedly is to consider the world only as appearance (which is not the same as assuming that it is only appearance), while the discussion of the subject can, and does, shift between regarding it as a phenomenon or as something beyond appearances – but this distinction is not cleanly maintained, since sometimes (e.g., in the consideration of the simplicity of the components of the world) arguments about cosmology introduce non-phenomenal considerations (albeit usually in a way to be criticized – but the same is true in the Paralogisms), and sometimes (in the Second and Third Antinomies, e.g., A 463/B 491) they consider psychological examples after all.

These oddities do not present a very severe problem as long as it is not assumed that the three Ideas need to be approached in fully parallel ways. And in fact this is not a fair assumption since Kant makes clear that he has very different views about the Ideas. Whereas he argues that rationalist claims about the self are fallaciously inflated, he does not do much to rule out the possibility of a consistent, albeit very formal and negative, pure theory of the ultimate nature of the self, for example, as necessarily immaterial and rational. Cosmological claims, in contrast, supposedly lead to contradictory theses that are resolvable only by transcendental idealism. According to the result of the Antinomies, it is wrong to say determinately that the sensible world is of either necessarily finite or given infinite magnitude, although supposedly arguments for each of these would succeed if transcendental realism were true.[16] Here the main problem is not a lack of knowledge or detail. Rather, for certain questions – for example, "How old is the spatiotemporal world in itself?" – there is supposedly no sensible answer at all since there is no quantity for a whole of this sort "in itself." But this pattern of argument applies at best to only the first antinomy; for most cosmological issues, a fairly extensive rational doctrine (of phenomenal laws and noumenal possibilities) is allowed and is outlined in part in the *Metaphysical Foundations of Natural Science*.[17] Finally, the theological Idea is like the psychological Idea in not leading to contradictions, but also somewhat like the cosmological Ideas in providing a relatively full doctrine of attributes, although for Kant their instantiation is left without support until one shifts from theoretical to moral-practical considerations. We thus gain from rational theology the "transcendental ideal" of a perfect and necessary being, even if speculative arguments all fail to establish its existence.[18] Even on a charitable reading that accepts the validity of all of its particular arguments, the Dialectic excludes only a very specific set of claims and not the truth of all traditional metaphysical doctrines.

III. THE RESULT OF THE DIALECTIC: HOW MUCH DID IT "ANNIHILATE"?

In addition to the various limitations just noted in Kant's treatment of *specific* theoretical claims in the Dialectic – limitations implying that for Kant many of the notions of traditional rational psychology, cosmology, and theology can still be very useful for ordering our *thinking* about issues in these fields – there are some *general* limitations in his own position on the limitations of reason. What is clearly distinctive about Kant's criticism is that it is an argument about principled limitations in principle of *theoretical* reason as constitutive.[19]

Kant distinguishes two fundamental uses of reason, practical and theoretical (or "speculative"), and it can never be emphasized enough how often he stresses that our reason *can* establish practically all the most important claims that he says it *cannot* establish theoretically. According to all three *Critiques*, pure practical reason turns out to be right in its basic conclusions that we should believe there is a God, absolute freedom of choice, an immortal soul, and a "highest good" involving a providential end for those who act properly (cf. *Critique of Practical Reason* [5:122–34] and *Critique of the Power of Judgment*, §87). These claims are not merely to be treated as true, with a literal personalist and theist meaning; Kant also goes out of his way to try to show that they are grounded in adequate considerations of *reason*.

Kant calls his postulates "practical" simply because they have the peculiarity of resting on (a) at least one essential premise that asserts an irreducible pure normative truth (that there are categorical obligations in Kant's sense), something resting ultimately on a pure practical "fact of reason" for which he thinks no purely theoretical or even practical-prudential basis is possible.[20] Kant's position also depends on (b) the theoretical truth of transcendental idealism, which he believes provides the only way to protect our metaphysical commitment to (a) from what would otherwise be a sufficient ground to defeat it – namely, the claim that the laws of nature entail we are absolutely determined and hence not free moral agents. (This is apparently the only such ground that Kant believes we have an evident theoretical need to defeat, although there are other problems, such as fear of a fatalistic theology, that he treats as worth at least neutralizing.) Recall that a transcendental realist reading of the results of the Transcendental Analytic (in particular, the Second Analogy) entails that all the states of our life fall under *and only* under deterministic spatiotemporal laws of nature. For this reason the Third Antinomy of the Transcendental Dialectic is constructed to show that the transcendental ideality of space and time established earlier in the *Critique* leaves room for us to continue nonetheless to regard our actions as, for all we know, the result of an absolutely spontaneous non-spatiotemporal ground, a moral will freely following a moral law. Hence, even if our actions, in their spatiotemporal side, are all in accord with natural laws and conditions, the main implications of the *Critique's* theoretical philosophy is that they might *also* fall under non-natural laws and conditions.

All this shows that Kant's Dialectic does indeed have a complicated structure, with mixed positive/negative and practical/theoretical aims. Hamilton's suspicions are thus easily understandable, for with such a complex "body" of metaphysics undergoing dissection in such a complex way, it is not surprising that some "germ" or "spectre" of the "older metaphysic" might seem able to escape. But there are very different diagnoses possible of the most relevant danger here. For some, a "visionary" residue may seem to be present if any non-empiricist claims are allowed at all. But it has been already noted that the very first steps of the transcendental philosophy must leave room for making some pure theoretical claims that go beyond experience in some sense, and especially beyond any mere contingent summation of impressions. To disallow this much would be to take back all of the Analytic and to undercut any distinctive positive value in the *Critique's* project.

A more appropriate worry concerning the "visionary" would focus on the core *spiritualist* claims of the older metaphysic. That worry would be warranted if the *Critique* in any way encouraged theoretically establishing something like a Cartesian or Crusian dualism, a Malebranchian occasionalism, a Leibnizian pre-established harmony of monads, or a Berkeleyan spiritualism. It should be clear by now, however, that the *Critique* is directed entirely against all arguments for determinate claims such as these, even if it might not unconditionally demonstrate that they all must be false.[21]

There remain, nonetheless, at least two other very relevant notions that are directly connected with the Dialectic and that can raise (and have raised) understandable worries about a relapse to a "visionary" metaphysics, namely, the notions of *idealism* and the *unconditioned*. The strategy of the Dialectic is precisely to stress that reason by its very nature makes a demand for the unconditioned, and that Critical philosophy responds best to that demand by validating a distinctive form of idealism (cf. *Critique of Practical Reason*, Book Two, and *Critique of the Power of Judgment*, §57, Observation 2). This is enough to suggest that, at least at a first glance, some concern about a "spectre of the absolute" can seem proper after all.

The worries about the unconditioned and about idealism need to be dealt with separately, although they also turn out to have important connections with one another. In presenting his position specifically as "transcendental idealism," Kant repeatedly explains that his is a merely "formal" variety of idealism, meaning that there is an irreducible reality of "stuff" that remains completely independent of "us," even though the specific *a priori* forms of our experience, and all that depends on them, do not (see *Prolegomena* [4:337] and B 519n.). The *Critique* never denies that there are items other than our mind, and it even notes that what we at first characterize as a mind can have an underlying reality that is not psychological at all (B 427–8) since the transcendental ideality of space and time entails that in itself our self definitely cannot be mental in its ordinary temporal sense. It is precisely for that reason that the indirect argument for transcendental idealism relies on considerations concerning only the relational characterizations of the sensible world through determinations of space and time.

It should be obvious that the ideality of such relational properties does not immediately endanger the reality of the intrinsic non-relational features of things. But worries that the *Critique* still involves a radical and "spectral" type of idealism can arise from understandable sources. First, the most relevant "cousins" to Kant's philosophy here, the views of Leibniz and Berkeley, combine a claim of the non-ultimacy of spatiotemporal determinations with a position that does not leave any kind of nonmental things as ultimate realities. This position, however, is commonly understood as relying on a peculiar insistence on the reducibility of spatiotemporal determinations to intrinsic mental properties (perception and appetition in monads for Leibniz, perceptions within individual spirits for Berkeley) that Kant consistently and emphatically *denies*.²² This is an important reminder of how, given the specific character of Kant's unusual position, the unattractive idealist consequences of other philosophies that are critical of the reality of the spatiotemporal as such should never be projected directly onto him.

Nonetheless, there is an understandable second worry that arises from a comparison with Kant's other philosophical cousins, the naturalist heirs of Locke and the scientific revolution. Modern scientific realists welcomed the non-reality of secondary qualities precisely because they held that spatiotemporal qualities could adequately secure and characterize the independent reality of matter alone (i.e., "matter" not merely in a general philosophical sense but in the specific physical sense that modern science uses). Hence, any philosophical doubts about these qualities can still seem to undermine any notion of mind-independent reality as such. There are various ways for Kantians to respond to this worry. One strategy would be to note that science itself can and has entertained the possibility of *other nonmental* primary qualities that could underlie the relational determinations of the space-time that we know – and there is no reason that Kant's ontology cannot be understood as leaving room for an analog of this position.[23]

Alternatively, it has been proposed by some interpreters that Kant's distinction between the in itself and the ideal is nothing more than the distinction between the relational and the intrinsic. On this "humble" reading, the Critical ideality of features such as space and time need not have anything to do with specifically mentalistic forms of idealism, and so there is nothing to be feared by a sophisticated scientific realist. For this view, transcendental idealism simply expresses a kind of "humility" about our not being able to penetrate, in any of our actual explanations, which are all relational, to the ultimate and underlying intrinsic features of things.[24] A hint of something close to, but not quite the same as, this kind of view can be found in a passage of the *Critique* that stresses that things cannot be understood as composed of relational properties *alone* (A 49/B 66). This point does not go far enough, however, and aside from a lack of adequate support elsewhere in the *Critique*, the "humble" interpretation has, I believe, the weakness of encouraging an overly "optimistic" reading of Kant's views of body and the material domain as such. The Critical Kant (in contrast to some of his pre-Critical views) does not suggest that there could be any kind of intrinsic and *literally* bodily, and in *that* sense material, character for things in themselves – and for an obvious reason, since for him spatiality is not only relational and ideal but also essential to the very definitions of our notions of body and matter.[25] Nonetheless, the *Critique* does leave room for some other (for us unimaginable) kind of non-mental stuff to compose things in themselves, and so some kind of non-"haunted" Kantian realism could remain even without the "humble" interpretation.

This interpretation is also suspect because it is not true in any case that Kant's position requires the features of things in themselves as such to be only intrinsic rather than also relational. It is precisely at the level of things in themselves, after all, that Kant is most concerned with allowing relations of grounding and free

causing: between us and our temporal effects or empirical character, between things in themselves and our "affected" perceptions,
and also between God and other things, especially as a condition
for the realization of the highest good. The obvious way for Kant to
understand the crucial characteristic of absolute freedom of choice
is precisely as relational, and it is clear that for him this must be
a characteristic concerning things in themselves, rather than mere
phenomena, since according to the Second Analogy phenomena as
such must remain described simply by laws of nature.

The preceding considerations introduce one of the most common
of all objections to Kant's metaphysics: The *Critique's* transcendental idealism can seem able to escape skeptical or mentalistic absurdi-
ties only at the cost of introducing causal relations between things in
themselves and phenomena, relations that directly conflict with the
Critique's own transcendental limitations on what we can mean and
know. This objection, however, commonly presupposes that Kant
can allow only concepts of causality that are spelled out entirely in
spatiotemporal terms. This presupposition involves a conflation of
pure and (spatiotemporal) schematized senses of the categories. The
presupposition is defeated by Kant's explicit and repeated reminder
that we have a pure notion of cause, one that derives from general
logical features of the understanding and that need not be *defined* in
terms of any specific forms of sensibility, let alone space and time
in particular (cf. *Critique of Practical Reason*, 5:50–7).

A fallback form of the objection is to contend that even if non-
spatiotemporal causality could make some sense, it still would be
wrong for Kant to allow the *assertion* of such relations, since this
would go beyond the restriction of our theoretical *knowledge* to spatiotemporal determinations. This is a shrewder objection, but there
is a response to it once it is understood that Kant does not present or
need to understand the assertion of the mere existence of pure causal
relations between things in themselves and phenomena (which he
explicitly suggests our considering at A 534/B 562ff., and in many
later discussions of our free action as moral agents) as grounded in a
theoretical *inference within* his system. It is perfectly open to him
to *begin*, as he in fact does, with various common pre-philosophical
notions, such as that we all allow that we have common forms
of sensibility (see e.g., A 42/B 59, "to be sure, it pertains to every
human being"); that we all are finite receptive subjects, *"receptive"*

to something existent that we are not responsible for; and that we all may continue to assume this (as we all do[26]), without any ground to believe otherwise – and then to say, *later*, because of transcendental idealism, that this independent being must have some non-sensible features.

Starting from such common assumptions still leaves a lot for philosophy to do. There remains the task of working out the Analytic of the specific structures within our experience, and there is also the general philosophical question of what to say about whatever exists in itself. This question can be properly pursued by recalling the general pure ("non-schematized") features of the categories and by considering what properties we definitely should *not* attribute to the in itself as such, given what the *Critique* teaches about our pure forms of experience and the possible ways of explaining them. Here the main implication of Kant's idealism is simply that the structures of spatiotemporality *cannot* be used to determine the in itself. Given the clarifications made earlier, there is nothing in this result concerning the ideality of the mere forms of space and time that suggests, let alone entails, that we should give up thinking that there is some reality, aside from our own mind, responsible for our encounter with experience. Moreover, if it were supposed that we may assert only items that are licensed by scientific spatiotemporal determinations, then, in Kant's view, we would absurdly also have to forfeit our constant thought of ourselves as spontaneous agents.

Note that the crucial pre-philosophical thought of our free causality fits in with, but is not prior to, the thought of our being receptive.[27] The thought of our freedom takes the natural form, after all, of asking about how we should choose among some options that we understand as precisely given rather than created by us. Note also that this acceptance of a thing in itself grounding our experience, which Kant repeatedly asserts,[28] is in no tension at all with the specific negative conclusions of the Dialectic. We have not "flown" to any *determination* of the in itself in terms of a specific quantity or quality (simple, or endlessly complex), and we have not made any theoretical claims about it as rooted in an uncaused causing rather than only caused causings, or in a necessary being rather than something contingent. We also do not claim to know theoretically if it is some kind of special mind-like (mental in some way, but not non-temporal in itself) finite being after all, or how, if at all, it is related to some kind of infinite being. The upshot of the *Critique* is therefore a kind of realism combined with theoretical agnosticism on most traditional positive claims in psychology, cosmology, and theology. Nonetheless, this is a metaphysical position and not an entirely contentless "standpoint," not a mere allowance that there is some X that could be anything. It involves a commitment to some absolute truths: The in itself is definitely not spatial, temporal, material, or mental in any ordinary (temporal, natural) sense, and yet it must be such as to allow for a form of experience that has very specific *a priori* structures for a receptive subject. Moreover, whatever is in itself must be compatible with the general categories of thought, which, Kant insists, allows for considerable practical determination by us.

All this may show that, even when Kant's particular version of idealism is given a somewhat non-humble metaphysical interpretation, it still need not engender the specific worries that apply to other forms of idealism. But it does not follow that the actual legacy of the *Critique*, that is, the way it was taken up by its best known successors, was not determined by these worries. In general, it is possible for the most common appropriations of a highly original and complex philosophy to be based on significant misunderstandings, and this seems to be the case with Kant's philosophy. It is also quite possible that reactions to Kant's metaphysics that did not involve an entirely correct understanding of him led to many important philosophical insights that may not have occurred otherwise. Developments in the aftermath of the *Critique* were heavily affected by a host of progressive and epochal changes. Events such as the French Revolution, the Weimar renaissance, and the general upheavals of late eighteenth-century German social and university life played a role in Kant's reception that often outweighed the intricate and rarely followed technicalities of the Critical texts.[29] There is, however, one "technical" concept right at the center of the *Critique* itself that figured heavily in the reaction to these events and had a central influence in shaping thought after Kant. This is the troublesome notion mentioned earlier of the unconditioned, which can no longer be avoided.

IV. THE POISON OF KANT'S CRITIQUE: THE DEMAND FOR THE UNCONDITIONED

In the second edition Preface to the *Critique* Kant directly connects the concept of the unconditioned not only with the traditional demands of the "older metaphysic" but also with reason as such: "that which necessarily drives us to go beyond the boundaries of experience and all appearances is the *unconditioned*, which reason necessarily and with right demands in things in themselves for everything that is conditioned" (B xx). He goes on to explain that his transcendental idealism will dissolve the antinomies and show that "*the contradiction disappears*; and consequently that the unconditioned must not be present in things insofar as we are acquainted [*kennen*] with them (insofar as they are given to us), but rather in things insofar as we are not acquainted with them, as things in themselves" (B xxi). And he adds, clearly having in mind the positive results of the second *Critique*, "what still remains for us is to try whether there are not data in reason's practical data for determining that transcendent rational concept of the unconditioned, in such a way as to reach beyond the boundaries of all possible experience, in accordance with the wishes of metaphysics, cognitions *a priori* that are possible" (B xxi). In other words, Kant is not only saying that the "unconditioned" is demanded by reason "with right," but he is also immediately and explicitly indicating that it is present within his own system. He does not refer merely to a spurious unconditioned in the thoughts of other systems or in the mistakes of some kind of totally suspect faculty. The issue he focuses on, remarkably, is *not* the mistake of affirming the unconditioned as such but instead that of treating what is sensible as if *it* could be unconditioned.[30] Given passages like this, and what we know of philosophy immediately after Kant, it can again seem that Hamilton was on to something in speaking of a "germ" in the "bosom" of Kant's own philosophy, something with some role in the development of the "more visionary doctrine of the absolute" that came to "haunt the schools of Germany even to the present day."

There are, nevertheless, enormous differences between the Critical affirmation of the unconditioned and its role in other philosophies. Kant immediately restricts "determination" of it to the "the practical standpoint," and he continually emphasizes that using it to characterize anything empirical is definitely improper and leads to contradiction. Nonetheless, a natural way to read his discussion as a whole is to take it as saying that things in themselves definitely must be thought as unconditioned, that something conditioned is given to us, and that, given any conditioned item, reason must regard "the series of conditions as completed" (B xx). Nowhere does Kant take

away the presumption that we are confronted with something literally "conditioned." This is not a minor point. A Humean might say,
for example, that an impression simply exists. It may be contingent
in the sense that it is not contradictory for it not to have existed. But
this does not mean that it is literally "given" in the sense of having
to be "conditioned," that is, depending on something else. Even if it
is analytic that whatever is called "conditioned" requires "a condition," it is not analytic that what confronts us is "conditioned." And
yet, *that* the given is conditioned does seem to be a constant *theoretical* position for Kant. We are finite, *receptive* minds that take
data to be not simply present but to be given to us (see, e.g., A 19/
B 33, the first paragraph of the *Critique* proper), and ultimately, given
transcendental idealism, we have to regard them as themselves conditioned in a more than empirical sense.[31] Some might wish that
Kant had held to the thought that what is empirical is conditioned
in a merely empirical sense (and so might not need, as the syllogism
goes, a non-empirical condition), but in fact he does not restrain
himself in this way. He speaks, for example, of "the existence of
appearances not grounded in the least within itself but always conditioned" (A 566/B 594), and he says, "appearances [that] do not
count for any more than they are in fact, namely not for things in
themselves ... must have grounds that are not appearances" (A 537/
B 565). That is, the empirical data require something conditioning
them, something thought of as itself not empirically conditioned,
and hence something that is in that sense unconditioned.[32] There is
a "smoking gun" in the text after all, a kind of "spectre" that is not
fully "exorcised."

For some, the unconditioned might seem more palatable if we
keep in mind that Kant explains that reason can think of it as taking
the form of either an unconditioned complete series of beings or a
single being that is unconditioned (A 409/B 436f; A 483/B 511), and
so it by no means has to be a *typical* "spectral" being. The general
idea here seems to be simply that, in order for something to be, it
must "completely" or "absolutely" have "whatever it takes" to be.
After all, how could something hold in reality while the "complete"
conditions needed for it to be, *whatever they are*, would not hold? In
particular, how would that be possible with what we really are given?
It is true that, since the conditioning relation is naturally thought of
as a relation between two distinct items, then, given the definition

of a particular thing or state that is conditioned, it is a logically synthetic and uncertain claim that some other *particular kind* of thing or state exists as its condition. But *as long as* the *Critique* holds that for us the sensible as such is *given* in the sense of being itself *conditioned*, and that the domain of spatiotemporal sensibility by itself can never constitute a "complete" ground that does the conditioning, then it does appear to require *something else* "with right" for what is given to us.

This conclusion leaves open, of course, exactly what it is that is needed. Perhaps there is some non-sensible, but finite and single feature or act or being that conditions the relevant conditioned item, or perhaps there is an endless (non-sensible) sequence of conditions for the conditioned. It does not follow that this unconditioned is anything very remarkable, for example, mental, absolutely necessary, or God-like. Kant is perfectly willing to call items "unconditioned" that are unconditioned only in a specific respect and not altogether, and he nowhere gives a general argument that something could not simply have a finite property F "without condition." One can imagine some traditional philosophers saying that something could not simply be F without some greater G making it be that way, but Kant's arguments do not have this kind of general pattern. He starts with the fact that we see particular temporal or spatial or causal "slices" of something conditioning something else, and so on and on, and hence we naturally look for further conditions of that type in each case, but he does not presuppose that properties as such must be really conditioned simply because they are properties. (Kant does hold that the *concept* of each finite property can be regarded as a limitation of the concept of the properties of an *ens realissimum*, but his theoretical philosophy does not claim that there really must be such a being, or that in general there must be more eminent properties than the ones we are actually acquainted with.)

From all that has been presented here it also does not follow that Kant was clearly right in his own considerations to insist that no sensible features, either those that seem finite or those that seem infinite, could themselves provide something unconditioned. This has to be settled by an evaluation of all the specific arguments of the Antinomies, which cannot be attempted here. Any proper evaluation of them, however, would have to keep in mind that Kant goes so far as to contend that the problem with sensible appearances is *not*, as some might suspect, basically a matter of their being *not all given to* any actual finite mind like ours. Kant states that the fact that appearances are not an "absolute whole" or thing in itself follows *even if* you "assume that nature were completely exposed to you; that nothing were hidden to your senses and to the consciousness of everything laid before your intuition" (A 482/B 510). For him there is something about the content of "empirical cognition" *as such* that precludes a "consciousness of its absolute totality" (A 483/B 511), which in turn precludes its being a thing in itself. In other words, the problem with sensible appearances does not seem to be that we do not have a kind of "God's eye view" on them. We ourselves might well have something like that view insofar as we could, with Kant's encouragement, imagine *them all* "laid before" us so that nothing is hidden. The problem is not so much with *our view* but with *them*.[33] That is, the kind of whole that they would constitute even on a clear and complete view would still not be "an absolute whole," and "it is really this whole for which an explanation is being demanded in the transcendental problems of reason" (A 484/B 512). Kant also expresses his view by saying, "with all possible perceptions, you always remain caught up in *conditions*, whether in space or time, and you never get to the unconditioned" (A 483/B 511). Here, contrary to our contemporary inclinations, I take him not to be expressing skepticism about the unconditioned as such but to be allowing reason to hold that there is something unconditioned, and then to be stressing that no set of spatiotemporal features could ever reveal it as such. The error of dogmatism (or "transcendental realism") then is not a general matter of holding on to an affirmation of things in themselves and of something in some sense "unconditioned"; it is rather a specific matter of trying to *determine* the in itself by making spatiotemporal features ("forms of sensibility") themselves into something unconditioned.

This may seem to be an unusual charge, but in fact it is directly relevant to all of Kant's major opponents: Leibniz, Newton, Berkeley, and Hume. He charges all of them, quite understandably, with making such features into (in principle) transparent beings of a particular unconditioned kind. For these philosophies the features do in fact exist either as mental items on their own, as with Hume's impressions, or as determinate ultimate features of reality simply by being components of a mind. For Berkeley, they exist in our mind; for

Newton, in God's mind; and for Leibniz the features are themselves
taken to be relational, but the intrinsic features that they reduce to
upon "clarification" turn out to be properties of independent monads. For Kant, in contrast, the spatiotemporal sensible features we
are acquainted with require a condition in a being that, whatever
it is, is definitely unlike them.[34] The characterization of the thing
in itself as unconditioned is thus compatible with the transcendental ideality of the spatiotemporal and conditioned – and can even be
understood as part of the Dialectic's very argument for this ideality –
and yet this characterization is also a reminder of how Kant's position is not at all a "visionary" idealism, or speculative mentalistic
view like that of his main predecessors. The position is also a form
of realism insofar as it definitely asserts that there is something concrete distinct from us that is precisely not to be understood as the
mere product of a mind – our individual or group mind, or even the
divine mind.

On this reading it turns out that there is a very close relationship
between Kant's two key notions, the unconditioned and the ideal,
a relationship that is very helpful in understanding how things in
themselves relate to appearances. If causal and other relations are
possible here after all, one might wonder about the point of making
such a sharp, metaphysical distinction in terminology. My proposal
is that we understand the relation between the sensible and transcendentally ideal, on the one hand, and the thing in itself on the
other hand, as just what Kant repeatedly indicates it is, a relation of
several kinds between the conditioned and unconditioned. This sort
of relation allows the peculiar "intimacy" that Kant needs if he is to
keep to the language that he uses about a "ground" of appearances
and about our freedom acting as an intelligible cause on sensible
effects. At the same time, the special meaning of "unconditioned"
allows for the unique heterogeneity that Kant clearly takes to hold
between things in themselves and appearances. This heterogeneity is
in fact very helpful because it implies that the sensible items that are
appearances in a transcendental sense do *not* stand to be "corrected"
in any internal *epistemic* way by the notion of things in themselves
(and so there is no "God's eye view" that is a "measure" of them)[35] –
unlike appearances in an empirical sense, which can be corrected by
other sensible appearances, so that we come to a proper objective
view of spatiotemporal phenomena as such. Items that are called

appearances in a transcendental sense simply have to be understood as having to have "complete" grounds beyond themselves – in some cases grounds that allow empirical givenness to occur at all, in other cases grounds that may allow specific relations such as free causality to take place. The point of calling something a mere appearance in this sense is to claim not that it fails to exist at all but is rather to say that it (including all our empirical mental properties) requires something else, something of a much more fundamental kind, to exist as it does.

This point is not a matter of how the term "appearance" is understood in general. The term can also be used in a different way, say by phenomenologists, as designating a kind of sheer presence, without any contrast with things in themselves. Kant's main use of the term, however, rests on reasons he gives for saying that the specific features we are given through our forms of sensibility are "mere appearances" *in the sense that* they cannot be self-grounded. The reasons are given in the arguments of the Aesthetic, Analytic, and Dialectic to the effect that any non-spatiotemporal properties that we can determine must depend on spatiotemporal ones, and that (especially because of the First Antinomy) these properties in turn must depend on something else. The cogency of this argument is not transparent, but my main point is simply that it is the natural way to understand the main point at the heart of the *Critique*'s Dialectic, and that it alone leaves Kant with enough of a non-humble metaphysics to have the chance he needs for preserving his own very substantive practical views. The argument's exposition admittedly involves terminological complications that can understandably give rise to the kinds of "visionary" notions that later interpreters demanded – and then regretted – but it also leaves Kant's own system at least free of the troubles of the mentalistic versions of idealism with which it is often confused.

V. KANTIAN POSTLUDE: THE LEGACY OF THE "SPECTRE" OF THE UNCONDITIONED

To indicate that this reading is not as far-fetched as it might seem to analytic readers, I turn to a brief sketch of the (still relatively little known) immediate impact of Kant's critique of metaphysics. The quotations that have been given concerning the unconditioned may seem to rely on unusual passages. In Kant's own time, however, there was no more common concern among philosophers than precisely the unconditioned, or, as it came to be more commonly called, "the absolute." As many scholars have documented, the search for the unconditioned was the dominant agenda of the generation of the Pantheism Dispute, the controversy awakened by Jacobi's reading of Lessing, Spinoza, Hume, and Kant.[36] "We seek everywhere the unconditioned [*das Unbedingte*] and find only the conditioned [*Dinge*]" became the watchword for post-Kantians of every stripe.[37] One might at first suppose that this concern was something that Kant came to only with the remarks about the Dialectic cited earlier from the second edition Preface of the *Critique* (1787), which appeared just a couple years after the height of the Pantheism Dispute (1785). In fact, however, the crucial idea that in sensible experience we "always remain caught up with *conditions*," was, as just noted, already explicit and central in the first edition *Critique* (A 483/B 511). What Kant's successors did was combine this thought with a host of their own pressing concerns. Five major strands of reaction to Kant's notion of the unconditioned can be distinguished: Jacobi, Reinhold-Fichte, Early Romanticism, Schelling-Hegel, and neo-Kantianism.

Friedrich Heinrich Jacobi dominated the first phase of reaction, which colored all the rest even long after the details of his work were forgotten. It was Jacobi who combined the interest in an unconditioned with the attitude of what he called faith [*Glaube*] and a dismissive view of all forms of modern non-theist theoretical philosophy. For the improper reasons noted earlier, he took the notion of the thing in itself to be directly contrary to the main doctrines of the Critical philosophy, and he suggested that Kant's theoretical account of experience could at best amount to little more than a Hume-like cavalcade of private ideas, ideas that happen to be tied together by the laws of the Analogies and hence leave us subject *a priori* to determinism or worse. Given this bleak view of theoretical philosophy, Jacobi preached the alternative of a return to revelation and intuition. His engaging personal manner, his Hume-like emphasis on the feelings of the common man and the limits of reason (in contrast to "belief," *Glaube*), his highly popular literary efforts, and his intense religiosity of a kind peculiar to the modern German tradition, all gave him an influence that goes far beyond what one might expect from a study of his philosophical texts alone.[38] His role in bringing to light the significance of Spinoza's philosophy, even if he was ultimately unsympathetic to it, also made it a major task for other readers of the time to find some way to relate Spinoza's appealing naturalistic interest in an unconditioned to the mysterious uses of this term in Kant's texts. In the end, Jacobi represents the option of what can be called a *non-philosophical flight to the unconditioned*, one that replaces Kant's detailed arguments for making a nuanced distinction between apparent and underlying features with a hasty and non-rational affirmation of a truly "visionary" absolute. It is no surprise that Jacobi would also have an influence on the genuinely "spectral" strands of later continental thought.

A second main line of reaction was ushered in by Karl Leonhard Reinhold and Johann Gottlieb Fichte. They sought to overcome Kant's indeterminate theoretical notion of the thing in itself by finding a privileged form of representation that would allow a completely unified and systematic type of immanent metaphysics. For them, the unconditioned stands not for a special transcendent *thing* that is a metaphysical condition for sensible appearances but instead for a transparent philosophical *principle* of subjectivity that can ground a totally autonomous philosophical science.[39] They followed Jacobi in taking a transcendent and causal thing in itself to be literally impossible for any post-Critical thought, but they resolved not to abdicate the priority of rationalist philosophy itself, while also not allowing any kind of non-libertarian metaphysics, or falling back into a position that would be vulnerable to skepticism or reduce to a form of subjective idealism.[40] In Fichte's most significant phase, the unconditioned reveals itself in forms of immediate self-consciousness and categorical commands of morality that supposedly do not require, as an *a priori* theoretical argument for their possibility, the "letter" of Kant's metaphysics of transcendental idealism. The existence of the subject's absolute freedom, and then of a social and natural world to accommodate its aims, was taken to be a first certainty. Since Fichte rejected Kant's thing in itself while holding on to the language of idealism, English readers, until recently, have tended to misunderstand his view as a form of subjective idealism.[41] This is highly unfair since Fichte's system is adamantly committed to presenting knowledge of a thoroughly objective domain, and it is even more radical than Kant's in rejecting any possibility of literally spiritual and transcendent entities. Nonetheless, in placing so much emphasis, for methodological purposes, on considerations of self-consciousness and morality, Fichte played into the hands of opponents even within his own tradition. His absolute is "visionary" not in a literally transcendent sense but because it involves an overly ambitious secular version of Kant's doctrine of the postulates of pure practical reason, a version that makes reality necessarily and fully transparent (albeit asymptotically) to human efforts. The main danger of the Fichtean option is that it neglects a detailed reconsideration of the full theoretical and natural *prerequisites* of the very substantive practical-rational claims needed in any truly Critical philosophy.

A third broad reaction to the Kantian metaphysics of the unconditioned, which can be touched on only very briefly here, consists in the sketches offered by the "Jena circle" of philosophers such as Johann Benjamin Erhard and the Early Romantic figures Friedrich von Hardenberg (Novalis) and Friedrich Schlegel. Unlike the other reactions, the members of this group were willing to accept a fundamentally agnostic metaphysics without either abandoning philosophy altogether or claiming it could ever be organized into a complete foundational system.[42] Since, at their best, they each in their own way allowed a non-sensible thing in itself without claiming any uniquely privileged and transparent moral, religious, or aesthetic determination of it and without demeaning the robust empirical realism and categorial organization of nature that Kant also wanted to emphasize, it can be argued that they are the closest interesting heirs of the Critical philosophy, even if it has taken centuries to recognize them as such.

A fourth immediate reaction to Kant was the "absolute idealism" developed originally in the work of the early Friedrich Wilhelm Joseph Schelling and Georg Friedrich Wilhelm Hegel and their project of a constitutive and organic *Naturphilosophie*.[43] Schelling is particularly relevant because he was the first of the Tübingen trio (Schelling, Hegel, and Hölderlin) to gain influence by publishing his systematic views. The main theme of his first writings is the project of uniting "dogmatism and criticism," that is, of combining the appealing naturalistic metaphysics of the unconditioned that he takes Spinozism to represent with a more modern account of the dynamic faculties of mind that Kant, Reinhold, and Fichte develop in their concern with autonomy. Schelling strongly encouraged Hegel to jettison all notions of a transcendent thing in itself, just as the "Earliest System Program of German Idealism" (1796 or 1797) expressed the Tübingen trio's commitment to hastening a completely immanent realization of Kant's postulates of pure practical reason.[44]

What distinguishes the approach of Schelling and Hegel is an insistence on returning theoretical metaphysics to a position of methodological primacy and exhaustive "scientific" systematicity. Each claims in his own way to give a rational derivation of the necessary development of self-determination throughout the objective realm, especially in detailing the non-mechanistic aspects of nature and the positive dialectical aspects of history that Kant and Fichte neglect. Their position is called "absolute idealism" not because it makes everything "ideal" in some literally mental sense but because it holds that what is "absolute," that is, unconditioned, is simply the *whole* of (broadly) natural reality, and that this whole can be proven to have a fundamentally rational and teleological, and in that sense "ideal," structure.[45] Like Kant, they also call space, time, and sensible features "mere appearances," and like him they take this to signify not that these items are private or merely psychological but that they have a ground in some more basic entity, an entity that is not literally a monad-like mind.[46] The difference is that their unconditioned, unlike Kant's, cannot be a particular thing in itself, or group of them, but must be an all-inclusive whole, an absolutely unconditioned structure that allows us to determine it, that is, to know and fulfill it. An advantage of their position is that it blocks all transcendent mysteries and fits more closely with the now-common unrestricted understanding of the term "unconditioned." A problem for their position (eventually emphasized by Schelling himself), aside from the details of the particular arguments they present, is that the core content of their program seems directly to threaten the very commitment to absolute individual freedom that was the prime motive for developing a Critical philosophy in the first place. This alone does not show that their position involves more of a relapse into dogmatism than does Kant's, but it does indicate one reason why the presentation of their view is much more esoteric than the *Critique*. Even if absolute idealism does not deserve blame for being "visionary" in the full sense that Hamilton implied, it still makes that blame understandable.

The fifth line of reaction to Kant's critique of metaphysics has a character very unlike the others. This broadly scientific line does not necessarily deny Kant's interest in the thing in itself, or his underlying moral motivations, but what it takes to heart most seriously is the lesson that there is definitely a systematic problem in continuing metaphysics in the old style, with the assertion of absolute necessities of any kind. For these later Kantians, the best tactic is always to begin, as Kant himself did, by considering what structures are required by the most advanced exact sciences of one's time, and then reflecting astringently on what, if anything, remains left over for philosophy once all these structures are characterized with full precision and generality.

This approach is most familiar to us now from neo-Kantians of the late nineteenth century such Hermann Cohen, Alois Riehl, and Heinrich Rickert, but it can also be found in earlier strands of thought such as the school of Johann Friedrich Fries (who taught in Heidelberg in 1805 and was called to Jena in 1816), which was developed further by Leonard Nelson.[47] More recently, Michael Friedman has reinvigorated this tradition by explaining how Ernst Cassirer, Moritz Schlick, Hans Reichenbach, Rudolf Carnap, and other leading twentieth-century figures can be understood as having developed a rigorous new kind of Kantian program that uncovers principles that are *a priori* in the significant but limited sense of being constitutive rules for a basic scientific framework within a particular era.[48] This way of continuing Kant's critique of metaphysics obviously seems less likely to make the mistake, which dogged Kant's immediate successors, of falling back into the clutches of introducing questionable "visionary" metaphysical programs. It has not itself, however, been free of excessive optimism about being able to present a fully unified account of science and philosophy. A further disadvantage of the approach is that it has tended to lose touch with Kant's concerns with ordinary experience, which clearly interested him as much as any particular scientific developments, and which still might yield some most general "life-world" structures that can remain constant throughout scientific change. Edmund Husserl's later work moved in this broadly Kantian direction at the same time that the deep historicism of his student, Martin Heidegger, pushed most Continental philosophy in the opposite direction, away from any genuinely Kantian approach.[49]

Neo-Kantianism based entirely on a reconstruction – or critique – of current scientific frameworks tends not to have much to say in detail about classical metaphysical problems such as the philosophical thematization of a general distinction between appearances and things in themselves. To the extent that these kinds of problems do continue to animate contemporary analytic discussions (see, e.g., Wilfrid Sellars, Peter Strawson, Hilary Putnam, Barry Stroud, and John McDowell) of transcendental arguments in a fruitful way that does not depend on specific problems of current scientific frameworks, it can be said that at least some of the underlying spirit of Kant's critique survives in our own time – even while what may have mattered most to him in the Dialectic, the discussion of the unconditioned, stays in the shadows.[50]

In retrospect: Kant's own Critical metaphysics, with its full arsenal of serious commitments to transcendental idealism, transcendental freedom, and a complete transcendental philosophy that "will come forward as a science," has few "bosom" companions. His modern predecessors were all too mentalist; the empiricist ones too skeptical and psychological, the rationalist ones too dogmatic and spiritual. His best-known German successors created a new idealism that avoids these flaws, but they and their followers gave up too soon on either a genuine metaphysics of nature (Reinhold, Fichte) or a genuine metaphysics of individual freedom (Hegel). The scientific neo-Kantians have tended not only to go beyond the specific errors of past groups but also to give up on classical metaphysics altogether. This leaves only the figures of the Jena circle and Early Romanticism – but although they are not anti-systematic as such, their fragments introduce a deep sense of history and relativity that surely takes them beyond Kant's own strict program as well.[51] A supposedly childless professor, Kant the metaphysician left behind a fertile family of illegitimate heirs.

NOTES

1. Sir William Hamilton, *Discussions on Philosophy and Literature*, ed. Robert Turnbull (New York, 1861), p. 25. Cited in Manfred Kuehn, "Hamilton's Reading of Kant: A Chapter in the Early Scottish Reception of Kant's Thought," in *Kant and his Influence*, ed. G. M. Ross and T. McWalter (Bristol, 1990), pp. 305–47, at p. 335.

2. Passages from the first *Critique* are all cited as translated by Paul Guyer and Allen W. Wood, *Critique of Pure Reason* (Cambridge, 1998).

3. See my *Kant and the Fate of Autonomy: Problems in the Appropriation of the Critical Philosophy* (Cambridge, 2000), ch. 2; *Between Kant and Hegel: Texts in the Development of Post-Kantian Idealism*, rev. edition, ed. G. di Giovanni (Indianapolis, 2000); and Dieter Henrich, *Between Kant and Hegel: Lectures on German Idealism* (Cambridge, 2003).

4. See *Kant's Early Critics: The Empiricist Critique of the Theoretical Philosophy*, ed. B. Sassen (Cambridge, 2000); cf. John Findlay, *Kant and the Transcendental Object* (Oxford, 1982).

5. See my *Interpreting Kant's Critiques* (Oxford, 2003), Introduction.

6. See, for example, Rudolf Makkreel, *Imagination and Interpretation in Kant* (Chicago, 1990); and Thomas Wartenberg, "Reason and the Practice of Science," in *The Cambridge Companion to Kant*, ed. P. Guyer (Cambridge, 1992), pp. 228–48.

7. This idea is stressed by interpreters such as Gerold Prauss, Henry E. Allison, and Robert Pippin. I note some problems with early uses of the idea in *Kant and the Fate of Autonomy*, ch. 5.

8. See, for example, Michael J. Loux, *Metaphysics: A Contemporary Introduction* (London, 1998).

9. For a good treatment of Kant's appreciation of the meaningfulness of metaphysical concepts, see James Van Cleve, *Problems from Kant* (New York, 1999).

10. See *Hegel: The Essential Writings*, ed. F. Weiss (New York, 1974), p. 26 (*Encyclopedia Logic*, Introduction, §6); for a Kantian critique of Hegel, cf. my *Kant and the Fate of Autonomy*, ch. 6; and Paul Guyer, "Absolute Idealism and the Rejection of Kantian Dualism," in *The Cambridge Companion to German Idealism*, ed. K. Ameriks (Cambridge, 2000), pp. 37–56.

11. For more details, see Michelle Grier, *Kant's Doctrine of Transcendental Illusion* (Cambridge, 2001); and Henry E. Allison, *Kant's Transcendental Idealism*, rev. edition (New Haven, 2004).

12. For a comparison of Kant's account with the "genealogies" presented by later philosophers, see Alain Renaut, "Transzendentale Dialektik. Einleitung und Buch I," in *Immanuel Kant/Kritik der reinen Vernunft*, ed. G. Mohr and M. Willaschek (Berlin, 1998), pp. 353–70.

13. See my *Kant's Theory of Mind: An Analysis of the Paralogisms of Pure Reason*, 2nd ed. (Oxford, 2000), and "Apperzeption und Subjekt. Kants Lehre vom Ich," in *Warum Kant heute? Systematische Bedeutung und Rezeption seiner Philosophie in der Gegenwart*, ed. D. Heidemann and K. Engelhard (Berlin, 2004), pp. 76–99.

14. Kant treats the second antinomy, unlike the last two, as involving a "heterogeneous" as opposed to a "homogeneous" series, but it is not clear that the traditional notion of an underlying simple being is best thought of as homogeneous with a series of divisible parts. See A 414/ B 441.

15. See Paul Guyer, "The Unity of Reason: Pure Reason as Practical Reason in Kant's Early Concept of the Transcendental Dialectic," *Monist* 72 (1989): 139–67, reprinted in his *Kant on Freedom, Law, and Happiness* (Cambridge: Cambridge University Press, 2000).

16. For more detail on the arguments of the Antinomies, see my "The Critique of Metaphysics: Kant and Traditional Ontology," in *The Cambridge Companion to Kant*, p. 272, n. 5, and p. 275, n. 15, and my *Interpreting Kant's Critiques*, ch. 3; Eric Watkins, "The Antinomy of Pure Reason, Sections 3–8," in *Immanuel Kant/ Kritik der reinen Vernunft*, pp. 447–64; and Henry E. Allison, "The Antinomy of Pure Reason, Section 9," ibid., pp. 465–90.

17. See *Kant and the Sciences*, ed. E. Watkins (Oxford, 2001).

18. See Allen Wood, *Kant's Rational Theology* (Ithaca, 1978), and *Kant* (London, 2004).

19. See above, n. 6, for literature on Kant's regulative/constitutive distinction.

20. See my *Interpreting Kant's Critiques*, ch. 10.

21. For more details, see my "The Critique of Metaphysics: Kant and Traditional Ontology," pp. 255–72.

22. Cf. my "Idealism from Kant to Berkeley," in *Eriugena, Berkeley and the Idealist Tradition*, ed. S. Gersh and D. Moran (Notre Dame, forthcoming).

23. This line of thought is suggested by ideas from Wilfrid Sellars, and, more recently, Daniel Warren, *Reality and Impenetrability in Kant's Philosophy of Nature* (London, 2001).

24. See Rae Langton, *Kantian Humility* (Oxford, 1998).

25. See my *Interpreting Kant's Critiques*, ch. 5.

26. See, for example, Immanuel Kant, *Lectures on Metaphysics*, ed. K. Ameriks and S. Naragon (Cambridge, 1997), p. 226 (29:928), "This error [that bodies do not exist] is likewise refutable neither from experience nor *a priori*." For another perspective, cf. Paul Guyer, "Kant on Common Sense and Scepticism," *Kantian Review* 7 (2003): 1–37.

27. Manfred Frank notes that the Jena romantics used this Kantian idea against Fichte. See his *Selbstgefühl* (Frankfurt, 2002), p. 37, and cf. his *'Unendliche Annäherung': Die Anfänge der philosophischen Frühromantik* (Frankfurt, 1997).

28. See even Kant's late work (1804), *What is the Real Progress that Meta-physics Has Made in Germany since the Time of Leibniz and Wolff?*, ed. F. T. Rink (20:290); and *Lectures on Metaphysics*, p. 213 (29:857), "They show us merely the appearances of things. But these are not the things themselves. They indeed underlie the appearances"; and p. 217 (29:861), "But there still must be a transcendental cause from which this appearance arises. This cause is unknown to us since it does not belong to the sensible world."

29. See especially Karl Reinhold, *Letters on the Kantian Philosophy*, ed. K. Ameriks (Cambridge, 2005).

30. "All antinomies rest on this, that we seek the unconditioned in the phenomenal world, which simply will not do." *Lectures on Metaphysics*, p. 362 (28:661); cf. 28:658.

31. Kant does not logically exclude the idea that this condition might be a greater being that includes, and so is not really distinct from, us, but in fact he never expresses sympathy with this Spinozist alternative.

32. Note that for Kant the real feature of being conditioned is not the same thing as contingency. A main point of the Fourth Antinomy is precisely that, for all we know, something conditioned might – or might not – depend on a being that is necessary, and that all that this being conditions might then necessarily follow from it as well (A 562/B 590; A 564/B 592). Thus, something could be, in a sense, both conditioned and necessary; "empirical contingency" is not proof of "intelligible contingency," that is, metaphysical non-necessity.

33. Here Kant is actually agreeing with something that Hegel wanted him to say. See above, n. 10, and cf. my *Kant and the Fate of Autonomy*, pp. 301–2.

34. Kant begins also with the thought that the thing in itself of appearances is not God, since his theoretical perspective by itself provides no grounds for even introducing an assertion of God's existence; and so later, when through practical reason he does assert God's existence, he does so in a context where it is presumed that God as a thing in itself is not identical with the thing in itself underlying appearances. Cf. *Critique of Practical Reason* (5:102).

35. This is a worry, for example, in Allison, *Kant's Transcendental Idealism*, Introduction; and John McDowell, *Mind and World* (Cambridge, 1994), pp. 3–6 and 41–4.

36. This point has been emphasized often by Dieter Henrich and Manfred Frank. See also *Friedrich Heinrich Jacobi: The Main Philosophical Writings and the Novel Allwill*, ed. G. di Giovanni (Montreal, 1984); Frederick Beiser, *The Fate of Reason: German Philosophy from Kant to Fichte* (Cambridge, MA: Harvard University Press, 1987), ch. 2; and

Paul Franks, "All or Nothing: Systematicity and Nihilism in Jacobi, Reinhold and Maimon," in *The Cambridge Companion to German Idealism*, pp. 95–116.

37. Novalis, *Pollen*, #1, as translated in *The Early Political Writings of the German Romantics*, ed. F. Beiser (Cambridge, 1996), p. 9. Cf. Charles Larmore, "Hölderlin and Novalis," in *The Cambridge Companion to German Idealism*, pp. 141–60.

38. See, for example, Nicholas Boyle's account of Jacobi's encounter with Goethe, in *Goethe: The Poet and the Age*, vol. 1 (Oxford, 1992), pp. 182–4.

39. See Henrich, *Between Kant and Hegel*, chs. 8–18.

40. The problem of skepticism was acute at this time because of G. E. Schulze's *Aenesidemus* (1792), which conflated Kant and the early Reinhold and attacked them for not having an adequate response to skepticism. See Daniel Breazeale, "Fichte's 'Aenesidemus' Review and the Transformation of German Idealism," *Review of Metaphysics* 34 (1980/1): 545–68.

41. See, for example, George Santayana, *Egotism in German Philosophy* (New York, 1915), ch. 6.

42. See especially Frank, *Unendliche Annäherung*.

43. See Frederick Beiser, *German Idealism: The Struggle Against Subjectivism, 1781–1801* (Cambridge, MA: Harvard University Press, 2002), Part IV; and Robert Richards, *The Romantic Conception of Life: Poetry and the Organic in the Age of Goethe* (Chicago, 2001).

44. The authorship of this piece is much disputed. See the translation by Daniel Dahlstrom in *The Emergence of German Idealism*, ed. M. Baur and D. Dahlstrom (Washington, 1999), pp. 309–10. Cf. Klaus Düsing, "The Reception of Kant's Doctrine of Postulates in Schelling's and Hegel's Early Philosophical Projects," ibid., pp. 201–37.

45. Cf. Hans-Joachim Glock, "Vorsprung durch Logik: The German Analytic Tradition," in *German Philosophy since Kant*, ed. A. O'Hear (Cambridge, 1999), p. 145.

46. See Hegel, *Encyclopedia*, §§45 and 50; and cf. my *Kant and the Fate of Autonomy*, p. 276, n. 18.

47. See Leonard Nelson, *Socratic Method and Critical Philosophy* (New York, 1965). Cf. Klaus Köhnke, *The Rise of Neo-Kantianism: German Academic Philosophy between Idealism and Positivism* (Cambridge, 1991); and Otfried Höffe, *Kants Kritik der reinen Vernunft* (Munich, 2003), p. 221.

48. See Michael Friedman, *Dynamics of Reason* (Stanford, 2001), and *A Parting of the Ways: Carnap, Cassirer, and Heidegger* (Chicago, 2000).

49. A significant exception is Gerold Prauss, *Die Welt und wir*, 2 vols. (Stuttgart, 1990–1999). On Heidegger's misreading of Kant, see Dieter Henrich, "Über die Einheit der Subjektivität," *Philosophische Rundschau* 3 (1955): 28–69.

50. See however Paul Franks, *All or Nothing: Systematicity, Transcendental Arguments, and Skepticism in German Idealism* (Cambridge, MA: Harvard University Press, 2005).

51. On the relation of Kant and the romantics, see my "Hegel's Aesthetics: New Perspectives on its Response to Kant and Romanticism," *Bulletin of the Hegel Society of Great Britain* 45/46(2002): 72–92; as well as *Novalis: Fichte-Studies*, ed. J. Kneller (Cambridge, 2003); and Fred Rush Jr., "Kant and Schlegel," in *Kant und die Berliner Aufklärung. Akten des IX. Internationalen Kant-Kongresses* (Berlin/New York, 2001), vol. 3: 622–30.

9   Philosophy of natural science

A serious and detailed engagement with the natural science of his time was a hallmark of Kant's long intellectual career. Kant's earliest "pre-critical" writings were almost wholly devoted to this subject, including such works as *On the True Estimation of Living Forces* (1747), his doctoral dissertation *Meditations on Fire* (1755), his ground-breaking formulation of the nebular hypothesis (now often known as the Kant-Laplace hypothesis) in the *Universal Natural History and Theory of the Heavens* (1755), and his early formulation of a so-called dynamical theory of matter in the *Physical Monadology* (1756). In all of these works we see Kant striving, in particular, to reconcile his firm commitment to Newtonian physical theory (including such controversial doctrines as action at a distance) with the Leibnizean metaphysical tradition that was dominant in mid-eighteenth-century Germany. And these concerns with contemporary natural science and its metaphysical foundations are by no means absent in the "critical" period, which begins with the publication of the first edition of the *Critique of Pure Reason* in 1781. On the contrary, Kant's most developed philosophical exploration of the foundations of natural science, the *Metaphysical Foundations of Natural Science* (1786), appears at the height of this period. Moreover, the influence of this work is clearly visible in the revisions Kant made in the second edition of the *Critique* (1787); and a renewed emphasis on the problem of natural science more generally is evident in the way in which both the *Prolegomena to Any Future Metaphysics* (1783) and the Introduction to the second edition of the *Critique* now reformulate the "main transcendental question" addressed by the critical philosophy – "how are synthetic *a priori* judgements possible?" – in terms of the two subquestions "how is pure mathematics possible?" and "how is pure natural science possible?"[1]

All of this is clear and uncontroversial. What is less clear is the precise character and significance of Kant's engagement with natural science and its metaphysical foundations, in both the pre-critical and critical periods. In particular, while there is no doubt that Kant was just as firmly committed to Newtonian physical theory in the critical period as he was in the pre-critical period, it is quite controversial how central this commitment is in the system of the critical philosophy as a whole. Whereas, for example, Kant clearly uses fundamental principles of Newtonian mechanics (such as the law of inertia and the equality of action and reaction) to illustrate the presence of synthetic *a priori* judgements within "pure natural science" in the Introduction to the second edition of the *Critique* (§§V, VI; B 17–21), one may very well wonder whether Kant's defense of the synthetic *a priori* depends on these particular illustrations. For, if it does, then it would seem that Kant's critical philosophy as a whole stands or falls with the truth – and, indeed, synthetic *a priori* truth – of the fundamental principles of Newtonian mechanics. Since we now believe that precisely these Newtonian principles are actually in need of revision, this conclusion may appear especially unwelcome to those convinced of the enduring significance of the critical philosophy. It is very tempting, therefore, to view such examples from Newtonian natural science (together with the examples from Euclidean geometry illustrating the question "how is pure mathematics possible?") as *merely* illustrative. Kant is only truly committed to much more general synthetic *a priori* principles – such as the spatial character of experience in general, say, together with a similarly general principle of empirical lawlikeness – but not to the more specific principles of Euclidean geometry and Newtonian physics to which he happens to appeal.

I will address these questions in the following way. After a discussion of the intellectual background to and early development of Kant's philosophy of natural science, I will turn to his most developed articulation of the concept of pure natural science in the *Metaphysical Foundations of Natural Science*. I will discuss, in particular, the relationship of this work to both Kant's pre-critical writings and the *Critique of Pure Reason*. I will then consider the significance of Kant's views on pure natural science for the critical philosophy as a whole. My own view – which is quite controversial – is that Kant is committed to the synthetic *a priori* status of specific principles of Euclidean geometry and Newtonian physics, and, indeed, that without this commitment some of Kant's most important more general doctrines (for example, his "answer to Hume" concerning the necessity of causal laws of nature) simply become unintelligible. Nevertheless, despite the fact that these particular principles have since been revised in the course of further progress in the natural sciences after Kant, it does not follow that the critical philosophy as a whole is deprived of enduring significance. I approach this last issue by examining some post-Kantian developments in both natural science and its philosophical foundations that were explicitly inspired by Kant, and I conclude with some brief remarks about the significance of Kant's philosophy of natural science today.

I. BACKGROUND TO KANT'S METAPHYSICAL FOUNDATIONS OF NATURAL SCIENCE

What we now call modern philosophy was intimately connected with the scientific revolution of the sixteenth and seventeenth centuries. Descartes, in particular, was centrally involved with both revolutionary enterprises, which were by no means clearly distinguished at the time. Indeed, throughout the sixteenth, seventeenth, and early eighteenth centuries, what we now call "natural science" was still often called "natural philosophy." For example, Descartes' major contribution to what we now call natural science is entitled *The Principles of Philosophy* (1644), and Newton's great culminating work of the scientific revolution is entitled (apparently partly in reaction to Descartes) *Mathematical Principles of Natural Philosophy* (1686). In the case of Descartes, what he called "philosophy" was divided into two subdisciplines: "natural philosophy" or "physics" and "first philosophy" or "metaphysics." Physics dealt with the visible or corporeal part of the universe, and its distinctive task was to describe all phenomena in this part of the universe in terms of the motions and interactions of tiny parts of matter or corpuscles – which, in turn, possess only the purely geometrical properties (later called "primary qualities") of extension, figure, and motion, and interact with one another (and thereby change their states of motion) only by impact (whereby the speed and direction of one such corpuscle is changed by collision with another). The discipline of metaphysics, by contrast, dealt with the invisible and incorporeal part of the universe, namely, God and the soul, and so Descartes' fundamental distinction between extension and thought is precisely mirrored in this disciplinary distinction. Nevertheless, there is still an intimate relationship between the two disciplines, in that physics receives its ultimate foundations from metaphysics. For example, the basic law of nature governing all changes of motion of matter – the conservation of what Descartes called the total "quantity of motion" – is ultimately grounded in the unity and simplicity of God, whereby God continually recreates the entire material universe at each instant while constantly expressing the very same divine essence.[2]

From the point of view of most later thinkers, however, the Cartesian system turned out not to be fully satisfactory, and it failed to solve, in particular, two especially fundamental problems faced by the new natural science (or natural philosophy). In the first place, Descartes had failed to formulate the basic laws of motion in an adequate way; and, in fact, it appeared that an additional dynamical quantity (which we now take to be the quantity of mass, together with the closely related quantity of momentum) – one that is *not* reducible to the purely geometrical properties of extension, figure, and motion – is actually required (see note 2). In the second place, although the Cartesian system had indeed instituted an essential relation between God and nature, it appeared that nature might still not be related to God in the right way. For, given the basic laws of motion, all changes in the visible or material world then proceed purely mechanically, with no reference whatsoever to purpose, value, intention, or choice. What room is left, therefore, for moral or spiritual values *within* extended nature? What room is left, more specifically, for the exercise of human moral freedom of choice?[3] And, in this connection, it is important to remind ourselves that, although these questions may seem somewhat quaint and old-fashioned from the point of view of contemporary philosophy of science, they were absolutely central for the natural philosophy of the time. Indeed, it is not too much to say that the most fundamental task of the scientific and philosophical revolution initiated by Descartes was precisely to show how the new mechanical physics is, after all, fully compatible with (and, in the end, in fact best adapted to) both the spirit and the letter of the Christian religion.

From our point of view, the most important post-Cartesian thinker to react to these problems was Leibniz. Leibniz began, in fact, by reacting to the first problem: Descartes' failure adequately to formulate the basic laws of motion and interaction that were supposed to govern, according to the then-dominant paradigm of the "mechanical natural philosophy," all phenomena in the material or corporeal world. Leibniz responded to this problem by emphasizing the importance of a new, essentially dynamical quantity, which he called *vis viva* or living force (mv² or what we now call [twice the] kinetic energy), where the basic law of motion is now formulated as the conservation of the total quantity of *vis viva*. Moreover, Leibniz also strongly emphasized that this quantity is not purely geometrical or mechanical, so that, in particular, this quantity (unlike Descartes' purely mechanical "quantity of motion") reintroduces an element of Aristotelian teleology into the mechanical philosophy. For *vis viva* or living force, on Leibniz's view, is the counterpart of the Aristotelian notion of *entelechy*: namely, that internal (non-spatial) principle by which an ultimate simple substance or monad determines (by a kind of "appetition") the entire future development of its own internal state. In this way, an element of intention or value is reintroduced into the mechanical worldview quite generally; and Leibniz then makes the point perfectly explicit in his doctrine of divine creation as God's choice of the best among all merely logically possible worlds. The distinction between what is logically possible and what is actual – between all merely thinkable worlds available to the divine intellect and the best and most perfect of these worlds as determined by the divine will – then corresponds to the distinction between principles of pure mathematics (including geometry), on the one side, and principles of natural science or physics (i.e., the laws of motion), on the other. The laws of motion, unlike the merely mathematical laws of pure geometry, thereby precisely express the divine wisdom in actualizing or creating the best and most perfect of all possible worlds.[4]

Leibniz's system of natural philosophy was thus a major improvement on Descartes' with respect to both of the two problems sketched above. First, Leibniz succeeded in formulating the basic laws of motion of the mechanical philosophy – the laws of impact – in a much more adequate way; and, second, Leibniz thereby also established a more satisfactory relationship between God and nature, whereby divine wisdom and value are clearly and explicitly reintroduced *within* the divine creation. Once again, however, from the point of view of most later thinkers, Leibniz had still not solved either problem completely. In the first place, Newton soon formulated the basic laws of motion in a way that generalizes and extends the mechanical philosophy in a quite essential (and also quite controversial) way. For Newton, the fundamental dynamical quantity governing all changes of motion is momentum (mass times velocity or mv),[5] and the fundamental dynamical quantity causally responsible for such changes was "impressed force" – where this refers to any action of a second body on the body in question by which a change of momentum of the first body is produced. Force, in the Newtonian sense, is thus an external action of one body on another, not an internal principle like Leibnizean *vis viva*; and, what is worse, the action of this kind of force is not intrinsically limited to the condition of contact. On the contrary, the principal instantiation of this concept, in Newton's *Principia*, is precisely the force of universal gravitation, whereby one body attracts another (as in the sun's gravitational attraction of the earth) immediately and at a distance (at least to all appearances).[6] In the second place, however, even if we ignore the later development of physics and the laws of motion in the work of Newton, it seemed that Leibniz had still not made sufficient room for *human* moral freedom of choice. To be sure, God in some sense freely chooses (in a way that exceeds the bounds of purely geometrical necessity) the best of all possible worlds. But what is the sense in which we human creatures – whose lives, in particular, are apparently completely determined by God's prior choice – are similarly morally free? Leibniz struggled mightily with this remaining moral and theological problem, but no fully satisfactory solution (from the point of view of most later thinkers) was in fact ever achieved.

The early eighteenth century witnessed a great stage-setting intellectual debate, the famous correspondence between Leibniz and Clarke of 1715–16, which sharply focused attention on the opposition between the Leibnizean and Newtonian natural philosophies with respect to all of the above questions. This debate paid equal attention to both technical problems in physics and natural science (such as the laws of impact and the nature of matter) and very general issues within metaphysics and theology (such as the principle of sufficient reason and God's choice to create our world).[7] Leibniz objected to the Newtonian doctrine of direct divine intervention in the phenomena of the material universe – such as specially adjusting the orbits in the solar system, for example, so as to ensure that they all lie in approximately the same plane – and defended his own version of the principle of sufficient reason, whereby God's creative activity is exercised only in his initial choice of the best of all possible worlds. Clarke (representing Newton) replied that this would entail an unacceptable limitation on God's freedom of action, and, in particular, he defended Newtonian absolute space against Leibniz's use of the principle of sufficient reason to argue that such a space is impossible because God would then have no reason to place the material universe in one position rather than another within absolute space. In mid-eighteenth-century Germany this great debate between Leibnizeans and Newtonians dominated the intellectual agenda within both natural science and metaphysics, and Kant himself was no exception. As I have already suggested, his earliest writings were overwhelmingly concerned with problems of natural philosophy in general and the project of reconciling Leibniz and Newton in particular.

Two of Kant's most important pre-critical writings in this connection were the *Universal Natural History and Theory of the Heavens* and the *Physical Monadology*. In the first work, as already noted, Kant developed one of the earliest versions of the nebular hypothesis. He formulated the idea that the band of stars visible as the Milky Way consists of a rotating galaxy containing our solar system and that other visible clusters of stars also consist of such galaxies. Moreover, according to the hypothesis in question, all such galaxies originally arose from rotating clouds of gas or nebulae whose centrifugal force of rotation caused a gradual flattening out in a plane perpendicular to the axis of rotation as they cooled and formed individual stars and planets. The laws of such galaxy formation, for Kant, proceed entirely in accordance with "Newtonian principles." At the same time, however, since our solar system has the same nebular origin as all other galactic structures, we are able to explain one important feature of this system for which the Newtonians had invoked direct divine intervention – the fact that all the planets in our system orbit in approximately the same plane – from purely mechanical natural laws after all, precisely as the Leibnizeans had maintained.[8]

The question dominating the *Physical Monadology* concerned a specific metaphysical problem arising in the debate between Leibnizeans and Newtonians. If the ultimate constituents of matter are absolutely simple elementary substances or monads, as the Leibnizeans contend, how can this be reconciled with the geometrical infinite divisibility of space? It would appear that by dividing the space filled or occupied by any given piece of matter, however small, we would also eventually divide the elementary material substances found there as well – contrary to the assumed absolute simplicity of such substances. So how can an elementary constituent of matter or "physical monad" possibly fill the space it occupies, without being infinitely divisible in turn? Kant's answer (in 1756) is that physical monads do not fill the space they occupy by being immediately present in all parts of this space; they are not to be conceived, for example, as bodies that are solid through and through. Physical monads are rather to be conceived as point-like centers of attractive and repulsive forces, where the repulsive force, in particular, generates a region of solidity or impenetrability in the form of a tiny "sphere of activity" emanating from a central point. Geometrically dividing this region of impenetrability in no way divides the actual substance of the monad, but merely the "sphere of activity" in which the point-like central source manifests its repulsive capacity to exclude other monads from the region in question. So the Leibnizean commitment to ultimate simple substances or monads is perfectly consistent with the infinite divisibility of space after all – but (and here is Kant's characteristic twist) it can only be maintained by explicitly adopting the Newtonian conception of forces acting at a distance (in this case a short range repulsive force acting at a very small distance given by the radius of its "sphere of activity").[9]

Kant's conception in the *Physical Monadology* is thus an early example of a dynamical theory of matter, according to which the basic properties of solidity and impenetrability are not taken as primitive and self-explanatory, but are rather viewed as derived from an interplay of forces – here, more specifically, the two fundamental forces of attraction and repulsion, which together determine a limit or boundary beyond which repulsion (and thus impenetrability) is no longer effective and attraction (representing Newtonian gravitation) then takes over unhindered. This kind of theory exerted a powerful influence in the later part of the eighteenth century, in the work of such thinkers as Boscovich and Priestley, for example, and it can appropriately be viewed as an anticipation, of sorts, of the field-theoretic approach to physics developed in the nineteenth century beginning with the work of Faraday and culminating in Maxwell's theory of electricity and magnetism. In this sense, Kant's own contributions to a dynamical theory of matter had a significant impact on the development of natural science itself, quite apart from the original, more metaphysical setting within which it was first articulated.[10]

I will return to the influence of Kant's dynamical theory of matter in the philosophy and science of the early nineteenth century below. But I here want to emphasize that Kant's own original motivations, in the *Physical Monadology*, were indeed primarily metaphysical. In particular, Kant's incorporation of Newtonian action-at-a-distance forces within the framework of a Leibnizean monadology served to unify the intrinsically non-spatial (and thus essentially mental or spiritual) realm of ultimate simple substances lying at the basis of corporeal nature with what was now generally believed to be the correct Newtonian formulation of the laws of motion. As Kant makes clear in the complementary metaphysical treatise framing the *Physical Monadology*, the *New Elucidation of the First Principles of Metaphysical Cognition* (1755), the primary motivation for creating his dynamical theory was to accept the Leibnizean doctrine of the fundamentally internal intrinsic natures of the ultimate simple substances themselves, while simultaneously granting that they have essentially external or relational determinations as well. It is precisely these external determinations, by which the monads are set into genuine relation with one another, that are now phenomenally manifested as the fundamental forces of repulsion and attraction; and Newtonian absolute space, in particular, is nothing but the phenomenal expression of these relations. Thus, we can accept the Newtonian formulation of the laws of motion (and, moreover, we can accept universal gravitation as a genuine action at a distance) while also retaining the Leibnizean reconciliation of the corporeal and spiritual realms – which Leibniz himself termed the realm of nature and the realm of grace.[11]

2. PURE NATURAL SCIENCE IN THE CRITICAL PERIOD

The *Metaphysical Foundations of Natural Science* appeared, as I have said, in 1786 and thus at the height of the most creative decade of Kant's critical period – which includes, besides the two editions of the first *Critique* and the *Prolegomena*, the *Groundwork for the Metaphysics of Morals* (1785), the *Critique of Practical Reason* (1788) and the *Critique of the Power of Judgment* (1790). The appearance of the *Metaphysical Foundations* at this point shows, more specifically, that the deep (and in part extraordinarily innovative) concerns with fundamental questions in the natural science and natural philosophy of the time characteristic of Kant's pre-critical period were also very salient in the critical period. In particular, the *Metaphysical Foundations* continues, and also attempts to integrate, two separate lines of thought from the pre-critical period: the extension of Newtonian gravitational astronomy to cosmology first suggested in the *Theory of the Heavens*, and the further development of a dynamical theory of matter as first sketched in the *Physical Monadology*. At the same time, however, Kant now frames both developments within the radically new context of his critical philosophy.[12]

The critical version of the dynamical theory of matter is developed in the longest and most complicated part of the *Metaphysical Foundations*, the second chapter or Dynamics. As in the *Physical Monadology*, Kant here views the basic properties of matter – impenetrability, solidity, hardness, density, and so on – as arising from an interplay of the two fundamental forces of attraction and repulsion. In sharp contrast to the *Physical Monadology*, however, Kant abandons the idea of smallest elementary parts of matter or physical monads, and argues instead that all parts of matter or material substances, just like the space they occupy, must be infinitely divisible. Indeed, in the course of developing this argument, Kant explicitly rejects the very theory of physical monads he had himself earlier defended (in 1756). A space filled with matter or material substance, in Kant's new theory, now consists of an infinity or continuum of material points, each of which exerts the two fundamental forces of attraction and repulsion. The "balancing" of the two fundamental forces that had earlier determined a tiny (but finite) *volume* representing a "sphere of activity" of impenetrability around a single point-like central source now determines a definite *density* of matter at each point in the space in question effected by the mutual interaction of attraction and repulsion.

Thus, in the *Metaphysical Foundations*, as in the first *Critique*, material or phenomenal substance is no longer viewed as simple and indivisible, but is instead a genuine continuum occupying all the (geometrical) points of the space it fills. Accordingly, the problem posed by the infinite divisibility of space that the *Physical Monadology* had attempted to solve by invoking finite "spheres of activity" is now solved, in the Dynamics of the *Metaphysical Foundations*, by invoking the transcendental idealism articulated in the Antinomy of Pure Reason of the first *Critique* – and, more specifically, the argument of the Second Antinomy resolving the apparent incompatibility between the infinite divisibility of space and the presumed absolute simplicity of the material or phenomenal substances found in space. Matter or material substance is infinitely *divisible* but never, in experience, ever infinitely *divided*; hence, since matter is a mere appearance or phenomenon and is thus given only in the "progress of experience," it consists neither in ultimate simple elements nor in an actual or completed infinity of ever smaller spatial parts. Therefore, it is only by viewing matter as a thing in itself or noumenal substance (which would be necessarily simple) that we obtain a genuine contradiction or antinomy; and so, by an indirect proof or *reductio ad absurdum*, we have a further argument in support of Kant's characteristically critical doctrine of transcendental idealism.

The cosmological conception presented in the *Theory of the Heavens* had also included a striking vision of how the various galactic structures are distributed throughout the universe. The smallest such structure (due to nebular formation) is our own solar system, consisting of the sun surrounded by the six then-known planets. The next larger structure is the Milky Way galaxy, in which our solar system as a whole orbits around a larger center together with a host of other stars and (possible) planetary systems. But the Milky Way galaxy itself, for Kant, is then part of an even larger rotating system consisting of a number of such galaxies; this system is part of a still larger rotating system; and so on *ad infinitum*. The universe as a whole therefore consists of an indefinitely extended sequence of ever larger rotating galactic structures, working its way out from our solar system orbiting around its central sun, through the Milky Way galaxy in which our solar system is itself orbiting around a galactic center, then through a rotating system of such galaxies, and so on. Moreover, this indefinitely extended sequence of galactic structures reflects a parallel indefinitely extended sequence of nebular galactic formation, as the structures in question precipitate out from an initial uniform distribution of gaseous material sequentially starting from the center.

The *Metaphysical Foundations*, unlike the *Theory of the Heavens*, is not a work of cosmology. But the cosmological vision of the *Theory of the Heavens* is still centrally present there, transposed, as it were, into a more epistemological key. The very first explication of the *Metaphysical Foundations*, in the first chapter or Phoronomy, defines matter as the *movable* in space; and, as Kant immediately points out, this inevitably raises the difficult question of relative versus absolute motion, relative versus absolute space. Kant firmly rejects the Newtonian conception of absolute space as an actual "object of experience," and he suggests, instead, that it can be conceived along the lines of what he himself calls an "idea of reason." In this sense, "absolute space" signifies nothing but an indefinitely extended sequence of ever larger "relative spaces," such that any given relative space in the sequence, viewed initially as at rest, can be then viewed as moving with respect to a still larger relative space found later in the sequence. In the final chapter or Phenomenology, which concerns the question of how matter, as movable, is possible as an object of experience, Kant returns to this theme and develops it more concretely. He characterizes absolute space explicitly as an "idea of reason" and, in this context, describes a procedure for "reducing all motion and rest to absolute space." This procedure then generates a determinate distinction between true and merely apparent motion – despite the acknowledged relativity of all motion as such to some given empirically specified relative space. The procedure begins by considering our position on the earth, indicates how the earth's state of true rotation can nonetheless be empirically determined, and concludes by considering the cosmos as a whole, together with the "common center of gravity of all matter," as the ultimate relative space for correctly determining all true motion and rest.

What Kant appears to be envisioning, then, is an epistemological translation of the cosmological conception of the *Theory of the Heavens*. To determine the true motions in the material and thus empirically accessible universe, we begin with our parochial perspective here on earth, quickly move to the point of view of our solar system (where the earth is now seen to be really in a state of motion), then move to the perspective of the Milky Way galaxy (where the solar system, in turn, is itself seen to be in motion), and so on *ad infinitum* through an ever widening sequence of ever larger galactic structures serving as ever more expansive relative spaces. What Kant calls the "common center of gravity of all matter," relative to which all the motions in the cosmos as a whole can now be determinately considered, is never actually reached in this sequence; it is rather to be viewed as a forever unattainable regulative idea of reason towards which our sequence of (always empirically accessible) relative spaces is converging. In this way, in particular, we obtain an empirically meaningful surrogate for Newtonian absolute space using precisely the methods used by Newton himself (in determining the true motions in the solar system in the *Principia*, for example). At the same time, we preserve the fundamental Leibnizean insight that any position in space, and therefore all motion and rest, must ultimately be determined, in experience, from empirically accessible spatio-temporal relations between bodies.[13]

Kant's conception of absolute space in the *Metaphysical Foundations* therefore corresponds – in the more specific context of a consideration of matter as the *movable* in space – to his famous attempt in the *Critique of Pure Reason* to depict his own doctrine of the transcendental ideality of space as the only possible middle ground between the two untenable extreme positions of Newtonian "absolutism" and Leibnizean "relationalism." It also corresponds, even more directly, to Kant's conception of the extent of the material or empirical world in space articulated in the First Antinomy, according to which there is indeed no limit to this extent at any particular finite boundary, but, at the same time, the world cannot be conceived as an actually infinite completed totality nonetheless. In the end, there is only the purely regulative requirement or demand that, in the "progress of experience," we must always seek for further matter beyond any given finite limit and, accordingly, accept no such given boundary as definitive. We must seek, in the terminology of the *Metaphysical Foundations*, for ever larger relative spaces encompassing any given relative space; and, in this way, Kant's conception of absolute space as an idea of reason is the complement, from the point of view of the critical doctrine of transcendental idealism, of his new version of the dynamical theory of matter as consisting of a potential (but not actual) infinity of ever smaller spatial parts. Both are thus now firmly embedded, as we have said, within the radically new critical perspective of "transcendental philosophy."

But it is in Kant's third chapter or Mechanics that we find the most developed and explicit correspondence between the pure natural science of the *Metaphysical Foundations* and the transcendental philosophy of the first *Critique*. The main business of this chapter is establishing what Kant calls the three "laws of mechanics." These are, first, a principle of the conservation of the total quantity of matter in the universe, second, a version of the law of inertia, and third, the law of the equality of action and reaction. So it is precisely here that Kant actually derives the principles of pure natural science he uses, in the Introduction to the second edition of the *Critique*, to illustrate the presence of synthetic *a priori* judgments in this science.[14] We find a very explicit correspondence, in particular, between these three laws of mechanics and the categories of relation and accompanying principles (i.e., the analogies of experience). The principle of the conservation of the total quantity of matter corresponds to the more general transcendental principle established in the first *Critique* – the permanence of *substance* in all changes in the (phenomenal) world; the law of inertia corresponds to the category, and accompanying principle, of *causality;* and the law of the equality of action and reaction corresponds to the category, and accompanying principle, of thoroughgoing dynamical interaction or *community.* Thus, in considering material substances or bodies as interacting with one another through their fundamental forces and, as a result, thereby standing in relation to one another in a community of what Kant calls their inherent motions (i.e., momenta), we are, at the same time, applying the categories or pure concepts of relation (and their accompanying principles) to these same bodies.

More specifically, it is precisely by applying Kant's three laws of mechanics that we are then able, in the Phenomenology, to implement the procedure of "reducing all motion and rest to absolute space" described earlier. In particular, the most important step in this procedure depends on Kant's proof of the equality of action and reaction in the Mechanics. Kant there explicitly chides Newton for attempting to derive this law from experience, and what Kant proposes instead is an a priori proof from the concepts of absolute motion and rest. In any interaction between two bodies whereby they stand in a community of their fundamental forces (repulsion in impact or attraction in gravitation), there is a privileged relative space or reference frame for considering the resulting changes of motion: namely, the center of mass frame of the two bodies, in which the two corresponding momenta (and their changes) are necessarily equal and opposite. The principle of the conservation of momentum therefore necessarily holds in this frame, together with the equality of action and reaction. We then implement the procedure described in the Phenomenology by a kind of successive iteration of this argument to wider and wider systems of bodies: we move from the center of mass of the solar system, to the center of mass of the Milky Galaxy, to the center of mass of a system of such galaxies, and so on *ad infinitum*. Absolute space, as we have seen, is thus no actual space at all but rather a forever-unattainable regulative idea of reason – given, in the end, by the "common center of gravity of all matter" – toward which our procedure is converging.

Kant's proof of his second law of mechanics, a version of the law of inertia, marks a further fundamental break with the pre-critical conception of the *Physical Monadology*. For Kant now formulates the law of inertia as the proposition that "every change of matter has an *external* cause" (my emphasis), where the ground of proof of this proposition is precisely that "matter has no essentially internal determinations or grounds of determination" (4:543). But the whole point of the *Physical Monadology*, as we have seen, was to combine a Leibnizean insistence on the essentially internal intrinsic natures of the ultimate simple substances lying at the basis of corporeal reality (i.e., the physical monads) with a Newtonian physical description of this same reality. Indeed, in the pre-critical period, Kant goes so far as explicitly to associate the internal or intrinsic determinations of the ultimate simple substances with the Newtonian force of inertia or *vis insita*. Now, in the *Metaphysical Foundations*, Kant decisively rejects this force of inertia, and he decisively rejects, at the same time, the "hylozoism" characteristic of Leibnizean natural philosophy. Just as, in the critical period, there is no longer any room for the simplicity of phenomenal substance, there is similarly no longer any room for attributing a purely internal (and thus mental or spiritual) nature to such a substance. Kant's earlier attempt to combine the

Leibnizean realms of nature and grace within a single metaphysical description of the corporeal or material universe must now be seen as a failure.[15]

Indeed, according to the transcendental idealism characteristic of the critical philosophy, no reconciliation or unification of these two realms – which Kant now calls the realm of nature and the realm of freedom – within a single picture of reality is possible at all, at least from a purely theoretical point of view. And, as is well known, further reflection on the problem of human moral freedom, as expressed, for example, in the Third Antinomy of Pure Reason, is what primarily drives Kant to this conclusion. What Kant now proposes, in particular, is that we must sharply distinguish between theoretical and practical reason, where the former is confined to knowledge of spatio-temporal phenomena and only the latter can meaningfully grasp the supersensible. But practical reason "grasps" the supersensible solely from a practical point of view, in terms of directives regulating our conduct. In the end, the three most fundamental ideas of reason – the ideas of God, freedom, and immortality – function as the ultimate and most general regulative principles guiding and framing all human conduct whatsoever, including the conduct of theoretical natural science itself. The indefinitely extended sequence of stages of inquiry governing our progressive investigation into both smaller and smaller parts of matter (in accordance with Kant's critical version of the dynamical theory of matter) and larger and larger regions of space (in accordance with Kant's critical doctrine of absolute space) must in turn be entirely subordinated, by what Kant now calls the priority of practical reason, to humanity's morally necessary progression toward the Highest Good.[16]

3. THE SIGNIFICANCE OF PURE NATURAL SCIENCE WITHIN THE CRITICAL SYSTEM

What we have just seen is that the system of pure natural science Kant develops in the *Metaphysical Foundations* is a specific realization or instantiation of the transcendental philosophy expounded in the *Critique of Pure Reason* and other critical works. Whereas the first *Critique* describes a "nature in general," that is, a world of spatio-temporal substances standing in thoroughgoing interaction with one another so as mutually to determine their resulting changes of state in accordance with the analogies of experience (and other principles of pure understanding), the *Metaphysical Foundations* describes a "corporeal nature" of material bodies filling the spaces they occupy by their impenetrability and weight, and thereby standing in thoroughgoing interaction with one another by the two fundamental forces of repulsion and attraction so as mutually to determine their resulting changes of motion in accordance with the three laws of mechanics (and other principles of pure natural science).[17] Similarly, whereas the transcendental idealism of the first *Critique* depicts nature in general in space and time as an appearance rather than a thing in itself, and, in particular, as a potentially infinite "progress of experience" rather than a completed (finite or infinite) totality, the application of this doctrine to specifically corporeal nature depicts the ultimate constituents of matter in terms of an indefinitely extended regress into progressively smaller spatial parts (in explicit opposition to the ultimate simple substances of Kant's pre-critical physical monadology) and explains Newtonian absolute space as a regulative idea of reason.

The crucial question, however, concerns how central this specific instantiation of the critical system is for the system as a whole. Does Kant's system of transcendental philosophy – and, in particular, his answer to the question "how are synthetic *a priori* judgements possible?" – essentially depend on this specific example? Or, on the contrary, is Kant only committed to much more abstract and general principles, such that the critical system can still easily survive if the more particular principles of pure natural science are no longer accepted as valid? Is the specific realization of transcendental philosophy presented in the *Metaphysical Foundations* a central and indispensable instantiation, without which Kant's critical system loses its force? Or, on the contrary, is it rather simply one instantiation among others, which can easily be dropped if the need arises?

The specific realization presented in the *Metaphysical Foundations*, under the rubric of pure natural science, is a precise mathematical one, described, at the level of physics itself, by Newton's mathematical theory of motion. Indeed, in the Preface to the *Metaphysical Foundations* Kant explicitly distinguishes between "special metaphysics of corporeal nature" and "general metaphysics" or "transcendental philosophy" by the idea that the former is necessarily mathematical while the latter is not.[18] It is tempting, then,

to institute a parallel distinction between precise and mathematical scientific experience, whose possibility is explained in the *Metaphysical Foundations*, and the looser and less exacting ordinary experience or experience in general, whose possibility is explained in the
first *Critique*. Whereas scientific experience, for Kant, is naturally
described by the best mathematical science of his own time, ordinary
experience or experience in general need not be. On the contrary,
from the point of view of the distinction we are now considering,
the conditions of the possibility of experience in general are then
viewed, as I have already suggested, as themselves much looser and
more general – involving only the spatial character of experience
in general, for example, as opposed to the much more precise and
exacting principles of Euclidean geometry, and only the lawlikeness
of experience in general as opposed to much more precise and exacting principles of Newtonian mathematical physics.[19]

My own view, as I have also already suggested, is that this
particular way of explaining Kant's distinction between the special
metaphysics of corporeal nature and general metaphysics or transcendental philosophy will not work, and, in particular, that Kant's
explanation of the possibility of synthetic *a priori* knowledge in
general actually depends on the specific (mathematical) examples
of such knowledge comprising what he calls pure natural science.
This view, as I say, is quite controversial, and I have argued for it
in detail elsewhere; so I will only briefly summarize what I take
to be the most important arguments for it here. In the first place,
although there is no doubt that the principles of pure understanding
presented in the *Critique* are much more abstract and general than
the principles of pure natural science presented in the *Metaphysical
Foundations*, the former are by no means as loose and unexacting
as the appeal to ordinary (or commonsensical) experience implies.
For example, Kant does not simply argue that there are more or less
universal regularities governing our experience of nature in general;
he argues that there are absolutely exceptionless laws possessing
both necessity and "strict universality." And Kant does not simply
argue that there are more or less enduring substances underlying our
experience of change; he argues that substance as such is absolutely
permanent, necessarily enduring throughout all of time. Thus, on the
one hand, the more abstract and general synthetic *a priori* principles
defended in the first *Critique* are just as subject to refutation by the

further progress of empirical natural science as are the more specific and explicitly mathematical principles defended in the *Metaphysical Foundations*, and, on the other, it is very hard even to understand Kant's arguments for the still quite rigorous and exacting principles articulated in the former work without giving a central position to the latter.[20]

In the second place, there are very clear textual indications that pure natural science is not simply one instantiation among others of transcendental philosophy, but is, rather, the primary and indispensable instantiation. Thus, the Preface to the *Metaphysical Foundations* distinguishes between general metaphysics and the special metaphysics of corporeal nature (or "doctrine of body") by the idea that the latter is limited to the objects of specifically outer (i.e., spatial) intuition while the former is not. But Kant also emphasizes that general metaphysics or transcendental philosophy must *necessarily* take its instantiation from the doctrine of body (4:478): "It is also indeed very remarkable (but cannot be expounded in detail here) that general metaphysics, in all instances where it requires examples (intuitions) in order to provide meaning for its pure concepts of the understanding, must always take them from the general doctrine of body, and thus from the form and principles of outer intuition; and, if these are not exhibited completely, it gropes uncertainly and unsteadily among mere meaningless concepts."[21] This passage from 1786 is then closely mirrored by a corresponding passage from the General Remark to the System of Principles added to the second edition of the *Critique* in 1787, where Kant similarly emphasizes that only outer (i.e., spatial) intuitions can verify the objective reality of the categories.[22] In this same passage Kant further emphasizes, in particular, that the pure intuition of *motion* (of a mathematical point) exhibited in the drawing of a straight line is what he calls the "figurative" representation of time; and this idea also plays a prominent role in §24 of the second edition transcendental deduction of the categories, where precisely this representation of motion is used to illustrate what Kant calls the "figurative synthesis" or "transcendental synthesis of the imagination" through which the understanding first "determines" inner sense (i.e., time). Since natural science, according to the Preface to the *Metaphysical Foundations*, is "either a pure or applied *doctrine of motion*" (4:477), and since the transcendental synthesis of the imagination, according to §24 of the second edition, is "an action of the understanding on sensibility and its first application to objects of an intuition possible for us (and at the same time the ground of all other applications)" (B 152), what these texts all suggest, I believe, is that the application of the categories to objects of experience in general is only possible by means of, and, as it were, *through* their prior application to pure natural science.[23]

Nevertheless, if pure natural science is the first and primary instantiation of the categories and principles of the understanding, it by no means follows that it is the only such instantiation. On the contrary, according to Kant's philosophy of natural science more generally, what he calls pure natural science is only a part (albeit a central and indispensable part) of natural science in general. Pure natural science articulates the metaphysical foundations of the Newtonian mathematical theory of motion, but this theory, in turn, has been thus far applied (in the late eighteenth century) to only a tiny fraction of the phenomena of nature. In particular, thermal phenomena, electrical and magnetic phenomena, and chemical phenomena – not to mention biological, anthropological, and psychological phenomena – remain, thus far, almost entirely unaccounted for. What Kant appears to be envisioning, therefore, is an open-ended and essentially incompletable process of natural scientific development, which begins with the application of pure natural science in Newtonian mathematical physics and then proceeds successively to incorporate more and more natural phenomena along the way. This procedure is guided, in accordance with the doctrine of the regulative use of pure reason articulated in the Appendix to the Dialectic of the first *Critique*, by the idea of the *systematicity* of nature – according to which all lower-level empirical concepts and laws are eventually unified in a system under the highest-level empirical concepts and laws, where these latter, in turn, directly stand under the categories.[24]

Thus, for example, the (empirical) concept of matter lying at the basis of the pure natural science expounded in the *Metaphysical Foundations* would represent the very highest empirical concept in a classificatory system of such concepts, and this concept would directly instantiate the categories. The categories would then apply to all lower-level empirical concepts (and thereby to all more specific regions of experience) by means of (or *through*) the highest-level (empirical) concept of matter, insofar as this concept is successively specified and articulated in the course of the indefinitely unfolding progress of natural science. So it is not as if the categories could apply to experience in general (nature in general) entirely independently of their application in pure natural science, so that the latter could simply be dropped from the critical system if the need arises. Rather, the sense in which nature in general necessarily exceeds the bounds of pure natural science is that experience in general and as a whole comprises the ideal limit of scientific inquiry as natural science continually approaches – but never actually reaches – an ideal state of systematic completeness.[25]

We saw, at the end of the last section, that one of the central new ideas of the critical philosophy is a sharp distinction between theoretical and practical reason, together with a doctrine of the priority of the latter. According to this doctrine, the regulative use of theoretical reason, as described in the Appendix to the Dialectic of the first *Critique*, is itself subordinated to humanity's morally necessary progression towards the Highest Good – so that, in particular, the examination of theoretical reason in the first *Critique* is subordinated to the examination of practical reason in the second. This distinction between theoretical and practical reason, together with the subordination of the first *Critique* to the second, now sheds further light on the fundamental distinction in point of view between the general metaphysics or transcendental philosophy presented in the first *Critique* and the special metaphysics of corporeal nature presented in the *Metaphysical Foundations*. More specifically, the categories and principles of pure understanding play a central and indispensable role in both types of metaphysics, but from two very different points of view.

In the *Metaphysical Foundations* the categories and principles of the understanding are taken simply as given, as premises for the further derivation of principles of pure natural science from them: from the permanence of substance we derive the conservation of matter, from the principle of causality we derive the law of inertia, from the principle of community we derive the equality of action and reaction, and so on. The principles of the understanding, through this application to specifically outer (i.e., spatial) objects, thereby necessarily acquire a determinate mathematical content: a determinate connection, that is, with the Newtonian mathematical theory of motion. But the derivation of the principles of pure understanding themselves in the first *Critique* is prior to this procedure. In particular, the principle of the transcendental unity of apperception – the very highest point of the transcendental deduction, from which all principles of pure understanding ultimately derive – is an essentially non-mathematical *a priori* principle.[26] Indeed, it characterizes what Kant calls an intellectual rather than a sensible (i.e., spatiotemporal) synthesis, of which the understanding "is conscious even without sensibility, but through which it is capable of determining sensibility inwardly with respect to the manifold, however [the manifold] may be given to it in accordance with the form of [the manifold's] intuition" (B 153). The unity of apperception thus has meaning – but of course no determinate application to objects of knowledge – entirely independently of space and time. In considering the principles of understanding as derived from the spontaneity of the subject (from the "I think" expressing the transcendental unity of apperception), we are necessarily considering these principles from a transcendental rather than mathematical point of view.

According to the Paralogisms of Pure Reason, especially as revised in the second edition of the *Critique,* the spontaneity of the subject expressed in the "I think" cannot, by itself, determine this subject of experience as an object of experience as well: it cannot inwardly determine the subject as an existing thing in space and time. This, in fact, is one of the main points in the Refutation of Idealism also added to the second edition, according to which my cognition of my own self as determinately existing in time necessarily requires the perception of (material) things existing outside me in space. However, as Kant also explains in the second edition Paralogisms, we have another form of spontaneity by which we can indeed inwardly determine our own existence: a "certain inner faculty" by which "we are *legislative* completely *a priori* with respect to our own *existence,* and thus also determinative of this existence" (B 430–1). The inner faculty in question is pure practical reason, and the determination of our existence Kant has in mind here is our self-legislation of the moral law – through which we determine the actuality of our *will* by viewing ourselves, entirely independently of the sensible world, as members of an ideal realm of ends. In this way, the spontaneity of pure practical reason, in sharp contrast to the spontaneity of pure understanding in the representation "I think," can determine our existence as subject (including our existence as members of the sensible world) with no need of mediation from either pure or empirical

intuition. Whereas the pure categories and principles of the understanding, including even the principle of pure apperception itself,
require application to both pure and empirical intuition (and thus,
in my view, to pure mathematics and pure natural science) in order
to have determinate *theoretical* content, the *a priori practical* principles generated by the faculty of (pure practical) reason are quite independent of such application. Nevertheless, nature in general and our
experience as a whole are still entirely subordinated to these same
practical principles.[27]

The Preface to the *Metaphysical Foundations*, in the course of
sharply distinguishing between general metaphysics or transcendental philosophy and the special metaphysics of corporeal nature,
explains that an "important reason for detaching [the doctrine of
body's] detailed treatment from the general system of metaphysics,
and presenting it systematically as a special whole" is that "[general]
metaphysics has busied so many heads until now, and will continue to do so, not in order thereby to extend natural knowledge
(which takes place much more easily and surely through observation, experiment, and the application of mathematics to outer
appearances), but rather so as to attain cognition of that which lies
wholly beyond all boundaries of experience, of God, Freedom, and
Immortality" (4:477).[28] The general metaphysics or transcendental
philosophy advanced in the first *Critique* (and then further articulated in the second and third) does indeed portray nature in general
and human experience as a whole as necessarily framed by essentially non-mathematical *a priori* principles extending far beyond the
boundaries of all theoretical science of the natural world. This world
is thereby seen to be much more than a theater for objective human
experience and knowledge (which, in my view, are necessarily constrained, from the point of view of the understanding, by the *a priori*
concepts and principles of Newtonian mathematical exact science);
it is also, and primarily, a vehicle for the realization of the moral law.

4. PHILOSOPHICAL FOUNDATIONS OF NATURAL
SCIENCE AFTER KANT

In considering the question of the enduring significance of Kant's
philosophy of natural science – its significance, in particular, for
our post-Newtonian world – there is no better route, I believe, than

a consideration of how the philosophy of natural science actually developed after Kant, in response to both perceived problems within Kant's original system and new developments within the mathematical and physical sciences themselves. This story, which spans most of the nineteenth and early twentieth centuries, is naturally extremely complex, but there are two nineteenth-century developments that are particularly salient from our point of view: the development of *Naturphilosophie* within early post-Kantian idealism, especially as represented by Friedrich Wilhelm Joseph Schelling, and the development of a new type of "scientific philosophy" by philosophically minded natural scientists and mathematicians in the mid to late nineteenth century, especially as represented by Helmholtz. This latter development formed the immediate background to the philosophy of logical empiricism arising in the early twentieth century, which, in turn, constitutes the immediate background to our present situation within what we now call philosophy of science.

We have seen that for Kant there is a fundamental distinction between regulative principles guided by ideas of reason, such as the principle of systematic unity within an ideal complete science of nature, and constitutive principles derived from the concepts or categories of pure understanding, such as the principles of substance, causality, and community. The latter are necessarily instantiated within our sensible experience in space and time; the former can never be fully realized within sensible experience, but serve only to guide this experience, by way of a never actually completed sequence of approximations, toward an ideal state of completion. We have also seen that, from Kant's own point of view in the late eighteenth century, only a tiny fraction of the phenomena of nature have been so far objectively grounded by the constitutive principles of the understanding originating in the first *Critique* and further specified in the pure natural science of the *Metaphysical Foundations*. In particular, Kant explicitly denies, in the latter work, that chemistry has yet become a science strictly speaking, and he uses examples from contemporary chemistry, in the former work, as primary illustrations of the regulative use of reason. The main problem, as Kant also clearly explains, is that chemical phenomena have not yet (and perhaps never will be) constitutively grounded in the fundamental forces of matter – in the way, for example, that gravitational phenomena have now been successfully so grounded in the work of Newton.[29]

From the point of view of post-Kantian idealism, however, we are therefore left with a quite intolerable form of (Humean) skepticism concerning most of the phenomena of nature; for only very few of these phenomena are actually constitutively grounded in the *a priori* principles of the understanding (and are therefore governed by necessary laws), while, for the rest, we have at best the otherwise entirely indeterminate hope that they might be constitutively grounded someday. Indeed, for the case of biology, as is well known, the situation is even worse – for we shall never achieve, according to Kant, a genuinely constitutive grounding of the properties and behavior of even a single blade of grass. It appears, then, that the vast majority of natural phenomena are not (and most likely never will be) objectively grounded at all, and our claims to have rational or objective knowledge of nature are accordingly cast into doubt.[30] Schelling's decisive contribution to this situation was radically to transform Kant's own formulation of a dynamical theory of matter in the *Metaphysical Foundations* so as, in particular, to erase the sharp distinction between constitutive and regulative principles. For Schelling, transcendental philosophy, the story of how human reason successively approximates to a more and more adequate picture of nature, has a necessary counterpart or dual, as it were, in *Naturphilosophie*, the story of how nature itself successively unfolds or dialectically evolves from the "dead" or inert matter considered in statics and mechanics, to the essentially dynamical forms of interaction considered in chemistry, and finally to the living or organic matter considered in biology. Since nature, on this view, dialectically unfolds or successively evolves in a way that precisely mirrors the evolution or development of our rational conception of nature, it follows that there is no possible skeptical gap between nature itself and our conception of it, or, in Kantian terminology, between the constitutive domain of the understanding and the merely regulative domain of reason. All the phenomena of nature – including, in particular, both chemical and biological phenomena – are rationally or objectively grounded in the same way.[31]

The key to Schelling's conception is the idea that Kant's own dynamical theory of the most general properties of all matter (which embraces, therefore, even the "dead" or inert matter considered in statics and mechanics) had already introduced an essentially dialectical element into nature, insofar as the dynamical constitution of matter in general proceeds from the positive reality of expansive force (repulsion), through the negative reality of contractive force (attraction), to the limitation or balance of the two in a state of equilibrium. Moreover, we now know, as Kant himself did not, that chemistry can be dynamically grounded by a dialectical continuation of this same progression – as we proceed, more specifically, from the magnetic, through the electrical, to the chemical (or galvanic) forms of the basic or original dynamical process grounded in the fundamental forces of attraction and repulsion. And, once we have gone this far, it is then a very short step (particularly in view of the newly discovered parallel interconnections among electrical, galvanic, and biological phenomena) to view biology, too, as a further dialectical continuation of the same dynamical process. Biology, too, can be a science, for all rational science, as Kant did not and could not see, is grounded in a single dynamical evolutionary dialectical progression. The whole of nature, in this sense, is at once both rational and alive; and this means, in particular, that there actually is life – objectively, not merely regulatively – in even the very simplest forms of organized matter. In the end, it is precisely by rejecting the fundamental Kantian contention that all matter in general and as such is essentially lifeless that Schelling, from his point of view, has finally overcome any possibility of a skeptical gap between our rational conception of nature and nature itself.[32]

In the system of absolute idealism first developed by Schelling (and later further elaborated by Hegel) we saw a self-conscious return to the metaphysical approaches to nature characteristic of the pre-Kantian period, as exhibited in such thinkers as Leibniz and Spinoza; for *Naturphilosophie* had now rediscovered a way – taking full account, as well, of the fundamental contributions of Kant – to combine mechanism and life, matter and mind, nature and spirit within a single overall vision of reality.[33] Kant's own delicately balanced distinctions between appearances and things-in-themselves, constitutive and regulative principles, theoretical and practical reason, the realm of nature and the realm of freedom had now been effectively erased, and the way was once again opened up for a unified metaphysical system of the totality of human experience.[34] Yet it was precisely this grand metaphysical vision that violently repelled the next generation of philosophers of natural science. These thinkers, as I have suggested, had their main intellectual roots within the natural sciences, and they conceived their primary mission as one of reclaiming the philosophy of natural science for the sake of the natural scientists themselves. In particular, perhaps the most important representative of this movement, Hermann von Helmholtz, took his starting point from an explicit rejection of what he took to be the entirely speculative systems of *Naturphilosophie* due to Schelling and Hegel, and he called, accordingly, for a return to the more sober and scientific preoccupations of Kant himself – who, in Helmholtz's opinion, "stood in relation to the natural sciences together with the natural scientists on precisely the same fundamental principles."[35]

Helmholtz's call for a return to Kant was by no means uncritical, however. On the contrary, the Kantian philosophy needed to undergo adaptation and modification as new developments within the mathematical natural sciences required it. For example, Helmholtz, too, embraced a central contention of Kant's dynamical theory of matter, the thesis that all forces and powers of matter are to be explained by attractive and repulsive forces depending only on distance; but he also adapted it to a radically new scientific situation, the discovery of the conservation of energy, and he used it, accordingly, to combat the "vitalism" characteristic of *Naturphilosophie*.[36] But by far the most important and dramatic modification of Kant arose from the discovery of non-Euclidean geometries. Helmholtz had encountered these geometries in the course of his own psycho-physiological work on the problem of space perception, and he then quickly became the leading advocate on behalf of their revolutionary philosophical importance. Helmholtz argued, in particular, that Kant was simply wrong to take specifically Euclidean geometry as the necessary form of our spatial intuition or perception. The new non-Euclidean geometries are not only logically possible, they are also perceptually or intuitively possible as well, in that we can very well imagine what our perceptual experience would be if we lived in a non-Euclidean world. The necessary form of our spatial intuition, Helmholtz concluded, was therefore the much more general structure common to the three classical geometries of constant curvature (Euclidean, hyperbolic, and elliptic); and this structure was described, accordingly, not by the specific axioms of Euclid, but rather by the much more general principle of what Helmholtz called "free mobility" permitting arbitrary continuous motions of rigid bodies.[37]

Helmholtz did not live to see the new non-Euclidean geometries actually applied to the science of nature in Einstein's general theory of relativity in the early years of the twentieth century. It was Moritz Schick, the founder and guiding spirit of the Vienna Circle of logical empiricists, who, against the background of Helmholtz's earlier modifications of Kant, seized on Einstein's theory as his philosophical model and used it, in particular, to argue that nothing was left of Kant's conception of synthetic *a priori* judgements at all – neither within pure mathematics nor within mathematical physics.[38] It was at precisely this point, therefore, that our contemporary worries about the compatibility of Kant's doctrine of the synthetic *a priori* with post-Newtonian scientific developments first crystallized. And it was at this point, too, that philosophical exploration of the foundations of natural science in the tradition explicitly inspired by Kant decisively broke away from the larger ethical, spiritual, metaphysical, and even theological questions that had framed the philosophy of natural science from Descartes through Schelling and Hegel (and including Kant himself). For it quickly became a key doctrine of logical empiricism that ethical, spiritual, theological, and metaphysical questions are one and all "cognitively meaningless." The only (cognitively) meaningful factual or synthetic statements are those of the empirical natural sciences themselves; the only other (cognitively) meaningful statements are the purely formal or analytic sentences of logic, mathematics, and the logical analysis of the natural sciences. Philosophical exploration of the foundations of natural science had now become what Rudolf Carnap called *Wissenschaftslogik* (the logic of science) – which soon became officially known as philosophy of science.[39]

The last stage of this history is now very well known. The American philosopher W. V. Quine, who had earlier studied with Carnap in Vienna, famously opposed what he called the "two dogmas of empiricism" – the doctrine of a clear and sharp distinction between analytic and synthetic statements, and the complementary idea that individual "empirical meanings" can be assigned to the statements of even the very best examples of natural science.[40] We are left, according to Quine, with a pragmatic and holistic form of empiricism, in which the totality of our beliefs forms a vast and intricate web that only comes into contact with sense experience along its edges. Any belief in this system – even the most centrally located sentences of logic and mathematics – can be revised in response to "recalcitrant experience," and there is thus no difference in principle between beliefs that were traditionally thought to be *a priori* (like those of logic and mathematics) and those that are paradigmatically empirical (like those of biology, say). It was precisely here, then, that a position wholly antithetical to Kant had finally been reached. For, although Carnap, for example, had indeed rejected the Kantian synthetic *a priori*, he still retained the fundamentally Kantian idea that there is a philosophically central difference in principle between the formal statements of logic and mathematics, which frame empirical natural science and thereby make it possible, and the factual statements of the empirical natural sciences themselves.[41]

It is less well known, however, that there was also an explicit attempt to preserve elements of the original Kantian *a priori* in the early years of logical empiricism. Hans Reichenbach, like Schlick, was one of the initial philosophical defenders of Einstein's theory of relativity, and, in his first book on the subject, published in 1920, Reichenbach explicitly criticized Schlick for entirely rejecting Kant's doctrine. For Reichenbach, the great lesson of the theory of relativity was that we must now distinguish two different aspects of the *a priori* originally combined in Kant: necessary and unrevisable, fixed for all time, on the one side, and what Reichenbach called "constitutive of the concept of the object," on the other. The theory of relativity has indeed shown that principles Kant had assumed were eternally fixed and necessary – like the principles of Euclidean geometry and the Newtonian laws of motion – are, after all, revisable. Yet it does not follow that they are not, in the Kantian sense, *constitutive*: that is, conditions of the possibility of the properly empirical statements and principles (such as the Newtonian law of universal gravitation) also contained in the best scientific theory of Kant's time. What Kant did not and could not see, rather, is that precisely such constitutive principles change and develop as empirical natural science progresses – so that, for example, although specifically Euclidean geometry is no longer constitutively *a priori* in the context of the general theory of relativity, the more general geometrical framework assumed by Einstein (the Riemannian theory of metrical manifolds) plays an analogous constitutive role within Einstein's new theory.[42]

I have recently attempted to revive this (early) Reichenbachian emphasis on the importance of constitutively *a priori* principles within mathematical natural science. By paying detailed attention to the development of, and interaction between, both scientific philosophy from Kant through the early twentieth century and the mathematical and natural sciences themselves, I have attempted further to develop Reichenbach's idea, to defend it against Quinean holism, and to apply it to the issue of conceptual relativism arising from Thomas Kuhn's theory of scientific revolutions.[43] Here is clearly not the place to go into these matters in more detail. My own conclusion, however, is that central and important aspects of Kant's original philosophical conception – including, in particular, the distinction between *a priori* formal principles framing our empirical knowledge of nature and this empirical knowledge itself, together with the related distinction between constitutive *a priori* principles (framing our natural scientific theorizing at a given stage of development) and regulative a priori principles (governing the entire never-to-be-completed progression of such stages in the limit) – are still very much alive.

NOTES

1.   For Kant's intellectual development see E. Cassirer, *Kant's Life and Thought* (New Haven: Yale University Press, 1981); and, for a more detailed recent treatment, M. Kuehn, *Kant* (Cambridge: Cambridge University Press, 2001). For Kant's early work in metaphysics and natural philosophy see A. Laywine, *Kant's Early Metaphysics and the Origins of the Critical Philosophy* (Atascadero, CA: Ridgeview, 1993); M. Schönfeld, *The Philosophy of the Young Kant* (Oxford: Oxford University Press, 2000); and the Introduction to my *Kant and the Exact Sciences* (Cambridge, MA: Harvard University Press, 1992). Many of the most important of Kant's pre-critical works (with the exception of the *Theory of the Heavens*) are translated in D. Walford, ed., *Immanuel Kant: Theoretical Philosophy, 1755–1770* (Cambridge: Cambridge University Press, 1992). For a translation of part of the *Theory of the Heavens* see M. Munitz, ed., *Universal Natural History and Theory of the Heavens* (Ann Arbor: University of Michigan Press, 1969). For the *Metaphysical Foundations of Natural Science* see my translation in the series *Cambridge Texts in the History of Philosophy* (Cambridge: Cambridge University Press, 2004).

2.   By "quantity of motion" Descartes meant speed multiplied by "size." This differs from our modern (Newtonian) conception of quantity of motion or momentum in being a scalar rather than vector quantity, and

also by involving no articulated concept of mass or quantity of matter. For a discussion of Cartesian physics in the context of his metaphysics see D. Garber, *Descartes' Metaphysical Physics* (Chicago: University of Chicago Press, 1992).

3. These problems became most acute in the philosophy of Spinoza, who argued that the purely geometrical or mechanical character of Cartesian physics entails not only the complete elimination of Aristotelian teleology but also that of human freedom of the will.

4. Leibniz first articulated his criticism of Descartes concerning *vis viva* in "A Brief Demonstration of a Notable Error of Descartes and Others Concerning a Natural Law" (1686), and he developed the wider metaphysical implications of *vis viva* in his "Discourse on Metaphysics," published in the same year. Both of these, together with a very wide selection of Leibniz's works, are translated in L. Loemker, ed., *Leibniz: Philosophical Papers and Letters* (Dordrecht: Reidel, 1969).

5. Compare again note 2. Thus, Newtonian quantity of motion is a vector rather than scalar quantity (involving the vector velocity rather than the scalar speed). Leibnizean *vis viva* (mv^2) is also a scalar quantity, although Leibniz himself is perfectly clear and explicit that the fundamental law governing (what we now call perfectly elastic) impact involves both the conservation of (vector) momentum and the conservation of (scalar) *vis viva* (inelastic impact, by contrast, involves the former but not the latter).

6. As is well known, Newton himself expressed serious doubts about action at a distance and preferred to leave open the question whether the action of gravity might be due to the pressure of an external aether. This is one place where Kant explicitly criticizes Newton: for details see my *Kant and the Exact Sciences* (note 1 above), and "Kant and Newton: Why Gravity is Essential to Matter," in P. Bricker and R. Hughes, eds., *Philosophical Perspectives on Newtonian Science* (Cambridge, MA: MIT Press, 1990).

7. See H. Alexander, ed., *The Leibniz-Clarke Correspondence* (Manchester: Manchester University Press, 1956). A classical discussion of the underlying issues is A. Koyré, *From the Closed World to the Infinite Universe* (Baltimore, MD: Johns Hopkins University Press, 1957).

8. As Kant explains in the Preface, he was inspired by ideas of the English astronomers Bradley and Wright. Kant's contemporary (later friend and correspondent) J. H. Lambert published similar ideas, independently of Kant, in his *Cosmological Letters* (1761). The nebular hypothesis was given its most developed formulation in the eighteenth century by Laplace in his *Système du Monde* (1796).

9. See the translation in the volume edited by Walford cited in note 1 above. It is noteworthy that this same solution to the problem of absolute simplicity of substance versus geometrical infinite divisibility of space is found in the *Inquiry concerning the Distinctness of the Principles of Natural Theology and Morals* (1764), where it appears as an "example of the only certain method for metaphysics illustrated by reference to our cognition of the nature of bodies": see Walford, *Immanuel Kant*, pp. 259–63.

10. For discussion of the development and influence of eighteenth-century dynamical theories of matter see P. Harman, *Metaphysics and Natural Philosophy* (Sussex: Harvester Press, 1982); and *Energy, Force, and Matter* (Cambridge: Cambridge University Press, 1982); as well as E. McMullin, *Newton on Matter and Activity* (Notre Dame: University of Notre Dame Press, 1978), chapter 5. Boscovich's *Theory of Natural Philosophy*, appearing in 1758, was much more widely influential than Kant's *Physical Monadology* – where it again appears that the work of Boscovich and Kant were entirely independent of one another.

11. The *New Elucidation* is also translated in the volume edited by Walford cited in note 1. For further discussion of Kant's early (quasi-Leibnizean) metaphysics see the secondary sources cited there.

12. For a fuller discussion of both the *Metaphysical Foundations* and its pre-critical background see the Introduction to my translation (see note 1), upon which I am drawing here.

13. For further discussion (in connection, specifically, with Newton's argument for determining the true motions in the solar system in Book III of the *Principia*) see my contribution to P. Guyer, ed., *The Cambridge Companion to Kant*, 1st ed. (Cambridge: Cambridge University Press, 1992), and (for even more details) my *Kant and the Exact Sciences*.

14. Here they are cited as the laws "of the permanence of the same quantity of matter, of inertia, [and] of the equality of action and reaction" (B 20n).

15. For "inertial force [*vis inertiae*]" or "innate force [*vis insita*]" in the pre-critical period compare the *New Elucidation* at 1:408 with the *Physical Monadology* at 2:485. Kant rejects this force of inertia, in the *Metaphysical Foundations*, in the two remarks to his proof of his third law of mechanics. The rejection of "hylozoism" occurs in the remark to the proof of the second law (4:544): "The inertia of matter is, and means, nothing else than its *lifelessness*, as matter in itself. *Life* is the faculty of a *substance* to determine itself to act from an *internal principle*, of a *finite substance* to change, and of a *material substance* [to determine itself] to motion or rest, as change of its state. Now we know no other internal principle in a substance for changing its state except *desiring*, and no other internal activity at all except *thinking*, together with that

which depends on it, the *feeling* of pleasure or displeasure, and *desire* or willing. But these actions and grounds of determination in no way belong to representations of the outer senses, and so neither [do they belong] to the determinations of matter as matter. Hence all matter, as such, is *lifeless*... The possibility of a proper natural science rests entirely and completely on the law of inertia (along with that of the persistence of substance). The opposite of this, and thus also the death of all natural philosophy, would be *hylozoism*. From this very same concept of inertia, as mere *lifelessness*, it follows at once that it does not mean a *positive striving* to conserve its state. Only living beings are called inert in this latter sense, because they have a representation of another state, which they abhor, and against which they exert their power." Thus, Kant here closely associates life with mentality ("thinking"), and his rejection of "hylozoism," accordingly, appears to be directed at Leibnizean "panpsychism." Compare the discussion of the Leibnizean monadology and what may be internal to substance in the Amphiboly of the first *Critique* at A 265–6/B 321–2.

16. The doctrines of the priority of pure practical reason and of the Highest Good are developed in the Dialectic of Pure Practical Reason in the second *Critique*. The subordination of all regulative teleology to what Kant calls "ethico-theology" is developed in the Methodology of Teleological Judgment in the third *Critique*. The distinction between the realm of nature and the realm of freedom is emphasized in the Introduction to the third *Critique*. Kant then uses his doctrine of practical or rational faith [*Vernunftglaube*] to provide a detailed reinterpretation of Christianity in *Religion within the Boundaries of Mere Reason* (1793). For discussion of Kant's moral religion see A. Wood, "Rational Theology, Moral Faith, and Religion," in P. Guyer, ed. (note 13), and *Kant's Moral Religion* (Ithaca, NY: Cornell University Press, 1970).

17. The contrast between "a *nature in general*, as the lawlikeness of appearances in space and time" and the "particular laws" of nature governing "empirically determined appearances" is made in §26 of the second edition transcendental deduction (B 165). In the Preface to the *Metaphysical Foundations* Kant describes an analogous distinction between "general" and "special" metaphysics (4:469–70): the former "treat[s] the laws that make possible the concept of a nature in general, even without relation to any determinate object of experience, and thus undetermined with respect to the nature of this or that thing in the sensible world, in which case it is the *transcendental* part of the metaphysics of nature," whereas the latter "concern[s] itself with a particular nature of this or that kind of things, for which an empirical concept is given, but still in such a manner that, outside of what lies in this concept, no other empirical

principle is used for its cognition (for example, it takes the empirical concept of matter or of a thinking being as its basis, and it seeks that sphere of cognition of which reason is capable *a priori* concerning these objects), and here such a science must still always be called a meta-physics of nature, namely, of corporeal or of thinking nature."

18. See the continuation of the discussion quoted in note 17 (4:470): "[A]lthough a pure philosophy of nature in general, that is, that which investigates only what constitutes the concept of a nature in general, may indeed be possible even without mathematics, a pure doctrine of nature concerning *determinate* natural things (doctrine of body or doc-trine of soul) is only possible by means of mathematics. And, since in any doctrine of nature there is only as much proper science as there is *a priori* knowledge therein, a doctrine of nature will contain only as much proper science as there is mathematics capable of application there." It turns out, in the following discussion (4:471), that there is no science of the soul, properly speaking, since "mathematics is not appli-cable to the phenomena of inner sense and their laws." Thus, the only pure doctrine of nature, strictly speaking, is that of material or corporeal nature.

19. I think it is fair to say that this point of view has been dominant in twentieth-century Kant scholarship. It is articulated most clearly, per-haps, by Gerd Buchdahl, in his *Metaphysics and the Philosophy of Sci-ence* (Oxford: Blackwell, 1969), in terms of a fundamental distinction between "experience" and "systematic experience," "nature" and "the order of nature." Nature as constituted by the understanding consists of a plurality of spatio-temporal particulars, which is only subsequently transformed by the regulative use of reason into an order of nature gov-erned by systematic scientific laws. It is thus only at the level of the order of nature or systematic experience that particular mathematical-physical theories, such as Newton's, come into play, whereas the expe-rience due to the understanding is constituted entirely independently of all mathematical-physical theorizing, and thus comprises "the straight-forward things of commonsense" bereft of all "scientifico-theoretical components" (Buchdahl, *Metaphysics*, pp. 638–9, note 4).

20. For a detailed discussion of laws of nature and the principle of causality see my "Causal Laws and the Foundations of Natural Science," in P. Guyer, ed. (note 13), which also contains an examination of Buchdahl's views in particular (for citation, see 19). With respect to the principle of the permanence of substance, note that Kant explicitly reformulated this principle in the second edition as a quantitative conservation law – "[i]n all change of the appearance substance is permanence, and its quan-tum in nature is neither increased nor diminished" (B 278) – thereby

explicitly mimicking the principle of the conservation of the total quantity of matter proved in the *Metaphysical Foundations*.

21. The passage continues: "And so a separated metaphysics of corporeal nature does excellent and indispensable service for *general* metaphysics, in that the former furnishes examples (instances *in concreto*) in which to realize the concepts and propositions of the latter (properly speaking, transcendental philosophy), that is, to give a mere form of thought sense and meaning." (4:478).

22. This passage begins (B 291): "It is even more remarkable, however, that, in order to understand the possibility of things in accordance with the categories, and thus to verify the *objective reality* of the latter, we require not merely intuitions, but always even *outer intuitions*. If, for example, we take the pure concepts of *relation*, we find, first, that in order to supply something *permanent* in intuition corresponding to the concept of *substance* (and thereby to verify the objective reality of this concept), we require an intuition *in space* (of matter), because space alone is determined as permanent, but time, and thus everything in inner sense, continually flows."

23. For further argument and discussion of these texts see my "Transcendental Philosophy and Mathematical Physics," *Studies in History and Philosophy of Science* 34 (2003): 29–43, which also contains an analysis of the structure of the second edition transcendental deduction from this point of view.

24. For further discussion of the role of the regulative use of reason in relation to pure natural science see my "Causal Laws" (note 20), and "Kant on Science and Experience," in V. Gerhardt et al., eds., *Kant und die Berliner Aufklärung*, vol. I (Berlin: de Guyter, 2001), pp. 233–45. As I point out in this latter work, the present conception is therefore the reverse of Buchdahl's (note 19). On my view, the understanding can *constitutively* ground objective experience only through or by means of the mathematical exact sciences, and it is reason, as opposed to the understanding, which then supplies essentially non-mathematical *regulative* principles so as, in particular, to accommodate the more ordinary or commonsensical experience that does not yet have a scientific grounding.

25. For further discussion of the empirical concept of matter and its relation to both the categories and the indefinite further development of natural science see my "Matter and Motion in the *Metaphysical Foundations* and the First *Critique*," in E. Watkins, ed., *Kant and the Sciences* (Oxford: Oxford University Press, 2001).

26. See §17 of the second edition deduction (B 137): "The first pure cognition of the understanding, on which the entire rest of its use is based,

and which is also wholly independent from all conditions of sensible intuition, is the principle of the original *synthetic* unity of appercep-tion." Compare also §19, which explains that "principles of the objec-tive determination of all representation, insofar as cognition can arise therefrom" are "all derived from the principle of the transcendental unity of apperception" (B 142).

27. For further discussion of the Paralogisms in this context see my "Science and Experience" (note 24), upon which I am drawing here.

28. This passage is closely followed by the passage (to which note 21 above is appended) concerning the need general metaphysics has for "exam-ples (intuitions)" provided by the doctrine of body "in order to provide meaning for its pure concepts of the understanding."

29. For Kant's denial of strict scientific status to chemistry in the *Meta-physical Foundations* see 4:470–1: "So long, therefore, as there is still for chemical actions of matters on one another no concept to be discov-ered that can be constructed, that is, no law of the approach or with-drawal of the parts of matter can be specified according to which, per-haps in proportion to their density or the like, their motions and all the consequences thereof can be made intuitive and presented *a priori* in space (a demand that will only with great difficulty ever be fulfilled), then chemistry can be nothing more than a systematic art or experi-mental doctrine, but never a proper science, because its principles are merely empirical, and allow of no *a priori* presentation in intuition." For Kant's discussion of contemporary chemistry in the first *Critique* see the examples – drawn from Stahlian phlogistic chemistry – sketched in the Appendix to the Dialectic (A 647–7/B 673–4, A 652–3/B 680–81). For further discussion of these examples see chapter 5 of my *Kant and the Exact Sciences*.

30. This kind of (Humean) skepticism within the tradition of post-Kantian idealism is most clearly and explicitly represented by Salomon Mai-mon. See P. Franks, "What should Kantians learn from Maimon's Skepticism?" in G. Freudenthal, ed., *The Philosophy of Salomon Mai-mon and its Place in the Enlightenment* (Dordrecht: Kluwer, 2003). I am indebted to Franks's interpretation of Maimon in my own formu-lation of the skeptical problem in question, although Franks does not emphasize, as I do, the distinction between constitutive and regulative principles – he instead formulates what I take to be essentially the same problem by means of a distinction between scientific judgements and everyday or ordinary judgements.

31. See *Ideas for a Philosophy of Nature* (1797, 1803), E. Harris and P. Heath, trans. (Cambridge: Cambridge University Press, 1988). For further dis-cussion and references see my "Kant – *Naturphilosophie* – Electromag-netism," in R. Brain and O. Knudson, eds., *Hans-Christian Oersted and*

the Romantic Legacy in Science (Dordrecht: Kluwer, 2005), upon which I am drawing here.

32. Schelling is here self-consciously returning to precisely the Leibnizean "hylozoism" Kant explicitly rejects in his own discussion of the law of inertia (see note 15, together with the paragraph to which it is appended). As I explain in detail in the work cited in note 31, Schelling's conception was fueled by a number of new discoveries in electro-chemistry arising from the invention of the Voltaic pile in 1800 – which discoveries strongly suggested, in particular, that chemical forces (affinities) were ultimately electrical in nature. This gave Schelling good reason to think that chemistry could be grounded in the fundamental forces of matter after all (contrary to Kant's own skepticism as expressed in note 29). Moreover, although Kant had been converted to Lavoisier's new antiphlogistic chemistry by the late 1790s (contrary to his earlier adherence to Stahl), and he had then granted scientific status to chemistry (on somewhat different grounds from his earlier denial in 1786), Kant never came to terms with the new electro-chemistry that flourished around the turn of the century. In this sense, it was Schelling's radical transformation of Kant's dynamical theory of matter, rather than Kant's original theory, which actually stood in the immediate background to the field-theoretic physics developed by Faraday and Maxwell later in the nineteenth century (see note 10, together with the paragraph to which it is appended); in particular, Oersted's seminal discovery of electromagnetism was directly inspired by Schelling's transformation of the Kantian theory.

33. In this sense, one can view absolute idealism as a synthesis of Spinoza's monistic conception of the relationship between matter and spirit with Leibniz's emphasis on teleology and life (compare note 3, together with the paragraph to which it is appended and the succeeding paragraph). For further discussion see F. Beiser, *German Idealism: The Struggle against Subjectivism, 1781–1801* (Cambridge, MA: Harvard University Press, 2002), and *The Romantic Imperative: The Concept of Early German Romanticism* (Cambridge, MA: Harvard University Press, 2003). Absolute idealism also adds an essentially new element – a dialectical evolutionary conception of the development of spirit and life from the fundamental forces of matter – due ultimately to Schelling's transformation of Kant's dynamical theory.

34. For the elimination of Kant's "dualisms" see P. Guyer, "Absolute Idealism and the Rejection of Kantian Dualism," in K. Ameriks, ed., *The Cambridge Companion to German Idealism* (Cambridge: Cambridge University Press, 2000).

35. This passage comes from Helmholtz's celebrated address, "Über das Sehen des Menschen" (On Human Vision), delivered at the dedication

of a monument to Kant in Königsberg in 1855 – reprinted in *Vorträge und Reden* (Braunschweig: Vieweg, 1903), vol. I, p. 88. This address became a model for philosophers who wished to turn away from the "metaphysics" of post-Kantian absolute idealism to a new type of scientific "epistemology" inspired by Kant – particularly for those in what then became the neo-Kantian tradition. See E. Cassirer, *The Problem of Knowledge: Philosophy, Science, and History since Hegel* (New Haven: Yale University Press, 1950), and K. Köhnke, *The Rise of Neo-Kantianism: German Academic Philosophy between Idealism and Positivism* (Cambridge: Cambridge University Press, 1991).

36. See "On the Conservation of Force" (1847), translated in R. Kahl, ed., *Selected Writings of Hermann von Helmholtz* (Middleton, CT: Wesleyan University Press, 1971). Although, as we have seen, Helmholtz is fundamentally unfair in his contention that the *Naturphilosophie* of Schelling and Hegel is entirely speculative and unscientific (see note 32), the discovery of the conservation of energy had indeed essentially reconfigured the debate over vitalism. For this discovery showed that all the fundamental forces or powers of matter (mechanical, thermal, electrical, chemical, and so on) are mutually intertransformable and that there is a *constant* quantity of energy preserved in all such transformations. Helmholtz (along with many others) took this decisively to undermine the "emergentist" picture of life defended by *Naturphilosophie*. In the case of biology, in particular, Helmholtz (along with many others) later took Darwinian natural selection as a decisive argument against all essentially teleological conceptions of evolution.

37. See "On the Origin and Significance of the Axioms of Geometry" (1870) and "The Facts in Perception" (1878), both translated in P. Hertz and M. Schlick, eds., *Hermann von Helmholtz: Epistemological Writings* (Dordrecht: Reidel, 1977). For further discussion see J. Richards, "The Evolution of Empiricism: Hermann von Helmholtz and the Foundations of Geometry," *British Journal for the Philosophy of Science* 28 (1977): 235–53, and my "Geometry, Construction, and Intuition in Kant and His Successors," in G. Scher and R. Tieszen, eds., *Between Logic and Intuition: Essays in Honor of Charles Parsons* (Cambridge: Cambridge University Press, 1999).

38. See *Space and Time in Contemporary Physics* (1917), translated in L. Mulder and B. van de Velde-Schlick, eds., *Moritz Schlick: Philosophical Papers* (Dordrecht: Reidel, 1977); *General Theory of Knowledge* (1918), A. Blamberg, trans. (La Salle, IL: Open Court, 1985). For detailed discussion of Schlick and his relation to Helmholtz see my "Helmholtz's *Zeichentheorie* and Schlick's *Allgemeine Erkenntnislehre*: Early Logical

Empiricism and Its Nineteenth Century Background," *Philosophical Topics* 25 (1997): 19–50.

39. See "Overcoming Metaphysics through Logical Analysis of Language" (1932), translated as "The Elimination of Metaphysics Through Logical Analysis of Language" in A. J. Ayer, ed., *Logical Positivism* (New York: Free Press, 1959); *Logical Syntax of Language* (1934), A. Smeaton, trans. (London: Kegan Paul, 1937); *Philosophy and Logical Syntax* (London: Kegan Paul, 1935). The first work contains Carnap's famous attack on Heidegger, which I discuss, in the context of the neo-Kantian background to the work of both men, in *A Parting of the Ways: Carnap, Cassirer, and Heidegger* (Chicago: Open Court, 2000). See also my *Reconsidering Logical Positivism* (Cambridge: Cambridge University Press, 1999) for further perspective on the development of logical empiricism.

40. See "Two Dogmas of Empiricism" (1951), reprinted in *From a Logical Point of View* (New York: Harper, 1961), and *Word and Object* (Cambridge, MA: MIT Press, 1960).

41. See, for example, "Formal and Factual Science" (1935), translated in H. Feigl and M. Brodbeck, eds., *Readings in the Philosophy of Science* (New York: Appleton-Century-Crofts, 1953).

42. See the translation of *The Theory of Relativity and A Priori Knowledge* (Los Angeles: University of California Press, 1965). Reichenbach's criticism of Schlick sparked a correspondence between the two, and Reichenbach eventually renounced the Kantian conception of the (constitutively) *a priori* in favor of Poincaré's notion of convention. For further discussion see chapter 3 of my *Reconsidering Logical Positivism* (cited in note 39).

43. See my "Philosophical Naturalism," *Proceedings and Addresses of the American Philosophical Association* 71 (1997): 7–21; *Dynamics of Reason: The 1999 Kant Lectures at Stanford University* (Stanford: CSLI, 2001); "Kant, Kuhn, and the Rationality of Science," *Philosophy of Science* 69 (2002): 171–90.

10 The supreme principle of morality

I. WHAT IS "THE SUPREME PRINCIPLE OF MORALITY"?

In the Preface to his best known work on moral philosophy, Kant states his purpose very clearly and succinctly: "The present ground-work is, however, nothing more than the search for and establishment of the supreme principle of morality, which already constitutes an enterprise whole in its aim and to be separated from every other moral investigation" (*Groundwork*, 4:392). This paper will deal with the outcome of the first part of this task, namely, Kant's attempt to formulate the supreme principle of morality, which is the intended outcome of the search. It will consider this formulation in the light of Kant's conception of the historical antecedents of his attempt.

Our first task, however, must be to say a little about the meaning of the term "supreme principle of morality." For it is not nearly as evident to many as it was to Kant that there is such a thing at all. And it is extremely common for people, whatever position they may take on this issue, to misunderstand what a "supreme principle of morality" is, what it is for, and what role it is supposed to play in moral theorizing and moral reasoning. Kant never directly presents any argument that there must be such a principle, but he does articulate several considerations that would seem to justify supposing that there is. Kant holds that moral questions are to be decided by reason. Reason, according to Kant, always seeks unity under principles, and ultimately, systematic unity under the fewest possible number of principles (*Pure Reason*, A 298–302/B 355–9, A 645–50/B 673–8). Where systematicity is being given to empirical data, this may result in an irreducible plurality of principles, but the fact that moral questions are to be decided by reason gives us grounds for thinking that here there must ultimately be only a single principle. For this means that we must suppose there is an objective answer to them, an answer valid for all possible agents or inquirers (whether or not we are ever able to find that answer or agree on it) (*Groundwork*, 4:442, *Morals*, 6:207; cf. *Lectures on Ethics* 27:276, 29:621, 625–6). It is familiar enough in everyday life, of course, that moral considerations are sometimes plural and mutually conflicting, but if there were no single principle to which they could be traced back, then necessarily there would be no objectively correct answer to moral questions whenever opposing answers could be made to rest each on its own ultimate, incommensurable principle. In that case it is not even clear that we could consider the different conflicting answers to the same question, or consider there to be a specifically *moral* point of view, or even any determinate *moral* questions at all, since each of the irreducibly plural principles would define a distinct practical viewpoint and a distinct set of practical questions, and no communication would be possible between these points of view concerning what, in the end, we *ought to do* or how we *ought to live*. This would spell the end of all moral objectivity, perhaps even of all morality, period.[1]

That there is a supreme principle of morality, however, does not mean that there cannot be moral questions that are difficult to decide in practice, or that there must be an easy resolution to all moral conflicts and dilemmas. Nor does it mean that moral decisions are always, or even typically, to be made by referring them directly to the supreme principle. This is the mistake made by all those who think of Kantian ethics as recommending that we make all our decisions merely by applying Kant's famous formula of universal law, asking ourselves "What if everybody did that?" Kant may have let himself in for such a mistaken reading when he said:

Thus I need no well-informed shrewdness to know what I have to do in order to make my volition morally good. Inexperienced in regard to the course of the world, incapable of being prepared for all occurrences that might eventuate in it, I ask myself only: Can you will also that your maxim should become a universal law?   (*Groundwork*, 4:403)

However, the context of this remark must be carefully considered. Kant's only aim in the passage is to draw a clear distinction between the prudential question whether it is safe to make a false promise for immediate gain and the moral question whether it is permissible to do so. He has just been observing that whether it is in our long-term self-interest to make a false promise is often a nice question, hard to decide on account of the conflicting considerations of momentary advantage and possible long-term risk. His point in this remark is that the same subtleties do not afflict the question whether it is morally right to make a false promise, since he thinks it is obvious that we could not rationally will that others should be allowed to perpetrate such deceptions on us, or fail to believe our promises – as they obviously would if everyone were permitted to adopt the policy of making any promise they liked with no intention of keeping it. It is not at all clear, however, that the obvious generalization suggested by Kant's remark is true, or is anything he would want to support. About many decisions made every day in the business world, for example (in particular, decisions about how far to be wholly frank with people and when to let them act on false beliefs), it is easy to see that these decisions are both safe and profitable, but a subtle and difficult question whether they are morally right. We would seriously misunderstand Kant's ethics if we concluded from this passage that he has some deep theoretical reason for wanting to deny this obvious fact. The fact even further supports his main conclusion by showing another way moral questions can be easily distinguished from prudential questions.

Even more harmful and misleading, however, is the extremely common thought that Kant is recommending here that every decision we make in life should be prompted by asking ourselves whether some maxim or other can be willed as a universal law. This thought is responsible for so many misunderstandings, and there are so many things wrong with it, that it is hard even to know which ones to list first. This thought ignores the fact that, as we shall see below, the formula of universal law is only the first step in the process of formulating the supreme principle of morality, and consequently ignores Kant's other, richer, and more definitive formulations of this principle. It does not consider that the formula of universal law provides only a negative test for maxims (a way of rejecting some as impermissible), but could never tell us in positive terms that we ought to follow any specific maxim. It disregards the fact that Kant never presents, and never uses, the formula of universal law as a general moral decision procedure. In any case, although the universalizability test may be suited to illustrate the specific examples to which Kant applies it, it would be radically defective as a general moral criterion, since it systematically yields both false positives and false negatives when we try to employ it generally.[2]

Against the general thought that the supreme principle of morality is to be used directly to make moral decisions, what is said by J. S. Mill might just as well have been said by Kant:

> It is a strange notion that the acknowledgement of a first principle is inconsistent with the admission of secondary ones...Men really ought to leave off talking nonsense on this subject, which they would neither talk nor listen to on other matters of practical concernment...Whatever we adopt as the fundamental principle of morality, we require subordinate principles to apply it by; the impossibility of doing without them, being common to all systems, can afford no argument against any one in particular.[3]

In the case of Kant, he indicates clearly that the supreme principle of morality requires for its application a "practical anthropology" (*Groundwork*, 4:388), so that we may determine what this highest principle – so abstract and removed from ordinary decision making that the search for and establishment of it must "constitute an enterprise whole in its aim and to be separated from every other moral investigation" – requires of us under the actual conditions of human life. When we turn to Kant's actual account of ordinary moral reasoning in the Doctrine of Virtue, we see that it turns not on figuring out which maxims are universalizable, but on reasoning from a system of duties – juridical and ethical, to ourselves and others, of respect and of love. Some of these duties are "perfect," "narrow" or "strict," requiring particular actions or omissions from us; most of them, however, are "imperfect," "wide" and "meritorious," requiring only that we set certain ends, and leaving it up to us to decide the priority among them and the specific actions that we will take toward them. Kant clearly recognizes that there can be conflicts between the different "obligating reasons" that arise from our various ends (*Morals*, 6:224), and he worries a good deal (under the heading of "Casuistical Questions") about cases in which special circumstances might make it necessary to modify or make exceptions even to moral rules that are taken to be of strict obligation (see *Morals*, 6:423–4, 426, 428, 431).

The role of a supreme principle of morality is not to dictate what we do in every particular case, but rather to stand behind and justify such a system of general moral rules or duties, and to provide a general rationale for deciding cases where reasons derived from them either collide, or leave it indeterminate what to do, or require us to make alterations in their demands to fit unusual situations. We would look in vain in the *Metaphysics of Morals* for any rigorous inferential route from the supreme principle of morality (in any of its formulations) to the specific duties Kant identifies. Only one of them is based on anything like the formula of universal law; all the others rest on appeals, usually both brief and casual, to the formula of humanity as an end in itself.[4] But it is clear enough how the system reflects the general ideas of rational autonomy, the dignity of every rational being as an end in itself, and the laws by which every human being could rationally will that all should conduct themselves.

The function of a supreme principle of morality, then, is *not* to tell us directly, from day to day and minute to minute, through some uniform canonical process of moral reasoning to be applied in exactly the same way to all situations, exactly which actions we should (and should not) be performing and precisely how we should be spending our time. In this respect, we ought to ask far less of a supreme principle of morality than philosophers are in the habit of asking. But in another respect, we ought to ask a good deal more of such principles than is often asked. Analytical philosophers often aim at producing moral principles that may be very complex in structure, full of subclauses and qualifications, because these principles enable them to capture "our moral intuitions" and the precisely worded epicyclic subclauses enable us to deal cleverly with threatened counterexamples of various kinds. (Kant's Formulas of Universal Law and the Law of Nature, when subjected to sophisticated interpretations that are intended to deal with all the troublesome counterexamples, are easily twisted into principles of this kind.) But the resulting principles often do more to disguise than to state the fundamental value basis on which decisions are to be made. The right interpretation of Kant's formulation of the supreme principle of morality, by contrast, will be one that exhibits the principle as less concerned with generating results for all cases that accord precisely with our so-called "intuitions," and more concerned with identifying perspicuously the ultimate value on which moral rules and duties may be grounded.

2. FORMULATING THE SUPREME PRINCIPLE

In the *Groundwork*, Kant formulates the supreme principle of morality in conscious contrast to what he sees as the entire philosophical tradition of thinking on the topic. Further, in the twentieth century there was one interesting attempt to interpret the *Groundwork* as a conscious response to one influential historical text, namely, Cicero's *On Duties*, especially as it had recently been interpreted by Kant's contemporary Christian Garve. But it will prove to be more perspicuous if we postpone such historical reflections until after an exposition of the procedure through which Kant develops his formulations of the supreme principle.

Duty and respect for law

Kant develops the moral principle twice in the *Groundwork*, using first a more commonsensical starting point in the First Section, then a more philosophical starting point in the Second Section, leading to a more complete formulation. In the first section, the starting point is "common rational moral cognition." The aim here is to enlist what Kant regards as certain of our most deeply held rational beliefs about morality on behalf of his new conception of the moral principle. He begins by focusing on the "good will," which, he claims, we recognize as good in itself and as having a special place among goods in that it is the only thing good in itself whose goodness cannot be augmented or diminished by its combination with other good or bad things. Kant then attempts to forge a special connection between the good will and the idea of "acting from duty" – that is, acting with inner rational moral constraint, motivated solely by the thought of following a moral principle. The crucial claim is that we think there is something uniquely worthy of esteem about a person who fulfills duty in the absence of (or even in opposition to) all other inducements of inclination or self-interest, solely out of respect for the moral law.

In the light of over two hundred years of lively controversy over Kant's assertions in the opening pages of the *Groundwork*, it is hard to resist the thought that Kant overestimated the extent to which the truth of his claims is available to all of us through "common rational moral cognition." Our purpose here, however, is to see how he uses these claims to derive a formulation of the supreme moral principle. His central argument is that when we act from duty, even in opposition to all inclination, the only thing left that could motivate us is the purely rational appeal of a universally valid practical principle. This leads him to his first formulation of what we may call the Formula of Universal Law (FUL): "I ought never to conduct myself except so *that I could also will that my maxim become a universal law*" (*Groundwork*, 4:402). In other words, the special motive of duty, which has a special affinity with the good will because it alone can rationally constrain us to a course of action even in opposition to all our empirical desires or inclinations, can be nothing else but the unconditional worth of following a principle that binds us solely on account of its source in our own rational willing – in the fact that we regard it as a principle fit for being legislated to ourselves merely as rational beings, hence for being legislated universally to all rational beings.

Although Kant uses these thoughts only to reach FUL, they contain at least implicitly all the main ideas he goes on to develop, resulting in an entire system of different (yet, he argues, essentially equivalent) formulas of the supreme principle of morality. This more systematic exposition of the supreme principle of morality takes place in the Second Section of the *Groundwork*.

The categorical imperative

Crucial to the Second Section's formulation of the principle is the idea of a "categorical imperative," which can best be understood in connection with an entire philosophical theory of rational agency, presented very succinctly by Kant at *Groundwork*, 4:412–21.

Kant's theory takes us to be agents who are self-directing in the sense that we have the capacity to step back from our natural desires, reflect on them, consider whether and how we should satisfy them, and be moved by them only on the basis of such reflections. An inclination (or habitual desire we find in ourselves empirically) moves us to act only when we choose to set its object as an end for ourselves, and this choice then sets us the task of selecting or devising a means to that end. If I see an apple up in a tree and a desire to eat it occurs to me, then I will eat it only if I first decide to make eating it my *end*, and then devise a *means* (such as climbing the tree, or reaching for the apple with a stick, or knocking it to the ground by throwing something at it) to achieve the end. In acting on my inclination,

I thus make a series of decisions and create in myself a set of new desires (to climb the tree, or find a suitable stick) whose source is not merely the original desire I am trying to satisfy, but even more the exercise of my own capacities to set ends, devise means, and hold myself to some self-chosen plan for applying the means. Our desires, then, do not simply push us around like the levers and pulleys of a machine, but rather provide inputs into a rational process of self-direction involving our adoption and recognition of rational norms and the decision to follow or not follow the norms we recognize.

Setting an end is the most basic normative act, since (Kant holds) there is no action without an end to be produced by it. This act involves the concept of an object (or state of affairs) to be produced and also the concept of some means needed to produce it. Setting an end thus subjects me to a normative principle commanding me to perform the action required as a means to the end. Kant calls this principle a "hypothetical imperative." It is called an "imperative" because it is a command of reason requiring the agent to do something; it is "hypothetical" because the command governs our action only on the condition that we will the end in question. By contrast, an imperative that has no such condition would be called a "categorical imperative."[5]

Kant thinks that if the good will that acts from duty has the characteristic that it follows a rational principle even when all empirical incentives oppose it, then such a will should be understood as following a categorical imperative. For to act from duty is to follow a moral principle whether or not doing so achieves some antecedently desired end.[6] Therefore, if acting from duty is what is most essential to morality, then the moral law should also be characterized as a categorical imperative. Thus the supreme principle of morality, whatever else it is, must be conceived as a categorical imperative.

First formula: Universal law and the law of nature

As these considerations might lead us to expect, Kant now proceeds to derive essentially the same formula we saw at the end of the First Section, namely, the Formula of Universal Law (FUL), which is now stated as: "*Act only in accordance with that maxim through which you can at the same time will that it become a universal law*" (*Groundwork*, 4:421). By a "maxim," Kant means a normative principle, which a subject lays down for itself with the intention of acting according to it. It perhaps involves a degree of idealization to represent agents as acting on "maxims," since people do not typically recite to themselves (even silently) some general principle on which they are acting before they act. But the degree of idealization involved is not so great when we consider that understanding an action at all normally involves understanding the agent's intention, and the intention with which an agent acts is essentially such a subjectively adopted norm, usually also permitting us to form generalizations about what actions, consistent with this intention, the agent will perform or would perform under various counterfactual circumstances.

FUL provides us with a test for permissibility of maxims. It tells us that it is permissible to act only on those maxims we could will to be universal laws. The criterion of possibility here seems to be the absence of contradiction or conflicting volitions. It is not possible for me to will my maxim as a universal law if I cannot consistently think both of myself acting successfully on the maxim and also of its being a universal law, or if the volition that the maxim be a universal law would conflict either with the volition to act on the maxim or else with some other volition that I, as a rational being, necessarily have.

The term "universal law," as used in FUL, appears also to carry a normative force. That is, the question we are asking about our maxim is whether we could will that everyone (at least, everyone in our present circumstances) should be permitted to act on it. This is clearly the way Kant applies FUL in the First Section to the maxim of making the false promise: "Would I be able to say that anyone may make an untruthful promise when he finds himself in embarrassment which he cannot get out of in any other way?" (Groundwork, 4:403). In other words, FUL invites us to consider which maxims we can will to be morally permissible for all, and commands us to restrict ourselves only to those maxims.

Apparently, however, Kant thinks it is easier (or more intuitive) to apply a different permissibility test to maxims, asking ourselves not which ones we can will to be universally *permissible*, but rather which ones we can will to be *actually followed as universal laws of nature*. (Again, the criteria of possible volition seem to be the absence of contradictions or conflicting volitions.) For in the Second

Section, he immediately proposes this variant of FUL, which we may call the Formula of the Law of Nature (FLN): "*So act as if the maxim of your action were to become through your will a **universal law of nature**" (*Groundwork*, 4:421). That is, we are to imagine a world in which, with the regularity of a natural law, the maxim we are considering is followed by everyone (in relevantly similar circumstances to the ones we are in). FLN, not FUL, is the formula Kant actually uses in illustrating his first formulation with reference to the four much-discussed examples, organized according to the taxonomy of duties through which Kant structures his more fully developed moral theory (that is, duties to ourselves and to others, perfect duties and imperfect duties).

Once Kant has completed his exposition of the supreme principle of morality, he tells us that the three formulas he has developed represent the moral principle from three different points of view: "form," "matter," and "complete determination" (*Groundwork*, 4:436).[7] The version of the first formula he identifies with "form" is again FLN: "That the maxims must be chosen as if they are supposed to be valid as universal laws of nature" (*Groundwork*, 4:436). Both FUL and FLN may be regarded as identifying the "form" of the supreme principle of morality in the sense that they seek to specify a formal property of maxims such that having that property makes them compatible with the moral principle. This form consists in a certain relation to the rational will of the agent who proposes to act on the maxim, namely, the capacity of that agent to will that the maxim be a universal law of nature (or, in the FUL version, to will that its universal permissibility should be a valid norm for all rational beings).

Second formula: Humanity as an end in itself

Kant's choice to begin by expounding the supreme principle of morality has been fateful regarding the misunderstandings and consequent (misguided) criticisms that it has provoked. Many, perhaps most, readers of the *Groundwork* have behaved as though Kant had intended his presentation of the moral principle to be complete at *Groundwork* 4:425. His further development of the supreme principle of morality in the *Groundwork* has been treated as a mere set of afterthoughts, not regarded as essential to interpreting the content of FUL and FLN or determining their role in Kant's conception of the moral principle. It is no exaggeration, however, to say that when the *Groundwork* is read in this way, its basic aims and contentions have been fundamentally misunderstood.

For example, Kant's entire approach to ethics has been (and still is) widely described as "formalistic." He has been criticized for not providing (or even for not allowing the possibility of) any substantive value lying behind the moral principle, or providing the rational will with any ground for being able to will one maxim, and not another, to be a universal law (or law of nature). The very concept of a categorical imperative has sometimes been rejected as nonsensical, on the ground that this concept precludes our having any substantive reason for obeying such an imperative. Schopenhauer, for instance, explained the alleged incoherence of Kant's thinking by attributing to him an ethics of divine command but without admitting a divine lawgiver to back up the command.[8]

Such criticisms are obviated, however, at least in the form they are usually presented, as soon as we turn from Kant's first to his second formulation of the moral principle. For it deals explicitly with the "matter" of the principle, by which Kant means the "end" for the sake of which it is supposed to be rational to follow a categorical imperative. Kant's "formalism" applies only to the first stage of his development of the principle; it is complemented immediately by considering the principle from the opposite, "material" point of view, in which Kant inquires after our rational motive for obeying a categorical imperative, and locates this motive in the distinctive value that grounds morality, which he identifies with a kind of *end*.[9]

Here too, however, Kant's procedure was revolutionary, from a historical point of view, rejecting the standard picture of the kind of substantive value that might ground a moral principle and also the traditional conception of the sorts of things that can count as ends of human action. This radically new conception of the fundamental end of morality perhaps explains the incredulity that has often greeted the *Groundwork* on this point. The traditional view is that what grounds any principle must be an end to be produced, a state of affairs whose desirability gives us a reason to follow principles whose execution is conducive to bringing it about. As we have already noted, Kant accepts the traditional idea that every action has an end to be produced, but insists that the setting of such ends must be consequent on moral principles, not their ground. He rejects the thesis that any end to be produced grounds the supreme principle of morality, arguing that this would turn the principle into a merely hypothetical imperative, and deprive it of its status as a categorical imperative. The question then is: What sort of substantive value could give us reason to follow a principle without appealing to any end to be produced by following it?

Kant's answer to this question is found in the following remark, presented first in the form of a mere *supposition*: "But suppose there were something *whose existence in itself* had an absolute worth, something that, as an *end in itself*, could be a ground of determinate laws; then in it and only in it alone would lie the ground of a possible categorical imperative, i.e. of a practical law" (*Groundwork*, 4:428). In other words, the substantive value grounding a categorical imperative cannot be the value of something future to be brought about as a consequence of our obeying it, but rather the value of something already in existence, which grounds our obedience to the imperative because such obedience serves to manifest or express our recognition of that value. Such an existent value is an end in the sense that it is that *for the sake of which* it is rational for us to act.

Going beyond the mere supposition of something with this sort of value, Kant next presents his thesis in the form of an *assertion*: "Now I say that the human being, and in general every rational being, exists as an end in itself" (*Groundwork*, 4:428). He then proceeds immediately to support the assertion by presenting, first, a series of arguments eliminating other possible candidates for what might exist as an end in itself: the objects of empirical desires or inclinations, the inclinations themselves, and nonrational beings (*Groundwork*, 4:428). He follows this up with a brief, obscure, but crucial positive argument that only "humanity," understood in the technical Kantian sense of rational nature regarded as the capacity to set ends, can qualify as an end in itself: However we interpret this argument, the gist of it seems to be that we do value our own existence as an end in itself, but we do so *rationally* only insofar as we value the existence of other rational beings in precisely the same way.[10]

Rational nature as an existent end in itself is distinct from all ends to be produced, but it stands in a determinate relation to them. All ends to be produced are set as ends by rational beings, since only rational nature has the capacity to regulate itself by rational norms, the most basic of which is the setting of ends and the selection of means to them (*Groundwork*, 4:437). There are, in Kant's theory, two basic kinds of ends to be produced that the supreme principle of morality requires us to set: our own perfection and the happiness of others (*Morals*, 6:386–8, 391–4; cf. *Groundwork*, 4:423, 430).[11]

Regarded from the standpoint of its "matter," then, the supreme principle of morality rests on the absolute worth of rational nature in the person of each human being, and leads to the second main formula of the moral principle, the Formula of Humanity as End in Itself (FH): "*Act so that you use humanity, as much in your own person as in the person of every other, always at the same time as an end, never merely as a means*" (*Groundwork*, 4:429). As I have already mentioned, this is the formula of the moral law to which Kant most consistently appeals when he derives the duties belonging to the system he expounds in the *Metaphysics of Morals*.

Third formula: Autonomy and the realm of ends

Kant has now derived two distinct formulas of the supreme principle of morality, both from the concept of a categorical imperative. The first was derived from the concept of a maxim that is compatible with this kind of imperative, and the general form that such a maxim would have to have. The second was derived from the concept of the substantive value (or the end) that could give us a rational ground to follow a categorical imperative. These two lines of argument from the concept of a categorical imperative are quite independent of each other, and lead to distinct formulations of the moral principle, even if (as Kant thinks) there is no conflict between these distinct formulas, and they can be treated as merely different ways of expressing "precisely the same law" (*Groundwork*, 4:436). Kant's next step, however, is to combine the two ideas behind these first two formulas to derive a third formula:

> The ground of all practical legislation, namely, lies *objectively in the rule* and the form of universality, which makes it capable of being a law (at least a law of nature) (in accordance with the first principle), but *subjectively* it lies in the *end*; but the subject of all ends is every rational being as an end in itself (in accordance with the second principle): from this now follows the third practical principle of the will, as the supreme condition of its harmony with universal practical reason, the idea of the *will of every rational being as a will giving universal law*. (*Groundwork*, 4:431)

The third formula combines the conception of a law valid universally for all rational beings (in FUL) with the conception of every rational nature as having absolute worth, to get the idea of the will of every rational being as the source of a universally valid legislation. The term "idea" used in this formulation should be understood in Kant's technical sense: an "idea" is a concept of reason to which no empirical object can ever correspond, but which we use regulatively in arranging our cognitions in a system (*Pure Reason*, A 312–20/B 368–77, A 642–704/B 670–732). Thus, to regard the legislator of the moral law as the *idea* of the will of every rational being is not to say that the law is given by your arbitrary will or mine (for our wills are corrupt and fallible), but rather that the law is regarded as having been legislated by each of our wills insofar as it corresponds to an ideal rational concept of what it ought to be (but always falls short of being).

"The idea of the will of every rational being as a will giving universal law" is Kant's initial presentation of the Formula of Autonomy (FA). It is also stated more directly, like the first two formulas, in the form of an imperative: "Do not choose otherwise than so that the maxims of one's choice are at the same time comprehended with it in the same volition as universal law" (*Groundwork*, 4:440). Or again: "Act in accordance with maxims that can at the same time have themselves as universal laws of nature for their object" (*Groundwork*, 4:437). In these formulations, FA may sound superficially like FUL (or FLN), but in fact it is a formula quite distinct from either of them, making a much stronger demand on maxims and yielding much stronger conclusions about what we ought to do.

Where FUL and FLN provide a mere condition of permissibility for maxims, consisting in its being *possible* (without contradiction or conflicting volitions) for you to will the maxim as a universal law, FA tells you *positively to follow* those maxims which *actually contain in themselves the volition* that they should be universal laws. FUL (or respectively, FLN) counts a maxim as permissible if there would be no contradiction or conflicting volitions in willing it to be a universal law (or law of nature); but a maxim might pass this purely negative test without containing in itself the volition that it should actually be a universal law (or law of nature). So the criterion on maxims proposed in FA is significantly stronger than the criteria of universalizability proposed in either FUL or FLN. And it justifies a correspondingly stronger conclusion about maxims, telling us not merely which ones are permissible and which not, but also which ones we have a positive duty to adopt because they are part of a system of universal moral legislation given by our own rational will.

Of course FA does not pretend to offer us any *test* to discriminate maxims that have this property from maxims that do not. But as I have already said, it would be an error to think that the universalizability tests present in FUL or FLN are intended (even as permissibility tests) to apply to all conceivable maxims, so there is really nothing they can do that FA cannot. Both FUL and FA, rather, should be seen as indicating the spirit of a universal moral principle, and defining a task for reasoning: namely, in the case of FUL, that of deciding which maxims are compatible with a system of universal law (which maxims do not violate the laws of such a system), or, in the case of FA, which ones belong to that system as part of its actual legislation as given by the idea of the will of every rational being.

FA combines in itself the main idea of FUL and the main idea of FH. Kant indicates this later when he says: "The three ways mentioned of representing the principle of morality are, however, fundamentally only so many formulas of precisely the same law, of which one of itself unites the other two [*deren die eine die anderen zwei von selbst in sich vereinigt*]" (*Groundwork*, 4:436). This last clause has been mistranslated as "each of them unites the others in itself" or "any one of them of itself unites the other two in it."[12] Both these translations say, as the original does not, that it is *equally* true of *each* of Kant's three formulas that it unites the other two. However, it is only of FA that Kant ever explicitly claims that it unites the other two in itself; no such claim is ever made about FUL or FH. Consequently, I think we should regard FA as having a special status among the three formulas: FA is the formula that unites and sums up the others. It should be regarded as the definitive formulation of the principle of morality, insofar as there is one.

Just as Kant earlier provided a more "intuitive" version of FUL in the form of FLN, so here he also provides a more intuitive variant of FA, the Formula of the Realm of Ends (FRE): "Act in accordance with maxims of a universally legislative member for a merely possible realm of ends" (*Groundwork*, 4:439). FRE provides a new characterization of the system of legislation referred to in FA, by describing the nature of the community that is to result from it. It calls this community a "realm of ends" (*Reich der Zwecke*). By a "realm" Kant means "a systematic combination of various rational beings through communal laws," or again, "a whole of all ends in systematic connection" (*Groundwork*, 4:433). In other words, a collection of ends constitutes a "realm" if these ends are not in conflict or competition with one another, but are combined into a mutually supporting system. The laws of a realm of ends are those that, if followed, would bring the ends of rational beings (both the existent ends that are the rational beings themselves according to FH, and the ends set in the maxims chosen by those rational beings) into a mutually supporting harmony with each other. FRE commands us to follow maxims involving ends that belong to this mutually supporting system, and forbids us to adopt ends that fall outside it.

Kant sometimes looks upon this system (or "realm") of ends as something like a single overarching end, and thinks of following the principle of morality (as formulated in FRE) as joining with others in the shared pursuit of this collective end (or system of ends). The key terms Kant uses to express this idea are "system" (*System*) and "combination" (*Verbindung*). Thus, at the conclusion of the *Anthropology*, he speaks of human progress from evil toward good as achievable only "through progressive organization of citizens of the earth in and to the species as one system, cosmopolitically combined" (*Anthropology*, 7:333). Kant's two main conceptions of what it is to act empirically according to the idea of a realm of ends are the relation of friendship, in which the happiness of both friends is "swallowed up" in a common end that includes the good of both, and the religious community, which in Kant's view should be bound together fundamentally not by creeds or scriptural traditions but by the shared pursuit of the highest good as a common end.[13]

If this is right, then one interesting consequence is that FRE gives priority to securing human community or harmony over maximizing human welfare or satisfaction. We should avoid all patterns of end-setting that involve fundamentally competitive relations between different rational beings, and we are forbidden to engage with others in ways that require the frustration of some people's deepest ends. Conflict or competition between human ends is permissible only if it is in service of a deeper systematic unity among all human ends, a system in which no member of the realm of ends is left out. The moral law commands us, in other words, to seek only that degree and kind of welfare for ourselves, and for others, that can be made to cohere with and support everyone's pursuit of the common welfare of all. If this means less total welfare than could be gotten by permitting fundamental conflicts between the ends of different rational beings, then lesser, not greater, total welfare is what the moral law commands us to seek.

The "universal formula"

At this point, let us summarize the three (or five) formulas of the moral law, the system of which constitutes the result of the *Groundwork's* search for the supreme principle of morality:
First formula:

FUL   *The Formula of Universal Law*: *"Act only in accordance with that maxim through which you at the same time can will that it become a universal law"* (*Groundwork*, 4:421; cf. 4:402);

with its more "intuitive" variant,

FLN   *The Formula of the Law of Nature*: *"So act, as if the maxim of your action were to become through your will a* **universal law of nature**" (*Groundwork*, 4:421; cf. 4:436).

Second formula:

FH   *The Formula of Humanity as End in Itself*: *"So act that you use humanity, as much in your own person as in the person of every other, always at the same time as an end and never merely as a means"* (*Groundwork*, 4:429; cf. 4:436).

Third formula:

FA   *Formula of Autonomy*: *"*. . . the idea *of the will of every rational being as a will giving universal law"* (*Groundwork*, 4:431; cf. 4:432) or "Not to choose otherwise than so that the maxims of one's choice are at the same time comprehended with it in the same volition as universal law" (*Groundwork*, 4:440; cf. 4:432, 434, 438);

with its more "intuitive" variant,

FRE   *The Formula of the Realm of Ends*: "Act in accordance with maxims of a universally legislative member for a merely possible realm of ends" (*Groundwork*, 4:439; cf. 4:433, 437, 438).

As we have already noted, at *Groundwork* 4:436 Kant presents the three formulas as a system, characterizing FLN as giving us the "form," FH the "matter," and FRE the "complete determination" of maxims under the moral law. He apparently chooses FLN over FUL and FRE over FA here because, as he says, his aim at this point is to "bring an idea of reason nearer to intuition (in accordance with a certain analogy) and through this, nearer to feeling" (*Groundwork*, 4:436). He apparently means that FLN, using the analogy of practical laws with laws of nature, and FRE, characterizing the system of laws in FA through the analogy with an ideal community or realm of ends that is to result from it, have greater appeal to us, thereby (as he elsewhere puts it) "providing entry" (into the human heart) for the precepts of morality (*Groundwork*, 4:405). But after presenting his system of formulas with this intention, he points to the limits of his aim in the following remark: "But one does better in moral judging always to proceed in accordance with the strict method and take as ground the universal formula of the categorical imperative: '*Act in accordance with that maxim which can at the same time make itself into universal law*' (*Groundwork*, 4:436–7).

The main point Kant seems to be making here is that the way of thinking (closer to "intuition" and "feeling") that is best for animating human hearts and actions on behalf of morality is not the same as the way of thinking that is best when it comes time to pass critical judgment either on the actions we have performed or on the maxims we are proposing to adopt. For this latter task, apparently, a more austere and abstract principle is better because, flawed human nature being what it is, the same feelings and intuitions that may make us enthusiastic friends of virtue also make us more susceptible to self-deception and make it easier for us to pass off corrupt actions and maxims as morally commendable ones. (In other words, those sentimentalists who think that what satisfies the heart, but not the head, represents greater moral purity, have things exactly wrong: where the head has been corrupted, it was the heart that corrupted it; and the first remedy for the corruption of our hearts is to learn to think in an enlightened way, with our heads, about what to do, and which feelings we should allow to influence us.)

In light of the systematization of the three formulations of the moral principle Kant has just presented, however, what are we to make of his reference to "the universal formula of the categorical imperative"? Is this intended to be the same as one of the other formulas already derived? The most common interpretation is that the "universal formula" is FUL (perhaps because "universal formula" is, carelessly, thought to be shorthand for "formula of universal law"). Most who adopt this reading do so as if it were not the least bit problematic, as though it were simply what the text itself says.[14] But of course it is not. I fear this reflex reaction on the part even of many distinguished commentators is due to the pernicious influence of the traditional but deeply false idea that FUL is the primary (or in fact even the *only real*) Kantian formula of the moral principle.

Another (deeper and more interesting) thought is presented by Klaus Reich (in an article whose main contentions we will be examining in the next section). This is that the "general" (or "universal" – *allgemein*) formula is yet a fourth (or a "sixth") formula, distinct from all the "particular" formulas derived earlier in the Second Section and then systematized at *Groundwork* 4:436.[15] This suggestion is interesting, and it gains some support from the fact that in Kant's other two most important ethical works, *The Critique of Practical Reason* and the *Metaphysics of Morals*, the moral law is also represented by a single "universal formula" whose statements are very similar to that given at *Groundwork* 4:436–7: "So act that the maxim of your action could always at the same time hold as a principle of universal legislation" (*Practical Reason*, 5:30) and "Act upon a maxim that can also hold as a universal law" (*Morals*, 6:225). But Reich's suggestion raises the question where this new "general" formula is supposed to have come from, and in what way it is more "general" than the formulas already derived and explained.

Surely it is more natural to suppose, as the most common interpretation does, that the "universal formula" is one of the formulas already derived. The question, though, is: which one? There seem to me several reasons for thinking that it is to be identified not with FUL, but with FA. For one thing, the "universal" formula occurs in the same paragraph devoted to FRE (which is the more "intuitive" version of FA). Then too, as we have seen, FA is the formula that combines the other two in itself, and in which, in that sense, the search for the supreme principle of morality culminates. Further, the universal formula as presented in the *Critique of Practical Reason* is said reciprocally to imply freedom of the will (*Practical Reason*, 5:28–30), but FA is the only formula in the *Groundwork* about which this claim is made (*Groundwork*, 4:446–9). But the best reason is found simply in what the "universal formula" *says*: It tells us to act on that maxim that can *make itself* into a universal law. If a maxim "can make itself into a universal law" by "containing in itself the volition that it should be a universal law," then this makes the "universal formula" equivalent to FA in several of its formulations. (If a maxim is able to "hold" or be "valid" [*gelten*] as a universal law whenever it contains in itself the rational volition that it should hold as a universal law, then the universal formulas of the moral law found in the *Critique of Practical Reason* and the *Metaphysics of Morals* can also be seen to be versions of FA.) By contrast, FUL tells us only to restrict ourselves to maxims that can (without contradiction or volitional conflict) be thought as universal laws; it does not tell us positively to act on maxims that can make themselves into such laws. The most compelling reading of *Groundwork* 4:436–7, then, is that the Second Section culminates in a system of mutually complementary formulas for the supreme principle of morality with each formula viewing the principle from a different standpoint. The universal formula, in which the others are combined and summed up, and which is the best standard to be used in moral judging, is FA.

3. KANT'S GROUNDWORK AND CICERO'S *ON DUTIES*

Having now examined Kant's attempt to develop a formulation of the supreme principle of morality, we turn next to a consideration of this attempt in relation to its historical antecedents. Our first task must be to evaluate the claim, which found considerable favor among some Kant scholars in the last century, that the *Groundwork*'s formulation of the moral principle was consciously based on a particular ancient text, which was well known and influential in Kant's day, namely, Cicero's treatise *On Duties*.

Kant probably began composing the *Groundwork* in 1783, after fifteen years of promising to write a "metaphysics of morals." In that year, the Berlin philosopher Christian Garve published a new translation of *On Duties* and also a set of critical notes on it. Kant's brilliant but eccentric friend J. G. Hamann reports in correspondence that the philosopher began writing about moral philosophy about this time in order to provide an "anticritique" of Garve's book on Cicero, and then that by Spring, 1784, he was at work on a "*Prodromus der Moral*" (though terms like "anticritique" and "prodromus" sound more like Hamann's peculiar uses of language than they do like Kant) (4:626–8). But these facts might lead us to wonder how far the *Groundwork* might have been influenced by Cicero's treatise *On Duties* (or by Garve's presentation of it).

During the twentieth century, reflections on this question led to some historical speculations about the genesis of some of the main ideas in the *Groundwork*, and the historical reference of Kant's formulations of the moral principle in it. Their source was an article by Klaus Reich, published in *Mind* in 1939. But Reich's speculations also influenced other scholars of the *Groundwork*, most notably H. J. Paton and A. R. C. Duncan.[16] Some of Reich's claims are quite plausible, such as that Kant was thinking of the classical list of virtues (justice, wisdom, courage, and self-control), which he probably would have known about through Cicero, when he denies unqualified worth to both courage and self-control in the opening pages of the *Groundwork* (*Groundwork*, 4:394; cf. Cicero, *On Duties* 1.15).[17] Reich's most significant theses, however, concern the supposed sources in Cicero, and in the Stoic philosopher Panaetius of Rhodes, on whom Cicero was depending, for Kant's three main formulas of the moral principle as they are presented systematically at *Groundwork* 4:436. Specifically, Reich identifies FLN with the Stoic formula *convenienter naturae vivere* ("live according to nature") (Reich, p. 455; Cicero, *On Duties* 3.3), FH with Cicero's admonition that injuring another human being *omnino hominem ex homine tollit* (in Garve's translation, *im Menschen die Menschlichkeit aufhebt*, "abolishes humanity in the human being," Reich, p. 458; Cicero, *On Duties*, 3.5), and FRE with the Stoic formulas *communis humani generis societas* ("the society common to the human race," Reich, p. 459; Cicero, *On Duties* 3.5), *commune tanquam humanitas corpus* ("a community like a body of humanity," Cicero, *On Duties*, 3.6), and *deorum et hominum communitas et societas inter ipsos* ("the community and society of gods and men with one another," Cicero, *On Duties*, 1.43). Though Reich never quite puts it in this way, he writes as if in formulating the principle of morality, Kant was thinking of a series of Stoic formulations presented by Cicero early in Book Three of *On Duties* (and perhaps also of Garve's thoughts about them).

As Reich himself observes, there are no explicit references to either Cicero or Garve anywhere in the *Groundwork*. From this he rightly concludes that "in deciding on passages in which Kant took account of this work the greatest caution must naturally be exercised" (Reich, p. 447). Duncan is if anything even more explicit: Reich's conjecture, he says, is "no more than a hypothesis," even a hypothesis that "cannot be established beyond reasonable doubt" (Duncan, pp. 178–9). The interest of this unprovable historical hypothesis, it seems to me, depends almost entirely on how much light it sheds on the philosophical content of the *Groundwork*. In other words: How much *philosophical* interest is there in the thoughts we entertain if we suppose that Kant's formulations of the moral principle were inspired by reflections on the opening sections of Book Three of Cicero's *On Duties*?

Judged by this criterion, I do not think Reich's hypothesis fares well at all. There is (as Reich himself points out) a wide gulf separating the Stoic maxim "live according to nature" and FLN, which tells us instead to live according to laws we could will to be laws of nature. The thought that in injuring another I am removing or abolishing his humanity is not at all the same as, and it does little or nothing to illuminate, the thought that humanity, in the sense of rational nature, is an end in itself, and the fundamental value motivating obedience to all moral laws. (The comparative philosophical illumination of the two thoughts in relation to each other seems to be just the reverse: The Kantian thought would show why removing or abolishing someone's humanity would be removing or abolishing something of great value. This might be implied by Cicero's formulation, but it is not even explicit in it, much less subjected to philosophical elucidation.) There is certainly ethical as well as historical interest in the fact that the Stoics thought of humanity, or even gods and men together, as a single social body, but nowhere in this thought is there the crucial Kantian idea that the laws governing this body should be seen as proceeding from the idea of the will of each and every one of its members, so that in obeying them, each is really obeying only himself. Regarding all three formulas, you need have the Kantian thought clearly in mind already before you can recognize anything like it in Cicero, and what you find in Cicero teaches you nothing at all philosophically about the essential Kantian thought.

We are no better off regarding the systematic connection between Kant's formulas. Although the quotations cited by Reich all occur within a relatively short space of text, as do the three formulas developed in the Second Section of the *Groundwork*, there is no suggestion in Cicero that these particular sayings constitute a single system defining the foundations of moral duty. On the contrary, they occur, along with many other thoughts, as part of Cicero's wide-ranging rhetorical argument in Book Three, whose main thesis is that there can never really be any conflict between rectitude or honor and mere expediency, but rather that the expedient or advantageous thing to do must always be the same as the right or dutiful thing to do (Cicero, *On Duties*, 3.4).[18] On this point, however, far from its being true that Kant might have been inspired by Cicero, it would be no exaggeration to say that the emphatic repudiation of Cicero's thesis is one of the most persistent themes throughout the entire *Groundwork*. Yet it is hard to convince oneself even that Kant was setting out to argue against Cicero in particular here. For in the *Groundwork* there are no references to Cicero's defense of this thesis, and no discernible attempt to address any of his particular arguments in favor of it.

Thus, looking at the matter from every point of view, and even supposing for the sake of argument Reich is correct in conjecturing (on the basis of no real evidence worthy of the name) that Kant had Cicero's treatise in mind while he was composing the *Groundwork*, it still seems that the argument of the *Groundwork*, regarding what is philosophically interesting in it, proceeds very much as if Kant had not been thinking about Cicero or Garve at all. In other words, we learn virtually nothing of philosophical interest about Kant's formulation of the supreme principle of morality from reflecting on this fact about his private mental history (again assuming, with no explicit evidence, that it is a fact). This makes it very hard to concur with Duncan's insistence that "No one who undertakes to write about Section II [of the *Groundwork*] can afford to neglect [Reich's article in *Mind*]" (Duncan, p. 175). Or at least, speaking only for myself, I must confess that I have learned practically nothing about the philosophical content of the *Groundwork* by attempting to reflect on Reich's unprovable historical speculations. (If others more discerning or imaginative than I am are capable of finding these conjectures more philosophically illuminating than I have, then more power to them.)

If we are to understand the relation of Kant's search for the supreme principle of morality to its historical antecedents, I think we would do better to look at this in the light of Kant's own explicit statements about it – in the *Groundwork*, in the *Critique of Practical Reason*, and elsewhere. That is what we will do in the final section.

4. KANT'S CRITIQUE OF PREVIOUS ATTEMPTS TO DISCOVER THE SUPREME PRINCIPLE OF MORALITY

Ancient ethics did not talk much of "moral principles" but oriented itself either toward conceptions of human virtue or conceptions of the human good. During the twentieth century, there arose among moral philosophers a fashionable view – combining, with an appearance of inconsistency that merely added to its attractiveness, the appeal of iconoclasm with that of piety toward what is old – that this point represents an advantage of ancient over modern ethics, perhaps even showing that there is something misguided about modern moral philosophy as a whole. According to one seminal and influential presentation of this view, that of G. E. M. Anscombe, the modern conceptions of "obligation," "ought," and "moral principles" are dependent on a "law conception of ethics," which in turn makes sense only within a religious view of the world in which God is thought of as the moral lawgiver.[19] But it is precisely this conception, she claims, that modern moral philosophy has given up. So it finds itself working with a set of conceptions that, apparently through some sad fit of absent-mindedness on the part of virtually all modern moral philosophers, have managed to survive "the framework of thought that made [them] really intelligible" (Anscombe, p. 31).

Since Kant's moral philosophy would seem to be sitting right in the bull's-eye of the target at which such polemics are aimed, it might surprise their proponents to learn that he accepts the historical side of their contentions, at least up to a point.[20] According to Kant, the question of "the basis of morality," which asks about "the principle of morality," "has been investigated in the modern age" (*Lectures on Ethics*, 29:620). In place of this, by contrast, he says, the ancients asked about the *summum bonum*, the highest good (*Lectures on Ethics*, 27:247, 29:599; cf. *Practical Reason*, 5:111ff.).

Ancient ethics: "The ideal"

In Kant's view, the highest good was conceived by the ancient schools in a variety of ways. All of them were oriented primarily to "the ideal," that is, the "pattern, idea or archetype" of what a human being can be. For some (but not all) of the ancients, the ideal was also associated with a conception of happiness. Among the ancients, Kant distinguishes the following theories of the ideal:

1. The Cynic ideal (of Diogenes and Antisthenes), which is *natural simplicity*, and happiness as the product of nature rather than of art.
2. The Epicurean ideal, which is that of the *man of the world*, and happiness as a product of art, not of nature.
3. The Stoic ideal (of Zeno), which is that of the *sage*, and happiness as identical with moral perfection or virtue.
4. The mystical ideal (of Plato), of the visionary character, in which the highest good consists in the human being seeing himself in communion with the highest being.
5. The Christian ideal of holiness, whose pattern is Jesus Christ. (*Lectures on Ethics*, 27:247–50; 29:602–4).

The first three ideals place the incentive to morality in happiness, but the last two do not (*Lectures on Ethics*, 27:250). The Cynics and Epicureans think of happiness as an *effect* of achieving the ideal (hence they think of moral virtue – conceived alternatively as natural simplicity and worldly wisdom – as a *means* to happiness), while the Stoics think that happiness is *identical* with achieving the ideal (*Lectures on Ethics*, 27:250–1; *Practical Reason* 5:111–12).

There is another general criticism that Kant addresses against ancient ethics as a whole: It fails to distinguish principles of right from those of morality, and treats both under the common heading of ethics. It is noteworthy that Kant selects Cicero's *On Duties* as the chief target of this criticism (*Lectures on Ethics*, 27:481–2). Perhaps it is even more noteworthy that the position Kant is here criticizing in the ancients is one frequently attributed nowadays to Kant himself, by those who hold that for Kant right is subordinated to ethics and that Kant's principle of right is derived from his principle of morality.[21]

Modern ethics: Principles of morality

The highest good may have seemed to the ancients like a natural starting point for ethics, but Kant thinks that it treats as primary what is really secondary, and more fundamentally, it fails to ask the basic question. For, he contends, "the concept of good and evil must not be determined before the moral law (for which, it would seem, this concept would have to be the foundation), but only...after it and by means of it" (*Practical Reason*, 5:63). The moderns, therefore, are asking the right question in inquiring after the basis of morality in its supreme principle. Some of their answers to this question, in his view, are non-starters because they substitute mere analytic judgments for a principle that must be synthetic if it is to ground the activity of practical reason. Other answers are faulty because they have not separated themselves far enough from the ancient standpoint. And all previous answers remain unsatisfactory to the extent that they have proposed a basis for morality in principles of heteronomy.

Analytic principles

Kant considers several ethical principles that he rejects because they attempt to pass off an analytic judgment as if it were more than that:

1. Do good and avoid evil (Wolff).
2. Act according to the truth (Cumberland).
3. Act according to the mean between vices (Aristotle). (*Lectures on Ethics*, 27:264, 276–77).

"Do good and avoid evil" is trivial because the concept of a good action is simply that of an action that is to be done, and the concept of an evil action is that of one that is to be omitted. The principle attributed here to Richard Cumberland is actually one that is held, in various forms, by virtually all adherents of the British rationalist tradition in ethics, including Ralph Cudworth, Samuel Clarke, William Wollaston, and Richard Price.[22] It holds that actions have a real nature, and are involved with real relations to things and to other actions. In virtue of these natures and relations, it is *true* of some actions that they are *right* or *to be done*, and of others that they are *wrong* and *to be avoided*. Presumably Kant's criticism of the principle that one should act in accordance with such *truths* is that this principle actually says no more than Wolff's principle does (for it tells us only to perform those actions of which it is *true* that they are right and ought to be performed). It is curious that Kant should have listed Aristotle's principle of the mean along with principles of the moderns, and curious also that Aristotle finds no place in Kant's account of the ancient schools. But his criticism is no doubt that, like Wolff's principle, it tells us only to do those actions that fall under the concept "to be done."[23]

Principles of heteronomy: Kant's taxonomy

Kant criticizes the moral principles proposed by previous philosophers by characterizing them as "heteronomous" in contrast to his own principle of autonomy (in the form of FA). In the *Groundwork*, his taxonomy of such principles distinguishes "rational" principles from "empirical" principles; in the *Critique of Practical Reason*, the same distinctions are made, but this time between "determining grounds" of moral principles, and the distinction is between "objective" (instead of "rational") and "subjective" (instead of "empirical") grounds. There, each of these groupings is further divided, in a way that cuts across this first distinction, into "external" and "internal" grounds. The second *Critique*'s taxonomy (*Practical Reason*, 5:40) thus looks like this:

Subjective	
External	Internal
Education (Montaigne, [Mandeville]) Civil Constitution (Mandeville, [Hobbes])	Physical feeling (Epicurus, [Hélvetius]) Moral feeling (Hutcheson, [Shaftesbury])

Objective	
Internal	External
Perfection (Wolff, the Stoics, [Baumgarten, Cumberland])	The will of God (Crusius, the theological moralists, [Baumgarten])

(The names inserted in brackets are found in Kant's lecture presentations of the distinctions, not in the *Critique of Practical Reason*; see *Lectures on Ethics*, 27:253, 510, 29:621–2, 625–7.)[24]

It is significant (and clarifying) that in the *Critique of Practical Reason*, Kant treats this as a taxonomy not of moral *principles* but of moral "determining grounds" – that is, of proposed *grounds for following* moral principles. The association between the two is in any case quite natural in most cases. To view (with Montaigne) custom and education as providing the source of moral duties naturally goes along (at least in Kant's view) with viewing the moral ground as "imitation" or "example" – morality consists in doing what one has been taught by custom to do simply because it is what others in one's society do (and are approved for doing); likewise, to think (with Mandeville or Hobbes) of moral principles as those legislated in civil constitutions is to treat the coercive force of the sovereign as one's ground for following them (*Lectures on Ethics*, 27:253, 29:621). To make the moral principle happiness or moral feeling is to treat the desire for happiness or moral sentiments of approval and disapproval as the ground for complying with these principles. Theological ethics, making God's will the moral principle, treats either fear or love of God as the ground of morality, while the principle of perfection takes the value of perfection as our ground for following the principle.

Kant's critique of principles of heteronomy

The shift is also significant because Kant's critique of these alternative principles, both in the *Groundwork* and elsewhere, also focuses essentially on issues raised by these grounds for following them. Crucial to Kant's criticism of these alternative principles is his claim that each of them takes some object of the will as the determining ground of the rule that is to govern the will. The principle of education takes the imitation of examples as such an object, the principle of civil constitution takes the fear of the sovereign's sanctions, the principle of physical feeling takes the enjoyment of pleasure, the principle of moral feeling takes the feeling of approbation (or the avoidance of feelings of disapprobation), the theological principle takes conformity to God's will, the principle of perfection takes the achievement of perfection. But, Kant argues, if the determining ground is an object of the will, then the imperative grounded on it can be only hypothetical, since the validity of the imperative for the will is conditional on achieving that object:

Wherever an object of the will is to be taken as the ground in order to prescribe the rule determining that will, there the rule is nothing but heteronomy; the imperative is conditioned, namely: *if* or *because* one wills this object, one ought to act thus or so; hence it can never command morally, i.e. categorically.   (*Groundwork*, 4:444)

This argument needs to be understood against the background of what Kant thinks he has already established in the *Groundwork*, namely, that if morality is not a mere cobweb of the brain, then its supreme principle is a categorical imperative, and such a principle can be comprehended, in its most developed and universal form, as autonomy of the will (FA). The ultimate value on which this principle rests is the dignity of the rational will as capable of giving universal law to itself and to all other rational wills. The advantage of the principle of autonomy is that it enables us to conceive the validity of the moral principle as independent of any object of the will. All objects of the will (such as the "ideals" of ancient ethics, or their conceptions of happiness, or any of the objects providing the determining grounds involved in the taxonomy of modern ethical principles) are thereby shown to be inadequate grounds for morality, in contrast to the principle of autonomy, which alone can be made consistent with the idea of a categorical imperative.

Once the force of this argument is appreciated, it is easy to understand why partisans of the various ethical principles Kant rejects should react to it by attempting to discredit the very concept of a categorical imperative. For in the light of this argument, that concept seems to set up a hurdle that their favorite principle can never jump. The most obvious first reaction is therefore to criticize the demand itself as unreasonable and the concept supporting it as nonsensical. However, contrary to this first reaction, we can see fairly easily that none of these theories turns for its defensibility on the question whether the notion of a categorical imperative makes sense. For, as I will now argue, those principles that *must* hold that it does not are indefensible even if we reject that notion, while the rest can, contrary to Kant's contention, meet his demand that they be understood as categorical imperatives. Empiricist theories, namely, are hopeless even apart from Kant's criticisms, while rationalist theories are quite defensible against them.

The strategy of denying that the notion of a categorical imperative makes sense is the only one available to those defending *empirical* principles, or *subjective* determining grounds for the moral principle.

For they are committed to saying that in the end, the only reason we can give for following the moral principle is that we are *so built by nature* that we have certain *desires* (to imitate others, to avoid the sanctions that the sovereign might impose, to feel pleasure). Or at most, they can say that we are so built that we *count* something *as a reason* (a feeling of approval or disapproval). Such empirical desires or dispositions to take something as a reason are necessarily only contingent features of our nature, without which the principle in question would have no validity for us. At most, then, they could supply us only with hypothetical imperatives. Partisans of such views often announce this point themselves, insisting that to ask for more than this is to indulge in metaphysical nonsense. (You can always tell when the hollowness of an empiricist view is in danger of exposure by the empiricist's desperate resort to the accusation that you are committing "metaphysics.")

Yet the problem with such views seems to me to go even deeper than Kant's criticism reveals. For even if we do not insist that moral principles are categorical imperatives, we ought at least to insist that there must be *some genuine reason* (categorical or not) for us to follow them, and none of the empirical theories seem consistent with meeting even that minimal requirement. For the fact that we are so built that we desire something does not give us a reason to desire it, nor a reason to satisfy the desire that we may have for it. Nor does the fact that we are so built that we take some feeling to be a reason for doing something amount to there really being a reason for us to do it. For as rational beings, we are also so built that we are capable of requiring genuine reasons for doing what we do, and also capable of recognizing bogus substitutes for reasons as bogus.[25] (If it takes "metaphysics" to acknowledge that there are genuine reasons, then that is about as good a defense as "metaphysics" could ever hope for, since then it would then be self-contradictory for anyone to claim they had a genuine reason to reject "metaphysics.") The empirical theories are therefore indefensible even apart from the Kantian worry that they cannot treat moral principles as categorical imperatives.

The rational principles are not so badly off. In fact, I do not think that rationalists necessarily need to attack the idea of a categorical imperative to save themselves from Kant's criticism. Theological moralists (at least a certain kind of rationalistically minded theological moralist) may say that we are obligated to obey the divine will because that will is perfect, and hence what it wills or commands really is right in itself, independently of whether or not obeying the command achieves any further object of the will. But, if we allow the notion of a categorical imperative, then that is just to say that the commands of a perfect (divine) will are categorical imperatives. Likewise, a defender of the principle of perfection may say that this principle means only that we have a reason to act according to the idea of a perfect will, simply because perfection of will is intrinsically good – again quite apart from whether so acting achieves any other object. That allows the perfectionists to say that their principles are categorical imperatives (again, assuming we accept the idea of a categorical imperative). The British rationalist variant of this is that we are obligated to do those actions whose nature marks them out as right or to be done, while we are obligated to refrain from those actions whose nature makes them wrong or not to be done.[26] Again, the reason for doing and refraining lies in the nature of the actions themselves, and is not dependent on whether the doing or refraining achieves any other object of the will. There is nothing in this that is inconsistent with regarding the principle of morality as a categorical imperative.[27] Ancient "ideal" theories of ethics may be defended in the same way, as long as their ideals are interpreted in a rationalist rather than an empiricist way. This is perhaps unpromising for the Epicurean ideal and probably also for the Cynic ideal since they seek either worldly virtue or natural simplicity as means to happiness, but can in principle give no account of why we have a genuine reason to want to be happy. But it seems quite possible for the Stoic, mystical (or Platonic), and Christian ideals to be framed in terms that are compatible with understanding morality as grounded on a categorical imperative. With the ancients, then, as with the moderns: Rationalism is defensible, empiricism, indefensible, whether or not we decide the notion of a categorical imperative makes sense.

Thus, we arrive at the following conclusion concerning Kant's critique of the conceptions of the supreme principle of morality that preceded his own in the history of ethics: Kant is right in rejecting empirical moral principles, but he does not need to assume the idea of a categorical imperative to do so, for they are quite hopeless even apart from that idea; on the other hand, his arguments do not necessarily discredit rational moral principles, since these can be so understood that they can be just as easily brought into harmony with the idea of a categorical imperative as can Kant's own principle of autonomy.

NOTES

1. No doubt these radical-sounding thoughts are sufficiently titillating and have sufficient resonance with many frustrating practical dilemmas and intractable moral disagreements that trouble us, that some people find in them enough appeal to be worth a defense. To most sober-minded people, however, the appeal of such thoughts does not last long, because the apparently exciting new vistas they appear to offer moral thinking turn out to be far less liberating than they at first seemed to be, once they have been surveyed with even minimal care and seriousness. In any case, our inquiry here must begin with the recognition that Kant's reflection on morality begins with their resolute rejection.

2. There are false negatives whenever we are dealing with a maxim (such as: "Give more to charity than the average person does") that does not violate universal moral laws, but could not itself be made into a law without contradiction. We can generate false positives by framing maxims that include enough specific information that the maxim would no longer have unwillable consequences if made into a universal law, but remains a morally objectionable maxim nonetheless – for instance, "If you are in need of money, borrow it from someone named Hilly Flitcraft on a Tuesday in August by promising to repay him, even though you have no intention of doing so." For a further discussion of these issues, see my book *Kant's Ethical Thought* (New York: Cambridge University Press, 1999), pp. 97–107. Self-appointed defenders of Kant ("self-appointed" because Kant never tries to use the universalizability test as a general moral criterion in the way they are trying to defend) will probably never abandon the noble, Grail-like quest for an interpretation of the universalizability test that enables it to serve this purpose, despite the history of miserable failure that has always attended this quest. I regard their attempts as worse than a waste of time, since they encourage critics of Kant's ethics to continue thinking, falsely, that something of importance for Kantian ethics turns on whether there is a universalizability test for maxims that could serve as such a general moral criterion.

3. John Stuart Mill, *Utilitarianism*, ed. George Sher (Indianapolis: Hackett, 1979), p. 24.

4. For documentation of this claim, see *Kant's Ethical Thought*, pp. 139–41.

5. It is the prior setting of an end as the condition of the imperative's validity for me that makes the imperative hypothetical in Kant's sense. "If you make a promise, keep it" is not a hypothetical imperative because the if-clause does not refer to an end that conditions the validity of the imperative. Likewise, categorical imperatives are categorical because their validity is not conditional on some end. A moral imperative may be conditional in other ways – for instance, there may be implied conditions that release us from a promise, in which case there is no categorical imperative at all to keep it under those conditions – but a valid moral imperative is always categorical in the sense that its rational validity does not depend on some prior setting of an end. The word "prior" is crucial here, since categorical imperatives, in commanding us to act, also thereby always command us to set ends (according to Kant's theory, our own perfection and the happiness of others are the kinds of ends that are also duties). The thought that categorical imperatives command us to act without having any end at all is a nonsensical thought.

6. Since for Kant every action has an end to be produced, following a moral principle will always involve setting and achieving some end – for instance, fulfilling a promise will involve accomplishing the thing you promised to do. So it is just plain silly to represent Kantian ethics as caring nothing about the consequences of our actions – as is commonly done by those who do not understand the first thing about Kant's ethics, such as John Dewey (*Human Nature and Conduct* [1922] [New York: Random House, 1957], pp. 225–7). Nor do Kantian principles preclude using hypothetical reasoning about consequences – for instance, what would happen if anyone were permitted to make a promise without intending to keep it – from figuring in the reasoning that justifies the moral principle (ignoring this point frequently leads to a charge of inconsistency against Kant, as in Dewey, *Human Nature*, p. 226.) The point is rather only that the validity of a moral principle, such as "Keep your promises," is not dependent on the actual achievement of any particular end to be produced by following the principle. Such criticisms of Kant are more often symptoms of an inconsistent procedure on the part of the critics. Starting from the mistaken idea that all practical reasoning is instrumental in nature, and inferring from this that all moral reasoning must be justified by the particular consequences of the action, philosophers then see that there are clear counterexamples to this consequence. So they try to save their original dogma by appealing not to actual consequences but to the expected consequences of a principle's being generally followed or to the imagined consequences of its being followed or not followed under certain ideal counterfactual circumstances (in other words, using the same kind of reasoning that Kant uses). They then

conclude that maybe there is something right in Kant's theory after all (see Dewey, *Human Nature*, pp. 226–7); but they erroneously regard it as consistent with their own dogma that all practical reasoning is instrumental and oriented toward actual consequences, and inconsistent with Kantian principles. But the incoherence is in their views, not in Kant's.

7. This triad represents the three conditions Kant places on concept formation, with the third condition applying only to the concepts of individuals. "Form" refers to the kind of generality involved in a concept, a generality created by the understanding according to the judgment-forms and categories; "matter," to the intuitive content or possibility of providing a sensible object for a concept. "Complete determination" means that for every pair of contradictory predicates, one and only one of them belongs to the concept. When a concept is completely determined, it is (according to Leibnizian doctrine) the concept of an individual rather than a universal concept. Why does Kant choose this triad, drawn from his logic of concepts, to systematize the formulas for the supreme principle of morality? I have attempted to answer this question in "The Moral Law as a System of Formulas," in H. Stolzenberg and H. F. Fulda, eds., *Architektonik und System in der Philosophie Kants* (Hamburg: Felix Meiner Verlag, 2001).

8. Schopenhauer, *The World as Will and Representation*, tr. E. J. F. Payne (New York: Dover, 1958), 1:514–26; *On the Basis of Morality*, tr. E. J. F. Payne (Indianapolis: Bobbs-Merrill, 1965), pp. 53–5.

9. Kant himself may have made it difficult for readers to see this point, by insisting in the *Critique of Practical Reason* that morality must countenance only "formal principles" and eschew "material principles" that presuppose an end (*Practical Reason*, 5:27). But here he is using "end" and "material principles" in the traditional sense only. It should be appreciated that already in the *Groundwork*, he distinguished "formal principles" from "material principles" precisely in terms of the kind of motive (or end) on which they were grounded (*Groundwork*, 4:427–8). A formal principle is *never* for Kant a principle that is not grounded on any end as its motive. Here the overemphasis on FUL and FLN again does mischief, by persuading people that we may identify a "formal" principle simply using the universalizability tests, without recourse to any substantive value or end to serve as the motive for following such a principle. A careful reading of *Groundwork* 4:427–9 reveals this reading of Kant to be quite mistaken.

10. For a fuller account of my interpretation of this argument, see *Kant's Ethical Thought*, pp. 124–32. A similar interpretation has been defended by Christine Korsgaard, *Creating the Kingdom of Ends* (Cambridge: Cambridge University Press, 1996), pp. 106–33.

11. Why not also our own happiness and the perfection of others? We honor rational nature as an end in itself by making it our end to increase its capacity rationally to set and pursue ends, and the general name for this capacity is "perfection." We honor it also by making our end the ends set through its exercise, and the name for the totality of ends a rational being proposes for itself is its "happiness." We honor rational nature in others only to the extent that we further the perfections in themselves that they also set as ends, so morality bids us to pursue their perfection only insofar as it falls under the heading of their happiness. We need no moral constraint to pursue our own happiness except insofar as we are tempted to make ourselves less perfect by neglecting it, so morality bids us pursue our own happiness only insofar as it falls under the heading of our perfection.

12. The first of these translations is Lewis White Beck's (*Foundations of the Metaphysics of Morals* [Indianapolis: Bobbs-Merrill, 1959], p. 54), the second is Mary Gregor's (Kant, *Practical Philosophy* [New York: Cambridge University Press, 1996], p. 85). My own translation (*Groundwork of the Metaphysics of Morals* [New Haven: Yale University Press, 2002], p. 54) is also a bit less literal than the one I have just presented: "one of which unites the other two in itself." But it does capture the feature of the passage to which I am calling attention. It is true that the original text can be read so that it does not positively exclude the possibility that each of the three formulas unites the other two. If I say of the three musketeers: "One of them would give his life for the other two," it is natural to understand me to be saying not only of one specific musketeer but of *each* of the three, Athos, Porthos, and Aramis, that he would give his life for his two comrades. But this is only because we have no reason to single out any one of them as more self-sacrificing than the other two, and so we have reason to treat "one" in this context as meaning "each one." However, in the *Groundwork* Kant has already singled out FA by saying that it follows from FUL and FH, but he has not made any comparable claim about either FUL or FH. So it is not natural to read "one" (*die eine*) here as if it were equivalent to "each" (*jede* or *irgend eine*). If Kant had meant *jede* or *irgend eine*, he could have said so. The (mis)reading of the passage is normally used to suggest, at the outset, a kind of equality of status between the three formulas, but usually this is nothing but a front for the common reading that privileges FUL over the other two formulas. That in turn usually goes along with treating FUL as a universal moral criterion, or interpreting it as a procedure for "constructing" the entire content of ethics, or a lot of other false and philosophically indefensible notions that fundamentally misunderstand Kant's moral philosophy.

13. For more on Kant's views about friendship and religion, see *Kant's Ethical Thought*, pp. 274–82, 309–20. The spirit of Kantian ethics has often been characterized as "individualistic" on account of the priority Kant gives to the value of autonomy or self-legislation, to individual rights and freedom, to thinking for oneself, and because Kant regards only individuals, never groups of people, as bearing moral responsibility (though – what is seldom appreciated – he does regard both the cause and the cure for moral evil as social). Yet once we see that the fundamental principle of morality, formulated as FRE, gives absolute priority to achieving a community, that is, a convergence or consilience, among all the ends of all rational beings, we should also recognize that the spirit of Kantian ethics is, at a very fundamental level, exactly the reverse of individualistic.

14. Examples are H. J. Paton, *The Categorical Imperative* (London: Hutcheson, 1947), p. 130; Onora O'Neill, *Constructions of Reason* (Cambridge: Cambridge University Press, 1989), p. 127; Paul Guyer, "The Possibility of the Categorical Imperative," in Guyer (ed.) *Groundwork of the Metaphysics of Morals: Critical Essays* (Lanham, MD: Rowman and Littlefield, 1998), p. 216.

15. Klaus Reich, "Kant and Greek Ethics II," *Mind* 48 (1939), pp. 452–3. Cited parenthetically as "Reich," followed by page number.

16. See previous note; also A. R. C. Duncan, *Practical Reason and Morality* (London: Nelson, 1957), pp. 175–82, cited parenthetically as "Duncan." See also H. J. Paton, "The Aim and Structure of Kant's *Grundlegung*," *Philosophical Quarterly* 8 (1958), pp. 112–30, and Brendan Æ. Liddell, *Kant on the Foundation of Morality* (Bloomington: Indiana University Press, 1970), pp. 138–40.

17. Cicero, *On Duties*, cited by book and section. Cicero, *De officiis*, Scriptorum classicorum bibliotheca Oxoniensis (Oxford: Clarendon Press, 1994). For a recent English translation, see Cicero, *On Obligations*, translated by P. G. Walsh (Oxford: Oxford University Press, 2000).

18. Reich relies on Garve's account of Cicero's intention, which is that Cicero was trying to "resolve the apparent conflict between duty and interest" (Reich, p. 455). But this is surely misleading, for it suggests that it was Cicero's aim to devise strategies for making the (apparent) conflict disappear, whereas the plain import of *On Duties* is that there is no such conflict, and it is only human error or vice that leads people to think there is. Of course, Kant is even less interested than Cicero in the project Garve describes. For it is his view that when people take steps to reduce the "apparent" conflict of duty and interest (which in Kant's view is sometimes not apparent but quite real), they do so mainly by deceiving themselves about what duty demands, and

softening these demands so that they do not infringe on self-interest. Kant is as far as it is possible for anyone to be from wanting to help them to do this.

19. G. E. M. Anscombe, "Modern Moral Philosophy," *Philosophy* 33 (1958), reprinted in Roger Crisp and Michael Slote, eds., *Virtue Ethics* (Oxford: Oxford University Press, 1997), cited parenthetically in the latter source, by page number, as "Anscombe."

20. Of course he does not accept – and has no reason to accept – Anscombe's contention that a "law conception of ethics" makes sense only in a framework of thought where a divine legislator is thought of as the source of moral obligation; still less does he accept Anscombe's contention that "the idea of 'legislating to oneself' is absurd," because "the concept of legislation requires a superior power in the legislator" (Anscombe, p. 27). We find as far back as Socrates the idea that the most important ruler-ruled relationship is the relationship to oneself (Plato, *Gorgias* 491d5–10); the idea of constraint through laws and principles makes just as much sense when the constraint is conceived as self-constraint through reasons as when it is conceived as coercive constraint through external force. Simply to assume the opposite without argument is simply to dismiss out of hand, and for no good reason, the most basic idea of Kantian ethics.

21. For example, Paul Guyer, "Kant's Deduction of Principles of Right," in Mark Timmons, ed., *Kant's Metaphysics of Morals: Interpretive Essays* (Oxford: Oxford University Press, 2002), pp. 23–64; Bernd Ludwig, "Whence Public Right? The role of Theoretical and Practical Reasoning in Kant's Doctrine of Right," in Timmons, ed., *Kant's Metaphysics of Morals*, pp. 159–84. The other side of this interpretive dispute, the one apparently supported by Kant's criticism of Cicero, is defended in this same volume by me, "The Final Form of Kant's Practical Philosophy," pp. 5–10, by Markus Willascheck, "Which Imperatives for Right? On the Non-Prescriptive Character of Juridical Laws in Kant's Metaphysics of Morals," pp. 65–88, and by Thomas Pogge, "Is Kant's *Rechtslehre* a 'Comprehensive Liberalism'?," pp. 133–58. There is some connection, but by no means an identity, between the issue being debated here and the older controversy in the German literature between defenders of what has been called the "independence thesis" (such as Julius Ebbinghaus, Klaus Reich, and Georg Geismann) and critics of it (such as Wolfgang Kersting and Bernd Ludwig). A good discussion of this issue is found in Pogge, "Kant's *Rechtslehre*," pp. 150–1.

22. The emphasis on truth is especially identified with Wollaston, whose views were prominently criticized (though not using his name) in Hume's *Treatise of Human Nature*, edited by L. A Selby-Bigge

(Oxford: Clarendon Press, 1967), p. 461. It is even a bit odd that Kant should identify this view with Cumberland (even though it is stated prominently in the opening chapter of *De Legibus Naturae* [1672]), since Cumberland is more often thought of as an ethical eudaimonist. The probable explanation is that Cumberland is the only one of these authors who wrote in Latin, and Kant did not read English.

23. In the *Metaphysics of Morals*, Kant criticizes Aristotle's principle not on the ground that it is analytic, but on the ground that it is *false*, since (he argues) it gives a false account of what virtue is (*Morals* 6:404).

24. The fact that some names appear more than once (when the *Lecture* versions of Kant on the history of ethics are taken into account) should not disturb us. It is quite possible to interpret Epicurus, for instance, as a representative of the ancient "ideal" conception of ethics and also to realize that his views can be (and are) appropriated by moderns to support a principle of hedonistic eudaimonism. In some philosophers, such as Mandeville and Baumgarten, it is easy enough to find endorsements of both of the views with which Kant associates their respective names. (If there is an inconsistency here, the blame lies at their door rather than at Kant's.) And it is quite possible to interpret the British rationalist principle of truth either as an analytic claim or (more sympathetically) as a version of rational perfectionism.

25. The problem is that there are just too many ways in which we could come to desire things we have no reason to desire, be disposed to approve of things we have no reason to approve, and take as reasons things that are not genuine reasons at all. I will admit, or rather earnestly maintain, that our having a natural desire for something is good evidence that we have a reason to desire it, and even that it is good. (Thus J. S. Mill's much maligned argument to that effect in Chapter 4 of *Utilitarianism* seems to me a sound argument.) But then we have to suppose that there are good things, and genuine reasons for desiring or approving of good things, and that our natural dispositions somehow involve our being in contact with those reasons. The problem with empiricist theories is that when presented with this obvious point, the empiricists will not admit it. When you ask them to tell you what reasons we have for doing anything, and insist that they give you some answer that at least has the general form of being a genuine reason, they get all nervous and huffy and accuse you of metaphysics, obscurantism, and God knows what other misdemeanors. Accepting their theories apparently requires us either to stop asking for reasons at all or else to allow to count as reasons things that are transparently not genuine reasons at all. Such defensiveness is a sure sign that there is something deeply wrong with their position, and that at some level, they know it.

26. Of course, it is reasonable to ask the rationalist what these properties are, whether they are natural or non-natural properties, how we can know about them, and so forth. And it may be that their theories about these matters fall far short of being satisfactory. But at least their account of what reasons are has the virtue that what it says are reasons might actually be reasons. (That an action is right or good or ought to be done is a reason for doing it, whereas the fact that we are disposed to desire something is transparently not a reason for desiring it and that we are disposed to approve of something is transparently not a reason for approving it.) Some Kantians who like to call themselves "constructivists" think either that Kant has a superior theory to the rationalists on these points, or else at any rate that inspired by Kant, they have devised a superior theory. I think they are fooling themselves about this. Kant was perhaps a constructivist about mathematics in some intelligible sense, but no intelligible sense has yet been given to the term "Kantian constructivism" in ethics. As far as I can see, Kant has no better metaethical theory than the rationalists do, perhaps because he was interested only marginally, if at all, in the questions such theories are designed to answer.

27. Many of the ways that British moralists in the rationalist tradition anticipated Kant are explored in Stephen Darwall's excellent book, *The British Moralists and the Internal 'Ought' 1640–1740* (New York: Cambridge University Press, 1995).

11   Kant on freedom of the will

Although there can be no doubt regarding the centrality of the concept of freedom in Kant's thought, there is considerable disagreement concerning its proper interpretation and evaluation. The evaluative problem stems largely from Kant's insistence that freedom involves a transcendental or non-empirical component, which requires the resources of transcendental idealism in order to be reconciled with the "causality of nature." There is also, however, a significant interpretive problem posed by the number of different conceptions of freedom to which Kant refers.[1] In addition to "outer freedom" or freedom of action, and a relative, empirically accessible or "psychological" concept of freedom, which admits of degrees, Kant distinguishes between transcendental and practical freedom, both of which seem to involve indeterminism in the sense of an independence from determination by antecedent causes. Moreover, within this sphere he conceives of freedom as both absolute spontaneity (negative freedom), which is a condition of rational agency as such, and as autonomy (positive freedom), which is a condition of the appropriate moral motivation (acting from duty alone).

Given this complexity, the present discussion must be highly selective.[2] Specifically, it will focus initially on the nature of and relation between freedom as spontaneity and as autonomy. But since both of these senses of freedom affirm (albeit in different ways) an independence from natural causality, this necessitates a consideration of the relationship between freedom (in both senses) and transcendental idealism. And to situate Kant's views in their historical context, I shall frame the discussion with a brief account of the treatment of free will by some of his predecessors, on the one hand, and his idealistic successors, on the other.

In the German context, the agenda for the discussion of freedom of the will in the eighteenth century was set by Leibniz, who approached the topic in terms of his principle of sufficient reason. After Leibniz, the main participants in this discussion were Christian Wolff and Christian August Crusius. The former developed and systematized the Leibnizian position and the latter was its foremost critic. Accordingly, a brief consideration of the views of these three thinkers is essential to the understanding of Kant's position.

Gottfried Wilhelm Leibniz

Leibniz's philosophy is built on two great principles: contradiction (or identity) and sufficient reason. The former states that "a proposition cannot be both true and false at the same time"; the latter that "nothing happens without a reason why it should be so rather than otherwise."³ Whereas the first governs (logically) necessary truths, which hold in all possible worlds, the second governs contingent truths, which hold in the actual world. In addition to factual truths and laws of nature, the latter includes the basic propositions of Leibniz's metaphysics.

The principle of sufficient reason can have this metaphysical function, however, only because it involves a certain kind of necessity. Since God is a supremely perfect being, it follows (according to this principle) that God could choose only the best of all possible worlds. Already during his lifetime, Leibniz was attacked on this point for denying divine freedom, subjecting God to an overriding necessity or fate. Typically, he dealt with this problem by distinguishing between an absolute or logical necessity and a relative or hypothetical one: the former apply to necessary and the latter to contingent truths. Accordingly, Leibniz denied that it is absolutely necessary for God to create the best of all possible worlds, while also admitting that there is a sense in which he must choose the best, since anything else would constitute a violation of the principle of sufficient reason.

Leibniz applied the same general framework to the analysis of human freedom. Thus, he denied that the voluntary actions of finite rational agents are absolutely necessary, since their non-occurrence does not involve a contradiction, while insisting that their occurrence is certain (and is known timelessly by God), since their non-occurrence would violate the principle of sufficient reason.

So far it might seem that Leibniz had "saved" freedom only by contrasting contingent truths about the occurrence of human actions with logically necessary truths such as those contained in mathematics. This is obviously inadequate as an analysis of freedom, however, since (among other things) it fails to distinguish between voluntary actions and other occurrences in nature, which are causally rather than logically necessary. But Leibniz was well aware of this problem and attempted to deal with it by appealing to two more necessary conditions of a free act: spontaneity and choice (or intelligence). As he puts it at one point:

Aristotle has already observed that there are two things in freedom, to wit spontaneity and choice, and therein lies our mastery over our actions. When we act freely we are not being forced, as would happen if we were pushed on to a precipice and thrown from top to bottom; and we are not prevented from having the mind free when we deliberate, as we would be if we were given a draught to deprive us of discernment. There is contingency in a thousand actions of Nature; but when there is no judgment in him who acts there is no freedom.[4]

As this passage indicates, by "spontaneity" Leibniz understood the absence of compulsion by any external cause, and by "choice" (or "intelligence") the recognition (or at least belief) that a course of action is, in given circumstances, the best. Like contingency, spontaneity alone is insufficient for freedom since it characterizes some actions of inanimate objects (e.g., a ball which has been set in motion along a smooth trajectory) as well as the behavior of nonrational animals.[5] Thus, again following Aristotle, Leibniz thought that we can speak meaningfully of freedom only in the case of voluntary actions, in which an agent makes a conscious choice based on the perception of some good.

Although understanding freedom in this way enabled Leibniz to bring free actions under the principle of sufficient reason, it entails that, given a motive and a specific set of circumstances, an agent will invariably choose to act according to what is perceived to be the best. In other words, an agent could not have chosen otherwise under the same circumstances. Rather than denying this implication, however,

Leibniz attempted to reconcile it with freedom by appealing to his dictum that a reason or motive "inclines without necessitating."[6] He does not mean by this that free agents have a capacity to disregard their motives (that would constitute a violation of the principle of sufficient reason), but merely that being motivated to X does not render the performance of X anything more than hypothetically necessary. Consequently, freedom for Leibniz is compatible with a certain kind of necessity.

Christian Wolff

If Wolff may be said to have modified the Leibnizian conception of freedom at all, it is by emphasizing even more strongly its deterministic features and its intellectualism or anti-voluntarism. The first of these is a consequence of his attempt to derive the principle of sufficient reason from the principle of contradiction.[7] Since the former supposedly governs all that exists, its demonstration on the basis of the principle of contradiction threatens to reduce everything to a matter of logical necessity in the manner of Spinoza. Indeed, the charge that he taught a universal determinism was one of the main reasons for Wolff's expulsion from Halle in 1723.[8]

Nevertheless, Wolff did not think that the attribution of a logical necessity to the principle of sufficient reason entails that everything based on this principle is itself logically or "absolutely" necessary. Accordingly, he retained Leibniz's distinction between absolute and hypothetical necessity and subsumed free actions under the latter. Also, like Leibniz, he located the distinctive feature of free actions in the kind of grounds they have, not in their lack of sufficient determining grounds. Specifically, free actions for Wolff are those that are performed on the basis of what the intellect perceives to be best. Thus, rejecting the characterization of freedom as the capacity to choose either of two contradictory things on the grounds of its violation of the principle of sufficient reason,[9] he defined it instead as "the ability of the soul through its own power of choice to choose, between two equally possible things, that which pleases it the most."[10]

This conception of freedom must be understood in terms of Wolff's above-mentioned anti-voluntarism. Strictly speaking, there is only one mental faculty for Wolff: the cognitive. The other two traditionally conceived faculties (will and desire) are subsumed under it as reflecting different degrees in the distinctness of one's cognition.[11] Although it follows from this that an agent will necessarily "choose" what seems the best in a given situation, this does not undermine the freedom of choice. The latter is preserved because the action is determined intellectually by what is perceived (rightly or wrongly) to be the best rather than being the result of compulsion by external forces. Moreover, like many eighteenth-century thinkers (including Hume), Wolff insisted that such a conception of freedom is not only compatible with morality but required by it because its alternative (the so-called "liberty of indifference") effectively deprives an agent of any motive or reason to act.[12]

Christian August Crusius

As already noted, Crusius was the foremost opponent of Wolffian thought in Germany and, as such, exercised a major influence on Kant.[13] For present purposes at least, the focal points of his critique are the Wolffian understanding of the principle of sufficient reason and its intellectualism or anti-voluntarism. Not only did Crusius reject as spurious Wolff's attempt to demonstrate the principle of sufficient reason, he also repudiated the intellectualization of the real, that is, the equation of conditions of knowing (or consistent thinking) with ontological conditions. Against this virtual collapsing of ontology into epistemology or logic, Crusius (anticipating Kant) distinguished sharply between ideal and real grounds, between the logical relation of ground and consequent and the real relation of cause and effect. The latter has a kind of necessity, which Crusius never succeeded in explaining very well, but is quite distinct from the logical necessity based on the principle of contradiction.[14]

Armed with this sharp distinction between conditions of knowing and conditions of being, Crusius thought that he had created the conceptual space for a genuine freedom of the will. This is not only because the necessity governing the real is not a logical necessity, which even the Leibnizians acknowledged, but because the principle of sufficient reason governs our understanding of things rather than the things themselves. Thus, anticipating Kant, Crusius claimed that the endeavor to comprehend freedom leads to an unavoidable conflict of principles: on the one hand, we cannot conceive an action without a cause (which rules out freedom in a stronger-than-Leibnizian sense), while, on the other hand, we must

assume freedom (in a strong sense) in order to conceive of the possibility of moral agency.[15]

Crusius's basic claim is that the distinction between these two
kinds of conditions entails that our inability to understand or explain
freedom does not preclude its reality. On the contrary, he insisted on
the reality of freedom as a fundamental power of the soul, which
can be known to be actual, even though it remains inexplicable.
Within the framework of his epistemology, Crusius explained this
in terms of a distinction between two kinds of knowledge: symbolic
and intuitive.[16] The former comprehends things in terms of their
relations to something else and the latter consists in an immediate
awareness. Accordingly, we can have a direct assurance of realities
that we cannot understand. Freedom is one such reality.

Crusius's justification for this claim turns on his voluntarism.
Indeed, to underscore this point, he introduced a distinct science
("*Thelematologie*") whose special provenance is the will.[17] In this
context, Crusius defined the will as the power to act according to
one's ideas. His point is that a capacity for cognition does not entail
a capacity to act according to its determinations.[18] Since Crusius
thought that the will, as the chief power of the mind, has an executive
function that presupposes, but cannot be performed by, the intellect,
he denied that God would create a being with understanding but no
will.[19]

Moreover, for Crusius, this function of the will presupposes freedom in a strong sense. Consequently, the Wolffian account of freedom will not do since it is a thinly veiled determinism, which reduces
virtue to a matter of luck.[20] Against this, Crusius insisted that freedom must involve a capacity to choose between given alternatives
since it is only on the basis of this assumption that acts can be
imputed to an agent. As he puts it at one point, "A willing that
one could in identical circumstances omit or direct to something
else is called a free willing."[21] And later, in defining the most perfect
concept of freedom, he writes:

Whenever we freely will something, we decide to do something for which
one or several desires already exist in us....Freedom consists in an inner
perfect activity of the will, which is capable of connecting its efficacy with
one of the currently active drives of the will, or of omitting this connection
and remaining inactive or of connecting it with another drive instead of the
first one.[22]

For Crusius, then, rather than being determined by its strongest desire or, in the intellectualist version, by what is perceived to be the best, the will (or self) is conceived as somehow standing apart from its desires, with the capacity to determine which, if any, of them are to be acted upon. Such a conception of agency makes no sense from the Wolffian standpoint, with its reduction of all the powers of the mind to cognition, but Crusius thought that he was able to accommodate it by means of his sharp distinction between intellect and will.

II. KANT'S CONCEPTION OF RATIONAL AGENCY

Although Kant's eventual understanding of freedom of the will has strong affinities to Crusius's, his initial account is Wolffian. Thus, in his first metaphysical venture, Kant defends the distinction between absolute and hypothetical necessity against Crusius and, in good Wolffian fashion, insists that the question of freedom concerns the nature of the necessitating ground rather than the kind or degree of its necessitation (New Elucidation, 1:400). Accordingly, freedom of the will is said to consist entirely in its being determined by "motives of the understanding" rather than by external stimuli (New Elucidation, 1:400). Appealing to Leibnizian terminology, Kant defines spontaneity as "an action which issues from an inner principle," and remarks that "When this spontaneity is determined in conformity with the representation of what is best it is called freedom" (New Elucidation, 1: 402).

Remnants of this view are to be found in some of Kant's lectures on practical philosophy and associated Reflexionen, where he appeals to a relative, empirically based conception of freedom. In this context, he speaks of degrees of freedom, corresponding to degrees of rationality, and correlated with degrees of imputability. Indeed, as late as 1784–5, Kant is cited as claiming that, "The more a man can be morally compelled the freer he is; the more he is pathologically compelled, though this only occurs in a comparative sense, the less free he is" (Moral Philosophy Collins, 27:268). It is difficult to know what to make of such claims, particularly those stemming from the period after the initial publication of the first Critique. But since Kant used Baumgarten as his text and this remark (and many others like it) is taken from a student's notes, it seems plausible to assume that he was stating the latter's view rather than his own.

Be that as it may, in his metaphysical lectures of the seventies Kant repudiates the Wolffian conception of freedom on essentially Crusian grounds. Thus, he now distinguishes sharply between an absolute and a relative or conditioned spontaneity of the kind advocated by the Leibnizians. The former is claimed to be essential to freedom in the genuine or transcendental sense, while the latter is compared to that of a watch or turnspit (*Metaphysik L₁*, 28:267–8).[23] In fact, at one point Kant seems to have entertained a speculative proof of transcendental freedom that anticipates later idealistic accounts. According to this proof, the very conception of oneself as a thinking being proves one's transcendental freedom. As Kant puts it:

> When I say: I think, I act, etc., then either the word "I" is used falsely or I am free. Were I not free, I could not say: I do it, but rather I would have to say: I feel a desire in me to do, which someone has aroused in me. But when I say: I do it, that means spontaneity in the transcendental sense.
>
> (*Metaphysik L₁*, 28:269)

Nevertheless, even at that time Kant did not regard the self's transcendental freedom as unproblematic. Unlike his later treatments, however, its problematic feature is found in its apparent conflict with our ontological status as dependent beings.[24] The problem is to understand how such a being could have anything more than the relative spontaneity recognized by the Leibnizians. His resolution of the problem at this point is basically that of Crusius: we know *that* we are free in the transcendental sense, but we cannot explain *how* this is possible (*Metaphysik L₁*, 8:270–1).

The "critical" Kant retained the doctrine of the incomprehensibility of freedom, while denying its knowability. This denial is a consequence of the limitation of our cognition to phenomena, that is, to things as they appear in accordance with our forms of sensibility. Since the idea of transcendental freedom is the thought of an agency that is not determinable by sensible conditions, we cannot be said to know that we possess it. Kant also insists, however, on both the possibility and necessity of thinking our freedom, understood as an absolute spontaneity. Freedom, so conceived, is a transcendental idea (a necessary idea of reason), which is required for the thought of ourselves as cognizers and as agents.

The idea that even our capacity to think presupposes absolute spontaneity seems to have its roots in the speculative proof noted

above. As Kant develops it in his later writings, the basic point is
that to consider oneself as a cognizer is to assume such spontaneity.
This is because to understand or cognize something requires not simply having the correct beliefs and even having them for the correct
reasons, it also involves a capacity to take these reasons (whether
rightly or wrongly) as justifying the belief. In short, the thought of
ourselves as self-conscious cognizers is inseparable from the idea of
our absolute spontaneity.[25]

Kant recognized, however, that this is not sufficient to justify
freedom in the practical sense, that is, freedom of the will as it is
usually understood. The problem stems from the fact that our epistemic spontaneity appears to be self-certifying in a way in which
our practical spontaneity is not. The first part of this story is familiar, albeit hardly noncontroversial. Since spontaneity in the above-
mentioned sense is a necessary condition of thinking, I cannot think
of myself as thinking without attributing such spontaneity to my
mind. Expressed in Cartesian terms, I cannot coherently doubt that
I am a thinker because such doubt is itself an act of thinking. But
since it does seem possible to doubt that one has a will, or, equivalently, that one's reason is practical, this line of argument cannot be
directly carried over into the practical sphere. For all that we know,
we might be nothing more than thinking automata: beings who are
capable of thought, but whose actions are governed by instinct rather
than practical reason.

Here again, the influence of Crusius is evident. For both thinkers
it is the separation of intellect and will as distinct powers of the
mind that opens up the possibility, which is unintelligible from
the Leibnizian point of view, that we might have the former without
the latter. Unlike Crusius, however, Kant does not deny such a state
of affairs on theological grounds, but seems to have held that it is
a possibility that cannot be excluded by the resources of theoretical
reason.[26]

The main point, however, is that from the practical point of view,
this possibility is moot. At least from a first-person perspective,
while engaged in deliberation regarding the proper course of action,
we necessarily presuppose our freedom. To take oneself as a rational
agent capable of choice and deliberation is to assume that one's reason is practical or, equivalently, that one has a will. As Kant famously
puts it, "Now I assert that to every rational being having a will we

must necessarily lend the idea of freedom, also, under which alone he acts" (*Groundwork*, 4:448).

As we shall see below in connection with the Third Antinomy, this idea is that of an uncaused cause, that is, of an agency capable of making an "absolute beginning," by which is understood the capacity to initiate a causal series that is not itself determined by any antecedent condition. In its application to the human will and its practical freedom, this means that we are rationally constrained to regard ourselves as spontaneous initiators of causal series through our choices. Otherwise expressed, we cannot, at least from the first-person point of view, regard our choices as the predetermined outcomes of either the state of the world or of our own psychological state, including our beliefs and desires.

Perhaps Kant's best formulation of this conception of freedom is in a passage from *Religion*, where he writes:

[F]reedom of the power of choice [*Willkür*] has the characteristic, entirely peculiar to it, that it cannot be determined to action through any incentive except so far as the human being has incorporated it into his maxim (has made it into a universal rule for himself, according to which he wills to conduct himself); only in this way can an incentive, whatever it may be, coexist with the absolute spontaneity of the power of choice (of freedom).

(*Religion*, 6:24)

Although this characterization of the freedom of the power of choice is part of Kant's discussion of how the moral law can be an incentive for sensibly affected beings such as ourselves, it is noteworthy that he claims that it applies to any incentive (including those based on inclination). Consequently, it is best viewed as providing a model for the thought of free agency in general rather than merely moral agency. Nevertheless, its force is normative rather than descriptive. It is not the case that introspection invariably shows that we never act on an incentive without first "incorporating it into one's maxim"; it is rather that we necessarily conceive our agency according to this model insofar as we take ourselves to be acting on reasons. This act of incorporation may also be seen as the practical analogue of the spontaneity that we necessarily attribute to our understandings in cognition. Just as reasons to believe cannot function as reasons unless we take them as such, desires do not of themselves provide us with a sufficient reason to act. They can become reasons only insofar as we freely assign them this status, by subsuming them under a principle of action (maxim), which we likewise freely adopt.[27]

If we put this central Kantian idea into its historical context, it may be seen as a successor to the Leibnizian dictum that motives incline without necessitating. The difference is that, under the influence of Crusius, Kant construed the distinction between inclination and necessitation in much stronger terms than the Leibnizians. Whereas the latter meant by this merely that a strong inclination to X does not make it absolutely necessary that one will do X (though all things considered, it makes it certain), for Kant such an inclination does not, of itself, even give one a sufficient reason to X.

III. IMPUTABILITY AND AUTONOMY

Kant's account of the relationship between morality and freedom is complicated by the fact that it encompasses two issues: imputation and motivation. His treatment of the former consists in a relatively straightforward application of the general conception of rational agency to morally relevant acts. The basic idea is that the imputability of actions presupposes freedom in the strong sense of absolute spontaneity. Accordingly, unlike the Leibnizian view, for which a merely relative spontaneity, understood as a lack of external compulsion, suffices to ground responsibility, for Kant it requires that the agent is not predetermined at all. In other words, without violating the psychological continuity of the person, we must consider an imputable act as if it were an "absolute beginning."

Once again, this is close to the position of Crusius, who defended the traditional view that freedom involves a capacity to have chosen otherwise in a given set of circumstances. Kant, however, gives a somewhat different twist to this thought in the light of his conception of morality. Rather than defining freedom simply as the capacity to do otherwise in the sense of an ability to choose either for against the dictates of morality, Kant typically appeals to the principle that "ought implies can." Thus, the weight of his account falls on the idea that, no matter how dire one's circumstances, one is aware through one's consciousness of standing under the moral law that one *can* do what duty requires, simply because one *ought* to do so. Moreover, it is in this sense that we must understand Kant's claim, which may at first seem to conflict with the previous analysis of rational agency, that without the moral law such freedom would have remained unknown to the agent (*Practical Reason*, 5:30).[28] It is not that the consciousness of the moral law first makes us aware of our rational agency, since insofar as we take ourselves to be acting we are necessarily conscious of that. It is rather that this consciousness makes us aware of a capacity to disregard all our inclinations, even our natural love of life, when duty requires it.

This conception of freedom rests on the assumption that moral considerations give one a sufficient reason to act or, as Kant usually puts it, that the moral law serves as an incentive. To understand this, however, we need to consider the doctrine of the autonomy of the will. As introduced in the *Groundwork*, autonomy is defined as "the property of the will by which it is a law to itself (independently of any property of the objects of volition)" (4:440). It is contrasted with the principle of heteronomy, which denies that the will can give itself the law and assumes that the object (whatever happens to be desired) must give the law to the will (4:441). Consequently, to attribute heteronomy to the will is not to claim that it is causally determined, but rather that it requires some antecedent desire in order to have a reason to act.

Kant claimed that the will's heteronomy was presupposed by all previous moralists, including voluntarists such as Crusius (*Practical Reason*, 5:39). His basic objection is that it is incompatible with the possibility of the categorical imperative since the latter not only determines what our duty is in given circumstances, but requires us to act *from* duty, which is possible only on the assumption that the will is autonomous. Thus, unlike most present-day conceptions of autonomy, Kant's is an all-or-nothing affair: either the will has it or it does not. Moreover, if it does not, morality must be rejected as a phantom of the brain (*Groundwork*, 4:445).

In the *Groundwork*, Kant argues also that the positive conception of freedom (autonomy) follows from the negative conception (spontaneity) and that given autonomy, "morality together with its principle follows from it by mere analysis of its concept" (4:447).[29] Or, as he puts it in the second *Critique*, "[F]reedom and unconditional practical law reciprocally imply each other" (5:529). Both formulations come to the same thing, namely, that freedom (construed as autonomy) is not only a necessary, but also a sufficient condition of morality.[30] Consequently, given the significance that Kant attributes to autonomy, it is no wonder that he devoted the third part of the *Groundwork*, which is intended to establish the reality of the categorical imperative, to a "deduction" of the autonomy of the will.

Although it is impossible to examine here this complex and difficult argument, which was replaced in the second *Critique* by an appeal to the "fact of reason,"[31] it is necessary to consider briefly Kant's distinction between *Wille* and *Willkür*, which is a central feature of his treatment of the will in his later writings. Whereas in the *Groundwork* Kant simply identified will (*Wille*) with practical reason, thereby equating the question of whether we have free will with the question of whether our reason is practical, in these later writings he introduces a more complex account of the will as containing both legislative and executive functions.[32]

In addition to creating problems for the translator since each of these terms can be rendered as "will," the situation is further complicated by the fact that *Wille* itself is taken in two senses: a broad sense in which it connotes the faculty of volition, or will as a whole, and a narrow sense in which it connotes the legislative function of this faculty. Accordingly, both *Wille* in the narrow sense and *Willkür*, which is here translated as "the power of choice," are aspects of *Wille* in the broad sense.

It is tempting to correlate these two aspects of will with the two conceptions of freedom (spontaneity and autonomy). In fact, this works nicely in the case of *Willkür*, the freedom of which consists in an absolute spontaneity. The situation is more complex in the case of the connection of *Wille* and autonomy, however, since Kant does not seem to have been of one mind on the matter. Thus, in the published text of the *Metaphysics of Morals*, Kant states that only *Willkür* can be regarded as free, whereas *Wille* must be thought to be neither free nor unfree since it is directed to giving law rather than to action (6:226). By contrast, in his unpublished preliminary notes (*Vorarbeiten*) for this work, Kant entertains the possibility that *Wille* might be free in a different sense than *Willkür* because it is law giving rather than law following (23:249). Perhaps the best way to render Kant consistent on this point is to keep in mind the distinction between the two senses of *Wille*. When Kant denied that *Wille* as such is either free or unfree, he had in mind the narrow sense of the term. *Wille*, so construed, may not be thought to be free with regard to the legislation of the categorical imperative, since this is its fundamental law. But, conversely, it does seem possible to attribute autonomy to *Wille* in the broad sense since it is conceived as legislating to itself.

IV. FREEDOM AND DETERMINISM

The centerpiece of Kant's account of freedom is the third antinomy in the *Critique of Pure Reason* and its attempted resolution through an appeal to transcendental idealism. Like each of the four antinomies, the third is presented as a conflict between cosmological ideas, that is, between ways of conceiving the world as a whole (as a totality of conditions). In this case, it is a conflict between the conception of the world as containing an infinite series of causal conditions, each of which is itself conditioned by its antecedent condition, and the conception of this series (and, therefore, the world as a whole) as anchored in something that is itself unconditioned. On Kant's analysis, each side is capable of demonstrating a contradiction in the opposed view. But since it is assumed by both parties that these alternatives are themselves contradictory, the refutation of one is seen as equivalent to the demonstration of the other.[33]

Insofar as this dispute is explicitly concerned with a cosmological issue regarding the need for (and possibility of) a first cause, its connection with the question of free will is not immediately evident. Kant's explanation turns on the conception of freedom as absolute spontaneity. As we have seen, to consider oneself as free in this sense is to conceive oneself as initiating through one's choice a fresh chain of events or an "absolute beginning." But the problem with such a conception of agency is that it appears to conflict with the principle of the second analogy: "Everything that happens (begins to be) presupposes something which it follows in accordance with a rule" (*Pure Reason*, A 189).

Kant's general approach to the antinomial conflict is to suggest that the appearance of a contradiction rests on a misunderstanding, which is itself a consequence of the transcendental realism assumed by both parties to the dispute. Since Kant regards such realism as the contradictory opposite of his own transcendental idealism, he defines it in relation to the latter. Underlying the contrast between the two forms of transcendentalism is the distinction between objects considered as they appear, that is, qua given under the subjective conditions of human sensibility (space and time), and these same objects considered as they may be in themselves, that is, qua thought independently of these conditions by some putative "pure understanding."[34] Whereas the transcendental idealist limits human cognition to objects considered in the former way, the transcendental realist ignores this distinction and assumes that our cognition, even of the spatiotemporal objects of human experience, concerns objects considered in the latter way. In Kant's terms, the transcendental realist treats mere appearances as if they were things in themselves.

According to Kant, this confusion leads directly to the misunderstanding underlying the antinomial conflict as a whole and can be avoided only by replacing transcendental realism with transcendental idealism. This is because the transcendental realist is committed to the assumption that the totality of conditions must be "given" (at least for God) independently of our piecemeal and successive cognition of them. Consequently, such a realist necessarily assumes that this totality consists of either a finite or an infinite number of conditions. In the case of the third antinomy, the issue is whether there is a first, uncaused cause or an infinitely extended causal chain, every member of which is itself causally conditioned.

Things look rather different from the transcendentally idealistic point of view, however, since it is no longer assumed that there is some ultimate fact of the matter, not even one to be determined by God. The claim is rather that each position is legitimate, if relativized to a point of view. From the empirical point of view, every condition must itself be conditioned, which leaves no room for an absolute beginning or uncaused cause; whereas from the intellectualist point of view, which is concerned with the conditions of coherent thought rather than experience, it is necessary to assume some such cause in order to satisfy reason's demand for completeness. Kant's claim is that transcendental idealism (unlike transcendental realism) is able to reconcile these two points of view by introducing a distinction between conditions of experience and conditions of thought. This creates logical space for the possibility that both parties may be correct: the determinist with respect to objects of possible experience and the indeterminist with respect to merely intelligible objects.

In applying this schema to the human will, Kant invokes a distinction between empirical and intelligible character. The will in its empirical character is described as "nothing other than a certain causality of . . . reason, insofar as in its effects in appearance this reason exhibits a rule in accordance with which one could derive the rational grounds and the actions themselves . . . and estimate the subjective principles of his power of choice" (*Pure Reason*, A 549/B 577). Although it may appear strange to find the will in its *empirical* character described as a causality of reason, Kant's point is that, even at the empirical level, the voluntary actions of human beings exhibit a "character" that is distinct from that of physical occurrences since they reflect a set of underlying intentions. These intentions constitute the "subjective principles of the power of choice." They are empirical insofar as they can be inferred from overt behavior and used to explain past actions and predict future ones.

The notion of an empirical character therefore involves a deterministic, though not reductionistic, picture of human agency, and it is this picture to which Kant thinks we appeal when we are simply observing human behavior, "and, as happens in anthropology, . . . trying to investigate the moving causes of [a person's] actions physiologically" (A 550/B 578). It is also, in all essential respects, the view of such agency affirmed by the Leibnizians and most forms of compatibilism to the present day. Since agency, so conceived, is itself part of the natural order, there is no problem regarding its compatibility with this order. At least for Kant, however, the problem is that, under this assumption, there is also no freedom.

As Kant viewed the situation, freedom is required to account for the "ought" (both moral and prudential). Since this involves considering human actions normatively in relation to practical reason rather than descriptively in relation to the conditions of their experience and explanation, it requires a different conception of agency, one that allows us to conceive of the will as capable of an absolute beginning. The function of the notion of an intelligible character is to provide the requisite conception.

Kant's thesis that one and the same volition may be considered from these two apparently conflicting points of view and assigned two such characters has been deemed deeply paradoxical, if not outright incoherent, by many. Of particular concern is Kant's attempt to illustrate this thesis by means of the notorious case of the malicious lie. Faced with such an act, Kant suggests, we first enquire into its motive causes and then seek to determine the degree to which the act and its consequences may be imputed to the agent. In considering the former question, we naturally appeal to explanatory factors such as "bad upbringing, bad company...the wickedness of a natural temper insensitive to shame...carelessness and thoughtlessness, as well as to other occasional causes that may have intervened" (A 554/B 582). In short, it is assumed that the act can be fully explained in terms of a combination of environmental factors and character traits. But in spite of this, Kant maintains, we still blame the agent. Moreover, we do not do so on the familiar compatibilist grounds that the act is the consequence of the agent's own bad character. Rather, we do so because we presuppose that:

[i]t can entirely set aside how that life was constituted, and that the series of conditions that transpired might not have been, but rather that this deed could be regarded as entirely unconditioned in regard to the previous state, as though with that act the agent had started a series of consequences entirely from himself. (A 555/B 583)

If one is to avoid reducing Kant's account to sheer nonsense, this claim must be considered with great care. First, we must keep in mind its context, which is that of a critique of the attempt to conceive imputation solely in terms of a Leibnizian-type view of agency. As Crusius had already claimed, this view is inadequate because it reduces one's virtue or viciousness to a matter of luck. But if this is to be avoided, it does seem necessary to regard an agent as acting in a way that is not determined entirely by character and circumstance, that is, as capable of initiating an absolute beginning.

Second, in spite of Kant's language, we need not take him as affirming the utterly implausible view that one's past behavior, disposition, and circumstances play no role in governing one's actions, as if one's present self were discontinuous with one's past self. This would amount to a form of the liberty of indifference, justly ridiculed by the Leibnizians and many others. Consequently, Kant is not claiming that, all things considered, it would be equally easy for the liar to speak the truth on that occasion. He is claiming rather that he could have done so. Or, perhaps better, that we must presuppose that he could have done so if we are to blame him for the lie.

Third, we must keep in mind the status of freedom as a transcendental idea, which, as such, has no explanatory role. It is not that in some cases we appeal to freedom of the will in order to explain an action, while in others we judge that the agent had no choice in the matter. Certainly, we often distinguish actions in these terms, considering the former voluntary and the latter involuntary, and Kant has no problem with this distinction. His point is rather that it applies only within the explanatory framework of empirical character and does not touch on the transcendental question. The latter concerns the very conception of a voluntary action insofar as it is deemed imputable. And it is to resolve this question that transcendental idealism is required.

Considered as a whole, Kant's account may be seen as an attempt to reconcile two apparently conflicting principles: 1) the deterministic principle of the second analogy, which holds that every occurrence (including the voluntary actions of rational agents) has an antecedent condition from which it follows according to a rule; and 2) the thesis that the conception of ourselves as genuine agents to whom actions are imputed requires the attribution to the will of freedom in a strong (indeterminist) sense. Given this problematic, transcendental idealism is presented as the only hypothesis on the basis of which both of these principles can be maintained.

Nevertheless, such a resolution appears vulnerable at three points. One is the coherence of its proposed solution. If transcendental idealism is, as many critics charge, itself incoherent, then appealing to it to reconcile these principles is of no greater import than appealing to the concept of a round square would be with regard to the question of how a figure can be both round and square. The other two points concern each of these principles taken singly. For if we abandon (or modify) either the deterministic principle of the second analogy or Kant's essentially Crusian conception of freedom, then the need to appeal to transcendental idealism apparently disappears.

Although some defenders of Kant have chosen the first route, which involves the reduction of the causal principle to a merely regulative status,[35] the usual move is to take the second, which amounts to an appeal to some form of compatibilism. Whether at the end of the day this provides an adequate conception of freedom remains an open question that cannot be decided here. What should be clear, however, is that Kant rejected the compatibilist conception of freedom as he understood it. On this issue, Kant stands firmly with Crusius rather than the Leibnizians. Thus, while defending the general thesis that freedom is compatible with causal determinism, which is the defining mark of compatibilism, he rejected the conception of freedom in terms of which this compatibility is usually understood. This is the source of both the complexity and much of the interest of Kant's account.

V. FREEDOM OF THE WILL IN KANT'S SUCCESSORS

This final section will discuss briefly the concept of free will in three of Kant's idealistic successors: Fichte, Hegel, and Schopenhauer. Although other thinkers, for example, Schelling, undoubtedly could have been included, these three arguably provide the most interesting case studies of the development and criticism of Kant's thought on the topic.

Johann Gottlieb Fichte

Whereas for Kant and his predecessors freedom is a problem (albeit a vitally important one) for philosophy, for Fichte it provides the foundation of philosophy. This is reflected in Fichte's characterization of his own position as a "system of freedom,"[36] which he also misleadingly describes as nothing more than the Kantian philosophy "properly understood."[37]

Fichte's creative reconstruction of the Kantian philosophy is articulated in various versions of his *Wissenschaftslehre* and related writings, which he composed in the middle and late 1790s. It is based largely on two principles, each of which breaks with orthodox Kantianism. The first is that the absolute autonomy (independence) of the I is the mandatory starting point of philosophy in the sense that everything is to be explained in terms of the I and its conception of itself, while this self-conception is not itself to be explained in terms of anything more fundamental.[38] The second is that the I is not a thing or substance (a Cartesian *res cogitans*) but an activity. Specifically, it is the activity of self-determining or self-positing, which Fichte, following Kant, viewed as essential even to the theoretical use of intelligence. Accordingly, consciousness of self is just the consciousness of this activity, and the task of philosophy or *Wissenschaftslehre* is to spell out the necessary conditions and implications of this activity and the consciousness thereof.

Since to posit itself the I must confront an objective world (the not-I), which opposes and limits its activity, Fichte avoids what he takes to be the misguided appeal of some Kantians to a pregiven realm of things in themselves.[39] Instead, he "deduces" the reality of an external, physical world as a necessary condition of self-consciousness. Rather than a bizarre flight into metaphysical fancy, Fichte's position may be seen as grounded in a radical reinterpretation of Kant's distinction between two standpoints and his division of the philosophical terrain into transcendental idealism and transcendental realism. As already noted, for Kant the contrast between the two standpoints concerns two ways of considering things and events (including human actions): as they appear under the spatiotemporal conditions of sensibility and as they are thought through pure reason independently of these conditions. And for Kant at least one key difference between the two forms of transcendentalism is that the former allows for the distinction between the two standpoints, whereas the latter denies its legitimacy.[40]

Rejecting the appearance–thing in itself distinction as ordinarily understood, Fichte regards the contrast between the two standpoints as between the points of view of the philosopher and of ordinary consciousness. The latter is inherently and appropriately realistic (in the sense of Kant's empirical realism), with the result that the I is viewed as a being among beings. This may also be equated with the naturalistic standpoint assumed by science. For the philosopher, however (at least the idealistic philosopher), the mandatory starting point is the I itself, of which the philosopher becomes aware through a reflection on her own self-determining activity. Thus, it is from the standpoint of philosophy, and only from this standpoint, that primacy is assigned to this activity of the I and the objective world is viewed as existing only for and through it.

This is closely connected with Fichte's methodological dichotomy between idealism and dogmatism, which replaces the Kantian dichotomy between transcendental idealism and transcendental realism. Although clearly modeled on the latter, Fichte's understanding of the fundamental division of the philosophical terrain is oriented more to the question of the nature and status of the I than to the epistemological question of the conditions and limits of *a priori* knowledge. Put simply, whereas Fichtean idealism takes the I as starting point, dogmatism, in its various forms, starts with a pregiven world of beings (including human beings), and its project is to explain the possibility of the I, in both its cognitive and practical dimensions, on this basis. Not surprisingly, Fichte asserts that this project fails because dogmatism cannot account for the possibility of the I as self-reverting activity, whereas idealism, starting with the latter, can account for the experience of an objective world of things with which the dogmatist begins and which defines the standpoint of ordinary consciousness.

Even though the theoretical portion of the *Wissenschaftslehre* is devoted entirely to demonstrating the latter thesis, Fichte readily admits that the dogmatist will never be convinced by its argument.[41] More generally, he held that the conflict between idealism and dogmatism is irresolvable at the theoretical level. Nevertheless, Fichte thought that he could overcome this impasse through a radicalization of the Kantian principle of the primacy of practical reason. He does this by insisting that all reason is at bottom practical, which for Fichte means that practical considerations, that is, those concerning the conditions of the possibility of the I as self-reverting activity, constitute the ultimate court of appeal in philosophy.

Consequently, while Fichte agrees with Kant in denying the possibility of a theoretical proof of freedom, he has quite different reasons for doing so. One of these is the status assigned to freedom or self-determination, which, as inseparable from the thought of the I, itself serves as a first principle of philosophy and, as such, cannot be demonstrated. Although Kant, as we have seen, took freedom (in the sense of absolute spontaneity) to be inseparable from the thought of the I and at one time even used this as the basis for a demonstration of freedom, he never took the I as the first principle of philosophy in anything like Fichte's sense. Another, even more un-Kantian, reason is Fichte's pragmatic, even proto-existentialist, orientation. Anticipating themes developed in the past century, Fichte, with his doctrine of self-determination, not only regarded the existence of an I as prior to its essence (what the I makes of itself), he also seems to have divided all people (including philosophers) into two classes: those who affirm and those who attempt to deny their freedom. Accordingly, he suggests that the kind of philosophy one adopts (idealism or dogmatism) reflects the kind of character one has.[42] Idealists affirm their freedom, understood as the act of self-determination, while dogmatists deny it by conceiving of themselves as determined rather than as self-determiners. Thus, dogmatism is seen not merely as a defective philosophy but as the sign of a character defect as well.[43]

Considered from the practical point of view, this self-determining activity takes two forms and involves two conceptions of freedom, which correspond roughly to Kant's distinction between spontaneity and autonomy. In Fichte's preferred terminology, the former is characterized as "formal" and the latter as "material" or "absolute" freedom.[44] Each is made the central topic of a distinct work.

Formal freedom is the concern of the *Foundations of Natural Right* (*Grundlage des Naturrechts nach Principien der Wissenschaftslehre*) (1796), which contains the systematic statement of Fichte's legal and political philosophy. In the spirit of the *Wissenschaftslehre*, he attempts to "deduce" such freedom as a necessary condition of self-consciousness. The work is concerned, however, with a specific form of self-consciousness, namely, that of oneself as a particular individual with determinate desires and ends. Since this involves a conception of oneself as an end-setter, it is inseparable from the consciousness of one's capacity to set ends and to strive to realize them in the external world. Fichte's key claim here is that this consciousness is possible only insofar as one finds oneself as a finite rational agent among others. As he puts it at one point, "The human being...becomes a human being only among human beings."[45] Fichte develops this thought in connection with his conception of a "summons" (*Aufforderung*), which can stem only from another rational being. Since it is only through such a summons to do or refrain from a certain course of action that I can be aware of my capacity to choose, it becomes a necessary condition of my awareness of myself as a free, self-determining individual. But since in being aware of a summons one must also be aware of the free agency of the summoner, it follows that I can consider myself as free only insofar as I consider other finite rational beings as free in precisely the same sense, that is, as self-determining end-setters or free individuals.

Nevertheless, Fichtean formal freedom is a limited conception of freedom, which fails to do full justice to the self-determining activity of the I. This is because the kind of self-determination it requires consists merely in the setting of one's own ends as a rational agent. Confronted with alternative courses of action, I myself choose which one to adopt. Although equivalent to freedom of choice as traditionally understood, from the Kantian standpoint it provides a merely heteronomous conception of freedom. The problem is that, while attributing to rational agents a certain independence from their desires and a capacity to determine which ones to act on (spontaneity), it regards this choice as arbitrary rather than as norm-governed. Expressed in contemporary terms, the limitation of this conception of freedom as the basis for an adequate understanding of self-determination is that it does not "go all the way down." One may determine on which desires one chooses to act, but if one does not also determine the principles governing one's choice, one is not fully *self*-determined.

Fichte's account of material or absolute freedom, which is developed in *The System of Ethical Theory* (*Das System der Sittenlehre nach den Principien der Wissenschaftslehre*) (1798), takes the form of a reflection on the conditions of a complete self-determination (one that does go all the way down). Consequently, it is based on the questionable assumption that the latter is intelligible, that one can speak meaningfully of the I as constituting or determining itself, as it were, out of whole cloth. Fichte's basic claim, which provides the foundation of his ethical theory, is that such self-determination requires governing one's choice of maxims by a self-legislated principle. It turns out, however, that the only principle that qualifies in this respect is the demand to determine one's freedom solely in accordance with the idea of self-determination.[46] Or, as he also puts it, "The I shall be a self-determined I."[47] This amounts a radicalization of the Kantian principle of autonomy, as the result of which autonomy, understood as complete independence of any thing or value that is not rooted in the I and its self-determination, is reconceived as an infinite task rather than as a constitutive feature of the will. As moral agents, we are obligated to strive to attain full autonomy or self-determination even though, in virtue of our finitude, this can never be completely attained.[48]

Georg Wilhelm Friedrich Hegel

Like Fichte, Hegel granted a foundational role to the concept of freedom and equated it with self-determination. But whereas Fichte understood the latter as an apparently groundless act of self-positing, through which the I supposedly constitutes both itself and its other (the non-I), Hegel understood it in more "concrete" terms as a "being-with-oneself-in-an-other" (*Beisichselbstsein in einem Anderen*).[49] In terms of Hegel's dialectical logic, this means that freedom is attained through an overcoming of the otherness of the other, by which its otherness is negated, while its being is preserved. As Hegel shows graphically in his account of the life and death struggle in the *Phenomenology*, the latter is necessary because a simple, "abstract" negation (killing the other), does not leave an other in whom one's freedom can be actualized.[50] Consequently, the other must be negated in a way that preserves its being, that is, it must be "superseded" (*aufgehoben*). The famous master-slave dialectic in the *Phenomenology*, which immediately succeeds this struggle, is presented as the first and inherently flawed attempt to attain freedom so understood. Since the other (the slave) is conscious merely of his total dependence on the master, that is, of his unfreedom, the master is not able to find his freedom fully actualized in the slave's consciousness. The basic idea, which has clear affinities to Fichte's conception of a summons, is that one can find one's freedom only if it is freely (not slavishly) recognized by the other. Moreover, since only a free being can freely recognize the freedom of another, this means that no one is fully free unless all are free. Such a condition of universally recognized freedom is the goal of history, which, rather than being the infinite task it was for Fichte, Hegel believed to have been already attained (at least in principle) in the laws and institutions of post-revolutionary Western Europe.[51]

In the *Philosophy of Right*, this conception of freedom, the full attainment of which is identified with humanity's or "spirit's" self-realization, is applied to an analysis of the human will. Thus, it is here that Hegel's "speculative"-historical account makes contact with what is usually regarded as the problem of free will. Although this account involves the usual Hegelian obscurity, the basic goal is to analyze the problem in the light of the conception of freedom as being-with-oneself-in-an-other. This analysis begins with the concept of will, which, like Kant, Hegel identifies with practical reason or intelligence.[52] Also, like Kant, Hegel asserts that the will, so conceived, is inseparable from freedom. Accordingly, he claims that "freedom is just as much a determination of the will as weight is a basic determination of bodies." And, again, that "Will without freedom is an empty word, just as freedom is actual only as will."[53]

Hegel differs from Kant and stands much closer to Fichte in his understanding of practical reason. Whereas Kant begins with a separation of theoretical and practical reason and endeavors to unite them, Hegel rejects the Kantian dichotomy and begins instead with the idea of their inseparability. According to Hegel, neither will nor intelligence (thought) are possible apart from one another and the difference between them is simply between theoretical and practical attitudes. Thus, on the one hand, will is itself merely "a particular way of thinking – thinking translating itself into existence," while, on the other hand, it is only in thinking that one is with oneself and can, therefore, find oneself in another, which is the goal of the will as free.[54]

This interpenetration of thought and volition leads, in turn, to the most distinctive feature of the Hegelian conception of a free will, namely, its unification of apparently conflicting conceptions into a single concrete idea or "concept." In light of this concept, Hegel provides what amounts to a rational reconstruction of the concept of a free will in the Introduction to the *Philosophy of Right*, which he then uses in the body of the work as the basis for an analysis of the distinct spheres of right (Abstract Right, Morality [*Moralität*], and Ethical Life [*Sittlichkeit*]), each of which is viewed as the actualization of a particular dimension of concrete freedom.

The elements of this reconstruction are a set of interrelated dichotomies, which express in somewhat different terms what may be described as the subjective and objective poles of the concept of freedom. These include universality (or negative freedom) and particularity; infinitude and finitude; form and content; being for-itself and being in-itself. In each case, the first element stands for the moment of independence or indeterminacy. Thus, universality, or negative freedom, represents the indeterminacy through which consciousness stands apart from and above its particular contents. This indeterminacy is also expressed in the idea of the infinitude of the will, understood as its opposition to everything finite (including an agent's drives and inclinations). Similarly, this represents the "formal" side of willing, in contrast to the particular content chosen. Finally, it is also the free will as it is for-itself in contrast to this will as it is in-itself, that is, in its inherent nature, which consists in willing something determinate rather than in simply remaining indeterminate.

Since the first or subjective side of the dichotomy corresponds to what is usually thought to be the full or adequate characterization of free will, at least on an indeterminist account, Hegel argues, in effect, that this sense of adequacy is illusory because the conception it embodies is inseparable from, and dependent on, its polar opposite. Just as in the master-slave dialectic of the *Phenomenology*, the universality of the will turned out to be dependent on its particularity since the latter is the source of the content to be willed, the infinitude dependent on its finitude, and so forth. The lesson drawn from this is that an adequate understanding of freedom must integrate each of these opposing moments. In other words, the "truth" of freedom (in contrast to its "certainty") involves both universality and particularity, infinitude and finitude, form and content, and the will as it is both for and in itself. Thus, the initial elements in each of these pairings, which most previous philosophers have seen as both necessary and sufficient for freedom, are viewed by Hegel as merely necessary conditions, which, if not combined with their dialectical opposites, constitute merely the appearance or form of freedom.

This provides the justification for Hegel's definition of freedom as being-with-oneself-in-an-other since it supposedly shows that a freedom that does not somehow incorporate otherness is nothing more than an empty abstraction. Accordingly, the problem is to understand how otherness can lose its character of simple unfreedom and become dialectically transformed into an essential ingredient in freedom. Hegel's claim is that this is possible only if this otherness is itself an expression of freedom. Only then do we find freedom fully actualized as it is in-and-for-itself. Or, as Hegel also puts it, "The will in its truth is such that what it wills, i.e., its content, is identical with the will itself, so that freedom is willed by freedom."[55]

By understanding freedom in this way, Hegel may be said to have changed the subject, which is why here, as in other areas of philosophical inquiry, it is so difficult to juxtapose his views in a straightforward way to those of other thinkers. Thus, rather than worrying, as previous philosophers (including Kant and Fichte) had done, about the reconciliation of freedom with natural causality, Hegel's analysis focuses on the relation between a formally free choice and its content. Although Hegel would no doubt agree that in a sense he has changed the terms of the debate, he would also contend that this is the result of a dialectical analysis of the inadequacy of the way in which the problem has traditionally been framed. Indeed, he might suggest that this inadequacy consists precisely in an exclusive focus on the issue of the causal indeterminacy of a putatively free choice, thereby neglecting the substantive issue of the content of such a choice. His position seems to be that if the latter is ignored, one will be left with nothing more than an empty, abstract freedom, which is not worthy of the name and which corresponds to the so-called "liberty of indifference" that was dismissed by the Leibnizians and many others in the rationalist tradition.

Our present concern, however, is with Hegel's use of this analysis against Kant. According to Hegel, in virtue of his commitment to the categories of abstract understanding, which reflects a failure to attain Hegel's own speculative standpoint, Kant was led to conceive of freedom merely as "arbitrariness" (*Willkür*) or as a "formal self-activity," by which Hegel apparently understood simply the freedom to do as one pleases. Although the most common idea of freedom, it is also the least adequate since by viewing the content of the will's choice (provided by competing drives and inclination) as given to it from without, it reduces the will's freedom to a mere contingency. The latter is a moment of genuine freedom, but Hegel suggests that it is a delusion to take it as equivalent to freedom. And Kant, like all advocates of a "reflective," that is, nonspeculative, philosophy, is deemed subject to this delusion.[56]

Nevertheless, whatever the merits of Hegel's positive account, he seems to have seriously misrepresented Kant's view of free will. Expressed in Kantian terms, what Hegel is doing is characterizing Kantian freedom solely in terms of freedom of choice, thereby ignoring the intimate connection between *Willkür* and *Wille*.[57] In fact, properly understood, freedom for Kant does not consist in the sheer arbitrariness of choice, but in a choice governed by rational norms stemming from *Wille* or practical reason. Much as in Hegel, then, genuine Kantian freedom may be seen as involving a "synthesis" of form and content, with the former stemming from *Willkür* and the latter from *Wille*. The basic difference consists in the location of the source of these norms: in the autonomous pure practical reason of the agent for Kant, and in the objectively existing laws and institutions of a society for Hegel. Admittedly, this is an important difference, but it is one that cannot be considered here.

Arthur Schopenhauer

Schopenhauer's views on free will are of interest here for three reasons. The first is his uncompromising determinism with regard to particular actions, on the basis of which he dismisses a compatibilism such as Leibniz's as an inadequate, even duplicitous "middle way," which endeavors to preserve the term "free will" while emptying it of any sense.[58] The second is the connection of this determinism with a radical voluntarism, which effectively identifies ultimate reality (under the guise of the Kantian thing in itself) with will. The third is his use of Kant's contrast between empirical and intelligible character, which Schopenhauer describes as "the greatest of all achievements of the human mind," to offer an alternative conception of freedom.[59]

Schopenhauer's determinism is based on his appeal to the principle of causality, which he regards as one of the four distinct forms assumed by the principle of sufficient reason. As in Kant, nothing happens without a cause from which it follows necessarily. But rather than recognizing only the familiar mechanical, physical, and chemical causes, Schopenhauer assigned the causes of human actions to its motives insofar as they determine the will.[60] Consequently, Schopenhauer insisted that motives are every bit as much causes as any others since they involve the necessitation of their effects. He also thought that this is not always recognized, however, because of a confusion of the free with the voluntary.

The reason for this confusion is traced to self-consciousness, which makes one aware of a capacity to do as one wills: to choose either A or B, if one so wills. Schopenhauer acknowledged the genuineness of this awareness, but rejected its identification with a consciousness of freedom of the will. The latter concerns a supposed capacity to will what one wills, which he rules out on the grounds that it either directly violates the principle of sufficient reason (since it assumes that there could be a choice without a reason) or leads to an infinite regress, whereby an agent must be thought as willing to will, *ad infinitum*.

Although Schopenhauer regarded motives as causes, he did not view them as alone sufficient to determine the will. Since they always work in conjunction with character, the same motives could lead people with different characters to act in different ways under similar circumstances. Nevertheless, a person with a particular character will always act in the same way under the same circumstances. Thus, to claim that I (Henry Allison) could have acted differently is to say that I could have been a different person. Unfortunately, this is impossible since one can change one's behavior but not one's character, even though we can only discover this character after the fact by considering what we have done. Like many other thinkers, then, Schopenhauer located the ultimate determining ground of voluntary actions in a person's character because it determines the motives by which a person can be moved to act and to what extent that person is susceptible to these motives.

Perhaps the most striking feature of Schopenhauer's account lies in his near identification of character and will, which he viewed as the true core of the self. In other words, Schopenhauer is a voluntaristic determinist.[61] Like other voluntarists, for example, Crusius, he granted primacy to the will over the intellect. Indeed, Schopenhauer regarded the latter merely as an instrument or tool of the former, in the sense that its function is to determine which course of action is best suited to attain the ends projected by the will.[62] Unlike most voluntarists, however, he used this to deny freedom of the will. In fact, according to Schopenhauer, it is precisely the prioritizing of intellect to will in philosophers such as Descartes and Leibniz that led to their erroneous doctrines of free will. His point is that by making will subordinate to intellect, and even reducing volition to an act of thought, these intellectualists effectively reduced the question of what one is to what one knows, thereby assuming that by increasing one's knowledge one can change one's character.[63] Schopenhauer acknowledged that Spinoza did not come to such a conclusion, but he described him as a philosopher who reached the correct (deterministic) conclusion from false premises.[64]

Consequently, Schopenhauer's denial of freedom of the will rests not only on the universal scope of causality and the conception of motives as causes, but also on his core doctrine of the unchangeableness of character. According to Schopenhauer, our (empirical) character is something with which we are born and cannot change.[65]

Greater knowledge and experience may change how we act under given circumstances by making it clear that a certain course of action is good or harmful for us, but it does not fundamentally change who or what we are.

Nevertheless, Schopenhauer reconceived rather than denied freedom and, as noted above, did so by appealing to Kant's distinction between empirical and intelligible character. According to his reading of Kant, a person's empirical character (or will as phenomenon) is the necessary consequence of a timeless choice by the intelligible character (or will as noumenon). The choice must be timeless in order to be free because the principle of sufficient reason governs what occurs in time, and such a timeless choice is conceivable because time pertains merely to the phenomenal realm. Although Schopenhauer attributed this doctrine to Kant, he also suggested that it was anticipated, albeit in a mythopoetic manner, by Plato in his famous "Myth of Er" in the Republic.[66]

Schopenhauer apparently thought also that this doctrine of a timeless choice of character was required to do justice to our sense of moral responsibility. Even though we may know that our particular actions are determined by a combination of character and circumstances and that this character is itself fixed before birth, we nonetheless rightly hold ourselves responsible for our deeds.[67] But given the manner in which the issue is framed, the only way to save the freedom requisite for responsibility ("true moral freedom") is to regard ourselves as responsible for who we are, that is, for our character. And since the latter is innate and unchangeable, this means that we must conceive of our empirical character as the result of a timeless choice.

Although Schopenhauer, like Fichte, presented his view as a reformulation of Kant's position correctly understood, it is doubtful that Kant would have countenanced it. In fact, in spite of some indications to the contrary, it is clear from his example of the malicious lie that Kant would have rejected Schopenhauer's thesis that one chooses one's empirical character out of whole cloth and that freedom consists entirely in this choice. For Kant it is not only the case that such a person could have chosen not to be a liar but also that, given both his character and circumstances, he could at that moment have chosen not to lie. In short, Kant, unlike Schopenhauer, wished to preserve the freedom of particular acts. An agent must be deemed able to have chosen differently under the same circumstances because the categorical imperative dictates that he ought to have done so. But since Schopenhauer famously rejects Kant's conception of morality as based on a categorical imperative, arguing instead for an ethics of sympathy, he has neither need nor room for the Kantian conception of a free action.[68]

NOTES

1. For a systematic discussion of this issue, see Lewis White Beck, *A Commentary on Kant's "Critique of Practical Reason,"* Chicago: University of Chicago Press, 1960, pp. 176–208, and "Five Concepts of Freedom in Kant," *Philosophical Analysis and Reconstruction* (Festschrift for Stephan Körner), J. T. J. Srednick, ed., Dordrecht: Martinus Nijhoff, 1987, pp. 35–51.

2. For a fuller examination of these topics, the reader may wish to consult my *Kant's Theory of Freedom*, Cambridge: Cambridge University Press, 1990, esp. pp. 54–70, 85–106, and *Idealism and Freedom*, Cambridge: Cambridge University Press, 1996, pp. 129–42.

3. *The Leibniz-Clarke Correspondence*, ed. by H. G. Alexander, Manchester: Manchester University Press, 1956, p. 15 (Leibniz's Second Letter, §1). Leibniz refers to both principles, albeit often with somewhat different formulations, in virtually all of his philosophical writings.

4. Leibniz, *Theodicy*, §34, trans. by E. M. Huggard, London: Routledge & Kegan Paul, 1951, p. 143. See also §288, p. 303.

5. See Leibniz, *New Essays on Human Understanding*, Book II, Chap. xxi, §9, translated and edited by Peter Remnant and Jonathan Bennett, Cambridge: Cambridge University Press, 1981

6. Ibid., §8. The formula appears frequently in Leibniz and in the *Theodicy* (§43, p. 147) he suggests that it corresponds to the maxim of the astrologer's, "Astra inclinant, non necessitant."

7. Wolff, *Vernünfftige Gedancken von Gott, der Welt und der Seele des Menschen, Auch allen Dingen Überhaupt*, §31, 5th edition 1781, reprinted by Georg Olms, 1997, vol. 1, pp. 17–18.

8. See Beck, *Early German Philosophy*, Cambridge, MA: Harvard University Press, 1969, p. 259.

9. Wolff, *Vernünfftige Gedancken*, §511, vol. 1, pp. 312–13.

10. Ibid., §519, vol. 1, p. 317.

11. Ibid., §§878–9, vol. 2, pp. 544–6.

12. Ibid. §512, vol. 1, pp. 313–14. For a discussion of Wolff's ethics that highlights this point, see J. B. Schneewind, *The Invention of Autonomy*, Cambridge: Cambridge University Press, 1998, pp. 435–42.

13. The following discussion of Crusius is heavily indebted to Heinz Heimsoeth, *Metaphysik und Kritik bei Chr. A. Crusius*, Berlin: Deutsche Verlagsgesellschaft für Politik und Geschichte, 1926; Beck, *Early German Philosophy*, pp. 394–402; and Schneewind, *The Invention of Autonomy*, pp. 445–56.

14. See Beck, *Early German Philosophy*, pp. 396–7.

15. Ibid, p. 400.

16. Crusius, *Entwurf der notwendigen Vernunftwahrheiten*, §102, in *Die Philosophischen Hauptwerke*, vol. 2; Hildesheim: Georg Olms Verlagsbuchhandlung, 1964, pp. 171–3. See also Beck, *Early German Philosophy*, pp. 399–400.

17. Crusius, *Anweisung vernünftig zu leben*, §1; *Die Philosophischen Hauptwerke*, vol. 1, pp. 2–3.

18. Crusius, *Vernunftwahrheiten*, §427, pp. 826–7; §445, pp. 866–7; Beck, *Early German Philosophy*, p. 401.

19. Crusius, *Vernunftwahrheiten*, §445, pp. 866–7; §454, pp. 885–6.

20. Crusius, *Anweisung*, §40, p. 46; Schneewind, *The Invention of Autonomy*, p. 449

21. Crusius, *Anweisung*, §43, p. 54; Schneewind, *The Invention of Autonomy*, p. 449.

22. Crusius, *Anweisung*, §43, pp. 54–5; Schneewind, *The Invention of Autonomy*, p. 449

23. Kant later used the comparison to the freedom of a turnspit to denigrate the Leibnizian conception in *Practical Reason*, 5:97.

24. *Metaphysik L_1*, 28:268–70. Nevertheless, it should be kept in mind that Kant still wrestled with this problem in his "critical" period. See *Practical Reason*, 5:100–4.

25. See *Groundwork*, 4:448; *Review of Schulz*, 8:14. I discuss this issue in *Kant's Theory of Freedom*, pp. 37–9, and *Idealism and Freedom*, pp. 98–106; 130–4.

26. Nevertheless, there remains a teleological, if not theological, component in Kant's approach to the issue. For example, in the *Groundwork* he speculates that if nature had aimed at our happiness rather than our morality, it would have left things up to instinct rather than to practical reason (4:395).

27. Elsewhere I have termed this the "Incorporation Thesis." See *Kant's Theory of Freedom*, pp. 5–6 and passim, and *Idealism and Freedom*, pp. 118–23, 130–5, and 139–42.

28. See also Kant's earlier claim in the same work that the moral law is the "*ratio cognoscendi* of freedom" (*Practical Reason*, 5:4n).

29. Kant often contrasts a positive and a negative sense of freedom, albeit not always in the same terms. In the *Groundwork*, freedom in the

positive sense is identified with autonomy, while in its negative sense it is understood as the will's capacity to exercise its causality independently of determination by alien causes (4:446). The former is contrasted with heteronomy and the latter with natural necessity.

30. I have termed this the "reciprocity thesis." For my discussion of this thesis, see *Kant's Theory of Freedom*, pp. 201–13 and *Idealism and Freedom*, pp. 136–8 and *passim*.

31. I analyze this deduction and the subsequent doctrine of the fact of reason in *Kant's Theory of Freedom*, pp. 214–49.

32. For my discussion of this distinction, see *Kant's Theory of Freedom*, pp. 129–36

33. For my most recent analysis of the arguments of the third antinomy, see *Kant's Transcendental Idealism*, Revised and Enlarged Edition, New Haven and London: Yale University Press, 2004, pp. 376–84.

34. The reader should be apprised of the fact that the proper interpretation of Kant's transcendental idealism remains an extremely controversial matter. Although the basic issue is whether the appearance–thing in itself distinction is be understood as holding between two kinds of thing (the "two-world" view) or between two ways of considering the same thing (the "two-aspect" view), there are a number of other points in dispute (including the correct understanding of the latter view). I discuss this topic, including the relation between transcendental idealism and transcendental realism, in *Kant's Transcendental Idealism*, esp. pp. 20–73.

35. Most notably Beck, "Five Concepts of Freedom in Kant" and *The Actor and the Spectator*, New Haven: Yale University Press, 1975, and Stephan Körner, "Reply to Professor Beck," *Philosophical Analysis and Reconstruction*, pp. 52–8.

36. This is from the draft of a letter to Jens Baggessen, April/May 1795. The citation is from Daniel Breazeale, editor's introduction to J. G. Fichte, *Introductions to the Wissenschaftslehre and Other Writings*, translated and edited by Daniel Breazeale, Indianapolis: Hackett Publishing Company, Inc., 1994, p. vii note. Breazeale also cites similar claims from other letters.

37. *Zweite Einleitung in die Wissenschaftslehre, in Fichtes Werke*, herausgegeben von Immanuel Hermann Fichte, Berlin: Walter de Gruyter & Co., 1971, Band I, pp. 468–9. *Introductions to the Wissenschaftslehre and Other Writings*, p. 52.

38. According to Breazeale, Fichte initially affirmed this principle in his "Review of *Aenesidemus*." See Breazeale, editor's introduction to his edition and translation of *Fichte, Early Philosophical Writings*, Ithaca and London: Cornell University Press, 1988, pp. 14–16.

39. In the "Second Introduction to the *Wissenschaftslehre*," Fichte denied that such a doctrine was actually asserted by Kant himself. See *Fichtes Werke*, I, pp. 481–9; *Introductions to the Wissenschaftslehre*, pp. 66–76.

40. For Kant the distinction between the two standpoints is grounded in his foundational doctrine that there are two indispensable and irreducible sources of cognition: sensibility, through which objects are given in intuition, and understanding, through which they are thought by means of concepts (See *Pure Reason*, A 50–2/B 74–6). Although both are necessary for cognition, the understanding has a broader scope since it contains rules for the thought of "objects in general," regardless of how they may be given in sensibility. And for Kant this is what allows us to think, though not cognize, things as they are in themselves. I discuss the connection between Kant's two cognitive faculty doctrine, which I term the "Discursivity Thesis," transcendental idealism, and his critique of transcendental realism in the first two chapters of *Kant's Transcendental Idealism*.

41. *Fichtes Werke*, I, pp. 429–31; *Introductions to the Wissenschaftslehre*, pp. 15–16

42. *Fichtes Werke*, I, p. 434; *Introductions to the Wissenschaftslehre*, p. 20.

43. *Fichtes Werke*, I, p. 505; *Introductions to the Wissenschaftslehre*, p. 90.

44. I am here largely following the account of Frederick Neuhouser, *Fichte's Theory of Subjectivity*, Cambridge: Cambridge University Press, 1990, esp. pp. 121–31.

45. *Fichtes Werke*, III, p. 39; *Foundations of Natural Right*, edited by Frederick Neuhouser and translated by Michael Bauer, Cambridge: Cambridge University Press, 2000, p. 37.

46. *Fichtes Werke*, IV, p. 59.

47. Ibid., p. 212.

48. Ibid., pp. 66, 149, 229.

49. Hegel, *Grundlinien der Philosophie des Rechts* (*Elements of the Philosophy of Right*), §23. The following discussion is indebted to that of Frederick Neuhouser, *Foundations of Hegel's Social Theory: Actualizing Freedom*, Cambridge, MA: Harvard University Press, 2000, esp. pp. 18–54.

50. Hegel, *Phänomenologie des Geistes*, "Die Wahrheit der Gewissheit seiner Selbst," *Phenomenology of Spirit*, trans. by A. V. Miller, Oxford: Oxford University Press, 1977, p. 109–10, §§175–7.

51. This is the central theme of the various versions of Hegel's *Lectures on the Philosophy of World History*.

52. Hegel, *Elements of the Philosophy of Right*, §4.

53. Ibid., §4 *Zusatz*.

54. Ibid.

55. Ibid., §21 *Zusatz.*
56. Ibid., §15.
57. This misrepresentation is pointed out by Allen Wood in his editorial notes to the English translation of the text *Elements of the Philosophy of Right*, trans. by H. B. Nisbet, Cambridge: Cambridge University Press, 1991, p. 399n2.
58. Schopenhauer, *Essay on the Freedom of the Will*, trans. by Konstantin Kolenda, Indianapolis and New York: The Bobbs-Merrill Company, Inc., 1960, p. 15.
59. Schopenhauer, *Essay on the Freedom of the Will*, p. 15.
60. See Schopenhauer, *The Fourfold Root of the Principle of Sufficient Reason*, trans. by E. F. J. Payne, LaSalle, IL: Open Court Publishing, 1974, esp. pp. 70–2; and *Essay on the Freedom of the Will*, pp. 36–7.
61. Although some subsequent philosophers, most notably Nietzsche, who was himself deeply influenced by Schopenhauer, fit this category, most of his predecessors on this score appear to have been theologians, for example, Luther, intent on defending the doctrine of original sin.
62. See, for example, *Essay on the Freedom of the Will*, p. 101.
63. Schopenhauer, *The World as Will and Representation*, trans. by E. F. J. Payne, Indian Hills, CO: The Falcon's Wing Press, 1958, vol. 1, p. 292.
64. Ibid., p. 298.
65. Schopenhauer, *Essay on the Freedom of the Will*, pp. 54–5.
66. Schopenhauer, *On the Basis of Morality*, pp. 113–14.
67. Schopenhauer, *Essay on the Freedom of the Will*, pp. 91–9; *On the Basis of Morality*, pp. 112–13.
68. I wish to express my gratitude to Klaus Brinkmann for his helpful comments on a draft of the third part of this essay.

12 Mine and thine? The Kantian state

For if justice goes, there is no longer any value in human beings living on the earth.

(*Morals*, 6:332; 105)[1]

I

According to Kant, a

condition of the individuals within a people in relation to one another is called a civil condition (*status civilis*), and the whole of individuals in a rightful condition, in relation to its members is called a state (*civitas*).

(*Morals*, 6:311; 89)

A fuller definition of such a state or *civitas* follows.

A state (*civitas*) is a union of a multitude of human beings under laws of right. Insofar as these are *a priori* necessary as laws, that is insofar as they follow of themselves from concepts of external right as such (are not statuary), its form is the form of a state as such, that is, of the state in idea, as it ought to be in accordance with pure principles of right. This idea serves as a norm (*norma*) for every actual union into a commonwealth (hence serves as a norm for its internal constitution).

(6:313; 90)

This state is formally republican, in that the sovereign acts in the name of all subjects, and it should consist of a separation of (but not a true balance of) powers.[2] The state's main function is the protection of property rights and the regulation of disputes about property and contract, and its sovereignty is absolute (there is no "right of revolution"; revolution is always absolutely forbidden). Finally, citizen participation is strictly limited to what Kant calls active citizens, adult male property owners, and not women, domestics, nor "anyone whose preservation in existence... depends not on his management of his own business but on arrangements made by another" (6:314; 92).

However extreme these last two conclusions now strike us, this account of the state fits into a recognizable liberal tradition. The familiar problem concerns the use of coercion (the threat of violence) against individuals presumed to be autonomous, or capable of self-determination.[3] Kant's solution to that problem clearly follows one of the two familiar paths in liberalism designed to address it. As these quotations indicate, Kant does not directly link the state's function to the welfare, happiness, or security of its citizens, and does not link the claim to state authority to any implied or presumed act of consent.[4] Instead he ties the justification of its authority to the protection of the basic entitlements shared by all free rational beings. Such a right or entitlement claim – or rather the "one innate" or natural right according to Kant, freedom in its "external" manifestations – is said to place all others under an obligation, and this fact will ultimately form the basis of the state's authority. That authority is to be the authority of a noninstrumental practical reason (a stateless condition is wrong because, in a way that needs to be specified, it is irrational for rational free beings to accept or contrary to the demands of pure practical reason), but, as the second passage indicates, a "rightful" condition is to be determined by *pure* practical reason with *a priori* necessity, and so does not appeal to an instrumentally rational goal that all must be presumed to seek.

Such an empirically unaided reason is supposed to be able to justify two claims: why there ought to be such a rightful or just "union," a state, and what characteristics it must have. That is, Kant does not argue merely that a civil order is morally permissible, considered perhaps as a rational cooperation problem *consistent* with one's moral standing as a free, rational being. Rather, anyone willing to remain in a pre-civil state is not just an irrational noncooperator, but thereby does "*wrong* in the highest degree" ("*unrecht... im höchsten Grad*") (6:308; 86) and such a civil condition must be understood as some sort of *requirement* of pure practical reason. (It is practically necessary, not just permissible.) The problem is: *what sort of requirement is this?*[5] The duty to exit the state of nature (*exeundum e statu naturali*) is said to be a distinct duty of right (*Rechtspflicht*), not of virtue, and the claim itself (that there is a *duty* of justice) is integral to his defense of right, not supplemental to it.[6] I propose to discuss here how Kant thinks this justification works and what characteristics follow from it. This has become relatively familiar territory by now and the various alternatives are well known. But I also want to suggest that Kant's often meandering, confusing argument is, at its core, far more radical and suggestive than it has been given credit for, suggestive even of a wholly different strand of liberalism.

There are two main steps in the basic argument of the *Rechtslehre*. The first involves the status of this particular definition of the concept of right and so why it uniquely defines the requirement of pure practical reason among self-determining beings who can act externally, that is who can act in such a way that that action restricts the possible freedom of action another would otherwise have. The definition of the concept of right is: "the sum of the conditions under which the choice of one can be unified with the choice of another in accordance with a universal law of freedom" (*Morals*, 6:230; 24). An alternate version of the question would be why we are bound, constrained in our "external" actions, by this *Universal Principle of Right*:

Any action is right if it can coexist with everyone's freedom in accordance with a universal law, or if on its maxim the freedom of choice of each can co-exist with everyone's freedom in accordance with a universal law.

(6:230; 24)[7]

The second question involves the extraordinarily important role given *property* in the argument. The definition of the concept of right had referred to "the sum of conditions" in which a mutual exercise of freedom is possible (and without which is impossible). In the core argument of Private Right we learn that there is one condition essential to any principled establishment of such mutuality: an intelligible distinction between mine and thine, or the securing of property rights, and that this distinction can be made "*only*" in one way: "in a rightful condition," that is, "under an authority giving Laws publicly," that is, "in a civil condition," a state (6:255; 44). Clearly if the problem is figuring out the requirements of pure practical reason among beings who can act in such a way that their actions restrict the possible freedom of action another would otherwise have, the

solution is: mutually assured reciprocal observance of the boundary
between mine and thine. (We will obviously require an account of
why and how this reciprocal observance is to be assured.) The primary institution in modern bourgeois society as Kant sees it is private property, and the primary authority of the state stems from its
role in securing property rights. But we cannot deduce *a priori* what
is mine and what is thine, and that fact will lead Kant into some very
interesting, speculative claims about not just property but our social
or concretely practical identities as agents.

II

So Kant wants to claim that there is some condition under which the
claims of right – the claims of each to an exercise of external freedom
formally compatible with a like exercise by all – can be realized. This
condition is in general "the exit from the state of nature" (*exeundum
e statu naturali*), the rule of law, ceding the right to decide in your
own case to a public authority. In particular it involves the setting
of the boundaries between mine and thine, or moving from a provisional claim to property to a settled and certain claim. As noted,
his first problem is to make clear what sort of claim on each other
a claim of right is, especially since Kant wants, on the one hand, to
distinguish claims of right from general claims of moral entitlement
and moral duty. Most obviously compliance with claims of right may
and ought to be coerced, but ethical duties to others cannot and ought
not to be coerced. Coercing someone to adopt a morally obligatory
end is to fail to treat him as an end in itself, and Kant makes clear
frequently that he despises all forms of paternalism.[8] But coerced
compliance with claims of right involves no such lack of respect.
Quite the contrary, as we have seen, failing to compel or to support
a system of coerced compliance is a "wrong in the highest degree"
and would be to fail to accord another her proper status as a rational and free being, entitled to an external sphere where that freedom
may be exercised. And yet, on the other hand, despite this distinction between right and morality, the very form of the *Metaphysics
of Morals* suggests that claims of right are in some sense a *subset*
of our moral obligations to others, leading commentators to look for
some way to understand claims of right as an "application" of Kant's
highest moral principle, the categorical imperative, or in some other

way derived from the requirements of Kant's general moral theory. (Let us call these commentators the "derivationists.")

Kant's first official demarcation gives some comfort to the derivationists' claims about legal duties. Kant contrasts "laws of nature" with *all* "laws of freedom," and calls *all* of the latter "laws of morality." He then classifies, as subcategories of such *moral* laws, "juridical laws," those "directed merely to external actions," with respect to their mere conformity to law (6:220; 14).[9] And this classification introduces the most familiar opposition that Kant almost always appeals to in distinguishing these types of claims – external versus internal "use of choice" (*Gebrauche der Willkür*). They (all laws of freedom) are distinguished by the kind of "law-giving" appropriate to each, outer or inner, and he suggests that this alone might demarcate the types. So-called external laws are those for which external lawgiving (such as is created by the threat of punishment) is *possible*; in the case of moral or internally legislated laws, such external coercion is not possible (fulfillment of duties of virtue would not *be* fulfillment of the duty if motivated by fear of punishment; we would not have adopted the end). So if we make a promise, we would be dutybound, as a duty of morality, to keep the promise, even if there were no external constraint. But since such fulfillment involves actions in the "external domain," coerced compliance here is also possible and so Kant even says that "It is no duty of virtue to keep one's promises but a duty of right" (6:220; 21).

By saying that it is not a duty of virtue, he means that it is not a duty to adopt an end "internally," such as the perfection of our talents, or beneficence. But he still appears to have confused things by not noting that duties of virtue and enforceable rights claims do not exhaust all categories of obligation. There are, for example, perfect duties to oneself that need not involve such end-setting, but which are also forbidden by their very nature or form – such as suicide – compliance with which would still count as compliance even with no such internal motivation. Yet they do not seem a fit subject for criminalization. Likewise, there are some perfect duties to others that are forbidden by their very form, do not require the adoption of an end, but do not seem violations of juridical right. The cases of promising and truth-telling are the most obvious. I may refrain from lying when I could have lied, but from a nonmoral motive, with no internal legislation, and I would still have conformed to duty. And Kant himself admits that not all broken promises or lies are violations of right.[10] He notes that lies to others do not automatically count as violations of right because the addressee can choose to believe them or not, and we do not want a paternalistic state making those decisions for you. (It is when you count on a promise and suffer some harm from its nonfulfillment that the violation is a violation of right.) He thus admits in a footnote that there is indeed a boundary problem in drawing what he calls a "borderline" (*Grenzlinie*) between what belongs to *Ius* or right, and what to ethics.

It would take a separate article to sort out these various uses of "external" and "internal," but all we need to note here is that in this discussion of when lying should count as a violation of right, Kant points us in the important direction suggested earlier. He makes use of an interesting criterion in setting off as allowable an authorization "to do to others anything *that does not in itself diminish what is theirs*" (6:238; 30, my emphasis). This suggests again that if we want to know which sorts of claims on others are fit subjects of legislation, we will learn more from the concrete problem of determining the boundary between "mine and thine in the external sphere" than we will be able to see from the principle of right itself.

III

But the initial problem still remains: what *sort* of normative claim on others is a rights claim? There are three alternatives in the most recent literature, and I pause to summarize them here, mostly because I think they will again suggest that the alternative strategies all introduce more questions than they answer and so indirectly suggest that there might be much more to be learned from what I will call the "core" argument in the *Doctrine of Right*: about why it is "wrong" for free rational beings not to cede to a public authority the power to decide what is mine and thine.

As mentioned, there is first the direct "derivation" view, and we have already seen passages where Kant seems to subsume his principle of right under moral law and freely to apply moral notions of imperative and obligation in a political context.[11] Kant's moral theory defends the categorical imperative as the highest moral principle, and the very formulation of the Universal Principle of Right (with its reference to a universal law of freedom) strongly suggests that Kant is thinking of some derivation from that principle. And most of the standard commentaries on the *Doctrine of Right* defend some view of the claim that the highest principle of justice is derived in some way from the basic elements of Kant's moral theory. Otfried Höffe has argued that Kant's moral theory rests on a "general" categorical imperative, which then can be shown to have specific, demarcated forms: a formal rule of impermissibility in ethics, a "material" use in the specification of obligatory ends, as in the doctrine of virtue, and a juridical form, manifested in Kant's doctrine of Private Right and Public Right.[12] And so he claims that "however Kant separates Law from Ethics, he does not separate it from the moral point of view."[13] Wolfgang Kersting insists that "the justification of Kant's philosophy of right depends on his moral philosophy" and speaks regularly of "the categorical imperative of reason in the realm of right."[14] Mary Gregor has reasonably claimed that the central notion of Kant's political theory, right, since it means "capacity to place others under obligation," relies in a foundational way on a general moral notion of obligation.[15] Leslie Mulholland makes frequent, explicit use of the language of derivation and regularly invokes phrases like a "moral title to obligate others" when analyzing Kant on rights.[16] And there are many other such interpretations. (One might add to this list Bernd Ludwig, H.-F. Fulda, Roger Sullivan, Onora O'Neill, and Paul Guyer.)

Now, as far as I know, none of the major commentators who take this line make the mistake of thinking that the way in which the principle of right depends for its normative, binding status on moral principles means that Kant, in accounting for the obligatory character of right, is relying on some theory of moral motivation or requiring some moral acknowledgment of the claims of others. Everyone seems well aware of Kant's claim that no "internal legislation" is needed to account for our obligation to enter a civil order or to obey public law. The state makes no moral claim on its citizens, and the claim of right that is made must be accounted for as a distinct claim, even while still a *binding* rational requirement. Moreover, aside from Kersting, no one seems to think that Kant's position is like the one defended by Fichte in his 1793 remarks on the French Revolution – that, given our general moral obligations, we must do what we can to make the realization of our moral vocation more empirically, socially realizable; and that no one should be indifferent to the social conditions necessary for us to be able to do our duty more – rather than less – effectively. (We certainly *have* such duties for Kant, but in his account they are clearly imperfect ethical duties, not duties of right.)

But what is troubling for this position is that Kant nowhere argues for any such even indirectly moral status for principles of right. It appears that he attempts no derivation, works through no "application," and even though the *Groundwork* is supposed to be laying the foundation for the entirety of the *Metaphysics of Morals*, he suggests no direct route from the former to the latter. If we are supposed to think of the moral law as being "applied" to a sphere of human activity distinct enough to yield specific principles of right, our options seem quite limited. If the sphere is external exercises of will (the domain where my exercise of freedom restricts what you would otherwise be able to do), it would appear that such an application would just yield a prohibition on actions whose maxims cannot be universalized and a general imperfect duty not to ignore but to aid our fellow man. We might add a general right of self-defense, an "authorization" to resist those who illegitimately "hinder" permissible exercises of freedom, but we will have thereby not generated any requirement of public law.

All of which is grist for the mill of the "separationists." There are passages that seem to argue strongly for some sort of complete methodological autonomy for principles of right. Commentators like Allen Wood and Marcus Willaschek have noted that Kant (a) holds that the principle of right is analytic, which seems to mean that Kant is trying to present only the necessary form of rational free wills in external relations and is arguing that the authority to coerce compliance with this form follows analytically from the notion itself (that any "hindrance to the hindering" of freedom is permissible).[17] And (b) Kant calls the universal law of right a "postulate that is incapable of further proof" (6:231; 25), also suggesting he has no derivation in mind, despite his occasional "deduction" language. Finally, Kant says that the universal law of right,

is indeed a law that lays an obligation on me, but it does not at all expect, far less demand, that I myself should limit my freedom to those conditions just for the sake of this obligation; instead, reason says only that freedom *is* limited to those conditions in conformity with the idea of it and that it may also be actively [*tätlich*] limited by others.   (6:231; 25)

Claims like this have led Willaschek to argue that the realm of right is an "expression of human autonomy akin to, but independent of, the moral domain," and so that the principle of right is an "independent, basic law of practical rationality," a different sort of "expression of human autonomy."[18] And Wood has argued that, with this claim of analyticity, Kant seems "explicitly to discredit the whole idea that the principle of right is derived from the fundamental principle of morality"[19] with his claim about analyticity, and that juridical duties "belong to a branch of the metaphysics of morals that is *entirely independent* of ethics and also of its supreme principle."[20]

However, in the first place, the claims of analyticity and claims about postulates are not decisive evidence, as Paul Guyer has already shown. Analytic results based on spurious or arbitrary concepts do not establish anything of importance, and so Kant must understand his analysis of right to depend on what is already presumed in the "legitimate" concept of human freedom, namely, that we are subject to the requirements of pure practical reason, which is itself a synthetic claim.[21] Likewise, Kant does not claim that postulates require no proof, but that their proof is "constructive" (as in mathematics) rather than deductive, or, in the practical case, as making disputable claims about the conditions that, according to Guyer, are "necessary for the possibility of fulfilling a moral command."[22] Indeed the passage itself says that the law of right is a postulate incapable of *further* proof, implying that presenting a postulate *is* a proof of some kind. (Kant also says clearly that the authorization to acquire property and so impose an obligation on others that they would not otherwise have "could *not* be got from the mere concept of right as such" and for this reason is a "postulate" [6:247; 41; my emphasis].

Moreover, the passage quoted earlier (6:231) does insist that the law of right *lays an obligation on me* (something that would have ultimately to presuppose some synthetic claim) and carefully qualifies what is *not* laid on me by simply saying that duties of right do not, as moral duties do, require of us that we obey "for the sake of this obligation."[23] There is nothing surprising in such a claim. And in the light of all this it is hard even to understand Willaschek's position. It costs Kant no small amount of trouble to show that we are unconditionally obligated to the requirements of pure practical reason. If the principle of right is likewise such a rational requirement but not "covered" by that general argument, we would then face the task all over again, presumably in some completely independent, nonmoral way, of "deducing" or showing through the "exposition" of some new "fact of reason" that *those* requirements must also be conformed to.

This leaves us in a troubling aporia. The derivationists are right to insist that the principle of right be connected in some way with Kant's overall moral theory. Kant after all not infrequently notes that "all duties [*Pflichten*], just because they are duties, belong to ethics [*Ethik*]" (6:219; 21), and he says this a few pages before he introduces what he explicitly calls "duties of right" (6:236–7; 29). But such proponents cannot provide passages or reconstruct arguments that state and defend such a connection or subsumption (at least not without making political duties something like imperfect duties of virtue). The separationists, who want *Recht* and *Moral* strictly separate, are right that our obligation to leave the state of nature and our absolute duty to obey rightly constituted law are not moral duties as Kant normally understands them, and they make no appeal to "internal" legislation. Kant does after all *also* say, in glossing what he calls "strict right," that it "is not mingled with anything ethical" (6:232; 25). But that position still leaves us wondering what sort of claim on us *is* made by the rational form of free wills in external relations. Too much connection and derivation, and duties of justice look too much like moral duties or imperfect duties of virtue; too much distinctness and there seems to be no basis for Kant's claims about the "bindingness" (*Verbindlichkeit*, to use his explicit claim) of "duties of right."

Third, I note briefly one other, final variation on this theme, that suggested by Guyer in the article already noted, and in several others. (It is also exemplified in an interesting early article by Thomas Pogge.)[24] We might be going off track in this investigation of the normative authority of claims of right by trying to track exclusively the implications of the requirements of pure practical reason, by concentrating only on how our obedience to a moral law might be said to cover in a distinct way special cases where coercive compliance is warranted and required. We might do better by noting that it is essentially the rule of law that allows us to engage at all in an activity that Kant at least once defines as the distinguishing mark of humanity itself: the setting and pursuit of our own ends.[25] The argument might go: without giving up the right to determine mine-thine in one's own case and without the rule of law, this faculty cannot be effectively exercised and so our basic humanity would go unrealized. We would then have a natural contrast between political duties (rules necessary for the possible pursuit of *any* end) and broad, imperfect ethical duties to aid others in the pursuit of their actual ends. We could then understand right as "derived" from this broader concept of freedom and this suggested central place in the moral theory because it specifies the "conditions necessary for the instantiation of the concept of freedom in relations among persons."[26] The condition of right would be a "postulate" then in the same way that the Practical Postulates establish the conditions of belief necessary for the realization of our moral vocation.

This interpretation rests on too many controversial claims to be treated adequately here, but because it seems so natural to treat liberal politics as the protection of our entitlement to chart the course of our own life, where that ability must be of some serious moral significance, it deserves a brief hearing. The interpretation especially requires seeing the heart of Kant's moral theory not as obligation, law, and the formal constraints of pure practical reason, but as resting on "the unconditional value for human beings" of "the freedom of human choice and action itself,"[27] where this is understood as the power to set moral as well as nonmoral ends, and where adherence to the moral law is necessary only as (according to Guyer) a "means to the preservation and promotion of freedom."[28] The basic claim is: "only if we can find an objective and thus universally compelling end that can give rise to a universal law can we explain why rational beings should be bound by such a law in the first place."[29] Thus the position on right:

The fundamental principle of morality dictates the protection of the external use of freedom or freedom of action, as a natural expression of choice and thus as part of autonomy as a whole.[30]

So, freedom of choice in the external realm is to be understood as part of the "natural expression of autonomy" and we can thereby explain why a public coercive system, or the state's threat of punishment, is morally required to defend such a capacity, given that Kant so frequently extols the value and special status of human autonomy, and given that some expressions of freedom would restrict possibilities others would otherwise have. (Whether the exercise of such nonmoral freedom is actually such an "expression" or "part" of our *moral* capacity to act on the dictates of pure practical reason, and thereby anywhere near as valuable for Kant as moral autonomy, is another story. It is hard to see how the often banal and ordinary exercise of the freedom of choice alone is of the requisite Kantian awe-inspiring dimensions. And how can a nonautonomous exercise of *Willkür* be a "part" or "expression" of pure self-legislation or autonomy?) The doctrine of right can then on this account be connected with the moral theory, but only if we interpret that theory as a substantive value theory and only secondarily as a deontology. This would give us a much easier way of seeing what is our intrinsically valuable capacity and why it would be irrational not to secure the minimal conditions that would allow its exercise in a shared, finite world.[31]

There is not much textual evidence for this view in the *Doctrine of Right*, and most of its official formulations refer insistently, as we shall see, to the formal problems of rational consistency in the acquisition of rights and so to the formal requirements of law. There is very little evidence for much beyond such formulaic claims, and these alone do not get us very far. Guyer's reasonable point is that we will not understand what is *wrong* with ignoring such constraints unless we are able to see that adhering to them is the essential "means" for keeping faith with an intrinsic, supreme value. This all might lead one to think that Guyer has in mind a reconstruction of some Kantian, nonempirical case for this claim that freedom *is* an absolutely superordinate value, but Guyer honestly admits (i) that what looks like Kant's argument – that we can determine freedom (as the exercise of our rational capacities) to be the ultimate end or purpose "given" by nature to man – is unacceptable, and (ii) that there is, finally, no case at all in Kant for such a claim about freedom. The ultimate value of freedom is simply indemonstrable. He does say that Kant believes that "only by seeing ourselves as free can we import a source of unconditional value into the world,"[32] but wishing there were such an unconditional value, or noting what would be the case if there was not such a value, does not make it so.

Moreover, it *is* quite possible to summarize Kant's position by saying that human beings are the subjects of their own lives, and so cannot be objects in ours; they are ends in themselves and therewith possess "inestimable," incomparable worth. But what that *means* in the practical context – what it means that they have such worth – is just that one may not act in a way that arrogates to oneself a unique, exceptional status that cannot be accorded to all equally. And all *that* means is that we must adopt no maxim that could not be willed simultaneously by all or serve as a universal law of nature. It sends us in an ultimately non-Kantian direction to claim that a course of action is our duty *because* fulfilling that duty is a "means" to respect and realize freedom, primarily because it is already the case for Kant that we stand in an obligatory relation to such a status – we are duty bound to respect the status of each as an end in itself, a free being.[33] So Guyer's formulation would require that we say: we are obligated to the categorical imperative because it is the effective means to fulfill our obligation to the categorical imperative.

Finally, it is not at all clear whether this language of ultimate value and means to realize it can return us somehow to Kant's strict distinction between duties of right (which may be coercively enforced) and imperfect duties of virtue. It is quite reasonable to argue that we must not only exercise our own capacity of choice and do nothing to prohibit others from exercising theirs, but that we must do what we can to ensure the "conditions" under which all of us can so exercise our entitlement. And we could add that anyone hindering our exercise of such a right may be permissibly resisted, but we have yet no argument for the *exeundum e statu naturali* that Kant's case requires, and in form we seem to be arguing again only for imperfect duties, duties of wide latitude to do what we can to ensure that all may have a chance at securing their ends.

IV

One reason that it is so difficult to find an adequate account of the normative legitimacy of the state's monopoly on coercive violence is that Kant packs much more of his answer to this question deep in the details of his argument than he ever states programmatically. His "answer" is essentially contained not in the introductory material but in two dense paragraphs of the Private Right section, §8 and §9. These contain the core of his case. It amounts to: the unacceptability to free rational beings of *res nullius* (objects treated as if not capable of being property), and the claim that the state or the public rule of law is the "only" way (as he says in the title to §8) to ensure such intelligible possession, or "*possessio noumenon.*" (Kant is here making an unusual use of the distinction so important to the *Critique of*

Pure Reason. In that work, Kant had, he believed, fatally criticized the assumption on which all rational metaphysics had been built: that unaided pure reason is capable of determining the true nature of things as they are in themselves. He did not deny that reason could formulate a determinate view of how the world must be, or could not be, but he denied we could make defensible cognitive claims about these determinations. We know only "phenomena," objects subject to our cognitive conditions, namely, space and time and the pure categories of the understanding. However, this also meant that human reason was not capable of refuting, of adjudicating at all, theoretical claims about the nature of things. There might then be purely practical reasons for assuming something about the nature of things, which theoretical reason could neither refute nor confirm. In this case, Kant is pointing to the difference between physical possession, confirmation of which is simply a matter of empirical fact, and a relation to objects secured through a relation between rational wills. There is no possible empirical or metaphysical confirmation of such a property claim [and so it is "noumenal," a determination of pure reason], but according to Kant's critical philosophy, there could be a case made by pure practical reason for the possibility and even the practical necessity of such a relation, which case need fear no theoretical refutation. That is what he proposes to do next.)

So the unacceptability of *res nullius* and the state alone making possible *possessio noumenon* are the claims that reveal how Kant thinks his theory of justice relates to his moral theory, and why he thinks he can make this connection but yet still introduce the requirement of coercion for rights claims and so can defend the distinctness, the nonmoral yet "binding" status, of duties of right.

On the latter issue, it is useful to note first how different the formulations in the *Doctrine of Right* sound from Kant's earlier formulations. The key difference has to do with Kant's earlier (or *Groundwork*) position on the radical independence of the moral point of view and his later position on the social conditions necessary for an effective fulfillment of our general obligations to self and other. In the *Groundwork* (1785), writing about the end-in-itself formulation of the moral law, he had claimed,

But a rational being, though he scrupulously follow this maxim, cannot for that reason expect every other rational being to be true to it; nor can he expect the realm of nature and its orderly design to harmonize with him as a fitting member of a realm of ends which is possible through himself.... Still the law: Act according to the maxims of a universally legislative member of a potential realm of ends, remains in full force, because it commands categorically. And just in this lies the paradox that merely the dignity of humanity as rational nature without any end or advantage to be gained by it, and thus respect for a mere idea, should serve as the inflexible precept of the will.[34]

The overall drift here is clear. Respect for a "mere idea," obedience to the moral law, might mean you are the only rational being so constraining his will, and that might mean you are pretty bad off. But life is tough, and therein lies the glory of obedience anyway.

Twelve years later, Kant would write that, without the mutual assurances a state provides, each person or people or state "has its own right to do what seems right and good to it and not to be dependent upon another's opinion about this" (Morals, 6:312; 90). And in the state of nature, "human beings *do one another no wrong at all* when they feud among themselves" (6:308; 86; my emphasis). These are remarks that rest on Kant's original claim about external relations among free beings, that "I am not under obligation to leave external objects belonging to others untouched unless everyone provides me assurance that he will behave in accordance with the same principle with regard to what is mine" (6:255–6; 44). The gist here is clear too. Pure practical reason may be able to formulate the rational form of relations holding between free wills in external relations, but these cannot obligate me unless precisely that condition that, in the *Groundwork* quotation, Kant said we could not count on – that every other rational being would act likewise – be in fact *made something we can count on*. The principle of all external relations among rational wills is clear enough – respect the distinction between mine and thine – but its binding force is conditional: I will respect yours only if I can be assured that you will respect mine. (And this of course requires some reliable determination of what counts as mine and thine.)

But Kant has not really changed his mind about anything, just shifted emphasis. Consider the two parts of his case. First, he claims that objects belonging to no one would be "contrary to right" (6:251; 41). This is so because "freedom would be depriving itself of the use of its choice with regard to an object of choice." Objects that could be used in a way appropriate for beings responsive to reason, not just sensible determinations, would arbitrarily and irrationally not be so used. This would in effect "annihilate objects in a practical respect," and since there is nothing "in" objects that could be said to justify such a restriction, freedom would be denying its own capacity to make use of material objects, especially land, as rational means in the furtherance of its ends. It would be accepting a restriction – that nothing can be held in exclusive possession – that there is no reason, given the sort of being we are, for us to accept.

Further, a free being must be able to exercise this capacity *as such a free being*.[35] Not only must exclusive possession be possible for such a being, but nonphysical exclusive possession must be possible. This is possession not limited by the physical properties of nature, and this is necessary because acquisition and use of objects "has to do with a determination of choice in accordance with laws of freedom" (6:253; 43). Limiting rightful use to actual possession would also be to accept a limitation there is no reason to accept, one that unjustifiably contravenes the fact that agents can establish intelligible relations with one another (relations based on common recognition of an idea) and thereby intelligible relations with natural objects. The demonstration proceeds exactly in the unusual way Kant describes at the end of §7, that practical reason in this case – our attempt to determine what ought to obtain in the accomplishment of my ends, given that I am a being responsive to reasons – "extends" itself "without intuitions," simply by dropping or leaving out "empirical conditions" not appropriate as restrictions of a free rational being. By doing so, we end up with the social form that free beings must adopt in their pursuit of ends.

Such beings must be able to avail themselves of exclusive possession in the accomplishment of their ends, and that possession need not be restricted to the empirical conditions of physical possession or proximity. Given that I am a being that can institute rational relations with others, I ought to be able to secure such nonphysical ownership by such relations with others. But, Kant points out, I can not do that by a mere decree.

Now a unilateral will cannot serve as a coercive law for everyone with regard to possession that is external and therefore contingent, since that would infringe upon freedom in accordance with universal laws. So it is only a will putting everyone under obligation, hence only a collective general (common) and powerful will, that can provide everyone that assurance.   (6:256; 45)

Thus, Kant concludes with what is in effect the thesis of the work itself: "only in a civil condition can something external be mine or yours" (6:256; 45).

This then all amounts not to a shift in Kant's basic position, as if he is now arguing for empirical conditions of the possibility of moral duty as such. That remains unconditioned and categorical. But it is in effect Kant's way of addressing, *avant la lettre*, one of the oldest criticisms of his moral theory, that it is an empty formalism, and cannot be action guiding. Kant is here *himself* emphasizing that, on the one hand, pure practical reason can determine the necessary form of the relation of free wills in external relation – they must exercise their freedom in a way consistent with a like exercise of all. Then, with a wholly uncontroversial empirical addition – that the human world is finite – we can also stipulate that there will be actions that unavoidably limit what another would otherwise be able to do, and so the principle of right is a general, formal principle for resolving the unavoidable conflict between claims of mine and thine. And so we can rationally determine the general conditions of rightful acquisition, or what Kant calls original acquisition. Thus, we can conclude,

All men are originally in common possession of the land of the entire earth (*communio fundi originaria*) and each has by nature the will to use it (*lex iusti*) which, because the choice of one is unavoidably opposed by nature to that of another, would do away with the use of it if this will did not also contain the principle for choice by which a particular possession for each on the common land could be determined.   (6:267; 54)

This principle of choice must be a fully general will (not the will of one of the parties), powerful enough to establish the assurances that make any agreement to cede the right in one's own case actually reciprocal.

So far so good, but it is also now clear that Kant is insisting that in effect pure practical reason on its own is powerless to determine the *content* of any such resolution according to principle, and that that too has rational implications. The (rational) unacceptability of the state of nature is that it is a state of inteterminacy, that while we can clearly state that we are bound to respect the boundary between mine and thine, we have no way of deducing from our rational principle what *in concreto* is rightfully mine and thine. There may be minimal requirements for original acquisition (the land must not yet be claimed, for example; temporal priority gives title according to Kant [§14]), but any determinate acquisition can only be "provisional" and must be acquired in some "anticipation" of an eventual resolution of claims by a general will.

V

It is important to stress here that the unacceptability of the pre-civil situation is not discussed as a strategic or broadly pragmatic problem. The claim is that it is not *in principle* possible to establish *unilaterally* the intelligible possession that is a necessary condition of the exercise of our rational agency in a finite world populated by other agents. It is not that it is a practically difficult or insecure task without mutual assurance, or that it is simply not prudent for me to trust you until I can be assured you will respect what is mine. The problem lies much deeper – *there can be no "actually" determinate mine/thine distinction to protect* in the first place, about which to be prudent, without a genuinely "omnilateral" (*allseitiger*, §14) resolution of the merely provisional status of property claims. However, this resolution too would only be provisional and subject to constant challenge if we could not be supposed to have completely ceded our right to decide in our own case to such a general will, and *that* means granting such a sovereign real enforcement power and absolute sovereignty. The "assurance" required is thus necessary for any putative resolution of this indeterminacy *actually to be a resolution* of the rationally unacceptable condition of indeterminate property claims. That is, resting content with this indeterminacy would be inconsistent with our status as free rational beings and with the minimum necessary condition for the actual exercise of agency consistent with this status. It would thereby be, as Kant so explicitly insists, "*wrong* in the highest degree" (6:308; 86), not imprudent.[36] (In an unusual expression, Kant says that failing to institute rightful relations would be to "take" the "validity" away from right [*Gültigkeit nehmen*] and so act as if "savage violence were lawful" [*gesetztmäßig*] [6:308n; 86n]. I note too that it is here that Kant could have said, but does not, that lawless violence would make impossible the setting and pursuit of ends, or the realization of our humanity. But what is wrong is acting as if violence were *"gesetzmäßig"* when it is not.) Rational beings can interact rationally only as subject to the Universal Principle of Right, and this means that I am allowed to use what is mine under the condition: "to do to others anything *that does not in itself diminish what is theirs"*(6:238; 30). But we would be inconsistent if we acknowledged being bound to such a norm but also admitted that we are unable to determine in any rightful way what *is* yours or mine. This latter would be the case with only unilateral wills. There is only one other alternative. So, *exeundum e statu naturali.* QED.

This last point about "formally rational unacceptability" finally returns us to the question of the normative status of the Universal Principle of Right and therewith the Kantian state. *Has* Kant's core argument revealed anything about the question of the nature of the relation between *Recht* and *Moral?* To some degree it has, I think. The unacceptability of *res nullius* has returned us to the most basic issue in Kant's practical philosophy, namely, the authority of pure practical reason in its formal dimensions. That may finally be a dead end (I don't think it is), but that general claim to authority is clearing playing a continuous major role in the *Doctrine of Right.* Once we know that there is a condition that must be fulfilled to satisfy the requirements of the law of freedom among beings whose actions inhibit the range of possibilities others would otherwise have – the condition being intelligible possession – and that that cannot be realized without the creation of a genuine (forceful) common will, both the continuity and the distinctness of *Recht* and *Moral* will have been established. The continuity is a matter of being bound by the formal constraints of pure practical reason; the discontinuity appears in the special status of the condition required for the possibility of beings so constrained to interact rationally. This claim can be supported by a brief look at one last bit of text, perhaps the most mysterious passage in the *Doctrine of Right.*

The passage occurs as Kant tries to explain the "Division of the Doctrine of Right." He rather abruptly introduces a section called the "General Division of Duties of Right" and drags on stage, without any preparation or explanation, the third century Roman jurist Domitius Ulpianus[37] and three principles or formulae, the meaning of, Kant immediately admits, Ulpianus "may not have thought distinctly in them but which can be explicated from them" or, moving now to quite a radical hermeneutical principle, may be "put into them" (6:236–7, 29).[38] The "formulae" consist in (i) *Honeste vive*, or be an honorable human being, by which Kant means "assert your worth as a human being, never make yourself a means for others"; (ii) *Neminem laede*, wrong no one, to which Kant adds the unusual qualification, "even if, to avoid doing so, you should have to stop associating with others and shun all society"; and (iii) *Suum quique tribue*, or, if you cannot help associating with others, "enter into a society with them in which each can keep what is his." This is of course the core thesis, the unacceptability of remaining in a pre-civil world or the "exeundum" claim.[39]

The argument Kant seems to have in mind is best viewed as a kind of progression and it will immediately call to mind the argument just addressed in §8 and §9. His claim about "being the self-determining being you are" first appears to be simply a perfect duty to oneself, a sort of duty of moral integrity, and it is not immediately clear why it is included in the list of "duties of right." But as we have already seen, his main purpose appears to be to clarify the general "principle" on which political duties will eventually be derived. And this general requirement was indeed at work in the property argument – do not rest content with merely physically determined possession, or do not act as if you were the sort of being who could use property only while physically possessing it. *Honeste vive* will begin as: always act in a way consistent with the status of a being responsive to the demands of pure practical reason, and so in the "external" sphere, let no one take what is provisionally yours. However, to remain consistent, *honeste vive* will also have to end up as: in order to comply with this duty, establish the intelligible possession consistent with your status as a free rational being. Or it *will* have that meaning once we introduce the condition mentioned by the second duty.

This social dimension enters in the second duty, *neminem laede*. Wrong no one, *even if you must shun society to do so*. Clearly, Kant is implying (in a Rousseauian tone) that without a civil order, it will be difficult if not impossible to fulfill this duty with any determinacy. The only chance in the pre-civil world to keep faith with it is to shun society altogether – not a real alternative. The hypothetical is clearly unrealizable, just as it was for the Rousseau of the *Second*

Discourse. Rousseau worried about the inevitable dependence that would make any self-direction and thus worth in life impossible. Kant is not worried that it will be inevitable that we *will* harm each other (the state of nature is not a state of injustice, but just one devoid of justice), but he is noting that mutual charges of wrong or harm will be inevitable and in principle unanswerable on either side; there will be an absence of justice.

This consideration is what is supposed to move us to the conclusion *suum quique tribue*: in essence *resolve* the problem of an intelligible distinction between mine and thine by entering a civil order. The claims are that one cannot act consistently with the first duty without intelligible possession; one cannot establish intelligible possession in the state of nature without unavoidable charges of wrong against each other and so without possible violations of the second duty everywhere. Thus, to avoid what the second proscribes and yet to keep faith with the first, one must cede the right to decide in one's own case to some civil authority, to a sovereign power who must be presumed to speak for all in their claim to rights protection. We must enter a domain of external freedom "in which the choice of one can be united with the choice of another in accordance with a universal law of freedom." So it is in some way a matter of keeping faith with or remaining true to (consistent with) our status as free rational beings that makes entry into the civil order practically necessary. The wrongness of not doing so is, not surprisingly of course, the kind of wrongness *irrationality* is for Kant, the wrongness of relying on a condition necessary to act at all, but one that in our deed we effectively repudiate.

Kant is thus clearly attempting to show that in one area of our relations to others (mine/thine distinctions), to be the self-determining, reason-responsive beings that we are, we must respect a distinction that we cannot determine unilaterally, the content of which cannot be deduced as a law of pure practical reason.[40] This leads to nothing like an imperfect duty of virtue or the establishment of a condition necessary to make the setting and pursuit of ends more secure. The determinate boundary between me and others is at stake; there is no way to avoid setting such boundaries; we must set them as free rational beings, and there is only one solution for such beings – the establishment of a common will with coercive power.

This position still faces many objections. Indeed we can now see that it is because of this continual adherence to the authority of the formal dictates of pure practical reason that Kant is stuck with his "absolute sovereignty/no right of revolution" thesis. The solution to the problem of intelligible possession is not in the slightest substantive or dependent on some thesis about what by nature or by some other substantive standard you are entitled to. The problem is partly generated because reason has no insight into any such principle and therefore must opt for the formal solution of a final common will whose only function is to be final, to settle the boundary between mine and thine in ways that cannot be challenged. To reserve a right of revolution is thus formally and in effect to have refused to leave the state of nature. Or, in the words of *Perpetual Peace*, "*Any* legal constitution, even if it is only in a small measure lawful, is better than none at all."[41]

This form of reasoning is also partly why Kant faces so many other objections. Since the solution essentially amounts to there being a drawing of the mine/thine boundary, and since there is no substantive standard for doing this, Kant concludes that the sovereign has no choice but to start from the positions established provisionally in the state of nature. But since there can be no rational principle either provisionally or substantively guiding such acquisitions, Kant has to rely on a wholly empirical determination: you may acquire as much as you can defend. Your control of the ocean off your shore extends "as far as a cannon shot may reach" (6:265; 52). This is surprising since the unacceptability of *res nullius* and merely provisional possession was supposed to be the result of their inconsistency with our status as free rational beings. If the core argument rests on a claim that physical possession should not be a decisive criterion for rational beings, why allow the criterion of physical defensibility to set the extent of property for generations to come?[42]

VI

These problems can be multiplied and there are Kantian responses to many such charges, but I want to close by noting a few unusual features that distinguish Kant's "core" position, as laid out here. First, the narrative he sketches is in effect a narration of the transition from a merely empirical/sensible human status to "actual" status as an intelligible being located in a finite, unavoidably conflicted world. The latter is a status we must in some sense achieve and then sustain. (In the *Doctrine of Virtue*, Kant says that "a human being has a duty to raise himself from the crude state of his nature, from his animality [*quoad actum*], more and more toward humanity" [6:387; 151].) Of course, according to Kant's practical metaphysics, we simply *are* such intelligible, or reason-responsive beings, but this narrative suggests that such a capacity can also exist in an unrealized state, or in more speculative terms, that what it means to be such a subject is also to be able to fail *to take up such a status*, to fail to be one. Not acting to resolve provisional property claims is one such possibility. And what is especially interesting is that in this account, this dimension of that status – intelligible possession of property – is "actualized" in a distinctly social way as a result of the determinations of a general or common will and not a private, even privately rational (unilateral) will. There is something dramatically Rousseauian in the claim that our status as intelligible and even concretely free beings is a social achievement of some sort, that without this social determination, we are only "provisionally" and "anticipatorily" such intelligible subjects, subjects who, because of our deeds, can transcend what would otherwise be the empirical conditions and limitations of action.

Secondly – and this seems to me the most interesting result from what we have looked at – it is clear from this argument that the rule of law is not supposed to simply guarantee or secure what *is* mine and thine, given that Kant keeps insisting that without a legal order, or the institution of a genuinely common will, there is no conclusive mine and thine at all. Kant is supposed to be a liberal philosopher, constraining state activity for the sake of a private realm that is to be interfered with only to ensure a like domain for all, with state power limited by what all would rationally will, consent to, and so forth. But mine and thine, the basic boundaries of the private, are not treated as original starting points by Kant but as secondary and as some sort of socially mediated achievement. And this suggests that mine and thine are not properly descriptive terms but more like ascriptions of normative statuses, that they are not merely assured by a legal order but can finally only be said to exist within such a legal system of recognition, enforcement, and resolution of disagreement.

Now, at this point, we may seem to be drifting off here far too easily into the non-Kantian realms of Fichte's *Grundlage* and Hegel's *Phenomenology*, texts where the non-original and socially achieved status of individuality get their first truly modern (i.e., non-Aristotelian) hearing. Consider Fichte's famous claim from his *Grundlage*, where he says that

the concept of individuality is a reciprocal concept, can exist in a rational being only if it is posited as completed by another rational being . . . is never mine, rather it is . . . mine and his, his and mine; it is a shared concept within which two consciousnesses are unified into one.[43]

These are consistent with other claims like "the human being . . . becomes a human being only among human beings,"[44] and of course with very similar, more famous claims that Hegel makes in the *Phenomenology*, such as "Self-consciousness achieves its satisfaction only in another self-consciousness," "A self-consciousness exists for a self-consciousness," and his introduction of Spirit as an "I that is We and We that is I."[45]

Methodological individualism, rational egoism, and "rational will" theories of the state like Rousseau's and Kant's (in the official classification) are all supposed to be challenged by such accounts, and it might seem perverse to link *them* with Kant's *Doctrine of Right*. But I would note only that nothing said so far has drifted any significant distance from Kant's text. Kant too is treating "what is mine," what in effect counts as the actual or determinate me, and "what is thine," what counts as the actual or determinate you, not as some matter of independent fact, from which political reasoning begins. It is a socially dependent, variable, and negotiable boundary which exists by virtue of the mutual acknowledgment of both parties.

Of course, Kant is talking about property rights, not conditions for the possibility of any content for self-understanding, or for a "practical identity," and certainly not about the conditions for the possibility of determinate "self-consciousness," and so forth. Yet, given that for Kant my basic moral identity, my status as a rational free being, is an anonymous identity, essentially and indistinguishably one among many, Kant seems to realize that he also requires some sort of morally relevant account of "what we owe each other" (to coin a phrase) *qua the determinate concrete individuals we are*, or what we must "become" if such a mine-thine boundary is to be possible. The fact that he extends his moral theory in the way suggested by the Ulpian principles seems to me evidence of this concern.

The obvious question to ask about such claims for fundamental social dependence is: must we not already *be* determinate, self-aware rational beings in order to engage each other as such, to hear and properly respond to what Fichte called the demand or summons (*Herausforderung*) from an other? How can such claims for such dependence ever "get off the ground" if we can only be such subjects as a result? And yet here again, Kant's answer coincides with the way that question would be answered later in idealism – with this quasi-Aristotelian distinction between what is only provisionally (potentially) and so uncertainly posited as an identity or claim to "mine," open immediately to challenge and thus defeasible, and what can be mutually resolved and recognized as mine and thine. This is all admittedly speculative, builds on only a thin layer of Kant's ethical theory, and seems open to numerous qualifications. And, as indicated, Kant's formal conception of practical rationality and his general conception of practical philosophy will limit what he can say about all this, but it is not a wild stretch to say that Kant's *Doctrine of Right* might be characterized as post- or proto-Fichtean or proto-Hegelian in this (non-historical) sense, and thus suggestive of an alternative form of liberalism, one in which rational individuality is not ultimate, but derivative and an achieved social status.

NOTES

1. All references to Kant's *Metaphysics of Morals* (*Morals*) in the text are, first, to volume 6 of *Gesammelte Schriften* edited by Paul Natorp for the Königlich Preussischen Akademie de Wissenschaften (cited hereafter simply by volume and page) (Berlin and Leipzig: de Gruyter, 1900–), and are followed by a reference to Mary Gregor's translation (Cambridge: Cambridge University Press, 1996).

2. Kant believed that the sovereign must retain the right to dissolve or override the other branches in cases of irreconcilable conflict; otherwise we would not truly have left the state of nature. See the discussion in *Morals* §48 and especially in §49 on the *potestas executoria*.

3. Whereas the classical question had concerned "*who* should rule" and related questions about the best way to ensure the coincidence of wisdom and power and about the nature of the statesman's knowledge, the

modern question (Kant is typical) often concerns the very possibility of legitimate rule at all. Absent a successful answer, politics will come to look as it did to Nietzsche and Weber: the organized use of a monopoly of violence by one group against another.

4. Kant's position is sometimes called "contractarian," but empiricist or instrumentalist notions of original contract would not thereby be clearly enough distinguished. (I mean by the latter, Locke, Hobbes, Gauthier: people who believe that the interests satisfied by the rule of law, by giving up the right to decide in your own case, are so clear that one could never be said to exempt oneself from an implied agreement to satisfy those interests.) Kant appeals to an original contract only as an "idea" (§47), not an originating *source* of obligation. (And so Kant does not rely on claims like: "The law must be obeyed *because* we can be presumed to have *consented* to its enforcement.") Such a contract cannot be the source of legal obligation because, as noted below, Kant states clearly that we have a duty to exit the state of nature and form a civil condition (a duty "to contract," as it were). The *lex iustitiae* or third "duty of right," to enter the civil condition, is an obligation that obviously binds independently of the resulting contract itself. So, while Kant can state his basic notion of justice as having to do with the adoption of no law that "could not be willed by each," that is mostly a *façon de parler*. What effectively excludes a putative law on this principle is a familiar Kantian inconsistency in its universalized form, not an attempt to determine "what each *would* will." It would be clearer and more correct if Kant and the contractarians were classified as all "rational will" theorists of obligation, but that still leaves a lot unclear with regard to "rational." See the discussion in Leslie Mulholland, *Kant's System of Rights* (New York: Columbia University Press, 1990), pp. 278–80; pp. 280–93; and p. 385ff.

5. Kant even goes so far as to say that reason, "by a categorical imperative, makes it obligatory for us to strive after" a civil condition (*Morals*, 6:318; 95), and he explicitly lists a "duty of justice" (*lex iustitiae*) to enter a civil society (6:237; 29). He does not appear to be referring to a separately classifiable moral duty to obey principles of right (although there is one). At 6:220–1; 22, Kant notes that ethics "has duties in common with right" and that we have an ethical obligation to do our duty "wherever that duty comes from." So duties of right are also "indirectly ethical" duties as well.

6. Kant can be understood to be asking, "Exactly *why* must I restrict exercises of external freedom in consideration of the like exercise of external freedom by others?" The structure of the *Metaphysics of Morals* suggests right away that this restriction is not only our moral obligation (although it is *also* that), but a distinct and unique requirement of pure

practical reason. Indeed, it must be unique enough to permit and to require a collective attempt to *enforce* compliance by threat of punishment, something wholly inappropriate in the moral domain.

7. So Kant can certainly be enlisted in that *rational* natural right tradition that includes Rousseau, Fichte, and Hegel, as well as its most influential contemporary defender, John Rawls. But this is neither a contractarian tradition, as normally understood (see note 4), nor "rationalist" in the natural law sense – that pure reason can detect the order of normative nature. Kant believes that we are obligated only to what we obligate ourselves to, that the moral law is "self-legislated," a metaphor that has produced an endless stream of commentaries. See my "Über Selbstgesetzgebung," in *Deutsche Zeitschrift für Philosophie*, Bd. 6 (2003).

8. In the essay *Theory and Practice*, Kant calls a paternalistic government "the greatest despotism imaginable" (8:291). For the English, see "On the Proverb: That May Be True in Theory, But Is of No Practical Use," in Immanuel Kant, *Perpetual Peace and Other Essays*, trans. Ted Humphrey (Indianapolis: Hackett, 1983), p. 73.

9. He also suggests here a puzzling claim about moral duties: they always come in a dual form, commanding us both to obey the law and to make respect for the law itself our ground for action (a proposal that suggests an odd regress). See *Morals*, 6:391; 154 on the "universal ethical command" to "act in conformity with duty *from* duty."

10. The problems raised by violations of perfect duty that are not fit subjects for criminalization is ignored in Roger Sullivan's summary of Kant's argument in his Introduction to the Cambridge edition of *Morals*, p. xii. Guyer also sometimes writes as if the perfect duty category were congruent with duties of right. See his "Life, Liberty and Property," in *Kant on Freedom, Law, and Happiness* (Cambridge: Cambridge University Press, 2000), p. 278. For a fuller discussion of the issue, see my "On the Moral Foundations of Kant's *Rechtslehre*," chapter 3 in my *Idealism as Modernism: Hegelian Variations* (Cambridge: Cambridge University Press, 1997), pp. 56–91, and Guyer's more recent paper, "Kant's System of Duties," in his *Kant's System of Nature and Freedom* (Oxford: Oxford University Press, 2005), ch. 10.

11. Perhaps the clearest passage is at *Morals*, 6:239; 31: "we know our own freedom (from which all moral laws, and so all rights as well as duties proceed) only through the moral imperative, which is a proposition commanding duty, *from which the capacity for putting others under obligation, that is the concept of a right, can afterwards be explicated [entwickelt].*" ("entwickelt" is also often translated as "developed"; my emphasis).

12. Otfried Höffe, "Kant's Principle of Justice as Categorical Imperative of Law," in *Kant's Practical Philosophy Reconsidered*, ed. Y. Yovel (Dordrecht: Kluwer, 1989), pp. 146–67.

13. Ibid., p. 165.

14. Wolfgang Kersting, "Politics, Freedom, and Order: Kant's Political Philosophy," in *The Cambridge Companion to Kant*, ed. Paul Guyer (Cambridge: Cambridge University Press, 1992), p. 347. See also his more extensive treatment in *Wohlgeordnete Freiheit* (Berlin: de Gruyter, 1984).

15. Mary Gregor, "Kant on 'Natural Rights,'" in *Kant and Political Philosophy*, eds. Ronald Beiner and William James Booth (New Haven: Yale University Press, 1993), p. 53. (There is an especially helpful discussion in this article of the historical transition from the positions of Grotius and Pufendorf to Kant.)

16. Mulholland, *Kant's System of Rights*, p. 10, and pp. 167–98, especially his summary of the inseparability of law and "ethics" on p. 173, and the "derivation" itself, p. 181ff. See also the account and criticism of Mulholland, and an alternative account, in Katrin Flikschuh, *Kant and Modern Political Philosophy* (Cambridge: Cambridge University Press, 2000), pp. 157–68. As I will argue below, the problem of provisionality in acquisition is playing a larger role in the argument than these accounts credit.

17. See especially 6:396; 157–8: "It is clear in accordance with the principle of contradiction that, if external constraint checks the hindering of outer freedom in accordance with universal laws (and is thus a hindrance of the hindrance of freedom), it can coexist with ends as such. I need not go beyond the concept of freedom to see this; the end that each has may be what he wills. – The supreme principle of right is thus an analytic proposition."

18. Marcus Willaschek, "Why the Doctrine of Right Does Not Belong in the *Metaphysics of Morals*: On Some Basic Distinctions in Kant's Moral Philosophy," *Jahrbuch für Recht und Ethik*, 5 (1997): 208 and 223, respectively.

19. Allen Wood, "Kant's Doctrine of Right: Introduction," in *Metaphysiche Anfangsgründe der Rechtslehre*, ed. O. Höffe (Berlin: Akademie Verlag, 1999), p. 35.

20. Allen Wood, "The Final Form of Kant's Practical Philosophy," in *Kant's Metaphysics of Morals*, ed. Timmons, p. 9.

21. Cf. Mulholland on the difference between analysis of the concept of right and the synthetic claim that human beings have rights, *Kant's System of Rights*, p. 171.

22. Paul Guyer, "Kant's Deduction of the Principle of Right," in *Kant's Metaphysics of Morals*, ed. Timmons, p. 40 (reprinted in Guyer's *Kant's System of Nature and Freedom*.)

23. These two claims – that the universal law of right does "lay an obligation on me [*welches mir eine Verbindlichkeit auferlegt*]" and that its command is a command, but requires only obedience, not obedience from the motive duty – are, it seems to me, neglected in Wood's reading of the passage, with misleading consequences. See Wood, "The Final Form," p. 9.

24. Thomas Pogge, "Kant's Theory of Justice," *Kant-Studien*, 79 (1988): 407–33. The similar general claim proposed as a way of making duties of right clearer is what Pogge calls a principle that the state must also be understood as a "system of constraints" that are "optimally to promote the development and flourishing of reason." Even on its face, this clearly calls to mind an imperfect duty of virtue and there is little textual evidence to support any extension of the rights-protection function of the state into a "promoting the flourishing of reason" function.

25. "The capacity to set oneself an end – any end whatsoever – is what characterizes humanity (as distinguished from animality)" (*Morals*, 6:392; 154).

26. Paul Guyer, "Kant's Deduction of the Principles of Right," p. 43.

27. Paul Guyer, "Kantian Foundations of Liberalism," in his *Kant on Freedom, Law and Happiness* (Cambridge: Cambridge University Press, 2000), p. 237.

28. Ibid., p. 240.

29. Paul Guyer, "Morality of Law and Morality of Happiness," in his *Kant on Freedom*, p. 145. For a more detailed discussion of Guyer's position, see my "A Mandatory Reading of Kant's Ethics? Critical Study of Paul Guyer's *Kant on Freedom, Love and Happiness*," *The Philosophical Quarterly*, 51, 204 (July, 2001).

30. Guyer, "Morality of Law and Morality of Happiness," p. 243.

31. This sort of issue is also quite important in Wood's account. See my discussion in "Kant's Theory of Value: On Allen Wood's *Kant's Ethical Thought*," *Inquiry*, 43 (Summer, 2000).

32. Guyer, *Kant on Freedom*, p. 171.

33. I am only repeating here Kant's canonical formulation of what he calls this apparent "paradox" that "the concept of good and bad is not defined prior to the moral law, to which, it would seem, the former would have to serve as foundation; rather the concept of good and evil must be defined after and by means of the law" (5:62–3). English translation in *Critique of Practical Reason*, trans. L. W. Beck (Indianapolis and New York: Bobbs-Merrill, 1956), p. 65.

34. *Groundwork*, 4:438–9; 57.

35. Jay Wallace has pointed out to me that there is no particular reason that this *exeundum* argument should be tied tightly to the property issue. *Any* imagined situation in which rational beings do not establish with others the rational relations they are capable of would be a violation of the *"honeste vive"* requirement discussed below and thus unacceptable.

36. And again, this unacceptability is not said to be based on the inestimable "value" of "humanity," namely, our capacity to set ends for ourselves, as if security in property claims were a necessary practical condition for such a capacity (even though in some sense it clearly is). But the problem Kant is pointing to is the problem of *incompatible commitments* – on the one hand, inescapably, to intelligible possession, and so a solution to the mine/thine indeterminacy, but, on the other hand, to a restriction in the state of nature to a unilateralism that cannot establish this intelligible possession. Hence the *exeundum* claim.

37. Ulpianus (d. 228) is now mostly known because his commentaries on the civil law, *Libri ad Sabinum*, and his books on the praetorian edicts, *Libri ad edictum*, ended up forming the basis for about a third of Justinan's later (533) *Pandects*.

38. For a more detailed discussion of this passage, see my "Dividing and Deriving in Kant's *Rechtslehre*," in *Immanuel Kant, Metaphysische Anfangsgründe der Rechtslehre*, ed. Otfried Höffe (Berlin: Akademie Verlag, 1999), pp. 63–85.

39. He then adds that this list divides duties into internal and external duties and "duties that involve the derivation of the latter from the principle of the former by subsumption." He appears to mean that there are perfect duties to oneself (something like: be the self-determining being that you are) and perfect duties to others (harm no one, do not act as if others are not also such beings) and then a further class of external duties to others that are derived by subsuming this general duty to others, given a specific condition (the inescapability of contact with others) under the principle of the former, or *honeste vive* duty. That general principle would have to be the moral law in some form.

40. *Morals*, 6:263; 51.

41. 8:373n. English translation in *Perpetual Peace: A Philosophical Sketch*, in *Kant's Political Writings*, edited and translated by Hans Reiss (Cambridge: Cambridge University Press, 1970), 118n.

42. It is true, as Mulholland points out (*Kant's System*, p. 294), that the sovereign is given extraordinary leeway in redistributing originally acquired property once provisional becomes certain title, but it is an exaggeration to suggest that Kant's position is compatible with a *radically* redistributive politics. The necessity of moving from provisional

to certain title would be hard to understand if one could not assume that the sovereign would be in some sense guided by the results of original acquisition.

43. J. G. Fichte, *Grundlage des Naturrechts nach Principien der Wissenschaftslehre 1796* (Berlin: de Gruyter, 1971), p. 47; *Foundations of Natural Right*, ed. Frederick Neuhouser, trans. Michael Bauer (Cambridge: Cambridge University Press, 2000), p. 45.

44. Ibid., p. 37; English, p. 39.

45. G. W. F. Hegel, *Die Phänomenologie des Geistes* (Hamburg: Felix Meiner, 1999), p. 108; *The Phenomenology of Spirit*, trans. A. V. Miller (Oxford: Oxford University Press, 1998), p. 110.

13 Kant on sex and marriage right

Den Pakt zu wechselseitigem Gebrauch
Von den Vermögen und Geschlechtsorganen
Den der die Ehe nennt, nun einzumahnen
Ercheint mir dringend und berechtigt auch.

Ich höre, einige Partner sind da säumig.
Sie haben – und ich halt's nicht für gelogen –
Geschlectsorgane kürzlich hinterzogen:
Das Netz hat Maschen und sie sind geräumig.

Da bleibt nur: die Gerichte anzugehn
Und die Organe in Beschlag zu nehmen.
Vielleicht wird sich der Partner dann bequemen

Sich den Kontrakt genauer anzusehn.
Wenn er sich nicht bequemt – ich fürcht es sehr –
Muß eben der Gerichtsvollzieher her.
   ("On Kant's Definition of Marriage in the
   Metaphysics of Morals" by Bertolt Brecht[1])

Brecht's sonnet satirizes Kant's view of marriage as a legal contract between two persons for the legitimation of sex, and at the same time indicts bourgeois values according to which nothing is so sacred that it cannot be commodified.[2] Indeed, Kant's most important single statement on marriage, sex, and family is located squarely within his discussion of property rights in the "Doctrine of Right" in the *Metaphysics of Morals*. His language in this section, "On the Right of Domestic Society, Title I: Marriage Right," is that of contract and property law:

Sexual intercourse (commercium sexuale) is the reciprocal use that one human being makes of the sexual organs and capacities of another *(usus membrorum et facultatum sexualium alterius)*.   *(Morals, 6:277)*

Sexual intercourse in accordance with law is *marriage (matrimonium)*, that is, the union of two persons of different sexes for lifelong possession of each other's sexual attributes.   (6:277)

The natural use that one sex makes of the other's sexual organs is *enjoyment*, for which one gives itself up to the other. In this act a human being makes himself into a thing, which conflicts with the right of humanity in his own person. There is only one condition under which this is possible: that while one person is acquired by the other *as if it were a thing*, the one who is acquired acquires the other in turn; for in this way each reclaims itself and restores its personality. But acquiring a member of a human being is at the same time acquiring the whole person, since a person is an absolute unity. Hence it is not only admissible for the sexes to surrender and to accept each other for enjoyment under the condition of marriage but it is possible for them to do so *only* under this condition. That this *right against a person* is also *akin to a right to a thing* rests on the fact that if one of the partners in a marriage has left or given itself into someone else's possession, the other partner is justified, always and without question, in bringing its partner back under its control, just as it is justified in retrieving a thing.   (6:278)[3]

This text is the point of departure for Brecht's satire, and generations of Kantians and social philosophers have found Kant's position on marriage "an embarrassment," "shallow and repulsive," and "shameful."[4] Yet there is more to these passages than meets the eye that analyzes them only in terms of Kant's political and social writings, and in isolation from the political, historical, and philosophical context in which Kant wrote them. When Kant's views on sex and marriage are seen as framed by issues internal to his overall system and by external political and social concerns that occupied him, much of real philosophical interest comes to light. This is not to say that he is thereby exonerated of all these charges, of course. In what follows I will argue only that Kant's apparently simplistic contract-for-property model in the "Doctrine of Right" is actually infused with his philosophical commitments and a lively interest in social issues of the day. Although his views on the nature of women and their rights, or lack thereof, to full citizenship deeply compromise his account of marriage as a fair and equal bond, a close look at the assumptions and observations underlying this account render at least some standard objections to it less weighty. Moreover, Kant's treatment of the relation of the sexes is philosophically important inasmuch as crucial aspects of his philosophy of mind and morals, especially those involving the nature of individual persons and personhood in general, are profoundly problematized by human sexuality. Kant's attempt to legitimate sexual relations leads directly to some of the deepest puzzles in his philosophy.

What follows, then, will include a look at some of the prevailing attitudes of Kant's time on the relationship of the sexes and their relevance to the institution of marriage, including Kant's own pre-critical contribution to those attitudes. This will be followed by a closer look at the text of Kant's infamous statement on sex and marriage in the "Doctrine of Right." I will then suggest a reading of Kant's text here that draws on 1) the debate over the relationship of external and internal right in his political philosophy, and 2) what I will call Kant's "metaphysics of marriage," that is, his view of the metaphysics of personhood and the role this plays in his stance on marital relations in the "Doctrine of Right."

I. SEX DIFFERENCES AND THE POLITICS OF MARRIAGE IN KANT'S TIME

The views on the marriage contract mentioned earlier were first published in 1797 in the *Metaphysics of Morals*, but Kant had lectured and written on sex differences, sexual relations, and marriage far earlier. He was at least indirectly drawn into the debate over the nature of marriage in the 1780s, yet long before marriage became a political issue for him, Kant had established himself as a popular commentator on the differing natures of the sexes and the role of marriage in "unifying" them. One of the most successful popular pieces Kant ever wrote, *Observations on the Feeling of the Beautiful and Sublime*, was published in 1764 and contained a major section under the title "On the differences of the sublime and the beautiful in the relations between the sexes." This piece has since become notorious for what are clearly, by more enlightened standards, overtly sexist and racist views. It is an early, pre-critical and therefore non-definitive piece in terms of his philosophical enterprise. Thus, it would be tempting to dismiss it altogether were it not for the fact that much of what he claims about the nature of the sexes, taste, culture, and so forth appears again in his lectures over the years, and some of these even appear, albeit usually as examples, in his critical work as well.

Where gender relations are concerned, as with much else, Kant's debt to Rousseau is undeniable. In his "Remarks on the Observations" (notes written in his own copy of the *Observations*) Kant claimed that his reading of Rousseau "set him straight" about the relative value of humanity to knowledge, but it is also clear that Rousseau's story of the origin of human civilization and account of the relations between the sexes left a strong impression on him.[5] At the same time, Rousseau's influence on Kant's views on sex and marriage should not be *over*emphasized. If Kant echoes Rousseau's *The Origins of Inequality* when he says that "in the crude state of nature . . . the woman is a domestic animal, the man leads the way with weapons in hand, and the woman follows him, loaded down with his household belongings" (*Anthropology*, 7:304), he is also simply reiterating the old Germanic justification for sex-guardianship – the view that women are essentially wards of their fathers until they are transferred to husbands in marriage.[6] Rousseau might agree when Kant says that "It is by marriage that woman becomes free: man loses his freedom by it"(7:309), yet Kant is in fact simply stating the fact that by marriage under Prussian law a woman was freed from the guardianship of her father, which, were she to remain unmarried, would continue until his death.[7] Furthermore, Kant's "Rousseauian" account of women's subordination in the state of nature gives way to a more positive notion of women's role in civil culture than Rousseau allowed, if only because Kant was less skeptical than Rousseau about the benefits of civilization to humanity. For Kant, women have two natural purposes: "the preservation of the species and the cultivation of society and its refinement" (7:306). Kant viewed the education of women as to some extent (although less than for men) necessary. Women's natural tendencies are "more artful, fine and uniform (*regelmäßig*)" than men's, Kant says in one Reflection, and women therefore need less instruction. Nevertheless, they still should be educated in a way appropriate to the "vocation" (*Bestimmung*) of their sex. The fact that he adds that this method of education has not yet been found certainly suggests that he did not take Rousseau's views on the education of Sophie in *Émile* to be the last word on the problem (R 1303, 15:573).[8]

Kant's commitment to a two-track education for men and women was a view propounded by many during the Enlightenment and was based on what contemporary feminists call a theory of "natural complement."[9] Or, as Kant himself put it, the new was based on the desire to create "the unity that arises out of needs on both sides reciprocally complemented" (R 1296, 15:571). On this issue, as with his view of the "fair sex" more generally, Kant was no pathbreaker. English moralists, French philosophes, as well as early German Enlightenment figures like Johann Christoph Gottsched had long advocated for the "special" education of women. Although they represent a step forward in calling for the education of women at all, and although such views typically claim to value masculinity and femininity equally, natural complement theories also typically hold that women's value is expressed primarily in the sphere of the home and family. Thus, Kant had tradition on his side when he claimed that married women were sufficiently "glib" to represent themselves and their husbands in court, while at the same time affirming the sex-guardian laws that prevented them from doing so.[10]

Although generally speaking, complementarity theories provide an easy rationalization for the implicit or explicit exclusion of women from the public sphere, a remarkable exception to this is to be found in the work of Theodor Gottlieb von Hippel. In his work *On Improving the Status of Women*, Kant's close friend, former student, mayor of Königsberg, and pioneering advocate of women's equality adopted the view that women's special traits, such as "purity...tenderness, patience, endurance...sympathy, talkativeness," which "appear to be inherent in the female sex, and merely artificially acquired skills in the males," make them excellent teachers of both sexes.[11] He claims that the Socratic method, "which Socrates learned from his mother, a midwife (*sage femme*)...is doubtless peculiar to the opposite sex" and continues in a long, passionate discourse to reel off a list of women's characteristics and virtues, each of which reinforces his central claim that excluding women from the public sphere is a travesty of justice that prevents the advancement of humanity toward genuine civilization.[12] A brief excerpt from the beginning of the chapter on "Suggestions for Improvement" indicates the degree to which Hippel's views concerning women's rights surpassed those of even the greatest emancipatory male thinkers of his time:[13]

Is the opposite sex always to remain as it has been and is? Are the human rights so basely taken away from the women, the civil rights so indecently withheld from them to be lost forever? Are the women never to attain an absolute value *in* and *for* the state? Are they never to think and act *for* and *by* themselves? Will we seek the answers to these questions in a subtle and sophisticated Roman legal fiction or in ancient and traditional property rights and statutes of limitation, so that we may again reject such questions and force them into a state of distasteful silence? Will we even soothe our masculine consciences with misgivings concerning the possible consequences, with further abuses, or with whatever bugbears people use to frighten children and thus put off and put off again this concern of the entire human race? If so, then the glorious morning of redemption is not yet at hand. Will we be able to refrain from still calling ourselves Vandals and Goths – the names of our forefathers of old – if we do not seek to rectify this injustice, and the sooner the better?

Apart from the sheer boldness of his position, Hippel's treatises on women's rights and marriage are of interest for the fact that although published anonymously, they were clearly intended to influence political policy, and Hippel's positions were certainly the subject of discussion among Kant and his circle of friends, which included Hippel himself.

A third edition of *On Marriage* was prepared for quick publication in 1792 in hopes that the author's views (especially Hippel's opposition to sex-guardianship) would be incorporated in the Frederician Code revisions begun in the early 1780s. Early in 1780, the same year that he was appointed mayor and chief of police of Königsberg, Hippel was appointed by Frederick the Great to serve on the commission assigned the task of reforming the Prussian state legal code, for which "loyal services" he was decorated.[14] He continued to work officially on the reform of Prussian law throughout the decade, but his anonymous literary efforts in the early 1790s to establish equality of rights within marriage were frustrated by Frederick the Great's conservative successor, Frederick Wilhelm, and the new framers of the Code appointed by him. In the revised Code, as in the old, women were bound by the marriage contract to remain under the complete legal guardianship of their husband (even including his "right" to open her mail and permission to physically abuse her in certain cases).[15]

Hippel was a regular guest and discussant at Kant's dinner gatherings, held in his home from 1787 until 1793.[16] The fact that Hippel refers mockingly to sexist remarks made by Kant in the course of one of their dinner conversations is evidence that the issue of women's rights was among the many political and social topics discussed.[17] Probably the younger Hippel was not particularly surprised by his old professor's acceptance of the exclusion of women from the sphere of public affairs and from a scholarly education, nor by his persistent assumpton of their intellectual inferiority.[18] Yet, from the perspective of our own time it is hard to recognize these views as entirely consistent with those of the author that defined the Enlightenment in his 1784 essay on this theme as "mankind's exit from its self-imposed immaturity," where "mankind" is understood as "including the entire fair sex"(*Enlightenment*, 8:33–42). The implicit claim in this famous essay that women too could be lifted out of their situation of guardianship stands in stark contrast to Kant's rationalizations for the political subordination of women.

The tension between Kant's views on Enlightenment and his acceptance of sex-guardianship in marriage can in part be understood as part of the larger turmoil of opinions amongst intellectual policy makers of the 1780s and early 90s in Prussia. Legal institutions, including marriage, were undergoing change in Prussia and throughout Europe. A significant debate had emerged over the role of sex within marriage and had to do with the question of whether its sole justification was procreation, or whether the liberal Enlightenment view was justified, according to which love and sexual pleasure between married couples could be a legitimate end in its own right. Kant sided with the enlightenment view, indeed he assumed its truth in his descriptions of marriage:

> The end of begetting and bringing up children may be an end of nature, for which it implanted the inclinations of the sexes for each other; but it is not requisite for human beings who marry to make this their end in order for their union to be compatible with rights, for otherwise marriage would be dissolved when procreation ceases.[19]

Legally, reforms of Prussian civil law had included provisions for divorce on the grounds of infidelity, wrongful abandonment, and irreconcilable differences.[20] Kant repeats these provisions in his own accounts. Furthermore, as we saw, Kant was privy to some of the most radical thought on women's emancipation to come out of Europe in the eighteenth century in discussions with Hippel.

Perhaps most significant is the fact that the famous Enlightenment essay of 1784 was written as the direct result of a debate in the

Berlinischer Monatsschrift over whether the clergy should have an official role to play in civil union ceremonies. Kant's friend Johann Erich Biester, editor with Friedrich Gedike of the *Monatsschrift*, had written a critique of the role of the clergy in marriage, arguing that their real interest in performing marriage ceremonies was in the maintenance of their own power. The article, with the contentious title "Suggestion to the spiritual leaders not to trouble themselves anymore with marrying people," argued that marriage was simply a contract for civil union and that execution of a purely civil contract did not belong to the church but to the state.[21] The essay prompted the theologian J. F. Zöllner, in a subsequent attack on Biester's article published in the *Monatsschrift*, to castigate his contemporaries for their careless use of the term "enlightenment" and to ask the question "What is enlightenment?"[22] Biester decided to publish replies to this question and appealed to Kant to contribute one. Thus, Kant's renowned essay was in fact prompted by a debate over the nature of the institution of marriage, and it is important to understand his reference to "the entire fairer sex" in this context.[23] At the behest of his friend Biester, Kant's contribution represents an attempt to help lay the theoretical groundwork for the construction of an enlightened age by clarifying what it meant to live in an age of enlightenment, to use Kant's own distinction. Living in an "age of enlightenment" for Kant and his colleagues meant engaging in debates that could reconfigure state power and law. Kant was well aware of the impact his views could have on the powers that be in Prussia, and his discussion of the marriage contract is surely written in full awareness of Hippel's views on the need to balance the scales of equality that were tipped against women at the time. Kant's views on marriage laid out in the *Metaphysics of Morals* were published at the very end of Kant's career, shortly after Hippel's death and after the revision of the Frederician Code. They should certainly be read with this history in mind.[24]

II. SEXUAL RELATIONS AND MARRIAGE RIGHT

Kant's account of marriage was known to students in his Ethics courses and is available in the form of some of their lecture notes over the years dating from 1762 (Herder) to 1794 (Vigilantius). Kant's own, more concise account was published in a section of the first half of his *Metaphysics of Morals*, the "Doctrine of Right," in 1797.

To understand his account of marriage it is necessary to make some preliminary comments about the context within which it is placed.

Under the "Doctrine of Right" Kant understands the systematic account of the conditions under which the choice of one can be harmonized with others' choices. "An action is *right*," according to Kant's Universal Principle of Right, "if it can coexist with everyone's freedom in accordance with a universal law, or if on its maxim the freedom of choice of each can coexist with everyone's freedom in accordance with a universal law" (*Morals*, 6:230). An act is wrong in the case where it cannot so coexist, that is, if it hinders the rightful act or rightful condition of action of another (6:231). This system does not deal with internal incentives, or intentions, for Kant (that is covered in the "Doctrine of Virtue"). It is not, that is, about "internal" laws and law-giving, but about what actions may legitimately be governed by "external" law, apart from whether or not the agent is acting from a good will. In Kant's language it is about legality, or "juridical lawgiving, understood as imposing obligations on persons that, whether or not they impose them upon themselves as ethical duties, *can* be imposed on them by an outside authority" (6:219–20). At the same time, Kant's view of external lawfulness is rooted in the formula of universality, that is, the version of the categorical imperative that commands us to "Act only on that maxim through which you can at the same time will that it should become universal law" (*Groundwork*, 4:421).[25] Because the categorical imperative is a formula for testing one's intentions, and not (or not merely) an expression of intention, it can be put to external use as well. That is, it can be used in a context where individuals' actions, apart from their intentions, are to be judged by others. It commands that no action be performed that cannot be part of a system of freedom in accordance with universal law (4:402). Roger Sullivan puts the point as follows:

The categorical imperative determines which maxims are acceptable moral principles by their ability to serve as practical norms of conduct for everyone, that is, as laws within a civil community. Moral norms for conduct therefore are preeminently *public* laws, characterized by the universality of the obligations they impose, especially the obligation of reciprocity.[26]

In a civic legal system (and so in the "Doctrine of Right") the categorical imperative, the "principle of all maxims" (*Morals*, 6:231), is restricted in its application, as Sullivan puts it, to "external behavior between people."[27] With external right comes the authorization of external coercion, and it is with the latter that Kant is chiefly concerned in the "Doctrine of Right." Kant argues that if what is right is free choice that coexists with other's choices, and what is wrong is free choice that hinders other's freedom, then coercion is prima facie wrong.[28] But in cases where coercion is used to prevent the hindering of another's freedom, it thereby becomes legitimate. Coercive hindrance of one person's choice to hinder another's freedom resets the balance, as it were, and restores order.

Kant's version of the legitimation of state power is especially important in this context because Kant uses an analogue of this account to explain how the marriage contract reestablishes the equality of personhood that, he believes, sexual intercourse upsets. His discussion of the marriage contract falls under the heading of what he calls "private right," his contribution to the theory of property law. Rightful possession (where I have a claim to something even if I do not physically "hold" it), Kant says, may be divided into three subheadings depending on the three kinds of "external objects" I have the right to call mine. Any citizen may acquire 1) a physical object (primarily real estate), 2) another's choice to perform a task (e.g., the transfer of a thing to me, or performance of a service for me), 3) another's status in relation to me (as a wife, child, servant, or other) (*Morals*, 6:247ff).

Cases 2) and 3) explicitly involve contracts.[29] Contract right is the system of laws that governs "my possession of another's choice, in the sense of my capacity to determine it by my own choice to a certain deed in accordance with the law of freedom" (6:271). Kant defines the contract as "An act of the united choice of two persons by which anything at all that belongs to one passes to the other" (6:271). Kant's definition of the contractual process is important for understanding his view of marriage, and it can be glossed as follows: I can rightfully acquire the acts of another based on what is his, but not through any "negative" act, that is, through abandonment or renunciation. Rightful acquisition can involve only a positive act of *transference*, and that is only possible through a joint agreement – Kant calls it a "common will" – whereby the object passes from the control of one immediately to the other through a process of simultaneous giving up and acceptance on the part of both parties. The process of transfer or "giving up" one's possession to the other is "alienation";

and alienation in turn is the result of explicit agreement – a voluntary *act* of unification of wills of both parties. It is this act that Kant labels the "contract" (6:271).

A. Marriage right

Kant's account of the marriage contract itself occurs in the section on contract right in the "Doctrine of Right" under the heading "On Rights to Persons Akin to Rights to Things" ("*Von dem auf dingliche Art persönlichen Recht*," [6:276]). Such rights are not identical to original acquisition of land or to contracts for acquisition of things or services because they involve, in Kant's words, "possession of an external object as a *thing* and use of it *as a person*" (6:276). For Kant these contracts establish legal domestic relations and the terms of possession and use involved in spousal, parental, and domestic services.

This is the point at which Kant turns to the specific application of his definition of legal contract to the marriage contract, some of which we already saw: What is acquired in marriage is a right to an external object as a thing – the sexual organs and sexual capacities of another (*usus membrorum et facultatum sexualium alterius* [6:277]) and to use of that "thing" ("as a person") in sexual intercourse. What distinguishes this from the other cases of acquiring a particular control over persons is the fact that the marriage contract involves a giving up and receiving on the part of *both* parties, of one very personal "thing" – their bodies (or rather specific "organs and capacities") – in exchange for another very personal thing – their own individual pleasure. If this giving up and receiving is viewed as a form of simple reciprocity, it leads to the conclusion that Brecht had so much sport with: As with any acquisition, if one of the partners has run off with the "thing" it had contracted to exchange with the other partner, or if one of the partners has given that already contracted "thing" into the possession of someone else, then the wronged partner, in Kant's own words, "is justified, always and without question, in bringing its partner back under its control, just as it is justified in retrieving a thing" (6:278). Or, as Brecht said, if partners have been remiss and refuse to abide by the terms of the contract, there is nothing to be done but to confiscate the goods involved and haul the contract violator to court.[30] No wonder Kantians for two hundred years prefer to avoid altogether this little section of an otherwise reputable book. Kant is very clear that he views sex as both giving one's self up as a thing to be used as a means only, and using another as a means only. If he wants to maintain that legal right is grounded in any way in moral right, then obviously he must worry that sexual relations represent a double violation of the categorical imperative in the formula of humanity.[31] But why accept this account of sexuality? Is it even partially plausible? As Barbara Herman points out, a lot depends on how rosy one's view of sex is.[32] If one believes that sex can be and often is demeaning to both or one of the persons involved, one is more likely to follow Kant's argument. I believe Herman is right to argue that Kant's pessimism is worth taking seriously even in contemporary contexts. It should be added that his negative attitude is also not to be dismissed as just an artifact of a "puritanical" Pietist upbringing (although that surely plays a role). Kant was no libertine, to be sure, but he also was not the prudish crank that he is often caricatured as being.[33] Theoretically Kant cannot, and in his works he does not, deny the fact that sex is natural. He regards it as a fact, as an appetite of our bodily nature and as such as something that cannot be ignored nor, for that matter, condemned. We are animals and Kant is profoundly aware that as such, we humans are "beings of need." Still, sexual behavior for him is inherently degrading to our humanity in a way that the simple satisfaction of other bodily needs is not. Kant seemed truly to believe that during sex both partners reduce themselves to mere animals bereft of free will and responsibility. For him, a sign of this is the shame and secrecy attached to sexual activity. Kant says:

In the first place, sensual congress of the sexes is a phenomenon in man that is entirely similar in function to that of animals; this bodily act of physical nature also engenders shame and turns it into an obscene act, i.e., one that in public presentation would awaken repugnance, accompanied by the notion of [lewdness]. Now if the act of intercourse were permissible, in and for itself, there would be no explaining the shame; and it rests on nothing else but this, that in presenting ourselves to the other as an object of enjoyment we feel that we are demeaning humanity in our own person and making ourselves similar to the beasts.   (*Vigilantius*, 27:638)

Given the view that sexual relations necessarily involve a backslide down the evolutionary ladder, it makes some sense for Kant to insist that a remedy for this is either abstinence or that persons who plan to engage in this behavior at least promise beforehand not to abandon each other after the act. Marriage is a remedy in part because it involves this promise to stay together in perpetuity: Kant defines it as "the union of two persons of different sexes for lifelong possession of each others' sexual attributes" (6:277). The partners thus agree to use each other only on the condition that one or the other of them will never throw the other away, as he puts it, "as one throws away a lemon after sucking the juice from it" (*Collins*, 27:384). Sex outside of marriage involves no such lifelong commitment to the person, and so, for Kant, such relations cannot be morally redeemed over time. Similarly concubinage, or acquiring a mistress, is never a legitimate contractual arrangement because

nobody can make themselves into an object of the other's enjoyment if it is injurious to their personality, and . . . a strictly standing obligation to consummate a promise of carnal intercourse cannot be admitted. A contract for concubinage [*pactum concubinatus*] is [shameful], null and void and the concubine can therefore breach it at any time.   (*Vigilantius*, 27:638)

This last comment sheds light on at least part of Kant's own concerns, and suggests that he is sensitive to the fact that women (concubines were invariably women) stand to lose more than men in sexual relations. But considered from the eighteenth-century bourgeois woman's perspective, which Kant, probably thanks in large part to Hippel, seemed to have managed on occasion to do, things are indeed far from rosy where sex is concerned. Another example is Kant's comment on the special nature of the sexual contract in one of his lectures on ethics:

For the case [of sexual intercourse] is quite different from the permitted use of one's powers that is granted to the other [i.e., when one contracts to work for someone]. When a wife concedes the substance of her body to lust, she deteriorates through using up her forces in pregnancy; she subjects herself to the danger of dying in childbirth.   (*Vigilantius*, 27:637–8)

Here, at least, Kant explicitly recognizes the fact that women of his time stood to lose a great deal more than men in sexual partnership. Thus he told his students that the man must make up for his advantage by agreeing to be around for her during pregnancy, and if she survives that, to stay around even after her body and possibly her health deteriorate as a result. Even in Kant's time there were exceptions, as Kant was well aware,[34] but he clearly recognized that in his own time and station, women were less likely to flourish after being abandoned by their mate.

Dim as Kant's view of sex was, it is not indefensible by feminist standards. Not only are sexual partners subject to abandonment upon completion of the act, the weaker partner may be used and abused in other ways, both mental and physical. As Barbara Herman points out in her (mitigated) defense of Kant's views:

Objectification is plausibly problematic. If each sees the other as object – something for use–then strength (physical and social) can take the upper hand and domination follows.[35]

It was clear to Kant who the weaker partner typically was, and for this reason he stipulated that the marriage contract not only include a non-abandonment clause, but also that the partners share all assets in common:

For the same reasons [that partners are justified in retrieving each other where abandonment or infidelity occur], the relation of the partners in a marriage is a relation of *equality* of possession, equality both in their possession of each other as persons...and also equality in their possession of material goods. As for these, the partners are still authorized to forgo the use of a part, though only by a separate contract.   (6:278)

Because physical and social power differentials undermine the reciprocity relation in marriage, it is obvious on Kant's account that lifetime commitment, although necessary for preventing one-sided abandonment, is not sufficient to redeem sex. Abusive and disrespectful relationships can last a lifetime, a point Kant recognizes when he explicitly denies that marriages for money are moral, claiming instead they should be illegal (6:278-9). Equal access to internal resources would presumably mitigate an already bad situation.

In summary, the marriage contract institutes a system of relations that equalizes relations between wife and husband by requiring (1) exclusivity of use of the others' sexual capacities (2) over the course of the lifetime of each partner, with (3) equal division of property and other goods acquired during the course of the marriage. The marriage contract thus specifies a set of relations that can be upheld in a court of law, if need be. Yet the basis for entering such contract in the first place can only be mutual recognition of the personhood of the other. The marriage contract is premised on the willingness of both parties to recognize each other and themselves as persons.

B. The metaphysics of marriage

In the end, for Kant what redeems sex, what makes it human, is that it is a pact between free and equal *persons* for the "possession" of each other as persons over a lifetime. But the emphasis on personhood raises questions. It is one thing to point out with Gregor that Kant's extension of the categorical imperative to external relations between individual citizens can be made without appeal to internal states of those individuals, but it is another to explain how Kant can rely so heavily on a conception of respect for persons in his justification of marriage as a merely legal contract. Kant's discussion of marital relations appears to thoroughly confound his professed commitment in the *Metaphysics of Morals* to providing an account of the external regulation of relations among individuals. In a recent article on this topic, Allegra de Laurentiis argues that Kant favors "classifying the human body, its 'organs and capacities' (6:277), as a 'merely external' object," thereby paving the way for a purely private-property, contractarian account of marriage that is inconsistent with his ethical theory.[36] She argues that contemporary readings of Kant's views on marriage tend to conflate anthropological and moral theory with Kant's theory of right and therefore violate the letter and spirit of the latter.

Two points can be made by way of reply to this sort of objection. First, this section of the "Doctrine of Right" is framed in terms of rights to persons that "are similar to" rights to things (*Von dem auf dingliche Art persönlichen Recht*). As we already saw, Kant believed that marriage was an institution that should not be completely beyond or above the law. He therefore wanted to provide a legal definition of this bond that would make it accessible to judicial oversight and presumably provide protected legal "exit options" for victims of bad marriages.[37] Nevertheless, he was aware that he was stretching the notions involved to make them fit the contract model, and for this reason he explicitly argues for an *analogical* extension of marriage contract (and the parental and domestic employer bond) to property right. He discusses rights to persons that are like rights to things, while admitting that these will not be like other "things" that we possess because "whatever is acquired in this way is also inalienable and the right of possessors of these objects is the *most personal* of all rights" (6:277). (And recall the comment quoted above, that "the case [of sexual intercourse] is quite different from the permitted use of one's powers that is granted to the other" – women are not going to get an equal exchange merely because of mutual pleasure.) So from the very start of the discussion Kant warns that these "possessions" will differ dramatically from other physical possessions in that the "possessor" does *not* have the right to dispose of his or her "possession" as s/he sees fit (6:270).[38] The reference to the "most personal" nature of the acquisitions under discussion also clearly refers to the fact that "persons" in Kant's technical (i.e., moral and cognitive-theoretical) sense of the term is at issue and that he is consciously allowing this to inform his legalist account.

Second, there is good reason to take Kant's own claims to be presenting a formal, legalistic account of juridical right with a grain of salt, or several. The very notion of "contract" as defined by Kant can plausibly be interpreted as loaded with metaphysical meaning borrowed from his cognitive and moral theory. It involves "persons" and the unification of their "wills" to perform a joint "act." A strong case can be made for the point that Kant's moral theory and metaphysics are fundaments of his theory of right, not "incidental considerations."[39] In a book devoted to making this point, Katrin Flikschuh presents a sustained and compelling argument for the claim that "Kant's metaphysics of justice is based on the initial juxtaposition between the claims of freedom and the constraints of nature, and their eventual reconciliation by means of an act of practical political judgment." These three elements provide the "metaphysical framework which shapes Kant's political thought," she argues.[40] Although she does not focus on Kant's discussion of marriage, her characterization of the basis of the Doctrine of Right covers the marriage contract account perfectly, as will be seen in what follows. As for the objection that Kant's anthropology and social theory are irrelevant to his political theory, several authors have recently made strong arguments for the claim that Kant's anthropological writings also contain elements of a system of *a priori* principles and are not to be dismissed as extrasystematic collections of empirical data and anecdote.[41] Finally, the simple fact that Kant's lectures and reflections on ethics and anthropology contain repeated references to many, if not all, of the very points incorporated in his account of marriage in *Metaphysics of Morals* strongly suggests that the divide between ethics, culture, and legal right was not one he himself consistently saw the need to insist upon.

There is, I will argue, a strong element of metaphysics (in Kant's sense of a system of principles that hold *a priori* for possible experience, both cognitive and moral) in his account of marriage. The most important of these elements for this account is the concept of a person. Earlier in the *Metaphysics of Morals*, in a preliminary set of definitions for the book, he defines a person as "a subject whose actions can be *imputed* to him," and moral personhood as "nothing other than the freedom of a rational being under moral laws" (6:223). A "thing," on the other hand, is defined as "that to which nothing can be imputed, an object of free choice that itself lacks freedom." Kant speaks of sex as a violation of "a right of humanity in one's own person" because during sex we treat our own embodied person merely as a thing:

> Nobody, as such, has the [right to dispose over the substance of one's body], as over a thing that is owned, whereas anyone making themselves into an object of the other's lust is after all treating the substance of their body as a thing to be enjoyed, it seems as though all sexual inclination would run counter to morality.   (*Vigilantius*, 27:637–8)

But he refers to personhood (*Persönlichkeit*) also as an "absolute unity." Consistent with his critical philosophy, Kant's definition of "persons" in the "Doctrine of Right" involves a dual aspect conception: Persons are physico-psychological beings, on the one hand, and moral beings, on the other. Psychological personhood involves the capacity for consciousness of one's continued identity through time (*Pure Reason*, A 361), that is, it involves embodiment. What the marriage contract allows is the acquisition of whole persons, not just the parts. For Kant that is the only acquisition that is possible, metaphysically speaking, because persons cannot be divided: "Acquiring a member of a human being is at the same time acquiring the whole person, since a person is an absolute unity." When de Laurentiis accuses Kant of drawing the line between objects that may and may not be rightfully owned "right through the person," she is in one sense right. But the "line" itself is a metaphysical (i.e., transcendentally ideal) line. It is a line that points towards two aspects of the person, not a line that divides a person into ontologically distinct parts. Thus it is wrong to conclude as she does that his account of marriage right fails because of his "ultimate refusal to acknowledge that the body is an integral part of persons and therefore of their 'dignity,' 'worth,' or 'capacity for freedom.'"[42] Kant's views on the pleasures of sex may have been narrowly puritanical, but his notion of personhood is precisely that of an embodied subject.

In the Paralogisms in the first *Critique*, Kant defines the person as the capacity for consciousness of one's continued identity through time (A 361), and in the *Metaphysics of Morals* he reintroduces this "psychological" notion of the person as "merely the ability to be conscious of one's identity in different conditions of one's existence" (6:223). We might say that for Kant a person is, to coin a phrase, a physical substance that self-identifies as such. But in addition to his cognitive or physical account, Kant views persons also as conscious *agents*. He describes a person as a subject that is responsible for its own actions, and says that *personhood* (*Persönlichkeit*) is humanity in one's person. So "persons" for Kant are beings who are conscious of themselves as physical bodies and also as beings who are responsible for their actions. Persons are self-consciously physical substances: They identify themselves (but not exclusively) with their bodies. At the same time they feel responsible for their actions, which of course include the way they behave toward their own and others' bodies.

Given the identification of persons as embodied minds, it is not surprising that in his theory of property, we find Kant denying the principle of self-ownership.[43] Acquisition, he argues, is always of something external, of "things outside my person" (*Vigilantius*, 27:595). For this reason persons never legally "own" their body – it is not a possession. Hence, neither can they dispose of their own body. (This is part of his argument against suicide as well [27:603]. Bodies are not alienable: "A man cannot dispose over himself as over a thing" [27:602] – it is wrong to sell one's body parts, he says [teeth, hair], just as it is wrong to sell one's honor [e.g., to let oneself be called a liar for some gain or other]. Put simply, for Kant, my body is me, and I cannot sell myself and still be a person. If I do treat myself as a thing, I thereby *become* a thing.

Moreover, the integrity of the human person is reflected by the fact that both its aspects, not only body but also soul, are inalienable. In the Paralogisms in the *Critique of Pure Reason* he argues that we cannot own or "take possession of" [*in Besitz nehmen*] our souls as disembodied noumena (B 410). By limiting the very notion of an object to the conditions of possible experience, Kant forecloses the possibility that the soul (the non-physical self) is an object of my own or anyone else's possible experience. Since ownership requires that it be physically *possible* for me to use the thing I am claiming, and the existence of the thing would presumably be a condition for the possibility of using it, it follows from Kant's cognitive theory that my "soul" is not a possible object of ownership, for myself or anyone else. Thus a person cannot, Faust-like, dispose over their own agency "as over a thing" any more than they may do so with their bodies – this is why, as we saw, in his examples of specific parts of ourselves that we cannot sell, he includes our honor in the same list with hair and teeth. In marriage, that is in moral sexual relations, this means that we cannot subordinate the will of the other to our own, nor can we subordinate our will to the other without nullifying our personhood, thereby breaching the contract.

In summary, sexual relations pose a huge metaphysical problem for Kant because he has staked his philosophy on a distinction between our selves as we are in the world of nature and our selves as agents capable of improvement. Natural inclinations are not themselves evil or wrong, but human beings can and should control them. Kant's moral theory depends on the assumption that persons can be responsible because they can control their own behavior. Sex is a glaring instance of the tension, as Flikschuh puts it, "between the claims of freedom and the constraints of nature." It represents nature seemingly at its most intractable and uncontrollable: Every time we engage in it we relinquish our very personhood and ignore the personhood of another. For Kant it thus appears as a bodily inclination that is not merely animal but that is decidedly anti-rational and anti-human. Or put in political terms, it is a constantly recurring invasion of the state of nature into the midst of society. Sex represents the constant threat of moral devolution.

For Kant, civil control of the process via the marriage contract is the only answer because it sets the conditions under which it is possible for each partner to "relinquish" their whole person ("body and soul," as the song goes) and at the same time to "acquire" the whole person (body and soul) of the other. But if we are talking about "whole persons" in Kant's sense, that is, metaphysically and morally, the business of marriage ceases to look like business. It becomes apparent why Kant's account of sexual and marital relations is subsumed only *analogically* under his doctrine of property rights. They are not *identified* as rights to property, and the preceding discussion of the metaphysics of marriage should make it clear why there cannot be a property relationship, strictly speaking, between two human beings.

Some commentators suggest that Kant's decision to include marriage and family relations in this part of the "Doctrine of Right" at all is a matter of language dictated by the received conceptual framework of a newly emerging market-based economy:

> We need not be surprised that Kant uses the vocabulary of capitalist property relations in the context of relations between the sexes. All personal relationships were becoming more and more a matter of market relations [during Kant's time]. . . . It is only to be expected that the general patterns of social and economic life should be reflected in family life.[44]

This may be true, but Kant's account, as we have seen, takes into consideration aspects of the individuals involved that run deeper than mere contractarian equality. Given his notion of personhood, the exchange that takes place is in fact more akin to mutual giving and receiving, in which two people decide to give each other the very same thing – their "whole person," body and soul, such that over the course of a lifetime each "reclaim" themselves in the other. It is less like a contract and more like a gift exchange: The marriage pact involves two people "giving" themselves to each other for life and love.[45]

This is a romantic view of marriage that has wide acceptance today. It was and is deeply problematic, however, both now and in Kant's own time: There was no legal recourse in eighteenth-century society (nor is there in ours) for victims of gift exchanges in which one of the "givers" retracts, damages, or even destroys the other's gift. And Kant, being something of a pessimist about human relations, was keenly aware of the fact that mutual exchanges based on such ideals can and often do go very wrong. The rhyme in Brecht's poem is not just funny, it is true: Sometimes the law must be called in. Kant turns to property law as the only available remedy for righting wrongs and maintaining equality and reciprocity within the civil institution of marriage. But the application of these notions, or the conditions under which the law may intervene, are determined by his views on the metaphysics of personhood, and hence the metaphysics of the personal bond between two individuals in marriage.

CONCLUSION

Thus, the marriage contract is not simply an exchange of goods between individuals that leaves both unchanged except for the commodities they possess. It is rather a synthesis of a new, complex set of relations in much the same way that the social contract unifies the wills of many to form a new entity, the state. It perfectly illustrates Flikschuh's description of the "Doctrine of Right" as an account of the "reconciliation by means of an act of practical political judgment" of "claims to freedom and the constraints of nature." Consider what Kant has to say about domestic right:

> What is mine or yours in terms of [rights to persons akin to rights to things] is what is mine or yours *domestically*, and the relation of persons in the domestic condition is that of a community of free beings who form a society of members of a whole called a *household* (of persons standing in *community* with one another) by their affecting one another in accordance with the principle of outer freedom (causality).   (*Morals*, 6:276)

Kant goes on here to argue that no individual act of appropriation, nor even a contract can, by itself, make this special kind of "acquisition" possible:

> It must be a right lying beyond any rights to things and any rights against persons. That is to say, it must be the right of humanity in our own person, from which there follows a natural permissive law, by the favor of which this sort of acquisition is possible for us.   (6:276)

Exactly what Kant means by "permissive law" is obscure, having to do with a kind of empirical, preliminary judgment that allows for the provisional claim to something in a situation where nothing prohibits or commands it.[46] What is important here is that Kant appears to be using it exactly analogously to his account of "rightful presumption" preceding the social contract in the formation of the state. Kant says that an action that is prima facie wrong may be permitted *provisionally* if "it has in its favor the rightful *presumption* that it will be made into rightful possession through being united with the will of all in a public lawgiving" (6:257). Here in the section on marriage right, a right to "acquire" personal relations, in itself a violation of the right of humanity in a person, is permitted on the presumption that these relations will be redeemed by a "civil" condition: marriage.

Seen in this light, it is not surprising that Kant feels obliged to explain how equality is maintained within this civil union: Just as for the state, the question arises as to how this new entity is to be administered. Here, disappointingly, Kant's authoritarianism takes over. "If the question is therefore posed," says Kant,

> whether it is also in conflict with the equality of the partners for the law to say of the husband's relation to the wife, he is to be your master (he is to be the party to direct, she to obey): this cannot be regarded as conflicting with the natural superiority of the husband to the wife in his capacity to promote the common interest of the household, and the right to direct that is based on this can be derived from the very duty of unity and equality with respect to the *end*.   (6:279)

Kant's notorious "command" relationship between married couples is a rationalization of the ancient sex-guardian relations of Germanic law and a direct consequence of his deep-seated distrust of egalitarian rule. Kant simply assumes that someone has to have "supreme command" in any institution. His coy distinction between the wife's "reign" [*Herrschen*] and the husband's "governance" [*Regieren*] represents a rather desperate attempt to paper over this assumption with what he himself admits is only an illusion of equality.

This illusion of equality is simply not the equality of wills that his metaphysics of personhood requires of human couples in marriage, but this should come as no surprise when we consider the parallel claim he makes for the state, and what happens to citizens after the social contract is in place. Kant's account of the command system essentially tells wives the same thing that his "Enlightenment" essay told citizens: "Argue as much as you want, only obey!" Yet his theoretical account of the personal union forged by the marriage contract leaves open the possibility of filing for divorce (the analog of rebellion) not only under breach of the conditions of fidelity, non-abandonment, and shared property, but also under conditions of abuse, both physical and psychological. That Kant felt the need to conceal this possibility by a contorted defense of sex-guardianship is hard to explain except as an all-too-typical retreat to authoritarianism.[47]

Frederick Beiser has argued that Kant was a radical in theory but a conservative in practice. He claims that Kant had a "dated and restricted conception of political change" and that

such a narrow conception of political change clearly derived from the age of enlightened absolutism, which permitted at best only freedom of the press and which never dared to question the absolute sovereignty of the monarch.[48]

Although Kant appears to thoroughly commodify the partners and their "parts," his account of the internal workings of the institution of marriage is clearly modeled on his view of the state that emerges from his version of the social contract. Beiser points out that the only recourse Kant offers those who are oppressed by their monarch is resignation and the belief in the slow progress of nature or "providence" by way of unsocial sociability. Kant offers precisely the same advice to the wife in marriage, that is, she may argue all she wants and hope to change the mind of her husband through reason, but beyond that, she should accept her lot. It may well be that just as in the case of his stance on revolution, Kant denies wives the "right of rebellion" by making the false assumption that the institution is headed by a benevolent, enlightened monarch – every man a Frederick the Great in his own household – and hence simply assumes that reform "from above" is possible.[49]

Whatever the explanation, one thing is clear: The marriage contract presented by Kant in the *Metaphysics of Morals* recapitulates the deep tension between authoritarian and liberal egalitarian aspects of his theory of the state, or even more broadly, between Kant's commitments to hierarchically ordered systems, on the one hand, and to equality of persons, on the other. Although there is an interesting case to be made for viewing marriage as a form of "unsocial sociability" leading to progressively better forms of human intimate relationship,[50] cosmopolitan history is hardly going to remedy the injustice done to individual women suffering abusive relationships in the here and now. In the *Metaphysics of Morals* Kant's concern is with legal remedies for these individuals. He sketches a version of marital contract that, had he been able to conceive it without sex-guardianship, would have allowed women vastly greater exit options than they then possessed. Moved by calls from his compatriots for legal reform of the institution of marriage, Kant answered "No!" to Hippel's rhetorical question

Will we seek the answer to these questions [of women's equal civil status] in a subtle and sophisticated Roman legal fiction or in ancient and traditional property rights and statutes of limitation?

The account in *Metaphysics of Morals* is his contribution to this reform: an alternative to older legal standards. Unfortunately, Hippel's deeper questions – "Are women never to attain an absolute value *in* and *for* the state? Are they never to think and act *for* and *by* themselves?" – were answered by Kant only equivocally at best, and negatively at worst. From the materials of his own theoretical philosophy, Kant crafted a useful tool for building equality between the sexes, but he never really trusted it in the hands of ordinary citizens. Instead he locked it away in the cabinet of traditionalism by reaffirming the old institution of sex-guardianship. Kant's model of the marriage contract is for this reason likely to appear to us as an antique curio, but, as I hope to have shown, there is value in retrieving and reconsidering it even today.

NOTES

1. Bertolt Brecht, *Gesammelte Werke in acht Bänden*, IV, Redaction v. Elizabeth Hauptmann, Rosemarie Hill (Frankfurt am Main: Suhrkamp Verlag, 1967), p. 609. Following is a literal translation:

   The contract for the reciprocal use
   Of property and the sex organs
   That he calls marriage, seems to me
   Urgently to warrant securing.

   I hear that some partners are remiss.
   They have – and I don't doubt it –
   Recently evaded sex organs:
   The net has loopholes and they are large.

   So all that's left is to go to court
   And have the organs confiscated.
   Perhaps then the partners will trouble themselves

   To study the contract more closely.
   If they don't trouble themselves – and I'm afraid of that –
   Then the bailiff will just have to appear.

2. See Heiner Klenner's brief essay "Brechts Kant Falschung," *Deutsche Zeitschrift für Philosophie*, 26 (1978), pp. 1051–2.

3. Translations from the *Metaphysics of Morals* are from Mary Gregor, (Cambridge: Cambridge University Press, 1996).

4. The first is Susan Mendus's comment in "Kant: 'An Honest but Narrow-Minded Bourgeois'?," in *Essays on Kant's Political Philosophy*, ed. Howard Williams (Chicago: Chicago University Press, 1992), pp. 166–90; the second is quoted by Mendus in this article (p. 175) from Reinhold Aris's *History of Political Thought in Germany, 1789–1815* (London: George Allen & Unwin, 1936); the last is Hegel's comment, in *Philosophy of Right*, trans. T. M. Knox (New York: Oxford University Press, 1967) para. 75, Remark.

5. Kant was also a great fan of Rousseau's *Émile*. For a useful overview of European scholarship on the relationship of Rousseau's work to Kant's "Observations" and "Remarks on the Observations," see Richard Velkley's *Freedom and the End of Reason* (Chicago: University of Chicago Press, 1989), Chapter 2, pp. 41–52. Susan Shell, in "Kant's Political Cosmology: Freedom and Desire in the 'Remarks' Concerning *Observations on the Feeling of the Beautiful and the Sublime*," gives an extremely useful overview of Kant's early views on marriage as recorded in 1765. She points out rightly, I believe, that much can be learned about Kant's later philosophy from his views on resolving the "gap" between the sexes, especially the aesthetic difference between the beautiful and the sublime and his later, positive assessments of natural, unsocial sociability in historical development as well as the role of femininity and the appearance of morality. Shell's essay is found in *Essays on Kant's Political Philosophy*, ed. Howard Williams (Chicago: University of Chicago Press, 1992), pp. 81–119.

6. See Timothy F. Sellner's Introduction to Theodor Gottlieb von Hippel; *On Improving the Status of Women*, trans. Timothy F. Sellner (Detroit: Wayne State University Press, 1979), pp. 42ff. Sellner here offers a concise summary of the legal status of women in Germany based on Rudolf Huebner's *A History of Private Law*, trans. Francis Philbrick (Boston: Little, Brown, 1918).

7. Sellner's Introduction to Theodor Gottlieb von Hippel; *On Marriage*, trans. and ed. Timothy F. Sellner (Detroit: Wayne State University Press, 1994), p. 55.

8. Ursula Pia Jauch, in her excellent study *Immanuel Kant zur Geschlechts-differenz: Aufklärerische und bürgerliche Geschlechtervormundschaft* (Vienna: Passagen Verlag, 1988), to a certain extent *defends* the essay precisely for the reason that it is not a theoretical work. She argues that Kant never meant for it to be a philosophical treatise, but rather wrote it as a "pragmatic essay" (pp. 62–3) in which he

intentionally takes an androcentric standpoint (p. 66). She points to his explicit rejection of Rousseau ("I would certainly not have wanted to say what Rousseau so boldly asserts, that a woman never becomes anything more than a grown-up child" [2:247n, Goldthwaite trans., p. 102]) as a sign of Kant's already more enlightened view. Jauch then takes up the issue of the tension in Kant's essay between what she calls "equal value" theories of Rococo galantry and "equality theories" of the Enlightenment critique of prejudice. She argues that the "Observations" can be read as "an unmasking parody of the infantalizing consequences of the Rococo model of womanhood that was already socially enforced" in Kant's time (p. 82) and thus suggests that Kant was moving toward a more nuanced and enlightened position.

9. Ann Ferguson uses the term in "Does Reason Have a Gender?," *Radical Philosophy*, ed. Roger S. Gottlieb (Philadelphia: Temple University Press, 1983), pp. 21–47. See also Caroline Whitbeck, "Theories of Sex Difference," *Philosophical Forum*, 5, 1–2 (Fall/Winter 1973), pp. 54–80; Nancy Holmstrom, "Do Women Have a Distinct Nature?," *Philosophical Forum*, 14, 1 (Fall 1982), pp. 25–42.

10. *Anthropology*, 7:209. English translation in *Anthropology from a Pragmatic Point of View*, trans. and ed. Mary Gregor (The Hague: Martinus Nijhoff, 1974), pp. 79–80.

11. Theodor Gottlieb von Hippel, *On Improving the Status of Women*.

12. Ibid., p. 126. Hippel argues that women would not only be excellent educators, but also religious, moral, and political leaders, lawyers and judges, artists, musicians, physicians, and more. Indeed he often suggests that women are not only equally qualified for these professions, but that they are naturally equipped to be better at them.

13. It is important to note that he did not exceed Mary Wollstonecraft, who called for revolutionary changes in this respect. (See Sellner's introduction to *On Improving the Status of Women*, pp. 35ff., for a helpful comparison and contrast of the two treatises.) Hippel's strong rhetoric aside, in the end he called on women to be patient, to refrain from insisting on immediate change, and to wait for reform, both within marriage and the public sphere. (See *On Marriage*, pp. 178ff.) In this very passage Hippel makes the claim that a clever wife is "capable of training her husband in such a way that he merely commands what the wife in fact wishes herself" and at the beginning of the chapter states "If the *authority* in the household belongs to the man then it is the *governing* which falls to the woman; if the husband is *Director of the Household Judicial System*, then the wife is *Director of Police*" (p. 169). This is precisely the opposite of Kant's view that in a well-ordered marriage "the woman should *reign* and the man *govern* . . . he will be like a minister to

his monarch who thinks only of amusement...the monarch can do what [s]he wills, but on one condition: that [her] minister lets [her] know what [her] will is" (*Anthropology*, 7:309ff.). Indeed the metaphors are so similar that it is not unreasonable to suppose the two friends had debated precisely in these terms during one of their many private conversations.

14. Sellner, Introduction to Hippel's *On Improving the Status of Women*, p. 23; Jauch, *Immanuel Kant*, pp. 210–11.

15. Sellner, Introduction to Hippel's *On Marriage*, p. 53. See also Marianne Weber, *Ehefrau und Mutter in der Rechtsentwicklung: eine Einführung* (Tübingen: Mohr, 1907).

16. See Manfred Kuehn, *Kant: A Biography* (Cambridge: Cambridge University Press, 2001), p. 323.

17. Hippel, *On Marriage*, pp. 199 and 303–4n39. Also see Sellner's comments in his Introduction, p. 26.

18. See the infamous remark that "As for the scholarly woman, she uses her *books* in the same way as her *watch*, for example , which she carries so that people will see that she has one, though it is usually not running or not set by the sun" (7:307).

19. *Doctrine of Right*, 6:277–8. See also Jauch, *Immanuel Kant* pp. 156–7, 165–6.

20. See Jauch, *Immanuel Kant*, pp. 128ff., and Sellner, *On Marriage*, pp. 52ff.

21. *Berlinische Monatsschrift*, II/1783, pp. 265–76. Reprinted in *Was ist Aufklärung? Beiträge aus der Berlinischen Monatsschrift*, ed. Norbert Hinske (Darmstadt: Wissenschaftliche Buchgesellschaft, 1973), pp. 95–106.

22. *Berlinischer Monatsschrift*, II/1783, p. 516 (reprinted in Hinske, *Was ist Aufklärung?*, p. 115). Also see James Schmidt's introduction for details of the outcome of this question in the 1780s and beyond, in *What is Enlightenment? Eighteenth-Century Answers and Twentieth-Century Questions*, ed. James Schmidt (Berkeley: University of California Press, 1996), pp. 1–44.

23. For this reason too, the Enlightenment essay should be kept in mind when looking at the purely civil, legalistic account of marriage as contract that he gives in the *Metaphysics of Morals*. See Ursula Pia Jauch, *Immanuel Kant*, pp. 119ff.

24. No one has taken this more seriously to date than Ursula Jauch in *Immanuel Kant zur Geschlechterdifferenz*. See her chapters on Enlightenment and on Kant's complex theoretical and personal relationship to Hippel.

25. In "Kant's Deduction of the Principles of Right," Paul Guyer argues that the principle of right can be derived from the fundamental principle

of morality based on Kant's central assumption of the unconditional value of human freedom. (In *Kant's Metaphysics of Morals: Interpretative Essays*, ed. Mark Timmons [Oxford: Oxford University Press, 2002], pp. 23–64.) In an earlier article Guyer argues that the principle of right is deducible from the universalizability formulation of the categorical imperative and can be deduced from the formula of humanity as well. "Justice and Morality: Comments on Allen Wood," in *The Southern Journal of Philosophy*, 36, Supp. (1997), pp. 21–8, esp. pp. 23–4.

26. Roger J. Sullivan, Introduction to *Immanuel Kant: The Metaphsyics of Morals*, trans. and ed. Mary Gregor (Cambridge: Cambridge University Press, 1996), p. xii.

27. Ibid.

28. Kant actually argues that authorization to coerce follows *logically* ("by the principle of contradiction") from his claim that "a hindering of a hindrance to freedom is consistent with freedom" (6:231). As Guyer points out, the claim itself needs revision to make the argument plausible, see Guyer, "Kant's Deduction," p. 25.

29. I say "explicitly" because Kant held that *all* property relations are relations between or among subjects, even those that may appear to be direct claims of a subject to an object (as in the case of "original" ownership, where no prior competing claim exists) (6:268ff.).

30. Divorce is justified in these cases, as well as if there is failure to ever consummate marriage because of deceit about sexual capacities on entering into it.

31. Or a quadruple violation, if the contract is the unifying act of the wills of both partners!

32. Barbara Herman argues that Kant's views on sexuality bear striking resemblances to contemporary radical feminist views that focus on the objectification of women (although Kant worried about men being objectified as well) and the inequality that objectification produces. See her "Could It Be Worth Thinking About Kant on Sex and Marriage?" in *A Mind of One's Own: Feminist Essays on Reason and Objectivity*, eds. Louise M. Antony and Charlotte Witt (Boulder, CO: Westview Press, 1993), pp. 49–67.

33. Recent biographers have made this abundantly clear. See Manfred Kuehn's fascinating *Kant: A Biography* (Cambridge: Cambridge University Press, 2001), as well as Arsenij Gulyga's *Immanuel Kant and his Life and Thought*, trans. M. Despalatovic (Boston: Birkhauser, 1987).

34. See Kuehn, pp. 166–8, for an account of a scandal to which both Kant and Hippel were partisan witnesses. The story involves a couple with whom both Kant and Hippel were friends: a young wife leaves her well-respected older husband to marry another friend of Kant's.

35. Herman, "Could It Be Worth," p. 57.
36. Allegra de Laurentiis, "Kant's Shameful Proposition: A Hegel-Inspired Criticism of Kant's Theory of Domestic Right," *International Philosophical Quarterly*, 40:3, 159 (September 2000), pp. 297–312.
37. Susan Okin makes use of this notion, borrowed from the work of Robert Goodin and Albert O. Hirshman, in her *Justice, Gender, and the Family* (New York: Basic Books, 1991), Chapter 7, "Vulnerability by Marriage" (pp. 134–69). She goes far beyond the work of others on this topic by recognizing and detailing the degree to which women are forced to stay in bad marriages even where divorce is readily available. See also Robert Goodin, *Protecting the Vulnerable: A Reanalysis of Our Social Responsibilities* (Chicago: University of Chicago Press, 1985).
38. Susan Mendus's insightful article nevertheless does not take this aspect of Kant's view seriously enough, in my opinion.
39. De Laurentiis, "Kant's Shameful Proposition," p. 312.
40. Katrin Flickschuh, *Kant and Modern Political Philosophy* (Cambridge: Cambridge University Press, 2000), p. 6. See also Paul Guyer, "Justice and Morality."
41. See *Essays on Kant's Anthropology*, eds. Brian Jacobs and Patrick Kain (Cambridge: Cambridge University Press, 2003). See also H .L. Wilson, "A Gap in American Kant Scholarship: Pragmatic Anthropology as the Application of Kantian Moral Theory," in *Akten des Siebten Internationalen Kant-Kongresses, 1990*, ed. G. Funke (Bonn: Bouvier, 1991), pp. 403–19.
42. De Laurentiis, "Kant's Shameful Proposition," pp. 309, 310.
43. Susan Mendus's "'An Honest but Narrow-Minded Bourgeois'?" points out that this denial of the possibility of self-ownership is fundamentally at odds with "commodity morality" and undermines the claim that Kant's views on marriage are mere artifacts of his bourgeios allegiances (pp. 185–8).
44. Howard Williams, *Kant's Political Philosophy* (New York: St. Martin's Press, 1983), pp. 117–18.
45. Lara Denis, in "From Friendship to Marriage: Revising Kant" (*Philosophical and Phenomenological Research*, 63, 1 [July 2001], pp. 1–28), has explored a related theme in some detail, namely, that Kant's notion of marriage could be revised to accommodate his much richer and more egalitarian notion of friendship without undermining the fundamentals of his account of the former. As a reconstruction it seems promising, but it is questionable whether Kant himself could have envisaged such a fusion of what for him were two very different sorts of relationships. Sexuality aside, the mundane, constant physical intimacy of marriage alone would appear to be enough to disqualify it from the respectful and

prudent distance that was essential to Kant's personal ideal of friendship.

46. 6:223, and *Perpetual Peace*, 8:347n, 373n.

47. Susan Mendus explains the problem of Kant's autocratic version of marriage in terms of Kant's individualism, which she identifies, wrongly in
my view, as a version of atomic individualism that "cannot accommodate those institutions, such as the family, that transcend mere atomism" ("'An Honest but Narrow-Minded Bourgeois'?" p. 183). Hence
Kant, she argues, can see the family only as a single unit, governed by a
single head. To be sure, Kant's notion of marriage is based on his view
stated explicitly in the *Anthropology*, namely, "If a union is to be harmonious and indissoluble, it is not enough for two people to associate as
they please; one party must be *subject* to the other and reciprocally, one
must be the *superior* of the other in some way, in order to be able to rule
and govern him" (7:303). I believe it is Kant's authoritarian tendencies,
not necessarily a commitment to atomic individualism, that is at work
in these passages.

48. Frederick Beiser, *Enlightenment, Revolution, and Romanticism* (Cambridge, MA: Harvard University Press, 1992), p. 53.

49. Beiser makes this argument by way of explaining Kant's commitment
to reform that is *only* justified when instituted from above. Ibid., p. 56.

50. See Holly L. Wilson's essay "Kant's Evolutionary Theory of Marriage,"
in *Autonomy and Community: Readings in Contemporary Kantian
Social Theory*, eds. Jane Kneller and Sidney Axinn (Albany: State University of New York Press, 1998), pp. 283–306.

14 Kant's theory of peace

In the two centuries since its original formulation, Kant's theory of peace has lost none of its relevance. In fact, because of the recent resurgence of debates about globalization, about the role and mandate of the United Nations, and about the international order after the end of the Cold War, Kant's theory of peace has been steadily gaining attention since 1989.

Kant argues in *Perpetual Peace* and in the *Metaphysics of Morals* that true peace is possible only when states are organized internally according to "republican" principles, when they are organized externally into a voluntary league that promotes peace, and when they respect the human rights not only of their own citizens but also of foreigners. He regards these three main requirements as intrinsically connected and argues that they can be successfully met only jointly.

From the moment *Perpetual Peace* was published, Kant's ideal of a league of states was hotly disputed (when it was not rejected out of hand as wildly unrealistic). The formation of the League of Nations and later of the United Nations has not put an end to the debates. Points of contention persist as to whether the formation of a league of the kind envisioned by Kant is a good idea, and if so, what shape it should have; moreover, there is fundamental disagreement even on what exactly Kant's views are. Does he regard the league as the only form of international cooperation that is feasible and desirable, or does he actually see it as a step on the way toward a further goal, namely, that of an international federation of states with the authority to coercively enforce a common federal law?

More recently, there has been an upsurge in the attention paid to the other two requirements. Kant's claim that republics are more

477

peaceful than other kinds of states (nowadays usually discussed as the "democratic peace" thesis)[1] underwent renewed scrutiny when it was pointed out, in the 1980s, that the empirical record of the previous two centuries shows that democracies did indeed not wage war against each other during that time. Kant's theory of cosmopolitan right is enjoying growing interest because it addresses the rightful status of individuals vis-à-vis states of which they are not citizens. This is an issue that is increasingly relevant in a world full of individuals – from business travelers to refugees – who move (or attempt to move) across borders.

I. HISTORICAL CONTEXTS

Kant was by no means the first to develop a proposal for international peace.[2] He himself mentions the Abbé de Saint-Pierre and Jean-Jacques Rousseau as his predecessors.[3] Saint-Pierre had proposed that the Christian rulers of Europe form a federation with a permanent senate and an international court of arbitration, backed up by an international military force, to settle disputes between member states. Other key requirements mentioned by Saint-Pierre are the reduction of standing armies and the prohibition of territorial expansion and intervention in the internal affairs of other states. Rousseau had summarized the contents of Saint-Pierre's work and presented them to a broader audience.[4]

The first published essay in which Kant himself articulates the normative ideal of international peace and its requirements is the "Ideas toward a Universal History from a Cosmopolitan Point of View" (1784). The ideal of an international federation of states that Kant formulates here returns many times in later writings, for instance, in the *Critique of the Power of Judgment* (1790), *Theory and Practice* (1793), *Conflict of the Faculties* (1798), and most notably *Perpetual Peace* (1795) and the *Metaphysics of Morals* (1797).

Kant's views on peace undergo important modifications over time and move further away from Saint-Pierre's proposals in the process. During the 1780s Kant advocated the establishment of a strong federation of states with coercive authority at the federal level, and like Saint-Pierre, he appealed to the enlightened self-interest of rulers to defend the feasibility of this ideal. During the 1790s, however, Kant began to defend the establishment of a league without coercive powers (although he continued to mention the stronger form of federation as the ideal dictated by reason). Furthermore, he added the novel category of "cosmopolitan right" as the third kind of public right. To make the feasibility of his proposal plausible, Kant relied no longer merely on the self-interest of rulers. As he developed his republicanism, he mentioned a much broader set of natural forces that force humankind in the direction of peace, including the peaceful nature of republican states.

The changes in Kant's theory of peace are not unrelated to the historical developments at the time. Of the many events that could be mentioned here, the political events in France are probably the most important. During the French Revolution, the Ancien Régime was overthrown – or, according to Kant's preferred interpretation: Louis XVI handed sovereignty over to the people when he turned to them for financial help (Morals, 6:341–2). Subsequently, France was transformed into a republic, and from then on the republican ideal takes on a more and more central role in Kant's political thought. In the early 1790s, the new French republic employed an official rhetoric of wanting to "liberate" other peoples from their tyrants and form a fraternal alliance with the resulting states. Reality proved considerably more complicated, however. France was remarkably successful in its war against the large royalist alliance of European monarchies that aimed at reinstating the French monarchy. Yet it turned out that the people in most other countries did not regard the French invasion as their liberation. In 1795 France concluded peace with Prussia and Spain, but the end of the decade saw the rise of Napoleon and an increasingly successful French expansionism.

Kant seems to have always expected that the French republic would help the cause of international peace. This is implicit in his thesis, in *Perpetual Peace*, that republics are naturally more peaceful than despotic states. Moreover, he defends the feasibility of his own theory of peace by claiming that the French republic could become the center of a peace-promoting union that other states would then join (8:356). Toward the end of the decade he reportedly expressed the hope that Napoleon would bring about perpetual peace.[5]

Another historical process that is of importance for understanding Kant's views on peace is the spread of Europeans around the world. The European powers had of course been expanding their reach over the rest of the world for quite some time already, with different emphasis in different cases: from the establishment of trading posts to the control over natural resources elsewhere, the establishment of colonies, the slave trade, the exploitation of slaves on plantations, or the famous voyages of "discovery." Kant knew about all of this and followed reports about other continents with enormous interest. Although his attitudes towards non-Europeans are characterized, at least through the 1780s, by a good deal of ignorance, inconsistency, and harmful prejudice,[6] Kant was – unlike many others of his time – concerned with establishing peace not merely in Europe, but across the entire globe.

II. KANT'S THEORY OF PERPETUAL PEACE

In Kant's theory of international peace, all three parts of public right come into play. The rightful regulation of the interactions among individuals requires the rule of law within a rightful state; the rightful regulation of the interactions among states requires the rule of international right; and the rightful regulation of the interactions between states (or their representatives) and foreign individuals requires the rule of cosmopolitan right. Kant's theory of right is inherently cosmopolitan and includes not just a theory of the state, but also a theory of international right and cosmopolitan right.

All three parts of public right are grounded in the basic idea of external freedom. Kant argues that the notion of "right" derives from the concept of freedom as applied to the external relations among persons. *Right* is the "restriction of the freedom of each to the condition of its being compatible with the freedom of everyone, to the extent this freedom is possible in accordance with a general law; and *public* right is the sum of *external* laws that make such a universal harmony possible" (*Theory and Practice*, 8:289–90; see also *Morals*, 6:230.)

Public right requires, first of all, a state with just laws and the power to enforce them. In the absence of a just legal system with coercive authority, that is, in the state of nature, no one's right to external freedom can be secure against violence by others (*Morals*, 6:312). Kant is not here making the empirical assumption that people are in fact prone to violate the freedom of others (although he certainly believes they are); rather, he is assuming the *a priori* idea that people are free and that freedom implies the *possible* violation of the freedom of others. This posssibility alone is enough to require a system of laws and their enforcement to protect rightful freedom.

The only political system that is fully compatible with the requirements of public right is a republic. By "republic" Kant means a political system that is based on the principles of the freedom and equality of the citizens, and, depending on which text one reads, their independence as co-legislators (*Theory and Practice*, 8:294) or their dependence on a common legislation (*Perpetual Peace*, 8:349). A republic is governed by the rule of law, not the caprice of a despot. The laws of a republic are enacted by the citizens through their representatives. In a republic, the legislative, executive, and judicial branches of government are properly separated from each other. Finally, neither the territory of a republic nor the offices associated with its government are the personal property of the officers in function.

The ideal of the individual's freedom being "compatible with the freedom of everyone" transcends the level of the state, however. It also calls for the regulation of the behavior of states among each other and of individuals and states toward foreign individuals. This is because protecting external freedom at the state level alone is not enough to protect it completely. The latter also requires that states subject themselves to the rightful regulation of their interactions with each other. As long as states (republics or not) remain in the state of nature, in their interactions with other states, there is the threat of war, and war is a fundamental threat to the freedom of individuals – after all, the question of who wins a war is decided by might, not right.

Thus, it is not surprising that Kant often discusses the rightful regulation at the state level and at the inter-state level in tandem and that he regards the two as equally necessary. Beginning with the "Ideas toward a Universal History," he regards the solution of the one problem as dependent on the solution of the other. In this essay, he claims that the achievement of a perfect state constitution is not possible until rightful external relations among states (in an international federation) have been achieved (8:24). In later essays he turns the order around and claims that international peace will not be achieved until after states have become republics (e.g., *Theory and Practice*, 8:311). In *Perpetual Peace*, he argues that the two requirements stand in a reciprocal relationship (along with cosmopolitan right, about which more below) and that the one cannot be fully achieved without the other (8:349, note).

The thesis that states should leave the state of nature raises the question, however, of what peace at the global level requires. Kant's view on this matter evolves over time. Initially, in the "Ideas toward a Universal History from a Cosmopolitan Point of View" (1784), he argues that the situation of states in the state of nature is entirely analogous to that of individuals in the state of nature, and that just as individuals ought to leave the state of nature by subjecting themselves to common laws and law enforcement, states ought to form a global federation with coercive powers at the federal level. In this essay, Kant advocates a "cosmopolitan situation," which will come about once states form a federation "similar to a civil commonwealth" (8:25). They should "abandon the lawless state of savagery and enter into a federation of peoples in which every state, even the smallest, could expect its security and its rights, not from its own power or its own legal judgment, but rather solely from this great federation of peoples..., from a united power and from decisions based on laws of a united will" (8:24).[7]

Later, most clearly in *Perpetual Peace* and the *Metaphysics of Morals*, Kant defends a more complex view. In *Perpetual Peace*, Kant introduces a new and detailed set of conditions for attaining peace among states. First of all, he mentions a series of six negative conditions, in the form of "preliminary articles": Peace treaties should not contain secret reservations (as the 1795 Basel peace treaty between France and Prussia had contained); states should not be able to acquire other states (through inheritance, barter, purchase, or gift); standing armies should be phased out; states should not assume debts for the sake of foreign policy; states should not intervene with violence in the internal affairs (the constitution and government) of other states; and practices that undermine the possibility of mutual trust among states should be banned (such as employing assassins and recruiting traitors) (8:343–7).

Furthermore, Kant mentions three positive conditions, or "definitive articles": that states be internally organized in accordance with the principle of republicanism; that they pursue and honor the establishment of a league of states externally; and that states and individuals respect the principle of hospitality in their dealings with foreigners. Kant claims that all three are necessary conditions for peace. I will comment on each of these three in order.

Republicanism is important not only because it is the only constitution that is fully in accordance with external right, but also because it is the only constitution that by its nature leads to peace. Despots can easily burden their subjects with the costs of warfare without incurring direct costs to themselves. In republics, by contrast, the citizens' consent is required for the decision to go to war, and citizens themselves shoulder the burdens of warfare (financial and otherwise). Therefore, Kant claims, citizens are naturally disinclined to vote for a war and a republic is naturally inclined to be peaceful (8:352).

Kant's position on the regulation of the interactions among states is considerably less clear. Is his ultimate ideal a league of states? Or is this merely apparent and does he actually advocate the establishment of a federative union of states, as a few commentators have claimed? Or does he regard a league as the necessary first step on the road toward a federation of states? The standard view is the first. A small minority of commentators defends the second position, on the basis of the logic of Kant's overall position.[8] I believe there are good reasons (both textual and philosophical) to believe that the third alternative better represents Kant's view, that is, that Kant advocates the establishment of a noncoercive league of states (at least in his mature political writings such as *Perpetual Peace* and the *Metaphysics of Morals*), but that he does so because he regards it as the only possible road to the ultimate ideal, a state of states.

In the second "Definitive Article" of *Perpetual Peace*, Kant claims that international right should be based on the "federalism of free states" (8:354). Read in isolation, the statement may seem ambiguous. It may seem unclear whether the term "federalism" refers to a federation with coercive powers over the member states (analogous to a state) or to a looser confederation of independent states. Kant uses the word "Bund" to refer to both. Similarly, the term "free states" could refer to states that are not under binding international laws, or to states that enjoy the kind of rightful freedom analogous to the freedom enjoyed by citizens in a republic. When Kant's accompanying comments are taken into account, however, it becomes clear that he here advocates the establishment of a voluntary league of states, a league without any highest legislative or coercive authority (8:356; also *Morals* 6:351).

In both *Perpetual Peace* and the *Metaphysics of Morals*, however, Kant claims also that reason demands the formation of a state of states. In a notorious passage in *Perpetual Peace* he writes:

As concerns the relations among states, according to reason there can be no other way for them to emerge from the lawless condition, which contains only war, than for them to relinquish, just as do individual human beings, their wild (lawless) freedom, and to accustom themselves to public, binding laws, and to thereby form a (continually expanding) *state of peoples* (*civitas gentium*), which would ultimately comprise all of the peoples on earth. But they do not want this at all, according to their conception of the right of peoples (thus rejecting *in hypothesi* what is right *in thesi*);[9] therefore, instead of the positive idea of a *world republic* (if not everything is to be lost) only the *negative* surrogate of a lasting and continually expanding *league* [*Bund*] that averts war can halt the stream of law-shunning and hostile inclination, but with a constant threat of its breaking out.   (8:357)

This passage has caused considerable consternation among readers, as it seems to be an entirely uncharacteristic concession to realism on Kant's part. It is usually read as reducing what is normatively required (a state of states) to something more feasible (a league) on the basis of what states can be expected to want to join. This is then judged to be an inconsistent move because of Kant's own vehement and explicit opposition to theories that reduce what is normatively required on the basis of empirical data of the past or speculation of what is practically realistic (see especially his arguments in *Theory and Practice*).[10] Thus, on the standard reading, Kant contradicts himself fundamentally and blatantly, within one and the same section, and with regard to one of the most important issues of the book. Many commentators have argued that to be consistent, Kant should have advocated (or better: should have advocated *only*) the establishment of a federation of states (with coercive authority at the federal level over the member states), and not a league, as the proper way to overcome the state of nature. They argue that the logic of the argument is the same, whether it is states or individuals who leave the state of nature, and hence that the result should be the same in both cases: a state in the case of individuals, a state of states in the case of states.[11]

It is not necessary to read the quoted passage in this way, however, and there is an alternative reading that makes more sense both

textually and philosophically. Note first of all that the quote is not
a call to *reject* the ideal of a world republic. Furthermore, Kant does
not say that states *will never* want to join a federation but, rather,
that they *do not* want to do so because they (mis)interpret international right as a right to remain in the state of nature. As we shall
see, it is possible to read the quoted passage as saying that the only
way to leave the state of nature among states is by starting with a
league of states, while the federation remains the ultimate ideal.

What is necessary to make this reading plausible is an account
of how the states' not *wanting* to join a federation can be a valid
reason, according to Kant, for advocating a league. It is possible to
construct such an account, on the basis of an analysis of why the
analogy posited between the state of nature among individuals and
that among states is not in fact a perfect analogy. The considerable
difference is the following. When individuals leave the state of nature
to submit to the laws of a common state, the state they form may
not be perfect, but it will be better, normatively speaking, than the
state of nature that they left behind because before its creation there
was no rule of law at all. This is not true, however, in the case of
states leaving the state of nature.

In *Perpetual Peace* Kant explicates the difference, cryptically, by
stating that "states already have an internal legal constitution, and
thus they have outgrown the coercion of others to subject them to
a broader legal constitution according to their [viz., others'] conceptions of right" (8:355–6). In the *Vorarbeiten* (drafts and notes) for *Perpetual Peace*, he writes that states are allowed to resist the attempt
by others to force them to join a federative state of states "because
within them public right has already been established, whereas in the
case of individuals in the state of nature nothing of the kind takes
place" (23:168). Why would having an internal legal constitution
be a reason not to have to be forced into a state of states? The best
explanation is that forcing an unwilling state into a federation would
violate the autonomy of the individuals composing the state, collectively as co-legislating citizens. Kant defines the state as a union
of individuals under laws of right, and ideally as a union of politi-
cally autonomous individuals (see *Morals*, 6:313). Forcing them into
a state of states against their will would run counter to the basic idea
of political autonomy. Forcing individuals into a state, by contrast,
does not violate their political autonomy because, on the Kantian

account, they do not have political autonomy as long as they remain in the state of nature.

The problem with coercing unwilling states into a federation is not just that a despotic state of states could destroy the rights and freedoms that the citizens of a just republic had already secured internally (although this certainly is a problem too). The point is a deeper one. Even the individuals within currently despotic states may not want to join a federation of states if this has to happen on a conception of right that differs from their own.

One way to make this point clear is to think through what it would mean if we were to take the level of individuals and that of states in the state of nature as perfectly analogous. Most authors who claim that Kant should have argued in favor of the immediate establishment of a federative state of states do not themselves take this argument to its logical consequences; they inconsistently allow for voluntary joining and seceding. A few are more consistent, and then the results are propositions like the following:

> [I]f ... the creation of a world government would require that all nations have democratic or "republican" forms of government, then the prospects for the creation of a world government are not good. It may seem unlikely that all nations would ever agree to a particular form of a world government. But this is not necessary for the creation of a world government. It would be enough if all great powers (or all nuclear powers) agreed to the idea of a world state. They could then unite and compel other nations to join.[12]

Here the state of states is based on the sheer power of a few states with the weaponry that can compel all others, regardless of the others' "conception of right," to use Kant's words quoted above.[13] The despotic structure of this situation should be clear.

One might still wonder whether Kant should not make an exception for cases in which a state of states that is organized in accordance with principles of right coerces an oppressive despotic state into its organization, reorganizing the internal political structure of that state in the process and thereby improving the external freedom of the individuals within it. After all, it might seem that the freedom and political autonomy of these individuals would be only served in the process, as they would now receive rights and freedoms that they did not enjoy before. What is overlooked in this objection, however, is that this is an essentially paternalistic line of reasoning that passes over the political autonomy of the people it purports to serve. The people may well want to get rid of their despot, but it does not follow that they will want to join a particular state of states. Perhaps what they want most of all is to have a say in the matter. An analogy might help here. Imagine a state policy to the effect that when one spouse has been criminally abusive of the other and the victim wants to have the marriage dissolved, the state imposes a new marriage on the abused spouse, but this time to someone who is believed to observe principles of justice. It is clear that this kind of procedure would fail to treat the abused spouse as a person capable of autonomy and would be wrong for that reason. An analogous problem would occur if an otherwise justly ordered state of states coerced despotic states into its organization against their will, thereby failing to treat the peoples[14] involved as capable of political autonomy. There is good reason, then, given Kant's assumptions, to advocate not the coercive formation of a state of states but a league instead and to hope that the federation will subsequently become established voluntarily.

Kant's fear of despotism at the global level is also expressed in his opposition to the so-called "universal monarchy," which emerges when all states "fuse together" (8:367) by being absorbed into a single hegemonic superpower. This form of world goverment, based on one state's ability to overpower all other states, leads to "soulless despotism" (8:367).

Kant's opposition to a universal monarchy, however, is not inspired by a general opposition against states giving up their sovereignty.[15] States are allowed to join a federation when this happens voluntarily and with the preservation of the lawful freedom of their citizens. In fact, Kant believes that reason requires them to do so (8:357) and that there consequently is a moral duty to promote the establishment of a federative state of states (but *via* the establishment of a league).

Read in this way, there is no tension between Kant's advocacy of the league of states and the many other, oft-overlooked passages in *Perpetual Peace* and the *Metaphysics of Morals* in which Kant expresses the ideal of a state-like federation. For example, he expresses the hope that "distant parts of the world can peaceably enter into relations with each other, relations which can ultimately become publicly lawful and so bring humanity finally ever closer to a cosmopolitan constitution" (*Perpetual Peace*, 8:358). He writes that justice requires "an internal constitution of the state in accordance with pure principles of right, and then further, however, the union of this state with other neighboring or also distant states for the purpose of a lawful settlement of their conflicts" (*Perpetual Peace*, 8:379). And he writes in the *Metaphysics of Morals* that before states leave the state of nature all international right is merely "provisional," and that international right can come to hold definitively and establish a true perpetual peace only "in a universal union of states [*Staatenverein*] (analogous to that by which a people becomes a state)," a union that Kant on the same page refers to also as a "state of peoples" [*Völkerstaat*] (*Morals*, 6:350).

Thus, Kant endorsed the idea of a federative "state of states" throughout the 1780s and 1790s, but during the 1790s he began advocating the establishment of a league of states as the means to promote this ultimate ideal. It is possible that Kant made this change while observing France's behavior: Here was a republic that coercively incorporated unwilling states into its republican (and according to Kant as such correct) framework. Even though France dethroned their "tyrants," the populations of the conquered states turned out to be quite resistant to their self-proclaimed liberators. There were also cases, however, in which the French were (initially) welcomed, as with the Dutch Republic in early 1795. It is possible that Kant had these latter cases in mind when he voiced the hope that when a "powerful and enlightened people" can transform itself into a republic (a reference to France), this provides a core for other states to join and form a federative union (*Perpetual Peace*, 8:356).

"Cosmopolitan right" is the third category of public right, presented as such for the first time in *Perpetual Peace* and also included in the *Metaphysics of Morals*. Its discussion takes up just a few pages and it was hardly mentioned at all in the Kant literature until fairly recently, but it now enjoys considerable attention. Cosmopolitan right regulates the interactions between states and foreigners, for example, regarding migration, commercial ties, or attempts at colonial settlements.

In cosmopolitan right, "individuals and states who stand in an external relationship of mutual influence are regarded as citizens of a universal state of humankind [*allgemeiner Menschenstaat*] (*ius cosmopoliticum*)" (*Perpetual Peace*, 8:349, note). At its core is the right to hospitality. Despite the term, this right should not be understood as the right to be a guest. It is not even the right to enter foreign territory; rather, it is merely the right to *attempt* to be granted entry or establish relations with others elsewhere, the right to present oneself and make a request. Such a request may be denied, but not with violence, and not if this leads to the death of the individuals involved (8:358). Cosmopolitan right thus requires, for example, that states provide a safe haven for refugees in peril and that they and their inhabitants not intrude into or settle upon the territory of others without their explicit agreement. Kant strongly criticizes the colonial and international trading practices of his era, as the European powers in their attitudes towards non-Europeans made no distinction between visiting and conquering other territories and "held the inhabitants for nothing" (8:358). With this theory, Kant grants humans anywhere on earth certain basic rights. In contrast to Lockean theories, for example, Kant's theory grants nomads a rightful claim to land.

Kant writes that cosmopolitan right is grounded in the "common possession of the surface of the earth" (*Perpetual Peace*, 8:358) or the "original community of the surface of the earth" (*Morals*, 6:352), but he leaves much unclear as to the precise foundation and justification of cosmopolitan right. One possible articulation of what might be implicit here is the following: Originally, the earth was held in common, and the acquisition of particular parts of it by particular persons happened only at a later point in time. This implies that all parts of the earth have to be regarded as in principle acquirable by others, even if they currently have owners. To be able to try to acquire a piece of land, however, one needs to be able to get in touch with its owner. Hence, the in-principle acquirability of land implies a right to present oneself to others elsewhere. This is at least how Kant's argument was explicated by some of his followers at the time.[16]

If the argument is construed in this way, however, it provides at best a partial grounding for cosmopolitan right because it does not cover all the cases that Kant mentions as examples. It does cover attempts at certain commercial transactions, but not, say, the case of shipwrecked sailors (mentioned by Kant in the *Vorarbeiten to Perpetual Peace*, 23:173). After all, they are not attempting to acquire the beach where they wash ashore, but just to use it temporarily to save their lives. If cosmopolitan right is grounded in a theory about the origin of property rights, it does not address the question as to why and how cosmopolitan right would, in such cases, override the established property rights of the owners to determine the use of their land. Of course, the owner of the land would have a *moral* duty to help the hapless sailors, but when the question is what grounds the cosmopolitan *right* of the latter, Kant needs a different argument.

Kant could probably have developed such an argument from the "innate right to freedom" of which he speaks in the *Metaphysics of Morals* (6:237–8). This right includes the "right to be there where nature or chance (without [one's] will) has placed [one]" (6:262). Elsewhere, Kant motivates this by saying that being on land is necessary for the very existence of human beings, and thus, that people have a right to be on the land on which they are placed through no choice of their own, since denying them this right would mean denying them their existence and their freedom (23:318). As it stands, however, Kant does not use this argumentative strategy in his published discussion of cosmopolitan right.

III. THE PROCESS TOWARD PERPETUAL PEACE

Kant claims that the achievements in the three areas of public right hang together such that peace is attainable only if all three positive conditions have been satisfied (*Perpetual Peace*, 8:349, note; *Morals*, 6:311). He does not stipulate a temporal sequence among them (as if the league of states were possible only after all states have become republics, and cosmopolitan right were possible only thereafter).

This raises questions as to how Kant envisions the practical realization of what is normatively required according to his legal theory. He regularly criticizes thinkers who ground their normative theories on empirical considerations of what is feasible, but this should not lead one to think that he finds unimportant the empirical question of whether and how the normative ideals can be achieved. It is a question that can be posed correctly, however, only *after* the normative ideals have been formulated. Kant does find it important to show that although his ideals are grounded in pure reason, they are not unrealistic. In order to show this, he provides a teleological account of history that revolves around the assumption that nature is organized teleologically in such a way as to support the cause of law-governed peace and moral development.[17] "Nature" here includes both human and nonhuman nature – the teleological account encompasses everything from arrangements that enable humans to physically spread across the globe (driftwood that provides wood in icy regions, camels that can transport humans through the Sahara, etc.) to human psychological propensities, especially the "unsocial sociability" that drives humans to develop their rational potential.

As early as the *Critique of Pure Reason* Kant argues that teleological judgments can be justified as heuristic principles (A 687/B 715), and in the "Ideas toward a Universal History" he provides a teleological account of history on this basis. He proposes to regard history as progressing towards the "full development of all human predispositions" (*Universal History*, 8:27). A crucial part of this process is the development of a perfect internal state constitution as well as the establishment of an international federation of states. With these conditions in place, there will be room for moral education, culminating in the self-transformation of humanity into a "moral whole" (8:21). In the *Critique of the Power of Judgment*, Kant further develops his account of the epistemological status of teleological judgments and argues that all of nature can be regarded as teleologically oriented towards human "culture" (in its eighteenth-century meaning of "development"). This culture is itself subservient to the "final end of creation," which Kant determines as humans as moral beings (5:435–6). Finally, in the third *Critique*, too, we find the claim that legal progress will promote moral progress towards peace: Kant defends the assumption (not knowledge claim) that nature is organized in such a way that it "prepares (if not establishes) lawfulness combined with the freedom of states and thereby the unity of a morally grounded system of states" (5:433).

Of course this teleological account of history, developed in the "Ideas toward a Universal History" for the sake of presenting history as an orderly whole, can be put to use *also* in the service of moral theory. The assumption of progress is encouraging for the moral agent because it presents the normative ideals as not unrealistic. This does not of course mean that the moral subject can therefore become inactive and let nature do all the work. Duty remains duty even if natural forces lend a hand. What is more, nature *cannot* do all of the work. The full attainment of the final end requires morality itself, and morality can be the product only of genuinely free agency. Nature can, according to Kant, produce certain kinds of behavior in people, and insofar as right concerns the behavior of people (not their motivation), nature can bring about that which right requires and thus lead all the way to peace as defined in terms of right. For peace to be truly *perpetual*, however, it needs to be supported by *moral* dispositions (and this is of course also what morality requires). The fragile "natural" peace is itself conducive to its gradual and never-ending transformation into a perpetual "moral" peace, and this is how nature paves the way for morality without eliminating freedom, duty, and virtue.

With regard to the goal of peace specifically, Kant argues that self-interest drives humans in the direction of peace. Modern warfare is becoming so costly that states will find it prudent to strive for peace; and despotic states that fail to realize this and keep waging war will exhaust themselves. During the 1790s Kant begins to stress that when this happens, it opens up room for republicanization. Kant saw France as a good example of how despotic states are their own worst enemy. On his interpretation, Louis XVI, having exhausted all financial resources, had been forced to turn to the people and cede power in the process, thereby giving the people room to transform the state into a republic. Kant adds the view also that republics, because citizens decide whether there will be war or not, are by nature more peaceful. It is easy for despots to declare war because they hardly bear the consequences personally, shifting the actual dangers and burdens to their subjects. In a republic, by contrast, citizens will realize that war means higher taxes, personal risks, loss of liberties, and so on, and that this goes against their own interests. Either way, it is in every state's interest to avoid war, and hence it is in their interest to join a league that promotes peace.

Exactly how the league of states is supposed to promote further progress toward peace from there on is not particularly clear. Kant conceives of the league on the model of a congress of states, where delegates from the member states can bring complaints and submit conflicts to mediation and arbitration (*Morals*, 6:350). The league could, of course, encompass more than just a focus on conflict resolution, by, say, supporting other kinds of international programs that are conducive to mutual understanding and peace, such as educational programs, cultural cooperation, or mutual aid. Kant himself does not specify any of this, although these proposals would be compatible with his other views.

With regard to the mechanisms that further the realization of cosmopolitan right, Kant mentions the "spirit of trade." He maintains that this is essentially a force for peace because trade encourages people across the globe to entertain friendly relations with each other for the sake of mutually beneficial commercial interactions (*Perpetual Peace*, 8:368).

The peace that is established on the basis of self-interest is fragile, of course, and Kant is the first to admit this (8:357),[18] but he expects the legal peace (external freedom) to have a positive effect for morality (inner freedom). Even a peace based on sheer self-interest, he believes, makes it possible to expand human rights and interests and to divert resources to education and enlightenment instead of armament. In Kant's eyes this becomes a self-reinforcing process. When states improve internally as a consequence of peace, they provide even better environments for further political and even moral development. As a result, Kant believes, people gradually come to see the rightness of what they initially consented to only on the basis of self-interest. They will then come to accept peace as not merely prudent but right, and this will make the peace more and more stable. He expects that as a result of cultural development within states, people will gradually converge on moral and juridical-political principles, and that this will eventually yield an agreement to a peace that is durable (8:367; see also the earlier references to similar statements in *Universal History* and *Judgment*).

The most salient passage is probably the one found in the *Vorarbeiten* to the *Metaphysics of Morals*. Here Kant writes that when laws secure freedom externally, inner freedom (morality) will "come alive" and this, in turn, will enhance obedience to the laws. This self-reinforcing process gradually makes the legal peace ever more secure because peace becomes less a matter of mere self-interest and more a matter of moral disposition:

A firmly established peace, combined with the greater interaction among people [*Menschen*] is the idea through which alone is made possible the transition from the duties of right to the duties of virtue. Since when the laws secure freedom externally, the maxims to also govern oneself internally in accordance with laws can come alive; and conversely, the latter in turn make it easier, through their dispositions for lawful coercion to have an influence, so that peaceful conduct [*friedliches Verhalten*] under public laws and pacific dispositions [*friedfertige Gesinnungen*] (to also end the inner war between principles and inclinations), i.e., legality and morality find in the concept of peace the point of support for the transition from the Doctrine of Right to the Doctrine of Virtue.

(23:353–4, *Vorarbeiten* to the *Metaphysics of Morals*)

In the *Metaphysics of Morals* Kant emphasizes that this process will never completely reach its goal. He assumes that when the state of states becomes very large, it will no longer be able successfully to protect all of its members against other states. This problem cannot be solved by allowing multiple (smaller) states of states to keep the peace because these would themselves still exist in the state of nature. The political principle to *strive for* and *approximate* a state of states is not unfeasible, however, and therefore it remains a duty to continually approximate the idea of a single state of states.

IV. RECEPTION AND RESPONSE

Kant's first positive requirement for peace, namely, that every state be a republic (in Kant's sense of the term) because republics are naturally more peaceful, has provoked much discussion. It has led some theorists to assume that international peace, in the ideal at least, does not require any international institution with coercive powers to enforce international right. After all, if all states are republics (or, in current usage, democracies), and these do not wage war against each other, then international peace can be achieved via democratization.[19]

In its generality Kant's thesis has proven to be too strong, however. Democracies turn out not to be any less war-prone toward nondemocracies than nondemocracies are toward each other.[20] One explanation of why democracies wage war despite the fact that the citizens, who shoulder the burdens, have a say in the decision whether to go to war, may have to do with the role of power and the possibility of using ideology and manipulation to mobilize a civilian population to rally behind a war. Kant did not sufficiently take these factors into account. If the disinclination toward war, on the part of democracies, is merely an effect of their calculation of risks and benefits, then differences in power among the various states may lead to different results than Kant thought. The citizens of a very powerful state may well come to the conclusion that a successful war against a weaker state will serve their own long-term interests. Such citizens may feel comfortable undertaking war if they believe they are the strongest and they assess the risks as outweighed by the expected gains. Also, even in a representative democracy the decision to wage war is not necessarily made by those who shoulder the heaviest burdens (e.g., the representatives may not generally be from the same social class as those who risk their lives). Furthermore, citizens can be convinced by effective rhetoric or distorted information: Powerful interests may persuade them that war is a necessity to prevent a greater disaster in the future, that war will bring honor or take away shame, or that war is required to serve justice or God. Finally, perhaps part of the explanation of why democracies wage war is also that democracies more easily regard nondemocracies as a threat or an outrage.

When limited to the narrower thesis that democracies do not start wars against other democracies, however, the empirical evidence seems quite strong. As Michael Doyle has argued on the basis of a study of two centuries worth of wars, it does appear that democracies have started wars only against non-democracies.[21] Of course, one could wonder whether counterexamples to the thesis of the peacefulness of democracies towards each other could be found in acts of violence like, say, the 1973 assassination of Salvador Allende in Chile. Still, there is at least a striking pattern. Moreover, Kant's claim is not that republics *will never* wage war, but that they are significantly less likely to do so (not because they generally tend to act more in accordance with moral requirements, but because the citizens need to be convinced that war is necessary and they will have to shoulder the burdens of the war). And when narrowed to the behavior of democracies toward each other, this claim seems to have the statistics on its side.

One side effect of narrowing Kant's thesis in this way, however, is that it invalidates his general confidence in the pacific role of republics in the greater process of achieving worldwide peace. If democracies are no longer regarded as more pacific in general, just more peaceful toward fellow democracies, then it is no longer clear how the enlightened self-interest of the citizens of democracies helps to promote world peace, even if it helps reduce warfare among democracies themselves. After all, the narrowed thesis is compatible with the existing democracies jointly subjugating or exploiting the rest of the world. It might then still be true that a world of democracies would be peaceful, or in any event more peaceful, than the present world. But it would no longer be clear that democracies naturally play a crucial role in the process of bringing worldwide peace closer.

It is an indication of the importance of Kant's theory of international right, especially his advocacy for a league of states, that it has been the subject of intense debate for more than two centuries. "Realists" strongly reject it because they regard the normative principles expounded by Kant as inapplicable to the international arena. Kant's views have also found many supporters, however, and when states in the twentieth century moved to form first the League of States and then the United Nations, his defense of a league of states was often invoked – even if the resulting bodies only partially corresponded to the league proposed by Kant (most notably perhaps, standing armies were not abolished). Among recent political theorists, John Rawls is one who defends a voluntary league via an explicit appeal to Kant. Rawls often claims that he is "following Kant's lead" in his defense of a confederation of free and independent states ("peoples," in his terminology) and in his opposition against any form of world government.[22]

Kant's theory of international right has also, however, faced several criticisms from very early on. One point of contention has been whether Kant allows the league too much or too little coercive power to enforce its laws. From Johann Gottlieb Fichte to Jürgen Habermas, critics have asserted that Kant wrongly fails to extend coercive military powers to the league of states. Romantics, by contrast, starting with the young Friedrich Schlegel, have criticized Kant for including *any* power to coerce in his ideal of the good state.

According to the first tradition of critics, Kant is inconsistent in advocating the establishment of a voluntary league rather than a stronger form of federation of states. As explained above, the perception is that he reduces the normative requirement of a strong federation to the weaker requirement of a league, on the basis of the assessment that states are unlikely to *want* to join a federation that has the authority to coerce member states into compliance with its laws. This is just the kind of realist-empiricist move that Kant himself regularly denounces.

One reaction among Kantian theorists has been to try to rectify the perceived inconsistency by using Kant's own arguments against

Kant to advocate the establishment of an international federation with the authority and means to enforce its laws. Already in his *Grundlage des Naturrechts* of 1796, Fichte insists that the federation of states should have the power to enforce member compliance coercively because this is the only way to end war and provide a way to adjudicate conflicts in accordance with just laws. Member states in the federation ought to recognize each other through treaties, regard each other as equals, and treat each other's citizens rightfully. If a member state violates these rules, however, it is the task of the federation to punish this state.[23] In recent Kantian political theory one can similarly find appeals to strengthen the military powers of the United Nations, for example, in the work of Jürgen Habermas and Otfried Höffe.[24] If one reads Kant's texts according to the interpretation outlined earlier, however, there is actually no inconsistency to be corrected and the "amendment" appears in a different light. Given the standard reading, however, Kant has of course influenced the debate as one who advocates a voluntary league and opposes a stronger federation of states.

To more romantic readers, such as Friedrich Schlegel in his 1796 review of *Perpetual Peace*, the problem with Kant's theory is rather an empirically tainted and unduly pessimistic model of the state that carries over into his theory of international relations. Schlegel claimed that a truly pure concept of the state should not depend on the assertion that people will act against the law, and hence that the *ideal* of the state should not include "political power and dependence," for these are introduced into the concept of the state only on the assumption that people violate the law. "Therefore," says Schegel, "not *every* state includes the relationship between a superior and a subordinate, but only the state that is empirically determined by that actual fact." The ideal state, by contrast, is nonhierarchical and noncoercive. By extension, the same is true at the international level: The ideal should be a noncoercive, nonhierarchical republic of republics, characterized by the freedom and equality of the individual member states, who freely obey common laws.[25]

Interestingly, and perhaps even in response to Schlegel, Kant points out in the *Metaphysics of Morals* that it is "not experience" and "not a fact" that necessitates the coercive powers of the state, but rather the mere *possibility* that people violate each other's spheres of freedom. On Kant's own view this possibility is implicit in the very concept of the state of nature (*Morals*, 6:312). By extension, the same argument could be used with regard to the coercive powers of the federation of states.

A further standard criticism of Kant's theory in *Perpetual Peace*, likewise voiced already by early critics, such as Friedrich Gentz, is that the league of states would be *unable* to bring about peace. The charge is that if the league is merely voluntary and devoid of the authority to enforce compliance, states will join only if and as long as they are interested in peace. As soon as their perception of their interests changes, they will simply walk away from their "commitment" to peace, which therefore is no real commitment. Hence, the league makes no practical difference at all.[26]

While it is certainly true that Kant says surprisingly little about how he envisions the league to work, he does not actually claim that the league will by itself bring about durable peace (see, e.g., *Perpetual Peace*, 8:357), but rather that it is an important step on the way to a perpetual peace. If this is granted, the burden of proof can be shifted to the side of the critics, as they would now need to show that opening up channels of communication and negotiation does not help at all to further the cause of peace.

Finally, with regard to Kant's claim that peace at the legal level will have beneficial effects that will reinforce the stability of this peace over time, few if any current Kantians share all of Kant's views regarding the moral development of humankind. Yet significant aspects of Kant's view that legal peace is conducive to moral learning can still be found in the work of Kantian theorists. For instance, Rawls maintains that the more the "law of peoples," as specified in his own work, is observed, the more moral learning will take place. By the latter he means a psychological process by which peoples will tend to accept the law of peoples as an ideal of conduct. He expects this process to transform what once was a mere *modus vivendi* into something much more stable. Thus, Rawls too works with the assumption that a peace that is initially agreed to on the basis of self-interest can itself be conducive to a process that leads to its further stabilization, namely, the development of dispositions on the basis of which the peace is regarded as right, not just prudent.[27]

As for Kant's theory of cosmopolitan right, perhaps the most striking fact about its reception is the lack of it. Fichte gave cosmopolitan right a place in his *Grundlage des Naturrechts*, published between

Kant's *Perpetual Peace* and the *Metaphysics of Morals*. He transformed it into the most basic human right – the right to have and acquire rights. Anyone, stranger or not, has *"the right to have all human beings presuppose that they can enter into a legal relationship with him through treaties."*[28] Cosmopolitan right includes the conditions for the possibility of requesting entrance into a legal relationship with others anywhere on earth.[29] During the first decades of the nineteenth century, too, there were some Kantians who formulated their own versions of cosmopolitan right.[30] After that, interest waned, however, and in the reception of Kant's theory of peace cosmopolitan right generally stood in the shadow of his advocacy of the league of states.

Strikingly enough, however, developments in twentieth-century international law have gone quite far in the direction of implementing the requirements of Kant's cosmopolitan right. In particular, the status of individuals under international law has been expanded in an unprecedented way. International law now grants individuals certain rights as humans (i.e., rights that are not tied to a particular nationality). Examples of these are the refugee rights that were codified in the twentieth century.[31]

Moreover, Kant's introduction of cosmopolitan right into his theory of right shows that he realized that world peace requires not merely peace between states, but also peaceful behavior of states and foreign individuals towards each other. In this context, Kant himself referred, on the one hand, to the imperialism and colonialism of European states toward people who had not formed states yet, and, on the other hand, to what he regarded as the rightful prohibition by some foreign states against European trading companies entering their territories. In our own time, the international terrorist attacks by groups who are not acting as representatives of states but who direct their attacks against states and their citizens painfully underscore the truth of Kant's claim that world peace, that is, the security of the external freedom of all persons, requires more than peace among states.

Kant's confidence in the pacific nature of the "spirit of trade" (which he believes to show that cosmopolitan right can be realized) has proven to be too optimistic. Despite his claim that international commerce "cannot coexist with war" (*Perpetual Peace*, 8:368), the term "trade war" is not an oxymoron. Although commercial interests run counter to war sometimes, they do not always do so. Kant failed to take account of the struggles that develop in the competition over access to and control over markets or raw materials. As long as there are individual states, their interests can be expected to clash on occasion, and as a result states will be motivated to use the means at their disposal to get their way (when the issue is merely one of self-interested calculations). Second, the international arms trade has developed into a sizeable economic force (also in democracies, which house some of the world's largest arms producers). The production and sale of weapons are directly or indirectly a source of income and influence for a state, as well as employment for its citizens, which means that states have strong incentives to keep this going, but of course this supports exactly the kind of arms races that Kant regarded as so pernicious. This is not the same as saying that trade is necessarily a force for the worse. There are of course cases in which commercial interests avert a war or in which greed prompts a dictator to enact liberal reforms in order to attract foreign investment. Nevertheless, the relationship between international trade and peace is more complicated than Kant assumed.

The fact that Kant's views regarding the forces that promote peace are subject to considerable critique, however, does not mean that peace should be regarded as "unrealistic" and that the state of nature among states should simply be accepted. For one thing, none of what has been said earlier rules out that the ideal of peace can be approximated. From the Kantian point of view, this possibility in principle is all that is required to keep the striving for peace from turning into an empty irrational gesture. Thus, contemporary theorists in the Kantian tradition may be even less confident than Kant himself (who, in the *Metaphysics of Morals*, called perpetual peace an idea that could not be realized completely), but this need not affect their view that it *can* and *ought to* be a political principle to strive for peace. The interactions between states, as well as the interactions between states and foreign individuals, ought to conform to principles of justice and hence should be subject to proper regulation. The feasibility of increased transnational regulation is also underscored by the fact that it has in fact already increased enormously over the past century or so – think of the United Nations, the World Trade Organization, the International Criminal Court, and many other international organizations. What is more, rather than making Kant's theory of peace obsolete, the very difficulties that stand in the way of the real-ization of peace *underscore* the importance of proper international regulation. For those who do not just want to say that in the inter-national arena might makes right, Kant's theory of peace represents a classic theoretical framework for developing a set of normative ideals concerning international relations and the human rights of individuals.

NOTES

1.   The issue is nowadays discussed as a claim about democratic (rather than republican) states. This terminology is appropriate when what is meant is indirect, representative democracy. Kant ranked direct democ-racy as a form of despotism for lack of a proper separation of powers (*Perpetual Peace*, 8:352).

2.   See the texts collected in Kurt von Raumer, ed., *Ewiger Friede: Friedens-rufe und Friedenspläne seit der Renaissance* (Freiburg: Karl Alber Verlag, 1953).

3.   *Universal History*, 8:24; *Theory and Practice*, 8:313.

4.   Abbé Charles-Irénée Castel de Saint Pierre, *Projet pour rendre la paix perpétuelle en Europe* (1713). Jean-Jacques Rousseau, *Extrait du projet de paix perpétuelle de Monsieur l'Abbé de Saint Pierre* (1761) (*Oeuvres Complètes*, eds. Bernard Gagnebin and Marcel Raymond, vol. 3, 561–89). Rousseau did present some of his own thoughts as Saint-Pierre's: For a discussion of the differences between Saint-Pierre's account and Rousseau's presentation of it, see von Raumer, *Ewiger Friede*, 127–50. Rousseau's *Jugement sur la paix perpétuelle*, written around the same time as the *Extrait*, was first published posthumously in 1782 (*Oeuvres Complètes*, vol. 3, 591–600). Given that Rousseau distances himself clearly and explicitly from the Abbé's proposals in the *Jugement*, it does not seem that Kant had read this second text.

5.   Rudolf Malter, ed., *Immanuel Kant in Rede und Gespräch* (Hamburg: Felix Meiner Verlag, 1990), 459. Despite the fact that Kant denounced the execution of Louis XVI and the horrors of the period of Terror, he did not give up his admiration for the ideals of the French republic. See also *Conflict* 7:86, note.

6.   Although most of the texts in which Kant stipulates racial hierarcchies (with "whites" having the most talents and abilities) are from the pre-critical period (probably including the relevant passages in the lectures on physical geography), there are also later statements that refer to the inferior natural abilities of non-white races. An example of this is found

in the 1788 essay "On the Use of Teleological Principles in Philosophy" 8:174, including the note on that page. However, Kant seems to have developed a more egalitarian position during the 1790s, as can be seen in the discussion of cosmopolitan right in the present chapter.

7. See the lectures on anthropology from 1775–6: "Wir sehen daß sich Kriege erheben, und ein Staat den andern niederreißt, mit der Zeit werden die Fürsten den Nachtheil empfinden müssen, indem sie selbst im Frieden mit der Zurüstung eben solche Kräfte zu verwenden genöthiget sind, als im Kriege. Damit aber alle Kriege nicht nöthig wären, so müste ein Völkerbund entspringen, der alle Streitigkeiten der Völcker durch ihre Deputirte einen allgemeinen Volcker Senat constituirten, der alle Streitigkeiten der Völcker entscheiden müste, und dieses Urtheil müste durch die Macht der Völcker executirt werden, denn stünden auch die Völcker unter einem foro und einem bürgerlichen Zwange.... Wenn aber das ein Ende nimmt, so wird die Verbeßerung der inneren Regierung erfolgen" (25:676).

8. See Sharon B. Byrd, "The State as a Moral Person," in *Proceedings of the Eighth International Kant Congress*, ed. Hoke Robinson (Milwaukee: Marquette University Press, 1995), vol. 1.1., 171–89, esp. pp. 178–9; Sidney Axinn, "Kant on World Government," in *Proceedings of the Sixth International Kant Congress*, eds. G. Funke and Th. Seebohm (Washington, DC: University Press of America, 1989), 245–9.

9. In *Theory and Practice* Kant explains this terminology: "in thesi" means "in theory," "in hypothesi" is equivalent to "in practice" (*Theory and Practice* 8:276). On the states' interpretation of international right as a right to remain in the state of nature, see the *Vorarbeiten* to *Perpetual Peace*, 23:169.

10. For example, Allen Wood claims that the argument of *Perpetual Peace* would seem to require a state of states but that the account is riddled with perplexities. Thomas Pogge similarly calls Kant's account "extremely unsettled" and portrays Kant as experimenting with one argument after another without developing a single one successfully, trying to evade the demand for a world state that his theory commits him to. Thomas W. Pogge, "Kant's Theory of Justice," *Kant-Studien* 79 (1988): 407–33, esp. 427–33; Allen W. Wood, "Kant's Project for Perpetual Peace," in *Proceedings of the Eighth Kant Congress*, ed. Hoke Robinson (Milwaukee: Marquette University Press, 1995), vol. 1.1., 3–18, here p. 11. See also Thomas Carson, "*Perpetual Peace*: What Kant Should Have Said," *Social Theory and Practice* 14 (1988): 173–214; Georg Cavallar, *Kant and the Theory and Practice of International Right* (Cardiff: University of Wales Press, 1999), 113–32, esp. 123; Kevin Dodson, "Kant's Perpetual Peace: Universal Civil Society or League of

States?," *Southwest Philosophical Studies* 15 (1993): 1–9; Habermas, "Kant's Idea of Perpetual Peace with the Benefit of Two Hundred Years' Hindsight," in *Perpetual Peace: Essays on Kant's Cosmopolitan Ideal*, eds. James Bohman and Matthias Lutz-Bachmann (Cambridge, MA: MIT Press, 1997), 113–53 ; Otfried Höffe, "Some Kantian Reflections on a World Republic," *Kantian Review* 2 (1998): 51–71; Otfried Höffe, "Völkerbund oder Weltrepublik?," in *Immanuel Kant: Zum ewigen Frieden*, ed. Otfried Höffe (Berlin: Akademie Verlag, 1995), 109–32; Matthias Lutz-Bachmann, "Kant's Idea of Peace and the Philosophical Conception of a World Republic," in Bohman and Lutz-Bachmann, eds., *Perpetual Peace*, 59–77.

11. Kevin Dodson's formulation is representative: "This argument, however, explicitly accepts the subordination of considerations of justice to empirical judgments of what is realistic in the near future.... In putting forth this argument, Kant succumbs to the very same weakness that he so often warns us against" ("Kant's Perpetual Peace," 7).

12. Carson, *"Perpetual Peace,"* 211. The world government would have "military forces sufficient to dismantle and defeat any national army in the process of creation" (185 – note also the "far reaching intelligence network" of the world government, and Carson's assumption that one can prevent a military takeover just by having rules against it, 203–4). See also Axinn, "Kant on World Government," 249: "We may use violence to compel membership in an international federation. Things seem quite unKantian, yet we have merely put together Kant's own positions."

13. Commentators who criticize Kant's defense of the league of states on the grounds that the league is likely to have many flaws and who argue that only a state of states would be able to solve these problems often overlook the fact that the state of states itself, if pursued instead of a league, is also likely to be flawed.

14. "Peoples" here in the political, not nationalist sense.

15. I have argued this point at length in "Approaching Perpetual Peace: Kant's Defense of a League of States and his Ideal of a World Federation," *European Journal of Philosophy* 12 (2004): 304–25.

16. For example, Johann Heinrich Tieftrunk, *Philosophische Untersuchungen über das Privat- und das öffentliche Recht zur Erläuterung und Beurtheilung der metaphysischen Anfangsgründe der Rechtslehre vom Herrn Prof. Imm. Kant* (Halle: Rengersche Buchhandlung, 1798), vol. 2, 575–7.

17. See especially "Ideas toward a Universal History from a Cosmopolitan Point of View," the third essay in *Theory and Practice*, and of course the section "On the Guarantee of Perpetual Peace" in *Perpetual Peace*.

18. For further discussion, see Paul Guyer's explanation of why a republic is not sufficient for peace, in "Nature, Morality, and the Possibility of Peace," in Guyer, *Kant on Freedom, Law, and Happiness*, (Cambridge: Cambridge University Press, 2000), 408–34, here pp. 415–23.

19. Rawls defends a version of this view; see John Rawls, *The Law of Peoples* (Cambridge, MA: Harvard University Press, 1999), 8.

20. Michael W. Doyle, "Kant, Liberal Legacies, and Foreign Affairs," *Philosophy and Public Affairs* 12 (1983): 205–35 (part I) and 323–53 (part II).

21. Ibid.

22. See Rawls, *Law of Peoples*, pp. 10, 19, 21, 22, 36, 54.

23. *Fichtes Werke*, ed. Immanuel Hermann Fichte, vol. 3 (Berlin: Walter de Gruyter, 1971), 379.

24. Jürgen Habermas, "Kant's Idea of Perpetual Peace"; Otfried Höffe, "Völkerbund oder Weltrepublik?" and "Some Kantian Reflections on a World Republic."

25. "Versuch über den Begriff des Republikanismus" [1796], in Ernst Behler, ed., *Kritische Friedrich-Schlegel-Ausgabe* (München: Schöning, 1966), vol. 7, 11–25, here p. 13.

26. Friedrich Gentz, "Über den ewigen Frieden," *Historisches Journal* 2 (#3, Sept.–Dec. 1800), 710–90. Reprinted in Kurt von Raumer, ed., *Ewiger Friede: Friedensrufe und Friedenspläne seit der Renaissance* (Freiburg: Karl Alber, 1953), 461–97, here p. 479.

27. Rawls, *Law of Peoples*, 44–5.

28. Johann Gottlieb Fichte, *Grundlage des Naturrechts*, in *Fichtes Werke*, ed. Immanuel Hermann Fichte (Berlin: Walter de Gruyter, 1971), vol. 3, here p. 384.

29. Ibid. Fichte changed his view dramatically in 1800 with the publication of *Der geschlossene Handelsstaat*, in which he severely restricts individual mobility.

30. See, for example, Johann Heinrich Tieftrunk, *Philosophische Untersuchungen über das Privat- und öffentliche Recht zur Erläuterung und Beurtheilung der metaphysischen Anfangsgründe der Rechtslehre vom Herrn Prof. Immanuel Kant* (Halle, 1798), 583–4.

31. I have argued this point at greater length in "Kant's Cosmopolitan Law: World Citizenship for a Global Order," *Kantian Review* 2 (1998): 72–90. For other recent discussions, see Sankar Muthu, "Justice and Foreigners: Kant's Cosmopolitan Right," *Constellations* 7 (2000): 23–45; Seyla Benhabib, "Of Guests, Aliens, and Citizens: Rereading Kant's Cosmopolitan Right," in *Pluralism and the Pragmatic Turn: The Transformation of Critical Theory*, eds. William Rehg and James Bohman (Cambridge, MA: MIT Press, 2001), 361–87.

15   Kant's conception of virtue

VIRTUE ETHICS BEFORE KANT

Most ancient ethicists regarded virtues both as instrumentally valuable qualities of a person that enable her to live well, and also as valuable in themselves by being partly constitutive of happiness (*eudaimonia*).[1] The four cardinal virtues recognized by most ancient ethicists are courage, temperance, justice, and intelligence. Common among ancient theories of virtue are the following theses. First, the virtues are stable dispositions. For someone to be brave, she must be reliable and constant in her brave acts; they must be characteristic of her. Second, though ancient philosophers often described virtues as habits, they did not take them to be *mere* habits. Virtues are dispositions that require cultivation and involve choice.[2] Third, virtues involve reason. To be virtuous, a person must not only do or pursue the right things; she must know why they are the right things. The intellectual aspect of the virtues is illustrated by the common ancient view that virtues are a special kind of craft, or are formally similar to crafts in some ways.[3]

Fourth, for many ancients, virtue involves emotions. Plato (ca. 430–347 B.C.E.) and Aristotle (384–322 B.C.E.) took the soul to have both rational and non-rational parts, and virtue to involve both. Aristotle emphasized that the development of virtue requires not merely gaining control of one's emotions, but training them, bringing them into harmony with one's judgments about what is valuable and what virtue requires.[4] The virtuous person takes pleasure in performing right actions, and is pained by performing wrong ones. Furthermore, Aristotle's doctrine of the mean says that a virtuous person not only acts rightly, but also has the appropriate kind and intensity of feeling – feeling neither excessively nor deficiently angry at a particular injustice, for example.[5]

Stoicism (which originated ca. 300 B.C.E.) denied that the soul has both rational and non-rational parts, and that most emotions (passions) have a role in virtue.[6] Stoics understood the passions as unavoidably contrary to reason and virtue.[7] Stoics said that virtue motivates in itself; the virtuous person acts based on her judgment of what virtue requires, unimpeded by competing influences. For Stoics, passions are *misguided judgments*: unreflective judgments that attribute value to things other than virtue, and thereby hinder virtuous action. A fully virtuous person recognizes that virtue has a value incomparably higher than anything else.[8] Such a person would not feel grief at the death of a loved one, nor envy another's financial success. Thus, rather than train one's emotions, Stoics sought to etiolate them, advocating dispassion.[9]

While ancient ethicists generally agreed that virtue comprises the main part of happiness, they disagreed about whether virtue is *sufficient* for happiness. In *Republic* II, Plato argued only that one is always better off if one is just than if one is unjust. Aristotle argued that virtue is necessary for happiness, and the dominant part of happiness, but not sufficient for happiness. He emphasized that, as the final end, happiness must be a complete and self-sufficient good – a good that fulfills our desires, that lacks nothing.[10] Without "external goods" such as wealth, health, or family, even the person with a life of virtuous activity cannot be considered happy; he has reason to want more, to feel unsatisfied with his life.[11] Unlike Aristotle, Stoics and Epicureans argued – in different ways – that virtue is sufficient for happiness. Stoics held that virtue is valuable for its own sake, and indeed that it has such a special, high value that it cannot be made better or more complete by adding other things to it. For Stoics, happiness is constituted purely by a life of virtuous activity. No matter how poor, ill, or hated the virtuous person is, Stoics claimed she is happy. Thus, Stoics reduced Aristotle's "external goods" to "preferred indifferents," things reasonable to pursue so long as they accord with virtue, but not themselves necessary for happiness.[12] Epicurus (341–270 B.C.E.) conceived of happiness as pleasure, and took virtue to be valuable only as a means to happiness.[13] But Epicureans were not hedonists as we now commonly use the term, for they understood pleasure as an inner state of equanimity, which could obtain in the virtuous person no matter what hardships she suffered.[14]

With Christianity came increasing interest in understanding morality as commanded by God. Christian thinkers offered ethical interpretations of their New Testament, as well as of the Hebrew bible, developing, for example, the notion of original sin. Nevertheless, many medieval Christian philosophers retained aspects of ancient virtue ethics, which they transformed to accommodate their theological commitments. Saint Augustine (354–430), for example, followed the ancients in taking the ultimate end as central to morality.[15] But whereas the ancients saw virtues as at least largely constitutive of happiness in *this* life, Augustine and other Christians saw them as the basis for happiness in the *next* life; no one can be completely happy until united with God.[16] Augustine held that God rewards those who are virtuous in this life with happiness in the next. Yet he also claimed that God gives us virtues so that we can achieve this very salvation.[17] Finally, Augustine's view of the connection among the virtues had a distinctly Christian slant: all virtues express the love of God.[18]

Peter Abelard (1079–1142) defined virtues as dispositions to do good deeds, and vices as dispositions to do bad ones.[19] For example, Abelard described charity as the will's "consent" and "readiness" to aid the poor.[20] In keeping with his ethics of intention, Abelard took charity (and its moral value) to be independent of what a charitable agent accomplishes.[21] Moreover, Abelard considered struggle essential to virtue, rather than an accidental feature of it resulting from Adam's fall. For Abelard, without resistance from vice, there is no virtue; and the greater our internal opposition to virtue, the greater our merit before God in overcoming it.[22]

Saint Thomas Aquinas (ca. 1225–1274) understood virtues as habitual inclinations to act in accordance with the nature of a human being – that is, rationally, in control of one's passions.[23] Like Augustine and most of his other Christian predecessors, Aquinas accepted Aristotle's moral virtues of courage, temperance, intelligence, and justice, and added the theological virtues of faith, hope, and charity, which he thought were "infused" by God.[24] Whereas the four cardinal virtues aim at our earthly happiness as human beings, the three theological virtues aim at our "supernatural happiness," beyond the constraints of human nature. Thus, though altered considerably by the influence of Christianity, eudaimonistic virtue ethics remained important throughout the Middle Ages – and indeed through the Renaissance as well.[25]

Virtue had a much smaller role in the "natural law" philosophies that dominated in the seventeenth century, such as those of Hugo Grotius (1583–1645) and Samuel Pufendorf (1632–1694), which gave notions of duty, obligation, law, rights, and right action prominence.[26] Within the natural lawyers' philosophical framework, virtue was restricted to the class of "imperfect duties" – meritorious duties of indeterminate scope and requirement, which are not appropriately coerced, pertaining to and motivated by the good of others.[27]

In Thomas Hobbes's (1588–1679) moral theory, virtue was subordinate to self-interest.[28] Traits such as justice, mercy, and gratitude are moral virtues because they advance self-preservation. Hobbes understood the virtues as commanded by the laws of nature, yet he saw these laws as justified by consideration of what best promotes self-preservation. Although Hobbes took the laws of nature to be "immutable and eternal," he did not think it rational (or required) for people to follow them at the cost of their ability to protect themselves. Hobbes said the laws of nature always bind *"in foro interna"* (by demanding cultivation of certain desires, dispositions, or ends), but not always *"in foro externo"* (by demanding external actions).[29]

Virtue regained prominence with the "moral sense" theorists Anthony Ashley Cooper, Earl of Shaftesbury (1671–1713) and Francis Hutcheson (1694–1746). Moral sense theories of virtue tended to define virtue in terms of a *spectator* rather than of a deliberating agent.[30] Moral sense was said to be the faculty through which we perceive and judge people's moral qualities. What we love and approve in others' characters and motives, we call virtues; similarly, we call an act virtuous if it issues from a motive we love or approve.[31] Shaftesbury's work was motivated in part by his opposition to the portrayal of human nature as selfish found in Hobbes and Bernard de Mandeville (1670–1733). Although Shaftesbury believed that virtue is in the best interest of the virtuous person, and that this provides virtue's ultimate justification, he also believed that virtue leads people to act for the general good for unselfish reasons.[32] For Shaftesbury, a candidate for virtue must be a reflective being, able to order her own affections.[33] Virtue requires a self-authored, inner harmony. Shaftesbury's notion of virtue had a prominent aesthetic aspect: Moral goodness is a kind of beauty. Hutcheson rejected the psychological hedonism found in Hobbes and Shaftesbury. For Hutcheson, all virtues can, in some way, be understood as manifestations of benevolence. A virtuous person is one in whom universal benevolence reliably restrains lesser forms of benevolence ("kind affections" and "particular passions") and other passions, affections, and desires.[34]

Hutcheson's work greatly influenced David Hume's moral philosophy. According to Hume (1711-1776), virtues are whichever traits of character produce in observers the sentiment of moral approbation.[35] Hume thought that virtues are rooted in human nature: They develop naturally in us, are frequently manifested by us, and can be recognized and agreed upon by all who take up the "general point of view."[36] The basis for our shared reaction to people's traits and actions is the natural human tendency to care about the public good. Virtues were primary in Hume's understanding of moral action: We value virtuous actions *as expressions of virtuous character*.[37] Hume mentioned *many* virtues, which he divided into "artificial" and "natural" virtues.[38] Artificial virtues (e.g., fidelity, modesty, justice, and allegiance to one's government) develop in an organized social life and are necessary for the functioning of society. Such virtues may not please us in every manifestation of them; yet we recognize them as good on the whole. Natural virtues (e.g., good sense, wit, knowledge, eloquence, temperance, constancy, tenderness, discernment, veracity, frugality, and industry) enrich social life. Though less urgent for society's maintenance, they are more reliably pleasing than the artificial virtues. Hume rejected "monkish virtues," such as fasting, celibacy, mortification, penance, and self-denial.

Though Christian Wolff (1679-1754) and Christian August Crusius (ca. 1715-1775) opposed each other on many points, both heavily influenced Kant's ethics. Kant agreed with Wolff's secular leanings, including his view that morality is fundamentally independent of God. He also took up many of Wolff's positions about duties to oneself and duties to others. But Kant rejected Wolff's strong perfectionism as well as the consequentialism Wolff paired with it.[39] Wolff noted that a usual definition of virtue is a "[readiness] to direct one's actions according to the law of nature."[40] For Wolff, "the law of nature requires the perfection of us and our condition."[41] So Wolff ultimately defined virtue as "a readiness to perfect oneself and others as much as possible."[42] Crusius, a Pietist minister as well as a philosopher, defined virtue as "the agreement of the moral condition of a mind with the divine laws."[43] Crusius considered the love of God "the main virtue from which all others must flow."[44] Like Kant after him, Crusius distinguished between the form and the matter of virtue.[45] Crusius held that human beings have an innate drive to comply with duties of virtue, which comprise morality. Crusius also held that virtue makes one worthy of happiness, that God rewards the virtuous with proportionate happiness, and that the absence of such rewards in this life gives us reason to hope for immortality;[46] here Crusius's influence on Kant is evident.

KANT'S THEORY OF VIRTUE

Virtue

Kant's ethics contains several related theses concerning virtue. First, Kant describes virtue as a *disposition to do one's duty out of respect for the moral law*. Kant calls virtue "the morally good disposition" (*Groundwork*, 4:435) or "conformity of the *disposition* to the law of duty" (*Religion*, 6:37).[47] This disposition is a manifestation not of natural temperament but of will. This disposition implies a maxim (subjective principle) of acting as the moral law commands: "virtue consists in *rectitudo actionum ex principio interno* [rectitude of actions on an internal principle]" (*Collins*, 27:300; *Practical Reason*, 5:118; see also *Religion*, 6:23n. and *Morals*, 6:395) and "the persistent maxim of making [one's] will conform to the moral law" (*Mrongovius*, 29:611). Finally, this disposition reflects respect for the moral law: It is a disposition to comply with the moral law *out of respect for that law* (*Practical Reason*, 5:128, 160; *Collins*, 27:308; *Morals*, 6:387).

Second, Kant calls virtue a kind of *strength*. He defines virtue as "the concept of strength" (*Morals*, 6:392) and appeals to etymology: "The very Latin word *virtus* originally signifies nothing else but courage, strength, and constancy" (*Vigilantius*, 27:492); "the word *Tugend* [virtue] comes from *taugen* [to be fit for]" (*Morals*, 6:390; see also *Religion*, 6:57). In particular, virtue is "the strength of one's resolution" (*Morals*, 6:390), or still more precisely, "a moral strength of the will" (*Morals*, 6:405), "moral strength in pursuit of one's duty"

(*Anthropology*, 7:147). We can begin to understand Kant's conception of virtue as moral strength when we consider the context in which the agent strives to express her commitment to morality: one of inner conflict.

Third, then, Kant says that virtue *presupposes opposition and entails struggle* – struggle that calls for strength. Virtue is "moral disposition in conflict" (*Practical Reason*, 5:84), "the capacity and considered resolve to withstand a strong but unjust opponent ... with respect to what opposes the moral disposition *within us*" (*Morals*, 6:380). Kant often seems to identify our inclinations as the primary opponents of morality in us. For example, Kant calls virtue "the struggle of inclination with the moral law, and the constant disposition ... to carry out [one's] duties" (*Vigilantius*, 27:492; see also *Collins*, 27:465; *Vigilantius*, 27:570; *Groundwork*, 4:405). But his considered view is that inclinations are not the source of the problem.

Human beings do not have holy wills, wills "whose maxims are necessarily in accord with laws of autonomy (the moral law)" (*Groundwork*, 4:439), wills "incapable of any maxims which conflict with the moral law" (*Practical Reason*, 5:32). If we had holy wills, the moral law would not be an imperative for us. We would act rightly without moral obligation or struggle. According to Kant, we have a predisposition to moral goodness, but we also have one to evil. We can, and routinely do, act contrary to the moral law. Although this often amounts to satisfying inclinations at the expense of obedience to the moral law, the inclinations themselves are not to blame for this. We cannot be determined by an inclination unless we ourselves incorporate it into our maxim (*Religion*, 6:23–4). Thus, virtue's constant opponent is not self-love or inclination, but the *radical evil in human nature* – a propensity to give self-love (and inclinations generally) priority over the moral law in our maxims (*Religion*, 6:29, 35–7, 57n., 58; see also *Collins*, 27:463). Because of this ordering of our incentives, we find ourselves – as we have made ourselves (*Morals*, 6:394) – susceptible to temptations to violate the moral law or its purity in order to gratify our inclinations. It is because of this tendency, this radical evil, that virtue implies struggle and demands strength. Fundamentally, the goal of the virtuous person is to achieve the right ordering of her incentives, giving the moral law undisputed priority over self-love in her supreme maxim.

Thus, fourth, for Kant, virtue is *a feature of non-holy (e.g., human) rational beings*. Virtue is "a law-abiding disposition resulting from respect for the law and thus implying consciousness of a continuous propensity to transgress it, or at least to a defilement" (*Practical Reason*, 5:128). Moreover, "as a naturally acquired faculty, [virtue] can never be perfect" (*Practical Reason*, 5:33).

Fifth, Kant understands virtue as a form of self-constraint – *moral self-constraint* – "based on inner freedom" (*Morals*, 6:408). Inner freedom is motivational independence, the capacity to act on the autonomously chosen principles of morality, despite temptations to act otherwise.[48] Virtue does not tell us what the right thing to do is, but allows us to do what we recognize to be right, simply because it is right. "Virtue is . . . a self-constraint in accordance with a principle of inner freedom, and so through the mere representation of one's duty in accordance with its formal law" (*Morals*, 6:394). Similarly, "Virtue is . . . the moral strength of a *human being*'s will in fulfilling his *duty*, a moral *constraint* through his own lawgiving reason, insofar as this constitutes itself an authority *executing* the law" (*Morals*, 6:405).[49] For Kant, virtue not only expresses but also promotes inner freedom: The greater one's moral self-constraint, the more one acts based on one's judgments about what one ought to do, and the less one acts based on the strength of one's inclinations (*Morals*, 6:382 n.; *Collins*, 27:464). This notion of virtue fits well with what Kant calls the general obligation to virtue, the obligation to do all of our duties *from* duty (*Morals*, 6:410; *Vigilantius*, 27:541). It also explains one of Kant's main distinctions between duties of virtue and duties of right in the *Metaphysics of Morals*. Duties of virtue allow only for self-constraint, whereas with duties of right, external constraint is morally possible (*Morals*, 6:379–81, 394–5). The "Doctrine of Virtue" concerns inner freedom; the "Doctrine of Right," outer freedom.

Sixth and finally, Kant distinguishes between *phenomenal virtue*, "a facility in *actions* conforming to duty (according to their legality)," and *noumenal virtue*, "a constant disposition toward such actions from duty (because of their morality)" (*Religion*, 6:14). Phenomenal virtue, like noumenal virtue, reflects the agent's commitment to conform to the moral law. Purity of motivation, however, is an essential feature only of noumenal virtue: Phenomenal virtue "has the abiding maxim of *lawful* actions, no matter where one draws the incentives that the power of choice needs for such actions"

(*Religion*, 6:47). Yet although phenomenal virtue *can* exist without moral purity, Kant does not dismiss phenomenal virtue as a mere pretender. He instead describes it as virtue's "empirical character," meaning that phenomenal virtue is the form in which true virtue *appears to us* (*Religion*, 6:47; *Vigilantius*, 27:583).[50] Humans cannot cognize noumenal virtue (virtue's "intelligible character"); cognition of our supreme maxim is possible for God, but not for us (*Religion*, 6:47–8). Moreover, Kant is explicit that the duty to morally perfect oneself requires striving not only for the moral purity of noumenal virtue, but also for the success in fulfilling all one's duties characteristic of phenomenal virtue (*Morals*, 6:446–7).

Drawing all these theses together, we can understand Kant's conception of virtue as the form in which a rational being with a non-holy will expresses her supreme commitment to morality: as a continually cultivated capacity to master her inclinations so as to fulfill all her duties, a capacity whose cultivation and exercise is motivated by respect for the moral law.[51]

Vice

Kant distinguishes between vice and mere lack of virtue. Lack of virtue is the "*logical opposite*" of virtue, and vice virtue's "*real opposite*" (*Morals*, 6:384). Lack of virtue is weakness in duty, whereas vice implies "contempt for moral laws" (*Collins*, 27:463). An agent displays a lack of virtue when she has a commitment to morality, but is lax in her resolve to carry it out.[52] Kant associates lack of virtue also with not going very far in fulfilling flexible, meritorious, "imperfect" duties (i.e., promoting the obligatory ends of one's own perfection and the happiness of others), despite complying with strict, exceptionless, "perfect" duties. Vice, on the other hand, is a propensity to act contrary to the moral law (*Religion*, 6:37). It implies a problem not merely with resolve, but with maxims. One manifests "a true *vice*" when one allows oneself to dwell on feelings or impulses it would be wrong to act on, foster an interest in them, and then "take up what is evil (as something premeditated) into [one's] maxim" (*Morals*, 6:408). Similarly "it is when an intentional transgression has become a principle that it is properly called a *vice*" (*Morals*, 6:390). Kant associates vice with not merely failing to do much to fulfill imperfect duties, but with violating perfect duties – for example, duties not to degrade others (*Morals*, 6:464). These content-related distinctions may seem inconsistent with the more formal ones. But they make sense in the light of the fact that for Kant, the fundamental attitude of virtue is that of respect for the moral law itself and for its instantiation in individual rational beings. One may still respect rational nature even if one falls short of all one can do to honor it. But if one acts on maxims hostile to rational nature or its dignity, one's will is set against the moral law.

Virtue and the good will

Being virtuous is not the same thing as having a good will. Having a good will is simply a matter of having moral maxims, adopted for moral reasons; it is not a matter of strength and fitness in acting on them (*Groundwork*, 4:394, 399–400). A good will is not compatible with vice (cf. *Groundwork*, 4:455). It is, however, compatible with a lack of virtue. For example, Kant describes behavior manifesting a "lack of virtue" as "something childish and weak, which can indeed coexist with the best will" (*Morals*, 6:408). And Kant insists that "between maxim and deed there is still a wide gap" allowing an agent to fail to realize her good will in virtuous action (*Religion*, 6:47). So one could have the fundamental commitment to morality of a good will, and yet lack the strength of will in overcoming temptations that is part of virtue.

On the other hand, a good will is necessary for virtue. And virtue reflects the moral worth of a good will: "the dutifulness of our moral actions appears as *virtue*" (*Vigilantius*, 27:715). Finally, Kant explains the moral worth of a good will in terms of temptations to overcome, just as he explains virtue as strength (*Groundwork*, 4:397–403). If we understand moral worth as a property of agents and not of isolated acts, moral worth correlates with virtue. So although Kant's notions of virtue and a good will are conceptually distinct, they are intimately connected: The virtuous person has a good will; and it is through virtue that a good will finds expression.

Virtue and human agency

For a fuller understanding of Kant's conception of virtue, we must consider the virtuous agent's motivational structure. In particular, we should ask how moral motivation incorporates or rejects inclinations and emotions. As we have seen, virtue has its own motive: respect for the law (*Groundwork*, 4:426). For virtuous agents, respect for the moral law has priority over self-love in their supreme maxim. We now want to know what this implies for actual agents' particular acts of willing, given that there may be many layers of maxims between their supreme maxim and the maxim of any given action. Some of the answer must wait for our discussion of specific virtues and vices since part of a virtuous agent's motivational structure involves commitment to obligatory ends, cultivation of qualities that support promotion of these ends, and rejection of attitudes prohibited by the categorical imperative and hostile to obligatory ends. Yet we can answer part of the question now. We can say, for example, that respect for the moral law implies obedience to the categorical imperative, which tells us to respect rational nature in oneself and others. Therefore, if respect for oneself and others is grounded in this moral commitment, actions chosen in the light of this respect reflect moral goodness in the agent's willing. An agent need not be thinking explicitly about the moral law for her motivation to be pure.

Nevertheless, as human beings, we do not respond to others or the world in terms of respect for rational nature alone. According to Kant, we have three original predispositions, all of which supply drives, feelings, and impulses. The predisposition to *animality* "may be brought under the general title of physical or merely *mechanical* self-love, i.e., a love for which reason is not required" (*Religion*, 6:26); this predisposition contains drives for self-preservation, sexual reproduction and the care of offspring, and community with other humans, "i.e., the social drive." The predisposition to *humanity* "can be brought under the general title of a self-love which is physical and yet *involves comparison* [of our state with that of others] (for which reason is required)" (*Religion*, 6:27). The predisposition to *personality* "is the susceptibility to respect for the moral law *as of itself a sufficient incentive to the power of choice*" (*Religion*, 6:27; *Practical Reason*, 5:87).

Although the predisposition to personality is obviously morally crucial, all three predispositions are good; all encourage compliance with the moral law. The drives of humanity and animality, however, are susceptible to corruption. The drives of animality can have grafted onto them vices such as gluttony and lust. The drives of humanity can have grafted onto them vices such as jealousy, rivalry, and malicious glee. Thus, a large part of the struggle for virtue is the effort to harmonize these three predispositions so that personality develops fully, and humanity and animality develop in ways supportive of morally practical reason. The virtuous agent must find a way to use, transform, or conquer her natural tendencies as morality requires. The virtuous agent struggles both not to act on inclinations that it would be wrong to act on, and to turn what inclinations she can into means to moral ends. She realizes herself as a self-legislating and self-governing human agent by working on and with the natural stuff of which she is made. Indeed, when we look at particular virtues and vices, we will see that they have a lot to do with how to respect oneself and others as rational *human* beings – beings with legitimate drives of animality and humanity as well as personality. In discussions of duties to oneself, Kant (like Hume) rejects "monkish virtues"; he objects to their hostility to one's animal self (*Collins*, 27:379). The duty to perfect oneself involves cultivation of one's natural capacities – and not only so one can achieve narrowly moral ends (*Morals*, 6:387, 391–2, 444–6). When developed and expressed harmoniously with morality, animality and humanity are part of the flourishing of human beings.

Kant may sound as though he is condemning our animal selves in the form of our emotions when he urges apathy and self-mastery. Kant says, "unless reason holds the reins of government in his own hands, a human being's feelings and inclinations play the master over him" (*Morals*, 6:408). Apathy and self-mastery are essential for expressing and protecting inner freedom. In praising moral apathy, Kant advocates a way of being that is opposed not to our *having* emotions, but rather to our *determining our will* by whatever strong, fleeting feelings we happen to have: "in cases of moral apathy feelings arising from sensible impressions lose their influence on moral feeling only because respect for the moral law is more powerful than all such feelings together" (*Morals*, 6:408). Self-mastery is more comprehensive than apathy: "Since virtue is based on inner freedom, it contains a positive command to a human being, namely to bring all his capacities and inclinations under his (reason's) control and so to rule over himself" (*Morals*, 6:408; see also *Practical Reason*, 5:118; *Collins*, 27:360–9).[53] So in urging self-mastery, Kant recommends not that we rid ourselves of feelings and inclinations, but that we use them in ways that are compatible with – and perhaps even supportive of – morality. We are not completely passive with regard to our emotions (*Anthropology*, 7:254): They respond to our cultivation, and so are in part products of our choices (*Morals*, 6:402). Indeed, virtue involves feelings we have shaped in certain ways.[54]

Kant is explicit about at least three morally important roles for feelings of various kinds. First, he talks about certain emotions as naturally given feelings that we can use in the fulfilment of our duties and that we therefore have a duty to cultivate (*Morals*, 6:456–7, 458). For example, Kant says of sympathy, "it is ... an indirect duty to cultivate the natural ... feelings in us, and to make use of them as so many means to sympathy based on moral principles and the feeling appropriate to them" (*Morals*, 6:457). Among the ways we can make moral use of sympathy are as a means to understand what others' needs and desires are, as a means to communicate our concern for them and recognition of their wants and needs, as an incentive to facilitate helping others. Kant does not suggest we cultivate sympathy to take the place of moral motivation. He suggests, rather, that sympathy has epistemic, communicative, and subordinate motivational roles to play in agents who cultivate sympathy out of the motive of duty.

Second, Kant talks about moral feeling, conscience, love of human beings, and respect as special kinds of feelings that we are made aware of only though consciousness of the moral law (*Morals*, 6:399). These feelings are "moral endowments" that "lie at the basis of morality" and are "*subjective* conditions of receptivity to the concept of duty" (*Morals*, 6:399). It is not a duty to have these feelings; for if we did not have them, we would not be aware of any duties whatever. It is a duty to cultivate them, however, because of their moral usefulness.

Third, Kant talks about certain feelings as expressive of the attitude of a truly virtuous agent. He says "a heart joyous in the *compliance* with its duty ... is the sign of genuineness in virtuous disposition" (*Religion*, 6:24n.). There is an aesthetic temperament of virtue that is the result of reason working upon sensibility. The frame of mind emblematic of a virtuous agent is "*valiant* and *cheerful*" in fulfilling her duties (*Morals*, 6:484). So although Kant associates virtue with struggle, he denies that the virtuous agent will hate duty or be miserable in its fulfilment. The resolve, commitment, and appreciation for the value of virtue and the inner worth of the virtuous agent keep such an agent from resenting morality's commands, even when they conflict with her happiness. Indeed, the virtuous agent enjoys a sense of satisfaction in her hard-earned fitness to comply with morality's commands to the degree that she does (*Practical Reason*, 5:117–19).

So for Kant, virtue involves fostering morally useful aspects of our animality and humanity, besides constraining their expression in the light of the demands of morality. He recognizes the value of various emotions, feelings, and inclinations, as well as of prudence and peace of mind, which "are not sources of virtue, but merely aids to it" (*Collins*, 27:465).[55]

Virtues and vices

In addition to a conception of virtue and vice, Kant's moral theory includes many discussions of particular virtues and vices: "in its idea (objectively) there is only *one* virtue (as moral strength of one's maxims); but in fact (subjectively) there is a multitude of virtues, made up of several different qualities" (*Morals*, 6:447). These different qualities are required by, or facilitate fulfilment of, moral duties.

In the "Doctrine of Virtue" of the *Metaphysics of Morals*, Kant sets forth his taxonomy of directly ethical duties (duties of virtue) – duties for which no external compulsion is morally possible because they pertain to external actions only indirectly; they pertain directly to agents' maxims and ends (objects of choice), and thus are duties to which agents must constrain *themselves* through inner freedom. In presenting these duties, Kant primarily uses the formula of humanity (*Groundwork*, 4:429)[56] and the supreme principle of the doctrine of virtue:

Act in accordance with a maxim of *ends* that it can be a universal law for everyone to have. In accordance with this principle the human being is an end for himself as well as for others, and it is not enough that he is not authorized to use either himself or others merely as a means (since he could then still be indifferent to them); it is in itself his duty to make the human being in general his end.   (*Morals*, 6:395; see also 410)

Kant calls the "Doctrine of Virtue" a doctrine of ends. Duties of virtue do not merely restrict how agents may pursue their inclination-based ends; they also require agents to recognize their own and others' rational nature as ends more valuable than any inclination-based end. Consequently, duties of virtue require agents to adopt and promote the ends of their own perfection and the happiness of others because respect for the rational nature of finite, imperfect agents implies a commitment to foster and further their agency. Perfect duties to oneself, imperfect duties to oneself, duties of respect for others, and duties of love all follow from the requirement to make rational nature one's end.

Kant explains perfect duties to oneself and duties of respect in terms of vices to be avoided out of respect for rational nature. He explains duties of love, which follow from the obligatory end of the happiness of others, in terms of virtues to be cultivated and vices to be avoided: "To think of several virtues (as one unavoidably does) is nothing other than to think of the various moral objects to which the will is led by the one principle of virtue [to do all duties from respect for the moral law], and so too with regard to the contrary vices" (*Morals*, 6:406, see also 395). Vices are "the brood of dispositions opposing the law . . . monsters [the agent] has to fight" (*Morals*, 6:405). Each virtue and each vice has its own maxim (*Morals*, 6:404). An agent can have some virtues and lack others. If her virtues reflect a pure moral commitment, however, she will not also have *vices*, which imply maxims opposing the moral law (*Morals*, 6:447; *Religion*, 6:24–5).

Self-regarding duties require respect for oneself as a rational human being and promotion of one's natural and moral perfection. Perfect duties to oneself are defined primarily in terms of vices contrary to them. That is, Kant delineates his notion of proper self-respect largely in opposition to the maxims and attitudes one ought to avoid out of respect for oneself. Rarely does Kant explain perfect duties to oneself in terms of virtues – for example, humaneness, uprightness, or chastity (*Morals*, 6:443; *Collins*, 27:459–60; *Vigilantius*, 27:637, 699). One shows self-respect through how one treats one's body and its drives, as well as how one treats one's rational nature directly (*Morals*, 6:417–20). Kant calls suicide and self-mutilation (*Morals*, 6:421–4; *Collins*, 27:369–75; *Vigilantius*, 27:627–31), gluttony and drunkenness (*Morals*, 6:427–8; *Vigilantius*, 27:691), and sexual self-degradation (*Morals*, 6:424–6; *Collins*, 27:390–2; *Vigilantius*, 27:637–41) "vices contrary to perfect duties to oneself as an animal and moral being." He calls lying (to oneself and to others)

(*Morals*, 6:429–31; *Vigilantius*, 27:700–2), avarice (*Morals*, 6:432–4; *Collins*, 27:399–403), and servility (*Morals*, 6:434–7) "vices contrary to perfect duties to oneself as a moral being only." Kant's terminology here is unusual, for these "vices" are (on the face of it) not qualities or dispositions, but ways of acting: acting on various maxims that express disrespect for oneself. Calling these ways of acting "vices" makes sense, however, both because these are ways of acting that the agent must morally constrain herself to avoid (i.e., they are *vices* because they are contrary to duties of *virtue*), and because the qualities and dispositions for which we are morally accountable are those which are expressed in our maxims.

In the case of duties to oneself as an animal and moral being, disrespect for one's rational nature is shown by one's willingness to treat one's animal nature in a way destructive or disruptive to its reason-supporting role, directly or indirectly (e.g., through undermining our physical integrity or our organs' abilities to function), for an inclination-based end. So not every act of cutting off a limb amounts to the vice of self-mutilation. A maxim of removing an infected limb as a necessary means to save one's life is not vicious; but a maxim of surgically transforming one's body, regardless of the risks, in order to look as attractive as possible, is (*Morals*, 6:423). The first maxim reflects concern for one's continued existence as a rational human being, whereas the second reflects a willingness to endanger one's agency for the sake of beauty.

Avarice is an illuminating example of a vice contrary to one's duty to oneself as a moral being only. By "avarice" Kant means the hoarding of goods the agent would benefit from using. This hoarding amounts to a "slavish subjection of oneself to the goods that contribute to happiness, which is a violation of duty to oneself since one ought to be their master" (*Morals*, 6:434). Through a maxim of avarice, an agent degrades herself by treating her agency as a means to accumulating material goods – as though money or things have value above her own, or somehow give her life worth. Another important and illustrative duty to oneself as a moral being only is that of avoiding the vice of servility. Through maxims of servility, an agent treats herself, and encourages others to treat her, as though she were worth less than other rational human beings. Such a maxim is vicious because it contradicts the fundamental equality and dignity of each person as a rational being.

Difficult questions arise concerning which maxims manifest various vices opposed to perfect duties to oneself. It is sometimes hard to tell, for example, whether one is being merely polite or objectionably servile. In the "Doctrine of Virtue," Kant offers casuistical questions after his exposition of each of these duties, so that his readers can begin to make progress in their moral judgment.[57]

Kant has little to say about specific virtues to cultivate regarding the promotion of one's natural and moral perfection, perhaps because there are too many possible virtues to mention. To promote one's natural perfection, one must develop whatever excellences pertain to the abilities of mind, body, and spirit that one thinks it makes most sense to develop, given one's particular interests, desires, and talents. And to promote one's moral perfection, one must cultivate all the qualities one needs in order to purify one's moral motivation and to fulfill all of one's other duties to oneself and others (*Morals*, 6:386–7, 392–3, 444–7).

Duties of respect require treating others in keeping with their dignity.[58] As with perfect duties to oneself, Kant explicates duties of respect by discussing vices that respect precludes. Vices contrary to respect for others include arrogance, defamation, and ridicule. Arrogance is "the inclination to be always *on top*"; through maxims of arrogance, "we demand that others think little of themselves in comparison with us" (*Morals*, 6:465). Defamation is "the immediate inclination ... to bring into the open something prejudicial to respect for others" – even if true (*Morals*, 6:466). In defaming others, the agent makes herself feel better by making someone else look worse in others' eyes. Ridicule is "the propensity to expose others to laughter, to make their faults the immediate object of one's amusement" (*Morals*, 6:467). All these vices are contrary to proper respect for others, for all deny their targets the respect they deserve as equal, rational beings with dignity (*Morals*, 6:449, 462).

Kant explicates duties of love primarily in terms of other-regarding virtues, though he only rarely refers to them as virtues. Nevertheless, these are qualities it is our duty to cultivate as part of promoting the obligatory end of the happiness of others: beneficence (*Morals*, 6:448–54; *Collins*, 27:416–22), sympathy (*Morals*, 6:456–8), and gratitude (*Morals*, 6:454–6). The maxim of beneficence is one of "[promoting] according to one's means the happiness of others in need, without hoping for something in return" (*Morals*, 6:453). Cultivating love for other human beings is also part of the duty of beneficence (*Morals*, 6:402). The maxim of sympathy is one both of sharing actively in others feelings and of cultivating one's naturally sympathetic feelings to assist oneself in understanding their feelings and needs (*Morals*, 6:456–7). Gratitude likewise involves a maxim of not only "*honoring a person because of a benefit he has rendered us*" but also fostering feelings of appreciativeness for those that help us (*Morals*, 6:454–6). For Kant, promoting the happiness of others means helping them promote their permissible ends. Beneficence directly corresponds to this requirement; sympathy helpfully assists. Gratitude's relation is less direct: When we honor a benefactor and show her that we appreciate what she has done for us, we encourage her, and perhaps others, to continue helping others.[59]

Kant explicitly calls "vices" dispositions opposed to duties of love: "the loathsome family of *envy, ingratitude*, and *malice*" (*Morals*, 6:458–60; *Vigilantius*, 27:692–5). These vices are opposed to duties of love because they conflict with the commitment to promote the happiness of others.[60] For example, malice is "the direct opposite of sympathy" (*Morals*, 6:459), "malevolence or joy at another's misfortune," which may be "coupled with a desire to render the state of the other unhappy" (*Vigilantius*, 27:695). These and most other Kantian vices can be understood as perversions of natural human tendencies – that is, as vices grafted onto animality and humanity. Vices opposed to duties of respect and duties of love, for example, generally reflect the desire to see oneself as better or better off than one's neighbors. Ambition, lust for authority, greed, and vengeance emerge all too easily from human social interactions (*Anthropology*, 7:267–74).[61]

In addition to the virtues and vices corresponding to directly ethical duties, Kant discusses many traits that he stops short of calling virtues, or that he calls virtues only inconsistently. These qualities chiefly include dispositions that do not presuppose maxims grounded in respect for rational nature, but which often indirectly promote morality. Some traits do this by building people's trust in their community; others by reinforcing what morality demands;[62] others simply by making virtue seem attractive. Many of these qualities are ones Kant calls "virtues of social intercourse," such as "*affability, sociability, courtesy, hospitality*, and *gentleness* (in disagreeing without quarreling)" (*Morals*, 6:473). Some social virtues require "no great degree of moral resolution to bring them about" and so are not genuine (i.e., moral) virtues (*Collins*, 27:456). Yet we nevertheless have a duty of virtue to foster these traits "so to associate the graces with virtue" (*Morals*, 6:473):

> No matter how insignificant these laws of refined humanity may seem, especially in comparison with pure moral laws, anything that promotes sociability, even if it consists only in pleasing maxims or manners, is a garment that dresses virtue to advantage, a garment to be recommended to virtue in more serious respects too. The *cynic's purism* and the *anchorite's mortification of the flesh*, without social well-being, are distorted figures of virtue, which do not attract us to it. Forsaken by the graces, they can make no claim to humanity. (*Anthropology*, 7:282)

Finally, note that the discussion of virtues and vices in the "Doctrine of Virtue" is restricted to those pertaining to duties of one human being to another; it does not extend to discussions of duties and virtues for those of various ages, social positions, or sexes (*Morals*, 6:468–9). When Kant ventures into practical anthropology, however, he distinguishes between masculine and feminine virtues and vices (*Anthropology*, 7:303–8). For example, Kant describes courage as a masculine virtue, contrasting it with the feminine virtue of patience (*Vigilantius*, 27:645–6; *Anthropology*, 7:257). Tellingly, he also suggests that patience is only falsely considered a virtue (*Anthropology*, 7:149). In addition, Kant suggests that various races and nations have characteristic virtues and vices (*Anthropology*, 7:311–21).[63]

Virtue and the human good

In Kant's system, virtue is not the whole of the human good, which Kant follows many of his predecessors in calling "the highest good" (*summum bonum*). As the complete object of pure practical reason, the highest good is the systematic unity of those ends that pure practical reason takes to be good as ends (*Practical Reason*, 5:108). Thus, for Kant, the highest good consists not only in virtue, but in happiness as well. Virtue is the unconditioned element of the highest good; pure practical reason values virtue for its own sake, in every agent, in all circumstances (*Practical Reason*, 5:110; *Theory and Practice*, 8:278). Happiness, the natural good, which consists in the satisfaction of an agent's wants, wishes, and natural needs, is the conditioned element of the highest good. As the natural, finite rational beings that we are, we have our own happiness among our ends. When we constrain our pursuit of happiness by morality and commit ourselves to pursuing the happiness of others as well as ourselves, happiness becomes an object of pure practical reason (*Practical Reason*, 5:110; *Morals*, 6:453; *Religion*, 6:36–7; see also *Morals*, 6:451). Kant's views of virtue, happiness, and their relation within the highest good develop throughout his career.[64] In some versions of the highest good, happiness is conditioned by and consequent on virtue in such a way that happiness is perfectly proportionate to virtue. Each person gets as much happiness as she morally deserves, perhaps in the next life (*Morals*, 6:480–2; *Practical Reason*, 5:122–34). In other versions, the highest good is a shared, social good achieved through a historical and political progress, and a worldwide ethical community's moral striving (*Judgment*, 5:450, 453; *Religion*, 6:5, 93–100; *Theory and Practice*, 8:279, 307–12).[65] Whatever the details of Kant's account, however, he always insists on happiness as an ineliminable part of the highest good.

KANT'S CRITICISMS OF HIS PREDECESSORS

Kant criticizes Aristotle and seeks to distinguish his own theory of virtue from Aristotle's on several points. Most notably, Kant insists that Aristotle was wrong to think of virtue either as a habit or as a mean between two extremes. Kant defines habit as "a uniformity in action that has become a *necessity* through frequent repetition," "a lasting inclination apart from any maxim . . . a mechanism of sense rather than a principle of thought" (*Morals*, 6:407, 479). But, according to Kant, virtue presupposes a maxim, and precludes being fettered by sensibility. Virtue requires and promotes inner freedom. If virtue were a habit, "then, like any other mechanism of technically practical reason, it [would be] neither armed for all situations nor adequately secured against the changes that new temptations could bring about" (*Morals*, 6:383–4). More seriously, Kant warns, "if the practice of virtue were to become a habit the subject would suffer loss to that *freedom* in adopting his maxims which distinguishes an action done from duty" (*Morals*, 6:409). Thus, Kant insists that virtue is not simply a habit of acting in accordance with the moral law.

Nor, Kant claims, is virtue a mean: "The distinction between virtue and vice can never be sought in the *degree* to which one follows certain maxims; it must rather be sought only in the specific *quality* of the maxims (their relation to the law). In other words, the well-known principle (Aristotle's) that locates virtue in the *mean* between two vices is false" (*Morals*, 6:404). For Kant, virtue implies a moral maxim and a strength of resolution in acting on that maxim. Vice implies a choice to act against morality. Virtues are virtues because their maxims reflect respect for rational nature and are conducive to the fulfillment of one's duties. Vices are vices because their maxims show disrespect for rational nature and oppose the fulfilment of duties. Thus, Kant explains that a particular virtue, such as responsible management of one's resources, cannot be understood as arising from a reduction of one vice (prodigality) or an increase in its opposite vice (miserliness). Each virtue and each vice has its own "distinctive maxim" (*Morals*, 6:404, 432–3).

Kant says that ancient philosophers misunderstand the relation among virtue, happiness, and the human good.[66] Kant criticizes the Epicurean view this way: "The Epicurean had indeed raised a wholly false principle of morality, i.e., that of happiness, into the supreme one, and for law had substituted a maxim of free choice of each according to his inclination." Thus, Epicureans "degraded their highest good" (*Practical Reason*, 5:126). Kant contrasts the Epicurean approach with the Stoic position:

The Stoics, on the other hand, had chosen their supreme practical principle, virtue, quite correctly as the condition of the highest good. But as they imagined the degree of virtue which is required for its pure law as completely attainable in this life, they not only exaggerated the moral capacity of [the human being]...beyond all the limits of his nature...they also refused to accept the second component of the highest good, i.e, happiness, as a special object of human desire.   (*Practical Reason*, 5:126–7)

Kant claims that both Epicureans and Stoics went wrong in thinking we could achieve the highest good without God and through our freedom alone (*Practical Reason*, 5:125–6). More fundamentally, both went wrong in failing to appreciate the heterogeneity of the highest good and in taking the connection between virtue and happiness to be analytic rather than synthetic (*Practical Reason*, 5:112–13, 115–16). Epicureans mistakenly took happiness *as a means* to virtue, while the Stoics falsely thought that virtue *constitutes* happiness (*Practical Reason*, 5:24; *Mrongovius*, 29:623). Thus, the Epicurean conception of the highest good focused on happiness to the exclusion of (genuine) virtue, whereas the Stoic conception of the highest good focused on virtue at the expense of happiness (properly understood). Unsurprisingly, Kant sees the Stoic view as closer to the truth: Not only is virtue the unconditioned element of the highest good, but lasting happiness requires contentment with oneself (*Vigilantius*, 27:646–50; *Practical Reason*, 5:115–19).[67]

Most of Kant's criticisms of modern moral philosophers focus on their theories of obligation rather than their theories of virtue.[68] Kant argues that these philosophers err in setting forth material determining grounds for the principle of morality. All such approaches lead to heteronomy and are incapable of grounding a categorical imperative (*Groundwork*, 4:440–4; *Practical Reason*, 5:33–41; *Mrongovius*, 29:620–9). Kant quickly dismisses theories that ground morality in such circumstantially contingent sources as education (Montaigne) or civil constitution (Mandeville) (*Practical Reason*, 5:40–1). Kant argues that the feelings in which the moral sense theorists such as Hutcheson and Shaftesbury seek to ground moral obligation are contingent on our nature: Not all rational beings have these sentiments, and not all human beings have them to the same degree (*Practical Reason*, 5:38; *Mongrovius*, 29:625–6).[69] Although Kant shares Wolff's view that self-perfection is a crucial part of morality, Kant denies that the concept of perfection is adequate to ground the supreme moral principle. Among Kant's objections to the rational, non-theological concept of perfection is that it is indeterminate, even empty: To construct a morally relevant, robust conception of perfection, one would have to presuppose the very moral principle perfection is supposed to explain (*Groundwork*, 4:443; *Practical Reason*, 5:40–1). Similarly, one of Kant's reasons for rejecting attempts of theological moral philosophers, such as Crusius, to ground the supreme moral principle in the will of God is Kant's belief that one must already have a principle of morality in relation to which one recognizes God's perfection (*Groundwork*, 4:443; *Practical Reason*, 5:41; *Mrongovius*, 29:627–8).

RESPONSE TO KANT'S THEORY OF VIRTUE

Schiller

In his 1793 *On Grace and Dignity*,[70] Friedrich von Schiller (1759–1805) responds critically to Kant's account of virtue. Schiller associates grace with harmony between reason and sensibility, duty and inclination. He associates dignity with reason's oppression of sensibility, and duty's repression of inclination. Schiller argues that "what is demanded of virtue is not properly speaking dignity, but grace."[71] Thus, he argues that Kant errs in linking virtue so closely with dignity. Kant's conceptions of duty and virtue are too harsh, devoid of beauty and pleasure. In contrast to Kant, who so tries clearly to distinguish the moral spring of action from inclination, Schiller proclaims, "virtue is not anything else 'than an inclination for duty.'"[72] For Schiller, the inner struggle of a person who restrains inclination in order to do her duty is preferable to the chaos of one who lets inclination determine her actions unaided by reason. But the dignity of the former agent is nevertheless inferior to the grace of an agent whose sensibility and reason harmonize: "By the fact that nature has made of [the human being] a being both at once reasonable and sensuous ... it has prescribed to him the obligation not to separate that which she has united.... It is only when he gathers, so to speak, his entire *humanity* together, and his way of thinking in morals becomes the result of the united action of the two principles, when morality has become for him a second nature, it is only then that it is secure."[73]

Kant's response to Schiller's criticism is mixed. Kant reiterates views that Schiller finds unappealing, such as that virtue is the "struggle of inclination with the moral law and the constant disposition ... to carry out [one's] duties" (*Vigilantius*, 27:492), and that humans are not capable of doing their duties without inner coercion (*Vigilantius*, 27:491). Kant says, "I readily grant that I am unable to associate *gracefulness* with the *concept of duty*, by reason of its very dignity" (*Religion*, 6:23n.). Because of the self-constraint inherent in the ideas of duty and virtue, these notions call forth in us awe, the feeling of the sublime; one misrepresents them in aligning them with beauty and charm (*Religion*, 6:23n.; *Vigilantius*, 27:490). Still, Kant accepts, in his own way, some of Schiller's points. Kant agrees that we can take pleasure in virtue. But the sort of pleasure Kant thinks we take is that of satisfaction with ourselves for having done something difficult – namely, having equipped ourselves to fulfill our duties (*Vigilantius*, 27:490). As we have seen, too, Kant takes a cheerful heart to be a sign of true virtue (*Religion*, 6:23n.). Moreover, Kant agrees virtue can be associated with grace, though in a less immediate way than Schiller implies. For Kant, graces follow virtue because of virtue's often beneficent consequences. And although Kant sees social graces as proper accompaniments to virtue, making it more attractive and encouraging in people a sense of trust and hope in others' goodness, he does not conceptually associate virtue with grace, or claim that virtue requires grace: "virtue...does allow the attendance of the *graces*, who, however, maintain a respectful distance when duty alone is at issue" (*Religion*, 6:23n.)

Schopenhauer

Arthur Schopenhauer (1788–1860) spends much of *On the Basis of Morality* criticizing Kant's view of morality's foundation, structure, and content. Schopenhauer rejects Kant's rationalism, his account of moral worth, his taxonomy of duties, his notion of duties to oneself, and much else.[74] Schopenhauer also charges that Kant's conception of the highest good corrupts morality by making happiness the reward for virtue, and by rendering morality dependent on religion.[75] Schopenhauer accepts Kant's distinction between noumenal and phenomenal worlds. Yet Schopenhauer argues that, whereas people are individuals phenomenally, we are all one – as will – noumenally.[76] This metaphysical thesis is important for understanding Shopenhauer's view that compassion is the basis of morality and the only true moral incentive. Schopenhauer says that, in compassion, "I suffer directly with [another person], I feel *his* woe just as I ordinarily feel only my own; and, likewise, I directly desire his weal in the same way I otherwise desire only my own. But this requires that I am in some way *identified with him*, in other words, that this entire *difference* between me and everyone else, which is the very basis of my egoism, is eliminated, to a certain extent at least."[77] The compassionate person, then, perceives and responds appropriately to our noumenal unity, whereas others, egoists in particular, remain deluded by the appearance of plurality.[78] Compassion is the core of Schopenauer's (non-eudaimonistic) virtue theory. Schopenhauer holds that the virtues of justice and philanthropy follow from compassion, and that all other virtues flow from justice and philanthropy.[79] All vices, such as greed, lust, cruelty, and treachery, spring from the incentives of egoism and malice.[80] Schopenhauer is far more pessimistic than Kant about moral self-improvement.

Schopenhauer describes virtues and vices as "inherent and enduring qualities," and the goodness or badness of one's character as "innate and ineradicable."[81]

CONTEMPORARY VIRTUE ETHICS

Neither Kant's moral theory in general, nor his theory of virtue in particular, has been warmly received by contemporary virtue ethicists. Especially early on, contemporary virtue ethicists made the case for a return to virtue through critiques of the dominant moral approaches of Kantianism and utilitarian consequentialism.[82] G. E. M. Anscombe's "Modern Moral Philosophy,"[83] which is widely credited with reviving virtue ethics, does far more than criticize Kant. Certainly, however, one of the more influential claims of Anscombe's paper is that Kant's notion of self-legislation is inadequate to ground his system of duties. According to Anscombe, Kant's moral theory is incoherent: It portrays morality as independent of religion, and yet includes notions such as moral obligation and moral law that depend on a divine law giver. Anscombe argues that "the concepts of obligation, and duty . . . and of what is *morally* right and wrong, and of the *moral* sense of 'ought', ought to be jettisoned if this is psychologically possible; because they are survivals, or derivatives from survivals, from an earlier conception of ethics which no longer generally survives, and are only harmful without it."[84]

Many virtue-oriented critics of Kant have objected that his moral theory demands unreasonable impartiality, is hostile to emotions, and includes a conception of virtue that is impossibly demanding.[85] For example, in "Moral Saints,"[86] Susan Wolf draws on Kant's views of virtue and imperfect duties to sketch an account of a Kantian agent whose life is objectionably dominated by morality:

The Kantian would have to value his activities and character traits in so far as they were manifestations of respect for the moral law. If the development of our powers to achieve physical, intellectual, or artistic excellence, or activities directed towards making others happy are to have any moral worth, they must arise from a reverence for the dignity that members of our species have as a result of being endowed with pure practical reason. This is a good and noble motivation, to be sure. But . . . it is hardly what one hopes to find lying dominantly behind a father's action on behalf of his son or a lover's on behalf of her beloved.[87]

Some virtue-ethical criticisms of Kant regarding emotions and impartiality link virtue ethics to the ethics of care.[88] In this vein, Annette Baier suggests that a Humean virtue ethics better responds to the "different voice" captured by Carol Gilligan than do Kantian or consequentialist theories. In contrast to Kant, whose ethics Baier criticizes as too focused on rule-following, rationality, autonomy, equality, and interpersonal conflict, Baier sees Hume as offering a moral theory that recognizes the importance of character traits, the role of feeling in moral judgment, "fluid" boundaries between oneself and others, the moral significance of unchosen relationships (including those among nonequals), and intrapersonal conflicts.[89]

Because of the dominance of Kant's *Groundwork* and second *Critique* among Kant's ethical works in much of the English-speaking philosophical world, some criticisms of Kant's moral theory may well be made in ignorance of Kant's theory of virtue – or with a poor understanding of that theory. In contrast, Rosalind Hursthouse, a neo-Aristotelian familiar with a range of Kant's ethical writings, offers a fairly charitable appraisal of Kant's (and Kantian) ethics.[90] Hursthouse takes Aristotle's ethics to do better than Kant's in recognizing the moral significance of emotions and the relation between emotions and rationality. Yet she sees the potential for a more sophisticated Kantian account of emotions in the life of a virtuous person – perhaps to be constructed from Kant's own more thoughtful claims about emotions in the "Doctrine of Virtue."[91] We may reasonably hope that as Kantians further clarify Kant's theory of virtue, its richness will be more widely appreciated.[92]

NOTES

1. A *eudaimonistic* ethical theory takes happiness (or flourishing) as the ultimate end, and takes virtue to contribute to happiness.

2. See Aristotle's *Nichomachean Ethics* (NE), trans. T. H. Irwin (Indianapolis: Hackett, 1985), 1105a30–34, 1106b36–1107a2, 1144a14–20.

3. NE vi 4, and 1103a31–b1. For more on virtue and skill, see Julia Annas, *The Morality of Happiness* (New York: Oxford University Press, 1993) especially pp. 68–84.

4. NE 1102a13–1103a3, 1104b4–9.

5. NE 1106a14–b28.

6. They saw some calm emotions such as caution and reasonable wanting as consistent with virtue. See Diogenes Laertius 7.116 in *The Hellenistic*

Philosophers, vol. 1, trans., ed. A. A. Long and D. N. Sedley (New York: Cambridge University Press, 1987), p. 412.

7. Stobaeus 2.89, 8-90,6 in *The Hellenistic Philosophers*, pp. 410–11; see also Seneca, *De Clementia* II, v, in *Moral Essays*, vol. 1, trans. J. W. Basore (London: William Heinemann; Loeb Classical Library, 1928).

8. Cicero, *De Finibus Bonorum et Malorum* III, iii–iv, trans. H. Rackham (London: William Heinemann; Loeb Classical Library, 1914).

9. For a discussion of Stoics on emotion and virtue, including comparison with Kant, see Annas, *The Morality of Happiness*, pp. 53–66. For a variety of related papers, see *Aristotle, Kant, and the Stoics*, eds. Stephen Engstrom and Jennifer Whiting (New York: Cambridge University Press, 1996).

10. NE 1097a26–b22.

11. NE 1098a7–1100a9.

12. Cicero, *De Finibus* III, viii–ix.

13. For an explanation of, and challenge to, this common interpretation, see Annas, *The Morality of Happiness*, pp. 334–50.

14. Epicurus, *Letter to Menoeceus*, 127–32, in *The Hellenistic Philosophers*, pp. 193–4.

15. Augustine follows Aristotle regarding the relation between virtue and happiness. See *The City of God Against the Pagans*, trans. R. W. Dyson (Cambridge: Cambridge University Press, 1998), IX, 4, XIV, 8, pp. 361–5, 593–6. See also Bonnie Kent, "Augustine's Ethics," *The Cambridge Companion to Augustine*, eds. Eleanore Stump and Norman Kretzman (New York: Cambridge University Press, 2001), pp. 205–33.

16. *City of God*, XIX, 11, 20, 27, pp. 932–3, 949–50, 962–4.

17. *City of God*, IV, 20–1, pp. 165–8.

18. *The Catholic and Manichaean Ways of Life*, trans. Donald A. Gallagher and Idella J. Gallagher (Washington, DC: Catholic University of America, 1966), XV, 25.

19. *Ethics*, in *Ethical Writings*, trans. Paul Spade (Indianapolis: Hackett, 1995), pp. 1–2.

20. *Ethics*, p. 12.

21. *Ethics*, pp. 6–14, 23–4.

22. *Ethics* and *Dialogue Between a Philosopher, a Jew, and a Christian*, in *Ethical Writings*, pp. 2–3, 5–6, 111–14. Thanks to Bonnie Kent for her suggestions regarding Abelard.

23. *Summa Theologica* (ST), trans. Fathers of the English Dominican Province (Chicago: Encyclopedia Britannica, 1952), Part I of the Second Part, question 55, articles 1–4, and question 59, articles 1–5.

24. ST Part I of the Second Part, question 62, articles 1–4.

25. For a discussion of medieval ethics that challenges the centrality and acceptance of eudaimonism, see Bonnie Kent, "The Moral Life," in *The*

Cambridge Companion to Medieval Philosophy, ed. A. S. McGrade (New York: Cambridge University Press, 2003).

26. Grotius's main work is *On the Law of War and Peace*, trans. Francis W. Kelsey (Oxford: Clarendon Press, 1925). One of Pufendorf's most philosophical works is *The Law of Nature and of Nations*, trans. C. H. Oldfather and W. A. Oldfather (Oxford: Oxford University Press, 1934).

27. On natural law ethics, see Knud Haakonssen, *Natural Law and Moral Philosophy: From Grotius to the Scottish Enlightenment* (New York: Cambridge University Press, 1996), especially chapter 1. On natural law ethics and virtue, see J. B. Schneewind's "The Misfortunes of Virtue," *Ethics* 101 (1990): 42–63, especially 44–8. On natural law ethics and Kant, see Schneewind's "Kant and Natural Law Ethics," *Ethics* 104 (1993): 53–74.

28. See *Leviathan*, ed. Edwin Curley (Indianapolis: Hackett, 1994), chapters 8, 14, 15.

29. See, for example, *Leviathan*, chapter 15, pp. 99–100. Thanks to Dennis Klimchuk for his suggestions regarding this discussion.

30. See Hutcheson, *Illustrations on the Moral Sense*, excerpted in *British Moralists: 1650–1800*, ed. D. D. Raphael (Indianapolis: Hackett Publishing, 1991), vol. 1, pp. 305–6, 311.

31. For a study of British moral philosophy that bears on the development of Kant's thought, see Stephen Darwall, *The British Moralists and the Internal 'Ought': 1640–1740* (New York: Cambridge University Press, 1995).

32. See Shaftesbury, *An Inquiry Concerning Virtue, or Merit*, excerpted in *British Moralists: 1650–1800*, ed. D. D. Raphael (Indianapolis: Hackett Publishing, 1991) vol. 1, pp. 175–7. 186–8.

33. Shaftesbury, *An Inquiry Concerning Virtue, or Merit*, pp. 172–4.

34. See Hutcheson, *An Essay on the Nature and Conduct of the Passions and Affections*, excerpted in *British Moralists: 1650–1800*, vol. 1, pp. 303–4.

35. See Hume, *A Treatise of Human Nature* (T), eds. L. A. Selby-Bigge and P. H. Nidditch (Oxford: Clarendon Press, 1978), p. 498. See also *An Enquiry Concerning the Principles of Morals* (Enq.), ed. J. B. Schneewind (Indianapolis: Hackett Publishing, 1983), Appendix I, p. 85.

36. T III, 1, iii, pp. 581–2.

37. T III, 2, i, pp. 477–8.

38. T III, 2, i, pp. 477ff., and III, iii, 1, pp. 575ff. See also Enq. VI, p. 57, and VIII, pp. 68–72.

39. See *Reasonable Thoughts About the Actions of Men, for the Promotion of Their Happiness* (RT), excerpted and translated by J. B. Schneewind

in volume 1 of *Moral Philosophy from Montaigne to Kant* (New York: Cambridge University Press, 1990), para. 5, p. 335.

40. RT, para. 5, p. 335.
41. RT, para. 5, p. 335.
42. RT, para. 65, p. 338.
43. *Guide to Rational Living* (GRL), excerpted and translated by Schneewind in volume 2 of *Moral Philosophy from Montaigne to Kant* (New York: Cambridge University Press, 1990), para. 161, p. 577.
44. GRL, para. 240, p. 582.
45. GRL, para. 177, p. 579.
46. GRL, chapter II, pp. 581–2, and para. 372, p. 584.
47. I use the following translations of Kant's works: *Anthropology from a Pragmatic Point of View*, trans. Mary J. Gregor (The Hague: Martinus Nijhoff, 1974); *Critique of Practical Reason*, third edition, trans. Lewis White Beck (New York: Macmillan, 1993); *Critique of the Power of Judgment*, trans. Paul Guyer (Cambridge: Cambridge University Press, 2000); *Grounding for the Metaphysics of Morals*, trans. James W. Ellington (Indianapolis: Hackett, 1993); "Kant on the metaphysics of morals: Vigilantius's lecture notes," in *Lectures on Ethics*, trans. Peter Heath, ed. Peter Heath and J. B. Schneewind (Cambridge: Cambridge University Press, 1997); *Metaphysics of Morals*, in *Practical Philosophy*, trans., ed. Mary J. Gregor (Cambridge: Cambridge University Press, 1996); "Morality according to Prof. Kant: Mrongovius's second set of lecture notes (selections)," in *Lectures on Ethics*; "Moral philosophy: Collins lecture notes," in *Lectures on Ethics*; *Religion within the Boundaries of Mere Reason*, trans. Allen Wood and George di Giovanni (Cambridge: Cambridge University Press, 1998); "On the Common Saying, That May Be Correct in Theory, But It Is of No Use in Practice," in *Practical Philosophy*.
48. On inner freedom, see Stephen Engstrom, "The Inner Freedom of Virtue," in *Kant's Metaphysics of Morals: Interpretative Essays*, ed. Mark Timmons (Oxford: Oxford University Press, 2002).
49. Kant calls this "executive power" of the will "autocracy." See Henry Allison, *Kant's Theory of Freedom* (Cambridge: Cambridge University Press, 1990), pp. 164, 246, 285; and Anne Margaret Baxley, "Autocracy and Autonomy," *Kant-Studien* 94 (2003): 1–23.
50. There is much literature on whether the noumenal/phenomenal distinction, which runs throughout Kant's critical philosophy, is better understood as metaphysical or epistemological. For one view of this distinction in Kant's ethics, see Christine M. Korsgaard, *Creating the Kingdom of Ends* (Cambridge: Cambridge University Press, 1996), chapters 6 and 7.

51. For other analyses of Kant's conception of virtue, see Paul Guyer, *Kant on Freedom, Law, and Happiness* (Cambridge: Cambridge University Press, 2000), chapter 9, especially pp. 303–11; and Allen Wood, *Kant's Ethical Thought* (Cambridge: Cambridge University Press, 1999), pp. 329–33.

52. See Kant's discussion of *frailty* throughout part one of *Religion*.

53. For Kant on the passions, see *Anthropology*, 7: 265–7; *Morals*, 6: 407–8.

54. For discussion of Kant on emotions and apathy, see Lara Denis, "Kant's Cold Sage and the Sublimity of Apathy," *Kantian Review* 4 (2000): 48–73; Marcia Baron, *Kantian Ethics Almost without Apology* (Ithaca, NY: Cornell University Press, 1995), chapter 6; Nancy Sherman, "Kantian Virtue: Priggish or Passional?," in *Reclaiming the History of Ethics*, ed. Andrews Reath, Barbara Herman, and Christine M. Korsgaard (Cambridge: Cambridge University Press, 1997), pp. 270–96, and "The Place of Emotions in Kantian Morality," in *Identity, Character, and Morality*, ed. Owen Flanagan and Amelie Oksenberg Rorty (Cambridge, MA: MIT, 1990), pp. 149–70.

55. For Kant, virtue is not innate; it must be taught, cultivated, and practiced. On moral education and the development of virtue, see *Collins*, 27:463–5, 467–70; *Morals*, 6:477–80; and Kant's *Education*, trans. Annette Churton (Ann Arbor: University of Michigan Press, 1969), especially chapter 5.

56. See Wood, this volume.

57. For a more detailed discussion of duties to oneself, see Denis, "Kant's Ethics and Duties to Oneself," *Pacific Philosophical Quarterly* 78 (4) (1997): 321–48, and *Moral Self-Regard: Duties to Oneself in Kant's Moral Theory* (New York: Garland, 2001), especially chapter 4. For a wider-ranging discussion of Kant's system of duties as well as his particular ethical duties, see Mary J. Gregor, *Laws of Freedom* (Oxford: Basil Blackwell, 1963).

58. Jean-Jacques Rousseau (1712–1778) influenced Kant in many ways, including in helping him recognize the dignity of even the most common human beings. See Wood, *Kant's Ethical Thought*, pp. 5–9.

59. Kant sometimes calls these virtues "angelic"; other times, he rejects this terminology. See *Morals*, 6: 461; *Vigilantius*, 27:632, 699.

60. Kant discusses also the vice of scandal throughout his ethics. Through scandal, one indirectly encourages others to act wrongly through one's own (apparently) bad example. Kant does not neatly classify scandal in his taxonomy; he often aligns it with various other vices. See *Morals*, 6:394, 464, 474.

61. See Wood, *Kant's Ethical Thought*, pp. 259–75.

62. For example, Kant calls love of honor a constant accompaniment of virtue; yet love of honor can also lead people astray. See, for example, *Morals*, 6:334–6, 420.

63. Kant elaborates further on the character of the sexes, races, and nations in sections three and four of *Observations on the Feeling of the Beautiful and Sublime*, trans. John T. Goldthwait (Berkeley: University of California Press, 1965). Robert Louden considers the connection between work of this kind and Kant's more theoretical ethical writings in *Kant's Impure Ethics* (New York: Oxford University Press, 2000).

64. And with it, so does Kant's practical argument for the existence of God. On the practical argument, see Lara Denis, "Autonomy and the Highest Good," *Kantian Review* 10 (2005): 33–59, and "Kant's Criticisms of Atheism," *Kant-Studien* 94 (2003): 198–219. On the development of Kant's views on the highest good and the practical argument, see Eckart Förster's *Kant's Final Synthesis: An Essay on the Opus Postumum* (Cambridge, MA: Harvard University Press, 2000), chapter 5.

65. On proportionality, see Stephen Engstrom, "The Concept of the Highest Good in Kant's Moral Theory," *Philosophy and Phenomenological Research* 52(4) (1992): 747–80; cf. Andrews Reath, "Two Conceptions of the Highest Good in Kant," *Journal of the History of Philosophy* 26(4) (1988): 593–619.

66. See T. H. Irwin, "Kant's Criticisms of Eudaemonism" and Stephen Engstrom, "Happiness and the Highest Good in Aristotle and Kant," both in *Aristotle, Kant, and the Stoics*.

67. Kant admires the Stoics. His arguments regarding apathy, sympathy and other emotions, and suicide refer to Stoic positions (*Morals*, 6:422–3, 457; *Collins*, 27:368–9, 373–5). Kant appreciates Stoicism in large part for the dignity it attributes to humans as rational beings. Kant praises Epicurus for advocating moderation, resignation, and cheerfulness grounded in self-contentment (*Practical Reason*, 5:115–16; *Vigilantius* 27:648–9). Thanks to Dennis Klimchuk for his suggestions regarding this discussion.

68. See Wood, *Kant's Ethical Thought*, pp. 159–63. On Kant's relation and response to his modern predecessors, see J. B. Schneewind, *The Invention of Autonomy: A History of Modern Moral Philosophy* (Cambridge: Cambridge University Press, 1998), chapters 22 and 23. On pre-Kantian and Kantian theories of moral obligation, see Korsgaard, *The Sources of Normativity*, chapters 1–3.

69. Kant's notion of moral feeling, however, reflects his agreement with the moral sense theorists regarding the importance of feeling in moral motivation.

70. Schiller, "On Grace and Dignity" (GD), in *Essays: Aesthetical and Philosophical*, trans. various hands for Bohn's standard library (London: George Bell, 1875).

71. GD, p. 213.

72. GD, p. 199.

73. GD, pp. 199–200.

74. Schopenhauer, *On the Basis of Morality* (BM), trans. E. F. J. Payne (Indianapolis: Bobbs-Merrill, 1965), see especially part two.

75. BM, pp. 55–6. And see Schopenhauer, *The World as Will and Representation* (WWR), trans. E. F. J. Payne (New York: Dover Publications, 1969), vol. I, pp. 524–8.

76. See WWR, vol. I.

77. BM, pp. 143–4, and 138–47.

78. BM, pp. 199–214.

79. BM, pp. 134, 148–67.

80. BM, pp. 131–8, especially p. 136.

81. BM, pp. 196, 187.

82. Philippa Foot's work, such as the papers collected in *Virtues and Vices* (Berkeley: University of California Press, 1978), provides an example of early, constructive contemporary virtue ethics, drawing on Aquinas, the ancients, and others. Rosiland Hursthouse's *On Virtue Ethics* (New York: Oxford University Press, 1999) is an example of a constructive, neo-Aristotelian virtue ethics. Christine Swanton's virtue ethics, presented in *Virtue Ethics: A Pluralistic View* (New York: Oxford University Press, 2003) draws its inspiration from Nietzsche, as well as Aristotle and others.

83. *Philosophy* 33 (1958): 1–19.

84. "Modern Moral Philosophy," p. 1.

85. See, for example, Michael Stocker, "The Schizophrenia of Modern Ethical Theories," *Journal of Philosophy* 73 (1976): 453–66; and Bernard Williams, *Ethics and the Limits of Philosophy* (Cambridge, MA: Harvard University Press, 1985), for example, p. 181.

86. *Journal of Philosophy* 79 (1982): 419–39. Wolf's target is the meta-moral view that moral values and considerations are overriding. She does not take this Kantian "moral saint" to be the only possible interpretation of a virtuous Kantian agent.

87. "Moral Saints," p. 431.

88. See, for example, Lawrence Blum, *Friendship, Altruism, and Morality* (Boston: Routledge and Kegan Paul, 1980); and Michael Slote, "The Justice of Caring," in *Virtue and Vice*, eds. Ellen Frankel Paul, Fred D. Miller, Jr., and Jeffrey Paul (New York: Cambridge University Press, 1998).

89. "Hume, The Woman's Moral Theorist?," in *Women and Moral Theory*, eds. Eva Feder Kittay and Diana T. Meyers (Savage, MD: Rowman and Littlefield, 1987). See also "What Do Women Want in a Moral Theory?," chapter 1 of Baier's *Moral Prejudices: Essays on Ethics* (Cambridge, MA: Harvard University Press, 1994).

90. *On Virtue Ethics*, chapters 4–7.

91. Or by integrating an Aristotelian theory of emotions into a broadly Kantian ethics. See *On Virtue Ethics*, pp. 119–20.

92. Many thanks to Paul Guyer, Bonnie Kent, Dennis Klimchuk, and Roger Wertheimer for their comments on an earlier draft of this essay.

16 Kant's ambitions in the third *Critique*

Kant's ambitions in the *Critique of the Power of Judgment* are vast. The Introduction to the book, while setting the stage for the issues to be addressed in its two main parts, returns to an issue first broached in the Appendix to the "Transcendental Dialectic" of the *Critique of Pure Reason*, namely, the idea of a system of empirical laws of nature, but also suggests for the first time that their systematicity can ground the necessity of such laws, a clear addition to the theory of experience of the first *Critique*. The first main part of the book, the "Critique of the Aesthetic Power of Judgment," takes up a wide range of the topics debated in eighteenth-century aesthetics – including the ontological status of beauty, the universal validity of judgments of taste and the possibility of aesthetic criticism, the contrast between the beautiful and the sublime, the nature of genius, and the moral significance of aesthetic experience – and uniquely attempts to show that our aesthetic judgments and practices have a rational foundation even though they cannot be grounded on determinate principles. The second main part of the work, the "Critique of the Teleological Power of Judgment," takes up specific debates in contemporary biology, such as the controversy between epigenetic and preformationist theories of reproduction and the emerging debate over the possibility of speciation by evolution, while also tackling broader philosophical problems such as the possibility of comprehending organisms in general and the moral significance of nature as a whole. Above all, the third *Critique* argues that our pleasures in the beautiful and the sublime and our sense of the purposiveness of nature stemming from our experience of organisms can help bridge the "incalculable gulf fixed between the domain of the concept of nature, as the sensible, and the domain of the concept of freedom, as the supersensible" (*Judgment*, Introduction II, 5:175–6),[1] and thereby unify Kant's theoretical and practical philosophy in a single theory of human experience. In all of this, although he does not drop many names in the book, Kant also expressly or tacitly responds to a wide array of contemporary authors, learning from but also criticizing the empiricist theories of taste of Francis Hutcheson, David Hume, and Henry Home, the psychological analyses of our feelings of beauty and sublimity by Edmund Burke, the cognitivist aesthetics of Alexander Gottlieb Baumgarten and Georg Friedrich Meier, Alexander Gerard's argument that genius is manifest in both fine art and natural science, the preformationism of Albrecht von Haller and Charles Bonnet, the epigenesis of the Comte de Buffon, the *Bildungstrieb* of Johann Friedrich Blumenbach, and especially Leibniz's version of the preestablished harmony between the principles of nature and grace and Hume's critique of the argument from design in the *Dialogues concerning Natural Religion*.

So it would be impossible to discuss even just the major topics or the highlights of the historical context of the *Critique of the Power of Judgment* in a single essay, let alone both. At the same time, it would be profoundly misleading to attempt to reduce the topics of the book to a single idea (even though Kant himself attempts to do this with his new conception of "reflecting judgment") or to a response to a single author (as one author has done in seeing the whole work as an argument between Kant and his one-time student Johann Herder).[2] Nevertheless, just as it can be immensely helpful, especially to the Anglo-American reader, to interpret and evaluate the *Critique of Pure Reason* as a response to Hume's doubts about our ordinary conceptions of causation, external objects, and the self,[3] so I want to suggest here too that it can be illuminating to read much in the third *Critique* as a protracted argument with Hume. In this essay I will interpret and assess three of Kant's main topics in the work – the necessary truth of particular laws of nature, the universal validity of judgments of taste, and the moral significance of a teleological conception of nature – as attempts to provide *a priori* foundations for what Hume thought were matters of mere imagination and custom without relapsing into the rationalist metaphysics, aesthetics, and teleology of Leibniz, Christian Wolff, and Alexander Baumgarten. Hume gave a strictly empiricist explanation of our belief in the necessity of particular causal laws, of our confidence in the existence of a standard of taste, and of our belief in an intelligent designer and creator of nature. In the third *Critique*, Kant wanted to show that an *a priori* and transcendental (although regulative rather than constitutive) principle of the systematicity of nature underlies our belief in the necessity of particular causal laws; that an *a priori* principle underlies our claims of universal validity for our judgments of taste, although it cannot yield a standard of taste in the sense of rules for making those judgments; and that our experience of nature leads us to an *a priori* conception of its designer and his purposes, although that conception can be made determinate only by moral conceptions and can be put to use only for moral purposes.

I. HUME ON NECESSITY, TASTE, AND DESIGN

Hume's empiricist accounts of our belief in the necessity of particular causal laws, of the standard of taste, and of our belief in the intelligent design and creation of nature are well known and understood (except perhaps the last), so my account of these targets for Kant can be brief.

I. THE NECESSITY OF CAUSALITY. Hume raised three major questions about our belief in causation: What is the source of the idea of necessary connection that we include alongside of our ideas of spatial contiguity and temporal succession in our complex idea of causation?[4] Why do we believe the general principle "that *whatever begins to exist, must have a cause of existence*"?[5] And "*Why [do] we conclude that such particular causes must necessarily have such particular effects, and why [do] we form an inference from one to another?*"[6] In the *Treatise of Human Nature* (1739–40), where all three of these questions are explicitly raised, Hume says that it would be "more convenient to sink" the second of these questions into the third, and in the end much more clearly answers the first and third of his questions than the second. Kant is not supposed to have known the *Treatise*, however, only the abbreviated *Enquiry concerning Human Understanding* of nine years later (1748), where Hume does not clearly raise the second of these questions at all,[7] and so of course answers only the first and third. So one might think that in the *Critique of Pure Reason* Kant would have focused on those two questions, that is, the source of our idea of the necessity of causal connections and the basis for our belief in particular causal laws. In fact, however, in the first *Critique* Kant offers an elaborate theory of the origins of the category of causation and of our belief in the universal principle that "Everything that happens (begins to be) presupposes something which it follows in accordance with a rule,"[8] thus answering the second question that Hume had left largely unanswered, while ignoring the third question that Hume himself had attempted to answer in the *Treatise*. But in the Introduction to the *Critique of the Power of Judgment*, Kant does give his answer to Hume's question about our belief in particular causal laws; so for my purposes in this chapter I will focus on the first and third of Hume's questions.[9]

Hume's problem about the source of the simple idea of necessary connection that is an essential part of our complex idea of causation arises from the fundamental principle of his empiricism, *"that all our simple ideas in their first appearance are deriv'd from simple impressions, which are correspondent to them, and which they exactly represent."*[10] His argument is then that in any case of causation we can readily find the impressions of spatial contiguity and temporal succession that give rise to our ideas of those relations, but we can find no impression from which we might get the idea of necessary connection by means of which we are supposed to be able to distinguish a causal relation from a merely accidental juxtaposition of two objects or states of affairs – necessary connection is just not the sort of thing we can see or touch.[11] Hume's problem about our belief in particular causal laws, or in his terms particular causal inferences, is that they are clearly not what he calls truths of reason, or what Kant would call analytical truths, that is, the concept of the effect is not contained in the concept of the cause and cannot be inferred from it by purely logical methods, and of course we cannot infer the supposed effect from the supposed cause through the idea of necessary connection itself, because we do not yet have a source for that idea. Yet, if we turn to the only alternative to reason, namely, experience, more precisely our prior experience of the "constant conjunction" of pairs of objects or events, we could only infer that a new experience of a token of the type that we think of as the cause must be followed by a token of the type of effect we expect if we could proceed upon the principle *"that instances, of which we have had no experience, must resemble those, of which we have had experience, and that the course of nature continues always uniformly the same.*"[12] However, that principle is not a truth of logic, nor could it be inferred from prior experience without presupposing its own truth. Thus, we apparently have no adequate basis in either reason or experience for our particular causal inferences, or belief in particular causal laws.

Of course, Hume does not rest with skepticism about causation, which he in fact believes is the basis for all our knowledge of the external world, but instead offers a naturalistic explanation of both our idea of necessary connection and our belief in particular causal laws, indeed a single explanation of both of these. As he suggests, "'twill appear in the end, that the necessary connection depends on the inference, instead of the inference's depending on the necessary connexion."[13] His theory is that because of the way the imagination works, repeated experience of pairs of objects or events of a certain type creates both a tendency to have a vivid idea of the second member of the pair when presented with an impression of the first, an idea so vivid that it is as good as belief,[14] as well as a feeling of the transition of the mind from the impression to that vivid idea, "an internal impression of the mind, or a determination to carry our thoughts from one object to another," which is then transformed into an idea of necessity in the *object* because "the mind has a great propensity to spread itself on external objects, and to conjoin with them any internal impressions, which they occasion, and which always make their appearance at the same time that these objects discover themselves to the senses."[15] Repeated experience of constant conjunction thus gives rise to both causal inferences and our idea of necessary connection.

Now Hume himself recognized the empirical character of this answer to his first and third questions, that is, that it depends on *observation*[16] of how the mind itself *has* worked rather than on any reasoning about how it *must* work; at least that is what his designation of this account as a "Sceptical Solution" of his "Sceptical Doubts concerning the Operations of the Understanding" suggests.[17] Kant clearly found Hume's empirical account inadequate and tried to supply an *a priori* origin of our concept of causation in his theory of the categories and his derivation of the "synthetic principles of pure understanding" in the *Critique of Pure Reason*. In a nutshell, Kant's claims are that we can transform the purely logical concept of ground and consequence into the "schematized" category of cause and effect by interpreting it in the light of our equally pure and *a priori* intuitions of space and time, and that we can justify the synthetic *a priori* principle that every event has a cause by demonstrating that knowledge of particular causal laws is the condition of the very possibility of our knowledge of succession in objective states of affairs, a kind of knowledge that Hume never thought to doubt.[18] But in the first *Critique*, Kant offers no account of how we can come to know particular causal laws even though he clearly explains the role they play in our knowledge of change. His answer to this question comes only in the Introduction to the third *Critique*.

II. A STANDARD OF TASTE. Hume does not explicitly present it this way, but both his solution to the problem "Of a Standard of Taste" offered in his famous 1757 essay of that name and the theory of beauty dispersed throughout the *Treatise* and first *Enquiry* on which that solution rests are clearly intended to be empirical in character. Hume's theory of beauty is that in a certain number of cases our pleasure in an object is just an inexplicable response to certain features of its appearance or "*species*," while in a larger number of cases it is a response to the perception of its actual or apparent utility, which we enjoy either directly or else because of the imagination's tendency toward sympathy with the pleasure of others or its tendency to carry our response from actual utility over to merely apparent or imagined utility.[19] In all cases, "beauty is nothing but a form, which produces pleasure, as deformity is a structure of parts, which conveys pain; and since the power of producing pain and pleasure makes in this manner the essence of beauty and deformity, all the effects of these qualities must be deriv'd from the sensation." The beauty of mere appearance "is such an order and construction of parts, as . . . is fitted to give a pleasure and satisfaction to the soul" "by the *primary constitution* of our nature," while the beauty of actual or apparent utility, which is "a great part of the beauty, which we admire either in animals or in other objects, is deriv'd from the idea of convenience and utility," either our own, which we enjoy directly, that of another, which we enjoy by sympathy, or merely apparent utility, which we enjoy through the associative mechanisms of the imagination.[20] Kant will incorporate Hume's distinction between the two varieties of beauty in his own distinction between "free" and "adherent" beauty (*Judgment,*

§16), but what he will attempt to reject is Hume's strictly empirical observation that beauty and all of its effects are derived solely from sensations which are due to nothing more than the constitutions of our physiology and imagination.

Hume's theory of beauty is expounded only episodically in the *Treatise*, chiefly to illustrate points in his theory of the passions and moral philosophy, and is not accompanied with an explicit statement about its epistemological status. But the strictly empiricist character of Hume's methodology is explicit in "Of the Standard of Taste," his contribution to the eighteenth-century debate about the intersubjective validity of aesthetic judgments. Hume uses strictly empiricist language when he states that

It appears then, that amidst all the variety and caprice of taste, there are certain general principles of approbation or blame, whose influence a careful eye may trace in all operations of the mind. Some particular forms or qualities, from the original structure of the internal fabric, are calculated to please, and others to displease.[21]

Of course, people do not always agree in their pleasure in and approbation of particular objects, but Hume does not take that to imply that the "general principles of approbation" are merely statistical or probabilistic; rather, if these principles "fail of their effect in any particular instance, it is from some apparent defect or imperfection in the organ." Or as he puts it,

But though all the general rules of art are founded only on experience and the observation of the common sentiments of human nature, we must not imagine, that, on every occasion, the feelings of men will be conformable to these rules. Those finer emotions of the mind are of a very tender and delicate nature, and require the concurrence of many favourable circumstances to make them play with facility and exactness, according to their general and established principles.[22]

The project of the essay is then to determine the "favourable circumstances" that allow some people, the best qualified critics, to discern most reliably the pleasures that objects have to offer us and therefore to make judgments of taste that should be paradigmatic for the rest of us.[23] These "favourable circumstances" obtain when critics have "a perfect serenity of mind, a recollection of thought, a due attention to the object,"[24] or, more fully, delicacy of taste, practice,

opportunity for frequent comparisons among objects, and the freedom and good sense to "check" inappropriate prejudices and adopt
appropriate prejudices for the enjoyment of particular objects.[25] But
we need not worry about the details of these conditions here; the
chief point for us is simply that Hume is confident that the general
principles of taste, the mechanisms of physiology and imagination
that make them "tender and delicate,"[26] and the conditions for their
optimal operation are all "founded only on experience and on the
observation of the common sentiments of human nature." This will
be Kant's target in the "Analytic of the Beautiful" and the "Deduction of judgments of taste" in the third *Critique*.

III. DESIGN AND PURPOSE IN NATURE. Hume criticized the traditional argument from the apparent design of the natural world to an
omniscient, omnipotent, and benevolent God in Section 11, "Of a
Particular Providence and of a Future State," in the *Enquiry concerning Human Understanding*, which was known to Kant by the middle of the 1750s, and in the *Dialogues concerning Natural Religion*,
which were translated into German in 1781, very quickly after their
posthumous publication in English in 1779. It is easy to read Hume
as completely rejecting the argument from design, which was advocated by moderate and enlightened divines from the end of the seventeenth century until the end of the eighteenth, well after Hume's
own book.[27] In both the *Enquiry* and the *Dialogues*, Hume argues
that it is not rational to infer to a perfectly intelligent and purposive
creator from a nature that is clearly imperfect and often contrapur-
posive, at least as far as we can see. For example, in the *Enquiry*
the "friend" who seems to speak for Hume (unlike the rest of the
Enquiry, this section is written in dialogue form) says that

The Deity is known to us only by his productions, and is a single being in the
universe, not comprehended under any species or genus, from whose experienced attributes or qualities we can, by analogy, infer any attribute or quality
in him. As the universe shows wisdom and goodness, we infer wisdom and
goodness. As it shows a particular degree of these perfections, we infer a particular degree of them, precisely adapted to the effect which we examine. But
farther attributes or farther degrees of the same attributes, we can never be
authorized to infer or suppose, by any rules of just reasoning.... Every supposed addition to the works of nature makes an addition to the attributes
of the Author of nature; and consequently, being entirely unsupported by

any reason or argument, can never be admitted but as mere conjecture and hypothesis.[28]

And in the *Dialogues*, Hume's apparent spokesman Philo makes much sport with the argument, proposing that if we examine the world around us closely we might have to infer that it has just grown like a vegetable, or perhaps was designed by an immature god or a superannuated god or an ill-managed committee of gods. But it is important to note that throughout all of the fun Hume's apparent spokesmen deny the *rationality* of arguing for the existence of God by analogy with other forms of creation that we know, not the *naturalness* of the belief in an intelligent and purposive design and designer of the universe. In fact, Hume's spokesman Philo seems to allow that belief in the purposive design of the universe and the intelligence of its author is not only natural but also *useful*:

A Purpose, an Intention, a Design strikes every where the most careless, the most stupid Thinker; and no man can be so harden'd in absurd Systems, as at all times to reject it. *That Nature does nothing in vain*, is a Maxim establish'd in all the Schools, merely from the Contemplation of the Works of Nature, without any religious Purpose; and, from a firm Conviction of its Truth, an Anatomist, who had observ'd a new Organ or Canal, wou'd never be satisfy'd, till he had also discover'd its Use and Intention. One great Foundation of the *Copernican* System is the Maxim, *that Nature acts by the simplest Methods, and chooses the most proper Means to any End*; and Astronomers often, without thinking of it, lay this strong Foundation of Piety and Religion. The same thing is observable in other Parts of Philosophy: And thus all the Sciences almost lead us insensibly to acknowledge a first intelligent Author.[29]

As with causation in general, Hume in fact seems to think that our belief in God as the author of nature cannot be logically derived from reason or experience but is still a natural, irresistible, and useful product of the real source of our most fundamental beliefs, namely, the imagination. Kant will clearly *agree* with Hume that the conception of God is the source of useful strategies for the investigation of nature – indeed, Hume's use of the term "maxim" in this passage may make it a direct source for Kant's discussion of the maxims of scientific inquiry in the Introduction to the third *Critique* (Introduction V, 5:182). But he will equally clearly reject Hume's merely empirical recognition that the idea of an intelligent designer of nature comes to us through the ordinary mechanisms of the imagination. Kant will insist that the idea of God has an *a priori* origin in pure reason, although it has only heuristic value for the conduct of scientific inquiry and can be made *determinate* only from a moral point of view, indeed only to support *our own efforts* to comply fully with the demands of morality.

This will have to suffice for a sketch of Humean positions to which Kant will respond in the *Critique of the Power of Judgment*. Let us now turn to Kant's responses.

2. KANT ON THE NECESSITY OF THE LAWS OF NATURE

Kant presents the whole *Critique of the Power of Judgment* as a theory of "reflecting" rather than "determining" judgment, although this distinction seems to have come to him quite late in the development of his thought.[30] Judgment is "determining" when "the universal (the rule, the principle, the law) is given," and the power of judgment only "subsumes the particular under it." Judgment is "reflecting," however, when "only the particular is given, for which the universal is to be found" (*Judgment*, Introduction IV, 5:179). In other words, determining judgment seeks to apply a given universal to a particular, whereas determining judgment seeks to find an appropriate universal for a particular that is already given. Whether this conception of reflecting judgment fits all the cases of judgment that Kant discusses in the third *Critique*, especially the judgment of the beautiful, which Kant says "pleases universally without a concept" at all (*Judgment*, §9, 5:219), is debatable.[31] But it certainly fits the first use of the power of judgment that Kant describes in the Introduction to the third *Critique*, namely, the search for determinate empirical laws of nature by means of which the *a priori* but completely abstract principles established in the first *Critique* – such as the principle that "All alterations occur in accordance with the law of the connection of cause and effect" (B 232) – can be applied to particular objects of experience. There is an issue here because the concepts contained in such general principles are not specific enough to be applied directly to our empirical intuitions – the concept of causation, for example, is in fact only the abstract idea of "the succession of the manifold insofar as it is subject to a rule," or what Kant calls a "schema" for an empirical concept (A 144/B 183) – and there are in fact always a variety of conceivable ways in which such a general idea could be applied to particular sensory data, that is, a variety of hypotheses about causation that are equally consistent with the empirical data. Changes in the temperature of substances, for example, could be explained as the regular outcome of transfers of some substance distinct from that the temperature of which has changed (phlogiston) or as the regular outcomes of changes in the velocity of the particles of the same substance whose temperature has changed (the molecular theory of heat, which of course eventually won out over the phlogiston theory). But the general concept of causation or the general principle that every alteration has a cause does not by itself tell us which of these more concrete conceptions of causation to adopt.

This is at least the most obvious interpretation of the problem that Kant has in mind in the initial discussion of reflecting judgment in the first draft of the Introduction to the third *Critique*, which was apparently written in early 1789, about halfway through his composition of the book.[32] Here Kant writes thus:

With regard to the general concepts of nature, under which a concept of experience (without specific empirical determination) is first possible at all, reflection already has its directions in the concept of a nature in general, i.e., in the understanding.... But for those concepts which must first of all be found for given empirical intuitions, and which presuppose a particular law of nature, in accordance with which alone **particular** experience is possible, the power of judgment requires a special and at the same time transcendental principle for its reflection, and one cannot refer it in turn to already known empirical concepts and transform reflection into a mere comparison with empirical forms for which one already has concepts. For it is open to question how one could hope to arrive at empirical concepts of that which is common to the different natural forms through the comparison of perceptions, if, on account of the great diversity of its empirical laws, nature (as it is quite possible to think) has imposed on these natural forms such a great diversity that all or at least most comparison would be useless for producing consensus.   (*FI*, Section V, 20:212–13)

In other words, the problem is that on the basis of only the abstract laws of nature established in the first *Critique*, "we could not hope to find our way in a labyrinth of the multiplicity of possible empirical laws" (20:214).

Kant's response to this problem is that we must simply "presuppose that even with regard to its empirical laws nature has observed a certain economy suitable to our power of judgment and a uniformity that we can grasp, and this presupposition, as an *a priori* principle of the power of judgment, must precede all comparison" (20:213). In fact, we must not merely presuppose that the number of possible empirical concepts of nature is sufficiently small to be manageable by creatures with limited cognitive resources like ourselves; we must also presuppose the "general but at the same time indeterminate principle of a purposive arrangement of nature in a system, as it were for the benefit of our power of judgment, in the suitability of its particular laws (about which understanding has nothing to say) for the possibility of experience as a system" (20:214). By a system, Kant means "a hierarchical order of species and genera" (20:213). Such a system could be a system of concepts of natural *forms*, such as the Linnean taxonomy of plants and animals, which divides them into species, genera, families, orders, and so on on the basis of morphological similarities of parts such as reproductive organs, teeth, and the like, or a system of natural *laws*, or laws about natural *forces*, which subsumes more particular laws, such as the laws of chemistry, under more general laws, such as the laws of physics. Kant spells out this conception of a system in some detail (20:214–15) but does not actually explain in equal detail how presupposing that our concepts of forms and laws can be organized into systems will address the problem of the underdetermination of particular laws by the general laws of nature. But his idea seems to be that seeking to find "in the immeasurable multiplicity of things in accordance with possible empirical laws sufficient kinship among them to enable them to be brought under empirical concepts (classes) and these in turn under more general laws (higher genera) and thus for an empirical system of nature to be reached" (20:215) will help us by directing us to prefer among possible empirical concepts for some given data those that fit into a system with other empirical concepts we already have over those that do not, or those that fit better into a system over those that fit worse. With a guideline such as this, our search for empirical concepts to mediate between empirical intuitions and the general concepts of nature – the task of reflecting judgment – would not be "arbitrary and blind" (20:212).

Kant insists that we should not merely *strive* to find empirical concepts of nature that fit into a system, but that we must presuppose the "transcendental" principle

that nature in its boundless multiplicity has hit upon a division of itself into genera and species that makes it possible for our power of judgment to find consensus in the comparison of natural forms and to arrive at empirical concepts, and their interconnection with each other, through ascent to more general but still empirical concepts; i.e., the power of judgment presupposes a system of nature which is also in accordance with empirical laws and does so *a priori*, consequently by means of a transcendental principle.   (20:212)

The principle of reflecting judgment is not merely the "logical" or methodological prescription that *we* should prefer systematic over non-systematic empirical concepts, but the "transcendental" principle "of regarding nature *a priori* as qualified for a **logical system** of its multiplicity under empirical laws" (20:214), the principle that **"Nature specifies its general laws into empirical ones, in accordance with the form of a logical system, in behalf of the power of judgment"** (20:216). Contrary to Hume, Kant clearly maintains that we must make the *a priori* presupposition that nature itself is systematic, and that we can seek particular laws of nature, thus particular causal laws, only on this presupposition.

But why must we not just seek to introduce systematicity into our own concepts, and instead presuppose that nature itself is systematic? Several assumptions might account for such a claim. One would be the assumption of a correspondence theory of truth, on which a systematic set of concepts of nature could be true only if the forms or laws of nature are themselves systematic. Another would be an assumption about practical rationality, on which it is rational to seek to realize a goal only if we have some sort of guarantee that such a goal can actually be achieved – so that it would be rational to seek systematicity among our concepts of nature only if we have the guarantee that nature itself is systematic. Kant clearly holds a correspondence theory for empirical truths (see *Pure Reason*, A 59–60/B 84–5), and his doctrine of the postulates of pure practical reason is clearly based on the principle that it is rational to seek a goal only if we have a guarantee that the accomplishment of that goal is possible (although at least once he recognizes that if a goal is sufficiently important, as the goal of durable international peace certainly is, then it is entirely rational to pursue it as long as we just have sufficient reason to believe that its necessary conditions are *not impossible*).[33] So both of these could certainly be among Kant's motives for insisting that the principle of the systematicity of nature itself is not merely logical but transcendental, that is, an *a priori* principle about the object of our investigation.

In the published version of the Introduction, however, Kant makes a new point, missing from the first draft, which makes it clear that his conception of the systematicity of the forms and laws of nature is meant as a direct answer to Hume's problem about the *necessity* of causal laws – that is, not just the necessity that we know causal laws, but the necessary truth of those laws themselves. Kant here presents the fundamental problem for reflecting judgment as follow:

The determining power of judgment under universal transcendental laws, given by the understanding, merely subsumes; the law is sketched out for it *a priori*, and it is therefore unnecessary for it to think of a law for itself in order to be able to subordinate the particular in nature to the universal. – But there is such a manifold of forms of the universal transcendental concepts of nature that are left undetermined by those laws that the pure understanding gives *a priori* ... that there must nevertheless also be laws for it which, as empirical, may indeed be contingent in accordance with the insight of **our** understanding, but which, if they are to be called laws (as is also required by the concept of a nature) must be regarded as necessary on a principle of the unity of the manifold, even if that principle is unknown to us.

(*Judgment*, Introduction IV, 5:179–80)

Or as he formulates it a second time:

The understanding is of course in possession *a priori* of universal laws of nature, without which nature could not be an object of experience at all; but it still requires in addition a certain order of nature in its particular rules, which can only be known to it empirically and which from its point of view are contingent. These rules, without which there would be no progress from the general analogy of a possible experience in general to the particular, it must think as laws (i.e., as necessary), because otherwise they would not constitute an order of nature, even though it does not and never can cognize their necessity. Thus although it cannot determine anything *a priori* with regard to those (objects), it must yet, in order to investigate these empirical so-called laws, ground all reflection on nature on an *a priori* principle, namely, that in accordance with these laws a cognizable order of nature is possible – the sort of principle that is expressed in the following propositions: that there is in nature a subordination of genera and species that we can grasp; that the latter in turn converge in accordance with a common principle...; that since it seems initially unavoidable for our understanding to have to assume as many different kinds of causality as there are specific differences of natural effects, they may nevertheless stand under a small number of principles with the discovery of which we have to occupy ourselves, etc.

(*Judgment*, Introduction V, 5:184-5)

In response to this formulation of the problem, Kant then reformulates the transcendental principle of reflecting judgment thus:

Now this principle can be nothing other than this: that since universal laws of nature have their ground in our understanding, which prescribes them to nature (although only in accordance with the universal concept of it as nature), the particular empirical laws, in regard to that which is left undetermined in them by the former, must be considered in terms of the sort of unity they would have if an understanding (even if not ours) had likewise given them for the sake of our faculty of cognition, in order to make possible a system of experience in accordance with particular laws of nature.

(*Judgment*, Introduction IV, 5:180)

This obviously differs from the formulation of the principle in the first draft in making explicit Kant's assumption that all laws must originate in mind – what we might think of as a profoundly neo-Platonic assumption underlying Kant's entire philosophy – so if some laws do not originate in our mind, they must be thought of as if they originate in a mind more capacious than our own. But in context, it also makes it clear that laws must be thought of as part of a system in order to give them the necessity that they need to be laws at all but cannot otherwise possess.

What is Kant's idea here? Once again, he does not explain himself, but the most obvious interpretation of his idea would seem to be that a generalization that seems contingent when considered on its own can seem to be necessary when it is part of a system in which it is entailed by the higher-order generalizations under which it is subsumed and is the only candidate to entail the lower-order generalizations that are subsumed under it. If so, then looking for laws that are a part of a system is not just a heuristic for choosing among alternative hypotheses when our search would otherwise be blind and arbitrary, but a heuristic that has nothing to do with the modal status of the generalizations so found; rather, its position within a system would be precisely what gives a generalization the modal status of a law. Thus we could not leave acknowledgment of their position in a system behind once we have found our generalizations, as we could do with a mere heuristic; membership in a system would remain a condition of our recognition of our generalizations as laws. And since in Kant's way of thought the idea of the imposition of laws by a mind is in fact necessary to explain the *necessity* of those laws, it would be precisely by imposing on nature a *system* of laws that the understanding more capacious than our own, which we imagine in the principle of reflecting judgment, would impose the *necessity* on those particular laws that the categories of our own understanding are not sufficient to impose.

Now we can come back to the question of Kant's motivation for making the principle of reflecting judgment a transcendental rather than merely logical principle. It is just that there must be a source of the necessity of particular laws of nature when that source obviously cannot be our own minds, which can impose only the necessity of the general principles of the understanding on our experience of nature. In the first instance, we can think of that additional source of necessity as the systematicity of nature itself, although we might also go on to think, as Kant does in the published Introduction, that this systematicity must itself be imposed on nature by an understanding greater than our own. And the idea that we must presuppose the systematicity of nature in order to lend necessity to particular laws of nature can also explain what might seem another puzzle about Kant's account, namely, what good it could do us to suppose that these laws are "necessary on a principle of the unity of the manifold, even if that principle is unknown to us" (*Judgment*, Introduction IV, 5:180). The answer to this question is simply that we must be able to regard particular laws of nature as necessarily true even before we have discovered the whole system of them – which indeed we may never do at all – and we can do that only if we assume that the whole system of laws that makes the particular laws we know necessary exists, even if we do not know it. Thus we must suppose that the system of laws, beyond the bits of it that we happen to know, exists in nature itself (put there, if we want to follow the rest of Kant's thought, by an understanding greater than our own).

Thus Kant's thought is that the transcendental principle of the systematicity of nature provides an *a priori* basis for the objective necessity of causal laws instead of the subjective basis in the merely empirically known workings of the imagination, which was all that Hume could offer for the origin of the idea of necessary connection. Of course, now we must ask how plausible this response to Hume is.[34]

One question that naturally arises is how we could think that placing a particular law of nature within a hierarchical system of such laws could lend that law even an appearance of necessary truth when we might well be able to imagine whole other systems of laws consistent with other laws we take ourselves to know and the empirical observations we have made? Presumably Kant's assumption that nature itself is systematic is supposed to take care of this: If it is nature itself that is systematic, not merely our representation of nature through concepts and laws, then there must be some *one* way in which it is systematic (or some one system of organization that has been imposed on it by the understanding greater than our own). Of course, if we do not *know* what that whole system is, as Kant reasonably presupposes, then we can have no way of being certain that some particular law we are considering is actually a part of it, and thus no way of being certain that this law is in fact necessarily true. But that is not an objection if what Kant is offering is not an *epistemology* for necessary truth but more like a *metaphysics* for necessary truth, that is, a theory that explains how there can *be* necessary truth for particular laws of nature, not a method that guarantees that we can *discover* it. We can take Kant to be offering an account of how we can think that the particular laws we claim to know are necessarily true *if* they are in fact true at all. As our knowledge of the whole system improves, of course we may then have to revise our beliefs about *which* particular laws of nature are necessarily true because we will have to revise our beliefs about which of such laws are true at all.

Hume did not in fact ask how we can claim that one causal law rather than another is true, but how we can rationally believe that any generalization is necessarily true when we clearly cannot believe that on the basis of the finite number of cases we have sampled and any premise we could rationally add to those cases. So Kant's claim that we are entitled to the *a priori* supposition that nature itself is systematic at least answers the kind of question Hume actually asked. But now we must consider whether Kant's claim could possibly be a compelling answer to Hume's question. This seems dubious, for Kant seems to do the very thing he accused earlier respondents to Hume of doing, namely, of taking for granted precisely what Hume doubted.[35] Kant *begins* with the assumption that we must have a basis for regarding particular laws of nature as necessarily true, something we cannot do merely on the basis of our own pure understanding (and pure intuition), and then *presupposes* an *a priori* idea of the systematicity of nature to ground that initial assumption. It is not clear that Hume would have been much impressed with this move.

Does this mean that Kant's whole response to Hume's doubts about the necessity of causal laws is in vain? That would be too hasty a conclusion. There are two ways in which Kant clearly improves on Hume. First, by recognizing that we think of particular laws of nature as necessary only within the context of a whole system of laws, Kant changes what we might call the Humean psychology of doubt. Hume stirs our doubts about the rationality of particular causal inferences by considering them in isolation. For example, he imagines us being incapable of explaining why bread should nourish us rather than lions or tigers, thus appearing to make it reasonable to doubt whether we can know that the bread that has nourished us in the past will continue to do so in the future, by considering our claim to know that bread is nourishing for us in isolation from anything else we might know. But Kant makes it clear that we do not claim to know that such generalizations are necessarily true in isolation, but only as part of a whole system of natural laws, including more general ones that entail the particular one at issue. To doubt one causal law we would therefore have to doubt much else that we take ourselves to know, perhaps even the whole of the rest of our knowledge of nature. This may make doubting particular causal inferences much harder than Hume supposes.

More importantly perhaps, Kant's *a priori* idea that natural laws are always part of a system of such laws clearly offers a much richer heuristic for the conduct of scientific inquiry than Hume's. As we saw in an earlier quotation from the *Dialogues concerning Natural Religion*, Hume introduced the idea of a "maxim" for the conduct of inquiry that may well have influenced Kant. But he offered only one such maxim, namely, that nature always takes the shortest way. Kant's idea of a hierarchically ordered system of concepts or laws gives much more concrete guidance in searching for particular concepts or laws: A system is a well-ordered structure in which we can seek to fill particular gaps either by dropping specific predicates from our concepts in order to move upward or by adding predicates in order to move downward – a structure within which, in Kant's terms, we can seek both greater homogeneity and greater specificity for our concepts (see *FI*, Section V, 20:214–15 and *Pure Reason*, A 657–8/ B 685–6). Kant's conception of systematicity gives rise not just to the *lex parsimoniae*, "Nature takes the shortest way," but also to the *lex continui in natura*, that is, nature "makes no leaps, either in the sequence of its changes or in the juxtaposition of specifically different forms," and the *principia praeter necessitatem non sunt multiplicanda*, "the great multiplicity of its empirical laws is nevertheless unity under a few principles" (*Judgment*, Introduction V, 5:182). We may think of these as strictly heuristic or methodological principles, useful for the regulation of our inquiry but open to at least provisional refutation by the actual results of our inquiry; we may not be tempted by Kant's attempt to assign "transcendental" – although not quite "constitutive" – validity to these maxims. Nevertheless, Kant's a priori idea of systematicity clearly leads to a richer philosophy of science than Hume ever contemplated.

3. KANT ON THE *A PRIORI* PRINCIPLE OF TASTE

In the first half of the *Critique of the Power of Judgment*, the "Critique of the Aesthetic Power of Judgment," Kant touched on nearly every major issue discussed in eighteenth-century aesthetics. In the whole of his works, essays as well as treatises, Hume also managed to touch on a wide range of contemporary issues in aesthetics, but unlike most other philosophers of note in the period, he never wrote a systematic work on aesthetics,[36] and his signature work in the field, the essay "Of the Standard of Taste," is focused on the single issue of the conditions in which we may reasonably expect and secure agreement in judgments of taste. This was not in fact a major issue among German aestheticians, so Kant is clearly responding to Hume[37] when he makes this issue the focal point of the "Analytic of the Beautiful" (§§1–22), the first book of the "Critique of the Aesthetic Power of Judgment," and the subsequent "Deduction of judgments of taste" (§§30–40). My discussion of Kant's aesthetics here will focus on his theory of taste as an answer to Hume, even though this may not ultimately be the most important issue in aesthetics for Kant.[38]

As in his *Groundwork for the Metaphysics of Morals*, Kant's strategy in the "Analytic of the Beautiful" is to begin with an analysis of commonsense assumptions and then provide the philosophical theory that is necessary to support the assumptions revealed in this analysis.[39] Kant begins his analysis with the claim that "the satisfaction that determines the judgment of taste is without any interest" (*Judgment*, §2, 5:204), or is disinterested. By this he means that one's pleasure in a beautiful object is not a recognition that the existence of the object serves any merely physiological purpose, in which case it would be "agreeable" (§3), nor any moral purpose, in which case it would be "good" (§4), but concerns only one's response to the representation of the object: "It is readily seen that to say that [an object] is **beautiful** and to prove that I have taste what matters is what I make of this representation [of it] in myself, not how I depend on the existence of the object" (§2, 5:205). Kant supports this first step of his analysis not with any theoretical argument, but with an appeal to our response to an example:

If someone asks me whether I find the palace that I see before me beautiful, I may well say that I don't like that sort of thing, which is made merely to be gaped at, or, like the Iroquois sachem, that nothing in Paris pleased him better than the cook-shops; in true *Rousseauesque* style I might even vilify the vanity of the great who waste the sweat of the people on such superfluous things.... All of this might be conceded to me and approved; but that is not what is at issue here. One only wants to know whether the mere representation of the object is accompanied with satisfaction in me, however indifferent I might be with regard to the existence of the object of this representation.   (§2, 5:205)

Or even, one should add, however hostile to its existence I might be.

Kant next claims that the second "definition" (*Erklärung*)[40] of the beautiful as "that which, without concepts, is represented as the object of a **universal** satisfaction ... can be deduced from the previous explanation of it as an object of satisfaction without any interest," for "one cannot judge that about which he is aware that the satisfaction is without any interest in his own case in any way except that it must contain a ground of satisfaction for everyone" (*Judgment*,

§6, 5:211). Strictly speaking, this claim is a *non sequitur*: It does not follow from the fact that my satisfaction in an object is not caused by its satisfaction of either of the two kinds of interest identified in the previous section that it cannot be idiosyncratic in some other way, due perhaps to some personal and arbitrary association.[41] It also does not follow from the previously established claim that our pleasure in and therefore judgment of beauty must be independent of a concept of the object *as agreeable* or *good* that it must be independent of *any* concept whatsoever, as Kant's second "definition" seems to assert. But this is of little matter, because Kant's next moves are, first, once again to anchor the claim that a genuinely beautiful object should please everyone in an appeal to common sense, and then, second, to introduce a philosophical explanation of our pleasure in beauty that will both justify that claim to intersubjective validity and also explain why (and in what sense) that pleasure is independent of concepts.

Kant appeals to ordinary linguistic usage to anchor the claim that judgments of taste claim intersubjective rather than merely personal validity. "With regard to the **agreeable**," he says, "everyone is content that his judgment, which he grounds on a private feeling, and in which he says of an object that it pleases him, be restricted merely to his own person." Evidence for this is the fact that one "is perfectly happy if, when he says that sparkling wine from the Canaries[42] is agreeable, someone else should improve his expression and remind him that he should say 'It is agreeable **to me**'" (*Judgment*, §7, 5:212). But we do not accept this restriction when we call something beautiful: "It would be ridiculous if... someone who prided himself on his taste thought to justify himself thus: 'This object (the building we are looking at, the clothing someone is wearing, the concert that we hear, the poem that is presented for judgment) is beautiful **for me**." In calling something beautiful, we speak not with an individual but with a "universal voice" (§8, 5:216); we do not claim "objective universal validity," that is, that every object falling under some particular concept, or in a particular class, must please, but rather "subjectively universal validity," that is, that *this* object should please everyone (5:215); indeed, we even *demand* that others should take pleasure in that which we have found to be beautiful (§7, 5:213). Kant also puts this point by saying that there is a "necessity" in a judgment of taste that "can only be called **exemplary**, i.e., a necessity of the assent of **all** to a judgment that is regarded as an example of a universal rule that one cannot produce" (§19, 5:237) – a rule that cannot be produced because, as Kant has by that point more fully argued, although in a way we have not yet discussed, the pleasure in a beautiful object is not connected with its subsumption under any determinate concept.

Kant holds that a judgment of beauty is in a certain sense a synthetic *a priori* judgment rather than an empirical one. This is initially implicit in his claims that one "does not count on the agreement of others with his judgment of satisfaction because he has frequently found them to be agreeable to his own" (*Judgment*, §7, 5:213) and that we should not be deterred from demanding that others *should* agree with our judgments of taste even when, "as experience teaches," this assent "is often enough rejected" in practice (§8, 5:214). In calling something beautiful, we claim that everyone *would* take pleasure in it if everyone – I who make the judgment and the others who should agree with it – were in ideal or optimal circumstances to respond to the object, which is of course not always the case (Kant stresses that we are often mistaken in our own judgments of taste, thinking that an object has pleased us in a universally valid way when it has in fact pleased us only because of some hidden personal interest; see §8, 5:216, §19, 5:237, and §38, 5:290–1). But Kant makes the implication of his analysis explicit when he subsequently explains the question that needs to be answered by a "deduction of judgments of taste": "How is a judgment possible which, merely from **one's own** feeling of pleasure in an object, independent of its concept, judges this pleasure, as attached to the representation of the same object in **every other subject**, a priori, i.e., without having to wait for the assent of others?" (§36, 5:288). Because we cannot derive our pleasure in a beautiful object from any concept that applies to it, he assumes, it can only be "an empirical judgment that I perceive and judge an object is beautiful"; but because under appropriate circumstances I declare that my pleasure is valid for everyone else and demand that they should agree with my judgment, without having to wait for their assent and even in the face of their actual dissent (see also §32, 5:282), "it is an *a priori* judgment that I find it beautiful, i.e., that I may require that satisfaction of everyone as necessary." Put precisely, "it is not the pleasure but **the universal validity of this pleasure** perceived in the mind as connected with the mere judging of an object that is represented in a judgment of taste as a universal rule for the power of judgment, valid for everyone" (§37, 5:289).

Hume himself had argued that judgments of taste are not based on any determinate concepts of their objects and thus cannot be made in accordance with any determinate rules:

A man may know exactly all the circles and ellipses of the COPERNICAN system, and all the irregular spirals of the PTOLEMAIC, without perceiving that the former is more beautiful than the latter. EUCLID has fully explained every quality of the circle, but has not, in any proposition, said a word of its beauty. The reason is evident. Beauty is not a quality of the circle.... It is only the effect, which that figure produces upon a mind, whose particular fabric or structure renders it susceptible of such sentiments. In vain would you look for it in the circle, or seek it, either by your senses, or by mathematical reasonings, in all the properties of that figure.[43]

That is why he argues that we can look only to the particular judgments of critics who have formed their taste under optimal circumstances for our standard of taste, not to any rules that would say that any objects that have certain qualities are always beautiful. Kant fully endorses Hume's premise; in fact, he alludes to the very essay from which I have just quoted when he says that "although critics, as Hume says, can reason more plausibly than cooks, they still suffer the same fate as them" (*Judgment*, §34, 5:285),[44] the fate, that is, of not being able to defend their judgments by rational arguments from the concepts of their objects. But he self-consciously breaks with Hume when he insists that judgments of taste are *a priori* rather than merely empirical in the sense that he has specified. Of course, he recognizes that this analysis of what is claimed by a judgment of taste "must be grounded in something as an *a priori* principle, even if only a merely subjective principle," and that such a principle "also requires a deduction, by means of which it may be comprehended how an aesthetic judgment could lay claim to necessity" (§36, 5:288). This *a priori* principle and its deduction must be our next concern.

Kant attempts to discharge the burden of proof he has taken on in two main steps. The first step is to provide an *explanation* of our pleasure in beautiful objects, which will show that although this pleasure is not based on the subsumption of such objects under any determinate concepts, and therefore is not connected to the satisfaction of any interests that depend on a particular conceptualization of those objects, it is nevertheless connected to a certain state of our *cognitive powers*. The second step is to argue that the cognitive powers work the same way in every human being, so that if one person's pleasure is genuinely connected to this special state of his cognitive powers, then anyone else who is in optimal circumstances for the exercise of his cognitive powers should be able to feel the same pleasure.

The first step of this argument is Kant's theory that our pleasure in beautiful objects is due to a free yet harmonious "play" between the cognitive powers of imagination and understanding, where imagination has to be understood in a broad sense as the capacity to present imagery to the mind, thus as including both the capacity for present sensation that Kant ordinarily designates as "sensibility" and the capacity for the recall of past experiences and the anticipation of future ones that was ordinarily meant by "imagination" in the eighteenth century, and where understanding has to be understood in a broad sense as the capacity to find unity and coherence in the manifolds presented to us by imagination, whether through a concept or not. Kant states the essence of his theory in the Introduction to the third *Critique* when he writes that

If pleasure is connected with the mere apprehension ... of the form of an object of intuition without a relation of this to a concept for a determinate cognition, then the representation is thereby related not to the object, but solely to the subject, and the pleasure can express nothing but its suitability to the cognitive faculties that are in play in the reflecting power of judgment, insofar as they are in play, and thus merely a subjective formal purposiveness of the object. For that apprehension of forms in the imagination can never take place without the reflecting power of judgment, even if unintentionally, at least comparing them to its faculty for relating intuitions to concepts. Now if in this comparison the imagination ... is unintentionally brought into accord with the understanding ... through a given representation and a feeling of pleasure is thereby aroused, then the object must be regarded as purposive for the reflecting power of judgment.

(*Judgment*, Introduction VII, 5:189–90)

Kant further characterizes this idea of play between imagination and understanding in the first draft of the Introduction by saying that it is a state "which constitutes the subjective, merely sensitive condition of the objective use of the power of judgment in general (namely the agreement of those two faculties with each other)" (*FI*, Section

VIII, 20:223–4). If we think of the fundamental goal of the use of our cognitive powers as finding unity in the manifold of our experience, and think of the subsumption of objects under concepts as the objective way of attaining this goal, then we may think of the state in which it seems to us that our manifold of experience has been unified in a way that does not depend on the subsumption of its object under any determinate concept as the "subjective, merely sensitive condition" for the satisfaction of the ultimate goal of the use of our cognitive powers. And this interpretation in turn leads to Kant's explanation for why this peculiar state of mind should lead to a feeling of pleasure. Kant explicitly asserts that the "attainment of every aim is combined with the feeling of pleasure," and also seems to assume the converse, that every feeling of pleasure is connected with the attainment of some aim, but then adds that it is only when the attainment of the aim strikes us as "merely contingent" that the pleasure will be actually felt or "specially noticed" (*Judgment*, Introduction VI, 5:187–8). A state of mind in which it seems to us as if our fundamental cognitive goal of finding unity in our manifolds of experience has been achieved independently of the subsumption of the object of our experience under any determinate concept will surely strike us as a state in which the satisfaction of our goal is merely contingent, and our pleasure in this state will therefore be "specially noticed." Thus Kant's theory of the free play of our cognitive powers explains how we can be pleased with an object independently of its subsumption under a concept, and indeed entails the requirement of the independence of our pleasure from beauty that was initially merely assumed in Kant's exposition of the analysis of judgments of taste.

Now of course it is a matter of common sense (as well as an implication of Kant's theory of knowledge in the first *Critique*) that we are never conscious of an object without any concept altogether, and can never make a judgment about an object without using some concept to pick it out. This is true of aesthetic judgments as well; thus, even the most pedestrian aesthetic judgment, such as "This rose is beautiful," or, if you do not know what kind of flower it is, "This flower is beautiful," employs not only the concept of beauty itself as its predicate, but also some perfectly ordinary, at least relatively determinate concept such as "rose" or "flower" to designate its subject. So how can our pleasure in the object and our judgment that our pleasure is universally valid, and thus our application of the predicate "beautiful" to it, be independent of the subsumption of the object under any determinate concept? The answer to this question can only be that a beautiful object leaves the imagination and understanding room to play *beyond* what is regulated by the determinate concept or concepts that apply to it, in other words, that a beautiful object is one that gives us a feeling of unity and coherence that goes beyond the satisfaction of the conditions needed to satisfy the determinate concept that is applied to it. A beautiful rose is one that somehow gives us a greater sense of unity than a merely indifferent one, a degree of harmony in its shape or between its shape and color, or whatever, that is more than is needed just to count as a rose.[45]

This interpretation of what Kant means by the harmony of imagination and understanding, in addition to satisfying common sense and Kant's own epistemology, also has the virtue of explaining Kant's immediate expansion of the class of genuine aesthetic judgments beyond the case of simple judgments like "This rose is beautiful," which he designates as "pure" and subsequently "free" judgments of taste. Beyond these judgments, Kant recognizes at least four more classes of aesthetic judgments: judgments of "adherent" beauty, which do involve a concept of the purpose of their object; judgments about the "ideal of beauty," which involve a sense of harmony between the outward form and the invisible moral virtue of a human being; judgments of sublimity, which involve a feeling of harmony between the imagination and ideas of reason rather than understanding; and judgments about the beauty of fine art, which depend on a feeling of harmony between the form of a work of art and the special kind of content that Kant calls an "aesthetic idea." A discussion of Kant's theory of the sublime would exceed the boundaries of the present essay,[46] but some comments on the other cases will help illustrate the virtues of Kant's theory of the harmony of the faculties as an explanation of our pleasure in beauty.

Kant's distinction between "free" and "adherent" beauty is clearly his own version of Hume's distinction between beauty of appearance and beauty of utility.[47] In Kant's theory, free beauty involves a feeling of pleasure that is not connected to any concept by means of which the object is identified, while adherent beauty is *connected to* but not *determined by* the concept of its purpose that is implicit in the very concept by means of which an object is identified. When we call something an arsenal or a church, a race horse or even a human being, a concept of its purpose or in the case of a human being its moral vocation is implied, and this purpose places a *limit* on what forms we could possibly find acceptable in such an object – we cannot find an arsenal beautiful if it has light walls with many openings, nor, on Kant's views, is extensive tattooing consistent with the moral imperative always to treat one's body as well as one's personality as an end and not merely as a means (*Judgment*, §16, 5:230). But not every arsenal or human being that satisfies such constraints inherent in the concept of its purpose is beautiful; a beautiful one must be one that gives us a sense of unity or harmony that goes *beyond* what is necessary for satisfaction of its concept, or perhaps even an unusual sense of harmony *between* its purpose and its form, which it need not have merely in order to satisfy the concept of its purpose alone.[48] And this suggests that sometimes the free play of imagination can be a play *with* concepts, although not *determined by* concepts.

This is the possibility that Kant exploits in his brief treatment of the "ideal of beauty" and in his more extensive discussion of the traditional subject matter of aesthetics, namely, the fine arts. An ideal of beauty would be a "highest model" or "archetype" of taste. There is actually nothing in the logic of judgments of taste that requires such an ideal; the logic of taste requires ideal agreement about any beautiful object, but not any sort of hierarchy among beautiful objects. The requirement of an ideal of beauty comes instead from "reason's indeterminate idea of a maximum" (*Judgment*, §17, 5:232). Such an ideal arises when a human form is both judged to be beautiful, in a way that itself goes beyond any merely *normal, average,* or "correct" human form (5:234–5), and also felt to be in harmony with the "highest purposiveness" of a human being – "goodness of soul, or purity, or strength, or repose, etc." – in a way that cannot be derived from any determinate concept but instead requires both "pure ideas of reason and great imagination" (5:235). In other words, in judging a human being (or the depiction of one) to represent the ideal of beauty we judge it to have a beauty of form that goes beyond any determinate concept and a harmony between its form and central moral ideas that goes beyond any determinate concept.

Kant's theory of fine art depends also on the possibility of a harmony between the form of an object and concepts, in this case its content, which is not determined by those concepts.[49] Kant analyzes

a work of fine art as a product of human intentionality, which must
be guided by a concept, but which aims at producing a free play of
the imagination and understanding, and which therefore cannot be
fully determined by any concept (*Judgment*, §§43–4, 5:303–6). This
is why (successful) fine art must be the product of genius, which is
nothing less than a natural gift to produce something exemplary in
a way that uses rules (of technique, composition, and so on) but also
goes beyond them (§46, 5:307–8). Kant further assumes that a work
of art typically has a content – Kant did not yet envisage abstract
or "non-objective" art or see the need for defending the assumption
that all fine art is mimetic – but that its beauty consists precisely
in our sense of a free play *between* its content and its form. Thus
a work of artistic genius is an "aesthetic idea," a "representation of
the imagination that occasions much thinking without it being possible for any determinate thought, i.e., **concept**, to be adequate to it,
which, consequently, no language fully attains or can make intelligible" (§49, 5:313). An aesthetic idea is a conception for a work that
mediates between the rational ideas that are its theme and the form
and material of the work in a way that cannot be determined by any
rule but yet gives us the sense of harmony we need to find it beautiful. "If we add to a concept a representation of the imagination that
belongs to its presentation, but which by itself stimulates so much
thinking that it can never be grasped in a determinate concept, hence
which aesthetically enlarges the concept itself in an unbounded way,
then in this case the imagination is creative" (5:315).

Thus we can see how Kant's idea of the free and harmonious play
of imagination and understanding, which initially seems to explain
only a narrow range of aesthetic judgments such as "This rose is
beautiful," can illuminate the broad range of aesthetic judgments
that we actually make. But now we must return to the main thread
of our discussion and see whether this concept can provide the *a
priori* principle of taste that Kant needs to support his insistence
against Hume that judgments of taste can make an *a priori* claim to
universal validity even though they are not based on rules. This is
the burden of proof in Kant's "Deduction of judgments of taste."

The *a priori* principle underlying judgments of taste obviously
cannot be what Kant introduced as if it were the general principle of reflecting judgment in the Introduction to the third *Critique*,
namely, the principle that the particular empirical laws of nature

must be regarded as if they were part of a system of laws given by an understanding greater than our own but "for the sake of our faculty of cognition" (*Judgment*, Introduction IV, 5:180), because for reasons we have just seen aesthetic judgments do not depend on any concepts that classify their objects and thus neither depend on nor give rise to anything resembling particular empirical laws at all. But the *a priori* principle that Kant has in mind does concern "our faculty of cognition": it is nothing less than the *a priori* principle that we all have the same cognitive faculties and that they work in the same way, from which it should follow that an object that genuinely induces the free play of imagination and understanding in one optimally situated subject will induce it in any other such subject. Kant presents the argument for the principle as briefly as possible in the official "Deduction of judgments of taste" by saying that since a proper judgment of taste is based only on "the subjective conditions of the use of the power of judgment in general (. . . restricted neither to the particular kind of sense nor to a particular concept of the understanding)," it therefore involves only "that subjective element that one can presuppose in all human beings (as requisite for possible cognitions in general)," or that "In all human beings, the subjective conditions" of the aesthetic power of judgment, "as far as the relation of the cognitive powers therein set into action to a cognition in general is concerned, are the same, which must be true, since otherwise human beings could not communicate their representations and even cognition itself" (*Judgment*, §38, 5:290). The claim is that for different human beings to be capable of knowledge, they must all have all the faculties that are necessary for knowledge, and that each human being knows this *a priori* about all other human beings. It might be objected that one must *assume* this *a priori* in order for it to be rational to attempt to communicate one's knowledge to others, but that one could still be defeated in all of one's attempts to communicate knowledge to someone who seems to satisfy all imaginable criteria for being human, and thus that one's assumption is ultimately defeasible, thus not *a priori* but only empirical *knowledge*.[50] However, the more serious objection to Kant's argument would be that even if we are entitled to assume *a priori* that everyone has the same cognitive capacities, it does not follow that they must all work in exactly the same way, and in particular that they must all *play* in exactly the same way, or be set into play by the very same objects. After all, even people who do exactly the same job at work do not play the same games away from work!

Kant tries to address this objection in a preliminary version of the deduction in the "Analytic of the Beautiful."[51] In response to the question "Whether one has good reason to presuppose a common sense," Kant argues that we must assume not only that "if cognitions are able to be communicated, then the mental state, i.e., the disposition of the cognitive powers for a representation in general, and indeed that proportion which is suitable for making cognition out of a representation...must also be capable of being universally communicated," but further that "although this disposition of the cognitive powers has a different proportion depending on the difference of the objects that are given, nevertheless there must be one in which this inner relationship is optimal for the animation of both powers of mind" (*Judgment*, §21, 5:238). But Kant's pseudo-mathematical talk of an "optimal proportion" cannot mask the fact that he offers no basis for this assertion, no argument to bar the possibility that even if in some general way all human beings have the same cognitive capacities, different people might find that different objects set those faculties into free and harmonious play, even when personal interests in the agreeable, the good, and any other identifiably idiosyncratic association have been set aside. Kant's insistence that the cognitive powers of all humans must be alike both at work and at play seems more a matter of faith than a justifiable *a priori* principle.[52]

The empiricist premise of Hume's essay on taste could only have been that experience will reveal a high degree of agreement among the judgments of qualified critics, and that the rest of us will find that modeling our tastes on theirs largely optimizes our aesthetic experiences. In spite of his attempt to deduce an *a priori* principle of taste, Kant does not seem entitled to assume more than this. Does this mean that his entire effort at an aesthetic theory has been in vain? Not at all, because the explanation of our pleasure in beauty to which Kant has been led in his search for an *a priori* principle yields a far more systematic account of our aesthetic judgments than Hume had to offer. For Hume, there is no obvious connection between the two main species of beauty he recognized, the beauty of *species* and the beauty of utility, except perhaps the phenomenological claim that they yield the same feeling of pleasure, unlike any other kind of pleasure. He asserts that "the beauty of all visible objects causes a pleasure pretty much the same, tho' it be sometimes deriv'd from the mere *species* and appearance of the objects; sometimes from sympathy, and an idea of their utility," while "On the other hand, a convenient house, and a virtuous character, cause not the same feeling of approbation."[53] Kant, by contrast, assumes that *all* pleasures, whether in the agreeable, the beautiful, or the good, *feel* pretty much the same, although reflection can show them to have very different origins (see *Judgment*, §5, 5:209–10), but then uses the theory of the free play of imagination and understanding that he first proposes to explain our pleasure in free beauty to show the underlying resemblances between the superficially very different cases of free beauty, adherent beauty, artistic beauty, and more. This by itself is a theoretical gain over Hume. Further, Kant's theory that aesthetic judgment is not a form of cognition but nevertheless involves the cognitive powers should offer some guidance for aesthetic *discourse*, that is, for the conversations in which we may try to share our aesthetic judgments with each other or even to justify them to each other even though we have no *a priori* guarantee that we can succeed in doing so: We can point out how elements of a work seem to *cohere* with each other or *follow* from each other or fit together in any of the myriad ways in which components of cognition fit with each other, even though they do not do so literally. The rationality of seeking agreement in judgments of taste may not require an antecedent guarantee of success of the sort that would be provided by an *a priori* principle, but it is surely supported by the availability of a mode of discourse through which we might reach the desired end.

4. KANT ON THE PURPOSE OF NATURE

The "Critique of the Teleological Power of Judgment" can be read as Kant's reply to Hume's critique of the traditional argument from design.[54] Kant agrees completely with Hume that the thought that nature has been designed by an intelligent and purposive designer can never amount to theoretical cognition. But where Hume, or at least his apparent spokesman in the *Dialogues concerning Natural Religion*, seemed content to concede that we nevertheless have a natural and ineliminable tendency to believe that nature has such a designer, Kant argues that this thought is an *a priori* idea of pure reason that can be made more determinate by reflecting judgment and that has heuristic value in the conduct of scientific inquiry as well as moral value for our conduct in general. Kant makes it clear that the "physicotheology" (*Judgment*, §85, 5:436) that had been so thoroughly discredited – although not entirely eliminated – from human psychology by Hume can and should be replaced with an "ethicotheology" (§86, 5:442), but he also uses the idea of design for a richer philosophy of science than Hume had conceived.

Kant begins his argument with the statement that "the general idea of nature as the sum of the object of the senses" provides "no basis at all" for the specific idea "that things of nature serve one another as means to ends, and that their possibility itself should be adequately intelligible only through this kind of causality" (*Judgment*, §61, 5:359). He defends this general claim with two sorts of considerations. First, what appears to be "objective purposiveness" in the structure of organisms, such as "the structure of a bird, the hollowness of its bones, the placement of its wings for movement and of its tail for steering, etc.," can be taken as evidence of the *contingency* of the occurrence of such natural forms as easily as it can be taken as "being **necessarily** connected" with "objective purposiveness, as a principle of the possibility of the things of nature" (5:360); in other words, the very fact that the occurrence of such structures seems contingent relative to the basic "mechanism" of nature, the fundamental laws of motion and force, can just as easily argue against the idea that nature has been designed with an eye to such structures as for that idea. Second, Kant argues that natural forces and processes that turn out to be useful to us and to which we may therefore egocentrically assign "relative purposiveness," as if they had been designed for our benefit, can seem to have very different purposes or none at all if looked at from other points of view. We may think that plants exist to nourish herbivores that are of use to predators and ultimately to us – but we could just as easily think that all of these animals, even including ourselves, really exist only to encourage the growth and spread of the plants (§63, 5:367–8; §82, 5:427). Or we may think that ocean currents exist to bring driftwood to the human inhabitants of arctic regions and "great sea animals filled with oil" exist to bring them calories and lamp oil – but as soon as we ask "why human beings have to live" in such inhospitable regions at all any appearance of intelligent design in nature must quickly dissolve (5:369).

However, Kant next argues that there are specific things within nature that we inevitably experience as if they were products of design (namely, organisms) and that the "internal" purposiveness that we must ascribe to such things will in turn lead us to the idea that nature as a whole is a system that is purposive relative to some ultimate end or goal. Kant argues that we must experience organisms as "natural ends" that manifest intelligent design because there are various organic processes in which it seems that the whole of the organism is the cause of its parts as well as its parts being the cause of the whole, and that the only way in which *we* human beings, whose understanding of causality is ordinarily confined to the idea that the antecedent condition of parts explains the subsequent condition of the whole, can make any sense of this is by thinking of the parts of the organism as if they were the product of an antecedent design of the whole, and thus of a designer of the whole. Kant instances paradigmatic organic processes such as reproduction, in which one individual "generates itself" at least "as far the species is concerned," growth, in which the whole organism takes up "components that it receives from nature outside of itself" as new parts, and self-preservation, in which parts necessary for the survival of the whole, such as leaves for a tree, are themselves replaced or repaired by the whole organism (*Judgment*, §64, 5:371–2), as processes that we can make sense of only by conceiving of the whole as antecedently designed to produce the parts that can in turn produce or preserve the whole. Kant concludes that

Organized beings are thus the only ones in nature which, even if considered in themselves and without a relation to other things, must nevertheless be thought of as possible only as its ends, and which thus first provide objective reality for the concept of an **end** that is not a practical end but an end of **nature**, and thereby provide natural science with a basis for a teleology, i.e., a way of judging its objects in accordance with a particular principle the likes of which one would otherwise be absolutely unjustified in introducing at all.

(§65, 5:375–6)

This principle is that "**An organized product of nature is that in which everything is an end and reciprocally a means as well**. Nothing in it is in vain, purposeless, or to be ascribed to a blind mechanism of nature" (§66, 5:376). The idea of purposive design, and thus of an intelligent and purposive designer, is an idea that we must bring to our experience of nature in analogy with our own productive capacities (§65, 5:373–4); it is an idea that is thus *a priori* rather than merely copied from nature, but one that we are driven to apply to nature by our specific experience of organisms.

One might well ask what the principle of teleological judgment that Kant has just formulated has to do with his general conception of reflecting judgment. The answer seems to be that Kant intends this principle to serve as a heuristic to guide our search for *mechanical* explanations of natural phenomena, and thus ultimately as a help in bringing given particulars that initially seem resistant to scientific explanation into the system of our scientific concepts. To be sure, Kant's thought on this matter is involuted and hard to follow. He begins, as we have seen, with the clear idea that certain specific organic processes and structures defy our ordinary mechanistic model of explanation. But he quickly adds that it would be incoherent for us to explain the features or organisms by "two heterogeneous principles . . . jumbled together," so that once we have been forced to adopt the teleological point of view toward some features of organisms we must take it toward all and seek the purpose even of parts of organisms such as "skin, hair, and bones" that might readily seem explicable entirely on mechanical principles (*Judgment*, §66, 5:377). Yet very shortly Kant also insists that the concept of God as an intelligent designer should not be used *within* natural science and thus that "natural science must not jump over its boundaries in order to bring within itself as an indigenous principle that to whose concept no experience at all can ever be adequate and upon which we are authorized to venture only after the completion of natural science" (§68, 5:382). He thereby suggests that the idea of purposiveness should be used only to alert us to relations among parts of organisms that we might otherwise overlook but that we should then seek to explain along mechanistic lines. This impression is strengthened as Kant seems to shift his position from insisting that there are specific organic functions that we could never succeed in explaining to the more general claim that we cannot explain the origin of *life itself* in purely mechanical terms – at one point he suggests that the ability to originate motion, which is characteristic of life, is incompatible with the principle of inertia that is characteristic of matter under mechanical laws (§73, 5:394) – but that apart from this general restriction on the mechanical explanation of life there are no specific *a priori* limits to the mechanical explanation of organic functions. Indeed, Kant says that "It is of infinite importance to reason that it not allow the mechanism of nature in its productions to drop out of sight and be bypassed in its explanations; for without this no insight into the nature of things can be attained" (§78, 5:410); and he suggests that, once we have admitted the inexplicable fact of life and possibility of reproduction itself, then perhaps the immense variety of organic species could be entirely explained along mechanical lines, by such means as "the shortening of one part and the elongation of another, by the involution of this part and the evolution of another," allowing "the mind at least a weak ray of hope that something may be accomplished here with the principle of the mechanism of nature, without which there can be no natural science at all" (§80, 5:418).[55]

The shift in Kant's argument from the claim that there are very specific functions within nature that cannot be explained mechanistically to the idea that we should use the idea of an intelligent design for nature, which we are led to apply to nature by our experience of organisms only for guidance in seeking to expand the scope of our mechanistic explanations, also seems to be confirmed by the course of Kant's argument in the "antinomy" of teleological judgment (*Judgment*, §§69–78). Here Kant begins by suggesting that the thesis that "All generation of material things is possible in accordance with merely mechanical laws" and the teleological antithesis that "Some generation of such things is not possible in accordance with merely mechanical laws" would be in outright contradiction unless they are interpreted as merely regulative principles (§70, 5:387). The idea seems to be that if both of these principles are merely regulative then the full scope of *neither* is fully determinate, so no truly universal principle of mechanism will be violated if we come across something in nature that cannot be explained mechanistically. However, Kant then says that this is a merely "preparatory" resolution of the antinomy (§71, 5:388), and the real resolution of the antinomy seems to be the two-leveled, transcendental idealist solution that we must conceive of the designer of nature as existing *outside* of the appearances of nature and as accomplishing his purposes *through* the uniformly mechanistic laws of nature (§73, 5:395).[56] Kant's ultimate position thus seems to be that

Since it is still at least possible to consider the material world as a mere appearance, and to conceive of something as a thing in itself (which is not an appearance) as substratum, and to correlate with this a corresponding intellectual intuition (even if is not ours), there would then be a supersensible real ground for nature, although it would be unknowable for us, to which we ourselves belong, and in which that which is necessary in it as object of the senses can be considered in accordance with mechanical laws, while the agreement and unity of the particular laws and corresponding forms, which in regard to the mechanical laws we must judge as contingent, can at the same time be considered in it, as object of reason (indeed the whole of nature as a system) in accordance with teleological laws, and the material world would thus be judged in accordance with two kinds of principles, without the mechanical mode of explanation being excluded by the other, as if they contradicted each other.   (§78, 5:409)

Instead of the mechanical and teleological principles each having a potentially limited sphere, on this account each would have a potentially unlimited sphere of application: Everything in nature could potentially receive a mechanical explanation, while at the same time everything in nature could also potentially turn out to be purposive.

What does Kant think the value of such a twofold view of nature is? One point is already clear: The idea that everything in nature has a purpose that is to be achieved through mechanical laws can both spur us and guide us in the search for the mechanical means by which that purpose is achieved. The other point, of course, is that we must seek to comprehend, in terms accessible to us, what the purpose of nature could possibly be, and to guide our conduct in general and not just our conduct of scientific inquiry in the light of this conception of the goal of nature.

To understand this aspect of Kant's teleology, we must go back and retrace a step that was alluded to in the last quotation but has not yet been explained.[57] As we have seen, Kant has begun his train of thought with the idea that there are certain functions of organisms that lead us to think of them as if they have been designed. He has then added the idea that if we see some aspects of organisms as purposive, our predilection for unitary rather than heterogeneous models for explanation will lead us to the thought that every aspect of an organism must be purposive. But he applies this principle a second time when he proposes that once we have been led to think of some things in nature as if they were the product of purposive design, then it will be natural for us to think of the whole of nature as if it were a system designed in behalf of some end:

> It is therefore only matter insofar as it is organized that necessarily carried with it the concept of itself as a natural end, since its specific form is at the same time a product of nature. However, this concept necessarily leads to the idea of the whole of nature as a system in accordance with the rule of ends to which idea all of the mechanism of nature in accordance with principles of reason must now be subordinated (at least in order to test natural appearances by this idea).... By means of the example that nature gives in its organic products, one is justified, indeed called upon to expect nothing in nature and its laws but what is purposive in the whole.
>
> (*Judgment*, §67, 5:378–9)

Indeed, once we have been led by our experience of organisms as purposive systems to look at the whole of nature as a purposive system, it will also become natural for us to look on "even beauty in nature ... as an objective purposiveness of nature in its entirety, as a system of which the human being is a member" (5:380), even though this was not part of our aesthetic experience as originally analyzed.

Kant does not say what it is that "necessarily" leads us from the idea of organisms as purposive systems to the idea of nature as a whole as a purposive system, but it would seem to be the same rational idea of unitary explanation that he had appealed to in extending the teleological point of view from some functions of organisms to all of their parts. The next great step in Kant's argument is to infer, perhaps in analogy with our conception of our own rationality, that if the whole of nature is a product of intelligent design, then there must be some *point* or goal to the whole of nature, and to commence a search for what that goal might be.

As we saw earlier, it is natural enough for us egocentrically to suppose that we ourselves are the ultimate point of nature. But we also saw that such a thought, at least in isolation, is completely arbitrary. Moreover, if we assume it is our *happiness* as such that is the goal of nature, we are obviously in for a big disappointment:

> It is so far from being the case that nature has made the human being its special favorite and favored him with beneficence above all other animals, that it has rather spared him just as little as any other animal from its destructive effects, whether of pestilence, hunger, danger of flood, attacks by other animals great and small, etc.; even more, the conflict in the **natural**

predisposition of the human being, reduces himself and others of his own species, by means of plagues that he invents for himself, such as the oppression of domination, the barbarism of war, etc., to such need, and he works so hard for the destruction of his own species, that even if the most beneficent nature outside of us had made the happiness of our species its end, that end would not be attained in a system of nature upon the earth, because the nature inside of us is not receptive to that. (*Judgment*, §83, 5:430)

However, Kant supposes that we can conceive of a goal that is not so obviously at odds with the actual tendency of our own nature and also has more than the merely conditional value of happiness, namely, the unconditional value of morality itself, or of the human being as a moral value. Indeed, this is the only thing we can conceive to have unconditional value, and thus to be a proper end for the system of nature:

Now of the human being...as a moral being, it cannot be further asked...why (*quem in finem*) it exists. His existence contains the highest end itself, to which, as far as he is capable, he can subject the whole of nature...only in the human being, although in him only as a subject of morality, is unconditional legislation with regard to ends to be found, which therefore makes him alone capable of being a final end, to which the whole of nature is teleologically subordinated. (§84, 5:436)

Forced by our experience of organisms to think of the whole of nature as if it were purposive and by the character of our reason to think of a purpose for the whole of nature, the only thing we can conceive of as such an end is our own morality, our "supersensible faculty (**freedom**) and even the law of the causality together with the object that it can set for itself as the highest end (the highest good in the world)" (§84, 5:436).

Here, however, one will surely ask how Kant, who thinks that the freedom of the will can exist only in a noumenal realm, could conceive of human morality, which must be an expression of human freedom, and the highest good, which is human happiness achieved *through* human virtue and thus through human freedom,[58] as itself a product of *nature*, the phenomenal realm of deterministic law that is the very antithesis of freedom? This question must be answered in two steps. First, Kant does not in fact see the freedom of the human will as an end that can be directly achieved *within* nature; more precisely, it is "the culture of training (discipline), . . . the liberation of the will from the despotism of desires" (*Judgment*, §83, 5:432) that he thinks could be achieved within nature by entirely natural mechanisms, and this is more like a natural "condition of aptitude" for the exercise of genuine virtue than virtue itself – even once we have achieved such discipline, by natural means, we must still make the free choice to use it for the sake of morality rather than contrary to it. Second, although Kant cannot conceive of human freedom and morality properly speaking as something that can be realized entirely within nature, he can see the universal happiness not of the individual but of the species, which is to be included in the highest good, as the object and the product of our moral use of our freedom, and thus as something that can and indeed must be realized within nature.[59] So even though human happiness does not initially appear to be any special aim of nature, it can be seen as the final end of human morality to be realized within nature.

We must now take stock of Kant's teleology as briefly as we have expounded it. The most obvious internal question one might ask is how Kant's account of teleology and its principle comports with his original account of reflecting judgment and its transcendental principle. Initially, there seems to be a significant disanalogy. Kant's original principle postulated that nature can ground a system of *laws* (*Judgment*, Introduction IV, 5:180), whereas his account of our transition from the experience of organisms to a conception of nature as a whole and as a purposive system seems to concern *objects* in nature rather than laws. But as we saw in our discussion of the antinomy of teleological judgment, Kant's aim is to show how the mechanical laws of phenomenal nature can be reconciled with the teleological law that nature must have a purpose, and thus that those two forms of law can in fact comprise a single system. So if Kant's initial principle were modified to state that we must be able to consider particular empirical and moral laws as if they comprise a single system of laws given for the sake not just of our faculty of cognition but of our powers of mind as a whole, we could see a single principle of reflecting judgment at work. And Kant's idea that through teleological judgment we seek to find the moral purpose of nature can also be reconciled with his initial account of reflecting judgment. Whereas the conception of the moral end of nature must be regarded as given through pure reason and by no means completely unknown, what we actually seek to do through teleological judgment is to find a way to apply that idea of reason to nature as it is actually given to us, just as in the initial case of reflecting judgment we are actually given the pure concepts of the understanding but need to find the intermediate concepts of natural laws by which those pure concepts can be applied to nature as it is given to us. In these ways Kant's account of teleological judgment is more readily fit into his general model of reflecting judgment than is his account of aesthetic judgment.

But stepping outside of Kant's system, what can we make of Kant's teleology? Kant certainly seems to capture the systematic ambitions of practicing scientists: The twentieth-century revolutions in chemistry and genetics are clear cases of extending the scope of a unitary system of laws, and the continued search for a way to unify the four most fundamental kinds of physical force is completely within the Kantian spirit. At the same time, the Darwinian-Mendelian explanation of inheritance, together with the subsequent explanation of inheritance by the behavior of DNA, undermines any claim that we cannot understand organic processes in mechanical terms. The physical generation of mutations combined with their selection through reproductive success outlines precisely the sort of mechanical model of the kinds of processes that Kant seems to have thought must forever remain beyond the bounds of human comprehension. Further, Kant's idea that mechanical explanation, even if maximally extensive, must be completely consistent with the principle of purposiveness now seems hopeless. Whatever disagreements there may be among contemporary Darwinians, surely they all agree that not every trait that survives natural selection is purposive in the sense of being advantageous to the reproductive success of the organism, but that traits may survive as long as they are not reproductively *dis*advantageous and may do so particularly if they are mechanically linked to some other trait that is advantageous.

It is also unlikely that many will be convinced that we must conceive of nature as morally purposive unless they are already starting from a theological point of view, precisely what Kant was attempting to avoid. Nevertheless, most contemporary readers will agree with Kant that both our virtue and our happiness must be perfected within nature, not someplace else, and here Kant's teleological view of nature suggests some considerations of enduring value. One lesson that we can take from Kant's teleology is that it is only our own *moral* ends – and not our mere whims and lusts – that give us anything like a right to use the rest of nature as means. Thus, we might infer that it is morally permissible or even mandatory to use and destroy other animals to test medicines that may significantly alleviate human suffering, but impermissible to do so in order to test the efficacy or even the safety of cosmetics that will merely enhance our appearance. Second, the idea that nature is a system suggests that in any of our interventions in nature as we find it, even if undertaken for the most morally acceptable or even obligatory of reasons, our actions will have consequences far beyond our immediate concerns, and thus that we must always attempt to weigh the remote and long-term ecological consequences of our actions as well as their current value. Here is a point where Kant's insistence on the limits of the human powers of cognition seems entirely appropriate, and where we must limit our confidence in the rectitude of our goals with modesty in our claims to understand both the efficacy and the consequences of our means.

5. THE INFLUENCE OF KANT'S AESTHETICS AND TELEOLOGY

Kant's third *Critique*, even though often profoundly misunderstood, has been more influential on the subsequent history of aesthetics than any other single work. In the first period of its reception, lasting from its original appearance through the work of the young Friedrich Nietzsche, it was not so much Kant's formulation and solution to the problem of the universal validity of judgments of taste as his distinction between the beautiful and the sublime, his theory of fine art, his theory of genius, and his attempt to connect aesthetics with morality while preserving what is unique to each (a topic on which I have hardly touched in this essay) that were influential. Just to mention a few examples, Friedrich Schiller certainly developed Kant's thoughts on the connection between aesthetics and morality in his famous essay on "Grace and Dignity" (1793) and in his *Letters on the Aesthetic Education of Mankind* (1795); Friedrich Schelling's central idea that it is in the creation of art that the unconscious mentality of nature in general emerges into consciousness, the culminating idea of his *System of Transcendental Idealism* (1798) and the central theme of his *Lectures on the Philosophy of Art* (1803), undoubtedly comes directly from Kant's theory of genius; Hegel's idea that the beautiful is the sensible appearance of the Idea is unthinkable without Kant's theory of aesthetic ideas; and Nietzsche's central distinction between the Apollonian and the Dionysian in his *Birth of Tragedy* (1873) is clearly an heir to Kant's distinction between the beautiful and the sublime, even if a radical revision of it.

Arthur Schopenhauer's thesis that in the experience of beauty we are released from our ordinary concerns and their attendant pains into a state of "pure will-less, painless, timeless" subjectivity[60] is a distinctive interpretation of Kant's conception of the disinterestedness of the judgment of beauty, and is the origin of what later became known as "aesthetic attitude" theories in aesthetics, the most famous of which was perhaps offered by Edward Bullough at the beginning of the twentieth century.[61] Kant is often taken as the source for the idea of the autonomy of art or "art for art's sake," although his insistence that art that does not have moral content quickly becomes dissatisfying (*Judgment*, §52) would have become unwelcome to advocates of this view such as Oscar Wilde, and it should more properly be traced back to Karl Philipp Moritz's "Attempt at a Unification of all fine Arts and Sciences under the concept of *that which is perfect in itself*" (1785),[62] an essay that Kant himself clearly knew and to which he may have been responding with his insistence that the beauty of an object is its *subjective* purposiveness *for us*, not an *internal* purposiveness within *it* as Moritz had argued. Advocates of formalism in modern painting and other arts have also appealed to Kant as an authority, although to do so is to mistake Kant's initial analysis of free beauty, primarily in nature, with his subsequent account of the beauty of fine art proper as consisting in the interplay between form and content captured by his notion of the aesthetic idea.[63]

These references just begin to suggest the influence of Kant on subsequent aesthetics; a real history of that influence would be nothing short of a history of aesthetics since Kant. The history of the influence of Kant's thought about systematicity and teleology in the third *Critique* on subsequent thought would no doubt be much shorter. Whereas virtually all scientists tacitly accept the goal of the unity of the sciences, and that of course became a well-known theme for the philosophy of science in the 1930s, the Introduction to the third *Critique* no doubt played and plays very little role in this tendency of thought. Kant's apparent resurrection of a teleological conception of the organism may have had significant influence on the "vital-ist" tendency of some German biological thinking in the nineteenth century,[64] but as we have seen Kant himself pretty clearly intended his teleological conception of organisms only heuristically, and in any case vitalism soon fell, if not of its own weight, then under the weight of Darwinism.

Kant's argument that we must be led from our experience of organ-isms to a teleological, but ultimately "ethicotheological" view of nature as a whole has not had much impact on subsequent phi-losophy, or even received much attention in Kant scholarship. As I have briefly tried to suggest, however, Kant's thoughts on this sub-ject might provide important premises for an ethical, although thor-oughly non-theological, ecology. I am aware of only one work that has pursued this thought, a work by Lothar Schäfer that has received little notice.[65] Here much remains to be done, not so much by his-torians of philosophy as by philosophy itself.

NOTES

1. All references to the *Critique of the Power of Judgment* (*"Judgment"*) will be located by section number or other designation, then volume and page number as in *Kants Gesammelte Schriften*, edited by the Royal Prussian (later German, most recently Berlin–Brandenburg) Academy of Sciences (Berlin: Georg Reimer, subsequently Walter de Gruyter & Co., 1900–). Passages from Kant's first version of the introduction will be cited with the abbreviation *"FI."* Translations are from Immanuel Kant, *Critique of the Power of Judgment*, edited by Paul Guyer, translated by Paul Guyer and Eric Matthews (Cambridge: Cambridge University Press, 2000).

2. See John Zammito, *The Genesis of Kant's* Critique of Judgment (Chicago: University of Chicago Press, 1992).

3. See my "Objects, Self, and Cause: Kant's Answers to Hume," forthcom-ing in *Early Modern Metaphysics: Essay in Honor of Vere Chappell*, edited by Paul Hoffman, David Owen and Gideon Yaffe (Calgary: Broad-view Press, 2006).

4. David Hume, *A Treatise of Human Nature*, edited by David Fate Norton and Mary J. Norton (Oxford: Oxford University Press, 2000), 1.3.2, pp. 53–5.

5. Hume, *Treatise*, 1.3.3, p. 56.

6. Hume, *Treatise*, 1.3.3., p. 58.

7. See Hume, *Enquiry concerning Human Understanding*, edited by Tom L. Beauchamp (Oxford: Clarendon Press, 2000), Section 4, Part I, pp. 25–8.

8. Immanuel Kant, *Critique of Pure Reason*, edited and translated by Paul Guyer and Allen W. Wood (Cambridge: Cambridge University Press, 1998), A 188.

9. I have discussed the complex relations among Hume's three questions and Kant's answers to them in "Kant's Answer to Hume?," *Philosophical Topics* 31 (2003): 127–64.

10. Hume, *Treatise*, 1.1.1, p. 9.

11. See Hume, *Treatise*, 1.3.2, p. 55.

12. Hume, *Treatise*, 1.3.6, p. 62.

13. Ibid.

14. Hume, *Treatise*, 1.3.8, pp. 69–74.

15. Hume, *Treatise*, 1.3.14, pp. 111–12.

16. He in fact says that "'Tis a common observation, that the mind has a great propensity to spread itself." (*Treatise*, 1.3.14, p. 112).

17. See Hume, *Enquiry*, Section 5, pp. 35–45.

18. For a detailed account of these arguments, see my "Kant's Answer to Hume?" and "Self, Object, and Cause: Kant's Answers to Hume."

19. See Hume, *Treatise*, 2.2.5, p. 235, and 3.3.6, p. 393.

20. Hume, *Treatise*, 2.1.8, p. 195. I have given a detailed analysis of Hume's theory of beauty in "The Standard of Taste and the 'Most Ardent Desire of Society'," in *Pursuits of Reason: Essays in Honor of Stanley Cavell*, edited by Ted Cohen, Paul Guyer, and Hilary Putnam (Lubbock: Texas Tech University Press, 1993), pp. 37–66; reprinted in my *Values of Beauty: Historical Essays in Aesthetics* (Cambridge: Cambridge University Press, 2005), chapter 2.

21. Hume, "Of the Standard of Taste," in *Essays Moral, Political, and Literary*, edited by Eugene F. Miller, revised edition (Indianapolis: Liberty Classics, 1987), p. 233.

22. Hume, "Of the Standard of Taste," p. 232.

23. This is of course a simplification of Hume's strategy since it omits his recognition of the value that we place in the fact of consensus with others in addition to the pleasures that we may severally derive directly from objects. See again "The Standard of Taste and the 'Most Ardent Desire of Society'."

24. Hume, "Of the Standard of Taste," p. 232.

25. Hume, "Of the Standard of Taste," pp. 234–41.

26. A long debate on the adequacy of Hume's conditions for qualified critical judgment goes back to Harold Osborne, "Hume's Standard and the Diversity of Taste," *British Journal of Aesthetics* 7 (1967): 50–6, and

Peter Kivy, "Hume's Standard of Taste: Breaking the Circle," *British Journal of Aesthetics* 7 (1967): 57–66. For a review of the debate and discussion, see Astrid von der Lühe, *David Humes ästhetische Kritik* (Hamburg: Felix Meiner, 1996), pp. 207–35, and Dabney Townsend, *Hume's Aesthetic Theory: Taste and Sentiment* (London: Routledge, 2001), chapter 6, pp. 180–216.

27. William Paley published his *Natural Theology, or Evidences of the Existence and Attributes of the Deity collected from the Appearances of Nature*, as late as 1802. A list of both British and German works on the argument from design that would have been known to Kant is given in Johann August Eberhard, *Vorbereitung zur natürlichen Theologie* (Halle: im Waisenhause, 1781), §1, reprinted in the *Akademie* edition at 18:513–14. Kant's lecture notes on Eberhard's textbook are reproduced at 18:491–606. Eberhard does not mention Hume's *Dialogues*, which were translated into German only in the same year in which his own book was published.

28. Hume, *Enquiry concerning Human Understanding*, Section 11, pp. 108–9.

29. Hume, *Dialogues concerning Natural Religion*, Part 12; in David Hume, *The Natural History of Religion and Dialogues concerning Natural Religion*, edited by A. Wayne Colver and John Valdimir Price (Oxford: Clarendon Press, 1976), p. 245.

30. There is no hint of it even in the second edition of the *Critique of Pure Reason*, published in 1787.

31. In *Kant and the Claims of Taste*, originally published in 1979 (second edition, Cambridge: Cambridge University Press, 1997), I argued that the case of aesthetic judgment did not fit with Kant's general account of reflecting judgment (chapter 2, especially pp. 47–59). However, in "Kant's Principles of Reflecting Judgment," in *Kant's Critique of the Power of Judgment: Critical Essays*, edited by Paul Guyer (Lanham, MD: Rowman & Littlefield, 2003), pp. 1–61, I argued that aesthetic judgment could be counted as a case of reflecting judgment after all, as long as the conception of the universal that is to be sought is broad enough to include the intersubjective agreement itself that we seek to realize in a successful aesthetic judgment.

32. Kant set this draft aside and wrote a new version in March of 1790, as the rest of the book was already being set in type. Several years later, he gave it to his disciple Jakob Sigismund Beck, who was preparing several volumes of excerpts from Kant's philosophical works, telling him that he had decided not to use it in the published *Critique* only because of its length. Beck published some excerpts from the manuscript under

the title of "Philosophical Encyclopedia," and it was not recognized for what it was and published as the first draft of the Introduction to the third *Critique* until 1914. Since then it has been known as the "First Introduction" (*FI*) to the *Critique of the Power of Judgment*. For details, see my Editor's Introduction to the *Critique of the Power of Judgment*, pp. xli–xliii.

33. See "On the common saying: That may be correct in theory but it is of no use in practice," 8:312.

34. Sympathetic accounts of Kant's conception of systematicity as an answer to Hume's worries about inductions have been offered by Philip Kitcher, "Projecting the Order of Nature," in *Kant's Philosophy of Physical Science*, edited by Robert E. Butts (Dordrecht: D. Reidel, 1986), pp. 201–35, reprinted in *Kant's Critique of Pure Reason: Critical Essays*, edited by Patricia Kitcher (Lanham: Rowman & Littlefield, 1998), pp. 219–38; and Juliet Floyd, "Heautonomy: Kant on Reflective Judgment and Systematicity," in *Kants Ästhetik – Kant's Aesthetics – L'esthétique de Kant*, edited by Herman Parret (Berlin and New York: Walter de Gruyter, 1998), pp. 192–218. I have offered a critical response to these interpretations in "Kant's Answer to Hume?"

35. See Kant's scornful remark about the British "common-sense" philosophers (Thomas) Reid, (James) Oswald, (James) Beattie, and (Joseph) Priestly at *Prolegomena to any future Metaphysics*, Preface, 4:258.

36. Although he did identify "*Logic, Morals, Criticism*, and *Politics*" as the "four sciences" in which "is comprehended almost every thing, which it can in any way import us to be acquainted with" and which could be illuminated by his "Attempt to Introduce the Experimental Method of Reasoning into Moral Subjects" (*Treatise*, Introduction, pp. 4, 1).

37. And other British aestheticians who also made the problem of taste central to their work, including Edmund Burke, who added an "Introduction on Taste" to the second edition of his *Philosophical Enquiry into the Origin of our Ideas of the Sublime and Beautiful* (1759), no doubt in response to Hume's essay, which had appeared at the same time as Burke's first edition (1757), and Alexander Gerard, whose *Essay on Taste* also appeared in 1759. The 1762 *Elements of Criticism* by Hume's older cousin, Henry Home, Lord Kames, also concluded with a chapter on "The Standard of Taste." All of these works were widely known or known of in Germany. Burke's work was influentially reviewed by Moses Mendelssohn as soon as 1758, and Mendelssohn's friend Gotthold Ephraim Lessing began a translation, although in fact it was Christian Garve, later to become significant in Kant's career, who first published a translation of Burke, in 1773, with Kant's own publisher Hartknoch

in Riga. Gerard's essay, along with accompanying essays by Voltaire and d'Alembert drawn from the great French *Encyclopédie*, was translated into German in 1766.

38. My first work on Kant's aesthetics, *Kant and the Claims of Taste*, focused largely on the problem of the standard of taste. In *Kant and the Experience of Freedom* (Cambridge: Cambridge University Press, 1993), I focused largely on Kant's treatment of the connections between aesthetics and morality. A number of the essays in my *Values of Beauty: Historical Essays in Aesthetics* (Cambridge: Cambridge University Press, 2005) further explore Kant's account of the connections between aesthetics and morality, while several also discuss connections between beauty and non-moral utility. In "Bridging the Gulf: Kant's Project in the third *Critique*," forthcoming in *The Blackwell Companion to Kant*, edited by Graham Bird, I also focus on the connections between aesthetics and morality in a way I do not here. Among other work that stresses the connection between Kant's aesthetics and morality, Donald W. Crawford, *Kant's Aesthetic Theory* (Madison: University of Wisconsin Press, 1974), remains important.

39. See "The Strategy of Kant's *Groundwork*" in my *Kant on Freedom, Law, and Happiness* (Cambridge: Cambridge University Press, 2000), chapter 6.

40. This is actually a broader term than the English "definition," which could also be translated as "explanation," "exposition," "explication," or "declaration"; Kant himself points this out at *Pure Reason*, A 730/B 758. Perhaps "explication" would actually be the best translation in the present context.

41. See *Kant and the Claims of Taste*, second edition, pp. 118–19.

42. What we would call *cava*, although now it comes mostly from Spain.

43. Hume, "The Sceptic," in *Essays Moral, Political, and Literary*, p. 165.

44. See ibid., p. 163.

45. I have defended this interpretation in detail in "The Harmony of the Faculties Revisited," in *Values of Beauty*, chapter 3. There I respond to a number of alternative interpretations of Kant's concept of the harmony of the faculties, including Hannah Ginsborg, "Lawfulness without a Law: Kant on the Free Play of Imagination and Understanding," *Philosophical Topics* 25 (1997): pp 37–83; Fred L. Rush, Jr., "The Harmony of the Faculties," *Kant-Studien* 92 (2001): 38–61; and Henry E. Allison, *Kant's Theory of Taste: A Reading of the Critique of Aesthetic Judgment* (Cambridge: Cambridge University Press, 2001), especially chapters 5 and 8.

46. I have dealt with the sublime in a number of places, including "The Beautiful and the Sublime," chapter 6 of my *Kant and the Experience*

of Freedom (Cambridge: Cambridge University Press, 1993), and "Kant on the Purity of the Ugly," in *Values of Beauty*.

47. Recent discussion of Kant's distinction begins with Eva Schaper, "Free and Dependent Beauty," originally in *Akten des 4. Internationalen Kant-Kongresses*, Teil 1 (Berlin: Walter de Gruyter, 1974), pp. 247–62, reprinted in her *Studies in Kant's Aesthetics* (Edinburgh: Edinburgh University Press, 1979), pp. 78–98. I have discussed the distinction in more detail in two recent papers, "Beauty and Utility in Eighteenth Century Aesthetics," *Eighteenth Century Studies* 35 (2002): 439–53, and "Free and Adherent Beauty: A Modest Proposal," *British Journal of Aesthetics* 42 (October, 2002): 357–66, both reprinted in *Values of Beauty*.

48. I have discussed these three possibilities more fully in "Free and Adherent Beauty: A Modest Proposal."

49. I have discussed Kant's theory of fine art in "Kant's Conception of Fine Art," *Journal of Aesthetics and Art Criticism* (1994): 175–85, reprinted as chapter 12 of the second edition of *Kant and the Claims of Taste*. An interesting treatment of Kant's philosophy of art, which however implausibly argues that Kant placed more value on artistic than on natural beauty, is Salim Kemal, *Kant and Fine Art: An Essay on Kant and the Philosophy of Fine Art and Culture* (Oxford: Clarendon Press, 1986).

50. To be sure, some contemporary philosophers have accepted something like Kant's claim. Donald Davidson clearly accepted that we can only recognize something as another human being if we assign to it not only the same cognitive powers but the same fundamental conceptual scheme, thus that we cannot even understand the idea of *alternative* conceptual schemes, in his famous article "On the Very Idea of a Conceptual Scheme" (1974), reprinted in his *Inquiries into Truth and Interpretation* (Oxford: Clarendon Press, 1984), pp. 183–98.

51. In his treatment of the deduction, Henry Allison denies that Kant's discussion of "common sense" in §21 of the "Analytic of the Beautiful" should be regarded as a preliminary version of the deduction, but is only an attempt to display the intersubjective validity of the condition of cognition in general, which will only later become a premise of the deduction of judgments of taste (*Kant's Theory of Taste*, pp. 149–55). This seems to be incompatible with Kant's claim in this section, about to be explicated, that there is a unique proportion between imagination and understanding that can only be determined through *feeling* – the fundamental criterion of the *aesthetic* for Kant.

52. Kant's deduction has been defended by Karl E. Ameriks, "How to Save Kant's Deduction of Taste," *Journal of Value Inquiry* 16 (1982): 295–302, and "Kant and the Objectivity of Taste," *British Journal of Aesthetics* 23 (1983): 3–17, both reprinted in his *Interpreting Kant's* Critiques

(Oxford: Clarendon Press, 2003), as well as by Allison, *Kant's Theory of Taste*, pp. 184–92. Ameriks tries to defend the intersubjective validity of aesthetic judgment by assimilating it to empirical judgment in general, but does not show that we must all make the same empirical judgments under (ideally) similar conditions. Allison argues that our disagreements about particular judgments under *actual* conditions do not undermine the "normativity" of aesthetic judgments in general, but this seems to miss the point of my claim that Kant has not shown that our minds must all work the same way even under *ideal* conditions.

53. Hume, *Treatise*, 3.3.5, p. 393.
54. For an earlier reference to this connection, see Jerry E. Sobel, "Arguing, Accepting, and Preserving Design in Heidegger, Hume, and Kant," in *Essays in Kant's Aesthetics*, edited by Ted Cohen and Paul Guyer (Chicago: University of Chicago Press, 1982), pp. 271–305.
55. I have discussed Kant's several arguments for our necessarily teleological (although non-constitutive) conception of organisms in "Organisms and the Unity of Science," in *Kant and the Sciences*, edited by Eric Watkins (Oxford: Oxford University Press), pp. 259–81, reprinted in my *Kant's System of Nature and Freedom* (Oxford: Oxford University Press, 2005). In the Watkins volume, see also Hannah Ginsborg, "Kant on Understanding Organisms as Natural Purposes," pp. 231–58. Another important work on Kant's philosophy of biology is Peter McLaughlin, *Kant's Critique of Teleology in Biological Explanation: Antinomy and Teleology* (Lewiston: Edwin Mellen Press, 1990). The most detailed study of Kant's philosophy of biology in recent literature is Reinhard Löw, *Philosophie des Lebendigen: Der Begriff des Organischen bei Kant, sein Grund und seine Aktualität* (Frankfurt am Main: Suhrkamp Verlag, 1980).
56. I have defended this interpretation in more detail in "Purpose in Nature: What is Living and What is Dead in Kant's Teleology," in *Kant's System of Nature and Freedom*.
57. I have analyzed the following argument in more detail in "Purpose in Nature" as well as "From Nature to Morality: Kant's New Argument in the 'Critique of Teleological Judgment'," in *Architektonik und System in der Philosophie Kants*, edited by Hans Friedrich Fulda and Jürgen Stolzenberg (Hamburg: Felix Meiner Verlag, 2001), pp. 375–404, also reprinted in *Kant's System of Nature and Freedom*.
58. See especially *Critique of Pure Reason*, A 808–9/B 836–7, and "Ideas toward a Universal History from a Cosmopolitan Point of View," Third Thesis, 8:19–20.
59. See especially "On the common saying: That may be correct in theory but it is of no use in practice," Section I, 8:279–80.

60. *The World as Will and Representation*, Volume I, §34; in the translation by E. F. J. Payne (Indian Hills: Falcon Wing's Press, 1958), Volume I, p. 179.

61. "'Psychical Distance' as a Factor in Art and as Aesthetic Principle" (1912), reprinted in his *Aesthetics: Lectures and Essays*, edited by Elizabeth M. Wilkinson (Stanford: Stanford University Press, 1957), pp. 91–130.

62. Reprinted in Karl Philipp Moritz, *Werke*, edited by Horst Günther, 3 vols., second edition (Frankfurt am Main: Insel Verlag, 1993), vol. 2, pp. 543–48.

63. As was in fact recognized by Clement Greenberg, often thought of as the archformalist of mid-twentieth-century criticism; see Greenberg, *Homemade Esthetics: Observations on Art and Taste* (New York: Oxford University Press, 1999), pp. 113–14.

64. See Robert J. Richards, *The Romantic Conception of Life: Science and Philosophy in the Age of Goethe* (Chicago: University of Chicago Press, 2002), and Timothy Lenoir, *The Strategy of Life: Teleology and Mechanics in Nineteenth-Century German Biology* (Chicago: University of Chicago Press, 1989, originally Dordrecht: D. Reidel, 1982).

65. Lothar Schäfer, *Das Bacon-Projekt: Von der Erkenntnis, Nutzung und Schonung der Nature* (Frankfurt am Main: Suhrkamp Verlag, 1993); on Kant, see especially pp. 192–222.

17 Moral faith and the highest good

I. PROBLEMS OF INTERPRETATION

Any student who approaches Kant's philosophy of religion for the first time is bound to be daunted by the task. The obstacles are wide, deep, and long. They are wide because Kant thought about virtually every aspect of religion. They are deep because he thought through all these issues with systematic thoroughness and relentless rigor. And they are long because Kant began to think about religious issues as early as the 1760s, and his thinking underwent several transformations through the decades. If these challenges are not enough, Kant's thinking appears in a formidable corpus of writings. His mature religious philosophy is expounded in his three critical works, the Canon of the *Critique of Pure Reason*, the Dialectic of the *Critique of Practical Reason*, and the Doctrine of Method of the *Critique of the Power of Judgment*. The most important mature work, the only one entirely devoted to the philosophy of religion, is his 1793 *Religion within the Boundaries of Mere Reason*. Apart from these systematic works, there are several important essays of the 1780s and 1790s;[1] there are also the lectures on theology, and last but not least the lectures on ethics, which are crucial for their religious themes.

No short essay, at least from this author, can introduce all the major aspects of Kant's philosophy of religion.[2] My own aim is *per necessitatem* much more modest, though still much too ambitious. It is to explain just one of Kant's central doctrines: moral faith. This doctrine is the very heart and soul of Kant's mature philosophy of religion. Its exposition and defense was a central concern of Kant's in the late 1780s and early 1790s. The doctrine played a pivotal role in Kant's final sketches for a system of philosophy.[3]

588

To explain moral faith alone is, however, no easy task. Part of the problem is that the concept is so complex. It involves three basic components, each of which requires extensive analysis: (1) the ideal of the highest good; (2) the postulates of God and immortality; and (3) the concept of rational faith. Another part of the problem is that it is necessary to find one's way through the thicket and thistle of controversy. For no aspect of Kant's philosophy is more controversial than moral faith.

The basic source of controversy surrounding moral faith concerns its role in Kant's general philosophy. Some hold that it is central to his philosophy, the keystone of the entire critical edifice; others maintain that it is at best an afterthought, at worst a cancer. One can take three possible positions: that moral faith is necessary to, consistent with, or contrary to Kant's basic aims and principles. In the first fifty years of the reception of Kant's philosophy, all these positions had been taken; each has been revived many times since.

Since controversy is unavoidable, it is necessary to take a stand. So, in what follows I will defend the thesis that moral faith does play a pivotal role in Kant's philosophy in that it is not only consistent with but necessary to his basic aims and principles. We will see that moral faith is not guilty of two common charges of inconsistency: that it violates Kant's strictures against metaphysics, and that it undermines his ideal of moral purity. We will also see that it plays a fundamental role in Kant's philosophy, not in giving new content to its ethical principles, as is sometimes argued, but in explaining the possibility of moral action.

My defense of moral faith deliberately pushes the doctrine into waters where many contemporary Kant scholars fear to tread: the depths of metaphysics. Since the 1960s there has been a movement afoot in the Anglophone world to purge Kant's philosophy of all metaphysics, to make Kant scrubbed and sanitary for a more positivistic age.[4] It began with Kant's transcendental idealism; it then moved onto his ethics; but it has now dared to enter the inner sanctum itself: moral faith. True to their antimetaphysical programe, these scholars have defended a completely *secular* and *immanent* conception of the highest good, according to which it is simply a goal of human striving that need not involve the beliefs in the existence of God or immortality.[5]

Contrary to this trend, we will find that Kant's doctrine of moral faith is irreducibly metaphysical. It is metaphysical *not* in the sense that it makes implicit claims to knowledge of transcendent entities – if this were so it would be indeed inconsistent with Kant's critical principles – but in three other significant senses. First, Kant's ideal of the highest good is fundamentally Christian, indeed Protestant; it is utterly contrary to his intention to interpret it as secular and humanist. Second, it is impossible to separate the highest good from the postulates, the beliefs in the existence of God and immortality. Third, Kant's doctrine addresses a basic metaphysical problem: the connection between the noumenal realm of morality and the phenomenal realm of history. It was crucial for Kant to address this issue, we shall find, to explain the possibility of moral action.

Of course, in all these respects Kant will seem less relevant to our more secular and positivistic age. But we should beware of making Kant seem relevant at the cost of historical accuracy. We learn little from past thinkers when we make them caricatures of ourselves. My aim throughout is to restore the historical integrity of Kant's doctrine against those who would dismantle it for the sake of their own philosophical agenda.

2. MORAL FAITH IN CONTEXT

The best introduction to Kant's doctrine of moral faith is historical. Its purpose and structure become apparent only by seeing how it differs from, and takes issue with, Kant's predecessors and contemporaries. A fundamental, and still unfulfilled, desideratum of Kant scholarship is to specify the *individuality* of his doctrines, that is, what is original to and distinctive about them in the context of his age.

The central thesis of Kant's doctrine is that religious belief must be founded on practical reason alone. This was a very bold thesis, committing Kant to two very controversial propositions. First, the justification for religious belief must be based on reason alone. Kant therefore excludes the other competing criteria for "the rule of faith": apostolic and ecclesiastical tradition (Roman Catholicism), Scripture (orthodox Protestantism), and inspiration (the various Protestant sects). Second, the rational justification for religious belief cannot be theoretical but must be practical. In other words, we cannot demonstrate through reason the fundamental truths of natural religion, namely, the existence of God, providence, and immortality; rather, the only possible justification for these beliefs has to be moral. Kant could equate moral with rational justification through his moral philosophy, according to which the fundamental principles of morality are based on reason alone.

When we first place Kant's doctrine in its historical context, there does not seem to be anything especially new or original about it. Both propositions had become virtual commonplaces by the 1780s. The proposition that religious belief must be justified by reason alone had become familiar ever since the deist controversy of the 1690s and the freethinking campaign of the 1720s. And the proposition that religious belief must be defended essentially on moral grounds was as old as the latitudinarian movement of the 1660s; it was reaffirmed tirelessly by the Boyle lecturers and the freethinkers themselves in the first decades of the eighteenth century. All these developments in Britian were well known in Germany, where the writings of John Toland, Matthew Tindal, and Anthony Collins found a wide circulation.[6] Lessing had forced the German public to think about these propositions in the 1770s when he published Reimarus's writings and launched his famous dispute with Pastor Goeze.

What, then, one might ask, is new and original to Kant's doctrine of moral faith? The most plausible answer is simple and straightforward: Kant's ruthless, relentless, and indeed radical insistence that religious belief be justified *solely* by practical reason. This was a bold and original stand by the standards of the 1780s, even by those of the 1790s. This put Kant at odds with virtually every party in the religious controversies of his time. The demand that religious faith be defensible by reason put him at odds not only with the orthodox Lutherans, who stressed the authoritative role of Scripture, but also with the spiritualists, who valued mystical experience. The insistence that it be justifiable by *practical* reason alone set him against not only the traditional rationalist theologians, like Wolff, Mendelssohn, and Reimarus, but even some of the freethinkers, who, for all their skepticism about revealed religion and theism, continued to mount demonstrations for the truth of pantheism.

The full purport of Kant's doctrine became clear to himself and his contemporaries only in the late 1780s during the course of the

famous "pantheism controversy" between Moses Mendelssohn and
Friedrich Heinrich Jacobi. Kant's contribution to this controversy –
his 1786 essay "What Does It Mean to Orient Oneself in Thought?" –
revealed for the first time the distinctive outlines of his position
vis-à-vis his contemporaries. There were three competing positions
in this dispute. First, the metaphysics of the Leibnizian-Wolffian
school, represented by Mendelssohn, which held that it is possible
to provide theoretical demonstrations of the fundamental beliefs of
natural religion. Second, the fideistic philosophy of Jacobi, Hamann,
and Thomas Wizenmann, who held that religious belief cannot be
justified by reason but only by personal experience. Third, the free-
thinking Spinozists, especially Lessing and Herder. Although they
claimed that religious beliefs have to be justified by reason, they
denied the fundamental beliefs of traditional theism – a personal
God, providence, and individual immortality – and affirmed instead a
form of pantheism as the only religion of reason. Kant took issue with
all these positions. He differed from the rationalists in his demand
that rational justification be practical rather than theoretical; he
departed from the fideists in his demand for rational justification
and in his skepticism about personal experience; and he took issue
with the freethinkers in their persistent belief in the powers of
reason.

Although Kant's doctrine was very radical in some respects, it was
still conservative in others. In important respects his theological-
political doctrines belong to the older generation of *Aufklärer*, the
generation of Nicolai, Biester, Eberhard, and Garve. These thinkers
would have lost their wigs over Kant's purely practical defense of the
faith. But Kant still belongs among them in two respects: first, in his
defense of theism, especially the belief in a personal and supernatural
God; and, second, in his caution about enfranchising and enlighten-
ing the common people. In both respects the early romantics would
regard Kant as a relic of a bygone age. They would declare theism dead
and make pantheism *de rigeur*; and they were ready to enlighten and
enfranchise a broader segment of the people.

Still, in one respect the old fox of Königsberg would prove more
radical than the romantics themselves: in his suggestion that religion consists in a hypostatization of moral laws. This made Kant the
grandfather of Feuerbach, Marx, Stirner, and Bauer, the guiding spirit
behind the radical criticism of the 1840s. Radical critique of religion

in the name of liberation was the slogan of the young Hegelians; but that too was the legacy of Kant.

3. THE CITY OF GOD

Of the three basic components of the concept of moral faith, Kant's ideal of the highest good plays the central role. It provides the rationale for the postulates, which in turn provide the basis for the concept of rational faith. We should therefore begin our systematic analysis of moral faith with the highest good.

Kant's reflections on the highest good, which first appear in the Dialectic of the *Critique of Practical Reason*, are intelligible only when placed in a much broader historical context. They are part of a long history of thinking about this topic, a history consisting in bitter controversy and endless strife. Kant's reflections too are deeply partisan: He takes issue with some schools, he sides with others.[7] Their most striking aspect is Kant's self-conscious allegiance to the Christian, indeed Protestant, tradition. It is a point that cannot be stressed enough: Kant saw his ethics as Christian doctrine.

The problem of the highest good or *summum bonum* was first posed by Aristotle in the *Nicomachean Ethics*, where he raised the questions "What should be the fundamental goal of the good life?" and "What end in life makes it most worth living?"[8] These questions became the chief battleground between Stoics and Epicureans in antiquity. Whereas the Epicureans held that the highest good is pleasure alone, the Stoics taught that it consists solely in virtue. In the fourth century, the highest good became a matter of dispute between Christians and pagans. The dispute began when, in Chapter XIX of the *City of God*, Augustine argued that no pagan conception of the highest good – whether Epicurean or Stoic – is satisfactory, and that the highest good can be realized only in a Christian life. Famously, he taught that the highest good does not lie in the earthly city – in a world that man could know and create through his natural powers – but in the heavenly city alone – in a world known by divine revelation and established by divine grace.

In early modern philosophy the problem of the highest good had lost much of its importance. Some champions of the new natural philosophy – most notably, Hobbes and Locke – ridiculed the concept for its antiquated natural teleology and scholastic resonance.[9] When Kant introduced the topic in the second *Critique* he noted its unpopularity (5:64); but he was scarcely reviving a moribund issue.[10] The problem of the highest good had always been central to the *Aufklärung*. It became even a popular issue after J. J. Spalding's 1748 *Thoughts on the Vocation of Man*, which became one of the bestsellers of the age.[11] The problem was a source of much friction in the heated disputes between the Leibnizian-Wolffian school and the more freethinking members of the Prussian Academy. One of the major works in this dispute was Mendelssohn's 1755 *On the Sentiments*, which defended the perfectionism of the Leibnizian-Wolffian school against the "new fashionable Epicureanism" of the Prussian Academy.[12] Some answer to the problem of the highest good was *de rigeur* in eighteenth-century Germany; no respectable philosopher, least of all one of Kant's stature, could afford to ignore it.

What is most striking about Kant's treatment of the highest good in the second *Critique* is that he rejects both secular alternatives favored by the *Aufklärung* – Epicureanism and Stoicism – and reaffirms the traditional Christian view. Remarkably, in crucial respects, the precedent for Kant's argument is Augustine. Like his Christian forbear, Kant rejects Epicureanism and Stoicism for their worldly conceptions of the highest good, and he maintains instead that only Christianity has an adequate account of this ideal. His argument reaches its climax when he proclaims: "The doctrine of Christianity...gives a concept of the highest good (the kingdom of God) that alone satisfies the strictest demands of practical reason" (5:127–8). In making his case for Christianity, Kant reaffirms three of Augustine's central contentions against the pagans: that the highest good cannot be attained in this life; that we cannot attain it through our own efforts alone; and that justice prevails only in the heavenly city. Pivotal to Kant's argument is a conception fundamental to Augustine but alien to Epicureanism, Stoicism, and the entire Enlightenment tradition: the concept of sin. In going back to Augustine in all these respects, Kant proves to be deeply loyal to the Reformation, whose founding fathers, Luther and Calvin, found their inspiration in the same Augustinian doctrines.[13]

Kant's main account of the highest good is in the "Dialectic" of the *Critique of Practical Reason*. He begins his discussion there by making a distinction – one of evident Aristotelian provenance – between two senses of the concept (5:110). Kant explains that the highest good can be the *supreme* good, that is, the unconditionally good, or a good that is always an end and never a means and that is the condition under which anything else is good. But he adds that the highest good can also be the *perfect* good, that is, the whole or entire good, or a good that has other goods as its parts and that cannot be made better by adding another to it. Applying this distinction, Kant maintains that morality *alone* is the supreme good, and that happiness in accord with morality is the perfect good. Morality is the supreme good because it is an end in itself and the condition under which anything else is good. However, morality alone is not the perfect good, which also requires happiness. The perfect good cannot consist in morality alone – the achievement of perfect virtue – because it is possible to imagine a greater good: virtue with happiness.

Why must the highest good contain *both* happiness and virtue? Why should we recognize happiness as well as virtue as an element of the highest good? In the second *Critique* Kant explains that a perfectly rational being could never will that someone should need and deserve happiness yet never receive it (5:110). He also stresses that the need for happiness is "the necessary object of desire of any finite being" (5:25). Still, these points are not sufficient to explain why Kant thinks that happiness is a *distinct* element of the highest good. After all, the Stoics too saw happiness as part of the highest good; but they insisted that it is simply one part of, and consequent upon, the exercise of virtue. Their happiness is the inner tranquility and self-possession of the virtuous soul, which enjoys independence from fortune and the passions. This question becomes all the more puzzling when we find Kant himself expressing his admiration for the Stoic theory (5:117). Why, one wants to ask, did not Kant take the more Stoic view of the highest good, which, after all, seems to fit his moral rigorism?

It is interesting to note, therefore, that despite his admiration for Stoicism, Kant criticizes it all the same. The problem with Stoicism, he argues in the second *Critique*, is that it does not recognize the importance of "personal happiness" and fails to heed "the needs of our own nature" (5:127). Behind Kant's critique of the Stoics here it is possible to detect an old Christian complaint: that the Stoic sage possessed a heart of stone, sufficient to make him indifferent even to the death of wife and child.[14] The fundamental error of Stoicism, Kant further explains in *Religion*, is that it assumes the will itself is only a source of good and that the passions alone are evil (6:58n). With Augustine, Kant maintains just the opposite: that the source of evil lies in the will and that the passions alone are good.[15] Contrary to the Stoics, Kant finds it futile, even reprehensible, to attempt to eradicate natural desires and feelings. The Stoics ignored, he implies, what the Christians had rightly stressed: that evil comes from the spirit alone, which therefore stands in need of redemption.

Kant's arguments in the second *Critique* for making both happiness and virtue components of the highest good are all too sketchy and quick. Fortunately, though, we can understand much of his reasoning with the aid of his 1784–5 winter semester lectures on ethics. Here Kant equates the highest good with the ideal of the most perfect world and then argues that such a world must include both happiness and virtue. The highest good cannot be an amoral ideal, he argues, because we cannot conceive it simply as happiness; in that case we could still imagine something more to make it better: namely, the *worthiness* to be happy (27:247). Kant then asks his listeners to imagine two scenarios: a world where everyone is perfectly happy but no one is virtuous; and a world where everyone is perfectly virtuous but no one is happy. Neither of these worlds, he asserts, could be the highest good, the most perfect world. We could make the first world better by making its people virtuous; we could make the second world better by making its people happy. So the conclusion is inevitable: The highest good must include both happiness and virtue.

Assuming that the highest good consists in both virtue and happiness, how are we to connect these distinct elements? Kant joins them according to a principle of distributive justice: Happiness should be in direct proportion to merit. The highest good is therefore that ideal where everyone receives happiness in proportion to virtue, or where happiness is dispensed according to *the worthiness* to be happy. This is the ideal of "the moral world" expounded in the Canon of the first *Critique*: a world where moral agents are the *causes* of their own welfare and that of others, or where freedom under moral laws is the cause of the general happiness (B 837). Not surprisingly, Kant explicitly and frequently describes this ideal in religious terms: It is "the kingdom of God" or *"corpus mysticum."*[16] In *Religion* he identifies it with "a universal republic based on the laws of virtue," an ethical community whose single lawgiver is God alone (6:98–9). In the first *Critique* Kant betrays the immediate source of his ideal: It is the Leibnizian "city of God," a republic ruled by God himself, who governs all souls according to love and the strictest principle of justice (B 840).[17] The ultimate provenance for this view was, of course, Augustine. Kant knew this perfectly well; in the 1785 Mrongovius lectures he explicitly identifies his highest good with what "Augustine and Leibniz called... the kingdom of grace" (29:629).

Why must happiness and virtue be connected in this way? Why does Kant think that happiness *in proportion to* virtue is the highest good? Obviously, the question is basic and crucial; but in the second *Critique* Kant provides little explanation, perhaps because he took the Christian values behind it so much for granted. Crucial to his conception of the highest good is a powerful moral intuition, one central to the Judeo-Christian tradition. This is the ancient lament of Job: Life is unfair, and we live in an unjust world where the vicious prosper and the virtuous suffer. We think that there ought to be a causal connection between virtue and happiness, vice and misery; but in life there is nothing like it; indeed, almost the very opposite seems to be the case. Kant himself gave voice to this feeling in a striking passage from the *Critique of Judgment*:

Once people begin to reflect on right and wrong... they inevitably had to arrive at this judgment: that in the end it must make a difference whether a person has acted honestly or deceitfully, fairly or violently, even if to the end of his life he has received no good fortune for his virtues and no punishment for his crimes, at least none that we could see. It is as if they heard an inner voice that said: This is not how it should be.   (5:458)[18]

The underlying rationale behind this intuition, then, is nothing less than a principle of distributive justice: Rewards should be in proportion to merit. For Kant, this imperative of justice – the demand that the world itself be fair – is the great strength of the Christian conception of the highest good over its pagan competitors. The Stoic and Epicurean conceptions were fundamentally flawed because they never really considered the question of the *distribution* of the highest good. They saw the highest good as the virtue or happiness of the individual alone, of the solitary wise man, as if he could achieve it by his own efforts alone. But if this were so, the wise man could achieve the best life even in an unjust world! For Kant, as for Augustine, this was the *reductio ad absurdum* of all pagan conceptions.

Kant's vision of the highest good as justice made him take issue with the pagans in another crucial respect. The pagan conceptions of the highest good had always set a premium on the concept of self-sufficiency and moral independence. The great advantage of Stoic virtue and Epicurean happiness is that it gave the wise man freedom from the contingencies of life, independence from all the vicissitudes of fortune. The highest good could be achieved through sheer exercise of intelligence and bold resolve of the will, whatever might happen in the world. But, in seeing the highest good as a just world, Kant made it depend on fickle *fortuna* again, on factors beyond the control of the individual alone. No single individual alone, no matter how fortunate or virtuous, Kant argued, could ever be sure of taking one step toward the highest good. He could not know that others would assist him; and even if they did, he could not know that nature or fortune would ever cooperate. Last but not least, he could not even depend on his own will, which always strays from the path of righteousness. The achievement of the highest good, therefore, does not depend on the will alone, but on factors well beyond its control, on nothing less than the structure of the cosmos and the course of history itself. That was a fundamental gambit in Augustine's polemic against the ancient pagans; Kant now redeployed it against the modern pagans.

This point alone makes faith imperative in the moral life. It is the starting point of Kant's entire moral theology. In the Dialectic of the second *Critique* Kant will contend that the duty to seek the highest good is valid only in a moral universe. If we are to act morally, the universe itself must be designed for the achievement of moral ends; it must have indeed a final purpose, which is nothing less than the highest good, the kingdom of God itself. The city of God could be realized, Leibniz once taught, only if there is a harmony between the realms of nature and grace, only if "nature leads to grace, and grace perfects nature, by making use of it."[19] That, in a nutshell, was the Christian conception of the world. The purpose of Kant's moral theology was to vindicate it, though now on practical rather than theoretical grounds. We must now consider in more detail just how that was done.

Before we proceed, however, it is important to clarify one point that has been the source of much confusion about Kant's concept of the highest good. Scholars have debated the ontological status of Kant's ideal of the highest good, asking whether it is noumenal or phenomenal, transcendent or natural, other-wordly or this-worldly; many contend that Kant's ideal was originally transcendent and other-worldly but became increasingly phenomenal or this-worldly. But this entire discussion proceeds from a false premise, one that betrays ignorance of the Christian tradition. The false premise is the common assumption that these realms are exclusive. It is an assumption that would have aroused the indignation of the Bishop of Hippo, and that would have perplexed the sage of Königsberg himself. For it is central to Augustine's theory that the city of God does not exist in heaven, in some supernatural realm beyond the earth; rather, it exists on the earth and in this world; but on the earth and in this world insofar as it is *completely transformed by the second coming of Christ*.[20] We should view Kant's ideal of the highest good in a similar light. It always meant for him, as he described it in *Religion*, "the kingdom of God on earth." But this did not imply, as modern scholars believe, that the earth will remain natural; it means rather that the divine will come down to the earth, which will be completely transformed. Once we realize this simple point, we have no reason to think Kant is inconsistent, or that he changed his views in the 1790s. Kant's views were consistent and persistent. They were those of the Augustinian tradition.

4. THE METAPHYSICS OF MORALITY

Now that we have analyzed the concept of the highest good, it is necessary to examine the next essential component of moral faith: Kant's moral theology, the postulates of the existence of God and immortality. Kant thinks that there is an essential link between these components; if we accept the Christian concept of the highest good, we should also postulate the existence of God and immortality. For Kant, Christian morals and metaphysics are of a piece.

The starting point of Kant's argument for the postulates is a closer analysis of the Christian ideal of the highest good. It is crucial to and characteristic of that ideal, Kant maintains, that the two elements of the highest good are completely distinct and heterogenous.[21]

According to the Christian ideal, there is no necessary or analytic connection between moral virtue and happiness, but a causal or synthetic one. In other words, the Christian recognizes that in the earthly realm a person who is virtuous is not necessarily happy, and that a person who is happy is not necessarily virtuous. The problem with pagan conceptions of the highest good, Kant argues, is that they conflate the basic components of the highest good. They conceive the connection as analytic, as if one element were contained of necessity in the other. Thus, Epicureanism reduces virtue down to happiness by conceiving virtue as nothing more than prudence, the wisdom necessary to achieve happiness; and Stoicism reduces happiness down to virtue by interpreting happiness as nothing more than the self-possession of the sage.

This analytic conception of the connection between virtue and happiness, Kant maintains, is the crucial common premise behind the Stoics' and Epicureans' worldly or natural conceptions of the highest good (5:113). They assume that the highest good can be achieved by human action in this life only because they reduce it down to one element or the other. Hence the Epicureans think that virtue is attainable in this life because they see it as nothing more than prudence; and the Stoics assume that happiness is possible in this life because they regard it as nothing more than the contentment of the sage. But, Kant replies, the Epicurean concept of virtue is as false as the Stoic conception of happiness. Virtue is not simply prudence but the power of acting according to the moral law, which often brings us into conflict with our sensible desires and needs; and happiness is not simply the contentment of virtue because it also involves satisfying natural desires.

Nothing more clearly reveals Kant's affinity with the Christian tradition than his insistence in the second *Critique* that both Stoicism and Epicureanism suffer from a common failing: They assume that the human will can be "the sole and sufficient ground" of the possibility of the highest good (5:126). In other words, they wrongly hold that the highest good can be achieved "by the mere use of man's natural powers" (5:128n). What both ignore, Kant implies, is the radical evil of human nature, which makes us act contrary to the moral law even when we have the power to do so. The great strength of Christianity over Epicureanism and Stoicism, Kant argues, is that it fully recognizes weakness of will, the stubborn fact that we cannot achieve the ideal of morality through our own efforts alone (5:128n). The utmost that we achieve through our natural powers is a virtuous disposition, which, however, is always hedged and plagued by sensible temptations to act contrary to duty.

Having provided a closer analysis of the highest good, Kant proceeds to argue for the postulates themselves. The crucial moves take place in the "Antinomy of Practical Reason." This antinomy arises when the highest good seems both necessary and impossible: necessary, because practical reason demands that we realize the highest good; and impossible, because there is no means of joining together these distinct terms. We can join them together only if one is the condition of the other. There are only two ways in which this can be the case: Either the desire for happiness should be the motive for virtue; or the striving for virtue should be the cause of happiness. But, as we have seen, both alternatives are false. The first makes morality impossible by reducing it to prudence; the second makes happiness impossible by turning it into the contentment of virtue (5:113–14). Kant rejects the first alternative as *absolutely* false because happiness cannot be in any respect the condition for virtue; but he finds the second alternative only *conditionally* false. It is false *only if* I assume that my mode of existence in this phenomenal world is my only possible mode of existence. If, however, I assume that I have a noumenal will that acts on the phenomenal world, then I also have reason to assume that there is some transcendent cause that mediates between my noumenal will and its phenomenal effects (5:114–15). In a single dense sentence, Kant makes two fundamental moves. First, he introduces his noumenal-phenomenal dualism, as he does in the solution of other antinomies; and, second, he postulates a transcendent cause to mediate the connection between noumena and phenomena. Since virtue is noumenal and happiness phenomenal, this mediation will also join virtue and happiness. Though Kant's reasoning is dense and obscure, the fundamental point is plain enough. To connect virtue and happiness it is necessary to assume a transcendent cause, a moral being who has so designed nature that it is an instrument for the achievement of grace.

We need not go into details now about the structure of Kant's reasoning. The only point to note here is that Kant thinks the synthetic structure of the highest good – the contingent connection between virtue and happiness – presupposes the assumption of a moral world order, a realm of nature ruled by moral ends, which has its ultimate source in some "intelligible author." This is sufficient to show the link between his ethics and metaphysics, the connection between his Christian ideal of the highest good and his theism. The argument of the "Antinomy of Practical Reason" is indeed fundamentally metaphysical: that only a transcendent cause will bridge the gap between the realms of freedom and nature, noumena and phenomena; that only such a cause will explain the connection presupposed by the highest good.

But in what sense is this metaphysics? Kant stresses that the assumption of the transcendent cause has only a *practical* validity, that we have only *moral* reasons for believing in its existence; so in this sense he is definitely *not* engaging in metaphysics. Still, the underlying problem he is addressing, and the postulate he proposes to solve it, are metaphysical. If we were to purge metaphysics from the argument of the "Antinomy", Kant would have no basis to connect the realms of freedom and nature, no link between virtue and happiness. For Kant, this would be to undermine the very possibility of the highest good itself. In the end, then, to read the metaphysics out of Kant's concept of the highest good is only to beg the question of its possibility.[22]

A resolute secularist might still question why we need metaphysics. It is just a fact, he could say, that I have moral intentions and put them into effect by acting according to them. It is a mystery *how* this happens, perhaps, but it is not a mystery *that* it happens. Why, then, must we assume some transcendent cause to connect happiness and virtue? Why cannot the connection of these terms be at least approached, if not attained, by human striving alone?

It is important to see that, quite apart from the argument of the Antinomy, Kant had other powerful arguments against a purely secular and humanistic conception of the highest good. He was perfectly aware of such a conception and rejected it utterly. In some of his writings in the 1790s he gave at least three arguments against it. First, the individual efforts of finite human beings are not by themselves sufficient to bring about a collective result. We do not have reason to believe that others will share our own goals; and even if they do and we succeed in coordinating all our efforts, there is no reason to think that our efforts will succeed or last for long. There are too many contingencies in life and nature that might foil our best efforts.[23] Second, Kant does not think that human beings themselves are able to completely subdue radical evil, which constantly tempts them to except themselves from the moral law, even when it is contrary to their conscience. Although Kant does not think that grace is necessary for human beings to turn away from evil and toward the good, he still denies that they should have the confidence that they can ever redeem themselves before the sanctity of the moral law without grace.[24] Third, unlike his more idealistic successors, Kant does not think that the highest good can be a political ideal, one achieved through the state. The highest good demands that happiness be given according to virtue, which involves knowledge of a person's inner disposition and motives. But such an internal realm can never fall under the jurisdiction of the state, whose laws direct and control only external actions.[25] Kant thinks that these inner dispositions and motives can never be known by others, indeed even by the agent himself. What these motives are, and what precise reward they deserve, can be known only by an infinite moral being who has the power to peer into the human conscience.[26]

Ultimately, then, Kant's conception of both the world and humanity was far too pessimistic for him to believe that a Promethean humanity could approach, let alone attain, the highest good. In Part III of *Religion* he directly attacked this presumption, insisting that we could attain the goal of an ethical commonwealth only through divine aid (6: 100–1). "Out of such crooked wood as humanity is made," he asks, "how could one expect to construct something completely straight?" Kant staunchly denies, however, that such pessimism warrants fatalism, as if we have the right to stand by idly and wait for divine intervention. Although we human beings cannot create the kingdom of God through our own efforts, we still have to conduct ourselves as if everything depends on us. It is only if we work with all our effort toward this goal that we can ever have the right to expect divine aid (6:101). God, as the adage goes, will only help those who help themselves.

So, in the end, the highest good is indeed a goal of human striving; but the problem is that it cannot be approached, still less achieved, through human effort alone. What we also need, Kant believes, is that fundamental Christian virtue: hope, or faith in divine grace and providence. We can believe that all our efforts to create a better world will come to something, Kant argues, only if we also assume that there is a divine providence that has so organized nature and history that finite human efforts constantly progress toward their ultimate ideal. Without this faith all the labors of Prometheus will be no better than those of Sisyphus.

5. THE MORAL PROOF FOR THE EXISTENCE OF GOD

Kant's solution to the "Antinomy of Practical Reason" is only the beginning of his moral argument for the existence of God. That solution postulates only the existence of some "intelligible author of nature"; but it specifies nothing more about this author. In any case, it does not attempt to provide an explicit argument for belief in God, but only to specify the possibility of the highest good as a command of practical reason. Only in Section V of the "Dialectic" of the second *Critique* does Kant attempt to show that the existence of God is one of the fundamental postulates of practical reason. Kant has another formulation of the argument, with some significant variations, in §88 of the third *Critique*.

Put at its simplest and most schematic, Kant's argument in the second *Critique* takes the following form.[27] (1) We have a duty to promote the highest good. (2) We must assume the conditions for the possibility of this good. (3) God is a condition of the possibility of the highest good. Therefore, we have a duty to assume the existence of God. The general structure of this argument is what Kant calls an *absurdum practicum*; such an argument attempts to show that someone who denies its conclusion violates a duty. He contrasts it with an *absurdum logicum*, which is an argument that attempts to find some inconsistency in judgment.[28] This argument is an *absurdum practicum* because if we were to deny it we would violate our duty to pursue the highest good.[29]

The first premise is deeply problematic. Kant assumes that we have a duty to promote the highest good; but some skeptics question even this.[30] They find a circle in his reasoning: Kant reasons from the duty to the conditions of its possibility, which he must first prove before he can assume the duty.

Whatever its merits, this objection raises a controversial question: What is the basis for our duty to promote the highest good? Kant seems to think that such a duty follows straightforwardly from the categorical imperative; but he never provides a deduction of it. Some scholars contend that there cannot be, on Kant's own principles, any such duty;[31] others claim that it plays a fundamental role so that it cannot be derived from any higher principle.[32] One suggestion is that the highest good is really another version of Kant's ideal of the kingdom of ends.[33] This proposal too seems problematic because the highest good involves a principle of *distributive justice* not even implicit within the kingdom of ends.

The second premise also is troublesome. Its rationale is that if we assume we have a duty, we also must presuppose the conditions necessary to act on it. This is for the simple reason that "ought" implies "can." If we do not believe that we can do something, then we do not believe that we ought to do it. If, for example, I believe that it is impossible for me in a severe blizzard to rescue stranded mountaineers, I cannot also hold that I still have a duty (under these conditions) to rescue them. This is straightforward enough; but the problem with the premise is its moving from what I must presuppose to what I must believe. The argument wants to make it a moral duty for me *to believe* in the existence of the conditions necessary to realize my duty; but I do not have a duty *to believe* in the existence of these conditions unless I also *know* that they are conditions. This is why we cannot indict virtuous pagans. Although they accept their duties, they do not know, lacking the Christian revelation, the conditions for acting on them. Hence they cannot have a duty to believe in the existence of God. But if we must know these conditions, it seems we are again thrown back on the problem of having to establish the conditions of the duty before the duty itself.

The third premise also is problematic. Granted that we have a duty to the highest good, and that we must also believe in the conditions of such a duty, why must we assume that among these conditions is the existence of God? In Section V of the "Dialectic" in The second *Critique* Kant provides a very dense account of this premise. He explains that our finite human will cannot be a sufficient cause for happiness to correspond with morality, and that the only such cause would be an infinite *moral* being, that is, one having an infinite will, power, and intelligence (5:124–5). This still leaves Kant with Hume's objection: Even if we establish that nature conforms to ends, such that people receive happiness according to virtue, it does not follow that the source of this plan is a single *infinite* being. It is possible that it is created by a single powerful being, or by many such beings. In short, the existence of providence does not imply Christian monotheism.[34]

Apart from problems with specific premises, there are problems with the argument as a whole. Even if we admit the three premises, the argument seems strangely self-defeating. Assuming that the highest good exists and that it has some divine cause, we have no motivation to act on our duty to promote it. For if it already exists, why bother to do anything more in its behalf? Such was the objection of Hegel, which some find powerful.[35]

But Hegel's objection rests on a misunderstanding. What God creates is not the existence of the highest good itself – the reality of the moral world where happiness is in direct proportion to virtue – but simply the *plan* of nature or *purpose* of history. He designs everything in nature and history so that it can be a means or instrument for the realization of the highest good; but he does not realize this plan or purpose. Whether this plan or purpose is fulfilled depends on the choice or free will of finite agents themselves. So in creating simply the plan or purpose of creation, God lays down only its *enabling* conditions, leaving it to finite agents to act or not act on it.

Another general difficulty with the argument is that it seems, paradoxically, to sanction the immoralism of atheists. It makes the duty to promote the highest good depend on belief in the existence of God; so it seems that someone who denies the existence of God has the right to exempt himself from his duty to the highest good. Kant replies to this objection in §87 of the third *Critique*. He formulates it in these terms: If the moral law demands belief in the existence of God, then someone who denies God's existence exempts himself from the moral law. To that very suggestion Kant declares an emphatic *"Nein!"* (5:451). All that follows from his argument, he maintains, is that if we deny the existence of God, we do not have to strive for the highest good; but it does not follow that we are released from the moral law itself. An atheist is still obliged to obey the moral law because it is purely formal and commands unconditionally, regardless of any purposes, such as the highest good.

But here Kant is retreating from the *absurdum practicum* argument. The very heart of that argument, as he explains it in Chapter 2 of the "Dialectic" of the second *Critique*, is that the moral law demands that we should strive for the highest good, and that the condition for the fulfillment of that duty is belief in the existence of God. Kant is explicit and emphatic that the categorical imperative itself will be impossible if there is no obligation to the highest good (5:114).

What troubles Kant here is, partly, the idea that the atheist can slip out of his moral obligations simply by denying the existence of God. But this worry is needless, because the proper implication of Kant's argument is only the normative point that *we ought to* believe in the existence of God; even if someone denies the existence of God the obligation for him to believe in his existence remains all the same. There is another deeper worry, however, about the independence of moral obligations apart from religion. Kant wants to maintain that morality has an authority independent of religion, and that even if we are not religious the moral law has binding authority on us. He will soon reaffirm this view in the Preface to the first edition of *Religion*. There remains, then, a serious question of consistency: How can Kant maintain the *absurdum practicum* and the independent authority of the moral law apart from religion?

The apparent inconsistency disappears when we realize that moral law is dependent and independent from religion in different senses. Although the moral law is *epistemically* independent of moral faith, it still *logically* depends on it. In other words, it is possible to base the moral law on *evidence* that is completely independent of religion; hence I can *know* that the moral law binds my will even if I am an atheist. Nevertheless, the moral law logically depends on moral faith, according to the *absurdum practicum*, because if I cannot have moral faith I also cannot act on the moral law. This follows straightforwardly from the premises that (a) ought implies can, and that (b) moral faith is necessary for me to act on the moral law. This is the distinction between *ratio cognoscendi* and *ratio essendi*, which Kant applies elsewhere in the second *Critique*.

6. THE MEANING OF FAITH

Now that we have examined two elements of Kant's doctrine – the highest good and the postulates – it is necessary to consider the third and last, the concept of rational faith. With this concept Kant makes two very bold claims: first, that faith can be rational, and second, that faith has priority over knowledge. Since the first claim appears oxymoronic, and since the second smacks of irrationalism, Kant has some explaining to do.

Kant attempts to explain how faith can be rational in two crucial texts, Section III of the "Canon" of the first *Critique* and in the essay "What Does It Mean to Orient Oneself in Thought?" Here he sets forth a rather complex taxonomy of belief. He begins with a distinction between two forms of belief, or what he more exactly calls "holding something to be true" *(Fürwahrhalten)*. These forms of belief are conviction *(Ueberzeugung)* and persuasion *(Ueberredung)* (B 848). Conviction rests on grounds that hold for every intelligent being; persuasion, however, rests on grounds that hold only for the person having the belief. Kant thinks that persuasion is illusory because the subject thinks that its merely personal grounds should hold for everyone alike. The crucial distinguishing feature between these forms of belief is that conviction, unlike persuasion, is universally communicable and justifiable. Kant's insistence that conviction involves universal communicability and justifiability is already significant and controversial because it means – contrary to the mystics – that faith cannot be something inherently private and ineffable.

After distinguishing between conviction and persuasion, Kant then distinguishes between three different forms of conviction. There is *opinion, knowledge,* and *faith. Opinion* rests on insufficient subjective and objective grounds, that is, the person who has an opinion has insufficient evidence and also recognizes that it is insufficient. *Knowledge* rests on both sufficient subjective and objective grounds; but *faith* rests on insufficient objective but sufficient subjective grounds. The difference between *faith* and *opinion* seems to be that faith accepts a belief without accepting the possibility of its negation, whereas opinion admits that the the negation could also be true (B 849–51). In other words, opinion seems to permit doubt, faith to forbid it. Kant says that in *transcendental* questions opinion demands too little, knowledge too much. All that we can have about these questions is faith because they transcend experience and so we cannot attain evidence about them (B 851).

But in what sense can faith be rational? The crucial phrase is Kant's claim that, though it rests on insufficient *objective* grounds, faith still rests on sufficient *subjective* ones. What he means by this becomes evident only later: that even if the belief cannot be demonstrated on *theoretical* grounds, it is still possible to hold it on *practical* grounds. Here holding the belief on theoretical grounds means having evidence for its truth or falsity; and holding it on practical grounds means having reason to think that holding the belief is necessary to attain ends. The grounds are "subjective" not in the sense that they are sufficient for the particular person entertaining them – that would be only a form of persuasion again – but in the sense that, though they are valid for everyone alike as an intelligent being, they still do not provide insight into reality.

Kant's concept of rational faith therefore rests on the possibility of a pragmatic justification of belief. A pragmatic justification is one where, though we cannot demonstrate the truth or falsity of the belief by citing evidence, it is still defensible to hold the belief because it is a necessary or effective means to achieve an end. It is important, however, to be precise about the specific kind of pragmatic justification Kant warrants. He thinks that the ends in question must be moral, prescribed by practical reason; in the jargon of his moral theory, they should rest on categorical rather than hypothetical imperatives.[36] The practical justification of a belief must therefore fulfill two conditions: (1) holding the belief is a necessary condition of achieving the end, and (2) the end is necessary itself, resting on a *categorical* imperative.

It is important not to confuse Kant's concept of rational faith with other pragmatic justifications of faith. It was one of Hume's central contentions in the *Treatise of Human Nature* that some of our most fundamental beliefs are rationally indefensible but necessary to life and action. Hume defends these beliefs by appealing to human nature, to how we must feel and act. Kant departs from Hume in stressing that the practical justification of a belief must be *rational*. Hume equates *rational* justification of a belief with providing sufficient evidence for it, and so for him practical *excludes* rational justification. Kant questions this equation, stressing that all rational justification is not necessarily theoretical but can also be practical.

Some scholars have stressed the affinity between Kant's concept and Kierkegaard's defense of faith in *Concluding Unscientific Postscript*.[37] There are indeed some important similarities: Both think that faith cannot be justified on theoretical grounds and that the ultimate justification of faith lies in the autonomy of the thinking subject. Kant differs from Kierkegaard, however, in stressing the rational grounds of moral faith. Kant thinks that moral faith is obligatory, binding for every rational being, insofar as he must recognize the authority of the moral law. Although one still has the choice not to believe, one does so contrary to the imperatives of morality itself. This is very unlike, therefore, Kierkegaard's leap of faith, which is essentially an act of personal or individual decision.

There are also some affinities between Kant's moral faith and William James's pragmatic defense of faith in *The Will to Believe*. Both hold that we have a right, indeed a need, to hold beliefs where there is insufficient theoretical evidence, and that the reasons for holding a religious belief are practical. But, beyond this general affinity, the similarities rapidly dwindle away. James maintains that his beliefs are justified because of their consequences,[38] not because we have a duty to hold them; and he believes that it is "our passional nature" that is the source of our beliefs.[39] Again, the distinguishing feature of Kant's pragmatic defense of faith is its rational dimension.

7. THE PRIMACY OF PRACTICAL REASON

Kant's most striking statement of the second claim behind rational faith – that faith has priority over knowledge – is his famous confession in the Preface to the second edition of the *Critique* that he had to deny knowledge to make room for faith (B xxx). Kant's official explanation for this claim appears in Section III of Chapter II of the "Dialectic" of the second *Critique*, the section aptly entitled "On the Primacy of Practical Reason." It is necessary to consider this text in a little detail.

The primacy between two or more things connected by reason, Kant explains, is the *prerogative* by which one is the prime ground of its combination with others (5:119). In a narrower practical sense, primacy means the prerogative by which *the interest* of one faculty subordinates the interest of another. The interest of a faculty consists in "a principle which contains the condition under which alone its exercise is advanced" (5:119). The interest of theoretical reason consists in *knowledge*, or more specifically "the knowledge of objects up to its highest *a priori* principles"; the interest of practical reason consists in *action* and *direction of the will*, or more specifically in "the determination of the will with respect to the final and perfect end" (5:120). If practical reason cannot assume anything more than what can be known by speculative reason, then speculative reason has primacy over practical reason. But if the principles of practical reason demand that we hold certain beliefs that have no warrant in theoretical reason, then practical reason has primacy over theoretical reason (5:120). Hence the primacy of practical reason, as Kant explains it here, is *its right to make assumptions that cannot be established by theoretical reason*. If these assumptions do not contradict what is known by theoretical reason, they also cannot be demonstrated by it.

Kant gives primacy to practical reason only if there is no conflict between it and theoretical reason. Practical reason cannot command beliefs that contradict the evidence of theoretical reason; rather, they should be beliefs for which theoretical reason can give no evidence for or against, and which therefore transcend its jurisdiction. Hence Kant forbids Tertullian's maxim: *credo quia absurdam est*. If, following that maxim, we believe something absurd, that is because theoretical reason has evidence against it. Although the beliefs Kant allows might have no evidence for them, they still cannot have evidence against them. This requirement alone is sufficient for Kant to ward off charges of irrationalism.

Kant stresses that the primacy of practical reason is strictly limited; it has only a *moral* primacy over theoretical reason. It has the right to command beliefs only if they are necessary for action according to moral principles, and not if they are necessary for attaining happiness. Without this restriction, he argues, theoretical reason could be compelled to hold all kinds of beliefs, some of which are monstrosities, for example, Mohammed's paradise or the mystic's fusion with the deity (5:120–1). Kant envisages two possible conflicts between practical and theoretical reason. Practical reason can command beliefs, such as Mohammed's paradise, that are absurd according to theoretical reason; or theoretical reason can refuse to accept any belief except those for which it finds sufficient evidence. Kant thinks that the only way to avoid conflict is to give practical reason *moral* primacy over theoretical reason. If we give it more than moral primacy, then we foist absurd beliefs on theoretical reason; and if we do not give it any primacy at all, then practical reason must abandon some of its fundamental goals or ideals.

The primacy of practical reason is much more complex than Kant's official account suggests. There are at least three senses of the primacy of practical reason in the second *Critique* alone:

i) First, practical reason permits us to hold certain beliefs that we cannot demonstrate or refute by theoretical means. Such is the official account in the Dialectic.

ii) Second, practical reason can demonstrate the reality of its concepts through action. The concepts that cannot be demonstrated through theoretical reason can be demonstrated through practical reason when it makes them goals for action and realizes them in practice (5:3, 48, 66). Hence Kant states that the transcendent use of reason becomes immanent when reason becomes "in the field of experience an efficient cause through ideas" (5:48).

iii) Third, practical reason permits an extension of the categories beyond experience, which is not permitted in its theoretical employment. It can extend the category of cause to noumena, for example, so that we have the idea of a causality through freedom or a *causa noumenon*. Kant develops this sense of the primacy of practical reason in the Preface and Section II of Chapter 1 of the "Analytic," entitled appropriately "On the Right of Pure Reason to an Extension in its Practical Use which is not Possible to it in its Speculative Use" (5:51–8).

The crucial question remains: Why should practical reason have primacy over theoretical reason? The different senses of primacy in the second *Critique* complicate the answer to this question. The answer is obvious in the second sense because practical reason has a power to do something that theoretical reason cannot do, namely, to create the object of its belief. But it is not clear at all in the first and third senses. Why should practical reason have the right to extend the categories beyond experience? And why should it have the right to hold beliefs that are not demonstrated by theoretical reason? Kant suggests something of an answer to these questions in the "Canon of Pure Reason" in the first *Critique*. He explains that pure reason has an underlying *moral* interest: "The ultimate intention of nature in her wise provision for us has indeed, in the constitution of our reason, been directed to our moral interests alone" (B 829). We learn that the purpose of pure reason is to solve three fundamental problems: the freedom of the will, the immortality of the soul, and the existence of God. The solution of these problems is of no concern to theoretical reason, Kant maintains, because these ideas do not help it to explain any phenomenon in experience, and they do not increase our knowledge beyond experience (B 826–8). Hence the solution of these problems is of concern only to practical reason. The question is *"what ought we to do* if the will is free, if there is a God, and if there is a future world" (B 828). Although theoretical reason finds no explanatory value in these concepts, it still generates them. It must postulate the idea of the unconditioned to bring to completion the totality of the series of conditions. Theoretical reason is then caught in a quandary: It finds itself compelled to postulate ideas whose reality it cannot demonstrate, and whose value in explaining phenomena is nil. Since the reality of these ideas can be established only by practical reason, it turns out that theoretical reason *depends on* practical reason.

Practical reason has primacy over theoretical reason, then, because only practical reason establishes the reality of the ideas of theoretical reason. In other words, practical reason has the right to extend the categories beyond experience, and the right to hold beliefs not demonstrated by theoretical reason, because it alone gives reality to the ideas of theoretical reason itself. This dependence of the theoretical on practical reason is perfectly illustrated by Kant's argument in the "Dialectic" of the first *Critique* that the principles of reason be read in regulative (practical) rather than constitutive (theoretical) terms. Unless we put these principles to a regulative rather than a constitutive use, Kant argues, we end in antinomies, paralogisms, amphibolies, which are fallacies by the standards of theoretical reason itself. Hence practical reason *comes to the rescue* of theoretical reason, not only in giving reality to its ideas, a reality it cannot establish on its own, but also in resolving its own theoretical problems. Practical reason therefore has primacy over theoretical reason because theoretical reason *depends on* practical reason to ensure its own legitimacy.

8. MORAL FAITH AND AUTONOMY

Having analyzed the fundamental elements of moral faith, it is now time to turn to the controversial question of its place in Kant's

philosophy. Some critics have charged that the concept should play
no role at all in his philosophy because it is inconsistent with its general principles. They have found several sources of inconsistency.
One of the most basic, they argue, is that moral faith undermines
Kant's moral purity thesis.[40] According to that thesis, which Kant
expounds in Section One of the *Groundwork for the Metaphysics
of Morals*, the *sole* motive for a moral action should be duty alone,
independent of all motives of sensibility, where all such motives can
be subsumed under the head of happiness. The concept of moral faith
seems to compromise this thesis, however, by making the highest
good the end or object of practical reason. Since the highest good consists in happiness in accord with virtue, it seems as if Kant were recommending, or at least permitting, happiness as a motive for action;
whether this is in place of, or in addition to, morality, it still violates
the requirements of moral purity.

There is some textual evidence for this objection. Almost all the
evidence comes from *Reflexionen* of the late 1770s and the "Canon"
of the first *Critique*. In the late 1770s Kant became very worried
about the problem of the execution of the moral law, about whether
people would have sufficient incentive to act according to its rigorous
requirements.[41] While he affirmed that reason alone should provide
justification for an action, he doubted whether it alone could provide a sufficient *incentive* for the will to follow the moral law. If its
commands are to be acted on by finite human beings, Kant believed,
the moral law needs an incentive, which should derive from our sensibility, our desire for happiness. The idea of the highest good, by
bestowing happiness in proportion to virtue, seems to provide just
the required incentive. As Kant wrote in the "Canon":

Without a God, and a world of our hopes, which is not visible to us now,
the majestic ideas of morality can be objects of approval and admiration; but
they cannot be incentives of resolve and execution; for they would not fulfill
the entire end that is natural for every rational being.   (B 841)

The evidence seems even more compelling when Kant makes hope
of happiness the reward for moral action. Kant states that the fundamental issue for practical reason regarding the existence of God
and immortality boils down to the question "What may I hope?"
(B 833). He then explains that all hope concerns happiness, so that the
question of practical reason should be phrased: If I do what I should,

for what happiness may I hope? (B 833). Such hope, Kant later insists, is the necessary *incentive* for moral action (B 841). Thus, Kant seems to make the prospect of eternal reward the motive for doing my duty in this life.

Although these passages are perhaps difficult to square with the purity thesis, it is important to stress that when Kant wrote them he had still not formulated that thesis. These passages appeared in the first edition of the *Critique* (1781), and the *Groundwork* would not be published for another four years (1785). While Kant does have a view about moral purity in the first edition of the first *Critique*,[42] it is not developed with the clarity and emphasis of Section One of the *Groundwork*. Regarding the motives for morality, Kant's thinking was still very much in flux in the mid-1780s. Indeed, no one was more troubled by the apparent inconsistency than Kant himself. In the second *Critique* he goes to great pains to resolve it. In Chapter 3 of the Analytic he argues explicitly and emphatically, now perfectly in accord with the purity thesis, that "respect for the moral law is the sole and indisputable moral incentive" (5:78). Kant now fully realizes that his earlier doctrine of incentives not only sullies the motivation for moral action, but that it also endangers freedom itself by making sensible motives grounds for action. The central thesis of the second *Critique* – that pure reason alone can be practical – means not only that pure reason has the power to determine the laws of our actions, but also that it has the power to provide them with incentives. Accordingly, the concept of the highest good now takes on a new role in Kant's system. Its purpose is no longer to serve as an incentive for moral action but as the chief end or object of practical reason. All maxims require an end or object as well as a form, Kant now argues, and he then rationalizes the idea of the highest good as what gives systematic unity to all the objects or ends of practical reason. As if to thwart any suspicion of impurity, Kant makes it plain that the highest good, as the object of practical reason, does not precede but follows from the moral law (5:62–3).[43]

Although Kant does not explicitly discuss the inconsistency in the second *Critique*, he does so in the first section of his 1793 essay on theory and practice.[44] Kant now applies his reformulated theory in the second *Critique* to reply to the impurity charge. His response is to distinguish between the *motive* and the *object* or *aim* of morality. The motive is the reason for the action, which should be respect for the moral law alone; but the object or aim can be whatever is the purpose or end of the action, what it attempts to do. When we determine the morality of a maxim, Kant explains, we always abstract from its object or purpose. Although all maxims must have a content or aim, it is not this content that determines their moral worth but simply their suitability as universal laws. As the end or object of moral action, the highest good need not be the motive for moral action itself.

Kant's reply does go some way to clearing up the confusion. His critics have not been sufficiently observant of his distinction between motive and aim. Still, one could question that the issue has been entirely resolved. The problem is that if we make the highest good the end or object of morality, it is still possible for it to become a motive.[45] It seems that we are putting temptation into the path of those whose frail and fallible wills should be motivated by moral duty alone. For what is to prevent the extra hope for eternal happiness from becoming an element in the agent's motivation? If it becomes even *one* subconscious element, the purity of morality has been sullied. Kant prides himself on being a moral rigorist;[46] but in that case it would seem he should drop the highest good entirely as a danger to morals.

There are two questions here. One is the *moral* question whether happiness *ought* or at least *may* be a motive for morality? The other is the *psychological* question whether happiness might be a *motive* for morality? While the answer to the former question is a clear "No," the answer to the latter is an equally clear "Yes." The problem now is that Kant seems to be fostering a doctrine whose inevitable *psychological*, though not *logical*, consequence is to undermine his rigorism.

Even this problem begins to disappear, however, once we fully understand why Kant demands incentives for moral actions. What Kant is looking for is not rewards for moral intentions and actions, but the motivation to persist in moral action at all. His ultimate worry is (for lack of a better word) *existential*: the despair that comes from believing that all our moral efforts and strivings in the world are in vain. No less than Camus, Kant is haunted by the figure of Sisyphus, who rolls his boulder up the hill only for it to roll back down.[47] If we believe that all our actions will have no effect on the world – that all our efforts will come to nothing – then we will have no motivation to act at all. A Sisyphusian struggle might amuse the gods for a while; but the drama ends in farce when they see it repeats itself eternally. Though it appears mixed with the doctrine of rewards, this existential concern is already apparent in the "Canon" of the first *Critique* (B 838). It becomes much more explicit in Kant's writings after the second *Critique*. The problem is posed with great clarity in §87 of the third *Critique*, for example, where Kant imagines whether a righteous atheist – someone like Spinoza – would find sufficient motivation to act morally. He concludes that he would not have sufficient motivation, not because he would receive no reward for virtue – that possibility has already been excluded *ex hypothesi* – but because he would have no assurance that his efforts came to anything (5:452). A Spinozist has to reckon not with the prospect of divine punishment but sheer futility.

By the time he wrote *Religion* in 1793 Kant had completely reconceived the happiness of the highest good. He now stresses that the happiness of the highest good cannot be physical – for it makes no sense to talk about unregenerate sensibility in the kingdom of God – but that it has to be moral. Moral happiness consists in the serenity of knowing that one's moral disposition will remain firm and not relapse into temptation (6:67). To know this is to know that one's actions are pleasing to God, which is to enjoy the greatest bliss of all: the awareness of eternal salvation. Once happiness is conceived in such moralistic terms, it is difficult to make much sense at all of the impurity charge.

9. FAITH AND HYPOSTASIS

Another source of inconsistency is that moral faith seems to collide with Kant's critique of metaphysics. After having exposed the illusions of metaphysics in the "Dialectic" of the first *Critique*, these critics complain, Kant reestablishes it in the "Dialectic" of the second *Critique*.[48] There are various versions of this objection; but the most compelling is that there is an inconsistency between Kant's moral faith in the second *Critique* and his regulative strictures in the first *Critique*. We need to examine this inconsistency closely.

According to the second *Critique*, we have the right, indeed the duty, to believe in the *existence* of God and the immortality of the soul. Although we cannot prove their existence through theoretical reason, we have the right to believe in their existence through practical reason. Moral faith means, therefore, that God and immortality are legitimate *objects of belief*.[49] According to the "Dialectic" of the first *Critique*, however, reason – if it is to avoid its endemic and fatal fallacy of hypostasis – must read its constitutive principles as regulative. While a constitutive principle states that something exists, a regulative principle prescribes something only as a task. A constitutive principle assumes that if the series of conditions is *given*, the unconditioned is also given; but a regulative principle commands us only to *seek* the unconditioned for the series of conditions; in other words, the idea of the unconditioned should be taken not as an object of belief but only as a goal for action. When we apply this doctrine to the ideas of God and immortality, the objects of moral faith, the results are very disconcerting. Since Kant thinks that this fallacy can arise with all ideas of reason, and since he regards God and the soul as such ideas, the conclusion seems inescapable: It is hypostasis to believe in the existence of God and the soul. So, in all consistency, it seems, Kant should regard these ideas as goals for action rather than objects of belief. The most plausible explanation for Kant's inconsistency is that he had too tender a regard for the weaker consciences of the world, for all the Lampes of this world who still needed their faith in God (Lampe was Kant's supposedly simple manservant).

To assess this inconsistency, it is necessary to go back to the text where Kant first explains and justifies his idea of moral faith, Section Two of the "Canon" of the first *Critique*. Here Kant is perfectly mindful of his critical strictures in the "Dialectic"; but he expressly argues that they do not apply to the ideas of God and immortality. The central thesis of Kant's argument is that it is insufficient to grant these ideas merely a regulative status. More precisely, the regulative status of the idea of the highest good, its binding force as a duty of practical reason, requires that we give the ideas of God and immortality a constitutive status. Since, however, granting them constitutive status is justified only on *practical* grounds, the argument remains consistent with the Transcendental Dialectic, which forbids constitutive status only on *theoretical* grounds.

Kant begins his argument in Section Two by introducing the idea of a *moral world*. This is a purely noumenal realm, a *corpus mysticum*, which completely conforms to moral laws (B 836). He tells us that this is a world as it *can* be in accord with the freedom of rational beings, and as it *ought* to be according to the laws of morality. When Kant introduces this idea he makes it clear that we have a right only to assume its regulative status. He tells us repeatedly that "thus far" *(sofern)* it is only a practical idea whose validity rests on its use in experience, on its influence on our conduct in the sensible world (B 836). Although at one point he claims that this idea has an "objective reality," all that this means in the context is that we *give it* a reality through acting on it in the sensible world; we still do not know if it refers to something that exists because we do not have an intellectual intuition of such a realm. So far, then, Kant is self-consciously obeying the limits of his critical doctrine in the Transcendental Dialectic. But then the argument takes a surprising turn. Kant argues that we must go a step further. We must grant this idea, which thus far has only a regulative status, a constitutive validity too. His chief contention is that this idea has its regulative validity, which consists in its obligatory force as a moral principle, only if we also grant constitutive status to the ideas of God and immortality; in other words, the idea of a moral world remains problematic unless we also assume the *existence* of God and immortality.

But whence such a bold step? How does Kant justify it? He explains that the idea of a moral world can be realized only if *everyone* acts according to it, or only if we assume that "all actions of rational being occur as if they arose from a highest will that comprehends all private choice in or under itself" (838). The problem is that all my individual efforts will bear fruit only if others too act according to the same goal; but I have no guarantee that they will ever do so. There is no necessary connection between my efforts to create the moral world and the efforts of others; but it is only if we all work together in some coordinated manner that I have any reason to assume that my efforts will succeed. Without assuming the existence of some moral world order where my individual efforts are connected with the efforts of everyone else, there is no reason whatsoever to assume that all my strivings will have any effect on the world. We must assume, therefore, that there is some "highest reason," some moral cause of the world, that coordinates the efforts of all individuals among themselves so that their strivings to create a moral world produce a single collective result. We must assume, in other words, the *existence* of some moral world order where the striving of a morally perfect will creates happiness. It is only when we postulate the existence of the highest good, Kant contends, that reason can "find the ground" for the connection between morality and happiness presupposed in the idea of a moral world (B 838–9).

We can find many reasons for questioning Kant's argument. But the main point here is that we cannot accuse him – unless we beg the question – of a blatant inconsistency. Kant's central thesis is that we have a right on practical grounds to give an idea constitutive validity, whereas on theoretical grounds we have a right to give it only a regulative validity. The important points to see are that practical justification does not necessarily mean regulative status, and theoretical justification does not necessarily mean constitutive status. We must distinguish between the mode of justification of a proposition and its logical form, regulative or constitutive (declarative or imperative). The source of the confusion comes from not recognizing the specific logic of the concept of a postulate, which Kant explains explicitly in the second *Critique*. "By a postulate of pure practical reason," he explains, "I understand a theoretical proposition which is not as such demonstrable, but which is an inseparable corollary of an *a priori* unconditionally valid practical law" (5:122). Although it is justified only by a practical law, it is nevertheless a *theoretical* proposition, which means that it makes a statement about what exists.[50]

If this interpretation is correct, then Kant's moral theology and his critique of metaphysics are in perfect accord after all. This point has important implications for the general interpretation of Kant's moral postulates. It means that we cannot read them as if they were only regulative ideals, goals for action rather than objects of belief. Such a purely immanent and secular reading of Kant's ideals ignores the deeper problems he is attempting to address, namely, that these ideals cannot have their binding force unless we make definite constitutive assumptions about the moral structure of the world. Although Kant thinks that these assumptions are ultimately justified only on practical grounds, they are not simply imperatives or goals for action.

10. SYSTEMATIC PLACE OF MORAL FAITH

Although moral faith is perhaps consistent with Kant's philosophy, the question still remains whether it plays a crucial role within it.

Since the 1960s, much of the dispute surrounding the role of moral faith in Kant's philosophy has centered around the highest good. The main question has been whether this ideal plays a crucial role in Kant's ethics. Some scholars have argued that the highest good is essential to Kant's ethics because it alone provides some content or object for morality; others have held that the highest good adds no new content to Kant's ethics at all, its content being already contained within the moral law. The chief representative of the former view has been John Silber in some influential articles he wrote in the late 1950s;[51] the chief advocate of the latter view has been Lewis White Beck in his *Commentary on the Critique of Practical Reason*.[52] Their work has given rise to a much wider dispute in the scholarly literature.

This is not the place to assess the merits of the various positions in the Beck-Silber dispute. Although it has raised important issues, the dispute has now exhausted itself.[53] In any case, it really should lie behind us. For when we put the dispute into a broader perspective, it immediately becomes clear that it does not exhaust the more important general question about the role of the highest good in Kant's system. The dispute rather narrowly focused on the role of the highest good in Kant's ethics; but it is necessary to go further and to ask about its place in his system as a whole.

The importance of the highest good in Kant's thinking really lies elsewhere: in explaining the possibility of moral action.[54] When Kant first introduces the highest good in the "Canon" of the first *Critique*, it is to explain how moral intentions have their intended effect in the world (B 835). He makes it clear that the problem is not one of finding the content of moral principles but of explaining how anyone could ever act on moral principles assuming that their content is already found. Kant expressly brings this problem under the general rubric of transcendental philosophy, understanding it as part of its fundamental task of accounting for the possibility of experience. Kant explains that the experience in question here is not theoretical but practical; it concerns not knowledge of nature but action in history (B 835). This problem of moral action arises on at least two levels. It is partly the problem of straddling the gap between noumena and phenomena, of noumenal moral intentions and their phenomenal effects; and it is partly the problem of how the intentions of a single moral agent can have any valuable effect in history, given the contingencies of nature and fate, and given the lack of coordination between individual moral agents (B 838). Kant knew that much was at stake in this issue, namely, the very possibility of morality itself. If moral principles are to impose obligations on the will, the will must live and act in a world where it is possible for it to actualize its duties, where it is possible for its intentions to have the appropriate effect on nature. Unless we have reason to assume that the world too is compatible with moral ends, morality itself will become, as Kant puts it, "a mere figment of the brain" (*Hirngespinst*) (B 839).

Once we see the precise problem Kant is addressing with the highest good, its crucial importance in his system immediately becomes clear. The highest good provides the connecting link between the realms of freedom and nature, of noumena and phenomena, which in turn ensures the possibility of moral action itself.[55] To see why this is so, we only have to recall the basic structure of Kant's reasoning in the postulates. If we assume that we have a duty to promote the highest good, then such a duty is possible only if there is some intelligent moral cause of the world who has so designed nature that it can be the instrument and means for finite moral agents to realize their duties. The duty to promote the highest good demands that there be some coordination between happiness and virtue, which have no necessary connection with one another. Since we cannot forge that connection by our own efforts as finite beings, we must assume that there is some higher moral cause of the universe who makes it possible for them to be connected. This higher moral cause ensures both that noumenal causes can have phenomenal effects, and that individual moral actions will contribute toward progress in history.

Though the details and the emphasis often differ, Kant never ceases to follow the basic structure of this reasoning throughout the three *Critiques*.[56] The fundamental claim behind the concept, as Kant first explains it in the "Canon" of the first *Critique*, is that nature or the phenomenal realm is designed by a highest intelligence for the realization of moral ends (B 838). This highest intelligence has created the world according to moral ends, Kant explains, so that noumenal intentions can have phenomenal effects, and so that morally good intentions can create happiness. The pivotal role of the highest good is even more explicit in the second *Critique*, where Kant makes the synthetic connection between happiness and virtue in the highest good the basis for the postulate of "an intelligent author of nature" (5:115). In the third *Critique* the highest good continues to play the same fundamental role, only now it is even more explicit. Kant now argues that we must assume the highest good to be the final purpose of nature itself (§87, 5:447–53). The reason for making this postulate, we are told perfectly explicitly, is that only then do we have reason to assume that our moral striving will have some effect in the world (§86, 5:446). Since the moral law commands that we achieve happiness and morality, and since these are not connected through natural causes, we must assume some "moral cause of the world" (§87, 5:450).

That the highest good plays such a pivotal role in Kant's system might appear at first sight surprising because we are so used to the idea that Kant connects the realms of freedom and nature only in the third *Critique* with his organic conception of nature. Yet the "Canon" of the first *Critique* shows that both the problem posed by his dualism, and the rationale for forging a bridge to surmount it, was already formed before the third *Critique*. It would be a mistake to think, then, that Kant addressed these issues only in writing the third *Critique*. Whereas the idea of an organism is indeed crucial for bridging Kant's dualisms, it is important to see that Kant had developed this idea essentially for its moral or practical value and in the context of his reflections on the highest good. He had introduced the idea in the first *Critique* to explain the possibility of moral action (B 843–4); and he had developed a moral teleology in the third *Critique* to explain our duty toward the highest good (§§86–7).

Now that we have placed the highest good in its general context in Kant's system it should be clear that it is much more than a secular and immanent moral ideal. If we regard it in this light, then we strip it of its pivotal role in Kant's system as a whole, where it functions to hold together Kant's dualisms and to safeguard the possibility of moral action. Of course, on general philosophical grounds one might find reason to assume that all that is salvagable in Kant's philosophy is the purely moral and nonmetaphysical aspects of the highest good; but to proceed in this direction is to go beyond the interpretation of Kant; it is to engage in reconstruction of doctrines suggested by Kant. There is a danger in doing this: In shaping Kant according to our own antimetaphysical convictions we are in danger of begging the very questions that so deeply and rightly concerned him in the first place. It was a central insight of Kant's philosophy of religion that the question "What can I hope?" cannot be answered without a metaphysics, a moral view of the world. It was Kant's great merit to have seen the necessity of such a metaphysics and yet to have also placed it within regulative limits. His successors have yet to reach that point.

NOTES

1. The most important of these essays are "Conjectural Beginning of Human History," 8:107–24; "What Does It Mean to Orient Oneself in Though?," 8:131–48; "On the Failure of all philosophical Attempts at a Theodicy," 8:253–72; "The End of all Things," 8:325–40.

2. For an excellent attempt to provide extensive coverage, see Allen Wood's "Rational theology, moral faith, and religion," in Paul Guyer, ed., *The Cambridge Companion to Kant* (Cambridge: Cambridge University Press, 1992), pp. 394–416.

3. On its systematic role, see Paul Guyer, "The Unity of Nature and Freedom: Kant's Conception of the System of Philosophy," in Sally Sedgwick, ed., *The Reception of the Critical Philosophy: Fichte, Schelling, and Hegel* (Cambridge: Cambridge University Press, 2000), pp. 19–53; and Eckart Förster, *Kant's Final Synthesis* (Cambridge, MA: Harvard University Press, 2000), pp. 117–47.

4. In epistemology the major representative of this movement has been Peter Strawson, *The Bounds of Sense* (London: Methuen, 1966); and in ethics its chief advocate has been John Rawls, "Kantian Constructivism in Moral Theory," *The Journal of Philosophy* 77 (1980), 515–72.

5. For interpretations of moral faith along these lines, see Onora O'Neill, "Kant on Reason and Religion," *Tanner Lectures on Human Values* 18 (1997), 267–308; Richard Velkley, *Freedom and the End of Reason* (Chicago: University of Chicago Press, 1989), pp. 152–3; Klaus Düsing, "Das Problem des höchsten Gutes in Kants praktischer Philosophie," *Kant-Studien* 62 (1971), 5–42, esp. 41; Andrews Reath, "Two Conceptions of the Highest Good in Kant," *Journal of the History of Philosophy* 26 (1988), 593–619; Yirmiyahu Yovel, *Kant and the Philosophy of History* (Princeton: Princeton University Press, 1980), pp. 29–80, 118–21; and Thomas Pogge, "Kant on Ends and the Meaning of Life," in Andrews Reath, Barbara Herman, and Christine Korsgaard, eds. *Reclaiming the History of Ethics* (Cambridge: Cambridge University Press, 1997), pp. 361–87.

6. On the influence of these writers in Germany, see Hermann Hettner, *Geschichte der deutschen Literatur im Achtzehnten Jahrhundert* (Berlin: Aufbau, 1979), vol. 1, pp. 349–52.

7. This is fully apparent from Kant's lectures on ethics, especially the 1785 *Collins* lectures. Here Kant distinguishes the various schools of antiquity and subjects each of them to criticism. See 27:247–52.

8. See Aristotle, *Nicomachean Ethics*, Book I, chapters 2 and 5, 1094a 23–5 and 1095b13ff.

9. See Locke, *Essay concerning Human Understanding*, Book II, chapter 21, §§41, 53; Hobbes, *Leviathan* (Harmondsworth: Penguin, 1968), pp. 120, 160, 490–1.

10. *Pace* Düsing, "Das Problem des höchsten Gutes," pp. 5–6; and Wood, *Kant's Moral Religion* (Ithaca, NY: Cornell University Press, 1970), p. 90.

11. Johann Joachim Spalding, *Gedanken über die Bestimmung des Menschen. Von neuem verbesserte und vermehrte Auflage* (Leipzig: Weidmann, 1768). The book went through at least ten editions.

12. Mendelssohn's polemical intent is clear from the "Vorbericht" and "Anmerkung (g)." See *Über die Empfindungen, Gesammelte Schriften, Jubiläumsausgabe*, ed. Fritz Bamberger (Stuttgart Bad-Cannstatt: Frommann, 1971), I, 43–44, 312. See also his *Rhapsodie, Schriften* I, 402.

13. It is necessary to reassess Kant's relationship with Protestantism. Allen Wood's claim, *Kant's Moral Religion*, pp. 197–8n, that it is "harmful and misleading" to bring Kant within the Protestant tradition is harmful and misleading itself. A wise reader will also treat with caution Manfred Kuehn's statement that "It is absurd to claim that Pietism was a major influence on his moral philosophy." See his *Kant: A Biography* (Cambridge: Cambridge University Press, 2001), p. 54.

14. See Epictetus, *Encheiridion*, §11.

15. See Augustine, *City of God*, Book XIV, Chapter 3: "And it was not the corruptible flesh that made the soul sinful; it was the sinful soul that made the flesh corruptible" (Bettenson translation).

16. See *Practical Reason*, 5:128; *Religion*, 6:95, 101; *Pure Reason*, B 836.

17. On Leibniz's city of god, see *Discourse on Metaphysics*, §36, in *Die philosophischen Schriften*, ed. C. J. Gerhardt (Hildesheim: Olms, 1978) IV, 461–2; *Principes de la Nature et de la Grace*, §§15–18, VI, 605–6; *Monadologie*, §§86–90, VI, 621–23; and Leibniz to Arnauld, October 9, 1786, II, 124–5.

18. On these grounds it is essential to include justice within Kant's concept of the highest good. Its importance has been contested by Reath, "Two Conceptions," pp. 608–12, and Guyer, "Unity of Nature and Freedom," pp. 29, 52. But Kant's texts constantly and unequivocally insist

that happiness should be in accord with worthiness to be happy. More significantly, the notion of justice is essential to Kant's underlying intuition.

19. Leibniz, *Principes*, §15, VI, 605.
20. See Augustine, *City of God*, Book XX, chapters 17, 24.
21. This is especially clear from some *Reflexionen* from the late 1770s. See R 7060, 19:238; R 7312, 19:309; R 6611, 19:108–9.
22. I take issue here with Reath, "The Highest Good in Kant," pp. 594, 600; and O'Neill, "Kant on Reason and Religion," pp. 287–9.
23. See Kant's argument in section 3 of *Theory and Practice*, 8:308–12.
24. See Kant's argument in *Religion*, 6:72–6.
25. Ibid, 6:98–9.
26. Ibid, 6:21, 99.
27. See *Practical Reason*, 5:125, ll. 25–30. See also *Judgment*, §88, 5:455, ll. 5–12.
28. See the lectures on philosophical theology, 28:1083.
29. For a more detailed reconstruction and appraisal of this aspect of the argument, see Wood, *Kant's Moral Religion*, pp. 25–34.
30. The objection is very old. One of the first to make it was G. E. Schulze in 1793. See his *Aenesidemus*, ed. A. Liebert (Berlin: Reuther & Reichard, 1912), pp. 326–31.
31. L. W. Beck, *A Commentary on Kant's Critique of Practical Reason* (Chicago: University of Chicago Press, 1960), pp. 244–5.
32. John Silber, "Kant's Conception of the Highest Good as Immanent and Transcendent," *Philosophical Review* 68 (1959), 469–92.
33. Mary-Barbara Zeldin, "The Summum Bonum, the Moral Law, and the Existence of God," *Kant-Studien* 62 (1971), 43–54, esp. 49. One could argue that the highest good is implicit in the kingdom of ends, insofar as treating a person as an end in himself is to make that person's happiness one's own end. See Paul Guyer, "From a Practical Point of View: Kant's Conception of a Postulate of Pure Practical Reason," in *Kant on Freedom, Law, and Happiness* (Cambridge: Cambridge University Press, 2000), pp. 333–71, esp. 340–1. Though this might be the case, it still does not involve a principle of distributive justice.
34. Kant attempts to respond to this problem in §88 of the third *Critique* by claiming that there can be only moral or practical grounds for monotheism; but he does not specify these grounds.
35. Hegel, *Phänomenologie des Geistes*, ed. Johannes Hoffmeister (Hamburg: Meiner, 1952), pp. 274–82, 434–44. Wood, *Kant's Moral Religion*, p. 135, finds the objection "formidable." The same argument has been made by Beck, *Commentary*, pp. 244–5.
36. Kant states this restriction in *Practical Reason*, 5:120–1.

37. Wood maintains that faith for Kant and Kierkegaard is "a personal and 'subjective' matter." See *Kant's Moral Religion*, p. 16.

38. See William James, "The Will to Believe," in *The Will to Believe and Other Essays in Popular Philosophy* (New York: Longman & Green, 1897), p. 17.

39. Ibid, p. 11.

40. This objection was made as early as the 1790s. See Christian Garve, *Versuche über verschiedene Gegenstände aus der Moral, Litteratur und dem gesellschaftlichen Leben* (Breslau: Korn, 1792), pp. 111–16; and H. A. Pistorius, "Critik der praktischen Vernunft," *Allgemeine deutsche Bibliothek* 117 (1794), 78–105. It has been made often ever since. See, for example, Friedrich Paulsen, *Immanuel Kant: Sein Leben und seine Lehre* (Stuttgart: Frommann, 1899), pp. 323, 327; and Hermann Cohen, *Kants Begründung der Ethik* (Berlin: Cassirer, 1910), pp. 352–3. In the Anglophone world this objection found a prominent venue in Theodore Greene's Introduction to his translation of *Religion within the Limits of Reason Alone* (New York: Harper, 1960), pp. lxii–lxiii. The charge has been reaffirmed by Beck in *Commentary*, pp. 243–4 and Jeffrie Murphy, "The Highest Good as Content for Kant's Ethical Formalism," *Kant-Studien* 56 (1966), 102–10.

41. See *Reflexionen* 7097, 19:248; R 6858, 19:181; R 7303, 19:307; R 6876, 19:188.

42. See, for example, the passage in *Pure Reason*, B 841–2, and R 6858, 19:181.

43. Beck maintains that Kant never avoids the objection, even after the first *Critique*. He holds that Kant still retains the motivational thesis and cites as evidence the passages in *Practical Reason*, 5:132, 143, and *Religion*, 6:6n. See his *Commentary*, p. 243. However, when closely construed, these passages do not have the meaning Beck attributes to them. When Kant writes about the highest good as necessary for obedience to the moral law, he is not claiming that happiness must be a motive for the will but only that we must assume that our actions will have some effect in the world. Beck himself notes that Kant expressly denies in *Theory and Practice* that the highest good is necessary to give "firmness and effect to the moral disposition" (8:279). There is no reason to assume this passage is inconsistent with the others; they are all of a piece.

44. The importance of this passage is rightly stressed by Wood, *Kant's Moral Religion*, pp. 45–52. However, Wood regards this reply as conclusive, as if it should settle all doubts; and he treats the charge of inconsistency timelessly, as if it should apply to all or none of Kant's writings.

45. This problem was pointed out long ago by Schopenhauer, *Die Welt als Wille und Vorstellung* (Darmstadt: Wissenschaftliche Buchgesellschaft, 1968), I, 702. Schopenhauer notes that even though happiness is not supposed to be the motive for moral action, it still remains a silent inducement, serving like *"ein geheimer Artikel, dessen Anwesenheit alles übrige zu einem bloßen Scheinvertrage macht."*

46. See *Religion*, 6:22.

47. See *Theory and Practice*, 8:308.

48. The *locus classicus* for this charge is Heinrich Heine's *Zur Geschichte der Philosophie und Religion in Deutschland, Sämtliche Werke*, ed. Klaus Briegleb (Frankfurt: Ullstein, 1981), V, 604–5. Among more modern varients, see Beck, *Commentary*, p. 276; and Norman Kemp Smith, *A Commentary to Kant's Critique of Pure Reason* (New York: Humanities Press, 1962), p. 638.

49. Kant is very explicit about the point. See *Practical Reason*, 5:134, ll. 24–5; 5:135, ll. 6–7; 5:135, ll. 16, 21 and 27.

50. Admittedly, Kant does say at one point that "there cannot be any duty to assume the existence of a thing (since this pertains merely to the theoretical use of reason)" (*Practical Reason*, 5:125, ll. 33–4). What I think Kant meant to say here is that we have no duty to assume the existence of a thing *insofar as* it pertains to theoretical reason.

51. See Silber, "Highest Good as Immanent and Transcendent," "The Importance of the Highest Good in Kant's Ethics," *Ethics* 73 (1963), 179–95; and "The Copernican Revolution in Ethics: The Good Reexamined," *Kant-Studien* 51 (1959), 85–101. Silber's position has been sharply criticized by Jeffrie Murphy, "The Highest Good as Content for Kant's Ethical Formalism," *Kant-Studien* 56 (1966), 102–10; and Thomas Auxter, "The Unimportance of Kant's Highest Good," *Journal of the History of Philosophy* 17 (1979), 121–34.

52. Beck's interpretation has been countered by Wood, *Kant's Moral Religion*, pp. 95–9, and Mary-Barbara Zeldin, "The Summum Bonum, the Moral Law, and the Existence of God," *Kant-Studien* 62 (1971), 43–54.

53. The dispute continues. For an interesting attempt to sort out some of the issues, see Jacqueline Mariña, "Making Sense of Kant's Highest Good," *Kant-Studien* 91 (2000), 329–55.

54. This was the thesis of R. Z. Friedman, "The Importance and Function of Kant's Highest Good," *Journal of the History of Philosophy* 22 (1984), 325–42. Though I disagree with much in Friedman's general position, his central thesis is correct; and it was also timely, coming after decades of the Silber-Beck dispute.

55. This point has been stressed by others. See Guyer, "The Unity of Nature and Freedom," pp. 28, 40; and Phillip Rossi, "The Final

End of All Things: The Highest Good as the Unity of Nature and Freedom," in Phillip Rossi and Michael Wreen, eds., *Kant's Philosophy of Religion Reconsidered* (Bloomington: Indiana University Press, 1991), pp. 132–64.

56. The case for continuity in Kant's development in this regard has been argued in detail by Guyer, "The Unity of Nature and Freedom."

18 Kant's critical philosophy and its reception – the first five years (1781–1786)

Our understanding of any important work or body of works is determined to a large extent by its *Wirkungsgeschichte* or its "effective history." Kant's critical philosophy is no exception. If only for this reason, a better knowledge of the first reception of Kant's critical philosophy and his reactions to it would be of considerable value in understanding not just the man but also his work. It is, however, not just this that makes the early reception of Kant's works relevant. It is not just that we are influenced by the interpretations of others who came before us, as it is the case with any other work. It is rather that the way Kant's thinking developed between 1781 and 1800 was significantly shaped by the reactions of his contemporaries. His mature view is to a larger extent than is commonly realized determined by what his contemporaries in Königsberg and elsewhere thought, said, and wrote – at least that is what I would like to suggest in this chapter.

This period is sometimes called the *"aetas Kantiana."* Its history still has not been explored in its entirety. Though some parts of it are better known than others, there are also persistent myths that stand in the way of a better understanding. I would like to concentrate here on what I consider the more interesting episode in this development, namely, the first five years after the publication of his *Critique of Pure Reason* in 1781. This period saw not only the first reviews and discussions of the *Critique*, but also the publication of other Kantian works, namely the *Prolegomena to Any Future Metaphysics* (1783), the *Groundwork of the Metaphysics of Morals* (1785) and the *Metaphysical Foundations of Natural Science* (1786). But this was not all; Kant also published a number of important essays, such as the "Ideas toward a Universal History from a Cosmopolitan Point of View" (1784), "Answer to the Question: What is

Enlightenment?" (1784), the reviews of Herder's *Ideas* in *Allgemeine Literatur-Zeitung* (1785), "Observations on Jakob's Examination of Mendelssohn's Morning Hours" (1786), and "What Does It Mean to Orient Oneself in Thought?" (1786), to name just some of the most important. Kant wrote an incredible amount during this period. And he wrote so much, not just because he was afraid of dying before he had said all there was to say, but also because he thought that the other publications would support the claims made in the first *Critique*.

These first five years after the first *Critique* also saw three books by other thinkers that put forward Kantian ideas. The first of these was Johann Schultz's *Exposition of Kant's Critique of Pure Reason* (1784), the first defense of Kant's *Critique*. It was written by one of Kant's friends in Königsberg. The second book was Johann August Heinrich Ulrich's *Institutiones Logicae et Metaphysicae* (1785) in Jena and the third one Carl Christian Erhard Schmid's *Wörterbuch zum Gebrauch der Kantischen Schriften* (1786).

During this period Kant struggled to have his philosophical view recognized as the most important contribution to the philosophical discussion since the times of Locke, Leibniz, and Hume. He was convinced that the odds were not in his favor, as most of the leading thinkers of the period either ignored or openly argued against his philosophy. He became convinced only after 1787 that his thoughts were taken seriously and that his ideas would be successful.

Kant's own view about the early receptive history have been accepted to a large extent by historians of philosophy. But one may doubt whether Kant's own view is entirely correct. Although there can be no doubt that Karl Leonhard Reinhold's "Letters on the Kantian Philosophy," which first appeared during 1786 and 1787 in *Der teutsche Merkur*, played a significant role in changing the philosophical climate, and that after 1787 Kant's philosophy became all the rage among the younger students of philosophy, while at the same time becoming the target of criticism by "the establishment" of German philosophy, it would be a mistake to argue (as has frequently been argued) that this change in the climate of opinion was exclusively or even primarily due to Reinhold. Indeed, Kant's own books and essays clearly did more to convince the students at German universities to study his philosophy, even if – and sometimes just because – many of their teachers did oppose it. Two years after the appearance of the *Critique* Kant was well on his way to being recognized as the most important philosopher of the eighteenth century.

Whereas there are a number of papers and books on the first reception of Kant's philosophy, there is no discussion that concentrates explicitly and in a detailed way on the very beginnings of these developments. Indeed, most of them briefly discuss the review published by the *Göttingische gelehrte Anzeigen* in 1783 and then concentrate on the "more significant" developments that lead to "German Idealism," that is, the philosophy of Fichte, Schelling, and Hegel.[1] By contrast, I am going to concentrate only on the developments from 1781 to 1786, that is, from the time of the first appearance of the *Critique of Pure Reason* until the period during which Kant's thought became all the rage.[2] Although I will address the question of whether Kant was "ruthless," "exclusionary," and perhaps even not entirely truthful in the defense of his position at least indirectly, I will concentrate on what I take to be the philosophical consequences of this interaction with his contemporaries. In other words, I will try to reexamine the issue of what consequences the early reviews had for Kant's own philosophical development.

I. FOUR PUBLISHED REVIEWS AND KANT'S FIRST RESPONSES (1781–1782)

Kant sent the manuscript of his *Critique of Pure Reason* to the publisher at the end of September 1780. The book went into printing at the beginning of 1781, the first proof sheets arrived in Königsberg on April 6, 1781, other installments followed in quick order, and the book was published by the middle of July. Johann Georg Hamann, Kant's ambivalent friend and admirer in Königsberg, received a bound copy of the entire *Critique* on July 22.[3] Since he had already read the book in its entirety as the proofs arrived, he knew its contents well. At the beginning of May, he had already been complaining about the length of the work. "Such a fat book is neither fitting for the author's stature nor for the concept of pure reason, which he opposes to the lazy and *arse-like* (*ärschlich*) reason, that is, my very own reason, which loves the force of inertia and the *hysteron proteron* from taste and purpose."[4] But Hamann was not lazy in the ordinary sense of the word and wrote almost immediately a review of the *Critique* and somewhat later a short *Metacritique* (1783-4), which criticized Kant's approach in fundamental and interesting ways.

In his review Hamann calls special attention to Kant's intention to find a middle way between Leibniz and Locke, saying that "Leibniz intellectualized the appearance, Locke sensualized the concepts of the understanding," and then criticizes Kant for "assimilating appearances and concepts, the two basic constituents of all cognition, to 'a transcendental something = x of which we do not and cannot know anything in isolation of sensible data.'" He finds that Kant's distinctions between sensibility and understanding, between matter and form, and between the empirical and the transcendental are artificial and might lead to the destruction of both, and that Kant proceeds "arse-first," using the "weapons of light" to spread darkness or obscurity. If Kant is lucky, his work will be praised by some, known to all, and "as a mark of the highest authorship understood by bloody few" (*blutwenigen*).[5]

Hamann's main criticism in the *Metacritique* is that Kant completely ignores natural language, even though our "entire ability to think" rests on it. Furthermore, language is also the source of the problems Kant discusses in the Antinomies. This implies that philosophy cannot get beyond empirical knowledge, tradition, and doctrines accepted on faith. But his "transcendental superstition" and his hatred of anything "material" do not allow him to see that the "purifications of reason" are fundamental mistakes, leading to an idealism that is indebted to both Berkeley and Hume.[6] Hamann suppressed both the review and the *Metacritique* out of respect for Kant. The latter was published only in 1800, when Hamann was long dead and Kant himself past caring about the fate of his philosophical works. Accordingly, Kant never had the chance to respond to the charge that he ignored language and that this undercut his entire philosophy.

The rest of the literary world had, however, fewer reservations. Kant's *Critique* was reviewed just like any other book and the resulting reviews were friendly, if noncommittal. What Kant said was of some interest and should be taken into consideration by philosophers. Whether Kant's claim that a radical new beginning in philosophy was necessary was considered an open question. In any case, one had heard such claims before. Thus the first review, which appeared in the *Frankfurter gelehrte Anzeigen* of July 17 and 20,

1781, characterized Kant as one of the "most astute" philosophers. Since he had until then published only short works, the *Critique* was a new point of departure. It was not just a long book, but also one that was intended to change the philosophical discussion in fundamental ways. It proves that Kant is "a good German writer, who is free of all sectarian spirit."[7] After pointing out that the work purports to give an examination of the most basic principles of philosophy, the reviewer simply summarizes the main topics of the book without further commenting on the argument developed in it. This would have been asking too much, as the review appeared almost immediately after the book had appeared.

The reviewer of the *Neueste critische Nachrichten* (July 25, 1781) had little more time. He starts in a similar way, saying that Kant had published until then only short works, but that these had revealed him as someone "who went his own way" in philosophy – and this even though he lectured on "Meier's logic and Baumgarten's metaphysics." It seems he either knew Kant or someone who had studied with Kant. He then characterized the *Critique* as "logic in the genuine sense of the word," pointing out that it is far from unusual to call logic "critique" because the Stoics had already done this. Furthermore, Kant's conception of this logic as a doctrine that can teach speculative philosophers and pure mathematicians the proper method in pursuing knowledge that is independent of experience and entirely *a priori* points in the right direction. After a short indication of the contents of the book and a reference to Lambert's related views on the "Architectonic," the reviewer finds that it is "a work to be studied, not a work to be reviewed," wishing that it would be used in philosophical systems. The last sentence suggests that there is a problem, even though it also expresses optimism that it can be overcome: "Its penetrating and compressed style, combined with the depth of its subject matter demand considerable effort, which is, however, easily overcome on further use."[8]

This is, of course, the very problem with which the famous review of the *Göttingische Anzeigen von gelehrten Sachen* begins. It appeared in a supplementary issue, dated January 19, 1782, and is more extensive than the two earlier reviews. It is also more critical. The reviewer points out that the *Critique* is a work that always "exercises" the thought of its readers, even though it does not always "instruct" him and causes him to "strain his attention until he is tired." Nevertheless, the review also points out that sometimes there are happy illustrations and unexpected benefits. It characterized Kant's work as belonging to the tradition of idealism and skepticism in the British mode. Thus the only philosophers explicitly mentioned in the review are Berkeley and Hume. This gives a special significance to the claim that Kant wanted to offer a "system of higher, or... transcendental idealism." The suggestion is that the *Critique* is mainly "based on our concept of sensations as mere modifications of ourselves (on which Berkeley also primarily built his idealism)." Space and time are merely subjective receptacles of such sensations, even though Kant also wants to speak of "objects." Kant's objections to a substantial self were not original either, having already been used by Hume and others before him. Kant did not find the middle way between exaggerated skepticism and dogmatism, and his work does not lead his readers back to the most natural way of thinking. Rather, Kant's arguments are those of a *"Raisonneur"* who wants to leave common sense behind. He is therefore placed in the same tradition as other paradoxical thinkers. The invocation of Berkeley and Hume creates the appearance that there is hardly anything new in the *Critique*:

How does the reasoner lose his way? By opposing to each other two genera of sense: the inner and outer one, or by wanting to merge or transform these two into each other. When the form of internal sensation is changed into that of external sensation, or when it is mixed up with the latter, materialism, anthropomorphism, etc. result. Idealism is the product of contesting the rightful title of outer sense besides inner sense. Skepticism at times does the one and at other times the other in order to mix and shake everything into confusion. In some ways, our author does so as well. He does not recognize the rights of inner sensation. ... But his idealism still more contests the laws of external sensation and the resulting form and language natural to us.[9]

There is thus a contrast between the first two reviews and the one in the *Göttingische gelehrte Anzeigen*. Whereas the first two reviewers emphasize Kant's originality and are content to indicate the topics addressed by the book without criticism, placing Kant into the German philosophical context, the third review is not just longer but also more critical. Furthermore, the second reviewer mentions three philosophers as relevant for Kant: Baumgarten, Meier, and Lambert.

Though he does not explicitly state it, he clearly thinks that these thinkers provide the relevant background to Kant's own original contribution to the philosophical discussion. The third review, at least in the version that appeared in the *Göttingische gelehrte Anzeigen*, calls attention to two philosophers that had at that time a rather dubious reputation in Germany, and the author explicitly places Kant into the context of the discussion of skepticism and idealism. In doing so, the review characterizes Kant's philosophy in such a way that it would have been viewed by many as dangerous and something that needs to be avoided.

The review was by Christian Garve, but Georg Friedrich Heinrich Feder had heavily edited it. Of the 312 lines of Garve's original review, Feder took over unchanged only 76 lines; a further 69 lines were changed insignificantly, but the rest was changed significantly. Though one might say that Feder improved the readability of the review while at the same time being faithful to the intentions of Garve, he took some liberties with Garve's manuscript. Thus it was Feder who added the explicit comparisons between Kant, Berkeley, and Hume.[10] Whether this was distorting Garve's intentions may at the very least be doubted, as Garve characterizes (or misunderstands) Kant's idealism in the same way as Feder. And Feder never understood why his comparison of Kant's idealism with that of Berkeley upset Kant. Thinking that Kant was obviously as indebted to Berkeley as he was to Hume, he failed to understand why (or how) Kant wanted to put so much distance between his own thought and that of Berkeley.[11] For better or worse, this review set the tone and the agenda for the next decade or so. It became usual to view Kant as a skeptic in the Humean fashion, and to oppose him with appeals to language and common sense.

Later in 1782, in the August 24 issue of the *Gothaische gelehrte Anzeigen*, there was a review by one S. H. Ewald. It was more positive, but, like the first two reviews, offered only a short summary of the work, calling attention to Kant's theory of space and time in particular. The reviewer claimed that the *Critique* contributed to the "honor of the German nation" and was "a monument to the nobility and subtlety of the human understanding." He also pointed out, however, that its contents would be "incomprehensible for the greatest majority of the reading public." It clearly was intended mainly for "the teachers of metaphysics."[12]

Kant was, perhaps understandably, disappointed by the Göttingen review. He felt misunderstood. At the same time he also regretted the general lack of any response, even though this came not entirely unexpectedly. Still, he had expected that other philosophers would understand him and rally to support his project. After all, he had written the work partially as a response to earlier criticisms of Mendelssohn, Lambert, and Herz, and partially as a contribution to the philosophical discussion between Tetens, Lossius, and Feder. Whereas Lambert had died before the *Critique* was finished, Kant was very anxious to hear Mendelssohn's judgment about it. When he heard from Herz that Mendelssohn had put the book away and was not going to get back to it, he was "very uncomfortable," hoping it would "not be forever." Mendelssohn was, he thought, "the most important of all the people who could explain this theory to the world; it was on him, on Mr. Tetens and you [Herz], dearest man, that I counted most" (10:270). He also hoped to enlist Garve "to use [his] position and influence to encourage . . . the enemies of the book . . . to consider the work in its proper order" and to clarify the fundamental problem. "Garve, Mendelssohn, and Tetens, are the only men I know through whose cooperation this subject could have been brought to a successful conclusion before too long, even though centuries before this one have not seen it done" (10:341). In the same vein he wrote to Mendelssohn "to encourage an examination of [his] theses," because in this way "the critical philosophy would gain acceptability and become a promenade through a labyrinth, but with a reliable guide book to help us find our way out as often as we get lost" (10:345).

So Kant began to suspect soon after the appearance of the *Critique* that he was on his own and that none of those on whom he had counted would come to support him. He felt treated like an imbecile by those he did not respect and ignored by those he respected: "Mendelssohn, Garve and Tetens have apparently declined to occupy themselves with work of this sort, and where else can anyone of sufficient talent and good will be found?" (10:346). In some sense, he was correct. Mendelssohn himself claimed that a nervous disability had made it impossible for him to analyze and think through the works of "Lambert, Tetens, Platner, and even those of the all-crushing Kant." He claimed to know them only through reviews and from reports of his friends, and he said that philosophy for him "still stands at the point at which it stood in approximately 1775."[13] Garve had already spoken, even though Kant did not know it (and thought he was not interested at all). Tetens seemed to be no longer interested in philosophy and was occupied with other things. Platner did respond in time, but the response was rather muted. But this was not all. Kant was not satisfied with how he had expressed his view in the Critique. Advancing age and "worrisome illnesses" made him publish the book sooner than would perhaps have been advisable (10:273). So he declared as early as September 1781 to his publisher Hartknoch and his friend Hamann a willingness to write a "popular extract suitable for the general reader," or a book "in the popular style."[14] When he read the Göttingen review in January of 1782, the plan changed. Kant realized he had to take matters into his own hands. Accordingly, he gave up the plan of writing a mere "popular extract" and began to work on the "prolegomena of a still to be written metaphysics," which also was a response to the Göttingen reviewer.[15] But he responded also to the Gotha review, specifically pointing it out as an example of how his Critique should be reviewed. Furthermore, he praised the "learned public" for their silence, since this proves "suspension of judgment," and taking up the (Gotha) reviewer's claim that the Critique is a book for "teachers of metaphysics," he pointed out in the Preface that the Prolegomena is "not for the use of apprentices, but for future teachers" (4:380). Kant must have worked on the Prolegomena between January 1782 and September 1782, even though some of the preparatory work probably went back as far as September 1781. By late August 1782 Kant had essentially written it and his amanuensis was copying it. By September this copy was completed and sent to the publisher, but the publication of the work was delayed until April 1783.

2. THE *PROLEGOMENA* AS ANSWER TO THE GÖTTINGEN REVIEW (1782–1783)

How much the Göttingen review was on Kant's mind when he was writing the Prolegomena is shown not only by the so-called "Preliminary work on the Prolegomena," published in volume 23 of the Academy edition, but also by the Prolegomena itself (23:53–64).[16] Especially the Appendix shows how seriously Kant took the accusation that he was an idealist. The two sections entitled "Specimen of a judgment about the *Critique* which precedes the investigation" and "Proposal for an investigation of the *Critique*, after which the judgment can follow" make abundantly clear that Kant was engaging in polemics. Indeed, the first-mentioned section starts with a detailed reference to the review – something that occurs rarely in Kant's works – and takes the reviewer to task for the assertion that his *Critique* offers idealism, be it of the "higher," the "Cartesian," or the "Berkeleyan" variety. Accusing the reviewer of not having read the book carefully, Kant claims that he finds "nothing else worthy of note in the review." He challenges him to pick any one of the eight theses or antitheses in the chapter on the antinomy that he finds acceptable and to show why the proof of the antithesis offered in the *Critique* is unsound (4:376–7). But, he argues, the acceptance of this challenge would mean that the reviewer has "*to emerge from being incognito*" (4:379–80).

This is not all; the discussion of Hume's role in the origin and development of the *Critique* found in the Preface is clearly an answer to the claim that his philosophy amounts to (Humean) skepticism. Taking the side of Hume against his commonsense critics, Kant attempts to show how much actually separates the *Critique* from Hume's works. Hume's claim that reason cannot think the causal relation *a priori* and independently of experience reminded him to think harder about such relations and led to the conception of the categories. But, he argues, this generalization of Hume's problem cannot be reduced to Hume's suggestion.

If the only effect the Feder-Garve review had had was that Kant clarified his relationship to his philosophical predecessors, then it would be indirectly responsible for an interesting perspective on Kant's philosophical enterprise – no less, but also no more. I think, however, that one might argue it had an even deeper impact on Kant's thinking, one that Kant himself may not fully have understood in 1783, but one that did make him think again about the very nature of his philosophical enterprise and that ultimately led to the revisions he instituted in the second edition of the first *Critique* that appeared in 1787. Though Kant claims that these revisions concern only the style and not the substance of the book, not everyone has believed him.

One of the changes concerns the greater care with which he distinguishes already in the *Prolegomena* his own "critical idealism" from other kinds of idealism. This is just a question of emphasis.

In the *Prolegomena* and the second edition Kant emphasizes more emphatically the transcendental character of his idealism and its radical difference from empirical idealism. However, this greater emphasis on the transcendental character of his idealism goes with a more important change in the discussion of epistemological issues. Whereas the first edition of the *Critique* switches somewhat uncritically between the discussion of psychological and logical issues, the *Prolegomena* (and subsequent works) are rather more careful in this regard. Kant makes clear that the question is not "how the faculty of cognition is possible," but rather how certain kinds of judgment are possible. Indeed, the entire discussion of the possibility of metaphysic is now framed in those terms: "How are synthetic judgments *a priori* possible?" In the *Prolegomena* this question is closely bound up with the question concerning the difference between "judgments of perception" and "judgments of experience." And whether or not one finds this distinction useless and misleading, as most philosophical Kant scholars seem to do, or important and expressive of Kant's best intentions, as Gerold Prauss has argued, this way of framing the question is connected with the way that the Göttingen review forced on Kant the problem of the difference between appearance and reality.[17] There are, of course, many other changes in the *Prolegomena* and most of them have little to do with the review. But it appears to me that the connection between the Göttingen review and the later formulation of Kant's critical system deserves to be investigated further than it has been until now.

To return to the historical context, Garve took the bait Kant had planted in the Appendix to the *Prolegomena* and wrote to Kant on July 13, 1783, pointing out that he could not call the review his own because his manuscript had been changed significantly. Only some of his phrases had been retained, and some things had been interpolated. Indeed, he claimed that he was at least as angry at the review as Kant was. He also asked Kant not to make public use of the letter. It would be wrong to make difficulties for the editor since Garve had given him permission to revise and shorten the review and subsequently forgiven him for his heavy-handed changes. Kant intimated that he was satisfied. On August 7, 1783, he answered Garve, saying that he never believed that "a Garve" could have written the review. He also expressed his hope that Garve would help him in making clearer his goals to the enemies of the *Critique*.

The original text of the review appeared just a little later in the *Allgemeine deutsche Bibliothek*. When Kant received a copy of it on August 21, he was very disappointed. Garve's original review was really no better than the one that appeared in the *Göttingische Anzeigen*. It was just longer, and it did not mention Berkeley by name. Kant complained, and he felt he was being treated "like an imbecile."[18] Still, even in the eighteenth century the slogan that there is no such thing as bad publicity, only publicity, was not entirely inappropriate.

One might even say that Kant had emerged in the dispute with Garve and the *Göttingische Anzeigen* as the winner. The very fact that the *Allgemeine deutsche Bibliothek* published Garve's original manuscript is an indication of this. His *Critique* and his *Prolegomena* were now attracting a great deal of attention. Literary success was just around the corner.

Kant's *Critique* and *Prolegomena* were noted as important books in 1783. This is also shown by Johann August Eberhard's Preface to the new edition of a German translation of Baumgarten's *Metaphysica*, the very book Kant used in his lectures on metaphysics and anthropology.[19] Indeed, Eberhard calls explicit, if somewhat misleading attention to Kant, saying that such

an astute philosopher as Mr. Kant, who finds, as he expresses himself, only *analytic* judgments in contemporary metaphysics and requests that it must meet many other demands before he assigns to it the same scientific rank as pure mathematics, still recognizes A. G. Baumgarten as the first philosophical analyst. I cannot here give the reasons why I am convinced that the philosopher of Königsberg must give more credit to the one from Frankfurt [i.e. Baumgarten] with regard to metaphysics, as he seems to believe himself. First, there would have to be a decision about how justified Kant's demands concerning metaphysics are, how much has already been achieved in the present store of metaphysical cognitions and how much can still be achieved. Without investigating this now, we may say that the praise, which this competent and not easily satisfied judge gives to his predecessor, is of such great importance that it deserves the heartfelt approval of all seekers of truth.[20]

That Kant is here invoked as a witness for the (continuing) importance of Baumgarten certainly shows that it would be a mistake to think that Kant's *Critique* was still an unknown quantity.

This respect is also exhibited by the four other reviews published in 1783. The Hamburg *Altonaischer gelehrter Mercurius* published a longer notice of the *Prolegomena* on July 31, 1783 that amounted to a fairly detailed summary of its Introduction, and the issue of August 14 contained a short but substantial excerpt from the book itself, entitled "Is it Possible to Appeal to Common Sense in Metaphysics?" (4:369). The *Neueste kritische Nachrichten* of Greifswald, which had been the first to review the *Critique*, published a short notice of the *Prolegomena* on August 31, calling special attention to Kant's complaint that the Göttingen reviewer had not understood him. But the reviewer was not impressed: "If the honorable and witty man did not live so much in the clouds, if he did not use a terminology of his own and if his sentences were shorter and simpler, he might be less exposed to this danger."[21] The *Gothaische gelehrte Anzeigen* followed with a longer review on October 25 and 29. It consists mainly of a summary without commentary. But the book is introduced as one that deserves "the most strenuous examination of true philosophers" just because it concerns the conditions of the possibility of metaphysics. Though it has "not received this honor yet," the reviewer hopes that this will soon happen.

Still, Kant was not satisfied. He was worried and seems to have been suspicious. Hartknoch told Herder on a visit in 1783 that Kant believed the lack of attention to his first *Critique* was the result of Herder's influence.[22] Accordingly, he continued to work from Königsberg on the further spread of his philosophy. In particular, he began to lean on his friends. One of these was Johannes Schulz, a court chaplain with deep interests in mathematics and philosophy, who had already reviewed Kant's Inaugural Dissertation.

3. SCHULZ'S EXPOSITION OF THE *CRITIQUE* OF PURE REASON (1783–1784)

Kant had sent Schulz a copy of the *Critique* on August 3, 1781, saying that he admired his philosophical acumen as demonstrated in his review of the dissertation. Indeed, he said that Schulz had "penetrated the dry material best among all those who judged the book." This was high praise since the other three were Lambert, Mendelssohn, and Herz. Since Schulz had spurred him on to continue his thoughts, Kant was sending him the result, that is, the *Critique*, hoping that Schulz would have the time to examine and judge it. Schulz appears to have had little, for he answered Kant only two years later (on August 21, 1783), saying that he now had read the book and was willing to publish a review. In fact, he sent him a manuscript, which summarized the work and added a number of questions that he wanted to have clarified.[23] Kant answered on August 22 and sent him the Garve review for examination, saying it was better thought through than the one published in the *Göttingische Anzeigen*. He also said that he had heard through Jenisch, their common student, that Schulz had a draft of his evaluation, and he asked Schulz to hold off the review and to think about how to instruct others in how to approach the work. It would be a good thing if Schulz thought of his project as a book, rather than as a review. Just four days later, Kant wrote that Schulz had "penetrated deeply and correctly into the spirit of the project," and that Kant himself had "almost nothing to change" in the manuscript. If Schulz transformed the review into a book, then a few passages on the Dialectic should be inserted. Kant promised he would send Schulz some materials soon, but it took a long time for Kant to do this.[24] He wrote to Schulz only on the eve of publication, answering some of the questions Schulz had raised earlier, expressing his hope that Schulz could still use them to change the manuscript: "For nothing can be more desirable for the enemies than to find lack of uniformity in the principles" (10:367).[25] On October 26, 1783 Hamann wrote that Kant was lecturing on "philosophical theology" with an "amazing" number of students in attendance, while at the same time working on the "publication of the rest of his works" and "conferring with Magister and Court Chaplain Schulz, who also is writing about the *Critique*."[26] Late in 1784 Schulz's work was published as *Exposition of Kant's Critique of Pure Reason*, with the author's name spelled "Schultz" rather than "Schulz." Kant had his first defender – at least in Königsberg.

The book consists of two chapters. The first is an attempt to give a clear indication of the contents of the *Critique*, the second contains suggestions for its closer examination. There are, he says, five tasks that need to be addressed, namely,

(1) "To determine the true nature of sensibility, and its distinction from the understanding";

(2) "To seek out the complete supply of the original concepts...in our understanding";

(3) "To show in what way we are justified in ascribing objective
reality to these concepts";

(4) "Precisely in this way to determine the true limits of human
reason";

(5) "Finally, at the same time, to solve the riddle of why our reason is so irresistibly inclined to venture...beyond the limits
of possible reason."[27]

According to Schulz, Kant had solved all these problems in a completely satisfactory way. In particular, he had answered Hume's skepticism by fulfilling the first three tasks. Kant was by all accounts very
happy with Schulz's account.

The public viewed it basically as a Kantian work. There were two
reviews that dealt only with it.[28] Two other reviews discussed it
in connection with one of Kant's own works.[29] The very extensive
review and discussion of the *Exposition* in the *Allgemeine deutsche
Bibliothek* of May 1786 accords it the highest importance because
Kant himself approved this commentary.[30] It discusses the work as a
"commentary about the most important book that has been written
on metaphysics since the times of Aristotle."

4. KANT'S *GROUNDWORK* AND ITS RELATION TO GARVE'S CRITICISMS (1783–1784)[31]

In the summer of 1783 Kant was working on "a textbook of metaphysics in accordance with the...critical principles, compressed for
the purpose of academic lectures" (10:346). He hoped to finish the
first part on morals, but, as so often, this work developed along different lines. One of the external reasons for this was the publication
of Garve's *Philosophical Remarks and Essays on Cicero's Books on
Duties* in 1783, a work that brought home to Kant the philosophical
importance of Cicero as well as his continuing relevance for Kant's
German contemporaries.[32] Kant knew Cicero well, of course. He
always appreciated Cicero's style, arguing that "true popularity" in
philosophy could only be achieved by reading and imitating Cicero
(9:47). Even if he had not come close to this ideal in the first *Critique*,
Kant still hoped to accomplish it in his moral writings.

Furthermore, Garve was important. He had dared to criticize Kant's first *Critique*, and Kant was moved to criticize Garve in turn. Thus Hamann reported early in 1784 that Kant was working on a "counter-critique" of Garve. Though the title of the work was not determined yet, it was meant to become an attack not on Garve's review but on Garve's *Cicero*, constituting a kind of revenge.[33] Hamann, who took great interest in literary feuds, was initially excited. But he was soon disappointed. For six weeks later he had to report that "the counter-critique of Garve's *Cicero* had changed into a preliminary treatise on morals," and that what he had wanted to call first "counter-critique" had become a predecessor (*prodrome*) to morals, although it was also to have "a relation to Garve."[34] The final version did not explicitly deal with Garve. It is significant, however, that Kant read Cicero in Garve's translation, and that he carefully looked at Garve's commentary while writing the *Groundwork*. Though he might have been more interested in Garve than in Cicero, the latter had a definite effect on his views concerning the foundations of moral philosophy. But several scholars have argued that Garve's Cicero was actually important to Kant in dealing with fundamental moral issues.[35]

What was to be a mere textbook treatment of well-rehearsed issues became a much more programmatic treatise. It is therefore no accident that the terminology of the *Groundwork* turns out to be so similar to that of Cicero – that "will," "dignity," "autonomy," "duty," "virtue," "freedom," and several other central concepts play a similar foundational role in both Cicero and in Kant.[36] One of the most interesting things about Cicero's account in this context is that involves the claim that our own nature depends to a large extent on our social role. Sociability or communicability is for him the most important principle from which duty derives. This is clear from the very terms Cicero uses. "Honorableness" or "the honorable" are translations of "*honestas*" and "*honestum*." Both have to do with the holding of an office or an honor. Duties are thus essentially related to one's social standing. They are bound up with something that is public, part of the sphere of the *res publica* or the community. Duties make little sense outside society. They are not internal or subjective principles, but public demands on us. Insofar as some of these duties are based on sociability as such, some duties will be universal, but they remain duties we have as "citizens of the world."

Not only did Garve not have any fundamental objections to any of these aspects of duty in Cicero, but he endorsed the view that duty was ultimately based in human nature, that it could be traced back to the principles of self-preservation and human fellowship, and that happiness (*Glückseligkeit*) is not only at the root of duty, but is also always a motivating factor in moral decisions. Less clearly, he also views honor as one of the most fundamental concepts of morality. Indeed, when he summarizes the true content of human duties in a book that offers his own views on the most general principles of ethics, his first rule reads:

Act in such a way that you will appear in your conduct as a reasonable and noble man, and that you express the character of an enlightened and forceful mind.[37]

We must act with a view of how we will appear to others. To be sure, these "others" are perhaps best understood in terms of a disinterested spectator conceived after Adam Smith and David Hume, but it is society that is expressed in these others. What we may call Garve's "cosmopolitical imperative" is clearly meant to be an alternative to Kant's categorical imperative.

Honor was still important in eighteenth-century Germany. Indeed, it may be characterized as one of the central moral precepts of the Prussian *Ständestaat*. The estates and the guild system were pervaded by it just as much as was nobility. Honor may even have been more important to the citizens of the larger towns and cities in Prussia than it was to many members of the nobility. Without honor, the member of the guild was nothing. To be dishonored was to be excluded from the guild. *Ehrbarkeit* or honorableness was almost everything. So when Garve argued that each profession had its own moral code, that it should have its own code, and that philosophers should make distinct the "obscure maxims, which people of different professions follow," he seems to be endorsing a most important aspect of Prussian society.

Honor also always remained important for Kant.[38] Yet in the *Groundwork*, he argued that it could not be fundamental to morality. Honorableness or *Ehrbarkeit* was for Kant a *merely* external form of morality, or an *honestas externa* (6:236, 464). He realized clearly that it depended on the social order, and for this very reason he rejected it as the basis for our maxims. The ground of moral obligation must not be found "in the nature of man nor in the circumstances in which man is placed, but must be sought *a priori* solely in the concepts of pure reason" (4:389). Therefore, an ethics that remains founded on common life, expressed by such concepts as honor (*honestas*), faithfulness (*fides*), fellowship (*societas*), and seemliness (*decorum*) is too superficial and unphilosophical for Kant. For this reason he rejected not just Cicero, but all attempts to develop a Ciceronian ethics. Morality is about who we genuinely are or who we should be, and this has, according to Kant, nothing to do with our social status. In rejecting "honor," Kant also implicitly rejects one of the fundamental principles of the society he lived in. The distinction of different estates has no moral relevance. As moral agents we are all equal. Any attempt at defending or justifying social differences by appealing to morals must be rejected as well. The conservative *status quo* must be challenged. In the context of Prussia of 1785, these views must be called revolutionary.

Kant seems to be saying that we also must subordinate all personal considerations, self-love, and passions to the only goal to which it is worth aspiring, namely, to be moral. This has nothing to do with feeling and everything to do with reason and the "idea of another and far worthier purpose of one's existence" (4:396). One of the more important reasons that led Kant to reject honor as a genuine moral principle was his belief that anyone who relied on maxims of honor rather than on maxims of pure morality also relied on self-interest as a significant part in moral deliberations; and he was clearly right about this.

Kant's entire critical philosophy was meant to contribute to the formal aspect of science. His moral philosophy is no exception. It concentrates on the merely formal aspects of morality, leaving aside the empirical content, which belongs to anthropology, for Kant. This is odd, at least to some extent, as Kant had argued earlier that pure moral philosophy was not enough. Anthropology was also needed, since it

provides moral knowledge of man because we must find in it the motives (*Bewegungsgründe*) for morality and without it morality would be scholastic and not applicable to the world at all. It would not be pleasant for it. Anthropology is related to morality as spatial geometry to geodesics.   (25:1211)

Further:

Morality cannot exist without anthropology, for one must first know of the agent whether he is in a position to accomplish what is required of him.... One can...consider practical philosophy even without anthropology, or without knowledge of the agent, only then it is merely speculative; so man must at least be studied accordingly.   (27:244)

In the *Groundwork* it is "clear of itself from the common idea of duty and of moral law" that moral philosophy ultimately cannot have anything to do with empirical concerns (4:389). Whereas Kant argued earlier that we must differentiate between the *principium diiudicationis* and the *principium executionis* in morals and thought that the moral sense, moral feeling, or empirical considerations might well have to do with the latter, even if the former was purely moral, he now combined the two principles in one categorical imperative. Because the claims of moral philosophy are universal, the form of moral philosophy must be just as much *a priori* as that of theoretical philosophy. Still, the *Groundwork* was not designed to deliver all of the metaphysics of morals. Kant claims he sought only to describe and establish "the *supreme principle of morality*" (4:392). It should be clear that Kant's rejection of anthropological, social, or empirical considerations had to do at least to some extent with his studies of Garve and his *Cicero*. Even though it would be a mistake to view the *Groundwork* as a mere polemic against one of Kant's contemporaries, it would also be a mistake to overlook how important this background ultimately is. His categorical imperative is clearly also meant as an alternative to Garve's cosmopolitical considerations. Indeed, later developments clearly show that the dialogue between Garve and Kant continued. Garve later criticized Kant on just this problem, making powerful objections against the very possibility of acting from duty.[39] If the connection between Kant's own thinking and the reactions of his contemporaries is very apparent in the works we have discussed so far, it is even more apparent in the essays that he wrote between 1784 and 1786.

5. SOME ESSAYS ON ENLIGHTENMENT AND HISTORY (1784–1786)

As soon as the *Groundwork* was off his desk, Kant began to work on some contributions to the *Berlinische Monatsschrift*.[40] The first of these was his essay entitled "Ideas toward a Universal History from a Cosmopolitan Point of View," which appeared in the November issue of 1784 (8:15–31). The essay was a response to a remark published in the *Gothaische gelehrte Zeitungen* on February 11, in which it was claimed: "It is a favorite idea of Herr Professor Kant that the ultimate goal of the human race is the establishment of a perfect constitution. He desires that a philosophical historiographer would undertake it to write a history of mankind from this perspective in order to show whether mankind has come closer to this final goal at some time, has strayed from it at other times, and what still remains to be done to achieve it." Kant argues in the essay that such a historiography is possible only if we assume that nature (or perhaps better Nature) has certain characteristics. Put in another way, he claims that a certain idea of Nature is a necessary condition of "universal history from a cosmopolitan point of view." Therefore, we may say that if a "universal history from a cosmopolitan point of view" is legitimate, then a certain idea of Nature is also legitimate. Therefore we can also say that the "universal history" forms a "*justification* of Nature – or rather perhaps of *providence*." Indeed, Kant claims that such a project "is no mean motive for adopting a particular point of view in considering the world."

In December of 1784 he published another essay, "Answer to the Question: What is Enlightenment?" – again in the *Berlinische Monatsschrift*. Kant dated it September 30, 1784. The essay represents a response to a question by Johann Friedrich Zöllner (1748–1805), who was a member of a group of enlightenment thinkers centered in Berlin. In response to an article in the *Monatsschrift*, whose author had advocated that priests and ministers should no longer play a role in marriage, and that the religious ceremony of marriage contradicted the spirit of the enlightenment, Zöllner argued that the principles of morality were already in decline (*wankend*) and that the disparagement of religion could only accelerate this process. One should not "in the name of *enlightenment* confuse the heads and hearts of the people." In a note in the text, he asked: "What is enlightenment? This question, which is almost as important as 'What is truth?,' should really be answered before one starts to enlighten! And yet, I have not found an answer to it anywhere."[41] Kant was by no means the only one who addressed this question. Indeed, by the time he answered it, a dispute had already ensued and many philosophers had contributed to it. Kant's answer was, however, the most philosophical, or perhaps better, the most principled one (8:41–2).

He assigns to philosophy the role of bringing about in a state what nature's plan has been all along and argues that freedom of thought will lead to greater civil freedom. "The hindrances to universal enlightenment... are gradually becoming fewer." And enlightenment is for Kant "the human being's emergence from his self-incurred minority." Put positively, it is the stage of mankind's maturity. Minority is for Kant the "inability to make use of one's own understanding without direction from another. It is self-incurred when its cause lies not in a lack of understanding but in a lack of resolution and courage to use it without direction from another." We should have the courage to think for ourselves. This is expressed by the motto of the enlightenment – "*Sapere aude!*" or "Dare to be wise!" (8:35).

In 1784 a new journal was established that was to become most important in the further discussion of Kant's own philosophy, namely, the *Neue allgemeine Literaturzeitung* of Jena. Kant's former student Herder, who by this time had become a very famous German writer, published in the same year his *Ideas on a Philosophy of the History of Mankind* with the publisher of the first *Critique*. Kant was asked in July whether he would not be willing to make "at least a few contributions" and whether he was interested to review Herder's *Ideas* in particular (10:393–4). He agreed, probably after looking at Hamann's copy of the *Ideas*.[42] The review of Herder's book was to be "a trial." It was due on November 1, and it appeared in one of the first issues of the journal, namely on January 6, 1785 (10:396). As was customary, the review appeared anonymously.

Kant's judgment of this work of his former student was negative, and he did not hold back. Perhaps he even went out of his way to insult Herder. Thus, in the Introduction of the review, he did not talk so much about the book as about the author, saying that he was "ingenious and eloquent," demonstrating again his "renowned individuality," going on to note that "his is not logical precision in definition of concepts or careful adherence to principles, but rather a fleeting, sweeping view, an adroitness in unearthing analogies, in the wielding of which he shows a bold imagination... combined with a cleverness in soliciting sympathy for his subject – kept in increasingly hazy remoteness – by means of sentiment and sensations" (8:45).

After a detailed summary of the stages of Herder's argument in the *Ideas*, he summed up "the idea and final purpose of Part I" as follows:

The spiritual nature of the human soul, its permanence and progress toward perfection, is to be proved by analogy with the natural forms of nature, particularly their structure, with no recourse to metaphysics. For this purpose, spiritual forces, a certain invisible domain of creation, are assumed for which matter constitutes only the framework. This realm contains the animating principle that organizes everything, and in such a way that the schema of the perfection of this organic system is to be man. All earthly creatures, from the lowest level on, approximate him until finally, through nothing else than this perfected organic system, of which the essential condition is the upright gait of the animal, man emerged. His death can never more terminate the progress and enhancement of the structure already shown before copiously in other creatures. Rather a transcendence of nature to still more refined operations is expected, in order to further him thereby to yet higher grades of life, and so continuously to promote and elevate him into infinitude.

(8:52)

Kant did not understand the argument by analogy because what Herder stated as an analogy is a disanalogy. How can the similarity between man and all other creatures prove that man is immortal, or the middle link between mortality and immortality, when all other creatures decompose? Individuals are completely destroyed – or so it would seem. Herder's idea of a self-constituting organic system is an idea that lies entirely outside of the sphere of empirical investigation. It is mere speculation. The author may be praised for having thought for himself, and for a preacher this took courage. His "execution is only partially successful" (8:55). Kant closed by expressing his hope that philosophy would help Herder in "pruning... superfluous growth." Flighty imagination, "whether metaphysical or sentimental," will not get us anywhere.

Some have argued that Kant's review was essentially a personal reaction to Herder's lack of support. But this is probably not entirely correct. Kant also had deep philosophical reasons to oppose what seemed to him only unprincipled flights of imagination. Herder's book was not just a "superfluous growth," but a weed that needed to be rooted out. Furthermore, Kant himself did not seem to think the review was devastating. Nor did Hamann. He wrote to Herder just before the issue of the journal with Kant's review appeared, and he revealed that Kant was the author: "It will perhaps not be uncomfortable for you to know that our Kant reviewed you. In any case, keep it to yourself and do not reveal me."[43] Kant reviewed the second part of the *Ideas* in the *Allgemeine Literaturzeitung* of November 15, 1785. Again, he asks whether the poetic spirit of the book does not get into the way of the author's philosophy – "whether frequently the tissue of daring metaphors, poetic images and mythological allusions does not serve to conceal the corpus of thought as under a farthingale instead of letting it glimmer forth agreeably as under a translucent veil" (8:60). Of course, Kant thought they did; and he gave a number of examples to show this.

Herder did not like this installment of the review much better than the first.[44] He prayed: "God deliver us from this evil." Yet, Kant was not yet done with Herder. In November 1785, he published in the *Berlinische Monatsschrift* an essay on "The Definition of the Concept of the Human Race," which was, at least in part, an answer to Herder.[45] In it, he tried to show that race must be based on inherited traces, such as skin color, and he claimed that therefore there are just four races – namely, the white, yellow, black, and red. Furthermore, he argued that there are no characteristics other than color that are inevitably inherited. This also meant for him that children of mixed marriages necessarily inherit characteristics of both races, and that they will inevitably pass these characteristics on to their children. Kant rejected the idea that the different races originated from different kinds (*Stämme*) of people. There are no different species of humanity, only different races.

Whereas Kant declined to write reviews of the subsequent volumes of Herder's *Ideas*, he did publish another essay on a problem from Herder, namely, his "Conjectural Beginning of the Human Race." Its roots go back to the early seventies and Kant's correspondence with Hamann about *The Most Ancient Document of the Human Race*, but its immediate occasion was Book 10 of Herder's *Ideas*. Kant sent the essay to Berlin on November 8, 1785, and it was published in the January issue of the *Berlinische Monatsschrift* (8:107–27). In it he argued that conjecture about the beginning of the human race might be justifiable as "a history of the first development of freedom from its origins as a predisposition in human nature"

(8:109). Starting from Genesis, he argues that the first human being must have been able to "*stand* and *walk*; he could *speak*...and indeed *talk* – i.e., speak with the help of coherent concepts... – and consequently *think*" (8:110). At first, man only followed instinct, and he was happy. But "reason soon made its presence felt." With the help of the imagination, it invented desires without any natural basis. First, luxurious tastes developed; second, sexual fantasies made the fig leaf necessary, and "the first incentive for man's development as a moral being came from his *sense of decency*" (8:111). Next came the ability to anticipate future needs, and finally the realization that we are the "end of nature," that we are different from all other animals. This realization raises "man completely above animal society" and gives him a "position of *equality with all rational beings*...[as] *an end in himself*" (8:114). In a most characteristic passage, Kant claims that "Before reason awoke, there were no commandments or prohibition, so that violations of these were also impossible. But when reason began to function and, in all its weakness, came into conflict with animality in all its strength, evils necessarily ensued.... From the moral point of view, therefore, the first step...was a fall, and from the physical point of view, this fall was a punishment that led to hitherto unknown evils. Thus, the history of *nature* begins with goodness, for it is the *work of God*; but the history of *freedom* begins with evil, for it is the *work of man*" (8:115). Although this story shows that reason and freedom must look like a loss to the individual who must blame himself, they also are a cause for admiration and praise, if we take the point of view of the species. Our destiny is the progressive cultivation of the capacity for goodness.

These essays had a considerable effect. They showed that Kant was not just a dry metaphysician, whose ideas were of limited interest to some philosophers, but rather a public intellectual, who was able to talk about issues that concerned the average pastor and teacher and show to them that they have the deepest philosophical and historical significance. This certainly had an effect on how the *Critique*, the *Prolegomena*, and the *Groundwork* were seen. Whereas there had been only four reviews of the *Prolegomena* in 1783 and four more in 1784, the *Groundwork* received eleven between 1785 and 1786. Kant was a household name by this time.

One of the reasons why Kant wrote so many different things on so many different topics between 1783 and 1785 was certainly that he wanted to make an argument for the relevance and importance of his philosophical views and convince his contemporaries that the time had come to take a closer look at his critical enterprise.

6. METAPHYSICAL FOUNDATIONS OF NATURAL SCIENCE AND ULRICH'S INSTITUTIONES LOGICAE (1785–1786)

Kant pressed Johannes Schulz, his commentator, into other projects that would serve in the cause of the *Critique*. Thus he arranged for Schulz to publish reviews during the years following the publication of his *Exposition* on Kant and works relevant for Kant in the *Allgemeine Literatur-Zeitung*. And Schulz published at least seven such reviews.[46] The most important of these was perhaps the one of J. A. H. Ulrich's *Institutiones logicae et metaphysicae* that appeared on December 13, 1785.[47] Kant had asked Schulz to write this review because the work was clearly important for the further fate of the *Critique* since it advanced criticisms of the Transcendental Deduction. But far from decisively rejecting or refuting Ulrich's doubts, Schulz had added his own doubts, and Kant did not like it. Schulz pointed out that the book was important because it was up to this point the only one that thoroughly took Kant's system into consideration and even accepted a significant portion of it, and he rejected Ulrich's criticism that the Table of the Categories was incomplete because it did not include the heading "identity and difference." But he gave a qualified endorsement to Ulrich's doubts that "outside of the field of mathematics only those principles have *a priori* objective reality, which are required for the possibility of experience."[48] The principle of causality, for instance, is implied by the principle of sufficient reason and therefore dependent on it. We can perceive things without presupposing the causal principle, even though a judgment of experience presupposes it. Schulz adds to this that the transcendental deduction, which is fundamental to the whole system, could be clearer.

Hamann wrote to Herder on April 4, 1786 that Kant had been "in an extraordinarily bad mood" about the review, but that Schulz had defused the situation by visiting Kant first. They had a long conversation, and they parted on friendly terms. "The clergyman had looked into the philosopher's cards and Kant . . . was more bitter in the heat of the moment than he himself would have liked. This weakness was betrayed by his amanuensis and was afterwards covered up. In any case, Kant is in spite of his impetuousness (*Lebhaftigkeit*) a naïve (*treuherzig*) and innocent man. But he is ... [un]able to keep silent."[49] An answer to Schulz (and Ulrich) was necessary. This came in the *Metaphysical Foundations of Natural Science*, in which Kant put forward his philosophy of science. Although this text is driven to a large extent by Kant's systematic concerns and has little to do with the criticisms offered by other philosophers, there is in the text a long footnote in which he addresses the issue raised by his two critics:

I find doubts expressed in the review of Professor Ulrich's *Institutiones* ... not against [the] table of the pure concepts of the understanding, but to the conclusions drawn therefrom as to the limitations of the whole faculty of pure reason and therefore all metaphysics. In these doubts the deeply probing reviewer declares himself to be in agreement with his no less examining author. Since these doubts are supposed to touch the main foundation of my system ... they should be reasons for thinking that my system ... far from carried with it that apodictic conviction requisite for compelling an unqualified acceptance. (4:474n)

Kant tried his best to clarify the issue in the footnote and then again in the second edition of the *Critique of Pure Reason*, but it would be an exaggeration to say that he succeeded. But be that as it may, he did rise to the challenge posed to him by his contemporaries. Since he had already finished the *Metaphysical Foundations* during the summer of 1785, he probably added the footnote in the spring of 1786.

7. KANT'S INTERVENTION IN THE *PANTHEISMUS* DISPUTE

In August 1786 Kant submitted his essay "What Does It Mean to Orient Oneself in Thought?" to the *Berlinische Monatsschrift*. Ostensibly, the essay is a contribution to the so-called "*Pantheismus* Dispute" that had sprung up between Moses Mendelssohn and F. H. Jacobi after the death of Mendelssohn's lifelong friend Gotthold Ephraim Lessing. Jacobi had argued that all philosophy necessarily leads to Spinozism, that Lessing had conceded this to him, and that faith was the answer to whatever the problem was. Mendelssohn took up the defense of Lessing and philosophy. Kant, who had followed the dispute with great interest, was encouraged by the editor of the *Berlinische Monatsschrift* to intervene on Mendelssohn's behalf – especially because Jacobi was claiming that his position was close to Kant's (10:417–18, 433, 453–8). Kant was willing. He had already written to Herz that he had long planned to write something about Jacobi's oddity (10:442). Yet, far from simply defending Mendelssohn against Jacobi, he used the occasion to give another introduction to his own practical philosophy.

Taking as his point of departure Mendelssohn's heuristic principle (or maxim) that "it is necessary to orientate oneself in speculative reason...by means of a certain guideline which he sometimes described as common sense...sometimes as healthy reason, and sometimes as plain understanding" (10:133), Kant argued that this maxim undermines not only Mendelssohn's own speculative metaphysics but leads to zealotry and the complete subversion of reason. In other words, Mendelssohn's common sense is no better than Jacobi's faith. Both amount to one and the same thing.

Kant's project was thus to save Mendelssohn from himself, as it were, and to show against Jacobi that reason has the resources necessary for belief. We can orientate ourselves by a subjective means, namely, by feeling a need, which is inherent in reason itself. This need of reason can be theoretical or practical. The first, already explored in the *Critique of Pure Reason*, is expressed by the conditional that says that if you want to judge the first causes of things, then you must assume that God exists. But we have a choice in this matter, that is, it is not absolutely necessary to pass judgment on first causes. The practical need of reason, by contrast, is absolutely necessary and not conditional. In this case, Kant claimed, we must pass judgment. "For the purely practical use of reason consists in the formulation of moral laws," which lead "to the idea of the highest good that is possible in the world" (8:139). This highest good consists of a moral state in the world in which the greatest happiness coincides with the strictest observation of moral rules. It has thus two components for Kant. The first is morality in accordance with the categorical imperative (as already discussed in the *Groundwork*); the second is happiness in proportion to moral worth. But there is no necessary relation between morality and happiness. Indeed, often it seems the case that bad things happen primarily to good people. Yet, we must believe that eventually good deeds will make a difference in the world. Thus, reason needs to assume that happiness in proportion to moral worth is possible even though nature itself cannot be expected to bring it about. Only an intelligent and all-powerful moral agent can be expected to do this. Therefore, the highest good makes it necessary for a moral agent to assume that there is another cause that makes the highest good possible. This can only be a supreme intelligence that has moral concerns, that is, God. Therefore, we must assume the existence of God. The final point is new, and it anticipates a central argument of the *Critique of Practical Reason*. Rational belief should replace Mendelssohn's "healthy reason." It is what gives us orientation in speculation. This rational belief is not just a belief in certain articles of faith, recommended by reason; it is also a belief in reason itself.[50]

In 1786 there appeared the first lexicon explaining Kant's difficult philosophical terminology as part of a textbook on Kant's metaphysics. It was entitled *Critik der reinen Vernunft, im Grundrisse zu Vorlesungen, nebst einem Wörterbuche zum leichtern Gebrauch der Kantischen Schriften*, which was immediately reviewed, often with other works that had appeared on Kant, like Gottlob August Tittel's *Über Herrn Kants Moralreform* (1786), Adam Weishaupt's *Über den Materialismus und Idealismus: Ein philosophisches Fragment* (1786), and Jacob Freidrich Abel's *Über die Quellen der menschlichen Vorstellungen* (1786). The contributions to the "pantheism dispute," such as Moses Mendelssohn's *Morgenstunden* (1785) just as much as Thomas Wizenmann's anonymous *Die Resultate der Jacobischen und Mendelssohnischen Philosophie, kritisch untersucht von einem Freywilligen* (1786) and several other works, were often discussed with relation to Kant. Indeed, the review journals were full of discussions of books by, on, and relevant to Kant. When Reinhold's *Letters on Philosophy* began to appear at the end of 1786, the discussion of Kant's philosophy was already well on its way. Indeed, one may argue that Reinhold's *Letters* were themselves an effect of this discussion. One may perhaps say that they are philosophically more important than the reviews and the works that preceded them, but even that is something that can be disputed. In any case, while the earlier reviews and books may be shown to have had an effect on Kant that it may be worth while for philosophical scholars to investigate, Reinhold had less of an impact on Kant himself.

8. A NEW ERA?

On May 14, 1787 Daniel Jenisch wrote to Kant:

The *Letters* on your philosophy in the *Merkur* have made for a most impressive stir and all philosophical heads in Germany seem to have awakened from their indifference toward speculation and to the most lively sympathy for you, my dear professor, since the troubles with Jacobi, the *Results* and these *Letters*, in which Mendelssohn's *Morgenstunden* were generally mocked. It is incredible how little respect and influence Feder and Meiners have everywhere, i.e. even with those from Göttingen, of whom I have met...a considerable number. Everyone studies your *Critique* with the greatest possible industry, and many letters from Göttingen show that you are appreciated because you are understood. Campe, Trapp and Struve have been working on it for more than three months, and the latter recently told me that compared to your *Critique* all theodicies and Wolffian *volumina*. Jerusalem, being eighty-one years old, himself recently said to me: 'I am too old to engage in speculation á la Kant, but his essay in the *Berliner Monatsschrift* on orientation is the echo of my confession; Mendelssohn's proofs only tease the common sense that is vindicated by Kant.   (10:485)[51]

Jenisch goes on to talk about others who think highly of Kant's philosophy and points out that Kant is well known even in Holland. But his *Groundwork of the Metaphysics of Morals* finds "incomparably more resistance than the *Critique* among the scholars" Jenisch is acquainted with.

In other words, Kant is now at the stage where he seemed to want to be. He has many defenders. There are now "Kantians" everywhere. Many do not like them. Indeed, traditional enemies were united in this dislike. Herder calls them "an unphilosophical crew," Nicolai "idolatrous...worshippers," and Fichte "the shame of our century." But Kant is taken very seriously. His philosophy becomes most influential, if only for a relatively short time. For the defenders and expositors of Kant soon would become convinced that they could improve on his thoughts and developed their own systems – with Reinhold being not only the first but also the most frequent adopters of new Kantian "systems."

With these developments a new phase in the reception of Kant's philosophy begins, which is also by no means a phase in which critical thinking always keeps the upper hand. This is suggested by the *Analekten für Politik und Literatur* (Leipzig, 1787). Under the heading "Fights Among Students about Kantian Philosophy," it reports:

A student from the Mosel region defends the Kantian philosophy, resorting to violence against someone from lower Saxony, who studied in Göttingen. The Saxon was wounded and the student from the Mosel region incarcerated. He wrote to the academic senate from his cell that he knew he could only presume that there was a conflict of interest in the minds of the members of the senate because he did know that they disliked Kant's new philosophy. Therefore, no one could blame him, if he objected to their measures and judgments concerning his presumed misdeed. The senate decided that the case was so novel that it was almost necessary that all members (*Beysitzer*) of the senate would have to read Kant's *Critique of Pure Reason* and study it carefully.[52]

As the reporter speculates, this might mean that Kant's "abstruse work" was ultimately destined to become a piece of evidence at criminal court (*ein Prozeßaktenstück*) – presumably a different venue than the tribunal of pure reason.

NOTES

1. One of the first of these is Karl Rosenkranz, *Geschichte der Kant'schen Philosophie* (Leipzig: Leopold Voss, 1840), which appeared as vol. 12 of *Immanuel Kant's Sämtliche Werke*. Often, already the titles indicate this approach. George di Giovanni and H. S. Harris, *Between Kant and Hegel. Texts in the Development of Post-Kantian Idealism* (Indianapolis: Hackett, 2000; originally SUNY, 1985). See also Tom Rockmore, *Before and After Hegel. A Historical Introduction to Hegel's Thought* (Berkeley: University of California Press, 1993), pp. 4–38 and George di Giovanni, "The First Twenty Years of Critique: The Spinoza Connection," *The Cambridge Companion to Kant*, ed. Paul Guyer (Cambridge: Cambridge University Press, 1992), pp. 417–48. Brigitte Sassen, *Kant's Early Critics. The Empiricist Critique of the Theoretical Philosophy* (Cambridge: Cambridge University Press, 2000) also leaves out this part of the reception. I have covered some of these materials in a different way in Manfred Kuehn, *Immanuel Kant: A Biography* (Cambridge: Cambridge University Press, 2001).

2. Albert Landau, *Rezensionen zur kritischen Philosophie, 1781–87* (Bebra: Albert Landau Verlag, 1991). This is a very valuable collection not only of all the reviews of Kant's own works during the period but also of the works relevant for the spread of Kant's philosophy.

3. Johann Georg Hamann, *Briefwechsel*, vols. 1–7, ed. Walther Ziesemer and Arthur Henkel (Frankfurt am Main: Insel Verlag, 1955–1979), vol. 4, p. 312.

4. Hamann, *Briefwechsel* 4, pp. 292–3.

5. *Vom Magus im Norden und der Verwegenheit des Geistes. Ein Hamann Brevier*, ed. Stefan Majetschak (München: Deutscher Taschenbuch Verlag, 1988), p. 204.

6. *Vom Magus im Norden*, pp. 206–12. Hamann was, of course, aware of the Feder review by the time he wrote this. His pronouncements show that he basically endorsed Feder's point.

7. Landau, *Rezensionen*, p. 3.

8. Landau, *Rezensionen*, pp. 8–9.

9. Sassen, *Kant's Early Critics*, translates this passage in a slightly different way. See pp. 53–8, at p. 58 (*"gegen einander aufbringen"* cannot mean "bringing together"). She does not include the first two reviews here discussed, nor the next one.

10. See Emil Arnoldt, *Vergleichung der Garveschen und Federschen Rezension über die Kritik der reinen Vernunft*, in his *Gesammelte Schriften*, ed. Otto Schöndörffer, vol. 4 (Berlin, 1908), pp. 1–118. The two versions can be found in Immanuel Kant, *Prolegomena zu einer jeden künftigen Metaphysik, die als Wissenschaft wird auftreten können*, ed. Rudolf Malter (Stuttgart: Reclam Verlag, 1989). They are available in English translation in Sassen, *Kant's Early Critics*, pp. 53–77.

11. See Kurt Röttgers, "J. G. H. Feder – Beitrag zu einer Verhinderungsgeschichte eines deutschen Empirismus," *Kant-Studien* 75 (1984), pp. 420–41. Hamann was not the only one who would agree with Feder. Even today there are philosophical scholars who would argue that Kant's position is not that different from Berkeley's. See R. C. S. Walker, *The Ideal in the Real. Berkeley's Relation to Kant* (New York and London: Garland Publishing, Inc., 1989).

12. See Immanuel Kant, *Prolegomena*, ed. Malter, pp. 200–5 (Beilage 3: "Die Gotha Rezension").

13. Moses Mendelssohn, *Morgenstunden* (1785).

14. Hamann, *Briefwechsel* 4, p. 319 and 336, see also pp. 323, 331.

15. Hamann, *Briefwechsel* 4, pp. 376, 400, 418.

16. See also Kant, *Prolegomena*, ed. Malter, pp. 179–92.

17. Gerold Prauss, *Erscheinung bei Kant* (Berlin: Walter de Gruyter, 1971).

18. Hamann, *Briefwechsel* 5, p. 107.

19. Alexander Gottlieb Baumgarten, *Metaphysik*. Übersetzt von G. F. Meier. Anmerkungen von J. A. Eberhard (Halle, 1783).
20. Baumgarten, *Metaphysik*, p. v. Eberhard put this in a less flattering way later, claiming that whatever was interesting in Kant was already to be found in Leibnizian philosophy and that whatever was not already in Leibnizian philosophy was not worth anything. He published between 1788–92 *Das Philosophische Magazin* and between 1792–95 *Das Philosophische Archiv*. See also Henry E. Allison, *The Kant-Eberhard Controversy* (Baltimore: The Johns Hopkins University Press, 1973).
21. Landau, *Rezensionen*, p. 34.
22. Herder, *Sämtliche Werke* (Cotta, 1830) 3, p. 123; see also Vorländer, *Immanuel Kant*, I, p. 316.
23. The letters are translated in Johann Schultz, *Exposition of Kant's Critique*, ed. James C. Morrison (Ottawa: University of Ottawa Press, 1995), pp. 145–62. Schulz reveals in his Introduction that he read the *Critique* "only last summer."
24. For a more extensive discussion of this, see James C. Morrison, "Introduction," Johann Schultz, *Exposition of Kant's Critique*, pp. xi–xxxi. See also Kant's *Correspondence*, 10:351–3.
25. Hamann followed these developments with great interest and reported them to his friends. See Hamann, *Briefwechsel* 5, pp. 36, 71, 87, 108, 123, 131, 217, 227.
26. Hamann, *Briefwechsel* 5, p. 87.
27. Schultz, *Exposition*, pp. 188–9.
28. Landau, *Rezensionen*, pp. 140–2 and pp. 326–52.
29. Landau, *Rezensionen*, pp. 147–82 and 223–5.
30. Landau, *Rezensionen*, p. 326. The first review also has a very complimentary introduction and then quotes extensively from Schulz's Introduction. The second has a very extensive and interesting discussion of appearance and reality.
31. Kant sent the *Groundwork* to the publisher at the beginning of September 1784, but the book appeared only eight months later in April of 1785.
32. *Philosophische Anmerkungen und Abhandlungen zu Ciceros Büchern von den Pflichten.* This was a translation or adaptation of Cicero's *On Duties*.
33. Hamann, *Briefwechsel* 5, pp. 129f. He also reported: "but the title has not yet been formulated" and then that Kant wanted to send something "on Beauty" to the Berlin *Monatsschrift*. See also his letter to Hartknoch, March 14, 1784 (p. 131).
34. Hamann, *Briefwechsel* 5, pp. 134, 141.

35. The most extensive argument to this effect is to be found in Carlos Melches Gibert, *Der Einfluss Christian Garves Übersetzung Ciceros "De Officiis" auf Kants "Grundlegung zur Metaphysik der Sitten"* (Regensburg: S. Röderer Verlag, 1994). See also Johan van der Zande, "In the Image of Cicero: German Philosophy between Wolff and Kant," *Journal of the History of Ideas* 56 (1995), pp. 419–42. The Kant-Garve relation deserves, however, a more extended treatment.

36. See Klaus Reich, *Kant und die Ethik der Griechen* (Tübingen: J. C. B. Mohr [Paul Siebeck], 1935) (translated by W. H. Walsh as "Kant and Greek Ethics" in *Mind* 48 [1939]). Reich is criticized by Pierre Laberge in his "Du passage de la Philosophie Moral Populaire a la Métaphysique des Moers." *Kant-Studien* 71 (1980), pp. 416–44; comapare also Manfred Kuehn, "Kant and Cicero," *Proceedings of the 9th International Kant Congress in Berlin, April 2000*, ed. Volker Gerhardt, Rolf-Peter Horstmann, and Ralph Schumacher (Berlin/New York: Walter de Gruyter, 2001), pp. 270–8, and Allen Wood in chapter 10, above.

37. Christian Garve, *Eigene Betrachtungen über die allgemeinen Grundsätze der Sittenlehre. Ein Anhang zu der Übersicht der verschiedenen Moralsysteme* (Breslau 1798) p. 265, that is, *Garve's Übersicht der vornehmsten Principien der Sittenlehre von dem Zeitalter des Aristotles an bis auf unsere Zeit* . . . (Breslau, 1798). It was dedicated to Kant and included an extensive (and highly interesting) discussion of Kant's "system" (pp. 183–318).

38. Wasianski, *Immanuel Kant in seinen letzten Lebensjahren* (Königsberg, 1804), p. 245.

39. See Manfred Kuehn, "Einleitung" to Immanuel Kant, *Vorlesungen zur Moralphilosophie*, ed. Werner Stark (Berlin: de Gruyter, 2004), pp. vii–xxxv.

40. Hamann, *Briefwechsel* 5, p. 222; see also p. 238 (October 18, 1784), where he says that "Kant has until now worked hard for the *Berlinische Monatsschriften*."

41. Norbert Hinske, ed., *Was ist Aufklärung: Beiträge Aus Der Berlinischen Monatsschrift*, 4th ed. (Darmstadt: Wissenschaftliche Buchgesellschaft, 1981), p. 115. See also *What is Enlightenment? Eighteenth-Century Answers and Twentieth-Century Questions*, ed. James Schmidt (Berkeley: University of California Press, 1996).

42. Hamann, *Briefwechsel* 5, p. 175.

43. Hamann, *Briefwechsel* 5, p. 347 (February 3, 1785).

44. Hamann, *Briefwechsel* 6, pp. 212–13.

45. See also Hamann, *Briefwechsel* 6, p. 140.

46. See Stark, "Kant and Kraus," p. 179.

47. See Landau, *Rezensionen*, pp. 145–7.

48. Sassen, *Kant's Early Critics*, p. 211.
49. Hamann, *Briefwechsel* 6, p. 349; see also 6, p. 338.
50. The essay *Orientation* is closely related to Kant's "Some Remarks on L. H. Jakob's *Examination of the Mendelssohnian Morning Hours*," which appeared as a Preface to Jakob's book in 1786.
51. I quote this letter more fully because it is not translated in Arnulf Zweig's volume and because it is often taken to say that Reinhold's *Letters* were the only cause of the changed attitude in Germany.
52. Landau, *Rezensionen*, p. 766.

BIBLIOGRAPHY

The literature on Kant, as might be expected from both the range of his work and his centrality in the history of modern philosophy, is enormous. The following bibliography is necessarily selective, focusing on recent books and collections of articles, although including some older works that have attained classical status. An objective and meaningful selection of journal articles that have not been anthologized would be impossible, and articles are therefore excluded. This bibliography aims to be quite inclusive for books in English and to include many of the most important works in German; important works in French have also been included (for which I thank Béatrice Longuenesse), but none in other languages in which some important research on Kant is conducted, including Italian, Spanish, and Portuguese. Books that include especially extensive bibliographies are noted. Further bibliographical information can be found in the bibliographical surveys by Rudolf Malter and Margit Ruffing, which have been published since 1969 in *Kant-Studien*, the official journal of the Kant-Gesellschaft. More recently, bibliographical surveys prepared by Manfred Kuehn and G. Felicitas Munzel have been published in the newsletter of the North American Kant Society, also accessible at **www.naks.ucsd.edu**. An annnotated bibliography on Kant's ethics is *Kantian Ethical Thought: A Curricular Report and Annotated Bibliography* (Tallahassee: Council for Philosophical Studies, 1984). An extraordinary annotated bibliography of 2,832 items on Kant through 1802 (two years before Kant's own death!) edited by Erich Adickes was published in English in *The Philosophical Review* from 1893–96, and reprinted as *German Kant Bibliography* (New York: Burt Franklin, 1970). This is indispensable for studying the early reception of Kant. Many of the important works by Kant's early critics and admirers catalogued in this work were reprinted in the series *Aetas Kantiana* (Brussels: Culture et Civilisation, 1968–73).

The division of the following bibliography reflects the customary broad divisions in discussions of Kant's philosophy. More specialized works on

Kant's philosophy of physical science, politics, and biological science have been listed separately, but some of the more general works in the more general sections are also relevant to these areas. Many works fit even less neatly into these divisions, which are only intended to help the reader get started in further study of Kant.

I. KANT'S WORKS: GERMAN EDITIONS

The standard critical edition of Kant's works, the pagination of which is supplied by most contemporary translations of Kant, including the volumes of the *Cambridge Edition of the Works of Immanuel Kant*, and which is used by most contemporary authors on Kant, especially writers in English (German writers sometimes cite the pagination of Kant's original editions, which is itself given in the following edition), is:

Kant's gesammelte Schriften, edited by the Königlich Preußischen Akademie der Wissenschaften, subsequently the Deutsche and then Berlin-Brandenburg Akademie der Wissenschaften (originally under the general editorship of Wilhelm Dilthey). Twenty-nine volumes (twenty-eight thus far published) in thirty-seven parts. Berlin: Georg Reimer, subsequently Walter de Gruyter, 1900–. The edition is divided into four parts: *Werke* (volumes 1–9), that is, works published by Kant in his lifetime; *Briefe* (volumes 10–13), that is, correspondence; *Handschriftliche Nachlaß* (volumes 14–23), that is, posthumously published material in Kant's own hand, including notes and drafts (new editions of volumes 21 and 22, the *Opus postumum* or drafts for Kant's unfinished final work, are to be published by 2010); and *Vorlesungen* (volumes 24–29), consisting of lectures transcribed by students and copyists, on logic, anthropology, metaphysics and theology, ethics, and philosophical encyclopedia (volume 26, lectures on physical geography, is to be published by 2007). This edition is standardly referred to as the *"Akademie"* edition.

Other twentieth-century editions that are also sometimes cited are:

Ernst Cassirer, editor. *Werke*. Eleven volumes. Berlin: Bruno Cassirer, 1912–22.

Wilhelm Weischedel, editor. *Werke in sechs Bänden*. Wiesbaden: Insel Verlag, 1956–62. Reprinted in twelve volumes but with the original pagination by Suhrkamp Verlag, Frankfurt am Main, 1968. Unlike the *Akademie* edition, this contains German translations of Kant's several Latin works.

Editions of individual works are also published in the *Philosophische Bibliothek* of Felix Meiner Verlag, Hamburg. These include the standard edition of the *Critique of Pure Reason*, which is much easier to use than the unintegrated texts of the first and second editions of the first *Critique* in the

Akademie edition, and valuable new editions, also now preferable to the *Akademie* edition, of the second and third *Critiques*:

Immanuel Kant. *Kritik der reinen Vernunft*. Edited by Raymund Schmidt. Third edition, with a bibliography by Heiner F. Klemme. Hamburg: Felix Meiner Verlag, 1990, now supplanted by a new edition edited by Jens Timmerman, retaining the bibliography by Klemme (1998);

Immanuel Kant. *Kritik der praktischen Vernunft*. Edited by Horst D. Brandt and Heiner F. Klemme, with a bibliography by Heiner F. Klemme. Hamburg: Felix Meiner Verlag, 2003;

Immanuel Kant. *Kritik der Urteilskraft*. Edited with a bibliography by Heiner F. Klemme, with notes by Piero Giordanetti. Hamburg: Felix Meiner Verlag, 2001.

Three other volumes of special note in this series are:

Immanuel Kant. *Briefwechsel*. Edited by Rudolf Malter. Hamburg: Felix Meiner Verlag, 1986 (includes letters not in *Akademie* edition);

Malter, Rudolf, editor. *Immanuel Kant in Rede und Gespräch*. Hamburg: Felix Meiner Verlag, 1990 (supplements Kant's correspondence with passages about him in the correspondence of many contemparies);

Immanuel Kant. *Metaphysische Anfangsgründe der Rechtslehre: Metaphysik der Sitten, Erster Teil*. Edited by Bernd Ludwig. Hamburg: Felix Meiner Verlag, 1986 (proposes a new arrangement of some paragraphs of the previously accepted but corrupt text).

Another valuable edition of the first *Critique*, also including texts of the *Prolegomena* and the drafts for the essay *What is the Real Progress that Metaphysics has made in Germany since the Time of Leibniz and Wolff?* as well as extensive notes and commentary, is:

Immanuel Kant. *Theoretische Philosophie: Texte und Kommentar*. Edited by Georg Mohr. Three volumes. Frankfurt am Main: Suhrkamp Verlag, 2004.

The following volumes in the series *Kant-Forschungen*, begun by Reinhard Brandt, revise or add newly found material to the *Akademie* edition:

Brandt, Reinhard and Werner Stark, eds. *Neue Autographen und Dokumente zu Kants Leben, Schriften, und Vorlesungen*. Kant-Forschungen, Band 1. Hamburg: Felix Meiner Verlag, 1987.

Immanuel Kant. *Bemerkungen in den "Beobachtungen über das Gefühl des Schönen und Erhabenen."* Edited with commentary by Marie Rischmüller. Kant-Forschungen, Band 3. Hamburg: Felix Meiner Verlag, 1991.

Brandt, Reinhard and Werner Stark, eds. *Autographen, Dokumente und Berichte: Zu Edition, Amtsgeschäften und Werk Immanuel Kants*. Kant-Forschungen, Band 5. Hamburg: Felix Meiner Verlag, 1994.

Kowalewski, Sabina Laetitia and Werner Stark, eds. *Königsberge Kantiana* (*Immanuel Kant: Volksausgabe, Band I, ed. Arnold Kowalewski*). Kant-Forschungen, Band 12. Hamburg: Felix Meiner Verlag, 2000.
Another recent addition to Kant's lectures is:
Immanuel Kant. *Vorlesung zur Moralphilosophie*. Edited by Werner Stark, introduction by Manfred Kuehn. Berlin and New York: Walter de Gruyter & Co., 2004. This presents the previously unpublished transcription of Kant's lectures on ethics from 1777, and is more complete than any transcription of Kant's lectures on ethics heretofore published.

II. ENGLISH TRANSLATIONS

(1) The *Cambridge Edition*:
The *Cambridge Edition of the Works of Immanuel Kant*, which began appearing in 1992 under the general editorship of Paul Guyer and Allen W. Wood, provides new or revised translations of all of Kant's published works and extensive selections from his correspondence, posthumous materials, and lectures. The following volumes have been published to date:
Immanuel Kant. *Theoretical Philosophy, 1755–1770*. Edited and translated by David Walford in collaboration with Ralf Meerbote. Cambridge: Cambridge University Press, 1992.
Immanuel Kant. *Critique of Pure Reason*. Edited and translated by Paul Guyer and Allen W. Wood. Cambridge: Cambridge University Press, 1998.
Immanuel Kant. *Theoretical Philosophy after 1781*. Edited by Henry Allison and Peter Heath, translated by Gary Hatfield, Michael Friedman, Henry Allison, and Peter Heath. Cambridge: Cambridge University Press, 2002.
Immanuel Kant. *Practical Philosophy*. Edited and translated by Mary J. Gregor. Cambridge: Cambridge University Press, 1996.
Immanuel Kant. *Critique of the Power of Judgment*. Edited by Paul Guyer, translated by Paul Guyer and Eric Matthews. Cambridge: Cambridge University Press, 2000.
Immanuel Kant. *Religion and Rational Theology*. Edited and translated by Allen W. Wood and George di Giovanni. Cambridge: Cambridge University Press, 1996.
Immanuel Kant. *Lectures on Logic*. Edited and translated by J. Michael Young. Cambridge: Cambridge University Press, 1992.
Immanuel Kant. *Lectures on Metaphysics*. Edited and translated by Karl Ameriks and Steve Naragon. Cambridge: Cambridge University Press, 1997.
Immanuel Kant. *Lectures on Ethics*. Edited by Peter Heath and J. B. Schneewind, translated by Peter Heath. Cambridge: Cambridge University Press, 1997.

Immanuel Kant. *Notes and Fragments*. Edited by Paul Guyer, translated by Curtis Bowman, Paul Guyer, and Frederick Rauscher. Cambridge: Cambridge University Press, 2005.

Immanuel Kant. *Opus postumum*. Edited by Eckart Förster, translated by Eckart Förster and Michael Rosen. Cambridge: Cambridge University Press, 1993.

Immanuel Kant. *Correspondence*. Edited and translated by Arnulf Zweig. Cambridge: Cambridge University Press, 1999.

The remaining volumes in the series will be *Anthropology, History, and Education*, edited by Günter Zöller and Robert Louden; *Natural Science*, edited by Eric Watkins; *Lectures on Anthropology*, edited by Allen W. Wood and Robert Louden; and *Lectures and Drafts on Political Philosophy*, edited by Frederick Rauscher and Kenneth Westphal.

Several of the Cambridge translations have also been separately published in the *Cambridge Texts in the History of Philosophy* series. These include:

Immanuel Kant. *Prolegomena to Any Future Metaphysics, With Selections from the Critique of Pure Reason*. Translated and edited by Gary Hatfield. Revised edition. Cambridge: Cambridge University Press, 2004.

Immanuel Kant. *Metaphysical Foundations of Natural Science*. Edited and translated by Michael Friedman. Cambridge: Cambridge University Press, 2004.

Immanuel Kant. *Groundwork of the Metaphysics of Morals*. Edited and translated by Mary J. Gregor, with an introduction by Christine M. Korsgaard. Cambridge: Cambridge University Press, 1996.

Immanuel Kant. *Critique of Practical Reason*. Edited and translated by Mary J. Gregor, with an introduction by Andrews Reath. Cambridge: Cambridge University Press, 1996.

Immanuel Kant. *Metaphysics of Morals*. Edited and translated by Mary J. Gregor, with an introduction by Roger Sullivan. Cambridge: Cambridge University Press, 1997.

Immanuel Kant. *Religion within the Boundaries of Mere Reason and Other Writings*. Translated and edited by Allen W. Wood and George di Giovanni, with an introduction by Robert Merrihew Adams. Cambridge: Cambridge University Press, 1998.

Immanuel Kant. *Anthropology from a Pragmatic Point of View*. Translated by Robert Louden, with an introduction by Manfred Kuehn. Cambridge: Cambridge University Press, 2005.

(2) Other translations:

The following other translations are also still in use. Volumes of multiple works are listed first, followed by translations of individual works, listed in the chronological order of the originals.

Multiple Works

[Immanuel Kant.] *Kant's Latin Writings: Translations, Commentaries, and Notes*. Translated by Lewis White Beck, Mary J. Gregor, Ralf Meerbote, and John A. Reuscher. New York, Bern, Frankfurt, and Paris: Peter Lang, 1986.

Immanuel Kant. *Selected Pre-Critical Writings and Correspondence with Beck*. Translated by G. B. Kerferd and D. E. Walford, with a contribution by P. G. Lucas. Manchester and New York: Manchester University Press and Barnes & Noble, 1968.

[Immanuel Kant.] *Kant's Critique of Practical Reason and Other Works on the Theory of Ethics*. Translated by Thomas Kingsmill Abbott. Sixth edition. London: Longmans, Green and Co., 1909.

[Immanuel Kant.] *Kant's Critique of Practical Reason and Other Writings in Moral Philosophy*. Translated by Lewis White Beck. Chicago: University of Chicago Press, 1949.

Immanuel Kant. *On History*. Edited by Lewis White Beck, translated by Lewis White Beck, Robert E. Anchor, and Emil Fackenheim. Indianapolis and New York: Bobbs-Merrill, 1963.

Immanuel Kant. *Political Writings*. Edited by Hans Reiss, translated by H. B. Nisbet. Cambridge: Cambridge University Press, 1970.

Immanuel Kant. *Perpetual Peace and Other Essays on Politics, History, and Morals*. Translated by Ted Humphrey. Indianapolis: Hackett Publishing Company, 1983.

Individual Works

Immanuel Kant. *Universal Natural History and Theory of the Heavens*. Translated by W. Hastie, with a new introduction by Milton K. Munitz. Ann Arbor: University of Michigan Press, 1969.

Immanuel Kant. *The One Possible Basis for a Demonstration of the Existence of God*. Translated by Gordon Treash. New York: Abaris Books, 1979.

Immanuel Kant. *Observations on the Feeling of the Beautiful and Sublime*. Translated by John T. Goldthwait. Berkeley and Los Angeles: University of California Press, 1960.

Immanuel Kant. *Lectures on Ethics*. Translated by Louis Infield. London: Methuen & Co., 1930. Reprinted with an introduction by Lewis White Beck New York. Harper & Row, 1963 (now Hackett Publishing Company).

Immanuel Kant. *Critique of Pure Reason*. Translated by Norman Kemp Smith. Second edition. London: Macmillan & Co., 1933.

Immanuel Kant. *Critique of Pure Reason.* Unified edition. Translated by Werner Pluhar, introduction by Patricia Kitcher. Indianapolis and Cambridge: Hackett Publishing Company, 1996.

Immanuel Kant. *Prolegomena to Any Future Metaphysics.* Translated by Lewis White Beck. Indianapolis and New York: Bobbs-Merrill, 1950 (now Macmillan).

Immanuel Kant. *Groundwork for the Metaphysics of Morals.* Translated by Thomas K. Abbott (1873). Edited and revised by Lara Denis (with selections from Kant's other writings in moral philosophy). Peterborough, ON: Broadview Press, 2005.

Immanuel Kant. *The Groundwork of the Metaphysics of Morals* (originally *The Moral Law*). Translated by H. J. Paton. London: Hutchinson, 1948 (now Harper & Row). Reprinted in Immanuel Kant. *Groundwork of the Metaphysics of Morals in Focus* (with interpretative essays). Edited by Lawrence Pasternack. Routledge: London and New York, 2002.

Immanuel Kant. *Foundations of the Metaphysics of Morals and What is Enlightenment?* Translated by Lewis White Beck. Indianapolis and New York: Bobbs-Merrill, 1959 (now Macmillan).

Immanuel Kant. *Groundwork for the Metaphysics of Morals* (with interpretative essays). Edited and translated by Allen W. Wood. New Haven: Yale University Press, 2002.

Immanuel Kant. *Groundwork for the Metaphysics of Morals.* Translated by Arnulf Zweig and edited by Thomas E. Hill, Jr. and Arnulf Zweig. Oxford: Oxford University Press, 2002.

Immanuel Kant. *Metaphysical Foundations of Natural Science.* Translated by James Ellington. Indianapolis and New York: Bobbs-Merrill, 1970. Reprinted, with *Prolegomena*, in *Philosophy of Material Nature*. Indianapolis: Hackett Publishing Company, 1985.

Immanuel Kant. *Critique of Practical Reason.* Translated by Lewis White Beck. Indianpolis and New York: Bobbs-Merrill, 1956.

Immanuel Kant. *Critique of Practical Reason.* Translated by Werner Pluhar, with an introduction by Stephan Engstrom. Cambridge and Indianapolis: Hackett Publishing Company, 2002.

Immanuel Kant. *Kant's Critique of Aesthetic Judgement.* Translated with introduction, notes, and analytical index by James Creed Meredith. Oxford: Clarendon Press, 1911.

Immanuel Kant. *Kant's Critique of Teleological Judgement.* Translated with introduction, notes, and analytic index by James Creed Meredith. Oxford: Clarendon Press, 1928.

Both texts with indices only reprinted as:

Kant's Critique of Judgement. Translated by James Creed Meredith. Oxford: Clarendon Press, 1952.

Immanuel Kant. *First Introduction to the Critique of Judgment.* Translated by James Haden. Indianapolis and New York: Bobbs-Merrill, 1965.

Immanuel Kant. *Critique of Judgment: Including the First Introduction.* Translated by Werner S. Pluhar. Indianapolis: Hackett Publishing Company, 1987.

[Immanuel Kant.] *The Kant-Eberhard Controversy: An English translation together with supplementary materials and a historical-analytical introduction of Immanuel Kant's On a New Discovery According to which Any New Critique of Pure Reason Has Been Made Superfluous by an Earlier One.* Translated by Henry E. Allison. Baltimore: The Johns Hopkins University Press, 1973.

Immanuel Kant. *Religion within the Limits of Reason Alone.* Translated by Theodore M. Greene and Hoyt H. Hudson, with a new essay on "The Ethical Significance of Kant's *Religion*" by John R. Silber. New York: Harper & Row, 1960.

Immanuel Kant. *On the Old Saw: That May Be Right in Theory But It Won't Work in Practice.* Translated by E. B. Ashton. Philadelphia: University of Pennsylvania Press, 1974.

Immanuel Kant. *What Real Progress Has Metaphysics Made in Germany since the Time of Leibniz and Wolff?* Translated by Ted Humphrey. New York: Abaris Books, 1983.

Immanuel Kant. *Perpetual Peace.* Translated by Lewis White Beck. Indianapolis and New York: Bobbs-Merrill, 1957.

Immanuel Kant. *Metaphysical Elements of Justice: The Complete Text of the Metaphysics of Morals Part I.* Translated by John Ladd. Second edition. Indianapolis and Cambridge: Hackett Publishing Company, 1999.

Immanuel Kant. *The Metaphysical Principles of Virtue: Part II of the Metaphysics of Morals.* Translated by James Ellington. Indianapolis and New York: Bobbs-Merrill, 1964. Reprinted, with *Grounding for the Metaphysics of Morals,* in *Ethical Philosophy.* Translated by James Ellington. Second edition. Indianapolis and Cambridge: Hackett Publishing Company, 1995.

Immanuel Kant. *The Doctrine of Virtue.* Translated by Mary J. Gregor. New York: Harper & Row, 1964.

Immanuel Kant. *The Conflict of the Faculties.* Translated by Mary J. Gregor. New York: Abaris Books, 1979.

Immanuel Kant. *Anthropology from a Pragmatic Point of View.* Translated by Mary J. Gregor. The Hague: Martinus Nijhoff, 1974.

Immanuel Kant. *Anthropology from a Pragmatic Point of View.* Translated by Victor Lyle Dowdell. Carbondale: Southern Illinois University Press, 1978.

Immanuel Kant. *Logic.* Translated by Robert Hartmann and Wolfgang Schwarz. Indianapolis and New York: Bobbs-Merrill, 1974.

[Immanuel Kant.] *Kant on Education*. Translated by Annette Churton. London: Kegan Paul, Trench, Trübner, 1899; reprinted Ann Arbor: University of Michigan Press, 1960.

[Immanuel Kant.] *The Educational Theory of Immanuel Kant*. Translated by Edward Franklin Buchner. Philadelphia: J. B. Lippincott Company, 1904.

Immanuel Kant. *Lectures on Philosophical Theology*. Translated by Allen W. Wood and Gertrude M. Clark. Ithaca and London: Cornell University Press, 1978.

Immanuel Kant. *Kant: Philosophical Correspondence 1759–99*. Translated by Arnulf Zweig. Chicago: University of Chicago Press, 1967.

III. BACKGROUND, CONTEXT, AND RECEPTION

Ameriks, Karl. *Kant and the Fate of Autonomy: Problems in the Appropriation of the Critical Philosophy*. Cambridge: Cambridge University Press, 2000.

Beck, Lewis White. *Early German Philosophy: Kant and his Predecessors*. Cambridge, MA: Harvard University Press, 1969.

Beiser, Frederick C. *The Fate of Reason: German Philosophy from Kant to Fichte*. Cambridge, MA: Harvard University Press, 1987 (contains extensive bibliography of primary sources).

_____. *Enlightenment, Revolution, and Romanticism: The Genesis of Modern German Political Thought, 1790–1800*. Cambridge, MA: Harvard University Press, 1992.

_____. *German Idealism: The Struggle against Subjectivism, 1781–1801*. Cambridge, MA: Harvard University Press, 2002.

Buchdahl, Gerd. *Metaphysics and the Philosophy of Science: The Classical Origins Descartes to Kant*. Oxford: Basil Blackwell, 1969.

Cassirer, Ernst. *Freiheit und Form: Studien zur deutschen Geistesgeschichte*. Third edition. Darmstadt: Wissenschaftliche Buchgesellschaft, 1961.

_____. *The Philosophy of the Enlightenment*. Translated by Fritz C. A. Koelln and James P. Pettegrove. Princeton: Princeton University Press, 1951.

Cummins, Phillip D. and Guenter Zoeller, editors. *Minds, Ideas, and Objects: Essays on the Theory of Representation in Modern Philosophy*. North American Kant Society Studies in Philosophy, Volume 2. Atascadero: Ridgeview Publishing Company, 1992.

Easton, Patricia A., editor. *Logic and the Workings of the Mind: The Logic of Ideas and Faculty Psychology in Early Modern Philosophy*. North American Kant Society Studies in Philosophy, Volume 5. Atascadero: Ridgeview Publishing Company, 1997.

Emundts, Dina, editor. *Immanuel Kant und die Berliner Aufklärung.* Wiesbaden: Dr. Ludwig Reichert Verlag, 2000.

Hatfield, Gary. *The Natural and the Normative: Theories of Spatial Perception from Kant to Helmholtz.* Cambridge, MA: MIT Press, 1990.

Hunter, Ian. *Rival Enlightenments: Civil and Metaphysical Philosophy in Early Modern Germany.* Cambridge: Cambridge University Press, 2001.

Ross, George MacDonald and Tony McWalter, editors. *Kant and His Influence.* Bristol: Thoemmes, 1990.

Nelson, Leonard. *Progress and Regress in Philosophy: From Hume and Kant to Hegel and Fries.* Edited by Julius Kraft, translated by Humphrey Palmer. 2 vols. Oxford: Basil Blackwell, 1970–71.

Pinkard, Terry. *German Philosophy 1760–1860: The Legacy of Idealism.* Cambridge: Cambridge University Press, 2002.

Rosenkranz, Karl. *Geschichte der Kant'schen Philosophie.* Leipzig: Leopold Voss, 1840. Reprint edited by Stefan Dietzsch. Berlin: Akademie Verlag, 1987.

Rotenstreich, Nathan. *Reason and its Manifestations: A study on Kant and Hegel.* Stuttgart-Bad Canstatt: Fromman-Holzboog, 1996.

Sassen, Brigitte, editor. *Kant's Early Critics: The Empiricist Critique of the Transcendental Philosophy.* Cambridge: Cambridge University Press, 2000.

Schmidt, James, editor. *What is Enlightenment? Eighteenth-Century Answers and Twentieth-Century Questions.* Berkeley and Los Angeles: University of California Press, 1996.

Sedgwick, Sally S., editor. *The Reception of Kant's Critical Philosophy: Fichte, Schelling, and Hegel.* Cambridge: Cambridge University Press, 2000.

Schneewind, Jerome B. *Moral Philosophy from Montaigne to Kant.* 2 vols. Cambridge: Cambridge University Press, 1990.

———. *The Invention of Autonomy: A History of Modern Moral Philosophy.* Cambridge: Cambridge University Press, 1998.

Vuillemin, Jules. *L'Héritage Kantien et la révolution Copernicienne. Fichte, Cohen, Heidegger.* Paris: Presses Universitaires de France, 1954.

Wundt, Max. *Die deutsche Schulphilosophie im Zeitalter der Aufklärung.* Tübingen: J. C. B. Mohr, 1945.

IV. BIOGRAPHY, GENERAL WORKS, SINGLE- AND MULTIPLE-AUTHOR COLLECTIONS OF ARTICLE ON MULTIPLE ISSUES

Allison, Henry E. *Idealism and Freedom: Essays on Kant's Theoretical and Practical Philosophy.* Cambridge: Cambridge University Press, 1996.

Ameriks, Karl. *Interpreting Kant's Critiques.* Oxford: Clarendon Press, 2003.

Beck, Lewis White. *Studies in the Philosophy of Kant.* Indianapolis: Bobbs-Merrill Company, 1965.

_____. *Essays on Kant and Hume.* New Haven and London: Yale University Press, 1978.

_____. *Selected Essays on Kant.* Edited by Hoke Robinson. North American Kant Society Studies in Philosophy, Volume 6. Rochester: University of Rochester Press, 2002. Selected essays from the previous two volumes.

Beck, Lewis White, editor. *Kant Studies Today.* LaSalle: Open Court, 1967 (includes extensive bibliography).

Böhme, Hartmut and Gernot Böhme. *Das Andere der Vernunft: Zur Entwicklung von Rationalitätsstruckturen am Beispiel Kants.* Frankfurt am Main: Suhrkamp Verlag, 1985.

Buchdahl, Gerd. *Kant and the Dynamics of Reason: Essays on the Structure of Kant's Philosophy.* Oxford: Blackwell, 1992.

Caird, Edward. *The Critical Philosophy of Immanuel Kant.* 2 vols. New York: Macmillan and Co., 1889.

Cassirer, Ernst. *Rousseau, Kant, and Goethe.* Translated by James Gutmann, Paul Oskar Kristeller, and John Herman Randall, Jr. Princeton: Princeton University Press, 1949.

_____. *Kant's Life and Thought.* Translated by James Haden. New Haven and London: Yale University Press, 1981.

Chadwick, Ruth and Clive Cazeaux, editors. *Immanuel Kant: Critical Assessments.* 4 vols. London and New York: Routledge, 1992 (reprints of journal articles).

Cicovaki, Predrag. *Kant's Legacy: Essays in Honor of Lewis White Beck.* Rochester: University of Rochester Press, 2001.

Dancy, R. M., editor. *Kant and Critique: New Essays in Honor of W. H. Werkmeister.* Dordrecht: Kluwer Academic Publishers, 1993.

Delekat, Friedrich. *Immanuel Kant.* Second edition. Heidelberg: Quelle & Meyer, 1966.

De Vleeschauwer, H. J. *La Déduction Transcendentale dans l'oeuvre de Kant.* 3 vols. Antwerp, Paris, and the Hague: De Sikkel, Champion, and Martinus Nijhoff, 1934–37.

_____. *The Development of Kantian Thought: The History of a Doctrine.* Translated by A. R. C. Duncan. London: Thomas Nelson and Sons Ltd., 1962.

Den Ouden, Bernard and Marcia Moen, editors. *New Essays on Kant.* New York, Bern, Frankfurt, and Paris: Peter Lang, 1987.

Fenves, Peter. *Late Kant: Toward Another Law of the Earth.* New York and London: Routledge, 2003.

Ferrini, Cinzia. *Eredità Kantiane (1804–2004): Questioni Emergenti e Probleme Irrisolti*. Naples: Bibliopolis, 2004 (essays in English, German, and Italian).

Findlay, J. N. *Kant and the Transcendental Object: A Hermeneutic Study*. Oxford: Clarendon Press, 1981.

Förster, Eckart, editor. *Kant's Transcendental Deductions: The Three 'Critiques' and the 'Opus postumum.'* Stanford: Stanford University Press, 1989 (multiple-author anthology).

Fulda, Hans-Friedrich and Jürgen Stolzenberg, editors. *Architektonik und System in der Philosophie Kants*. Hamburg: Felix Meiner Verlag, 2001.

Gerhardt, Volker. *Immanuel Kant: Vernunft und Leben*. Stuttgart: Reclam, 2002.

Gerhardt, Volker and Friedrich Kaulbach. *Kant*. Erträge der Forschung, Band 105. Darmstadt: Wissenschaftliche Buchgesellschaft, 1979 (includes extensive bibliography emphasizing older as well as recent German literature).

Glock, Hans-Johann, editor. *Strawson and Kant*. Oxford: Clarendon Press, 2003.

Gram, Moltke S., editor. *Interpreting Kant*. Iowa City: University of Iowa Press, 1982.

Gulyga, Arsenij. *Immanuel Kant: His Life and Thought*. Translated by Marijan Despalatovic. Boston, Basel, Stuttgart: Birkhauser, 1987.

Guyer, Paul. *Kant's System of Nature and Freedom: Selected Essays*. Oxford: Clarendon Press, 2005.

———. *Kant*. London and New York: Routledge, 2006.

———, editor. *The Cambridge Companion to Kant*. Cambridge: Cambridge University Press, 1992.

Haering, Theodor. *Der Duisburg'sche Nachlaß und Kants Kritizismus um 1775*. Tübingen: J. C. B. Mohr, 1910.

Heidmann, Dietmar H. and Kristina Engelhard, editors. *Warum Kant heute? Systematische Bedeutung und Rezeption seiner Philosophie in der Gegenwart*. Berlin and New York: Walter de Gruyter, 2004.

Heimsoeth, Heinz. *Studien zur Philosophie Immanuel Kants*. Kant-Studien Ergänzungsheft 71. Bonn: Bouvier Verlag, 1956.

———. *Studien zur Philosophiegeschichte: Gesammelte Abhandlungen, Band II*. Kant-Studien Ergänzungsheft 82. Bonn: Bouvier Verlag, 1961.

———. *Studien zur Philosophie Immanuel Kants II*. Kant-Studien Ergänzungsheft 100. Bonn: Bouvier Verlag, 1970.

Heimsoeth, Heinz, Dieter Henrich, and Giorgio Tonelli, editors. *Studien zu Kants philosophischer Entwicklung*. Hildesheim: Georg Olms Verlag, 1967.

Heintel, Peter, and Ludwig Nagl, editors. *Zur Kantforschung der Gegenwart.* Darmstadt: Wissenschaftliche Buchgesellschaft, 1981 (contains extensive bibliography).

Henrich, Dieter. *The Unity of Reason: Essays on Kant's Philosophy.* Edited by Richard Velkley. Cambridge, MA: Harvard University Press, 1994.

Hinske, Norbert. *Kants Weg zur Transzendentalphilosophie: Der Dreißigjährige Kant.* Stuttgart: Kohlhammer, 1970.

Höffe, Otfried. *Immanuel Kant.* Translated by Marshall Farrier. Albany: State University of New York Press, 1994.

Horstmann, Rolf-Peter. *Bausteine kritischer Philosophie.* Bodenheim bei Mainz: Philo Verlag, 1997.

Hutter, Axel. *Das Interesse der Vernunft: Kants ursprüngliche Einsicht und ihre Entfaltung in den transzendentalphilosophischen Hauptwerken.* Kant-Forschungen, Band 14. Hamburg: Felix Meiner Verlag, 2004.

Irrlitz, Gerd. *Kant Handbuch: Leben und Werk.* Stuttgart: Verlag J. B. Metzler, 2002.

Kemp, John. *The Philosophy of Kant.* London: Oxford University Press, 1968.

Kennington, Richard, editor. *The Philosophy of Immanuel Kant.* Studies in Philosophy and the History of Philosophy, Volume 12. Washington, D.C.: The Catholic University of America Press, 1985.

Klemme, Heiner F. and Manfred Kuehn, editors. *Immanuel Kant.* 2 vols. Aldershot: Dartmouth/Ashgate, 1999 (selected journal articles).

Kojève, Alexandre. *Kant.* Paris: Gallimard, 1973.

Körner, Stephan. *Kant.* Harmondsworth and Baltimore: Penguin Books, 1955.

Kuehn, Manfred. *Kant: A Biography.* Cambridge: Cambridge University Press, 2001.

Laywine, Alison. *Kant's Early Metaphysics and the Origins of the Critical Philosophy.* North American Kant Society Studies in Philosophy, Volume 3. Atascadero: Ridgeview Publishing Company, 1993.

Lehmann, Gerhard. *Beiträge zur Geschichte und Interpretation der Philosophie Kants.* Berlin: Walter de Gruyter, 1969.

_____. *Kants Tugenden: Neue Beiträge zur Geschichte und Interpretation der Philosophie Kants.* Berlin and New York: Walter de Gruyter, 1980.

Melnick, Arthur. *Themes in Kant's Metaphysics and Ethics.* Studies in Philosophy and the History of Philosophy, Volume 40. Washington, D.C.: Catholic University Press of America, 2004.

Nagl-Docekal, Herta and Rudolf Langthaler, eds. *Recht – Geschichte – Religion: Die Bedeutung Kants für die Philosophie der Gegenwart.* Berlin: Akademie Verlag, 2004.

Neiman, Susan. *The Unity of Reason: Rereading Kant.* New York and Oxford: Oxford University Press, 1994.

Oberer, Hariolf and Gerhard Seel, editors. *Kant: Analysen – Probleme – Kritik.* 3 vols. Würzburg: Königshausen & Neumann, 1988, 1996, 1997.

Piché, Claude. *Kant et ses épigones. Le jugement critique en appel.* Paris: Vrin, 1995.

Prauss, Gerold, editor. *Kant: Zur Deutung seiner Theorie von Erkennen und Handeln.* Colgone: Kiepenheuer & Witsch, 1973.

Reich, Klaus. *Gesammelte Schriften.* Edited by Manfred Baum, Udo Rameil, Klaus Reisinger, and Gertrud Scholz. Hamburg: Felix Meiner Verlag, 2001.

Renaut, Alain. *Kant Aujourd'hui.* Paris: Aubier, 1997.

Rescher, Nicholas. *Kant and the Reach of Reason: Studies in Kant's Theory of Rational Systematization.* Cambridge: Cambridge University Press, 2000.

Riehl, Alois. *Der philosophische kritizismus.* 3 vols. Second edition. Leipzig: W. Engelmann, 1908.

Ritzel, Wolfgang. *Immanuel Kant: Eine Biographie.* Berlin and New York: Walter de Gruyter, 1985.

Rockmore, Tom, editor. *New Essays on the Precritical Kant.* Amherst, NY: Humanity Books, 2001.

Rotenstreich, Nathan. *Experience and Its Systematization: Studies in Kant.* Second edition. The Hague: Martinus Nijhoff, 1972.

Schaper, Eva and Wilhelm Vossenkuhl, editors. *Bedingungen der Möglichkeit: 'Transcendental Arguments' und transzendentales Denken.* Stuttgart: Klett-Cotta Verlag, 1984.

————. *Reading Kant: New Perspectives on Transcendental Arguments and Critical Philosophy.* Oxford: Basil Blackwell, 1989.

Schott, Robin May. *Cognition and Eros: A Critique of the Kantian Paradigm.* Boston: Beacon Press, 1988.

————, editor. *Feminist Interpretations of Immanuel Kant.* University Park: Pennsylvania State University Press, 1997.

Schönecker, Dieter and Thomas Zwenger, editors. *Kant verstehen/ Understanding Kant: Über die Interpretation philosophischer Texte.* Darmstadt: Wissenschaftliche Buchgesellschaft, 2001.

Schönfeld, Martin. *The Young Kant: The Precritical Project.* Oxford: Oxford University Press, 2000.

Schönrich, Gerhard and Yasushi Kato, editors. *Kant in der Diskussion der Moderne.* Frankfurt am Main: Suhrkamp Verlag, 1996.

Shell, Susan Meld. *The Embodiment of Reason: Kant on Spirit, Generation, and Community.* Chicago: University of Chicago Press, 1996.

Simon, Josef. *Kant: Die fremde Vernunft und die Sprache der Philosophie.* Berlin and New York: Walter de Gruyter, 2003.

Stark, Werner. *Nachforschungen zu Briefen und Handschriften Immanuel Kants.* Berlin: Akademie Verlag, 1993.

Vorländer, Karl. *Immanuel Kant: Der Mann und das Werk.* 2 vols. Leipzig: Felix Meiner Verlag, 1924.

———. *Immanuel Kants Leben.* Fourth edition. Edited by Rudolf Malter. Hamburg: Felix Meiner Verlag, 1986.

Walker, Ralph C. S. *Kant.* London, Henley, and Boston: Routledge & Kegan Paul, 1978.

Werkmeister, W. H. *Kant's Silent Decade: A Decade of Philosophical Development.* Tallahassee: University Presses of Florida, 1979.

———. *Kant: The Architectonic and Development of His Philosophy.* LaSalle and London: Open Court Publishing Co., 1980.

Werkmeister, W. H., editor. *Reflections on Kant's Philosophy.* Gainesville: University Presses of Florida, 1975.

Whitney, George Tapley and David F. Bowers, editors. *The Heritage of Kant.* Princeton: Princeton University Press, 1939.

Wolff, Robert Paul, editor. *Kant: A Collection of Critical Essays.* Garden City: Doubleday Anchor, 1967.

Wood, Allen W. *Kant.* Malden and Oxford: Blackwell Publishing, 2005.

Wood, Allen W., editor. *Self and Nature in Kant's Philosophy.* Ithaca and London: Cornell University Press, 1984.

Wundt, Max. *Kant als Metaphysiker: Ein Beitrag zur Geschichte der deutschen Philosophie im 18. Jahrhundert.* Stuttgart: Ferdinand Enke, 1924.

Zeldin, Mary Barbara. *Freedom and the Critical Undertaking: Essays on Kant's Later Critiques.* Ann Arbor: UMI Monographs, 1980.

V. THEORETICAL PHILOSOPHY: GENERAL EPISTEMOLOGY
AND METAPHYSICS

Abela, Paul. *Kant's Empirical Realism.* Oxford: Clarendon Press, 2002.

Adickes, Erich. *Kants Opus postumum.* Berlin: Pan Verlag, 1920.

———. *Kant und das Ding an sich.* Berlin: Pan Verlag, 1924.

———. *Kants Lehre von der doppelten Affektion des Ich als Schlüssel zu seiner Erkenntnistheorie.* Tübingen: J. C. B. Mohr, 1929.

Adorno, Theodor W. *Kant's Critique of Pure Reason.* Edited by Rolf Tiedemann, translated by Rodney Livingstone. Stanford: Stanford University Press, 2001.

Al-Azm, Sadik. *The Origins of Kant's Arguments in the Antinomies.* Oxford: Clarendon Press, 1972.

Allison, Henry E. *Kant's Transcendental Idealism.* New Haven and London: Yale University Press, 1983; revised edition, 2004 (includes extensive bibliography).

Allison, Henry E., editor. *Kant's Critical Philosophy. The Monist* 72 (April, 1989) (special issue multiple-author anthology).

Ameriks, Karl. *Kant's Theory of Mind: An Analysis of the Paralogisms of Pure Reason.* Oxford: Clarendon Press, 1982; new edition, 2000.

Aquila, Richard E. *Representational Mind: A Study of Kant's Theory of Knowledge.* Bloomington: Indiana University Press, 1983.

————. *Matter in Mind: A Study of Kant's Transcendental Deduction.* Bloomington: Indiana University Press, 1989.

Aschenberg, Reinhold. *Sprachanalyse und Transzendentalphilosophie.* Stuttgart: Klett-Cotta Verlag, 1982 (includes extensive bibliography).

Aschenbrenner, Karl. *A Companion to Kant's Critique of Pure Reason: Transcendental Aesthetic and Analytic.* Lanham: University Press of America, 1983.

Baum, Manfred. *Deduktion und Beweis in Kants Transzendentalphilosophie: Untersuchungen zur "Kritik der reinen Vernunft."* Königstein: Athenäum Verlag, 1986.

Bayne, Steven M. *Kant on Causation: On the Fivefold Routes to the Principle of Causation.* Albany: State University Press of New York, 2004.

Beck, Lewis White. *Kant's Theory of Knowledge: Selected Papers from the Third International Kant Congress.* Dordrecht: D. Reidel Publishing Company, 1974.

Becker, Wolfgang. *Selbstbewußtsein und Erfahrung: Zu Kants transzendentaler Deduktion und ihrer argumentativen Rekonstruktion.* Freiburg and Munich: Verlag Karl Albert, 1984.

Bennett, Jonathan. *Kant's Analytic.* Cambridge: Cambridge University Press, 1966.

————. *Kant's Dialectic.* Cambridge: Cambridge University Press, 1974.

Benoist, Jocelyn. *Kant et les Limites de la Synthèse.* Paris: Presses Universitaires de France, 1996.

Bieri, Peter, Rolf-Peter Horstmann, and Lorenz Krüger, editors. *Transcendental Arguments and Science: Essays in Epistemology.* Dordrecht: D. Reidel Publishing Company, 1979 (multiple-author anthology).

Bird, Graham. *Kant's Theory of Knowledge: An Outline of One Central Argument in the Critique of Pure Reason.* London: Routledge & Kegan Paul, 1962.

Böhme, Gernot. *Philosophieren mit Kant: Zur Rekonstruktion der Kantischen Erkenntnis- und Wissenschaftstheorie.* Frankfurt am Main: Suhrkamp Verlag, 1986.

Brandt, Reinhard. *D'Artagnan und die Urteilstafel: Über ein Ordnungsprinzip der Europäischen Kulturgeschichte.* Stuttgart: Franz Steiner Verlag, 1991.

_____. *The Table of Judgments: Critique of Pure Reason A 67–76/B 92–101.* Translated and edited by Eric Watkins. North American Kant Society Studies in Philosophy, Volume 4. Atascadero: Ridgeview Publishing Company, 1995.

Broad. C. D. *Kant: An Introduction.* Edited by C. Levy. Cambridge: Cambridge University Press, 1978.

Brook, Andrew. *Kant and the Mind.* Cambridge: Cambridge University Press, 1994.

Buroker, Jill Vance. *Space and Incongruence: The Origin of Kant's Idealism.* Dordrecht: D. Reidel Publishing Company, 1981.

Butts, Robert E. *Kant and the Double Government Methodology: Supersensibility and Method in Kant's Philosophy of Science.* Dordrecht: D. Reidel Publishing Company, 1984.

Butts, Robert E., editor. *Kant's Critique of Pure Reason, 1781–1981. Synthese* 47, 2 and 3 (1981) (special issues, multiple-author anthology).

Carl, Wolfgang. *Der schweigende Kant: Die Entwürfe zu einer Deduktion der Kategorien vor 1781.* Göttingen: Vandenhoeck & Ruprecht, 1989.

_____. *Die Transzendentale Deduktion der Kategorien in der ersten Auflage der Kritik der reinen Vernunft: Ein Kommentar.* Frankfurt am Main: Vittorio Klostermann, 1992.

Coffa, J. Alberto. *The Semantic Tradition from Kant to Carnap: To the Vienna Station.* Cambridge: Cambridge University Press, 1991.

Cohen, Hermann. *Kants Theorie der Erfahrung.* Second edition. Berlin: Dümmler, 1885.

Collins, Arthur. *Possible Experience: Understanding Kant's Critique of Pure Reason.* Berkeley and Los Angeles: University of California Press, 1999.

Cramer, Konrad. *Nicht-reine synthetische Urteile a priori: Ein Problem der Transzendentalphilosophie Immanuel Kants.* Heidelberg: Carl Winter Universitätsverlag, 1985.

Dicker, Georges. *Kant's Theory of Knowledge: An Analytical Introduction.* New York: Oxford University Press, 2005.

Dickerson, A. B. *Kant on Representation and Objectivity.* Cambridge: Cambridge University Press, 2004.

Dryer, Douglas P. *Kant's Solution for Verification in Metaphysics.* London: George Allen and Unwin, 1966.

Erdmann, Benno. *Kants Kriticismus in der ersten und in der zweiten Auflage der Kritik der reinen Vernunft.* Leipzig: Leopold Voss, 1878.

Ewing, A. C. *Kant's Treatment of Causality.* London: Routledge & Kegan Paul, 1924.

_____. *A Short Commentary on Kant's Critique of Pure Reason.* Chicago: University of Chicago Press, 1938.

Falkenstein, Lorne. *Kant's Intuitionism: A Commentary on the Transcendental Aesthetic.* Toronto: University of Toronto Press, 1995.

Fischer, Kuno. *A Commentary on Kant's Critick of Pure Reason.* Translated by John Pentland Mahaffy. London: Longmans, Green & Co., 1866.

Förster, Eckart. *Kant's Final Synthesis: An Essay on the* Opus postumum. Cambridge, MA: Harvard University Press, 2000.

Forum für Philosophie Bad Hamburg, editors. *Kants transzendentale Deduktion und die Möglichkeit von Transzendentalphilosophie.* Frankfurt am Main: Suhrkamp Verlag, 1988.

———. *Übergang: Untersuchung zum Spätwerk Immanuel Kants.* Frankfurt am Main: Vittorio Klostermann, 1991.

Gardner, Sebastian. *Kant and the Critique of Pure Reason.* London: Routledge, 1998.

Gram, Moltke S. *Kant, Ontology, and the A Priori.* Evanston: Northwestern University Press, 1968.

———. *The Transcendental Turn: The Foundations of Kant's Idealism.* Gainesville and Tampa: University Presses of Florida, 1984.

Gram, Moltke S., editor. *Kant: Disputed Questions.* Chicago: Quadrangle Books, 1967 (multiple-author anthology).

Greenberg, Robert. *Kant's Theory of A Priori Knowledge.* University Park: Pennsylvania State University, 2001.

Grier, Michelle. *Kant's Doctrine of Transcendental Illusion.* Cambridge: Cambridge University Press, 2001.

Grondin, Jean. *Kant et le Problème de la philosophie: l'a priori.* Paris: Vrin, 1989.

Gurwitsch, Aron. *Kants Theorie des Verstandes.* Edited by Thomas M. Seebohm. Dordrecht, Boston, London: Kluwer Academic Publishers, 1990.

Guyer, Paul. *Kant and the Claims of Knowledge.* Cambridge: Cambridge University Press, 1987.

Hahn, Robert. *Kant's Newtonian Revolution in Philosophy.* Carbondale and Edwardsville: Southern Illinois University Press, 1988.

Hanna, Robert. *Kant and the Foundations of Analytic Philosophy.* Oxford: Clarendon Press, 2001.

Harper, William A. and Ralf Meerbote, editors. *Kant on Causality, Freedom, and Objectivity.* Minneapolis: University of Minnesota Press, 1984 (multiple-author anthology).

Heidegger, Martin. *Die Frage nach dem Ding: Zu Kants Lehre von den transzendentalen Grundsätzen.* Tübingen: Max Niemeyer Verlag, 1962.

———. *Kant and the Problem of Metaphysics.* Translated by Richard Taft. Fifth edition, enlarged. Bloomington: Indiana University Press, 1997.

————. *Phenomenological Interpretation of Kant's Critique of Pure Reason*. Translated by Parvis Emad and Kenneth Maly. Bloomington: Indiana University Press, 1997.

Heidemann, Dietmar H. *Kant und das Problem des metaphysischen Idealismus*. Berlin and New York: Walter de Gruyter, 1998.

Heimsoeth, Heinz. *Transzendentale Dialektik: Ein Kommentar zu Kants Kritik der reinen Vernunft*. 4 vols. Berlin and New York: Walter de Gruyter, 1966–71.

Henrich, Dieter. *Identität und Objektivität: Eine Untersuchung über Kants transzendentale Deduktion*. Heidelberg: Carl Winter Universitätsverlag, 1976.

Heßbruggen-Walter, Stefan. *Die Seele und ihre Vermögen: Kants Metaphysik des Mentalen in der "Kritik der reinen Vernunft."* Paderborn: Mentis, 2004.

Hiltscher, Reinhard and Andre Georgi, editors. *Perspektiven der Transzendentalphilosophie im Anschluß an Kant*. Freiburg: Alber, 2002.

Hinsch, Wilfried. *Erfahrung und Selbstbewußtsein: Zur Kategoriendeduktion bei Kant*. Hamburg: Felix Meiner Verlag, 1986.

Hintikka, Jaakko. *Knowledge and the Known: Historical Perspectives in Epistemology*. Dordrecht: D. Reidel Publishing Company, 1974.

Höffe, Otfried. *Kants Kritik der reinen Vernunft: Die Grundlegung der modernen Philosophie*. Munich: C. H. Beck, 2003.

Hogrebe, Wolfgang. *Kant und das Problem einer transzendentalen Semantik*. Freiburg: Karl Alber Verlag, 1974.

Holzhey, Helmut. *Kants Erfahrungsbegriff*. Basel: Schwabe, 1970.

Hossenfelder, Malte. *Kants Konstitutionstheorie und die Transzendentale Deduktion*. Berlin and New York: Walter de Gruyter, 1978.

Howell, Robert. *Kant's Transcendental Deduction: An Analysis of Main Themes in His Critical Philosophy*. Dordrecht: Kluwer Academic Publishers, 1992.

Kaulbach, Friedrich. *Die Metaphysik des Raumes bei Leibniz und Kant*. Kant-Studien Ergänzungsheft 79. Bonn: Bouvier Verlag, 1960.

Keller, Pierre. *Kant and the Demands of Self-Consciousness*. Cambridge: Cambridge University Press, 2001.

Kemp Smith, Norman. *A Commentary to Kant's 'Critique of Pure Reason.'* Second edition. London: Macmillan & Co., 1923.

Kitcher, Patricia. *Kant's Transcendental Psychology*. New York: Oxford University Press, 1990.

Kitcher, Patricia, editor. *Kant's Critique of Pure Reason: Critical Essays*. Lanham: Rowman & Littlefield, 1998.

Klemme, Heiner F. *Kants Philosophie des Subjekts: Systematische und entwicklungsgeschichtliche Untersuchungen zum Verhältnis von*

Selbstbewußtsein und Selbsterkenntnis. Kant-Forschungen, Band 7. Hamburg: Felix Meiner Verlag, 1996.

Kopper, Joachim and Rudolf Malter. *Materialen zu Kants "Kritik der reinen Vernunft."* Frankfurt am Main: Suhramp Verlag, 1975.

Kreimendahl, Lothar. *Kant – der Durchbruch von 1769.* Köln: Dinter, 1990.

Langton, Rae. *Kantian Humility: Our Ignorance of Things in Themselves.* Oxford: Clarendon Press, 1998.

Longuenesse, Béatrice. *Kant and the Capacity to Judge.* Princeton: Princeton University Press, 1998.

_____. *Kant on the Human Standpoint.* Cambridge: Cambridge University Press, 2005.

Malzkorn, Wolfgang. *Kants Kosmologie-Kritik: Eine formale Analyse der Antinomielehre.* Kant-Studien Ergänzungsheft 134. Berlin and New York: Walter de Gruyter, 1999.

Marc-Wogau, Konrad. *Untersuchungen zur Raumlehre Kants.* Lund: Håkan Ohlssons Buchdruckerei, 1932.

Martin, Gottfried. *Kant's Metaphysics and Theory of Science.* Translated by P. G. Lucas. Manchester: Manchester University Press, 1955.

Mathieu, Vittorio. *Kants Opus postumum.* Edited by Gerd Held. Frankfurt am Main: Vittorio Klostermann, 1989.

Melnick, Arthur. *Kant's Analogies of Experience.* Chicago: University of Chicago Press, 1973.

_____. *Space, Time, and Thought in Kant.* Dordrecht: Kluwer Academic Publishers, 1989.

Meyer, Michel. *Science et Métaphysique chez Kant.* Paris: Presses Universitaires de France, 1988.

Mohanty, J. N. and Robert W. Shahan, editors. *Essays on Kant's Critique of Pure Reason.* Norman: University of Oklahoma Press, 1982 (multiple-author anthology).

Mohr, Georg and Marcus Willaschek, editors *Immanuel Kant: Kritik der reinen Vernunft.* Berlin: Akademie Verlag, 1998.

Nagel, Gordon. *The Structure of Experience: Kant's System of Principles.* Chicago: University of Chicago Press, 1983.

Natterer, Paul. *Systematischer Kommentar zur Kritik der reinen Vernunft: Interdisziplinäre Bilanz der Kantforschung seit 1945.* Kant-Studien Ergänzungsheft 141. Berlin and New York: Walter de Gruyter, 2003 (includes extensive bibliography).

Niquet, Marcel. *Transzendentale Argumente: Kant, Strawson und die sinnkritische Aporetik der Detranszendentalisierung.* Frankfurt am Main: Suhrkamp Verlag, 1991.

Parrini, Paolo, editor. *Kant and Contemporary Epistemology.* Dordrecht: Kluwer Academic Publishers, 1994.

Paton, H. J. *Kant's Metaphysics of Experience: A Commentary on the First Half of the Kritik der reinen Vernunft.* 2 vols. London: George Allen and Unwin, 1936.

Pippin, Robert B. *Kant's Theory of Form: An Essay on the Critique of Pure Reason.* New Haven and London: Yale University Press, 1982 (contains extensive bibliography).

Polonoff, Irving. *Force, Cosmos, Monads and Other Themes of Kant's Early Thought.* Kant-Studien Ergänzungsheft 107. Bonn: Bouvier Verlag, 1973.

Powell, C. Thomas. *Kant's Theory of Self-Consciousness.* Oxford: Oxford University Press, 1990.

Prauss, Gerold. *Erscheinung bei Kant: Ein Problem der "Kritik der reinen Vernunft."* Berlin: Walter de Gruyter, 1971.

―――. *Kant und das Problem der Dinge an sich.* Bonn: Bouvier Verlag, 1974.

Prichard, H. A. *Kant's Theory of Knowledge.* Oxford: Clarendon Press, 1909.

Proust, Joëlle. *Questions of Form: Logic and the Analytic Proposition from Kant to Carnap.* Translated by Anastasios Albert Brenner. Minneapolis: University of Minnesota Press, 1989.

Puech, Michel. *Kant et la Causalité: Etude sur la formation du système critique.* Paris: Vrin, 1990.

Reich, Klaus. *The Completeness of Kant's Table of Categories.* Translated by Jane Kneller and Michael Losonsky. Stanford: Stanford University Press, 1992 (German original reprinted in Reich, *Gesammelte Schriften*).

Robinson, Hoke, editor. *The Spindel Conference 1986: The B-Deduction. The Southern Journal of Philosophy* 25, Supplement (1987) (special issue multiple-author anthology).

Roussett, Bernard. *La Doctrine kantienne de l'objectivité.* Paris: J. Vrin, 1967.

Sacks, Mark. *Objectivity and Insight.* Oxford: Clarendon Press, 2000.

Savile, Anthony. *Kant's Critique of Pure Reason: An Orientation to the Central Theme.* Oxford: Blackwell Publishing, 2005.

Schaper, Eva and Wilhelm Vossenkuhl, editors. *Reading Kant: New Perspectives on Transcendental Arguments and Critical Philosophy.* Oxford: Basil Blackwell, 1989 (multiple-author anthology; includes extensive bibliography).

Schneeberger, Guido. *Kants Theorie der Modalbegriffe.* Basel: Schwabe, 1952.

Schultz, Johann. *Exposition of Kant's Critique of Pure Reason* (1784). Translated by James C. Morrison. Ottowa: University of Ottowa Press, 1995.

Schwyzer, Hubert. *The Unity of Understanding: A Study in Kantian Problems.* Oxford: Clarendon Press, 1990.

Sellars, Wilfrid. *Science and Metaphysics: Variations on Kantian Themes.* London: Routledge & Kegan Paul, 1968.

[Sellars, Wilfrid.] *Kant and Pre-Kantian Themes: Lectures by Wilfrid Sellars.* Edited by Pedro Amaral. Atascadero: Ridgeview Publishing Company, 2002.

[Sellars, Wilfrid.] *Kant's Transcendental Metaphysics: Sellars' Cassirer Lecture Notes and Other Essays.* Edited by Jeffrey F. Sicha. Ridgeview: Atascadero Publishing Company, 2002.

Smith, A. H. *A Treatise on Knowledge.* Oxford: Clarendon Press, 1943.

———. *Kantian Studies.* Oxford: Clarendon Press, 1947.

Smyth, Richard. *Forms of Intuition.* The Hague: Martinus Nijhoff, 1978.

Srzednicki, Jan T. *The Place of Space and Other Themes.* The Hague: Martinus Nijhoff, 1983.

Stern, Robert, editor. *Transcendental Arguments: Problems and Prospects.* Oxford: Clarendon Press, 1999.

Strawson, P. F. *The Bounds of Sense: An Essay on Kant's Critique of Pure Reason.* London: Methuen & Co., 1966.

———. *Entity and Identity and Other Essays.* Oxford: Clarendon Press, 1997.

Stuhlmann-Laeisz, Rainer. *Kants Logik: Eine Interpretation auf der Grundlage von Vorlesungen, veröffentlichten Werken und Nachlaß.* Berlin and New York: Walter de Gruyter, 1976.

Sturma, Dieter. *Kant über Selbstbewußtsein: Zum Zusammenhang von Erkenntniskritik und Theorie des Selbstbewußtseins.* Hildesheim: Georg Olms Verlag, 1985.

Thöle, Bernhard. *Kant und das Problem der Gesetzmäßigket der Natur.* Berlin and New York: Walter de Gruyter, 1991.

Tonelli, Giorgio. *Kant's Critique of Pure Reason within the Tradition of Modern Logic.* Edited by David H. Chandler. Hildesheim: Georg Olms Verlag, 1994.

Tuschling, Burkhard, editor, *Probleme der "Kritik der reinen Vernunft": Kant-Tagung Marburg 1981.* Berlin and New York: Walter de Gruyter, 1984 (multiple-author anthology).

Vaihinger, Hans. *Commentar zu Kants Kritik der reinen Vernunft.* 2 vols. Stuttgart: W. Spemann and Union Deutsche Verlagsgesellschaft, 1881–92.

Van Cleve, James. *Problems from Kant.* Oxford: Oxford University Press, 1999.

Walker, Ralph C. S. *The Coherence Theory of Truth: Realism, Anti-Realism, Idealism.* London and New York: Routledge, 1989.

Walker, Ralph C. S., editor. *Kant on Pure Reason.* Oxford: Oxford University Press, 1982 (multiple-author anthology).

Walsh, W. H. *Kant's Criticism of Metaphysics.* Edinburgh: Edinburgh University Press, 1975.

Watkins, Eric. *Kant and the Metaphysics of Causality*. Cambridge: Cambridge University Press, 2005.

Waxman, Wayne. *Kant's Model of the Mind: A New Interpretation of Transcendental Idealism*. New York and Oxford: Oxford University Press, 1991.

———. *Kant and the Empiricists: Understanding Understanding*. New York: Oxford University Press, 2005.

Weldon, T. D. *Kant's Critique of Pure Reason*. Second edition. Oxford: Clarendon Press, 1958.

Westphal, Kenneth. *Kant's Transcendental Proof of Realism*. Cambridge: Cambridge University Press, 2005.

Wike, Victoria S. *Kant's Antinomies of Reason: Their Origin and Resolution*. Washington, D.C.: University Press of America, 1982.

Wilkerson, T. E. *Kant's Critique of Pure Reason: A Commentary for Students*. Oxford: Clarnedon Press, 1976.

Winterbourne, A. T. *The Ideal and the Real: An Outline of Kant's Theory of Space, Time, and Mathematical Construction*. Dordrecht: Kluwer Academic Publishers, 1988.

Wolff, Michael. *Der Begriff des Widerspruches: Eine Studie zur Dialektik Kants und Hegels*. Meisenheim: Verlag Anton Hain, 1981.

———. *Die Vollständigkeit der kantischen Urteilstafel*. Frankfurt am Main: Vittorio Klostermann, 1995.

Wolff, Robert Paul. *Kant's Theory of Mental Activity: A Commentary on the Transcendental Analytic of the Critique of Pure Reason*. Cambridge, MA: Harvard University Press, 1963.

Zöller, Günter. *Theoretische Gegenstandsbeziehung bei Kant: Zur systematischen Bedeutung der Termini "objektive Realität" und "objektive Gültigkeit" in der "Kritik der reinen Vernunft."* Berlin: Walter de Gruyter, 1984.

VI. THEORETICAL PHILOSOPHY: PHILOSOPHY OF MATHEMATICS
AND PHYSICAL SCIENCE

Adickes, Erich. *Kants Opus postumum dargestellt und beurteilt*. Kant-Studien Ergänzungsheft 50. Berlin: Reuter und Reichard, 1930.

———. *Kant als Naturforscher*. 2 vols. Berlin: Walter de Gruyter, 1924.

Brittan, Gordon G., Jr. *Kant's Theory of Science*. Princeton: Princeton University Press, 1978.

Butts, Robert E., editor. *Kant's Philosophy of Physical Science: Metaphysische Anfangsgründe der Naturwissenschaft 1786–1986*. Dordrecht: D. Reidel Publishing Company, 1986 (multiple-author anthology).

Edwards, Jeffrey. *Substance, Force, and the Possibility of Knowledge: On Kant's Philosophy of Material Nature.* Berkeley and Los Angeles: University of California Press, 2000.

Emundts, Dina. *Kants Übergangskonzeption im Opus postumum.* Berlin and New York: Walter de Gruyter, 2004.

Enskat, Rainer. *Kants Theorie des geometrischen Gegenstandes.* Berlin and New York: Walter de Gruyter, 1978.

Falkenburg, Brigitte. *Die Form der Materie: Zur Metaphysik der Natur bei Kant und Hegel.* Frankfurt am Main: Athenäum, 1987.

_____. *Kants Kosmologie: Die wissenschaftliche Revolution der Naturphilosophie im 18. Jahrhundert.* Frankfurt am Main: Vittorio Klostermann, 2000.

Friedman, Michael. *Kant and the Exact Sciences.* Cambridge, MA: Harvard University Press, 1992.

Gloy, Karen. *Die Kantische Theorie der Naturwissenschaft: Ein Strukturanalyse ihrer Möglichkeit, ihres Umfanges und ihrer Grenzen.* Berlin and New York: Walter de Gruyter, 1976.

Holden, Thomas. *The Architecture of Matter: Galileo to Kant.* Oxford: Clarendon Press, 2004.

Hoppe, Hansgeorg. *Kants Theorie der Physik.* Frankfurt am Main: Vittorio Klostermann, 1969.

Koriako, Darius. *Kant's Philosophie der Mathematik: Grundlagen – Voraussetzungen – Probleme.* Kant-Forschungen, Band 11. Hamburg: Felix Meiner Verlag, 1999.

Martin, Gottfried. *Arithmetik und Kombinatorik bei Kant.* Berlin and New York: Walter de Gruyter, 1972.

Mudroch, Vilem. *Kants Theorie der physikalischen Gesetze.* Berlin and New York: Walter de Gruyter, 1987.

Parsons, Charles. *Mathematics in Philosophy: Selected Essays.* Ithaca: Cornell University Press, 1983.

Plaass, Peter. *Kant's Theory of Natural Science.* Translation, analytic introduction, and commentary by Alfred E. and Maria G. Miller, with an introductory essay by Carl Friedrich von Weizsäcker. Dordrecht: Kluwer Academic Publishers, 1994.

Pollok, Konstantin. *Kants Metaphysische Anfangsgründe der Naturwissenschaft: Ein kritischer Kommentar.* Kant-Forschungen, Band 13. Hamburg: Felix Meiner Verlag, 2001.

Posy, Carl J., editor. *Kant's Philosophy of Mathematics: Modern Essays.* Dordrecht: Kluwer Academic Publishers, 1992.

Schäfer, Lothar. *Kants Metaphysik der Natur.* Berlin: Walter de Gruyter, 1966.

Shabel, Lisa A. *Mathematics in Kant's Critical Philosophy: Reflections on Mathematical Practice.* New York and London: Routledge, 2003.

Tuschling, Burkhard. *Metaphysische und transzendentale Dynamik in Kants opus postumum.* Berlin and New York: Walter de Gruyter, 1971.

Van Cleve, James and Robert E. Frederick, editors. *The Philosophy of Right and Left.* Dordrecht: Kluwer Academic Publishers, 1991.

Vuillemin, Jules. *Physique et métaphysique kantiennes.* Paris: Presses Universitaires de France, 1955.

Warren, Daniel. *Reality and Impenetrability in Kant's Philosophy of Nature.* New York and London: Routledge, 2001.

Washkies, Hans-Joachim. *Physik und Physikotheologie des jungen Kant. Die Vorgeschichte seiner Allgemeinen Naturgeschichte und Theorie des Himmels.* Amsterdam: John Benjamins, 1987.

Watkins, Eric, editor. *Kant and the Sciences.* Oxford: Oxford University Press, 2001.

Wolff-Metternich, Briggita-Sophie von. *Die Überwindung des mathematischen Erkenntnisideals: Kants Grenzbestimmung von Mathematik und Philosophie.* Berlin and New York: Walter de Gruyter, 1995.

VII. PRACTICAL PHILOSOPHY: MORAL THEORY

Acton, H. B. *Kant's Moral Philosophy.* London: Macmillan & Co., 1970.

Albrecht, Michael. *Kants Antinomie der praktischen Vernunft.* Hildesheim: Georg Olms Verlag, 1978.

Allison, Henry E. *Kant's Theory of Freedom.* Cambridge: Cambridge University Press, 1990.

Allison, Henry E., editor. *Kant's Practical Philosophy. The Monist* 72 (July, 1989) (special issue multiple-author anthology).

Ameriks, Karl and Dieter Sturma, eds. *Kants Ethik.* Paderborn: Mentis, 2004.

Anderson-Gold, Sharon. *Unnecessary Evil: History and Moral Progress in the Philosophy of Immanuel Kant.* Albany: State University of New York Press, 2001.

Atwell, John E. *Ends and Principles in Kant's Moral Thought.* Dordrecht: Martinus Nijhoff, 1986.

Aune, Bruce. *Kant's Theory of Morals.* Princeton: Princeton University Press, 1979.

Auxter, Thomas. *Kant's Moral Teleology.* Macon: Mercer University Press, 1982.

Baron, Marcia W. *Kantian Ethics Almost Without Apology.* Ithaca, NY and London: Cornell University Press, 1995.

Baron, Marcia W., Philip Pettit, and Michael Slote. *Three Methods of Ethics.* Malden and Oxford: Blackwell Publishers, 1997.

Baumanns, Peter. *Kants Ethik: Die Grundlehre.* Würzburg: Königshausen und Neumann, 2000.

Baumgarten, Hans-Ulrich and Carsten Held, editors. *Systematische Ethik mit Kant.* Freiburg: Verlag Karl Alber, 2001.

Beck, Lewis White. *A Commentary on Kant's Critique of Practical Reason.* Chicago: University of Chicago Press, 1960.

Bielefeldt, Heiner. *Symbolic Representation in Kant's Practical Philosophy.* Cambridge: Cambridge University Press, 2003.

Bittner, Rüdiger. *What Reason Demands.* Translated by Theodore Talbot. Cambridge: Cambridge University Press, 1989.

Bittner, Rüdiger and Konrad Cramer, editors. *Materialien zu Kants 'Kritik der praktischen Vernunft.'* Frankfurt am Main: Suhrkamp Verlag, 1975 (selections from Kant's *Nachlaß* and early responses to Kant; includes extensive bibliography).

Böckerstette, Heinrich. *Aporien der Freiheit und ihre Aufklärung durch Kant.* Stuttgart and Bad Canstatt: Frommann-Holzboog, 1982.

Brender, Natalie and Larry Krasnoff, editors. *New Essays on the History of Autonomy: A Collection Honoring J. B. Schneewind.* Cambridge: Cambridge University Press, 2004.

Broad, C. D. *Five Types of Ethical Theory.* London: Routledge & Kegan Paul, 1930.

Carnois, Bernard. *The Coherence of Kant's Doctrine of Freedom.* Translated by David Booth. Chicago: Chicago University Press, 1987.

Cohen, Hermann. *Kants Begründung der Ethik nebst ihrer Anwendung auf Recht, Religion und Geschichte.* Second edition. Berlin: B. Cassirer, 1910.

Cohen-Halimi, Michèle, editor. *Kant: la Rationalité pratique.* Paris: Presses Universitaires de France, 2004.

Cox, J. Gray. *The Will at the Crossroads: A Reconstruction of Kant's Moral Philosophy.* Washington, DC: University Press of America, 1984.

Cummiskey, David. *Kantian Consequentialism.* New York and London: Oxford University Press, 1996.

Denis, Lara. *Moral Self-Regard: Duties to Oneself in Kant's Moral Theory.* New York and London: Routledge, 2001.

Duncan, A. R. C. *Practical Reason and Morality.* London: Thomas Nelson and Sons, 1957.

Engstrom, Stephen and Jennifer Whiting, editors. *Aristotle, Kant, and the Stoics: Rethinking Happiness and Duty.* Cambridge: Cambridge University Press, 1996.

Esser, Andrea Marlen. *Eine Ethik für Endliche: Kants Tugendlehre in der Gegenwart.* Stuttgart: Frommann-Holzboog, 2004.

Forschner, Maximilian. *Gesetz und Freiheit: Zum Problem der Autonomie bei I. Kant.* Munich and Salzburg: Verlag Anton Pustet, 1974.

Frierson, Patrick R. *Freedom and Anthropology in Kant's Moral Philosophy.* Cambridge: Cambridge University Press, 2003.

Gregor, Mary. *Laws of Freedom: A Study of Kant's Method of Applying the Categorical Imperative in the Metaphysik der Sitten.* Oxford: Basil Blackwell, 1963.

Guevara, Daniel. *Kant's Theory of Moral Motivation.* Boulder, CO: Westview Press, 2000.

Guyer, Paul. *Kant on Freedom, Law, and Happiness.* Cambridge: Cambridge University Press, 2000.

Guyer, Paul, editor. *Kant's Groundwork of the Metaphysics of Morals: Critical Essays.* Lanham, MD: Rowman & Littlefield, 1998 (includes extensive bibliography).

Hare, John E. *The Moral Gap: Kantian Ethics, Human Limits, and God's Assistance.* Oxford: Oxford University Press, 1996.

Herman, Barbara. *The Practice of Moral Judgment.* Cambridge, MA: Harvard University Press, 1993.

Hill, Thomas E., Jr. *Dignity and Practical Reason in Kant's Moral Theory.* Ithaca, NY, and London: Cornell University Press, 1992.

_____. *Human Welfare and Moral Worth: Kantian Perspectives.* Oxford: Clarendon Press, 2002.

_____. *Respect, Pluralism, and Justice: Kantian Perspectives.* Oxford: Oxford University Press, 2000.

Himmelmann, Beatrix. *Kants Begriff des Glücks.* Kant-Studien Ergänzungsheft 142. Berlin and New York: Walter de Gruyter, 2003.

Höffe, Otfried. *Ethik und Politik: Grundmodelle und -probleme der praktischen Philosophie.* Frankfurt am Main: Suhrkamp Verlag, 1978.

_____. *Categorical Principles of Law: A Counterpoint to Modernity.* Translated by Mark Migotti. University Park: Pennsylvania State University Press, 2002.

Höffe, Otfried, editor. *Grundlegung der Metaphysik der Sitten: Ein kooperativer Kommentar.* Frankfurt am Main: Vittorio Klostermann, 1989.

Höffe, Otfried, editor. *Immanuel Kant: Kritik der praktischen Vernunft.* Berlin: Akademie Verlag, 2002 (multiple-author commentary).

Hudson, Hud. *Kant's Compatibilism.* Ithaca, NY, and London: Cornell University Press, 1994.

Hutchings, Patrick Æ. *Kant on Absolute Value: A Critical Examination of Certain Key Notions in Kant's Groundwork of the Metaphysics of Morals and of His Ontology of Personal Values.* London: George Allen & Unwin, 1972.

Jones, Hardy E. *Kant's Principle of Personality.* Madison: University of Wisconsin Press, 1971.

Jones, W. T. *Morality and Freedom in the Philosophy of Kant.* Oxford: Oxford University Press, 1940.

Kaulbach, Friedrich. *Immanuel Kants "Grundlegung zur Metaphysik der Sitten": Interpretation und Kommentar.* Darmstadt: Wissenschaftliche Buchgesellschaft, 1988.

Kerstein, Samuel J. *Kant's Search for the Supreme Principle of Morality.* Cambridge: Cambridge University Press, 2002.

Köhl, Harald. *Kants Gesinnungsethik.* Berlin and New York: Walter de Gruyter, 1990.

König, Peter. *Autonomie und Autokratie: Über Kants Metaphysik der Sitten.* Berlin and New York: Walter de Gruyter, 1994.

Korsgaard, Christine M. *Creating the Kingdom of Ends.* Cambridge: Cambridge University Press, 1996.

———. *The Sources of Normativity.* With G. A. Cohen, Raymond Geuss, Thomas Nagel, and Bernard Williams. Edited by Onora O'Neill. Cambridge: Cambridge University Press, 1996.

Krüger, Gerhard. *Philosophie und Moral in der Kantischen Kritik.* Tübingen: J. C. B. Mohr, 1931.

Lo, P. C. *Treating Persons as Ends: An Essay on Kant's Moral Philosophy.* Lanham, MD: University Press of America, 1987.

Louden, Robert B. *Kant's Impure Ethics: From Rational Beings to Human Beings.* New York and Oxford: Oxford University Press, 2000.

Moore, A[drian] W. *Noble in Reason, Infinite in Faculty: Themes and Variations in Kant's Moral and Religious Philosophy.* London and New York: Routledge, 2003.

Mulholland, Leslie A. *Kant's System of Rights.* New York: Columbia University Press, 1990.

Munzel, G. Felicitas. *Kant's Conception of Moral Character: The "Critical Link" of Morality, Anthropology, and Reflective Judgment.* Chicago: University of Chicago Press, 1999.

Nell, Onora (O'Neill). *Acting on Principle: An Essay on Kantian Ethics.* New York: Columbia University Press, 1975.

Nelson, Leonard. *Die kritische Ethik bei Kant, Schiller, und Fries: Eine Revision ihrer Prinzipien.* Göttingen: Vandenhoeck & Ruprecht, 1914.

Nisters, Thomas. *Kants Kategorischer Imperativ als Leitfaden humaner Praxis.* Freiburg: Verlag Karl Albers, 1989.

O'Neill, Onora. *Constructions of Reason: Explorations of Kant's Practical Philosophy.* Cambridge: Cambridge University Press, 1990.

———. *Bounds of Justice.* Cambridge: Cambridge University Press, 2000.

Paton, H. J. *The Categorical Imperative: A Study in Kant's Moral Philosophy.* London: Hutchinson, 1947.

Potter, Nelson T. and Mark Timmons. *Morality and Universality: Essays on Ethical Universalizability.* Dordrecht: D. Reidel Publishing Company, 1985 (multiple-author anthology).

Prauss, Gerold. *Kant über Freiheit als Autonomie.* Frankfurt am Main: Vittorio Klostermann, 1983.

Rawls, John. *Collected Papers.* Edited by Samuel Freeman. Cambridge, MA: Harvard University Press, 1999. "Kantian Constructivism in Moral Theory." Pp. 303–58.

_____. *Lectures on the History of Moral Philosophy.* Edited by Barbara Herman. Cambridge, MA: Harvard University Press, 2000.

Reath, Andrews, Barbara Herman, and Christine M. Korsgaard, editors. *Reclaiming the History of Ethics: Essays for John Rawls.* Cambridge: Cambridge University Press, 1997.

Reiner, Hans. *Duty and Inclination: The Fundamentals of Morality Discussed and Redefined with Special Regard to Kant and Schiller.* Translated by Mark Santos. The Hague: Martinus Nijhoff, 1983.

Ross, Sir David. *Kant's Ethical Theory: A Commentary on the Groundwork of the Metaphysics of Morals.* Oxford: Clarendon Press, 1954.

Rossvaer, Viggo. *Kant's Moral Philosophy: An Interpretation of the Categorical Imperative.* Oslo, Bergen, and Tromso: Universitetsforlaget, 1979.

Sala, Giovanni B. *Kants "Kritik der praktischen Vernunft": Ein Kommentar.* Darmstadt: Wissenschaftliche Buchgesellschaft, 2004.

Schilpp, Paul Arthur. *Kant's Pre-Critical Ethics.* Second edition. Evanston: Northwestern University Press, 1960.

Schmucker, Josef. *Die Ursprünge der Ethik Kants in seinen vorkritischen Schriften und Reflexionen.* Meisenheim: Verlag Anton Hain, 1961.

Schnoor, Christian. *Kants Kategorischer Imperativ als Kriterium der Richtigkeit des Handelns.* Tübingen: J. C. B. Mohr (Paul Siebeck): 1989.

Schönecker, Dieter. *Kant: Grundlegung III: Die Deduktion des kategorischen Imperativs.* Freiburg: Verlag Karl Alber, 1999.

Schwaiger, Clemens. *Kategorische und andere Imperative: Zur Entwicklung von Kants praktischer Philosophie bis 1785.* Stuttgart: Frommann-Holzboog, 1999.

Schwemmer, Oswald. *Philosophie der Praxis. Versuch zur Grundlegung einer Lehre vom moralischen Argumentieren in Verbindung mit einer Interpretation der praktischen Philosophie Kants.* Frankfurt am Main: Suhrkamp Verlag, 1971.

Seidler, Victor J. *Kant, Respect and Injustice: The Limits of Liberal Moral Theory.* London, Boston, and Henley: Routledge & Kegan Paul, 1986.

Sherman, Nancy. *Making a Necessity of Virtue: Aristotle and Kant on Virtue.* Cambridge: Cambridge University Press, 1997.

Singer, Marcus G. *Generalization in Ethics.* New York: Alfred A. Knopf, 1961.

Stevens, Rex P. *Kant on Moral Practice.* Macon: Mercer University Press, 1981.

Seung, T. K. *Kant's Platonic Revolution in Moral and Political Philosophy.* Baltimore: Johns Hopkins University Press, 1994.

Stratton-Lake, Philip. *Kant, Duty and Moral Worth.* London and New York, 2000.

Sullivan, Roger J. *Immanuel Kant's Moral Theory.* Cambridge: Cambridge University Press, 1989 (includes extensive bibliography).

———. *An Introduction to Kant's Ethics.* Cambridge: Cambridge University Press, 1994.

Sussmann, David G. *The Idea of Humanity: Anthropology and Anthroponomy in Kant's Ethics.* New York and London: Routledge, 2001.

Timmerman, Jens. *Sittengesetz und Freiheit: Untersuchungen zu Immanuel Kants Theorie des freien Willens.* Berlin and New York: Walter de Gruyter, 2003.

Timmons, Mark, editor. *Kant's Metaphysics of Morals: Interpretative Essays.* Oxford: Oxford University Press, 2002 (includes extensive bibliography).

Tugendhat, Ernst. *Vorlesungen über Ethik.* Frankfurt am Main: Suhrkamp, 1993.

Velkley, Richard L. *Freedom and the End of Reason: On the Moral Foundations of Kant's Critical Philosophy.* Chicago: University of Chicago Press, 1989.

Voeller, Carol. *The Metaphysics of the Moral Law: Kant's Deduction of Freedom.* New York and London: Routledge, 2001.

Walker, Ralph. *Kant and the Moral Law.* New York: Routledge, 1999.

Ward, Keith. *The Development of Kant's View of Ethics.* Oxford: Basil Blackwell, 1972.

Wenzel, Uwe Justus. *Anthroponomie: Kants Archäologie der Autonomie.* Berlin: Akademie Verlag, 1992.

Wike, Victoria S. *Kant on Happiness in Ethics.* Albany: State University of New York Press, 1994.

Willaschek, Marcus. *Praktische Vernunft: Handlungstheorie und Moralbegründung bei Kant.* Stuttgart: Verlag J. B. Metzler, 1992.

Williams, T. C. *The Concept of the Categorical Imperative: A Study of the Place of the Categorical Imperative in Kant's Ethical Theory.* Oxford: Clarendon Press, 1968.

Wolff, Robert Paul. *The Autonomy of Reason: A Commentary on Kant's Groundwork of the Metaphysics of Morals.* New York: Harper & Row, 1973.

Wood, Allen W. *Kant's Ethical Thought.* Cambridge: Cambridge University Press, 1999.

———. *Unsettling Obligations: Essays on Reason, Reality and the Ethics of Belief.* Stanford: CSLI Publications, 2002.

Wood, Allen W. and Dieter Schönecker. Kants "Grundlegung zur Metaphysik der Sitten": Ein Einführender Kommentar. Padeborn: Friedrich Schöningh, 2002.

Yovel, Yirmiyahu, editor. Kant's Practical Philosophy Reconsidered: Papers Presented at the Seventh Jerusalem Philosophical Encounter, December 1986. Dordrecht: Kluwer Academic Publishers, 1989 (multiple-author anthology).

VIII. PRACTICAL PHILOSOPHY: POLITICAL PHILOSOPHY

Altmann, Alexander. Prinzipien politischer Theorie bei Mendelssohn und Kant. Trier: NCO-Verlag, 1981.

Anderson-Gold, Sharon. Cosmopolitanism and Human Rights. Cardiff: University of Wales Press, 2001.

Arendt, Hannah. Lectures on Kant's Political Philosophy. Edited by Ronald Beiner. Chicago: University of Chicago Press, 1982.

Batscha, Zwi, editor. Materialen zu Kants Rechtsphilosophie. Frankfurt am Main: Suhrkamp Verlag, 1976 (multiple-author anthology).

Baynes, Kenneth. The Normative Grounds of Social Criticism: Kant, Rawls, Habermas. Albany: State University of New York Press, 1992.

Beiner, Ronald and William James Booth, editors. Kant and Political Philosophy: The Contemporary Legacy. New Haven: Yale University Press, 1993.

Blumenberg, Hans, Jürgen Habermas, Dieter Henrich, and Jakob Taubes, editors. Kant/Gentz/Rehberg: Über Theorie und Praxis. Frankfurt am Main: Suhrkamp Verlag, 1967.

Bohman, James and Mathias Lutz-Bachmann, editors. Perpetual Peace: Essays on Kant's Cosmopolitan Ideal. Cambridge, MA: MIT Press, 1997.

Brandt, Reinhardt. Eigentumstheorien von Grotius bis Kant. Stuttgart and Bad-Canstatt: Frommann-Holzboog, 1974.

Brandt, Reinhardt, editor. Rechtsphilosophie der Aufklärung. Berlin: Walter de Gruyter, 1982 (multiple-author anthology).

Burg, Peter. Kant und die Französische Revolution. Berlin: Duncker & Humblot, 1974.

Busch, Werner. Die Entstehung der kritischen Rechtsphilosophie Kants 1762–80. Kant-Studien Ergänzungsheft 110. Berlin and New York: Walter de Gruyter, 1979.

Cavallar, Georg. Pax Kantiana: Systematisch-historische Untersuchung des Entwurfs "Zum ewigen Frieden." Vienna: Böhlau, 1992.

_____. Kant and the Theory and Practice of International Right. Cardiff: University of Wales Press, 1999.

Covell, Charles. *Kant and the Law of Peace: A Study in the Philosophy of International Law and International Relations*. Houndsmills: Palgrave Macmillan, 1998.

Deggau, Hans-Georg. *Die Aporien der Rechtslehre Kants*. Stuttgart and Bad-Canstatt: Frommann-Holzboog, 1983.

Easley, Eric. S. *The War over Perpetual Peace: An Exploration into the History of a Foundational International Relations Text*. Houndsmills: Palgrave Macmillan, 2004.

Ellis, Elisabeth. *Kant's Politics: Provisional Theory for an Uncertain World*. New Haven: Yale University Press, 2005.

Fleischacker, Samuel. *A Third Concept of Liberty: Judgment and Freedom in Kant and Adam Smith*. Princeton: Princeton University Press, 1999.

Flikschuh, Katrin. *Kant and Modern Political Philosophy*. Cambridge: Cambridge University Press, 2000.

Franceschet, Antonio. *Kant and Liberal Internationalism: Sovereignty, Justice, and Global Reform*. New York: Palgave Macmillan, 2002.

Franke, Mark F. N. *Global Limits: Immanuel Kant, International Relations, and Critique of World Politics*. Albany: State University Press of New York, 2002.

Gerhardt, Volker. *Immanuel Kants Entwurf "Zum Ewigen Frieden": Eine Theorie der Politik*. Darmstadt: Wissenschaftliche Buchgesellschaft, 1995 (includes extensive bibliography).

Höffe, Otfried. *"Königliche Völker": Zu Kants kosmopolitischer Rechts- und Friedenstheorie*. Frankfurt am Main: Suhrkamp Verlag, 2001.

Höffe, Otfried, editor. *Immanuel Kant: Zum ewigen Frieden*. Berlin: Akademie Verlag, 1995 (collaborative commentary).

———. *Immanuel Kant: Metaphysische Anfangsgründe der Rechtslehre*. Berlin: Akademie Verlag, 1999 (collaborative commentary).

Hüning, Dieter, and Burkhard Tuschling, editors. *Recht, Staat und Völkerrecht bei Immanuel Kant*. Schriften zur Rechtstheorie, 186. Berlin: Duncker & Humblot, 1998.

Hutchings, Kimberly. *Kant, Critique and Politics*. London and New York: Routledge, 1996.

Jahrbuch für Recht und Ethik/Annual Review of Law and Ethics. Volume 5. Special issue on 200th Anniversary of Kant's *Metaphysics of Morals*. Berlin: Duncker & Humblot, 1997.

Kaufman, Alexander. *Welfare in the Kantian State*. Oxford: Clarendon Press, 1999.

Kersting, Wolfgang. *Wohlgeordnete Freiheit: Immanuel Kants Rechts- und Staatsphilosophie*. Berlin and New York: Walter de Gruyter, 1984;

paperback edition with new introduction: Frankfurt am Main: Suhrkamp Verlag, 1993 (includes extensive bibliography).

_____. *Kant über Recht.* Paderborn: Mentis, 2004.

Kneller, Jane and Sidney Axinn, editors. *Autonomy and Community: Readings in Contemporary Kantian Social Philosophy.* Albany: State University of New York Press, 1998.

Kühl, Kristian. *Eigentumsordnung als Freiheitsordnung: Zur Aktualität der Kantischen Rechts- und Eigentumslehre.* Freiburg and Munich: Verlag Karl Albert, 1984 (includes extensive bibliography).

Küsters, Gerd-Walter. *Kants Rechtsphilosophie.* Darmstadt: Wissenschaftliche Buchgesellschaft, 1988 (includes extensive bibliography and review of literature).

Langer, Claudia. *Reform nach Prinzpien: Untersuchungen zur politischen Theorie Immanuel Kants.* Stuttgart: Klett-Cotta Verlag, 1986.

Ludwig, Bernd. *Kants Rechtslehre.* Kant Forschungen, Band 2. Hamburg: Felix Meiner Verlag, 1988.

Maus, Ingeborg. *Zur Aufklärung der Demokratietheorie: Rechts- und demokratietheoretische Überlegungen im Anschluß an Kant.* Frankfurt am Main: Suhrkamp Verlag, 1992.

Murphy, Jeffrie G. *Kant: The Philosophy of Right.* London: Macmillan, 1970.

Raulet, Gérard. *Kant, Histoire et Citoyenneté.* Paris: Presses Universitaires de France, 1996.

Reich, Klaus. *Rousseau und Kant.* Tübingen: J. C. B. Mohr (Paul Siebeck), 1936.

Riley, Patrick. *Will and Political Legitimacy: A Critical Exposition of Social Contract Theory in Hobbes, Locke, Rousseau, Kant, and Hegel.* Cambridge, MA: Harvard University Press, 1982.

_____. *Kant's Political Philosophy.* Ottowa: Rowman and Littlefield, 1983.

Ritter, Christian. *Der Rechtsgedanke Kants nach frühen Quellen.* Frankfurt am Main: Vittorio Klostermann, 1971.

Rosen, Allen D. *Kant's Theory of Justice.* Ithaca and New York: Cornell University Press, 1993.

Saage, Richard. *Eigentum, Staat und Gesellschaft bei Immanuel Kant.* Stuttgart: W. Kohlhammer, 1973.

Saner, Hans. *Kant's Political Thought: Its Origins and Development.* Translated by E. B. Ashton. Chicago: University of Chicago Press, 1973.

Sänger, Monika. *Die kategoriale Systematik in den Metaphysische Anfangsgründe der Rechstlehre: Ein Beitrag zur Methodenlehre Kants.* Berlin and New York: Walter de Gruyter, 1982.

Shell, Susan Meld. *The Rights of Reason: A Study of Kant's Philosophy and Politics.* Toronto: University of Toronto Press, 1980.

Symposium on Kantian Legal Theory. Columbia Law Review 87 (April, 1989). New York: Columbia Law Review.

Timmons, Mark, editor. *Kant's Metaphysics of Morals: Interpretative Essays.* Oxford: Oxford University Press, 2002 (includes extensive bibliography).

Van der Linden, Harry. *Kantian Ethics and Socialism.* Indianapolis and Cambridge: Hackett Publishing Company, 1988.

Vlachos, Georges. *La Pensée politique de Kant: Métaphysique de l'ordre et dialectique du progrès.* Paris: Presses Universitaires de France, 1954.

Williams, Howard. *Kant's Political Philosophy.* New York: St. Martin's Press, 1983.

———. *Kant's Critique of Hobbes.* Cardiff: University of Wales Press, 2003.

Williams, Howard, editor. *Essays on Kant's Political Philosophy.* Chicago: University of Chicago Press, 1992.

IX. THE THIRD CRITIQUE: GENERAL, AESTHETICS

Allison, Henry E. *Kant's Theory of Taste: A Reading of the Critique of Judgment.* Cambridge: Cambridge University Press, 2001.

Baeumler, Alfred. *Das Irrationalitätsproblem in der Ästhetik und Logik des 18. Jahrhunderts biz zur Kritik der Urteilskraft.* Second edition. Tübingen: Max Niemeyer Verlag, 1967.

Banham, Gary. *Kant and the Ends of Aesthetics.* Basingstoke: Macmillan Press Ltd, 2000.

Basch, Victor. *Essai Critique sur L'esthétique de Kant.* Second edition. Paris: J. Vrin, 1927.

Bartuschat, Wolfgang. *Zum systematischen Ort von Kants Kritik der Urteilskraft.* Frankfurt am Main: Vittorio Klostermann, 1972.

Böhme, Gernot. *Kants Kritik der Urteilskraft in neuer Sicht.* Frankfurt am Main: Suhrkamp Verlag, 1999.

Budd, Malcolm. *The Aesthetic Appreciation of Nature.* Oxford: Clarendon Press, 2002.

Burnham, Douglas. *An Introduction to Kant's Critique of Judgment.* Edinburgh: Edinburgh University Press, 2000.

Cassirer, Heinrich Walter. *A Commentary on Kant's Critique of Judgment.* London: Methuen & Co., 1938.

Caygill, Howard. *Art of Judgment.* Oxford: Basil Blackwell, 1989.

Cheatam, Mark A. *Kant, Art, and Art History: Moments of Discipline.* Cambridge: Cambridge University Press, 2001.

Cohen, Hermann. *Kants Begründung der Ästhetik.* Berlin: Dümmler, 1889.

Cohen, Ted, and Paul Guyer, editors. *Essays in Kant's Aesthetics*. Chicago: University of Chicago Press, 1982 (multiple-author anthology; includes extensive bibliography).

Coleman, Francis X. J. *The Harmony of Reason: A Study in Kant's Aesthetics*. Pittsburgh: University of Pittsburgh Press, 1974.

Courtine, Jean-François et al. *Of the Sublime: Presence in Question*. Translated by Jeffrey S. Librett. Albany: State University of New York Press, 1993 (multiple-author anthology).

Crawford, Donald W. *Kant's Aesthetic Theory*. Madison: University of Wisconsin Press, 1974.

Crowther, Paul. *The Kantian Sublime: From Morality to Art*. Oxford: Clarendon Press, 1989.

Dickie, George. *The Century of Taste: The Philosophical Odyssey of Taste in the Eighteenth Century*. New York and Oxford: Oxford University Press, 1996.

Dörflinger, Bernd. *Die Realität des Schönen in Kants Theorie rein ästhetischer Urteilskraft: Zur Gegenstandsbedeutung subjektiver und formaler Ästhetik*. Bonn: Bouvier Verlag, 1988.

Dumouchel, Daniel. *Kant et le Genèse de la Subjectivé Esthétique: Esthétique et Philosophie avant la Critique de la Faculté de Juger*. Paris: J. Vrin, 1999.

Dunham, Barrows. *A Study in Kant's Aesthetics: The Universal Validity of Aesthetic Judgment*. Lancaster: no publisher, 1934.

Esser, Andrea Marlen. *Kunst als Symbol: Die Struktur ästhetischer Reflexion in Kants Theorie des Schönen*. Munich: Wilhelm Fink Verlag, 1997.

Esser, Andrea, editor. *Autonomie der Kunst? Zur Aktualität von Kants Ästhetik*. Berlin: Akademie Verlag, 1995.

Feger, Hans. *Die Macht der Einbildungskraft in der Ästhetik Kants und Schillers*. Heidelberg: Universitätsverlag C. Winter, 1995.

Franke, Ursula, editor. *Kants Schlüssel zur Kritik des Geschmacks: Ästhetische Erfahrung heute – Studien zur Aktualität von Kants "Kritik der Urteilskraft."* Sonderheft des Jahrgangs 2000 der *Zeitschrift für Ästhetik und allgemeine Kunstwissenschaft*. Hamburg: Felix Meiner Verlag, 2000.

Fricke, Christel. *Kants Theories des reinen Geschmacksurteils*. Berlin and New York: Walter de Gruyter, 1990.

Fulda, Hans-Friedrich and Rolf-Peter, Horstmann, editors. *Hegel und die "Kritik der Urteilskraft."* Stuttgart: Klett-Cotta, 1990.

Gadamer, Hans-Georg. *Truth and Method*. Second revised edition. Translated by Joel Weinsheimer and Donald G. Marshall. New York: Continuum, 1999.

Gibbons, Sarah. *Kant's Theory of Imagination: Bridging Gaps in Judgment and Experience*. Oxford: Clarendon Press, 1994.

Ginsborg, Hannah. *The Role of Taste in Kant's Theory of Cognition*. New York: Garland Publishing Company, 1990.

Guyer, Paul. *Kant and the Claims of Taste*. Cambridge, MA: Harvard University Press, 1979; second edition, with additional chapter: Cambridge: Cambridge University Press, 1997.

———. *Kant and the Experience of Freedom*. Cambridge: Cambridge University Press, 1993.

———. *Values of Beauty: Historical Essays in Aesthetics*. Cambridge: Cambridge University Press, 2005.

Guyer, Paul, editor. *Kant's Critique of the Power of Judgment: Critical Essays*. Lanham: Rowman & Littlefield, 2003 (includes extensive bibliography).

Henrich, Dieter. *Aesthetic Judgment and the Moral Image of the World: Studies in Kant*. Stanford: Stanford University Press, 1992.

Huhn, Tom. *Imitation and Society: The Persistence of Mimesis in the Aesthetics of Burke, Hogarth, and Kant*. University Park: Pennsylvania State University Press, 2004.

Juchem, Hans-Georg. *Die Entwicklung des Begriffs des Schönen bei Kant: Unter besonderer Berücksichtigung des Begriffs der verworrenen Erkenntnis*. Bonn: Bouvier Verlag, 1970.

Kaulbach, Friedrich. *Ästhetische Welterkenntnis bei Kant*. Würzburg: Königshausen & Neumann, 1984.

Kemal, Salim. *Kant and Fine Art: An Essay on Kant and the Philosophy of Fine Art and Culture*. Oxford: Clarendon Press, 1986.

———. *Kant's Aesthetic Theory: An Introduction*. New York: St. Martin's Press, 1992.

Kern, Andrea. *Schöne Lust: Eine Theorie der ästhetischen Erfahrung nach Kant*. Frankfurt am Main: Suhrkamp Verlag, 2000.

Kirwan, James. *The Aesthetic in Kant: A Critique*. London: Continuum, 2004.

Krämling, Gerhard. *Die systembildende Rolle von Ästhetik und Kulturphilosophie bei Kant*. Freiburg and Munich: Verlag Karl Albert, 1985.

Kulenkampff, Jens. *Kants Logik des ästhetischen Urteils*. Second, expanded edition. Frankfurt am Main: Vittorio Klostermann, 1994.

Kulenkampff, Jens, editor. *Materialen zu Kant's 'Kritik der Urteilskraft.'* Frankfurt am Main: Suhrkamp Verlag, 1974 (original sources and multiple-author anthology).

Kuypers, Karel. *Kants Kunsttheorie und die Einheit der Kritik der Urteilskraft*. Verhandelingen der Koninklijke Nederlandse Akademie van

Wetenschappen afd. Letterkunde, Nieuwe Reeks, Deel 77-No. 3. Amsterdam and London: North Holland Publishing Co., 1972.

Lebrun, Gérard. *Kant et la fin de la métaphysique: essai sur la critique de la faculté de juger.* Paris: A. Colin, 1970.

Lyotard, Jean-François. *Lessons on the Analytic of the Sublime.* Translated by Elizabeth Rottenberg. Stanford: Stanford University Press, 1994.

Macmillan, R. A. C. *The Crowning Phase of the Critical Philosophy: A Study in Kant's Critique of Judgment.* London: Macmillan and Co., 1912.

Makkreel, Rudolf A. *Imagination and Interpretation in Kant: The Hermeneutical Import of the Critique of Judgment.* Chicago: University of Chicago Press, 1990.

Marc-Wogau, Konrad. *Vier Studien zu Kants "Kritik der Urteilskraft."* Uppsala Universitets Åarskrift 1938, 2. Uppsala: Lundequistka Bokhandeln, 1938.

McCloskey, Mary A. *Kant's Aesthetic.* Albany: State University of New York Press, 1987.

Meerbote Ralf, editor, and Hud Hudson, associate editor. *Kant's Aesthetics.* North American Kant Society Studies in Philosophy, Volume 1. Atascadero: Ridgeview Publishing Company, 1991 (includes extensive bibliography).

Menzer, Paul. *Kants Ästhetik in ihrer Entwicklung.* Abhandlungen der Deutschen Akademie der Wissenschaften zu Berlin, Klasse für Gesellschaftswissenschaften, Jahrgang 1950, No. 2. Berlin: Akademie-Verlag, 1952.

Mertens, Helga. *Kommentar zur ersten Einleitung zu Kants Kritik der Urteilskraft: Zur systematische Funktion der Kritik der Urteilskraft für die System der Vernunftkritik.* Munich: Berchmann, 1975.

Mothersill, Mary. *Beauty Restored.* Oxford: Clarendon Press, 1984.

Myskja, Bjørn K. *The Sublime in Kant and Beckett: Aesthetic Judgment, Ethics and Literature.* Kant-Studien Ergänzungsheft 140. Berlin and New York: Walter de Gruyter, 2002.

Nivelle, Armand. *Kunst- und Dichtungstheorien zwischen Aufklärung und Klassik.* Berlin: Walter de Gruyter, 1960.

Nuzzo, Angelica. *Kant and the Unity of Reason.* West Lafayette: Purdue University Press, 2005.

Parret, Herman, editor. *Kants Ästhetik – Kant's Aesthetics – L'esthétique de Kant.* Berlin and New York: Walter de Gruyter, 1998 (multiple-author anthology; extensive bibliography).

Pillow, Kirk. *Sublime Understanding: Aesthetic Reflection in Kant and Hegel.* Cambridge, MA: MIT Press, 2000.

Podro, Michael. *The Manifold in Perception: Theories of Art from Kant to Hildebrand.* Oxford-Warburg Studies. Oxford: Clarendon Press, 1972.

Pries, Christine. *Übergänge ohne Brücken: Kants Erhabenes zwischen Kritik und Metaphysik.* Berlin: Akademie Verlag, 1995.

Pries, Christine, editor. *Das Erhabene: Zwischen Grenzerfahrung und Größenwahn.* Weinheim: VCH, 1989.

Recki, Birgit. *Ästhetik der Sitten: Die Affinität von ästhetischem Gefühl und praktischer Vernunft bei Kant.* Frankfurt am Main: Vittorio Klostermann, 2001.

Rogerson, Kenneth F. *Kant's Aesthetics: The Roles of Form and Expression.* Lanham: University Press of America, 1986.

Saatröwe, Jürgen. *Genie und Reflexion: Zu Kants Theorie des Ästhetischen.* Karlsruhe: Schindele, 1971.

Savile, Anthony. *Aesthetic Reconstructions: The Seminal Writings of Lessing, Kant, and Schiller.* Aristotelian Society Series, 8. Oxford: Basil Blackwell, 1987.

———. *Kantian Aesthetics Pursued.* Edinburgh: Edinburgh University Press, 1993.

Schaper, Eva. *Studies in Kant's Aesthetics.* Edinburgh: Edinburgh University Press, 1979.

Scheer, Brigitte. *Zur Begründung von Kants Ästhetik und ihrem Korrektiv in der ästhetischen Idee.* Frankfurt am Main: Horst Heiderhoff Verlag, 1971.

Scherer, Irmgard. *The Crisis of Judgment in Kant's Three Critiques: In Search of a Science of Aesthetics.* New York, Bern, Frankfurt, and Paris: Peter Lang, 1995.

Schlapp, Otto. *Kants Lehre von Genie und die Entstehung der "Kritik der Urteilskraft."* Göttingen: Vandenhoeck & Ruprecht, 1901.

Schwabe, Karl-Heinz and Martina Thom, editors. *Naturzweckmäßigkeit und ästhetische Kultur: Studien zu Kants Kritik der Urteilskraft.* Sankt Augustin: Academia Verlag, 1994.

Taminiaux, Jacques. *Poetics, Speculation, and Judgment: The Shadow of the Work of Art from Kant to Phenomenology.* Translated and edited by Michael Gendre. Albany: State University of New York Press, 1993.

Uehling, Theodore E., Jr. *The Notion of Form in Kant's Critique of Aesthetic Judgment.* The Hague: Mouton & Co., 1971.

Wieland, Wolfgang. *Urteil und Gefühl: Kants Theorie der Urteilskraft.* Göttingen: Vandenhoeck & Ruprecht, 2001.

Zammito, John H. *The Genesis of Kant's Critique of Judgment.* Chicago: University of Chicago Press, 1992.

Zeldin, Mary Barbara. *Freedom and the Critical Undertaking: Essays on Kant's Later Critiques*. Ann Arbor: UMI Monographs, 1980.

X. THIRD CRITIQUE: TELEOLOGY AND PHILOSOPHY OF BIOLOGY

Dörflinger, Bernd. *Das Leben theoretischer Vernunft: Teleologische und praktische Aspekte der Erfahrungstheorie Kants*. Kant-Studien Ergänzungsheft 136. Berlin and New York: Walter de Gruyter, 2000.

Düsing, Klaus. *Die Teleologie in Kants Weltbegriff*. Kant-Studien Ergänzungsheft 96. Bonn: Bouvier Verlag, 1968.

Hermann, István. *Kants Teleologie*. Budapest: Akadémiai Kiadó, 1972.

Horkheimer, Max. *Gesammelte Schriften, Band 2: Philosophische Frühschriften 1922–32*. Edited by Gunzelin Schmid Noerr. Frankfurt am Main: Fischer Taschenbuch Verlag, 1987 (contains "Zur Antinomie der teleologischen Urteilskraft," 1922, and "Über Kants *Kritik der Urteilskraft* als Bindeglied zwischen theoretischer und praktischer Philosophie," 1925).

Löw, Reinhard. *Philosophie des Lebendigen: Der Begriff des Organischen bei Kant, sein Grund und seine Aktualität*. Frankfurt am Main: Suhrkamp Verlag, 1980 (includes extensive bibliography).

McLaughlin, Peter. *Kant's Critique of Teleology in Biological Explanation: Antinomy and Teleology*. Lewiston: Edwin Mellen Press, 1990.

———. *What Functions Explain: Functional Explanation and Self-Reproducing Systems*. Cambridge: Cambridge University Press, 2001.

McFarland, J. D. *Kant's Concept of Teleology*. Edinburgh: Edinburgh University Press, 1970.

Menzer, Paul. *Kants Lehre von der Entwicklung in der Natur und Geschichte*. Berlin: Georg Reimer, 1911.

Peter, Joachim. *Das transzendentale Prinzip der Urteilskraft: Eine Untersuchung zur Funktion und Struktur der reflektierenden Urteilskraft bei Kant*. Kant-Studien Ergänzungsheft 126. Berlin and New York: Walter de Gruyter, 1992.

Robinson, Hoke, editor. *System and Teleology in Kant's Critique of Judgment. Southern Journal of Philosophy* 30, Supplement, 1991.

Zanetti, Véronique. *La nature, a-t-elle une fin? Le problème de la téléologie chez Kant*. Brussels: Editions Ousia, 1994.

Zumbach, Clark. *The Transcendent Science: Kant's Conception of Biological Methodology*. The Hague: Martinus Nijhoff, 1984.

XI. PHILOSOPHY OF HISTORY AND ANTHROPOLOGY

Booth, William James. *Interpreting the World: Kant's Philosophy of History and Politics*. Toronto: University of Toronto Press, 1986.

Brandt, Reinhard. *Kommentar zu Kants Anthropologie in pragmatischer Hinsicht.* Kant-Forschungen, Band 10. Hamburg: Felix Meiner Verlag, 1999.

Fenves, Peter D. *A Peculiar Fate: Metaphysics and World-History in Kant.* Ithaca, NY, and London: Cornell University Press, 1991.

Galston, William A. *Kant and the Problem of History.* Chicago: University of Chicago Press, 1975.

Jacobs, Brian and Patrick Kain, editors. *Essays on Kant's Anthropology.* Cambridge: Cambridge University Press, 2003.

Jauch, Ursula Pia. *Immanuel Kant zur Geschlechtsdifferenz: Aufklärerische Vorurteilskritik und bürgerliche Geschlechtsvormundschaft.* Vienna: Passagen, 1988.

Kleingeld, Pauline. *Fortschritt und Vernunft: Zur Geschichtsphilosophie Kants.* Würzburg: Königshausen & Neumann, 1995.

Van de Pitte, Frederick P. *Kant as Philosophical Anthropologist.* The Hague: Martinus Nijhoff, 1971.

Weyand, Klaus. *Kants Geschichtsphilosophie: Ihre Entwicklung und ihr Verhältnis zur Aufklärung.* Kant-Studien Ergänzungsheft 85. Cologne: Kölner-Universitäts-Verlag, 1963.

Yovel, Yirmiahu. *Kant and the Philosophy of History.* Princeton: Princeton University Press, 1980.

Zammito, John H. *Kant, Herder, and the Birth of Anthropology.* Chicago: University of Chicago Press, 2002.

XII. PHILOSOPHY OF RELIGION

Bohatec, Josef. *Die Religionsphilosophie Kants in der "Religion innerhalb der Grenzen der bloßen Vernunft"* (1938). Hildesheim: Georg Olms, 1966.

Bruch, Jean-Louis. *La philosophie religieuse de Kant.* Paris: Aubier-Montaigne, 1968.

Despland, Michel. *Kant on History and Religion.* Montreal and London: McGill-Queen's University Press, 1973.

di Giovanni George, *Freedom and Religion in Kant and His Immediate Successors: The Vocation of Humankind, 1774–1800.* Cambridge: Cambridge University Press, 2005.

England, Frederick Ernst. *Kant's Conception of God: A Critical Exposition of its Metaphysical Development together with a Translation of the Nova Delucidatio.* New York: Dial Press, 1930.

Henrich, Dieter. *Der Ontologische Gottesbeweis: Sein Problem und seine Geschichte in der Neuzeit.* Second edition. Tübingen: J. C. B. Mohr (Paul Siebeck), 1967.

Laberge, Pierre. *La Théologie Kantienne précritique.* Ottawa: Éditions de l'Université d'Ottawa, 1973.

Michaelson, Gordon E., Jr. *The Historical Dimensions of a Rational Faith: The Role of History in Kant's Religious Thought.* Lanham, MD: University Press of America, 1979.

_____. *Fallen Freedom: Kant on Radical Evil and Moral Regeneration.* Cambridge: Cambridge University Press, 1990.

_____. *Kant and the Problem of God.* Oxford and Malden: Blackwell Publishers, 1999.

Reboul, Olivier. *Kant et la probléme du mal.* Montreal: Presses de l'Université de Montréal, 1971.

Ricken, Friedo and François Marty, editors. *Kant über Religion.* Stuttgart: Verlag W. Kohlhammer, 1992.

Rossi, Philip J. *The Social Authority of Reason: Kant's Critique, Radical Evil, and the Destiny of Humankind.* Albany: State University of New York Press, 2005.

Rossi, Philip J. and Michael Wreen, editors. *Kant's Philosophy of Religion Reconsidered.* Bloomington: Indiana University Press, 1991.

Sala, Giovanni. *Kant und die Frage nach Gott.* Kant-Studien Ergänzungsheft 122. Berlin and New York: Walter de Gruyter, 1989.

Schmucker, Josef. *Das problem der Kontingenz der Welt: Versuch einer positiven Aufarbeitung der Kritik Kants am kosmologischen Argument.* Freiburg, Basel, and Vienna: Herder, 1969.

_____. *Die Ontotheologie des vorkritischen Kants.* Kant-Studien Ergänzungsheft 110. Berlin and New York: Walter de Gruyter, 1979.

Schweizer, Albert. *Die Religionsphilosophie Kants von der Kritik der reinen Vernunft bis zur Religion innerhalb der grenzen der bloßen Vernunft.* Freiburg im Breisgau, 1899 (reprint: Hildesheim: Georg Olms Verlag, 1979).

Webb, Clement C. J. *Kant's Philosophy of Religion.* Oxford: Clarendon Press, 1926.

Wimmer, Reiner. *Kants kritische Religionsphilosophie.* Kant-Studien Ergänzungsheft 124. Berlin and New York: Walter de Gruyter, 1990.

Wood, Allan W. *Kant's Moral Religion.* Ithaca, NY, and London: Cornell University Press, 1970.

_____. *Kant's Rational Theology.* Ithaca, NY, and London: Cornell University Press, 1978.

XII. REFERENCE WORK AND SOURCES

Reference Works

Caygill, Howard. *A Kant Dictionary.* Oxford: Blackwell, 1995.

Eisler, Rudolf. *Kant-Lexikon: Nachschlagwerk zu Kants sämtlichen Schriften, Briefen und handschriftlichen Nachlaß.* Berlin: E. S. Mitter, 1930 (reprint: Hildesheim: Georg Olms Verlag, 1961).

Irrlitz, Gerd. *Kant Handbuch: Leben und Werk.* Stuttgart: Verlag J. B. Metzler, 2002.

Martin, Gottfried. *Sachindex zu Kants Kritik der reinen Vernunft.* Berlin: Walter de Gruyter, 1967.

_____. *Personenindex zu Kants gesammelte Schriften.* Berlin: Walter de Gruyter, 1969.

Mellin, G. S. A. *Encyklopädisches Wörterbuch der kritischen Philosophie.* 6 vols. 1797–1804 (reprint: Aalen: Scientia Verlag, 1970–71).

Ratke, Heinrich. *Systematisches Handlexikon zur Kritik der reinen Vernunft.* Hamburg: Felix Meiner Verlag, 1929.

Roser, Andreas and Thomas Mohrs, editors. *Kant-Konkordanz zu den Werken Immanuel Kants (Bände I–IX der Ausgabe der Preußischen Akademie der Wissenschaften).* 10 vols. Hildesheim: Georg Olms Verlag, 1992–.

Ruffing, Margit. *Internationale Kant-Bibliographie 1945 bis 1990.* Frankfurt am Main: Vittorio Klostermann, 1999 (a second volume, covering material published since 1990, is in preparation).

Schmid, Carl C. E. *Wörterbuch zum leichtern Gebrauch der Kantischen Schriften.* Fourth edition. Jena: Cröker, 1798 (reprint: Brussells: Aetas Kantiana, 1974).

Totok, Wilhelm, editor. *Handbuch der Geschichte der Philosophie.* Volume 5: Bibliography for eighteenth and nineteenth centuries. Frankfurt am Main: Vittorio Klostermann, 1986. Kant: pp. 44–145.

Journals

The leading journals for the publication of articles on Kant in English and German are:

Kant-Studien, founded in 1897, currently published by Walter de Gruyter & Co., and *The Kantian Review*, an annual published since 1997 by the University of Wales Press.

Kant Congress Proceedings

Since 1960, International Kant Congresses have been held under the auspices of the Kant-Gesellschaft every four or five years, and since the fourth Congress volumes of all the papers presented, both invited and submitted, have been published. There is naturally a wide range of quality among these papers, which are in German, English, and French, but these volumes contain many important works. They are:

Akten des 4. Internationalen Kant-Kongresses. Edited by Gerhard Funke and Joachim Kopper. Three Parts. *Kant-Studien* 65 (1975), Sonderheft.

Akten des 5. Internationalen Kant-Kongresses. Edited by Gerhard Funke, in collaboration with Manfred Kleinschneider, Ruldolf Malter, and Gisela Müller. Two Parts in three volumes. Bonn: Bouvier Verlag, 1981–2.

Proceedings of the Sixth International Kant Congress. Edited by Gerhard Funke and Thomas Seebohm. Two Volumes in three parts. Washington, D.C.: Center for Advanced Research in Phenomenology and University Press of America, 1989.

Akten des 7. Internationalen Kant-Kongresses. Two Parts in three volumes. Edited by Gerhard Funke in collaboration with Manfred Kleinschneider, Rudolf Malter, Gisela Müller, Ralf Müller, and Thomas M. Seebohm. Bonn: Bouvier Verlag, 1991.

Proceedings of the Eighth International Kant Congress. Edited by Hoke Robinson. Two volumes in five parts. Milwaukee: Marquette University Press, 1995.

Kant und die Berliner Aufklärung: Akten des IX. Internationalen Kant-Kongresses. Edited by Volker Gerhard, Rolf-Peter, Horstmann and Ralph Schumacher. Five volumes. Berlin and New York: Walter de Gruyter, 2001.

Another important volume of proceedings from a conference in 1974, in celebration of the 250th anniversary of the birth of Kant, is:

Actes du Congrès d'Ottowa sur Kant dans les Traditions Anglo-Américaine et Continentale/Proceedings of the Ottowa Congress on Kant in the Anglo-American and Continental Traditions. Edited by Pierre Laberge, François Duchesneau, and Bryan E. Morrisey. Ottowa: University of Ottowa Press, 1976.

Electronic Resources

Electronic links to Kantian texts and literature may be made at a number of websites. The website of the North American Kant Society, **naks.ucsd.edu**, contains many of these, including a link to an electronic version of the "Akademie" edition. The websites of the Kant Forschungstelle at the University of Mainz (**www.uni-mainz.de/~kant/kfs/**) and of the Kant research group at the University of Marburg, "Immanuel Kant Information-Online" (**www.uni-marburg.de/Kant**), contain many further links to electronic texts, bibliographical resources, and other websites.

INDEX

Abel, Jacob Friedrich, 657–658
Abelard, Peter, 507
action: and causation, 193; at a distance, 303, 310, 333; and reaction, 316–317, 323
aesthetic attitude, 579
aesthetic discourse, 568
aesthetic idea, 565
aesthetic judgment. *See* taste
agreeable, the, 558
agency: Kant's theory of rational, 348–349, 387–391; and virtue, 514–518
Alexander of Aphrodisias, 144
algebra, 100–101
Allende, Salvador, 495
ambition, 522
Amphiboly of the Concepts of Reflection, 86
Analogies of Experience, 14, 50, 193, 203–205. *See also* causation, community, conservation, interaction
analysis, 147
analytic judgments, 33–35; versus synthetic judgments, 55–56
analytic method, 132–133
Analytic of Principles, 47–48, 49; transcendental arguments in, 246. *See also* Axioms of Intuition, Analogies of Experience
animality, 515–516
animals, Leibniz on, 174
Anscombe, Gertrude Elizabeth Margaret, 229, 529

anthropology, practical, 345, 523, 647–648
Antinomy of Pure Reason, 15–16, 86, 276–277, 279, 286, 313, 315–316, 318, 390; determinism and freedom in, 394–399; and language, 633; and postulates of pure practical reason, 601–603
antinomy of teleological judgment, 572–573
Antisthenes, 366
apathy, 516
Apel, Karl-Otto, 262
appearances (phenomena), 10, 12, 71–72, 178, 211, 261, 290–291, 328. *See also* transcendental idealism
apperception: Leibniz on, 174–175, 186; unity of, 186–195, 224–225, 324, 325
a priori: Kant's concept of the, 28–60; epistemological conception of, 30–37, 43, 52, 56; ingredients as, 39–52; knowledge as, 24; marks of, 37–39, 43; weak vs. strong conceptions of, 33. *See also* explicit *a priori* knowledge, synthetic *a priori* knowledge, tacit *a priori* knowledge
apriority, in mathematics, 107–113. *See also a priori*
Aquinas, Thomas, Saint, 507
aquisition, original, 433
Aristotle: on categories, 129, 152; on freedom, 383; on highest good, 593; on logic, 144, 158; and principle of

Aristotle (*cont.*)
  non-contradiction, 240, 255–256; on
  synthesis, 147; on virtue, 367,
  505–506, 507, 524–525
arithmetic, 28, 99–100, 102–104, 112
Arnauld, Antoine, 137
arrogance, 25
art, fine, 563, 564; autonomy of, 579. *See
  also* aesthetic ideas, beauty, genius
association, 180
assurance, mutual, 430, 433
atheism, 606–607, 617
atomism, 63
Augustine of Hippo, Saint, 507, 593,
  594, 596, 597, 598, 599
autonomy: of art, 579; in Fichte, 399;
  and moral faith, 614–616; in
  morality, 26, 354–358, 360–361,
  370, 393, 485–486; of states, 487
avarice, 520
Axioms of Intuition, 47–48,
  118–119

Bacon, Francis, 177
Baier, Annette C., 530
Bauer, Bruno, 592
Baumgarten, Alexander Gottlieb, 6, 8,
  71, 635, 641; on aesthetics, 539; on
  morality, 368; on preestablished
  harmony, 67, 70
Beattie, James, 176
beauty, 21; adherent vs. free, 563–564;
  artistic, 20; Hume's theory of,
  543–544, 563; ideal of, 563, 564;
  Kant's theory of, 556–568; natural,
  20
Beck, Lewis White, 621
Beiser, Frederick C., 469
belief: Jacobi on, 292
beneficence, 521–522
Bennett, Jonathan F., and principle of
  significance, 273
Berkeley, George: and idealism, 281,
  289–290, 633, 635, 636; on vision,
  68
Biester, Johann Erich, 454, 592
biology, 327, 328. *See also* organisms,
  reproduction
Blumenbach, Johann Friedrich, 539
Bonaparte, Napoleon, 479

Bonnet, Charles, 539
Boscovich, Ruggiero Giuseppe, 311
Boyle, Robert, 62
Bradley, James, 333
Brandt, Reinhart, 164
Brecht, Bertolt, 447, 448, 457, 466,
  467
Brouwer, Luitzen E.J, 120
Buffon, Georges Louis Leclerc, comte de,
  539
Bullough, Edward, 579
Burke, Edmund, 539

calculus, propositional, 158, 160
Calvin, John, 594
Camus, Albert, 616
Carnap, Rudolf, 88, 296, 330–331
Cassam, Quassim, 250
Cassirer, Ernst: on Kant's conception of
  logic, 161; and relative *a priori*, 296
Castañeda, Hector-Neri, 199
casuistical questions, 345
categorical imperative, 16, 25, 461, 526;
  concept of, 348–349, 370–372; and
  sexuality, 458; and universal
  principle of right, 421–422, 455. *See
  also* morality
categorical judgment: Frege on, 161;
  Kant on 144–145
categories (concepts of pure
  understanding), 12, 13–14, 24–25,
  40, 47, 117–118, 129–152, 155, 168,
  224–225, 243, 244, 246; Heidegger
  on, 157; and ideas of pure reason,
  275; and natural science, 322–324,
  325, 326; table of, 146–147, 152. *See
  also* causation, community,
  interaction, magnitude, modality,
  substance
causal laws, 320
causation, 6, 7, 12, 14, 25, 45, 50, 134,
  150, 151, 272, 326; empiricist
  position on, 203; Hume on,
  540–543, 554–555; and inertia, 316,
  323; Kant's answer to Hume,
  215–217; Kant's proof of, 205–217;
  Leibniz's theory of, 212; modern
  developments in, 227–230; probable,
  229; rationalist position, 203–204;
  regularity theory of, 230; schema of,

166; and substance, 221–227; and transcendental idealism, 283

character, empirical and intelligible: Kant on, 19, 396; Schopenhauer on, 408

chemistry, 322, 326, 327, 328, 338, 577

choice, external use of, 420. *See also* will

Chomsky, Noam, 41

Christianity, 366, 372; and morality, 507–508

Cicero, Marcus Tullius, 347, 361–365, 644–647

Clarke, Samuel, 64–65, 67, 367. *See also* Leibniz-Clarke correspondence

coercion, 5, 417, 419, 420, 429, 456, 480, 496, 497–498

coexistence, 70, 131

Cohen, Hermann: and Heidegger, on Kant's conception of logic, 155–156, 157, 161; and relative *a priori*, 296

coherence theory of truth, 259

Coleridge, Samuel Taylor, 271

Collins, Anthony, 591

colonialism, 480, 499

community, category of, 323, 326

compassion, 528

compatibilism, 6, 398–399, 408

concept(s): Hegel's conception of, 405; vs. intuition, 133–135, 136; and judgments of taste, 562–563; and recognition of objects, 186; and rules, 182–183. *See also* categories

conceptual scheme, 258, 259

conflict, moral, 343

conscience, 517

consciousness, unity of, 156, 157. *See also* apperception, unity of

consent, 417

consequentialism, 509

conservation: of energy, 329; of matter, 14, 316, 323

constitutive principles, 22–24; and regulative principles, 326, 327, 328, 618, 620

construction: mathematical, 36, 98–101, 110–111, 112–113; ostensive, 100; symbolic, 100–101

contract, right of, 456–457

contractarianism, 441

contradiction. *See* non-contradiction

convenience, principles of, 10

conviction, 608

Copernican revolution, 223

cosmological argument, 7

cosmology: Kant-Laplace, 5, 303, 309–310, 312, 313–314; rational, 276–277. *See also* Antinomy of Pure Reason

cosmopolitanism, 478, 479, 488–490, 493

courage, 523

Crusius, Christian August, 6, 7, 8, 61; on freedom of the will, 382, 385–387, 388, 391, 397, 399; on God, 67–68; on intellect and will, 389; on monads, 71; on morality, 368, 509, 510, 526; on space, 67–68, 70, 71, 75; on truth, 241, 255; on voluntarism, 386, 392, 409;

Cudworth, Ralph, 367

Cumberland, Richard, 367, 368

Cynics, 366, 372

Davidson, Donald, and transcendental arguments, 253

decision, moral, 343–346

deduction. *See* metaphysical deduction, transcendental deduction

defamation, 521

deism, 591

democracy, and peace, 478, 494–496

Dennett, Daniel, 199

Descartes, René, 2, 8, 61, 62, 192, 409; on clear and distinct ideas, 241; on *Dioptrics*, 68; on foundations of physical science, 57, 305–307, 330; on geometry, 62–63, 66; Leibniz's critique of, 307; on metaphysics, 272; on mind, 170, 172; on natural light, 240; on scepticism, 255; on space, 62–63, 64

design, argument from: Hume on, 539, 545–546, 568–569; Kant on, 546–547

desire, 371

determinism, 6, 23, 386; and freedom in third Antinomy, 394–399; Schopenhauer on, 408

Dewey, John, 374–375

dignity, Schiller on, 527
Diogenes the Cynic, 366
disinterestedness, 557
disjunctive judgment, 144, 145
divisibility, infinite: Crusius on, 68 Kant on, 72, 313;
Doyle, Michael, 495
drunkeness, 519
dualism, 280
Duncan, A.R.C., 362, 363, 364
duty, 16; as motive for morality, 19; and respect for law, 325
duties: Kant's classification of, 16, 420–421; Kant's system of, 345, 354; of love, 519, 521; to oneself, 519–521; perfect vs. imperfect, 513; of respect, 519, 521

Eberhard, Johann August, 592, 641
education, and morality, 369, 526
egoism, rational, 439
Einstein, Albert, 88, 330, 331
electromagnetism, 339
empirical knowledge, Kant's conception of, 184–185
empirical realism, 400
empiricism, 28–29, 45, 180, 184, 199, 241, 242; on causation, 203; dogmas of, 330–331; logical, 326, 330; principle of, 541; on substance, 204. See also Berkeley, Hume, Locke, Quine
emotions: and moral motivation, 515, 516–518; Stoics on, 506
ends: and actions, 374–375; final, 22; rational beings as, 346, 352–354; realm of, 324, 354–362; setting of, 349, 374; and duties of virtue, 518–519; of system of nature, 574–577. See also humanity, purpose, purposiveness
energy, 228–229, 329
enlightenment, 4, 648–650
envy, 522
Epicureanism, 366, 372, 506, 525, 593, 594, 597–598, 600
Epicurus, 368, 506–507
epigenesis, 538, 539
equality, 468–469
Erhard, Johann Benjamin, 294

ethical life, Hegel on, 405
ethics, Kant's conception of. See also duties of virtue, virtue
Euclid, 97, 105, 107. See also geometry
Euler, Leonhard, 51
Evans, Gareth, 199, 246
evil, 511, 596, 603
evolution, 21, 538
Ewald, S. Hermann, 636
examples, in morality, 369
experience: Hermann Cohen's conception of, 155; independence from, 30–33, 42–43; judgments of, 155; and objectivity, 272; and science, 320; and transcendental arguments, 257–258
explicit *a priori* knowledge, 45

fact of reason, 393
Fair, David, 228
faith: and autonomy, 614–616; meaning of, 607–610; moral, 26, 588–592; and highest good, 593–599; and Kant's critique of metaphysics, 617–620; pragmatic justification of, 609; rational, 589, 590–592
Faraday, Michael, 311, 339
fatalism, 603
Feder, Georg Friedrich Heinrich, 636, 637, 638–642
federation, of states, 478–479, 482, 483, 488. See also league
Fermat, Pierre de, 51
Feuerbach, Ludwig, 592
Fichte, Johann Gottlieb: on freedom of the will, 399–403, 406; on French revolution, 422; on idealism and dogmatism, 400–402, 632; on intellectual intuition, 198; on international relations, 496, 497, 498–499; on "Kantians," 657–658; on political philosophy, 402–403, 439, 442; on primacy of practical reason, 401, 405; on self-positing, 244, 399, 403; on social dependence, 440; on things in themselves, 400; and transcendental arguments; and the unconditioned, 292, 293–294, 295, 297
Flikschuh, Katrin, 462, 465

forces: attractive and repulsive, 6;
Leibniz on, 64, 307; measure of, 5;
Newton on, 308, 310, 317
form, vs. matter of appearance, 77
formalism: in aesthetics, 579; in Kant's
moral theory, 432, 647–648
France, 479, 488, 492. *See also* French
revolution
Frederick the Great, 452
freedom: in Crusius, 382, 385–387, 388,
391; in Descartes, 306; and
determinism, 12–13, 394–399;
external, 26, 417, 420, 480; as idea
of reason, 388, 398;
incomprehensibility of, 388; inner,
524; and nature, 2, 6, 15–20, 21–24,
575–576; in Leibniz, 308; and moral
law, 4; proof of, 4, 263; in Reinhold
and Fichte, 293; as self-constraint,
512; and transcendental idealism,
284, 398; of the will, 6, 18–19, 26,
381–415. *See also* will
free-thinking, 591
Frege, Gottlob, 25, 33, 54–55, 120,
158–161
French revolution, 422, 479
Friedman, Michael, 296
Friedrich Wilhelm II, 452
friendship, 357–358
Fries, Jakob Friedrich, 296
Fulda, Hans-Friedrich, 422
function, Kant's concept of, 139–141,
150

Galen, 144
Galileo, Galilei, 39, 62, 155
Garve, Christian, 592 and review of
Critique of Pure Reason, 636, 637,
638–642; and Kant's *Groundwork*,
347, 361–362, 644–648
Gassendi, Pierre, 62, 63
Gauthier, David, 441
Gedicke, Friedrich, 454
general logic. *See* logic
genetics, 577
genius, 565
Gentz, Friedrich, 498
geometry, 28–29, 36, 55; construction in,
104–107, 110–111, 113; Descartes
on, 62–63; Euclidean, 82, 86, 304,

305, 320, 331; Leibniz on, 66;
necessity of, 75–77; non-Euclidean,
61, 82, 88, 120, 329–330; proofs in,
82, 104–107; as synthetic *a priori*,
13–14, 80, 81–83, 104–107. *See also*
Euclid, mathematics
Gerard, Alexander, 539
Gewirth, Alan, 262
Gilligan, Carol, 530
gluttony, 519
good will, 16, 347, 349; and virtue, 514
God: in Descartes, 306–307; existence
of, 7, 19–20, 589–590, 591, 599,
617–618; idea of, 277; Leibniz on,
64, 307, 308, 382; and morality, 368,
369, 372, 507–508, 526, 604–607.
See also cosmological argument,
ontological argument,
physicotheological argument
Goeze, Johann Melchior, 591
Gottsched, Johann Christoph, 451
grace: Kant on, 603; Schiller on, 527–528
gratitude, 521, 522
gravitation, 308
greed, 522
Gregor, Mary J., 422, 461
Grotius, Hugo, 508
*Groundwork of the Metaphysics of
Morals*, and Garve, 347, 361–362,
644–648
Guyer, Paul, 422, 424, 425, 426, 427–428

Habermas, Jürgen, 496, 497
habit, 524
Haller, Albrecht von, 539
Hamann, Johann Georg: on *Critique of
Pure Reason*, 632–633, 643, 654; and
fideism, 592; and Herder, 650, 652;
and Kant's *Groundwork*, 361–362,
645; and principle of significance,
273; and *Prolegomena*, 638
Hamilton, William, 269, 270, 280, 286
happiness: ancient views of, 366, 372,
506–507; Garve on, 646; in highest
good, 19–20, 523–524, 595, 596–598;
as moral principle, 369; not motive
for virtue, 601
harmony of cognitive powers, 561–565
Hartknoch, Johann Friedrich, 638,
642

Hegel, Georg Wilhelm Friedrich, 24–25; on beauty, 578–579; on freedom, 403–408; on highest good, 606; on idealism, 632; on Kant's conception of logic, 153–154; and metaphysics, 273; on natural rights, 442; on practical reason, 404–405; and principle of significance, 273; and science, 330, 340; on self-consciousness, 439; and the unconditioned, 292, 294–295

Heidegger, Martin, 25; historicism of, 296; on Kant's logic, 156–157

Helmholtz, Hermann, 88, 326, 329–330, 340

Helvétius, Claude Adrien, 368

Herbart, Johann F., 86–87

Herder, Johann Georg, 539, 592, 642, 654, 657–658; history in Kant and, 648

Herman, Barbara, 458, 460

Herz, Marcus, 82, 134, 138, 147, 243, 637, 642

heteronomy, principles of, 368–373, 392, 526

highest good, 19–20, 318, 323, 335; in antiquity, 365–366, 525–526, 593; happiness in, 523–524; and moral faith, 593–599; in Kant's moral theory, 621–624; and moral proof of God, 604–605; and postulates of practical reason, 593, 599–601; virtue in, 523–524

Hippel, Theodor Gottlieb von, 451–453, 454, 459, 470

history: and enlightenment, 648–650; Kant on Herder on, 648; reason in, 4; and peace, 478

Hobbes, Thomas, 2, 368, 369, 441, 508, 593

Höffe, Otfried, 422, 497

Hölderlin, Friedrich, 294

holiness, 366, 511–512

Home, Henry, Lord Kames, 539

honor, 645–647

humanity: in Cicero, 362–363; as end in itself, 16, 351–354, 358, 429–430; as basis for right, 425–428; predisposition to, 515–516; and virtue, 518

Hume, David, 2, 6, 7, 26, 196, 292; on argument from design, 539, 545–546, 568–569; on beauty, 539, 543–544, 563; on belief, 609; on bundle theory of mind, 175–176, 190–191; on causation, 205, 215–217, 230, 305, 540–543, 554–555; empiricist principle of, 591; on freedom, 385; and idealism, 289, 633, 635, 636; on imagination, 542; on morality, 509, 530, 646; on necessity, 540–543, 554–555; and skepticism, 241, 338, 639; on standard of taste, 543–545, 556–557, 560, 567–568; on substance, 204

Hursthouse, Rosalind, 530

Husserl, Edmund, 120, 296

Hutcheson, Francis, 8, 368, 508, 509, 526, 539

hylozoism, 334–335, 339

hypothetical imperatives, 369, 371

hypothetical judgment, 144, 145, 151, 160, 162

idea, Kant's concept of, 355

ideal of beauty, 563, 564

ideal of pure reason, 15

idealism: absolute, 294–295, 328, 632; critical, 639–640; in Fichte, 400–402; and Garve-Feder review, 634–636; refutation of, 6, 14–15, 324; post-Kantian, 327–329; and the unconditioned, 306. See also transcendental idealism

ideality, of space and/or time, 65, 74, 76–83, 242, 290–291. See also transcendental idealism

ideas of pure reason, 271, 272–275, 277–278; and categories, 275; deduction of, 247, 257; freedom as, 388; and syllogistic inference, 274–275; as regulative principles, 318

identity, principle of, 131, 382

imagination: free play of, 561–565; Heidegger on, 157; pure synthesis of, 225; transcendental synthesis of, 321

immortality, 8–9, 19–20, 589, 590, 591, 592, 599, 617–618

imputability, 387, 391–394
inclination, 348–349, 515
incongruent counterparts, 9, 72–75, 242
incorporation, 390–391
indeterminacy, Hegel's rejection of, 405–406
individualism, methodological, 439
inertia, 316, 317–318, 323, 334
inference, 144. *See also* syllogistic inferences
ingratitude, 522
innate ideas, Locke and Leibniz on, 173–174
inquiry, conduct of, 555–556
intelligible world, 178
interaction, 324; between mind and body, 65; between substances, 70, 92
international relations, 481. *See also* peace
intuition, 13, 77, 85–86, 114; vs. concepts, 133–134, 136, 162; empirical vs. pure, 109. *See also* space, time
intuitive knowledge, 386
irreversibility, 207–208

Jacobi, Friedrich Heinrich: fideism of, 592; and pantheism dispute, 292, 592, 655–657; and principle of significance, 273; and unconditioned, 292–293
James, William, 610
Jenisch, Daniel, 658
Jesus, 366
judgment: capacity for, 142, 146; determining vs. reflecting, 547–548, 571–572, 576–577; forms of, 14, 138–146; Kant's conception of, 138–146; principles of, 12, 13–14, 130; principles of, in natural science, 323–324; table of functions of, 142–143. *See also* taste, teleological judgment
justice: and highest good, 597. *See also* right

Kersting, Wolfgang, 421–422
Kierkegaard, Søren, 609–610

kingdom of ends. *See* realm of ends
knowledge: foundations of, 4; vs. opinion and faith, 608. *See also* synthetic *a priori* judgment or knowledge
Königsberg, 3
Kripke, Saul A., 56
Kuhn, Thomas S., 332

Lakatos, Imré, 120
Lambert, Johann Heinrich, 333, 634, 635, 637, 642
Laplace, Pierre Simon de, 333. *See also* cosmology
language: Hamann on, 633; ordinary, 158, 160; Wittgenstein on, 244
latitudinarianism, 591
Laurentiis, Allegra de, 461
Lavoisier, Antoine Laurent, 339
laws, scientific, 2, 12; necessary truth of, 553–555
league, of states, 492, 496–498. *See also* federation
legality, 455–456
Leibniz, Gottfried Wilhelm, 2, 3, 6, 10, 61, 196, 272, 277, 328, 539, 620; on apperception, 174–175, 186; on causation, 212; critique of Descartes, 307; on freedom, 308, 382–384, 408, 409; on geometry, 66; on God, 64, 307, 308, 309, 382; on innate ideas, 173–174; on life, 339; on mathematics, 95–96, 307; on mind, 173; on modality, 145; on monads, 64–65, 177, 195, 212; on motion, 307; on nature and grace, 597, 598; on necessity, 384; on pre-established harmony, 65, 70, 539; on space, 64–66, 69, 70, 71–72, 74, 75, 281; and the unconditioned, 289–290; on universal combinatoric, 132
Leibniz-Clarke correspondence, 62, 64–65, 66–67, 308–309
Lessing, Gotthold Ephraim: and free-thinking, 591; and pantheism dispute, 292, 592, 655–656
liberalism, 417–418
lexicon, 657
liberty of indifference, 397

Locke, John, 3, 175, 196, 281, 441, 633;
on highest good, 593; on innate
ideas, 173–174; on personal identity,
172–173, 192–193; on inner sense
and reflection, 170–172, 186, 187,
192–193
logic, Kant's conception of, 55, 135–138;
general vs. particular, 137–138;
general vs. transcendental, 135, 138,
145, 146–147, 152, 161; as
normative, 137
Lossius, Johann Christian, 176,
637
Lotze, Rudolf H., 86, 87, 88
Louis XVI, 478, 492
love, 517; duties of, 519, 521
Lovejoy, Arthur O., 206
Ludwig, Bernd, 422
Luther, Martin, 594
lying, 396–397, 410, 421, 519

McDowell, John, 297
McTaggart, John M.E., 228
Mackie, John, 227, 230
Maimon, Salomon, 197, 338
magnitude, 14, 150. *See also* Axioms of
Intuition
Malebranche, Nicolas, 272
malice, 522
Mandeville, Bernard de, 368, 369, 508,
526
marriage, 26, 447–476; in Prussia, 453;
right in, 454–461
Marx, Karl, 592
master-slave dialectic, 404
mathematics: construction in, 36,
98–101, 110–111, 112–113; Frege's
view of, 54; Kant's philosophy of,
94–128; method of, 8, 9, 132–133,
147–148; vs. physics in Leibniz, 307;
as synthetic *a priori* knowledge,
13–14, 24, 35–37, 45, 47–48, 50–51,
52, 53, 94, 97–107, 242; and
transcendental idealism, 114–119.
See also arithmetic, geometry
matter: concept of, 322–323; vs. form of
appearance, 77; Kant's dynamical
theory of, 303, 310–311, 312–313,
316, 327–328, 329; as the movable
in space, 314; Schelling on, 327–328

maxims, 18, 349–351; permissibility of,
355–356
Maxwell, James Clerk, 311, 339
mean, doctrine of, 367, 505
mechanics: Kant on, 316–318, 319;
Newtonian, 62, 304; Schelling on,
327. *See also* motion
Meier, Georg Friedrich, 539, 635
Mellor, David H., 228, 229
Mendelssohn, Moses: on Kant's critique
of metaphysics, 270; on
mathematics, 95, 96–97; in
pantheism dispute, 591, 592,
655–658; on perfectionism, 594; in
reception of *Critique of Pure
Reason*, 637, 642
Metaphysical Deduction, 14, 25,
129–155, 168; influence of, 152–161
metaphysics: Descartes' conception of,
306–307; and faith, 617–620; general
vs. special, 318–323; and highest
good, 602; Kant's critique of
traditional, 15–16, 25, 269–302; of
marriage, 461–467
method: mathematical, 81, 95–97, 98;
mathematical vs. philosophical, 8,
132–133, 147–148; rationalist, 7;
transcendental, 48–49; Wolff on,
95–96
Mill, John Stuart, 345
mind: Kant's early view of, 177–179;
Kant's philosophy of, 169–202
modality: Frege on, 159; functions of,
145
monads: Kant's view of, 71, 310, 311,
312, 317; Leibniz's view of, 64–65,
177, 195, 212
monarchy, 487
Montaigne, Michel de, 368, 369, 526
moral feeling, 369, 517
moral law, 342–380; formality of, 5; as
incentive, 392; and natural world,
325; and pure practical reason, 324;
purity of, 4; reality of, 18–19;
respect for, 515; and virtue, 510. *See
also* autonomy, humanity, nature,
universal law
morality: and atheism, 606–607;
foundation of, 9, 10–13;
fundamental and supreme principle

of, 16–17, 342–380; Hegel on, 405; Kant's critique of previous, 365–373; Kant's effect on, 3; modern theories of, 366; and nature, 575–576, 577–578; and peace, 492, 493–494; purity of motivation for, 8–9, 19, 614–616; relation to right, 419–428, 434–437

moral sense theory, 508–509, 526

moral world, 618–620

Moritz, Karl Philipp, 579

motion: absolute vs. relative, 314; experience of, 314–315; laws of, 63–64, 129–155, 168, 322, 331; Descartes on laws of, 306, 307; Leibniz on laws of, 307–308; Newton on laws of, 308, 316, 319, 323; and time, 321. See also mechanics, phenomenology, phoronomy

motives: purity of, 614–617; Schopenhauer on, 409

Mulholland, Leslie A., 422

Müller, Johannes, 87–88

nativism, in philosophy of mind, 170, 173

natural law, 508

natural rights, 442

nature: Kant's concept of, 318–323; formula of law of, 346, 358; and morality, 575–576, 577–578;

naturalism: in logic, 155, 158

Naturphilosophie, 326, 327, 328–329

necessity: Crusius on, 385–386, 387; Hume on, 540–543, 554–555; of judgments of taste, 558–559; Leibniz on, 384; as mark of the a priori, 37–39; and systematicity, 538, 540, 551–555

neglected alternative, 92

Nelson, Leonard, 296

neo-Kantianism: and the unconditioned, 292, 296–297. See also Cohen, Cassirer

Newton, Isaac, 2, 62, 63–64, 67, 73, 155, 289–290, 305, 315, 316, 319. See also mechanics, motion

Nicolai, Friedrich, 592, 657–658

Nicole, Pierre, 137

Nietzsche, Friedrich, 441, 578, 579

non-contradiction, principle of, 96, 131, 139, 240, 255

noumena, 10. See also things in themselves

Novalis (Friedrich von Hardenberg), 294

obligation: modern theories of, 526; and principle of right, 424–425

occasionalism, 280

objectivity, Kant's conception of, 205–206

Oersted, Hans Christian, 339

O'Neill, Onora, 422

ontological argument, 6, 7, 15

ontological relativity, 25

ontology: gives way to analytic, 130–131; vs. logic, 135–136

opinion, 608

opposition, logical and real, 7

organisms, 22, 139, 538; and purposiveness, 570–571

"ought implies can," 391–392, 605

Panaetius of Rhodes, 362

pantheism dispute, 292, 592, 655–657

Parfit, Derek, 199

Paralogisms of Pure Reason, 15, 179, 195–196, 275–276, 277, 324, 464

participation, in government, 416

paternalism, 419, 486

patience, 523

Paton, Herbert James, 270, 362

peace, 26, 477–504; definitive articles for, 482, 483; preliminary articles for, 482

perception: imagination and, 180–181; judgments of, 155

perfection, and morality, 10–13, 368, 369, 372, 509, 526

permanence, representation of, 218–221

permissibility: of maxims, 350–351, 355–356

permissive law, 467–468

person, Kant's definition of, 463–464

personality, 515–516

personal identity: Locke on, 172–173; Shoemaker on, 198

persuasion, 608

phenomena. See appearances

phenomenalism, 223–224, 226–227
phenomenology, in Kant, 314, 316, 317
phoronomy, 314
physicotheological argument, 7
physics, foundations of, 4, 5, 6, 323. *See also* force, mechanics, motion
Plato, 97, 241, 366, 372, 505, 506
pleasure, 562
Pogge, Thomas W., 425
Poincaré, Henri, 88
Port-Royal logic, 137, 147
possession, intelligible vs. physical, 428–429, 431–432, 433
postulates: of pure practical reason, 262, 279, 589, 590, 599–604, 617–620; and highest good, 593 of right, 423–424, 426. *See also* freedom, God, immortality
practical reason. *See* reason
pragmatic justification, 609
Prauss, Gerold, 640
pre-established harmony, 65, 67, 70, 280, 539
preformationism, 538
Price, Richard, 367
Priestley, Joseph, 311
private right, 456. *See also* property
progress, toward peace, 490–494
Prolegomena to any future metaphysics, and Garve-Feder review, 638–642
promising, 344
property: Kant's theory of, 416, 418–419; and state, 428–437
providence, 9
psychology, empirical vs. rational, 176–177, 179, 277; vs. philosophy, 196. *See also* Paralogisms of Pure Reason
Pufendorf, Samuel, 508
purpose, 22; in nature, 568–569. *See also* ends
purposiveness: objective, 569; principle of, 247; relative, 569–570
Putnam, Hilary, 297

qualities: primary vs. secondary, 62, 65
quantification, 158
Quine, Willard Van Orman, 25, 54, 56, 230–231, 330–331

radical evil, 511, 596, 603
rational being, as end in itself, 346, 520. *See also* humanity
rational psychology, 176–177, 179. *See also* Paralogisms of Pure Reason
rationalism, 7, 8, 45, 197–198; on causation, 203–204; on reason, 240; on substance, 204. *See also* Baumgarten, Descartes, Leibniz, Spinoza, Wolff
race, 523, 652
Rawls, John, 442, 496, 498
realism: about space, 78; transcendental, 115–116
realm of ends, 324, 354–362
reason: defense of, 240; fact of, 393; Fichte on primacy of practical, 401; Hegel on practical, 404–405; limits of, 185, 278; practical, 17–18, 279–280, 324–325, 417; practical, and religious belief, 590–592, 656–657; primacy of practical, 610–613; theoretical vs. practical, 318, 323, 328; and unity, 342–343
reciprocity thesis, 18
reflecting (reflective) judgment, 20, 547–548; and teleological judgment, 571–572, 576–577; transcendental principle of, 552–554
reflection, Locke on, 170–172
regulative principles, 22–24, 40, 248; absolute space as, 315, 317, 319; and constitutive principles, 326, 327, 328, 618, 620
Reich, Klaus, 360, 362–364
Reichenbach, Hans, 227, 296, 331–332
Reimarus, Samuel, 591
Reinhold, Karl Leonhard: and initial reception of Kant, 631, 657–658; and metaphysics, 270; and transcendental arguments, 249; and the unconditioned, 292, 293–294, 297
relations: categories of, functions of, 144–145, 316; logical vs. real, 132
relativity, theory of, 330, 331
reliabilism, 196
religion: Kant's philosophy of, 588–629; relation to philosophy, 4
reproduction, 538

republicanism, Kant's theory of, 416, 481; and peace, 477, 478, 479, 481, 482–483, 492
respect: and duty, 347–348; duties of, 519, 521; feeling of, 517; and virtue, 510, 515
reviews, of *Critique of Pure Reason*, 632–638
revolution, right to, 416, 437
Rickert, Heinrich, 296
ridicule, 521
Riehl, Alois, 296
right: cosmopolitan, 478, 479, 488–490, 493, 498–499; domestic, 467; duties of, vs. duties of virtue, 420–421, 425, 512; Hegel on abstract, 405; and humanity, 425–428; Kant's concept of, 418; private, 456; public, 480–481; relation to morality, 419–428, 434–437; to persons akin to things, 461–462; universal principle of, 418, 423–424, 434, 455
Romanticism, 292, 294, 297
Rorty, Richard, 273
Rousseau, Jean-Jacques, 176, 435, 439, 442; on gender, 450; on peace, 478
rules: and concepts, 182–183, 187, 188; and representation of objects, 205–207
Russell, Bertrand, 120

Saint-Pierre, Charles Irénée Chastel, Abbé de, 478
Salmon, Wesley P., 228
Schäfer, Lothar, 580
Schelling, Friedrich Wilhelm Joseph: on art, 578; and hylozoism, 339; and idealism, 632; on matter, 327–328; on science, 326, 327–329, 330, 340; and the unconditioned, 292, 294–295
schematism: of categories, 150, 230–231, 258; of causation, 166, 211; of empirical concepts, 547; Heidegger on, 157; in mathematics, 111–112
Schiller, Friedrich: aesthetics of, 578; on Kantian morality, 527–528;
Schlegel, Friedrich, 294, 496, 497
Schlick, Moritz, 296, 330, 331
Schmid, Carl Christian Erhard, 631

Schopenhauer, Arthur: on beauty, 579; on freedom of the will, 408–411; on Kant's ethics, 352, 528–529
Schulz, Johannes, 631, 642–644, 654–655
science: foundations of, 20, 25; foundations of, after Kant, 325–332; Kant's effect on, 3; Kant's philosophy of, 303–341, 655. *See also* biology, chemistry, physics
self: numerical identity of, 14; rationalist claims about. *See also* apperception, Paralogisms of Pure Reason, subject
self-consciousness, 194–195, 198. *See also* apperception
self-constraint, 512
self-contradiction, 256
self-defense, 423
self-degradation, 519
self-evidence, 241
self-interest, 492, 493, 508–509
self-love, 511, 515
self-mastery, 516–517
self-mutilation, 519, 520
self-ownership, 464–465
self-positing, 244, 399, 403
self-preservation, 508
self-respect, 519
Sellars, Wilfrid, 197–198, 297
sensation, 77, 178
sensible world, 178
sensibility, 13, 40, 77, 136, 197–198; manifold of, 148
servility, 520
sexuality, 26, 447–476
Shabel, Lisa A.,
Shaftesbury, Anthony Ashley Cooper, third Earl of, 368, 508–509, 526
Shoemaker, Sydney, 198, 199
Silber, John, 621
skepticism: and Hume, 241, 327, 639; and transcendental arguments, 239–240, 249, 255–256
Smith, Adam, 646
Smith, Norman Kemp, 212
social epistemology, 196
sociability, 645
Socrates, 451
soul, Kant's view of, 179, 192
sovereignty, of states, 487–488

space: absolute, 9–10, 62, 63–64, 72–76,
309, 314, 315, 316–317, 318, 319; as
appearance, 71–72; constructivist
theory of, 213–214, 272; not an
empirical concept, 78; ideality of,
74, 76–83, 242, 290–291; infinite
divisibility of, 72; as infinite given
magnitude, 79–80; Kant's early view
of, 69–72; Kant on perception of,
61–93; Leibniz on, 64–66, 70; as
necessary representation, 78–79; as
object, 83–86; pre-Kantian
metaphysics and epistemology of,
62–69; psychological views of,
87–88; as pure form of intuition, 13,
24, 36, 74–76, 79, 114, 129–130,
133–134, 321; reception of Kant's
view of, synthetic *a priori*
knowledge of, 86–89, 242–243;
visual, 89
Spalding, Johann Joachim, 594
Spinoza, Baruch (Benedictus de), 240,
292, 328, 333, 409, 617; and Jacobi,
293
spiritualism, 280
spontaneity, 26, 383, 387, 388–389, 392,
393, 394
Stahl, Georg Ernst, 39, 339
state: Kant's theory of, 416–446; and
property, 428–437. *See also* right,
public
Steinbuch, Johann Georg, 87
Stirner, Max, 596
Stoicism: on emotions, 506; on
happiness and virtue, 366, 368, 372,
506, 525–526, 593, 594, 595–596,
598, 600; on justice, 597–598; on
logic, 634
Strawson, Peter F.: on causation, 206; on
self, 199; on transcendental
arguments, 246, 249–250, 254, 255,
256, 260, 297; on visual space, 89
strength of will, and virtue, 510–511,
514
Stroud, Barry, 226; and transcendental
arguments, 250, 262–263, 297
struggle, and virtue, 511
subject, of cognition, 185–196, 248, 251;
as unconditioned, 275
subjectivity, in Reinhold and Fichte, 293

sublime, the: as aesthetic response, 20,
21, 563; as moral feeling, 527
substance, 25, 45, 50, 272, 326; and
causation, 221–227; in early Kant,
70; Herbart's view of, 86–87; in
*Metaphysical Foundations of
Natural Science*, 313, 316; Kant's
proof of, 217–227; Locke on, 172;
modern developments on, 230–232;
permanence of, 316, 320, 323;
rationalist position on, 204
succession: objective vs. subjective,
principle of, 70, 131, 206–210; as
schema of causation, 211
Suchting, W. A., 212
sufficient reason, principle of, 6, 64, 70,
131–132, 382, 383, 385
suicide, 519
Sullivan, Roger, 422, 455–456
Swedenborg, Emanuel, 8
syllogistic inference, 141, 143; and
derivation of ideas of pure reason,
274–275
symbolic knowledge, 20
sympathy, 517, 521, 522
synthesis, 83–86, 146, 181–182,
183–184, 188, 191–192, 194,
244–245; and categories, 147–149,
152; figurative, 321
synthetic *a priori* judgment or
knowledge: in mathematics, 13–14,
24, 35–37, 45, 47–48, 50–51, 52, 53,
94, 97–104, 107; in physics, 316,
320; possibility of, 29, 35–36,
129–130; rejection of, 330–331; of
space and time, 242–243; and taste,
559–560; transcendental, 321; and
transcendental arguments, 241–249
synthetic judgments, 55–56
synthetic method, 132–133
systematicity, 20–21, 26; of empirical
concepts, 549–551; of nature,
322–323, 574–577; and necessity,
538, 540, 551–555; and principle of
morality, 342

tacit *a priori* knowledge, 40–52, 53
talent, 521
taste: deduction of judgments of,
565–567; Hume on standard of,

543–545, 556–557, 560; Kant's theory of, 26, 556–568
teleological judgment, 4, 20, 21–22, 26, 491. *See also* teleology
teleology: antinomy of, 572–573; ethico-, 335; in history, 490–492; Kant on, 568–580; in Leibniz, 307
Tertullianus, Quintus Septimus Florens, 611
Tetens, Johann Nicolaus, 68–69, 637
theism, 592
things in themselves, 12, 17–18, 248; in Fichte, 400; and transcendental idealism, 284, 290–291
time: absolute, 62, 63–64; ideality of, 242; ideality of, 290–291; as pure form of intuition, 13, 24, 36, 114, 129–130, 133–134, 203–205, 213–215, 219; representation of, -series and causation, 207–215, 246, 321; synthetic *a priori* knowledge of, 242–243. *See also* transcendental idealism
Tindal, Matthew, 591
Tittel, Gottlob August, 657–658
Toland, John, 591
Torricelli, Evangelista, 39
Tourtal, Caspar Theobald, 87
trade, 493, 499–500
Transcendental Aesthetic, 13, 76–83, 245–246
transcendental arguments or proofs, 25, 187, 238–268; critique of, 249–254; and postulates of pure practical reason, 262; reconstruction of, 254–263; structure of, 253–254
Transcendental Deduction, 14, 25, 47, 83–86, 116–118, 129, 130, 223–227, 238–239, 244–246, 324, 654
Transcendental Dialectic, 15–16; structure of, 274–278. *See also* Antinomy of Pure Reason, God, Paralogisms of Pure Reason
transcendental freedom, 388. *See also* freedom
transcendental idealism, 24, 94, 589; and Antinomy of Pure Reason, 278, 279, 286, 394–395; and antinomy of teleological judgment, 572–573; as formal, 280–281; and freedom,

394–395, 398; as humility, 282–283; and mathematics, 114–119; in *Metaphysical Foundations of Natural Science*, 313, 316, 319; and postulates of pure practical reason, 279; and synthesis, 245; and theoretical vs. practical reason, 318; and things in themselves, 284; and transcendental arguments, 238, 240–241, 247–249, 262; and the unconditioned, 287, 290–291. *See also* idealism
transcendental knowledge, 48–49
transcendental logic, 135, 138. *See also* Metaphysical Deduction, Transcendental Deduction
transcendental philosophy, Kant's system of, 319
transcendental psychology, 45
transcendental realism, 289, 394–395
transcendentalism, 271
truth: coherence theory of, 259; correspondence theory of, 26; Kant's conception of, 205, 550

Ulpianus, Domitius, principles of, 434–436, 440
Ulrich, Johann August Heinrich, 631, 654
unconditioned, the, 274, 275, 280, 285–295
understanding, 77, 197–198; and judgment, 142, 146; synthesis of, 83–86
universal grammar, 41, 49
universal law, formula of, 344–345, 346, 348, 349–351, 355, 357–358, 359–360, 373, 423, 455
universal validity, of judgments of taste, 26, 544–545, 557–560
universality, as mark of the *a priori*, 37–39

vengeance, 522
verificationism, 250, 251
vice, 513–514, 519, 520, 522
virtue: and agency, 514–518; artificial vs. natural, 509; classical, 358–362; duties of, 5, 518–523; duties of, vs. duties of right, 420–421, 425, 512;

virtue (cont.)
and good will, 514; and happiness,
506, 601; in highest good, 19,
523–524, 596–598; and imperfect
duties, 508; Kant's conception of,
26, 510–513; as a mean, 524–525;
phenomenal, 512–513; pleasure in,
527–528; of social intercourse,
522–523. See also Aristotle
virtue ethics, 26; ancient, 505–506;
contemporary, 529–530;
pre-Kantian, 505–510
vision, pre-Kantian views of, 68–69
vitalism, 329, 580
voluntarism: in Crusius, 386, 392, 409;
in Schopenhauer, 408, 409–411

Walsh, William H., 270
war, 483, 492, 494–496
warrant, a priori, 32–33, 35
Weber, Max, 441
Weishaupt, Adam, 657–658
Wilde, Oscar, 579
will, 381–415; distinction between Wille
and Willkür, 393–394, 407–408;
general, 433, 438; strength of,

510–511, 514. See also freedom, of
will; good will
Willaschek, Marcus, 423, 424
Wittgenstein, Ludwig: on private
language, 244; and transcendental
arguments, 253
Wizenmann, Thomas, 592, 657
Wolf, Susan, 529
Wolff, Christian, 2, 6, 8, 10, 61, 131, 539;
on freedom of the will, 382,
384–385; on mathematics, 95–96;
on pre-established harmony, 70; on
principle of morality, 367–368,
509–510, 526; on rational
psychology, 176–177; on space and
time, 66–67, 68, 69–70, 71–72; on
theology, 591;
Wolff, Michael, 146, 163–164
Wollaston, William, 367
Wood, Allen W., 423, 424
world: moral, 618–620; sensible vs.
intelligible, 178
Wright, Joseph, 333

Zeno of Citium, 366
Zöllner, Johann Friedrich, 454